GOLF DAYS

GOLF COURSES IN SCOTLAND

SECOND EDITION

In this book is the priceless heritage of golf throughout Scotland. Over three hundred and ten courses, affiliated to the Scottish Golfing Union, that offer every conceivable golfing challenge.

Each course has its own special personality. Some are set amidst tranquil woodland with lakes giving beautiful reflections on still days; others enjoy breathtaking views over sea and strand with the benefit of in vigorating sea air.

The information you need to know is contained in this new edition covering so many clubs, from the world famous to the smallest nine holer. GOLF DAYS gives you all the golfing options and now you have the choice — all you have to do is enjoy this great game on some great courses.

FAMOUS
HIGHLAND
CHARACTER
THE FAMOUS GROUSE
FINEST SCOTCH WHISKY
PRODUCT OF SCOTLAND
QUALITY
IN AN AGE OF
CHANGE.

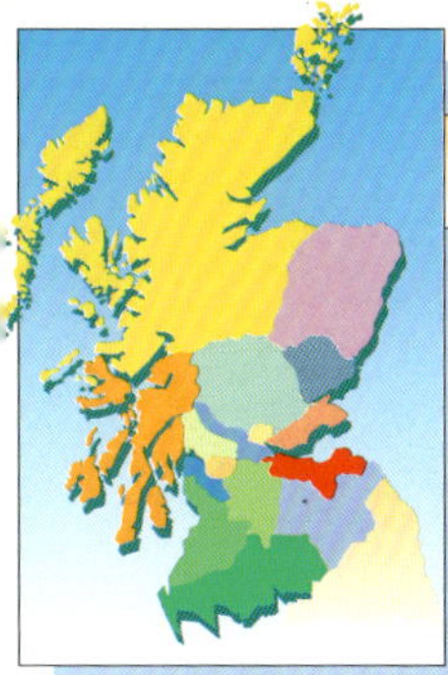

HOW TO USE THIS BOOK

GOLF DAYS SCOTLAND

The courses in this book are grouped in regions then listed alphabetically. The overall map at the front of the book displays the different regions along with their courses. The index at the back of the book lists all the courses in alphabetical order regardless of their region.

COURSE MAP

These are for general information and to provide a layout of the course. They are not intended for interpretation for scoring or competition purposes. In most instances bunker and tree positions are indicated to give players a feel for the course and are only for a general guide.

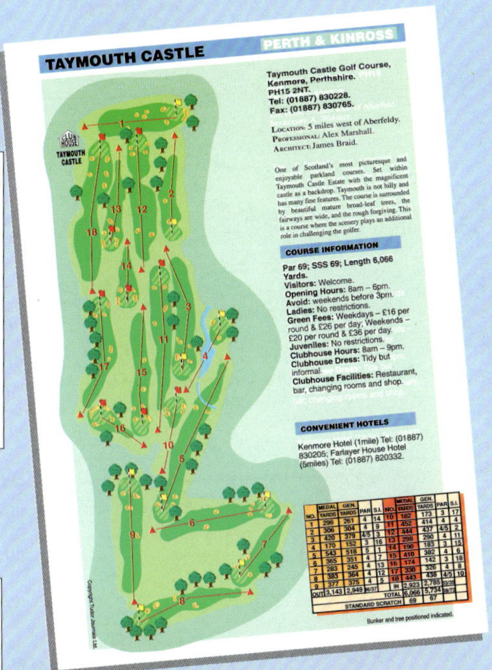

COURSE INFORMATION

This information has been provided by each club and readers are advised to check details in advance as the publishers cannot guarantee the accuracy. Most clubs will be only too glad to answer queries and telephone numbers for all the courses listed have been included for this purpose. **A telephone call can save a wasted journey.**

SCORE CARD

Some course cards are marked in metres, some in yards and some have both. Whatever method of distance that is currently used by each course, the same has been adopted in Golf Days to maintain the same standard of measurement. Some course lengths differ in text from course cards depending on whether Championship or Medal lengths are on the score card.

Cover Photo:
Stephen Marks (Image Bank).
Back Cover:
Scottish serenity (Eric Thorburn).

CONVENIENT HOTELS

The inclusion of Hotels is on the basis of convenience and *not* recommendation. Most establishments listed do however provide a good standard. Where no information appears, the course is usually sited in or adjacent to a town or city which has many such facilities.

QUICK REFERENCE GUIDE

Tudor 1969 1994 QUALITY & SERVICE Established 26 years

Published by
Tudor Journals Ltd
97 Botanic Avenue,
Belfast BT7 1JN. N. Ireland.
Telephone: (01232) 320088.
Fax: (01232) 323163.

Sales & Distribution
Tommy Mackin, Wayne Morgan & Deirdre Convery
Production
Angus McGuffin, Lesley Stevenson & Julie McBride
Assistant Publisher
Gary O'Hara
Publisher
Bill Campbell

Printed by W. & G. Baird Ltd.

GOLF CLUBS IN SCOTLAND

Affiliated to the Scottish Golf Union

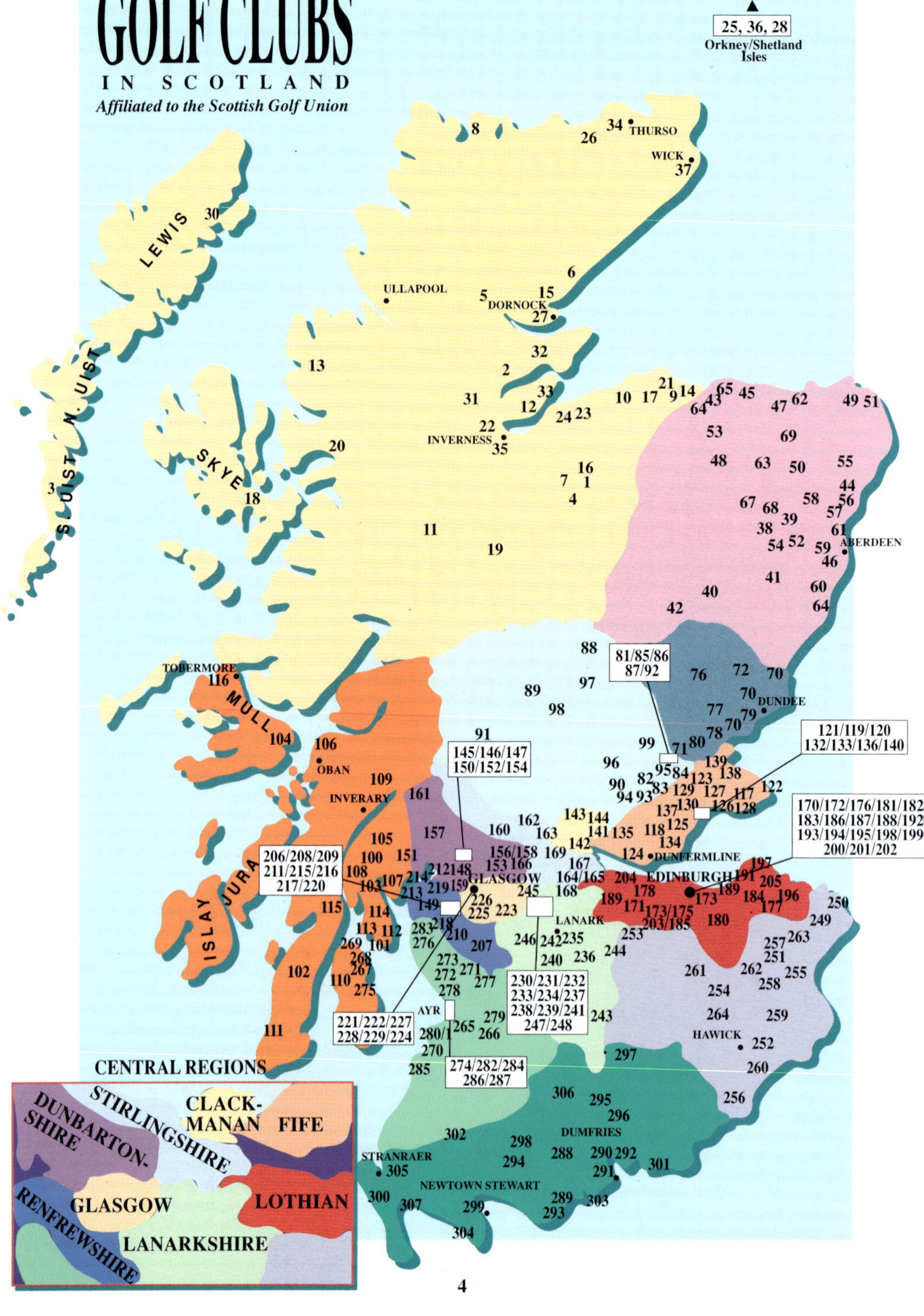

North

1 Abernathy
2 Alness
3 Askernish (S Uist)
4 Boat of Garten
5 Bonat Bridge (Ardgay)
6 Brora
7 Carrbridge
8 Durness
9 Elgin
10 Forres
11 Fort Augustus
12 Fortrose and Rosemarkie
13 Gairloch
14 Garmouth and Kingston
15 Golspie
16 Grantown-on-Spey
17 Hopeman
18 Isle of Skye
19 Kingussie
20 Lochcarron
21 Moray
22 Muir of Ord
23 Nairn
24 Nairn Dunbar
25 Orkney
26 Reay
27 Royal Dornoch
28 Shetland
29 Spean Bridge
30 Stornoway
31 Strathpeffer Spa
32 Tain
33 Tarbat
34 Thurso
35 Torvean
36 Whalsay
37 Wick

North East

38 Aboyne
39 Alford
40 Ballater
41 Banchory
42 Braemar
43 Buckpool
44 Cruden Bay
45 Cullen
46 Deeside
47 Duff House Royal
48 Dufftown
49 Fraserburgh
50 Insch
51 Inverallochy
52 Inverurie
53 Keith
54 Kemnay
55 McDonald
56 Murcar
57 Newmacher
58 Oldmeldrum
59 Peterculter
60 Portlethen
61 Royal Aberdeen
62 Royal Tarlair
63 Shiskine
64 Spey Bay
65 Stonehaven
66 Strathlene
67 Tarland
68 Torphons
69 Turriff

Angus

70 Arbroath Artisan
71 Brechin
72 Carnoustie
73 Downfield
74 Edzell
75 Forfar
76 Kirriemuir Players
77 Letham Grange
78 Monifeith
79 Montrose Courses
80 Panmure

Perth & Kinross

81 Aberfeldy
82 Auchterarder
83 Bishopshire
84 Blair Atholl
85 Comrie
86 Craigie Hill
87 Crieff
88 Dalmunzie
89 Dunkeld & Birnam
90 Gleneagles
91 Killin
92 King James VI
93 Milnathort
94 Muckhart
95 Murrayshall
96 Muthill
97 Strathtay
98 Taymouth Castle
99 The Green Hotel

Argyll & Bute

100 Blairmore & Strone
101 Bute
102 Carradale
103 Cowal
104 Craignure
105 Dalmally
106 Glencruitten
107 Innellan
108 Kyles of Bute
109 Lochgilphead
110 Machrie Hotel
111 Machrihanish
112 Millport
113 Port Bannatyne
114 Rothesay
115 Tarbet
116 Tobermory

Fife

117 Aberdour
118 Auchterderran
119 Balbirnie
120 Burntisland Golf House
121 Cowdenbeath
122 Crail Golfing Society
123 Cupar
124 Dunfermline
125 Dunnikler Park
126 Elie Golf House
127 Glenrothes
128 Kinghorn
129 Ladybank
130 Leslie
131 Lundin
132 Leven Golfing Society
133 Lundin
134 Pitreavie
135 Saline
136 Scoonie
137 Scotscraig
138 St Andrews
139 St Michaels
140 Thornton

Clackmannan

141 Alloa
142 Alva
143 Braehead
144 Tillicoultry

Dunbarton

145 Bearsden
146 Cardross
147 Clydebank Overtoun
148 Douglaston
149 Dunbarton
150 Hayston
151 Helensburgh
152 Hilton Park
153 Lenzie
154 Milnaganie
156 Palacerigg
157 Vale of Leven
158 Westerwood
159 Windyhill

Stirlingshire

160 Aberfoyle
161 Buchanan Castle
162 Callander
163 Dunblane New
164 Falkirk
165 Falkirk Tryst
166 Glenbervie
167 Grangemouth
168 Polmont
169 Stirling

Lothian

170 Baberton
171 Bathgate
172 Bruntsfield Links
173 Broomie Knowe
174 Dalmahoy East
175 Dalmahoy West
176 Duddingston
177 Dundbar
178 Dundas Parks
180 Gifford
181 Glen
182 Gogarburn Hospital
183 Gullane
184 Haddington
185 Harburn
186 Harrison
187 Hon. Company of Edinburgh Golfers
188 Kingsknowe
189 Linlithgow
190 Longniddry
191 Luffness New
192 Merchants of Edinburgh
193 Mortonhall
194 Murrayfield
195 Musselburgh
196 Niddry Castle
197 North Berwick New
198 Portobello
199 Prestonfield
200 Ravelston
201 Royal Musselburgh
202 Torphin Hill
203 West Linton
204 West Lothian
205 Winterfield

Renfrewshire

206 Barshaw
207 Bonnyton
208 Caldwell
209 Cochrane Castle
210 Eastwood
211 Erskine
212 Gleddoch House
213 Gourock
214 Greenock
215 Kilmacholm
216 Lochwinnoch
217 Old Ranfurly
218 Paisley
219 Port Glasgow
220 Ranfurly Castle

Glasgow

221 Bishopsbriggs
222 Cathcart Castle
223 Catkin Braes
224 Cawder
225 Cowglen
226 Haggs Castle
227 Linn Park
228 Littlehill
229 Pollock

Lanarkshire

230 Bellshill
231 Biggar
232 Blairbeth
233 Bothwell Castle
234 Cambuslang
235 Carluke
236 Carnwath
237 Crow Wood
238 Douglas Water
239 East Kilbride
240 Hollandbush
241 Kirkhill
242 Lanark
243 Leadhills
244 Mount Ellen
245 Shotts
246 Strathaven
247 Strathclyde Park
248 Wishaw

Border

249 Duns
250 Eyemouth
251 Galashiels
252 Hawick
253 Hirsel
254 Innerleithen
255 Kelso
256 Langholm
257 Lauder
258 Melrose
259 Minto
260 Newcastleton
261 Peebles
262 Selkirk
263 St Boswells
264 Torwoodlee

Ayrshire

265 Ayr Belleisle
266 Ballochmyle
267 Brodrick
268 Brunston castle
269 Corrie
270 Dallmilling
271 Hospitality Inn
272 Irvine
273 Kilbirnie Place
274 Kilmarnock (Barassic)
275 Lamlash
276 Largs
277 Loudown Gowf
278 Moor Park
279 New Cummock
280 Prestwick St Cuthbert
281 Prestwick St Nicholas
282 Royal Troon
283 Skelmorlie
284 Troon Municipal Courses
285 Turnberry
286 Western Gailes
287 West Kilbride

South

288 Castle Douglas
289 Colvend
290 Crichton Royal
291 Dumfries & County
292 Dumfries & Galloway
293 Kirkcudbright
294 Laggamore
295 Lochnaben
296 Lockerbie
297 Moffat
298 New Galloway
299 Newton Stewart
300 Portpatrick (Dunskey)
301 Powfoot
302 Sanquhar
303 Southerness
304 St Medan
305 Stranraer
306 Thornhill
307 Wigtownshire County

FLY DRIVE
FLY TO IRELAND FIRST CLASS WITH YOUR CAR & CLUBS
SeaCat
For reservations contact your local travel agent or telephone: 0345–523523
Passenger and Car from Stranraer — Belfast in 90 minutes.
SeaCat
THE FLYING BOAT

Getting
a round in
Northern
Ireland.

Long shadows on the 18th. Scottish Highland Photo Library.

GOLF DAYS™ SCOTLAND

ANGUS

Arbroath Golf Club, Elliot by Arbroath, Arbroath, Angus.
Tel: (01241) 72069.

LOCATION: 1 mile south of Arbroath.
SECRETARY: J. Lach-Szyrma.
Tel: (01241) 74874.
PROFESSIONAL: Les Robb.
Tel: (01241) 75837.
ARCHITECT: J. Braid.

A seaside Links course whose deceptive design appearance ruins many a complacent score-card. Not known as the 'windy links' for nothing, it is very rare indeed to play on a calm day, hence it presents a fair challenge to the average golfer.

COURSE INFORMATION

Par 70, SSS 69, Length 6,090 Yards.
Visitors: Welcome.
Opening Hours: 8am to 8pm.
Avoid: Saturday & Sunday.
Ladies: Welcome.
Ladies Day: Tuesday.
Fees: Weekdays £10, Day £16. Weekends £15, Day £24.
Juveniles: Permitted.
Clubhouse Hours: 11am to 11pm.
Clubhouse Dress: No shorts after 6pm, no loud T-shirts.
Clubhouse Facilities: Full catering facilities available.

CONVENIENT HOTEL

Seaforth, Inverpark — approximately 1.5 miles away.

NO.	YARDS	PAR	S.I.	NO.	YARDS	PAR	S.I.
1	371	4	10	10	412	4	4
2	481	5	3	11	321	4	15
3	344	4	12	12	310	4	11
4	153	3	16	13	376	4	2
5	396	4	1	14	236	3	14
6	374	4	7	15	355	4	8
7	162	3	17	16	167	3	18
8	367	4	5	17	495	5	6
9	365	4	9	18	405	4	13
OUT	3,031	35		IN	3,077	35	
				TOTAL	6,090	70	
				STANDARD SCRATCH	69		

Bunker and tree positions indicated.

BRECHIN

ANGUS

Brechin Golf Club, Trinity, Brechin, Angus, DD9 7PD.
Tel: (01356) 622383.

LOCATION: 1 mile North of Brechin on the Aberdeen Road (B966).
SECRETARY: A.B. May.
Tel: (01356) 622326.
PROFESSIONAL: S. Rennie.
Tel: (01356) 625270.

Rolling inland course, but no steep hills. Panoramic views of the Grampian Mountains. Very popular with visitors and parties.

COURSE INFORMATION

Par 72; SSS 69, Length 6,129 Yards.
Visitors: Parties over eight must book.
Opening Hours: 7.30am onwards.
Avoid: Saturdays. Sundays during competition hours.
Ladies: Welcome.
Ladies Day: Wednesday.
Fees: Weekdays: Round £13, Day £17. Weekends: Round £14, Weekends day £25.
Juveniles: Permitted only when times available.
Clubhouse Hours: 11am-11pm.
Clubhouse Dress: Informal (to a certain degree).
Clubhouse Facilities: All catering facilities are available throughout the week.

CONVENIENT HOTEL

Northern Hotel, Clerk Street, Angus.

NO.	MEDAL YARDS	GEN. YARDS	PAR	S.I.	NO.	MEDAL YARDS	GEN. YARDS	PAR	S.I.
1	429	407	4	7	10	204	181	3	14
2	317	306	4	13	11	215	206	3	8
3	124	120	3	18	12	259	201	4	17
4	492	430	5	1	13	282	259	4	16
5	183	168	3	15	14	486	481	5	4
6	389	358	4	5	15	429	417	4	6
7	487	472	5	3	16	494	479	5	2
8	301	288	4	9	17	277	264	4	10
9	437	348	4	11	18	318	294	4	12
OUT	3,159	2,897	36		IN	2,964	2,782	36	
					TOTAL	6,129	5,679	72	
STANDARD SCRATCH						69	69		

Bunker and tree positions indicated.

Carnoustie Championship Course,
Carnoustie Golf Links,
Links Parade, Carnoustie.
Angus, DD7 7JE.

Location: 11 miles northeast of Dundee.
Secretary: Earle J.C. Smith
Tel: (01241) 853789.

Described as one of the wonders of golf world, famous for the hardest finish of a British championship course. Voted as Britian's no.1 course by a panel of experts in Golf Monthly magazine in 1993, on the basis of its outstanding qualities as a test of golf.

COURSE INFORMATION

Par 72; SSS 74; Length 6,936 Yards.
Opening Hours: 9am-dusk.
Visitors: Welcome.
Green Fees: £40 per round and £70 per day or £50 to play both the Championship and Burnside Course.

Clubhouse Facilities: No catering. Several Golf Clubs in close proximity accept visitors.
Open Competitions: Northern Ladies – July; Craws Nest Tassie – September.

NO.	CHAMP YARDS	MEDAL YARDS	PAR	S.I.	NO.	CHAMP YARDS	MEDAL YARDS	PAR	S.I.
1	416	407	4	7	10	452	446	4	8
2	460	425	4	3	11	358	353	4	14
3	347	342	4	15	12	475	477	4/5	4
4	434	375	4	11	13	168	161	3	18
5	393	387	4	13	14	516	483	5	2
6	575	524	5	1	15	461	456	4	12
7	397	390	4	9	16	250	245	3	16
8	183	168	3	17	17	455	433	4	6
9	474	420	4	5	18	486	444	5/4	10
OUT	3,679	3,438	36		IN	3,621	3,498	36	
					TOTAL	7,300	6,936	72	
					STANDARD SCRATCH				

Bunker and tree positions indicated.

CARNOUSTIE (Burnside Course)

Burnside Course, Carnoustie Golf Links, Links Parade, Angus. DD7 7JE.

LOCATION: 11 miles northeast of Dundee.
SECRETARY: Earle J.C. Smith
Tel: (01241) 853789.

Links course. Shorter but subtler than the Championship Course.

COURSE INFORMATION

Par 66; SSS 64; Length 4,926 Yards, 5,418 metres.
Visitors: Welcome.
Opening Hours: 9am onwards.
Avoid: Before 1.30pm Saturday & before 11am Sunday mornings.
Ladies: Welcome.
Green Fees: £16 per round; £24 per day or £50 to play one round on both the Championship and Burnside Courses.
Juveniles: Welcome.
Clubhouse Facilities: No catering — but several Golf Clubs in close proximity accept visitors.
Open Competitions: Craw's Nest Tassie – September; Senior's September; Mixed Foursomes – May.

NO.	YARDS	PAR	S.I.	NO.	YARDS	PAR	S.I.
1	340	4	13	10	340	4	14
2	318	4	9	11	318	4	10
3	187	3	17	12	187	3	18
4	455	5	3	13	455	5	4
5	376	4	5	14	376	4	6
6	318	4	11	15	318	4	12
7	197	3	15	16	197	3	16
8	368	4	1	17	368	4	2
9	482	5	7	18	182	5	8
OUT	3,031	36		IN	3,031	36	
				TOTAL	6,062	72	
STANDARD SCRATCH							

Bunker and tree positions indicated.

DOWNFIELD

**Downfield Golf Club,
Turnberry Avenue,
Dundee, DD2 3QP.
Tel: (01382) 825595.
Fax: (01382) 813111.**

LOCATION: North of Dundee, off the A923.
SECRETARY: B.F. Mole.
Tel: As above.
PROFESSIONAL: Kenny Hutton.
Tel: (01382) 889246.

The venue of the Scottish Amateur Championship and the Amateur International (1993 Scotland v's France). This is an undulating, wooded Parkland Course with extensive practice areas.

COURSE INFORMATION

Par 73, SSS 73, Length 6,804 Yards, Metres 6,222.
Visitors: Pre-booking recommended. Weekends — call on day of play.
Opening Hours: Visitors: 9.30-12am, 2.00-3.30pm.
Avoid: Saturdays & Sundays am.
Ladies: Welcome.
Fees: Mon - Fri Round £25; Days £36; Sat, Sun & Bank Hols Round £30.
Juveniles: Welcome.

Clubhouse Hours: 11.00-11.00pm.
Clubhouse Dress: 'Smart Casual' — no jean, shorts, or T-shirts.
Clubhouse Facilities: Full catering facilities available, bar, snooker.
Open Competitions: August.

CONVENIENT HOTEL

Stakis Earl Grey; Swallow.

NO.	YARDS	PAR	S.I.	NO.	YARDS	PAR	S.I.
1	425	4	9	10	434	4	8
2	408	4	5	11	480	5	4
3	228	3	15	12	182	3	16
4	538	5	1	13	480	5	6
5	412	4	7	14	515	5	2
6	177	3	17	15	326	4	14
7	491	5	3	16	352	4	12
8	407	4	13	17	151	3	18
9	414	4	11	18	384	4	10
OUT	3,500	36		IN	3,304	37	
				TOTAL	6,804	73	
STANDARD SCRATCH					73		

Bunker and tree positions indicated.

Edzell Golf Club, High Street, Edzell, Angus.
Tel: (01356) 648235.

LOCATION: 6 miles North West of Brechin.
SECRETARY: J. M. Hutchison. Tel: (01356) 647283.
PROFESSIONAL: A. J. Webster. Tel: (01356) 648462.
ARCHITECT: Bob Simpson.

A heathland course in the foothills of the Grampians. A major tree planting programme has made it appear more parkland. This course has many interesting holes.

COURSE DESCRIPTION

Par 71; SSS71; Length 6,348 Yards.
Visitors: Welcome until 4.45 pm Mon - Fri; 10-12 & after 2pm Sat & Sun.
Opening Hours: Daylight.
Avoid: 4.45-6.15 pm Mon-Fri; 7.30-10.00am &12-2pm weekends.
Ladies: Welcome.
Ladies Day: Thursday.
Fees: £18.00 round and £27.00 day – £24 round; £36 day weekends.
Juveniles: Welcome.

Clubhouse Hours: 8.00am to 11.00pm.
Clubhouse Dress: Casual, but smart.
Clubhouse Facilities: Full meal bar service.

CONVENIENT HOTELS

Glenesk Hotel;
Central Hotel;
Panmure Arms Hotel.

NO.	MEDAL YARDS	GEN. YARDS	PAR	S.I.	NO.	MEDAL YARDS	GEN. YARDS	PAR	S.I.
1	312	304	4	17	10	369	316	4	12
2	446	436	4	1	11	433	424	4	2
3	310	300	4	13	12	361	336	4	14
4	370	340	4	9	13	415	405	4	6
5	429	425	4	3	14	155	145	3	16
6	178	166	3	11	15	338	300	4	8
7	385	375	4	5	16	316	302	4	10
8	354	342	4	7	17	191	178	3	4
9	478	452	5	15	18	508	496	5	18
OUT	3,262	3,140	36		IN	3,086	2,902	35	
					TOTAL	6,348	6,042	71	
					STANDARD SCRATCH	71	69		

Bunker and tree positions indicated.

Forfar Golf Club,
Cunninghill, Forfar.
DD8 2RL.
Tel: (01307) 462120.

Location: 1.5 miles East of Forfar.
Secretary: W. Baird.
Tel: (01307) 463773.
Professional: P. McNiven.
Tel: (01307) 465683.
Architect: James Braid.

Undulating parkland course with tree lined fairways.

COURSE INFORMATION

Par 69, SSS 70, Length 6,033 Yards.
Visitors: Welcome.
Opening Hours: 8am-dusk.
Avoid: Member competition times telephone in advance.
Ladies: Welcome.
Ladies Day: Tuesday.
Fees: £16 round, £24 day; Weekends £32 day.
Juveniles: Welcome.

Clubhouse Hours: 7.30am - 11pm.
Clubhouse facilities: Snacks anytime. Full catering - prior notice is required.

CONVENIENT HOTELS

Royal Hotel, Forfar Ives House, Letham.

NO.	YARDS	PAR	S.I.	NO.	YARDS	PAR	S.I.
1	341	4	15	10	359	4	7
2	354	4	12	11	352	4	11
3	381	4	5	12	444	4	1
4	393	4	3	13	154	3	18
5	200	3	8	14	478	5	6
6	376	4	10	15	412	4	4
7	404	4	2	16	153	3	16
8	395	4	13	17	344	4	9
9	164	3	17	18	329	4	14
OUT	3,008	34		IN	3,025	35	
				TOTAL	6,033	69	
STANDARD SCRATCH					70		

Tree positions indicated.

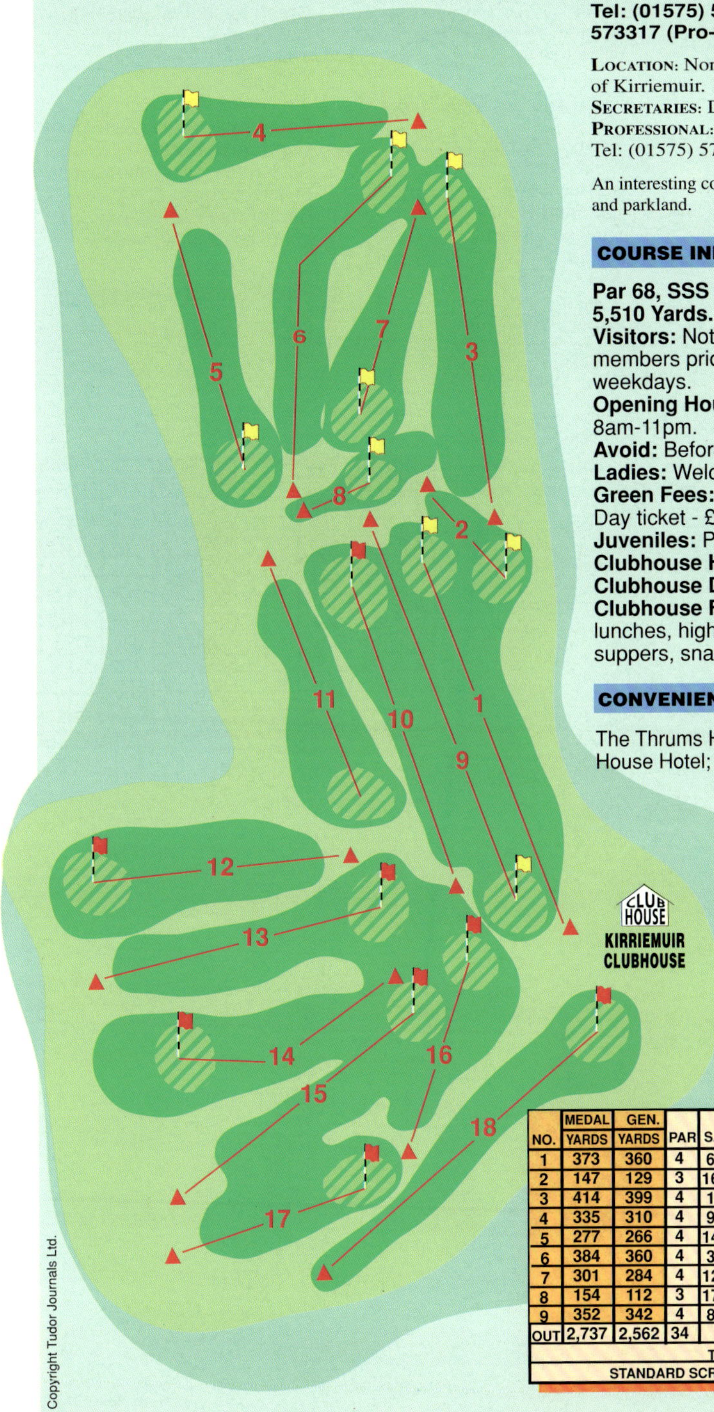

Kirriemuir Golf Club, Kirriemuir. Tel: (01575) 572144 (Clubhouse), 573317 (Pro-shop), Fax: 574608.

Location: North east outskirts of Kirriemuir.
Secretaries: Director of Golf.
Professional: A. Caira.
Tel: (01575) 573317.

An interesting course with a mixture of heath and parkland.

COURSE INFORMATION

Par 68, SSS 67, Length 5,510 Yards.
Visitors: Not allowed at weekends, members priority before 9.30am on weekdays.
Opening Hours: Clubhouse 8am-11pm.
Avoid: Before 9.30am weekdays.
Ladies: Welcome.
Green Fees: Round ticket - £14; Day ticket - £19.
Juveniles: Permitted.
Clubhouse Hours: 9am-11pm.
Clubhouse Dress: Sensible.
Clubhouse Facilities: Breakfasts, lunches, high teas, dinners, suppers, snacks.

CONVENIENT HOTELS

The Thrums Hotel; Castleton House Hotel; The Airlie Arms Hotel.

NO.	MEDAL YARDS	GEN. YARDS	PAR	S.I.	NO.	MEDAL YARDS	GEN. YARDS	PAR	S.I.
1	373	360	4	6	10	330	322	4	13
2	147	129	3	16	11	325	315	4	10
3	414	399	4	1	12	388	378	4	4
4	335	310	4	9	13	391	367	4	2
5	277	266	4	14	14	352	336	4	7
6	384	360	4	3	15	285	277	4	15
7	301	284	4	12	16	119	106	3	18
8	154	112	3	17	17	195	180	3	11
9	352	342	4	8	18	388	380	4	5
OUT	2,737	2,562	34		IN	2,773	2,661	34	
					TOTAL	5,510	5,223	68	
					STANDARD SCRATCH	67	66		

LETHAM GRANGE (New Course)

Letham Grange Golf Club, Colliston, Arbroath. DD11 4RL. Tel: (01241) 890373.

Location: 4 miles North of Arbroath on the A993.
Secretary: Miss Pamela Ogilvie. Tel: (01241) 890373.
Professional: David F.G. Scott. Tel: (01241) 890377.
Architect: T. MacAuley.

The New Course was officially opened in June 1991. In contrast to the Old Course it is shorter and slightly less demanding physically, but with narrow fairways and several cleverly positioned hazards, it proves to be a challenge to the intrepid golfer.

COURSE INFORMATION

Par 68, SSS 68, Length 5,528 Yards.
Visitors: Welcome every day.
Opening Hours: Sunrise-Sunset.
Avoid: Saturday & Sunday 8–9.00am and 1–2pm. Tuesday 9–10am.
Ladies: Welcome.
Ladies Day: Every Friday.
Green Fees: Weekday £13 per round & £19 per day; Weekend £16 per round & £26 per day.
Juveniles: Anytime.
Clubhouse Hours: 7am-11pm.
Clubhouse Dress: Restaurant jacket and tie/rest of hotel casual.
Clubhouse Facilities: Food from 7am till 9.30pm.

CONVENIENT HOTEL

Letham Grange Hotel.

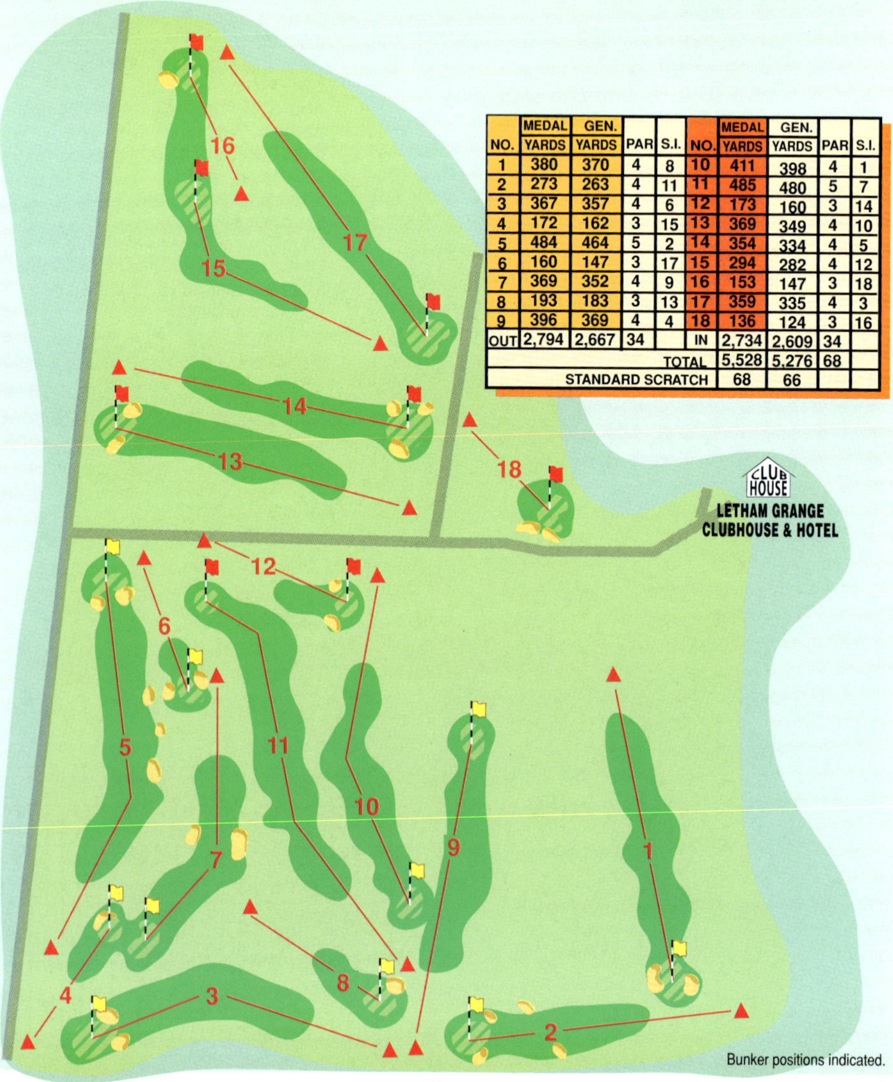

NO.	MEDAL YARDS	GEN. YARDS	PAR	S.I.	NO.	MEDAL YARDS	GEN. YARDS	PAR	S.I.
1	380	370	4	8	10	411	398	4	1
2	273	263	4	11	11	485	480	5	7
3	367	357	4	6	12	173	160	3	14
4	172	162	3	15	13	369	349	4	10
5	484	464	5	2	14	354	334	4	5
6	160	147	3	17	15	294	282	4	12
7	369	352	4	9	16	153	147	3	18
8	193	183	3	13	17	359	335	4	3
9	396	369	4	4	18	136	124	3	16
OUT	2,794	2,667	34		IN	2,734	2,609	34	
					TOTAL	5,528	5,276	68	
					STANDARD SCRATCH	68	66		

Bunker positions indicated.

LETHAM GRANGE (Old Course)

NO.	MEDAL YARDS	GEN. YARDS	PAR	S.I.	NO.	MEDAL YARDS	GEN. YARDS	PAR	S.I.
1	342	336	4	14	10	381	365	4	11
2	334	307	4	12	11	435	420	4	5
3	476	476	5	3	12	184	169	3	17
4	398	372	4	6	13	342	304	4	13
5	154	150	3	16	14	485	480	5	2
6	480	476	5	9	15	189	171	3	15
7	397	390	4	7	16	406	405	4	4
8	166	136	3	18	17	511	490	5	10
9	550	532	5	1	18	402	369	4	8
OUT	3,297	3,175	37		IN	3,335	3,173	36	
					TOTAL	6,632	6,348	73	
					STANDARD SCRATCH	73	71		

Letham Grange Golf Club, Colliston, Arbroath. DD11 4RL. Tel: (01241) 890373.

Location: 4 miles north of Arbroath on the A993.
Secretary: Miss Pamela Ogilvie. Tel: (01241) 890373.
Professional: David F.G. Scott. Tel: (01241) 890377.
Architect: D. Steel and K. Smith.

The course incorporates narrow, tree-lined holes and open rolling and undulating fairways. A constant, yet never extravagant feature is the intelligent use of water on 13 of the 18 holes. The 8th, and 10th holes are truly memorable — the par 3, 8th is played over a picturesque loch, to a green surrounded by mature trees and rhodendrons. Possibly the most spectacular hole is the 10th, which offers a challenge to the most experienced of golfers.

COURSE INFORMATION

Par 73, SSS 73, Length 6,632 Yards.
Visitors: Welcome every day.
Opening Hours: Sunrise-Sunset.
Avoid: Saturday & Sunday 8.00-9.30am and 12.30-2pm. Tuesday 9.00–10am.
Ladies: Welcome.
Ladies Day: Every Tuesday 9.00–10am.
Fees: Weekday £21 round; £32 day weekend, £32 round. No day ticket.
Juveniles: Not allowed before 4pm at weekends unless with an adult.
Clubhouse Hours: 7am-11pm.
Clubhouse Dress: Restaurant jacket and tie/rest of hotel casual.
Clubhouse Facilities: Food from 7am till 9.30pm.

CONVENIENT HOTEL

Letham Grange Hotel.

Bunker and tree positions indicated.

MONIFIETH

Monifieth Golf Links, Princes Street, Monifieth, Dundee.
Tel: (01382) 532767.

LOCATION: Six miles east of Dundee.
SECRETARY: H.R. Nicoll.
Tel: (01382) 535553.
PROFESSIONAL: I. McLeod.
Tel: (01382) 532945.

Links seaside course.

COURSE INFORMATION

Par 71; SSS 72; Length 6,651 Yards.
Visitors: Welcome.
Opening Hours: 9.30am – Dusk (summer); 10.30am – Dusk (winter).
Avoid: Saturdays before 2pm.
Ladies: Welcome.
Green Fees: Weekdays – £32 per round, £20 per day; Weekends – £36 per round, £36 per day. Juveniles – weekdays £11.
Juveniles: Welcome.
Clubhouse Dress: Casual.
Clubhouse Facilities: Yes.
Open Competitions: Links holiday Open – July; Monifieth Ladies Open – August; Seniors Open – June.

CONVENIENT HOTELS

Panmure Hotel, Monifieth (01832) 532911; Woodlands Hotel, Branhill, Dundee, (01832) 480033.

NO.	MEDAL YARDS	GEN. YARDS	PAR	S.I.	NO.	MEDAL YARDS	GEN. YARDS	PAR	S.I.
1	323	312	4	13	10	371	360	4	14
2	416	405	4	9	11	183	173	3	16
3	429	419	4	11	12	374	364	4	6
4	456	445	4	5	13	439	428	4	2
5	192	182	3	15	14	153	143	3	18
6	382	370	4	3	15	379	370	4	10
7	418	406	4	7	16	340	330	4	12
8	284	273	4	17	17	435	424	4	4
9	547	536	5	1	18	530	519	5	8
OUT	3,447	3,348	36		IN	3,204	3,111	35	
					TOTAL	6,651	6,459	71	
					STANDARD SCRATCH	72	71		

Bunker positions indicated.

MONTROSE LINKS TRUST

ANGUS

NO.	MEDAL YARDS	GEN. YARDS	PAR	S.I.	NO.	MEDAL YARDS	GEN. YARDS	PAR	S.I.
1	391	379	4	9	10	379	368	4	10
2	391	378	4	3	11	444	434	4	4
3	154	150	3	17	12	150	140	3	16
4	365	350	4	11	13	320	307	4	12
5	292	276	4	13	14	414	401	4	8
6	489	479	5	1	15	541	516	5	2
7	368	357	4	7	16	235	195	3	14
8	329	299	4	15	17	418	410	4	6
9	444	420	4	5	18	346	339	4	18
OUT	3,223	3,053	36		IN	3,247	3,110	35	
					TOTAL	6,443	6,470	71	
					STANDARD SCRATCH	72	70		

Bunker and tree positions indicated.

Montrose Links Trust, Traill Drive, Montrose, DD10 8SW.
Tel: (01674) 672932 Fax: 671800.

Location: 1 mile from Montrose on the A92.
Secretary: Mrs M. Stewart.
Tel: (01674) 672932.
Professional: Kevin Stables.
Tel: (01674) 672634.

Montrose True Links is believed to be 5th oldest in the world, with the existence of golf recorded as early as 1562. The 2nd fairway has one of the humpiest fairways ever encountered. The 17th hole par 4 is very difficult with it's raised green. Many great holes throughout this course; a true test of golf.

COURSE INFORMATION

Par 71, SSS 72, Length 6,470 Yards.
Visitors: Not allowed on Saturdays or before 10am Sundays.
Opening Hours: 7am-8pm.
Ladies Day: Monday and Thursday.
Fees: Mon-Fri £22, Sat-Sun £30.
Clubhouse Hours: 11am-11pm.
Clubhouse Dress: Smart Casual.
Clubhouse Facilities: In three member clubs ie: Montrose Caledonia, Montrose Mercantile and Royal Montrose.
Open Competitions: 5 Day Open Week, July; Ladies 36 Hole, June; Ladies Handicap, August; Seniors, September.

CONVENIENT HOTELS

Park Hotel, Links Hotel, George Hotel.

NO.	YARDS	PAR	S.I.	NO.	YARDS	PAR	S.I.
1	289	4	15	10	416	4	4
2	488	5	3	11	171	3	18
3	398	4	9	12	363	4	7
4	348	4	8	13	398	4	12
5	147	3	17	14	535	5	2
6	387	4	1	15	234	3	14
7	418	4	11	16	382	4	5
8	360	4	6	17	401	4	10
9	174	3	13	18	408	4	16
OUT	3,009	35		IN	3,308	35	
				TOTAL	6,317	70	
STANDARD SCRATCH					70		

Panmure Golf Club, Burnside Road, Barry, By Carnoustie. Tel: (01241) 853120.

LOCATION: 2 miles West of Carnoustie.
SECRETARY: Major G. Paton (retired).
Tel: (01241) 855120.
PROFESSIONAL: A. Cullen.
Tel: (01241) 852460.

Traditional links course providing an excellent test of golf for all handicaps. Used as a qualifying course for the 'Open', co-host with Carnoustie of the 1992 Amateur Championship qualifying rounds — venue for the Seniors Championship and other top amateur and professional competitions. Outstanding clubhouse.

COURSE INFORMATION

Par 70, SSS70, Length 6,317, Metres 5,776.
Visitors: No visitors on Saturdays.
Opening hours: 8am.
Avoid: Saturdays.
Ladies: Welcome, except on Saturdays.
Ladies Day: Tuesday.
Fees: £35 for day. £23 for round.
Juveniles: Allowed with a member.
Clubhouse Hours: 7.30am-11pm.
Clubhouse Dress: Mens bar: Casual. Lounge and Dining Room: Jacket and tie.
Clubhouse Facilities: Full catering facilities available.
Open Competitions: Seniors Open - May; Ladies Open - June.

CONVENIENT HOTEL

Broughty Ferry, Carnoustie.

GOLF DAYS™ SCOTLAND

ARGYLL & BUTE

BLAIRMORE & STRONE

**Blairmore & Strone Golf Club,
Strone, By Dunoon, Argyll,
Strathclyde.
Tel: (0136984) 676.**

LOCATION: High road Strone north of Dunoon.
SECRETARY: J. Clark.
Tel: (0136984) 467.

This is a hilly course with scenic views of the Firth of Clyde. The greens are small, requiring a certain degree of accuracy. This may explain why the current course record stands 63.

COURSE INFORMATION

Par 62; SSS 62; Length 4,224 Yards.
Visitors: Welcome.
Opening Hours: Sunrise – Sunset (Sunday 9am to Sunrise).
Ladies: Welcome.
Green Fees: £8 per day.
Juveniles: Welcome.

NO.	YARDS	PAR	S.I.	NO.	YARDS	PAR	S.I.
1	260	4	9	10	260	4	12
2	144	3	17	11	144	3	18
3	219	3	2	12	219	3	3
4	154	3	15	13	154	3	16
5	179	3	13	14	179	3	10
6	234	3	7	15	234	3	6
7	292	4	5	16	292	4	8
8	309	4	1	17	309	4	4
9	321	4	11	18	321	4	14
OUT	2,112	31		IN	2,112	31	
				TOTAL	4,224	62	
STANDARD SCRATCH					62		

Tree positions indicated.

BUTE

Bute Golf Club, Kingarth, Isle of Bute.

LOCATION: Stravanan Bay, off A845 Rothesay – Kilchattan Bay Road.
SECRETARY: J. Burnside.
Tel: (0170083) 648.

Flat links course with a beautiful view of the Isle of Arran. Fair number of natural hazards (bushes etc). Greens in excellent condition which tend to be on slow side.

COURSE INFORMATION

Par 64; SSS 64; Length 2,284 Metres 2,497 Yards .
Visitors: No play before 12.30 on Saturdays.
Opening Hours: Sunrise to Sunset.
Avoid: Saturday mornings.
Ladies: Welcome.
Ladies Day: Tuesday evenings and 1st Sunday of each month.
Green Fees: £6 daily.
Juveniles: £3 daily.
Open competitions: Kingarth open-2nd Sunday in May.

CONVENIENT HOTELS

Kingarth Hotel (1/2 mile from course.
St Blanes Hotel (Kilchattan Bay) 1/2 mile from course.

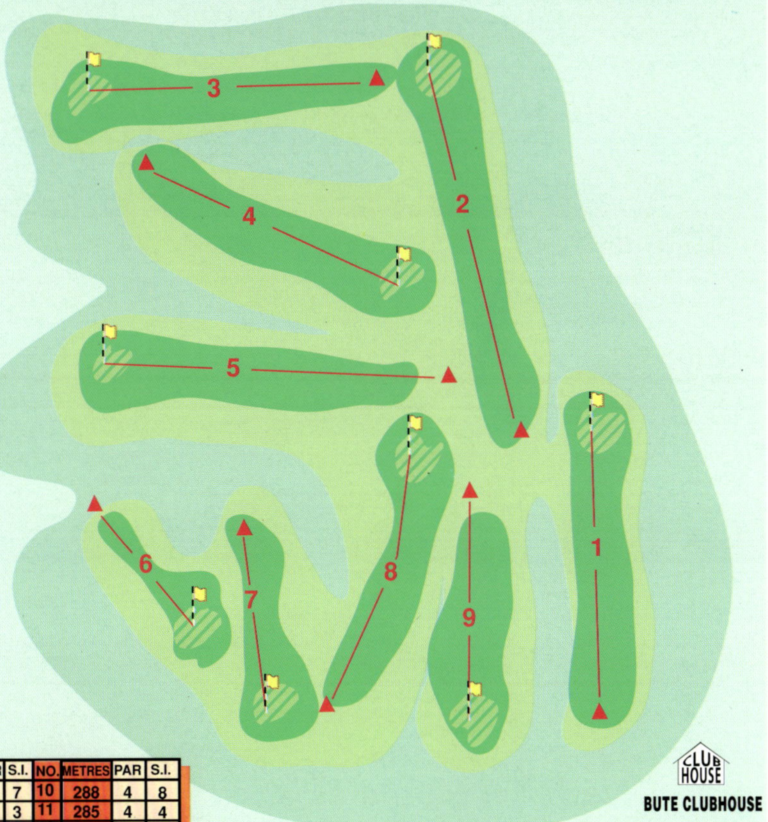

NO.	METRES	PAR	S.I.	NO.	METRES	PAR	S.I.
1	288	4	7	10	288	4	8
2	285	4	3	11	285	4	4
3	133	3	17	12	133	3	18
4	354	4	1	13	354	4	2
5	261	4	11	14	261	4	12
6	195	3	15	15	195	3	16
7	275	4	9	16	275	4	10
8	256	4	5	17	256	4	6
9	237	4	13	18	237	4	14
OUT	2,284	34		IN	2,284	34	
				TOTAL	4,568	68	
STANDARD SCRATCH					64		

**Carradale Golf Club,
Carradale, Argyll.
PA28 6QT.
Tel: (01583) 3387.**

LOCATION: 14 miles north of Campbeltown on the B842.
SECRETARY: J.R. Ogilvie.
Tel. (01583) 431643.

The course is short, built on a headland in the Kilbrannan Sound with magnificent views of Arran and Ailsa Craig. Heathland, fairly flat and a few sharp rises. Considerable difficulty off the medal tees, and the SS score has only been beaten once. This is a wonderful holiday course, ideal for children and beginners.

COURSE INFORMATION

Par 66; SSS 64; Length 4,784 Yards.
Visitors: Welcome.
Opening Hours: All day.
Ladies: Welcome.
Ladies Day: In Summer– most Thursdays there are Ladies Competitions.
Green Fees: £6 per day. Weekly & fortnightly rates for visitors. Country membership (1995 price £52 & £19 for juniors) allows entry to Club competitions.
Juveniles: No restrictions except July & August (afternoons only). Under 10's must be accompanied by an adult.
Clubhouse Hours: All day.
Clubhouse Dress: Shorts permitted with a shirt – no topless golf.
Clubhouse Facilities: Gents & Ladies changing rooms.
Open Competitions: Mens' Open 3rd Sunday in July & 1st Sunday in August.

CONVENIENT HOTEL

Carradale Hotel (at first tee) – all facilities available.

NO.	YARDS	PAR	S.I.	NO.	YARDS	PAR	S.I.
1	159	3	13	10	159	3	14
2	329	4	5	11	329	4	6
3	260	4	15	12	260	4	16
4	330	4	1	13	330	4	2
5	285	4	11	14	285	4	12
6	289	4	9	15	289	4	10
7	240	3	3	16	240	3	4
8	205	3	17	17	205	3	18
9	295	4	7	18	295	4	8
OUT	2,392	33		IN	2,392	33	
				TOTAL	4,784	66	
		STANDARD SCRATCH			64		

COWAL

Cowal Golf Club,
Ardenslate Road,
Dunoon, Argyle,
Strathclyde.
Tel: (01369) 705673.

LOCATION: North east boundary of Dunoon.
SECRETARY: Brian Chatham. Tel: (01369) 705673.
PROFESSIONAL: Russell Weir. Tel: (01369) 702395.
ARCHITECT: James Braid.

Founded in 1891, Cowal Golf Club overlooks the Firth of Clyde, one of the world's most beautiful estuaries, and the seaside town of Dunoon.

Cowal is a superb 18 hole, 6,251 yard course that skillfully exploits the wide variety of natural, and typically Scottish features, to produce an enjoyable a test of golf. On a clear day you'll see the Isle of Arran and the famous Ailsa Craig, rising out of the sea off the Ayrshire coast at Turnberry.

COURSE INFORMATION

Par 70; SSS 70; Length 6,251 Yards.
Opening Hours: Daylight hours.
Visitors: Welcome (special party rates).
Avoid: Members only times.
Ladies: Welcome.
Green Fees: Monday–Friday round £13; Day £20. Weekends round £20; Day £30.
Juveniles: Welcome; must be accompanied by an adult.
Clubhouse Dress: Smart/Casual.
Clubhouse Facilities: Daily catering available.
Open Competitions: Festival week – first week in June.

CONVENIENT HOTELS

Esplanade; St. Ives; West End; Kilmun House Hotel. All the above hotels and many more in the surrounding area offer special golf deals.

NO.	MEDAL YARDS	GEN. YARDS	PAR	S.I.	NO.	MEDAL YARDS	GEN. YARDS	PAR	S.I.
1	440	424	4	5	10	333	300	4	10
2	436	427	4	11	11	340	332	4	6
3	381	369	4	2	12	345	316	4	12
4	391	369	4	9	13	492	425	5	1
5	188	177	3	15	14	166	133	3	18
6	303	296	4	7	15	417	381	4	4
7	337	300	4	3	16	334	312	4	14
8	330	316	4	13	17	374	345	4	16
9	177	166	3	17	18	467	414	4	8
OUT	2,983	2,844	34		IN	3,268	2,958	36	
					TOTAL	6,251	5,802	70	
STANDARD SCRATCH						70	68		

Craignure Golf Club, Scallastle, Craignure, Isle of Mull Hotel, Isle of Mull.
Tel: (01680) 812370.

LOCATION: Craignure one mile.
SECRETARY: Mrs S. Weir.

12 years old nine hole links course in majestic surroundings of the hills of Argyll beside the Sound of Mull. Laid out towards the end of the last century and incorporating much of the original course it has,and is being moved with the help of substantial grant aid. Recently lengthened to incorporate par 5 seventh.

COURSE INFORMATION

Par 68; SSS 64; Length 4,926 Yards.
Visitors: Welcome.
Opening Hours: Daylight Hours – Honesty Box available.
Avoid: Competition start times.
Ladies: Welcome.
Green Fees: £8 (ticket can be obtained from Isle of Mull Hotel.
Juveniles: Welcome, reduced fee.
Clubhouse hours: Members and green keeper have keys to clubhouse.
Clubhouse dress: Informal.
Clubhouse facilities: It is hoped to have limited changing/toilet facilities available in th near future.
Open Competitions: August, September.

CONVENIENT HOTELS

Isle of Mull Hotel 3/4 miles away.

NO.	MEDAL YARDS	GEN. YARDS	PAR	S.I.	NO.	MEDAL YARDS	GEN. YARDS	PAR	S.I.
1	255	255	4	7	10	255	255	4	8
2	270	270	4	11	11	270	270	4	12
3	250	207	4	17	12	250	207	4	18
4	313	283	4	5	13	313	283	4	6
5	114	114	3	15	14	114	114	3	16
6	377	317	4	3	15	377	317	4	4
7	432	410	5	1	16	432	410	5	2
8	217	156	3	13	17	217	156	3	14
9	235	187	3	9	18	235	187	3	10
OUT	2,463	2,199	34		IN	2,463	2.199	34	
					TOTAL	4.896	4.398	68	
					STANDARD SCRATCH	64	64		

Bunker and tree positions indicated.

Dalmally Golf Club,
Dalmally, Argyll,
Strathclyde. TA33 1AR.
Tel: (018382) 00370.

LOCATION: One mile west of Dalmally on A85.
SECRETARY: A.J. Burke.
Tel: (018382) 370.

Dalmally Golf Club is a flat course surrounded by the River Orchy and mountains with many water hazards and trees testing a players ability.

COURSE INFORMATION

Par 64; SSS 63; Length 2,217 Yards.
Opening Hours: Daylight hours.
Visitors: Welcome.
Avoid: Sundays 9am - 10am; 1pm - 2pm.
Ladies: Welcome.
Green Fees: £7 per round: Juveniles – £3.00 per round.
Juveniles: Welcome; must be accompanied by an adult.
Clubhouse Hours: Weekends only.
Clubhouse Dress: Clean and Tidy.
Clubhouse Facilities: Limited facilities.
Open Competitions: Three man team Stapleford 4 July.

CONVENIENT HOTELS

Glen Orchy Lodge hotel; Orchy Bank Guest House.

NO.	MEDAL YARDS	GEN. YARDS	PAR	S.I.	NO.	MEDAL YARDS	GEN. YARDS	PAR	S.I.
1	166	154	3	14	10	166	154	3	11
2	360	290	4	1	11	360	290	4	5
3	158	149	3	6	12	158	149	3	8
4	294	241	4	2	13	294	241	4	4
5	135	126	3	18	14	135	126	3	15
6	284	244	4	12	15	284	244	4	13
7	147	110	3	17	16	110	147	3	16
8	311	256	4	7	17	308	311	4	10
9	402	390	4	3	18	402	390	4	9
OUT	2,257	1,960	32		IN	2,257	1,960	32	
					TOTAL	4,514	3,920	64	
					STANDARD SCRATCH	63			

Tree positions indicated.

GLENCRUITTEN

Glencruitten Golf Club, Oban, Argyll, Strathclyde. PA34 4BU.
Tel: (01631) 562868.

LOCATION: One mile from Oban.
SECRETARY: A.G. Brown. Tel: (016310) 64604.
ARCHITECT: James Braid.

A scenic course designed by James Braid. Includes 11 par 3 holes of varying degrees of difficulty. Though hilly, the course presents a challenge to even the low handicap golfer.

COURSE INFORMATION

Par 61; SSS 63; Length 4452 Yards.
Opening Hours: 8.30am - dusk.

Visitors: Welcome.
Avoid: Saturday morning and other Medal Days.
Ladies: Welcome:
Ladies day: Thursday afternoon.
Green Fees: Monday – Friday round £13, Saturday/Sunday round £12.50;
Juveniles: Welcome; Monday - Friday round £6.50, Saturday/Sunday round £7.50.
Clubhouse Hours: 10am - 11pm.
Clubhouse Dress: Informal/casual.
Clubhouse Facilities: Full catering facilities available.
Open Competitions: Held in August each year.

CONVENIENT HOTEL

Argyll Hotel.

NO.	MEDAL YARDS	GEN. YARDS	PAR	S.I.	NO.	MEDAL YARDS	GEN. YARDS	PAR	S.
1	445	432	4	2	10	150	141	3	[illegible]
2	170	163	3	17	11	238	205	3	[illegible]
3	167	160	3	13	12	410	373	4	[illegible]
4	271	271	4	8	13	185	176	3	[illegible]
5	163	148	3	18	14	318	310	4	[illegible]
6	228	215	3	7	15	178	151	3	[illegible]
7	219	205	3	10	16	313	313	4	[illegible]
8	263	263	4	5	17	180	180	3	[illegible]
9	197	187	3	14	18	357	357	4	[illegible]
OUT	2,123	2,044	30		IN	2,329	2,206	31	[illegible]
					TOTAL	4,452	4,250	61	[illegible]
					STANDARD SCRATCH	63	63		[illegible]

Tree positions indicated.

INNELLAN

Innellan Golf Club,
Innellan, Dunoon, Argyll.
Tel: (01369) 830242.

LOCATION: Four miles South of Dunoon at Dunoon ferry terminal.

Hilly panaromic views of the Firth of Clyde.

COURSE INFORMATION

Par ??, SSS 63, Length 4,686yds.
Opening Hours: 8.00am to dusk.
Visitors: Welcome.
Avoid: Mon evenings.
Ladies: Welcome.
Green Fees: Weekdays £8; weekends £10.
Juveniles: £4 per day.
Clubhouse Hours: 10.00am to dusk.

Clubhouse Dress: Casual.
Clubhouse Facilities: Catering on application.

CONVENIENT HOTELS

Royal Hotel; Roscairn Hotel; Braemar Hotel.

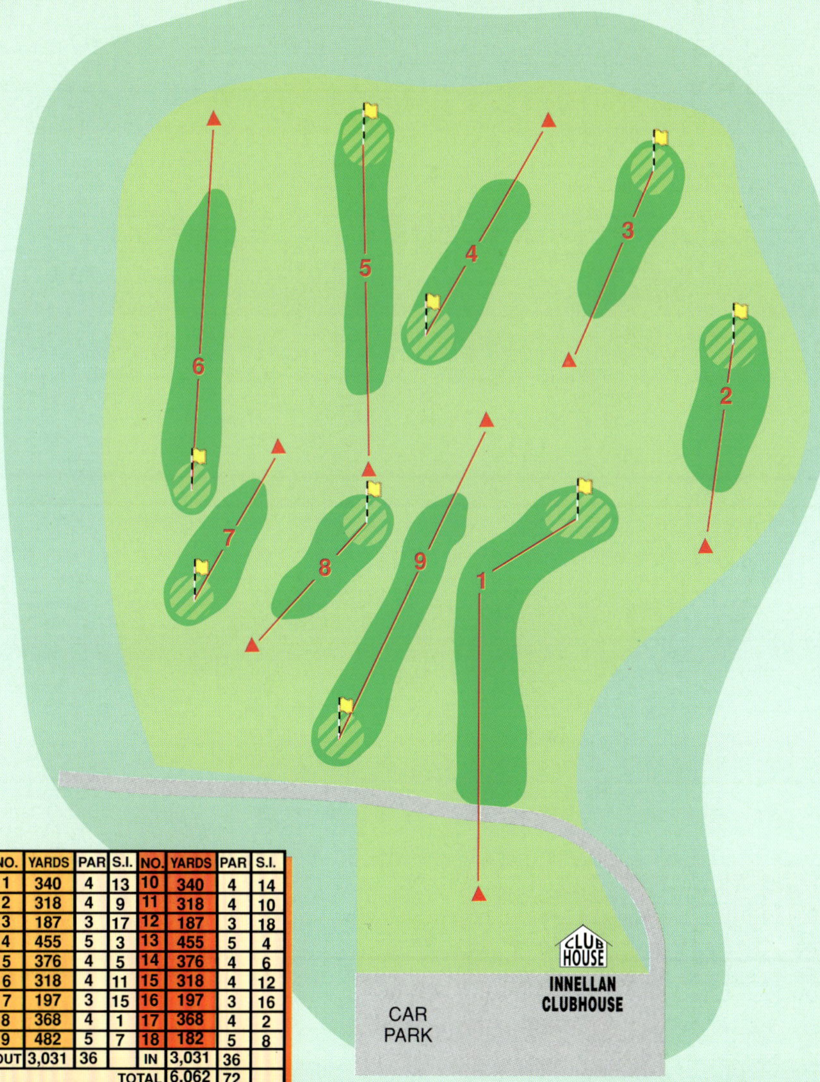

NO.	YARDS	PAR	S.I.	NO.	YARDS	PAR	S.I.
1	340	4	13	10	340	4	14
2	318	4	9	11	318	4	10
3	187	3	17	12	187	3	18
4	455	5	3	13	455	5	4
5	376	4	5	14	376	4	6
6	318	4	11	15	318	4	12
7	197	3	15	16	197	3	16
8	368	4	1	17	368	4	2
9	482	5	7	18	182	5	8
OUT	3,031	36		IN	3,031	36	
				TOTAL	6,062	72	
STANDARD SCRATCH							

KYLES OF BUTE

ARGYLL & BUTE

Kyles of Bute,
Tibhnabruaich, Argyll,
Strathclyde.
Tel: (0700) 811355.

LOCATION: 26 miles west of Dunoon.
SECRETARY: J.A. Carruthers.

A testing course for standards with excellent views over the Kyles of Bute.

COURSE INFORMATION

Par 66; SSS 62; Length 2,389 Yards.
Visitors: Welcome.
Opening Hours: No restriction.
Avoid: Thursday 6pm & Sunday 10am-12.
Ladies: Wednesday 3pm.
Green Fees: £6.
Ladies: Wednesday 3pm.
Green Fees: £6.
Juveniles: Welcome.
Clubhouse Dress: Casual.
Culbhouse Facilities: Tea/Coffee, Soft drinks, Confectionery.

CONVENIENT HOTELS

Kames Hotel; Royal Hotel, Kyles of Bute Hotel.

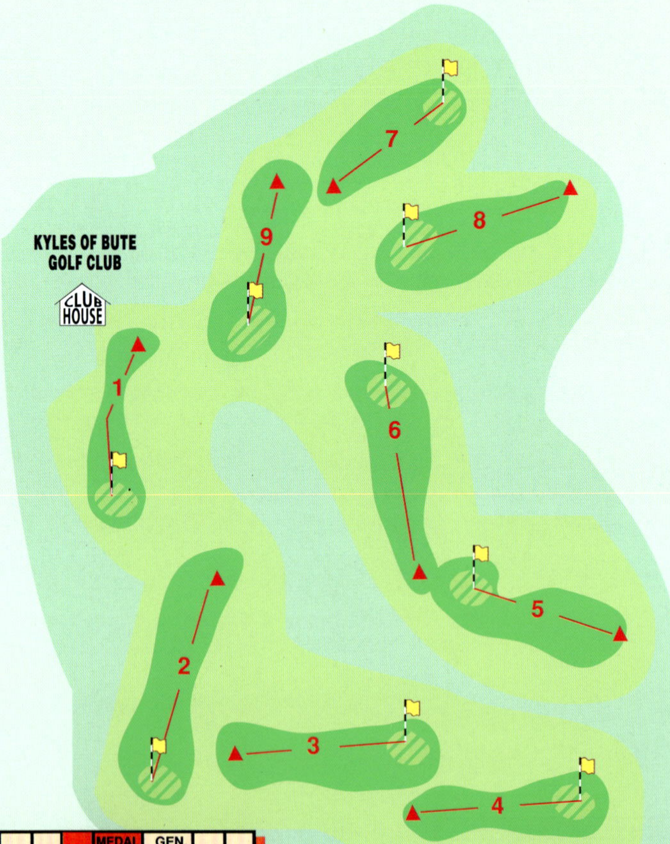

NO.	MEDAL YARDS	GEN. YARDS	PAR	S.I.	NO.	MEDAL YARDS	GEN. YARDS	PAR	S.I.
1	112	108	3	18	10	112	108	3	16
2	332	287	4	5	11	332	287	4	6
3	262	205	4	7	12	262	205	4	8
4	330	225	4	3	13	330	225	4	2
5	246	208	3	13	14	246	208	3	17
6	404	355	4	1	15	404	355	4	4
7	258	240	4	9	16	258	240	4	10
8	255	215	4	11	17	255	215	4	12
9	190	188	3	15	18	190	188	3	14
OUT	2,389	2,039	33		IN	2,389	2,039	33	
					TOTAL	4,778	4,078	66	
					STANDARD SCRATCH	64	66		

**Lochgilphead Golf Club.
Blarbuie Road,
Lochgilphead,
Argyll.
Tel: (01546) 602340.**

Location: Lochgilphead 1/2 mile adjacent to Argyll and Bute Hospital.
Secretary: Andrew Law.
Tel: (01546) 86302.

Lochgilphead's first golf club was established in 1891 on the site which is now Lochgilphead Caravan Park. The original course was also a nine hole course with holes varying from 130-290 yards, par 33. During the last 28 years the course has been modified to a testing hilly course on varied ground. It is hoped that it will be developed into an 18 hole in the near future.

COURSE INFORMATION

Par 64; SSS63; Length 4,484 Yards.
Visitors: Welcome.
Opening Hours: Dawn-dusk.
Avoid: Club Medal Play.
Ladies: Welcome.
Fees: £7.00 weekdays; £10.00 weekends.
Juveniles: Welcome.
Green Fees: £3.50 Mon-Fri, £5 Weekends.
Clubhouse Hours: Evenings on weekdays all day weekends.
Clubhouse Dress: Casual.
Clubhouse Facilities: Limited snacks at weekends.

CONVENIENT HOTELS

Stag; Victoria ; Empire Guest House.

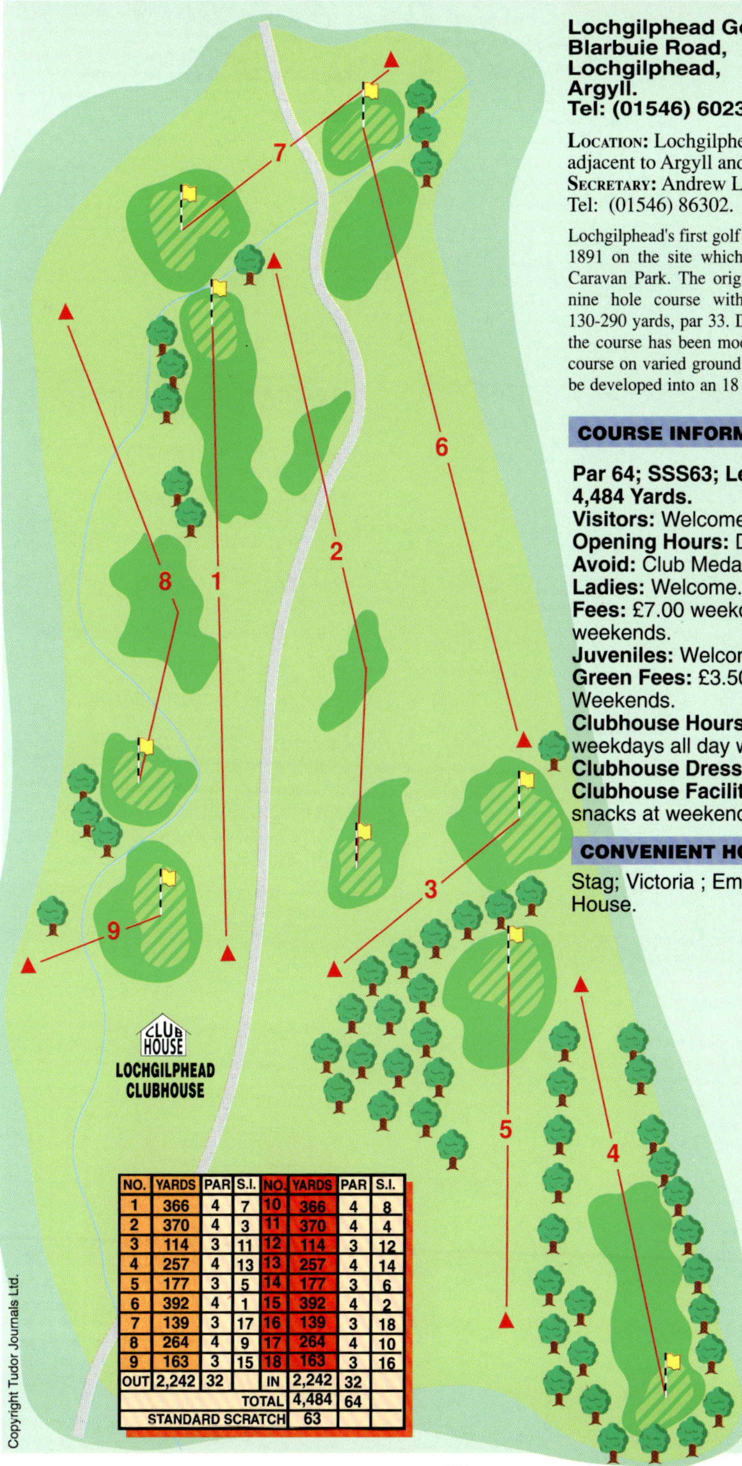

NO.	YARDS	PAR	S.I.	NO.	YARDS	PAR	S.I.
1	366	4	7	10	366	4	8
2	370	4	3	11	370	4	4
3	114	3	11	12	114	3	12
4	257	4	13	13	257	4	14
5	177	3	5	14	177	3	6
6	392	4	1	15	392	4	2
7	139	3	17	16	139	3	18
8	264	4	9	17	264	4	10
9	163	3	15	18	163	3	16
OUT	2,242	32		IN	2,242	32	
				TOTAL	4,484	64	
				STANDARD SCRATCH	63		

Tree positions indicated.

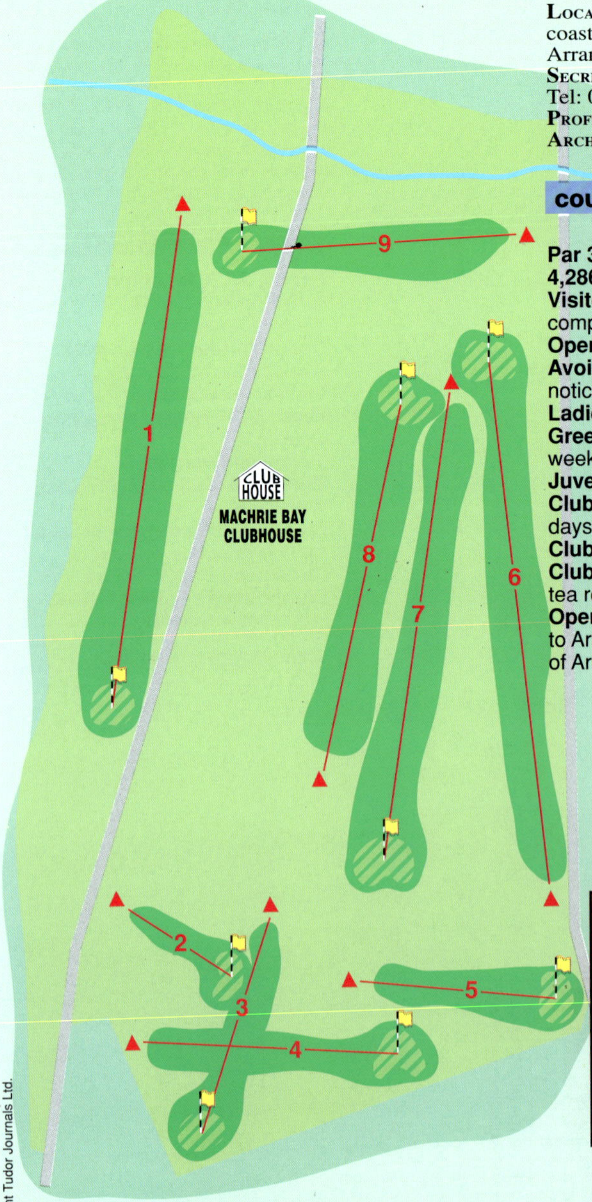

Machrie Bay Golf & Tennis Club,
Brodick,
Isle of Arran
KA27 8DZ.

Location: Seaside course on west coast 9 miles from Brodick, Isle of Arran.
Secretary: Mr A.M. Blair.
Tel: 01770 850 261.
Professional: W Hagan.
Architect: William Fernie.

COURSE INFORMATION

Par 32; SSS 61; Length 4,286 Yards.
Visitors: Welcome, avoid competitions dates.
Opening hours: Dawn to dusk.
Avoid: As advertised on noticeboards.
Ladies: Welcome.
Green Fees: £4 per day & £12 per week.
Juveniles: Welcome.
Clubhouse hours: 10am – 6pm 7 days April-September.
Clubhouse Dress: Informal.
Clubhouse facilities: Snacks in tea room April to September.
Open competitions: Applications to Arran Tourist Board, Brodick, Isle of Arran KA27.

NO.	YARDS	PAR	S.I.	NO.	YARDS	PAR	S.I.
1	314	4	2	10	314	4	11
2	185	3	4	11	185	3	13
3	165	3	9	12	165	3	18
4	278	4	6	13	278	4	15
5	205	3	1	14	205	3	10
6	256	4	8	15	256	4	17
7	268	4	5	16	268	4	14
8	220	3	3	17	220	3	12
9	252	4	7	18	252	4	16
OUT	2,143	32		IN	2,143	32	
				TOTAL	4,286	64	
STANDARD SCRATCH					61		

Machrihanish Golf Club,
Machrihanish, Campbeltown,
Argyll.
Tel: (01586) 810213.

Location: 5 miles west of Campbeltown.
Secretary: Mrs A. Anderson.
Tel: (01586) 810213.
Professional: Mr Ken Campbell.
Tel: (01586) 810277.
Architect: Tom Morris.

This course was designed in the words of Old Tom Morris by "The Almighty for Playing Golf". The excellent conditions of the course with its huge undulating greens and its romantic atmosphere provides a challenge for both high and low handicappers alike. The 1st hole is known world over offering a chance when the tide is in to drive over the Alantic Ocean.

COURSE INFORMATION

Par 70; SSS 71; Length 6,228 Yds.
Visitors: By arrangement with the professional.
Opening hours: Sunrise-Sunset.
Ladies: Welcome.
Fees: Mon – Fri Round £18 Day £28; Sat & Sun £32.
Juveniles: 9 hole course only.
Clubhouse hours: 11am-11pm.
Clubhouse dress: Informal.
Clubhouse facilities: Catering by arrangement with club steward.

CONVENIENT HOTELS

Argyll Arms Hotel; Seafield Hotel; White Hart Hotel.

NO.	MEDAL YARDS	GEN. YARDS	PAR	S.I.	NO.	MEDAL YARDS	GEN. YARDS	PAR	S.I.
1	423	423	4	3	10	497	497	5	10
2	395	395	4	5	11	197	197	3	8
3	376	376	4	11	12	505	505	5	6
4	123	123	3	18	13	370	370	4	12
5	385	385	4	7	14	442	442	4	1
6	315	315	4	13	15	167	167	3	16
7	432	432	4	12	16	233	233	3	4
8	337	337	4	9	17	362	362	4	14
9	354	354	4	15	18	315	315	4	17
OUT	3,140	3,140	35		IN	3,088	3,088	35	
					TOTAL	6,228	6,228	70	
					STANDARD SCRATCH	71	70		

Bunker positions indicated.

NO.	MEDAL YARDS	GEN. YARDS	PAR	S.I.	NO.	MEDAL YARDS	GEN. YARDS	PAR	S.I.
1	307	307	4	16	10	345	337	4	10
2	323	305	4	7	11	384	332	4	4
3	402	357	4	2	12	159	150	3	18
4	162	145	3	17	13	449	438	4	1
5	227	197	3	13	14	342	321	4	6
6	312	261	4	8	15	418	394	4	9
7	373	368	4	5	16	160	117	3	14
8	303	303	4	15	17	449	438	4	3
9	313	280	4	12	18	400	299	4	11
OUT	2,722	2,523	34		IN	3,106	2826	34	
					TOTAL	5,828	5,349	68	
					STANDARD SCRATCH	69	66		

Millport Golf Club, Millport, Isle of Cumbrae, KA28 0BH.
Tel: (01475) 530311.

LOCATION: Isle of Cumbrae. Car ferry from Largs.
SECRETARY: R.L.R. Hailstones.
Tel: (01475) 530306.
PROFESSIONAL: G. Docherty.
Tel: (01475) 530305.

Partially undulating and partially on hill side giving magnificent views over Bute to the Mull of Kintyre and up river to Ben Lomond. Ailsa Craig and Heads of Ayr and also Goat Fell on Arran are all visible. A pleasant well maintained course with water to all greens and a large practice area

COURSE INFORMATION

Par 68; SSS 69; Length 5,828 Yards.
Opening Hours: 8am – Dusk.
Visitors: Welcome.
Green Fees: Monday–Friday £15; Saturday/Sunday £20.
Juveniles: Welcome restricted July and August only.
Clubhouse Hours: 11am–11pm (in season).
Clubhouse Dress: Smart/Informal.
Clubhouse Facilities: Full bar and catering available.
Open Competitions: Cumbrae Cup – Mid Saturday of July.

Tree positions indicated.

Port Bannatyne Golf Club, Port Bannatyne, Isle of Bute, Strathclyde.

LOCATION: 2 miles n.orth of Rothesay.
SECRETARY: I.L.MacLeod.
Tel: (01700) 502009.

Port Bannatyne is a hill course with outstanding views of the mountains of Cowal, Kames Bay, the Kyles of Bute and Loch Fyne. It is unusual in having 13 holes then the first 12 are played, followed by the first 5 before a separate 18th.

COURSE INFORMATION

Par 68, SSS 63, Length 4,730 Yards.
Opening Hours: Dawn to dusk.
Visitors: Welcome.
Ladies: Welcome.
Ladies Day: Thursday.
Green Fees: £7.50 a day.
Juveniles: Welcome except some restrictions during important competitions.
Clubhouse Hours: Dawn to dusk.
Clubhouse Dress: Casual.

Clubhouse Facilities: Limited facilities. Catering by arrangement.

CONVENIENT HOTELS

Ardmory House; Port Royal; Port Inn.

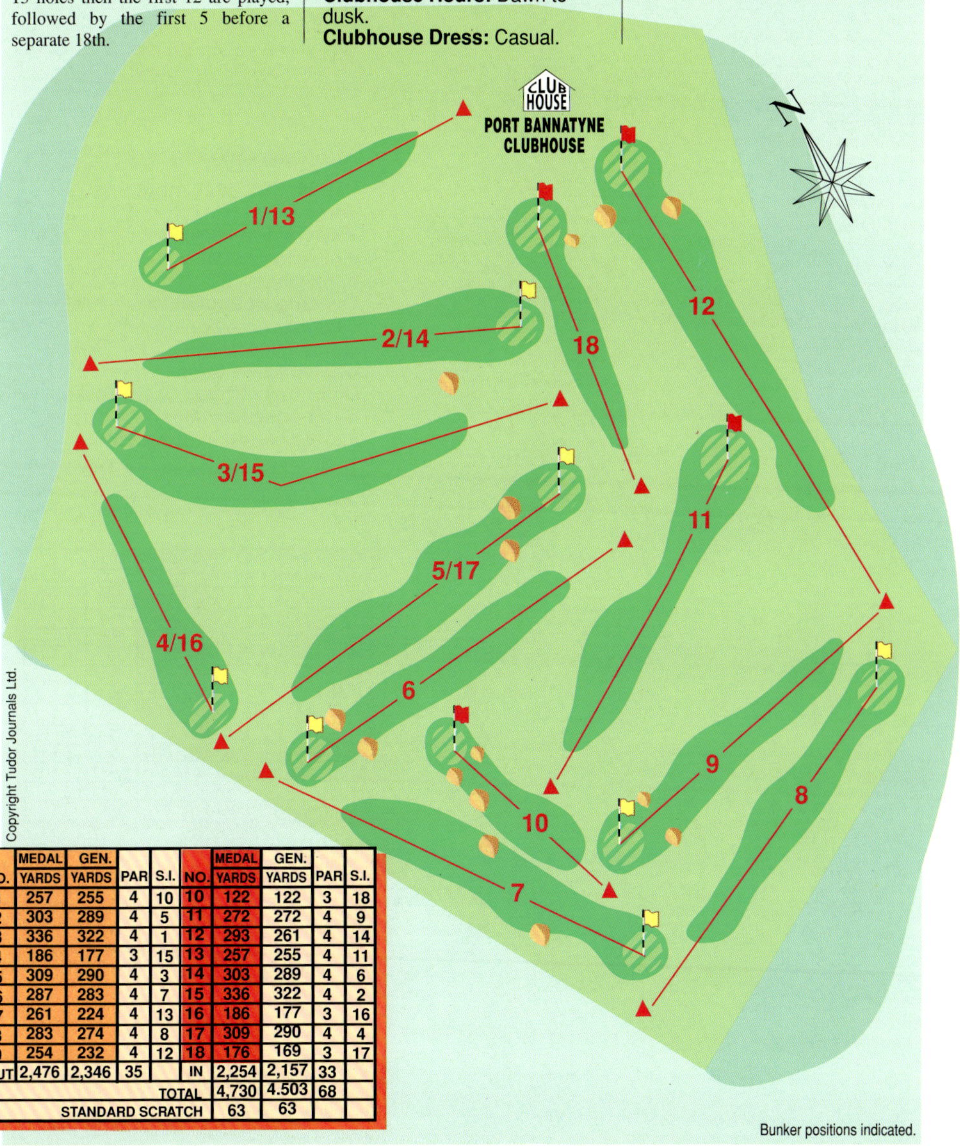

NO.	MEDAL YARDS	GEN. YARDS	PAR	S.I.	NO.	MEDAL YARDS	GEN. YARDS	PAR	S.I.
1	257	255	4	10	10	122	122	3	18
2	303	289	4	5	11	272	272	4	9
3	336	322	4	1	12	293	261	4	14
4	186	177	3	15	13	257	255	4	11
5	309	290	4	3	14	303	289	4	6
6	287	283	4	7	15	336	322	4	2
7	261	224	4	13	16	186	177	3	16
8	283	274	4	8	17	309	290	4	4
9	254	232	4	12	18	176	169	3	17
OUT	2,476	2,346	35		IN	2,254	2,157	33	
					TOTAL	4,730	4.503	68	
					STANDARD SCRATCH	63	63		

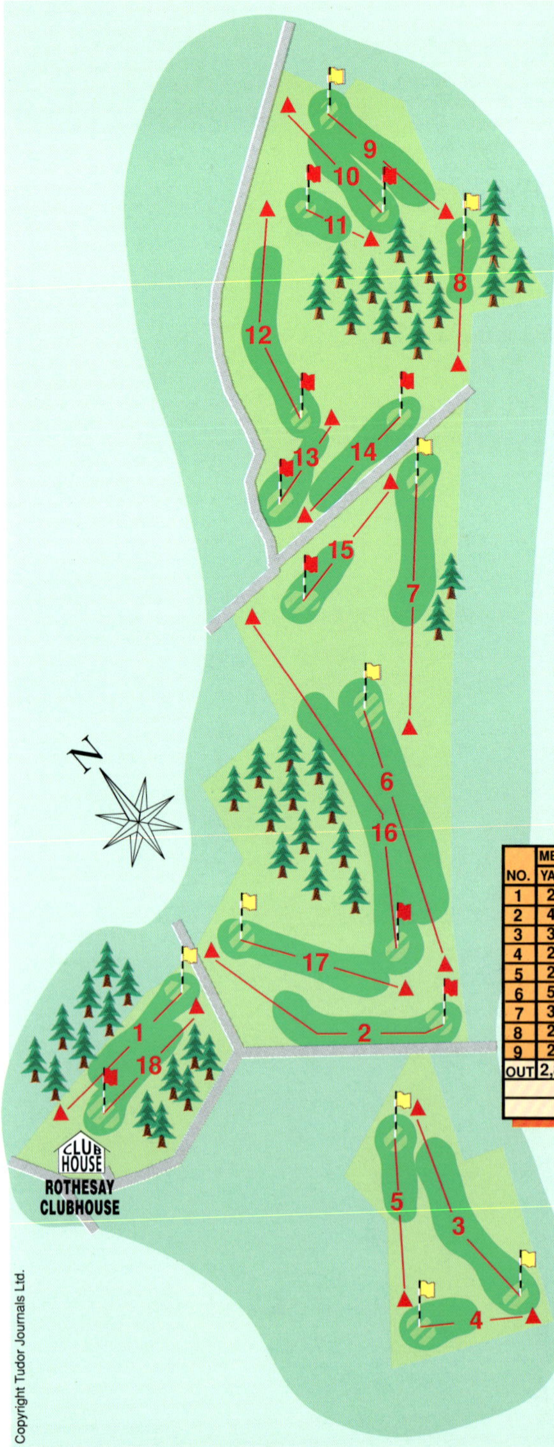

Rothesay Golf Club, Canada Hill, Rothesay, Isle of Bute. Tel: (01700) 2244.

Location: Island in the Firth of Clyde, Ferry Terminal Wemyss Bay, 35 Miles South West of Scotland.
Secretary: Alan Shore.
Tel: (01700) 3744.
Professional: J. Dougal.
Tel: (01700) 3554.
Arhitect: James Braid and Ben Sayers.

Moorland course with magnificent views of the Cowal Peninsula, The Firth of Clyde, The Cumbraes and the Isle of Arran.

COURSE INFORMATION

Par 69; SSS 67; Length 5,370 Yards.
Visitors: Pre-booking essential with professional at weekend (April – September).
Opening Hours: Sunrise-sunset.
Ladies: Welcome.
Green Fees: Mon/Fri £13; Sat/Sun £19 (bookings only).
Clubhouse Dress: Casual/Neat.
Clubhouse Facilities: Full catering mid April – end of September.

NO.	MEDAL YARDS	GEN. YARDS	PAR	S.I.	NO.	MEDAL YARDS	GEN. YARDS	PAR	S.I.
1	265	251	4	7	10	262	250	4	11
2	401	391	4	3	11	145	132	3	18
3	342	310	4	10	12	304	294	4	4
4	200	184	3	16	13	170	160	3	17
5	273	250	4	9	14	254	254	4	14
6	514	495	5	1	15	276	264	4	8
7	359	305	4	5	16	515	495	5	2
8	204	190	3	15	17	372	340	4	6
9	268	250	4	13	18	246	225	3	12
OUT	2,826	2,626	35		IN	2,544	2,417	34	
					TOTAL	5,370	5,043	69	
					STANDARD SCRATCH	67	65		

Tree positions indicated.

TARBERT

Tarbert Golf Club, Kilberry Road, Tarbert, Argyll.
Tel: (01880) 820565.

LOCATION: 1 mile west of Tarbert on B8024.
SECRETARY: Peter Cupples.
Tel: (01880) 820536.

This 9 hole course is attractively situated on the shores of West Loch Tarbert, is ideal for the player with perhaps a little time to spare before catching a ferry to Islay. The course is parkland in nature and affords spectacular views over the loch.

COURSE INFORMATION

Par 66; SSS 64; Length 4,460 Yards.
Visitors: Welcome.
Opening Hours: Sunrise-sunset.
Avoid: Saturday afternoons.
Ladies: Welcome.
Juveniles: Permitted.
Clubhouse facilities: Bar at weekend.

CONVENIENT HOTELS

Stonefield Castle Hotel; Tarbert Hotel; The Anchor Hotel.

NO.	YARDS	PAR	S.I.	NO.	YARDS	PAR	S.I.
1	264	4	8	10	264	4	7
2	295	4	12	11	295	4	11
3	145	3	16	12	145	3	15
4	160	3	14	13	160	3	13
5	332	4	2	14	332	4	1
6	303	4	10	15	303	4	9
7	324	4	4	16	324	4	3
8	128	3	18	17	128	3	17
9	279	4	6	18	279	4	5
OUT	2,230	33		IN	2,230	33	
				TOTAL	4,460	66	
STANDARD SCRATCH					64		

TOBERMORY

ARGYLL & BUTE

Tobermory Golf Club, Tobermory, Isle of Mull, Argyll, Strathclyde.

LOCATION: Tobermory, Isle of Mull.
SECRETARY: Dr.W.H. Clegg. Tel: (01688) 2020.
ARCHITECT: David Adams.

The course is physically demanding with heavy rough in places. The greens are small but good and there are exquisite views of sound of Mull.

COURSE INFORMATION

Par 64; SSS 64; Length 4,474 Metres.
Opening Hours: Daylight hours.
Visitors: Welcome.
Avoid: Open Competition days.
Ladies: Welcome, Ladies pm Wednesday.
Green Fees: £10.
Juveniles: Welcome.
Clubhouse Hours: Dawn – Dusk.
Clubhouse Dress: Informal.

Clubhouse Facilities: Changing room, toilet and lounge open to visitors. No catering facilities available.
Open Competitions: Mac Brayne Cup (36 Holes) – August.

CONVENIENT HOTEL

Fairways Guest House; Western Isles Hotel.

NO.	METRES	PAR	S.I.	NO.	METRES	PAR	S.I.
1	325	4	7	10	325	4	6
2	328	4	1	11	328	4	4
3	210	3	9	12	210	3	12
4	190	3	13	13	190	3	14
5	250	4	11	14	250	4	10
6	367	4	3	15	367	4	2
7	130	3	15	16	130	3	16
8	327	4	5	17	327	4	8
9	110	3	7	18	110	3	18
OUT	2,237	32		IN	2,237	32	
				TOTAL	4,474	64	
STANDARD SCRATCH					64		

GOLF DAYS™ SCOTLAND

AYRSHIRE

Out in one!

AYR BELLEISLE

AYRSHIRE

Bellisle Golf Course, Doonfoot Road, Ayr. KA7 4DU.
Tel: (01292) 441258. Fax: (01292) 442632.

Location: South of Ayr in Bellisle Park.
Manager: David Gemmell.
Tel: (01292) 441314.
Architect: James Braid.

Gently rolling parkland course with large well bunkered greens. The course is surrounded by mature trees which come into play on many of the holes. There are also great views over the Firth of Clyde to the majestic Isle of Arran and Ailsa Craig.

COURSE INFORMATION

Par 71; SSS 71; Length 6,477 Yards.
Visitors: Welcome.
Opening Hours: 7.30am – Dusk.
Avoid: No restricted times.
Ladies: Welcome.
Green Fees: £16.
Juveniles: Restricted.
Clubhouse Hours: As Hotel.
Clubhouse Dress: Casual.
Clubhouse Facilities: As Hotel.
Open Competitions: 1st full week in June.

CONVENIENT HOTELS

Bellisle House Hotel;
Carrick Lodge.

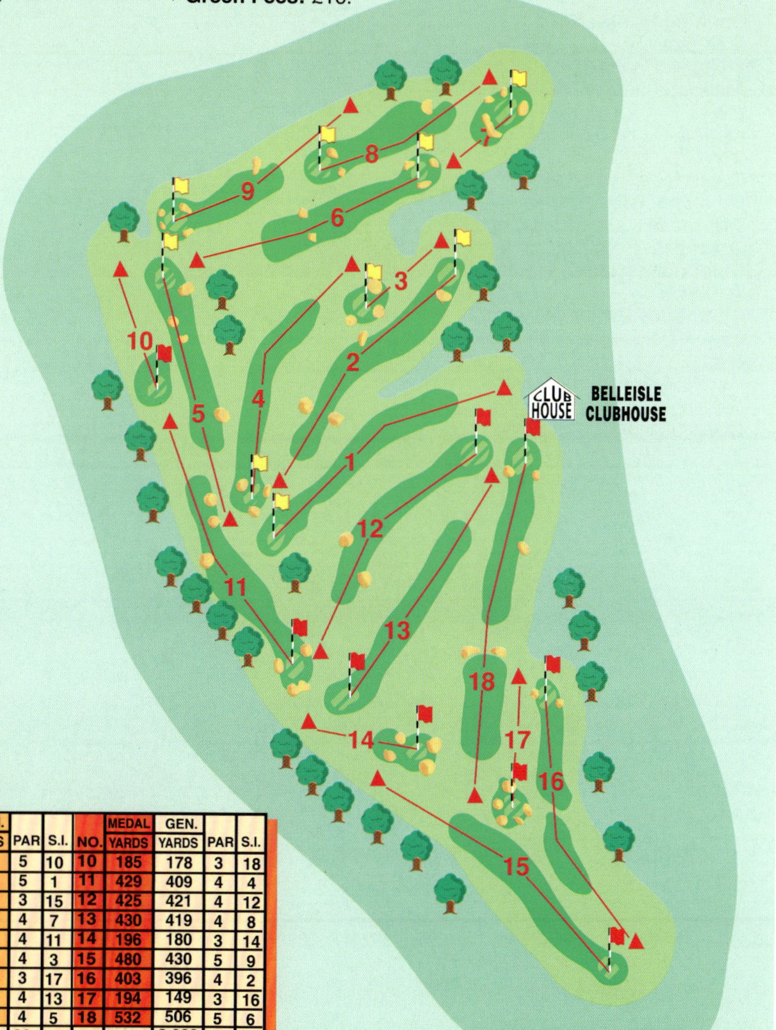

NO.	MEDAL YARDS	GEN. YARDS	PAR	S.I.	NO.	MEDAL YARDS	GEN. YARDS	PAR	S.I.
1	470	462	5	10	10	185	178	3	18
2	470	448	5	1	11	429	409	4	4
3	176	145	3	15	12	425	421	4	12
4	420	401	4	7	13	430	419	4	8
5	401	374	4	11	14	196	180	3	14
6	432	402	4	3	15	480	430	5	9
7	153	141	3	17	16	403	396	4	2
8	334	318	4	13	17	194	149	3	16
9	347	309	4	5	18	532	506	5	6
OUT	3,203	3,000	36		IN	3,274	3,088	35	
					TOTAL	6,477	6,088	71	
					STANDARD SCRATCH	71	70		

Bunker and tree positions indicated.

Ballochmyle Golf Club,
Mauchline, Ayrshire,
KA5 6LE.
Tel: (01290) 550469.

LOCATION: On B705 (off A76) 1 mile south of Mauchline.
SECRETARY: D.G. Munro.
Tel: (01290) 550469.

Inland parkland course with trees.

NO.	MEDAL YARDS	GEN. YARDS	PAR	S.I.	NO.	MEDAL YARDS	GEN. YARDS	PAR	S.I.
1	370	352	4	9	10	272	267	4	14
2	380	366	4	3	11	413	387	4	2
3	196	190	3	17	12	304	286	4	8
4	355	341	4	11	13	280	264	4	10
5	468	452	4	1	14	162	144	3	16
6	279	254	4	15	15	341	333	4	12
7	370	360	4	7	16	422	378	4	4
8	401	389	4	5	17	152	130	3	18
9	290	275	4	13	18	497	487	5	6
OUT	3,109	2,979	35		IN	2,843	2,676	35	
					TOTAL	5,952	5,655	70	
					STANDARD SCRATCH	69	68		

COURSE INFORMATION

Par 70; SSS 69; Length 5,952 Yards.
Opening Hours: 8.00am – 11.00pm.
Visitors: Phone in advance.
Avoid: Saturdays. Mondays in winter.
Ladies: No restrictions. Ladies day – Wednesday.
Green fees: Weekdays – £18 per round, £25 per day. Weekends £30 per day only.
Juveniles: Permitted.
Clubhouse Hours: 8.00am – 11.00pm.
Clubhouse Dress: No jeans, track suits, shorts, shirts without collars.
Clubhouse Facilities: Bar, catering, snooker.
Open Competitions: May.

Bunker and tree positions indicated.

BRODICK

Brodick Golf Club, Brodick, Isle of Arran.
Tel: (01770) 302349.

LOCATION: Brodick Pier 1 mile.
SECRETARY: H.M. MacRae.
PROFESSIONAL: P.S. McCalla.
Tel: (01770) 302513.

Approximately 1 mile north of ferry terminal. Flat parkland course adjoining Firth of Clyde with scenic views of the Bay and Goat Fell.

COURSE INFORMATION

Par 65; SSS 62; Length 4,405 Yards.
Opening hours: Sunrise - Sunset.
Visitors: Welcome; Parties by arrangement with Secretary.
Avoid: Club Competitions.
Ladies: Welcome.
Ladies Day: Tuesday.
Green Fees: Weekdays £10 per round; £15 per day. Weekends £15 per round; £20 per day.
Juveniles: Welcome; but restricted.
Clubhouse Hours: Seasonal.
Clubhouse Dress: Acceptable casual dress.
Clubhouse Facilities: Bar lunches available.

CONVENIENT HOTELS

Contact Isle of Arran Tourist Office, Brodick.

NO.	MEDAL YARDS	GEN. YARDS	PAR	S.I.	NO.	MEDAL YARDS	GEN. YARDS	PAR	S.I.
1	211	211	3	5	10	396	368	4	10
2	144	150	3	17	11	360	360	4	1
3	223	203	3	13	12	284	212	4	16
4	401	401	4	1	13	187	187	3	8
5	316	193	4/3	11	14	162	154	3	18
6	161	114	3	7	15	120	120	3	6
7	125	125	3	15	16	269	241	4/3	14
8	166	166	3	3	17	280	227	4/3	4
9	378	378	4	9	18	222	211	3	12
OUT	2,125	1,941	30/29		IN	2,280	2,080	32/29	
					TOTAL	4,405	4,021	62/58	
					STANDARD SCRATCH	62	58		

Tree positions indicated.

BRUNSTON CASTLE

Brunston Castle Golf Club, Bargany by Dailly, Ayrshire. KA26 9RH. Tel: (01465) 811471, Fax: (01465) 811545.

LOCATION: Adjacent to the village of Dailly, about 8 miles east of Girvan.
SECRETARY: I.F. Tennant. Tel: (01465) 714481. For bookings Telephone G. Ferguson (Clubmaster) at 01465 811471.
ARCHITECT: Donald Steel.

Parkland course in wooded area. Built on either side of the river Girvan. 9th & 18th greens are adjacent to the Clubhouse.

COURSE INFORMATION

Par 72; SSS 72; Length 6,792 Yards.
Visitors: Welcome.
Opening Hours: 8am – Dusk.
Avoid: Special competition days.
Ladies: No restrictions.
Green Fees: Weekdays £20 per round & £30 per day; Weekends £25 per round & £35 per day.(Buggies available £15 per round; Electric caddy cars £5 per round).
Juveniles: Under 14's accompanied by an adult.
Clubhouse Hours: 8am – Dusk.
Clubhouse Dress: No trainers, shellsuits, tracksuits or untidy jeans
Clubhouse Facilities: Snacks and lunch.

CONVENIENT HOTELS

Kings Arms, Girvan; Malin Court; Maidens; Heid Inn, Crosshill.

Bunker and tree positions indicated.

NO.	YARDS	PAR	S.I.	NO.	YARDS	PAR	S.I.
1	410	4	3	10	328	4	12
2	415	4	9	11	378	4	2
3	380	4	13	12	425	4	6
4	340	4	15	13	509	5	14
5	217	3	11	14	440	4	4
6	538	5	5	15	350	4	18
7	410	4	1	16	410	4	8
8	174	3	17	17	179	3	10
9	501	5	7	18	388	4	16
OUT	3,385	36		IN	3,407	36	
				TOTAL	6,792	72	
STANDARD SCRATCH					73		

A calm sea. Eric Thorburn.

CORRIE

AYRSHIRE

Corrie Golf Club, Sannox, Isle of Arran. KA27 8JD. Tel: (01770) 810223.

Location: 8 miles north of Brodick..
Secretary: Robert Stevenson. Tel: (01770) 810268.

Short nine hole course, full of character and very picturesque with some magnificent views.

COURSE INFORMATION

Par 62; SSS 61; Length 1,948 Yards.

Opening Hours: 8am – 8pm daily.
Visitors: Welcome; Cannot accept large groups.
Avoid: Course closed on Saturday afternoons.
Ladies: Welcome.
Ladies Day: Thursday afternoon.
Green Fees: £7 per day.
Juveniles: Welcome accompanied by an adult.
Clubhouse hours: 8am – 8pm.
Clubhouse Dress: Casual.
Clubhouse Facilities: Meals available from 8am till 8pm; 7 days from April to October.

CONVENIENT HOTELS

Ingledene Hotel, Sannox; Corrie Hotel, Corrie; Blackrock House Guest House.

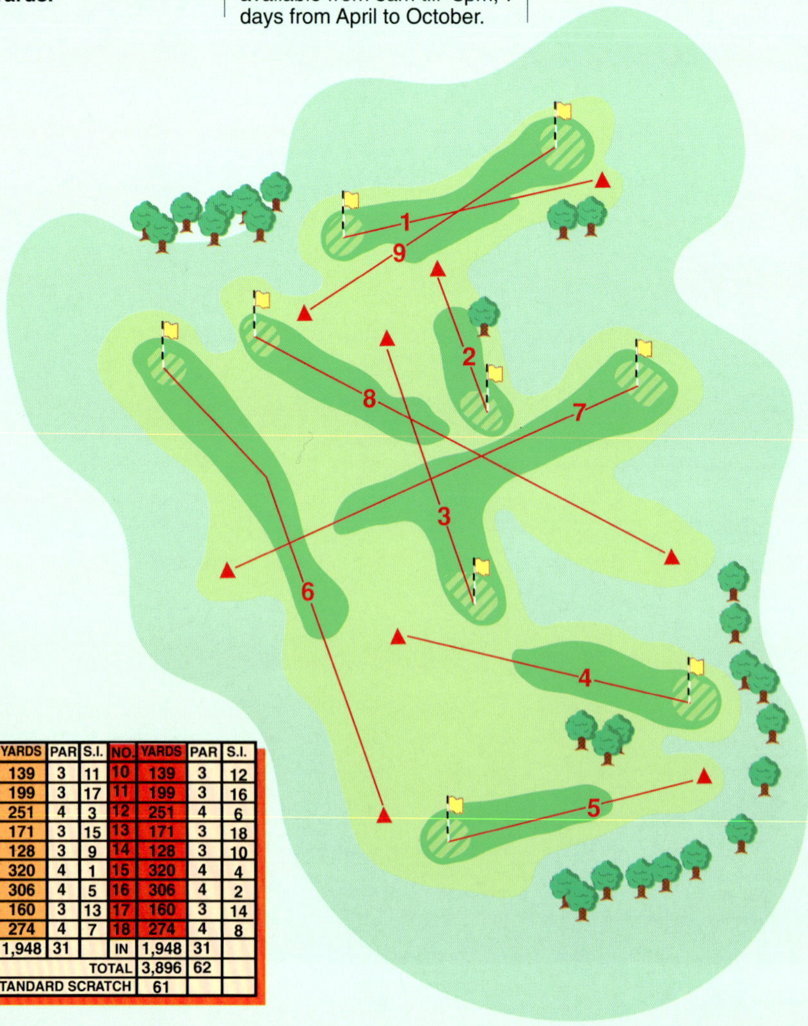

NO.	YARDS	PAR	S.I.	NO.	YARDS	PAR	S.I.
1	139	3	11	10	139	3	12
2	199	3	17	11	199	3	16
3	251	4	3	12	251	4	6
4	171	3	15	13	171	3	18
5	128	3	9	14	128	3	10
6	320	4	1	15	320	4	4
7	306	4	5	16	306	4	2
8	160	3	13	17	160	3	14
9	274	4	7	18	274	4	8
OUT	1,948	31		IN	1,948	31	
				TOTAL	3,896	62	
STANDARD SCRATCH					61		

Tree positions indicated.

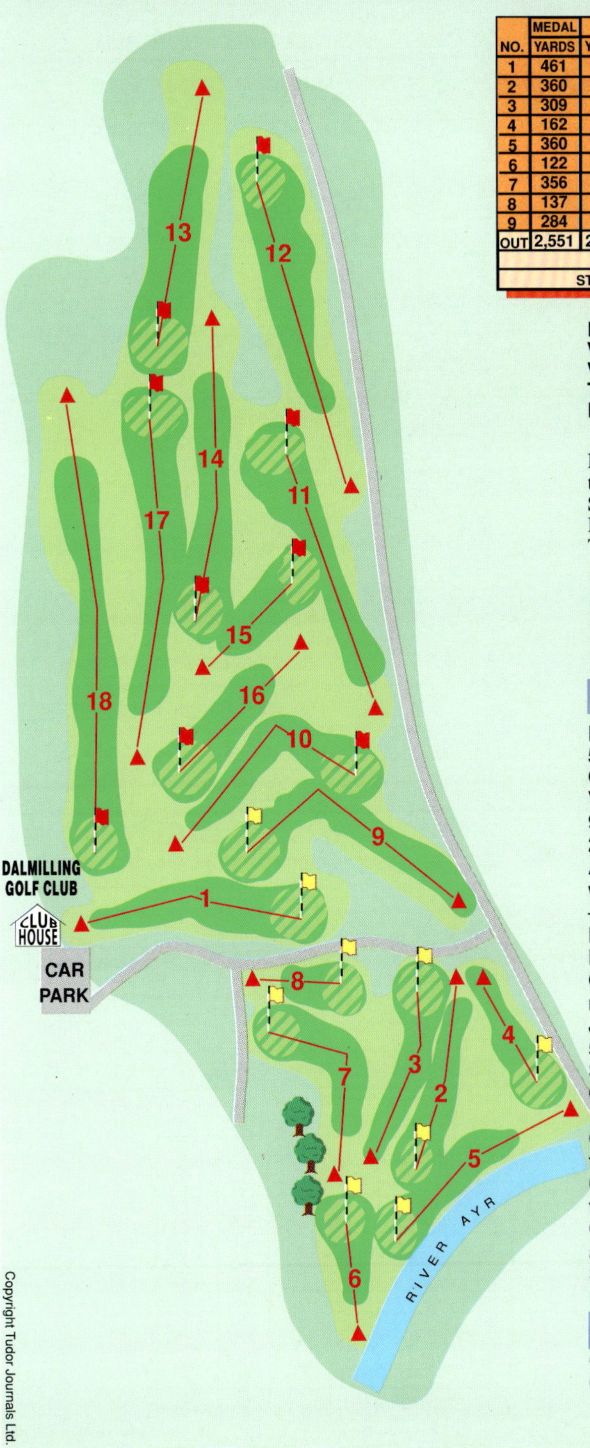

NO.	MEDAL YARDS	GEN. YARDS	PAR	S.I.	NO.	MEDAL YARDS	GEN. YARDS	PAR	S.I.
1	461	454	4	3	10	350	340	4	12
2	360	352	4	7	11	407	351	4	6
3	309	298	4	11	12	418	383	4	8
4	162	150	3	13	13	165	155	3	16
5	360	348	4	5	14	500	480	5	2
6	122	122	3	17	15	174	162	3	18
7	356	344	4	1	16	296	290	4	14
8	137	120	3	15	17	458	433	4	4
9	284	276	4	9	18	405	399	4	10
OUT	2,551	2,464	33		IN	3,173	2,993	35	
					TOTAL	5,724	5,457	68	
					STANDARD SCRATCH	68	66		

Dalmilling Golf Club,
Westwood Avenue,
Whitletts, Ayr, KA8 0QY.
Tel (01292) 263893.
Fax: (01292) 610543.

LOCATION: One mile north east of town centre off A77.
SECRETARY: Mr Stuart Graham.
PROFESSIONAL: Philip Cheyney.
Tel: (01292) 263893.

Gently undulating parkland course with several water hazards and the River Ayr as a boundary.Extensive work completed on revising and upgrading first 9 holes.

COURSE INFORMATION

Par 69; SSS 68; Length 5,724 Yards.
Opening Hours: 7.30am – Dusk.
Visitors: Welcome; Between 9.30am - 11.30am and from 2.15pm.
Avoid: Not before 9.30am, weekends and between 11.45am – 2.15pm.
Ladies: Welcome.
Ladies Day: Monday.
Green Fees: Mon-Fri £10 per round; £18 per day (seven days).
Juveniles: Weekdays before 5pm; Weekend after 12 noon Saturday & Sunday.
Clubhouse Hours: 10am – 10pm.
Clubhouse Dress: Informal at all times.
Clubhouse Facilities: All facilities by prior arrangements.
Open Competitions: August 22 and 23; Ayr Golf Week from 1st Sunday in June to following Friday.

CONVENIENT HOTELS

Carrick Lodge, Ayr;
Caledonian Hotel, Ayr.

Tree positions indicated.

IRVINE

AYRSHIRE

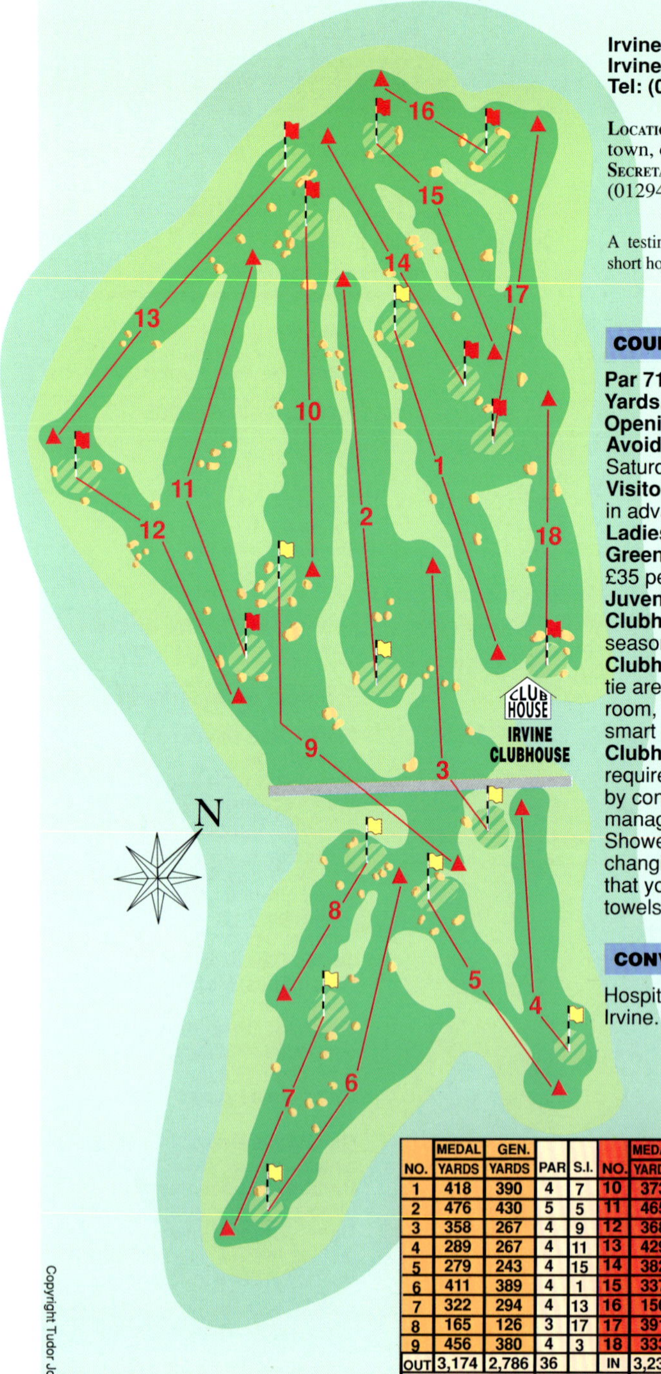

Irvine Golf Club, Bogside, Irvine.
Tel: (01294) 311347.

LOCATION: Bogside, North side of town, off the A737.
SECRETARY: A Morton Tel: (01294) 275979.

A testing links course with only two short holes.

COURSE INFORMATION

Par 71; SSS 71; Length 6,408 Yards.
Opening Hours: 8am – Dusk.
Avoid: May not play before 3pm Saturday and Sunday.
Visitors: Welcome (must contact in advance).
Ladies: Wecome.
Green Fees: £25 per round and £35 per day. Weekends – £35.
Juveniles: Welcome.
Clubhouse Hours: Varies on season.
Clubhouse Dress: Jacket and tie are required in the dining room, elsewhere in the clubhouse smart casual dress is allowed.
Clubhouse Facilities: Catering requirements may be arranged by contacting the catering manager (01294) 275979. Showers are available in the changing rooms, but recommend that your party bring their own towels.

CONVENIENT HOTELS

Hospitality Inn, Annick Road, Irvine.

NO.	MEDAL YARDS	GEN. YARDS	PAR	S.I.	NO.	MEDAL YARDS	GEN. YARDS	PAR	S.I.
1	418	390	4	7	10	373	360	4	10
2	476	430	5	5	11	465	405	4/5	2
3	358	267	4	9	12	368	303	4	14
4	289	267	4	11	13	429	380	4	4
5	279	243	4	15	14	382	348	4	12
6	411	389	4	1	15	337	310	4	8
7	322	294	4	13	16	156	137	3	18
8	165	126	3	17	17	391	382	4	6
9	456	380	4	3	18	333	276	4	16
OUT	3,174	2,786	36		IN	3,234	2,901	35	
					TOTAL	6,408	5,687	71/72	
					STANDARD SCRATCH	71	72		

Bunker positions indicated.

KILBIRNIE PLACE

Kilbirnie Place Golf Club, Largs Road, Kilbirnie, Ayrshire.
Tel: (01505) 683398.

LOCATION: 1/2 mile west of Kilbirnie.
SECRETARY: J.C. Walker.
Tel: (01505) 683398.

After occupying three other sites, Kilbirnie Place Golf Club moved in 1925 to 35 acres of land where the 9 holes laid out there still form part of todays course. The club continued to grow and in June 1977 the course was extended to 18 holes on which many hazards and burns exist.

NO.	MEDAL YARDS	GEN. YARDS	PAR	S.I.	NO.	MEDAL YARDS	GEN. YARDS	PAR	S.I.
1	139	134	3	16	10	262	252	4	15
2	319	309	4	6	11	394	260	4	3
3	468	448	4	1	12	317	297	4	8
4	321	278	4	4	13	484	484	5	2
5	161	156	3	18	14	196	181	3	9
6	335	275	4	11	15	268	253	4	14
7	367	357	4	7	16	316	304	4	12
8	207	205	3	10	17	514	500	5	5
9	309	289	4	13	18	144	134	3	17
OUT	2,626	2,451	33		IN	2,895	2,665	36	
					TOTAL	5,521	5,116	69	
					STANDARD SCRATCH	66	65		

COURSE INFORMATION

Par 69; SSS 66; Length 5,521 Yards.
Visitors: Welcome; except on weekends unless by prior arrangement.
Avoid: Weekends.
Ladies: Welcome; except after 4pm on Saturdays; Ladies competitions on Sundays.
Green Fees: Monday – Friday £10; Sunday £17.50.
Clubhouse Hours: 10am – 11pm (summer season).
Clubhouse Dress: Smart/Casual.
Clubhouse Facilities: Catering available.
Open Competitions: Gents Open – June; Ladies Open – July; Mixed Open – August.

CONVENIENT HOTEL

The Largs Hotel.

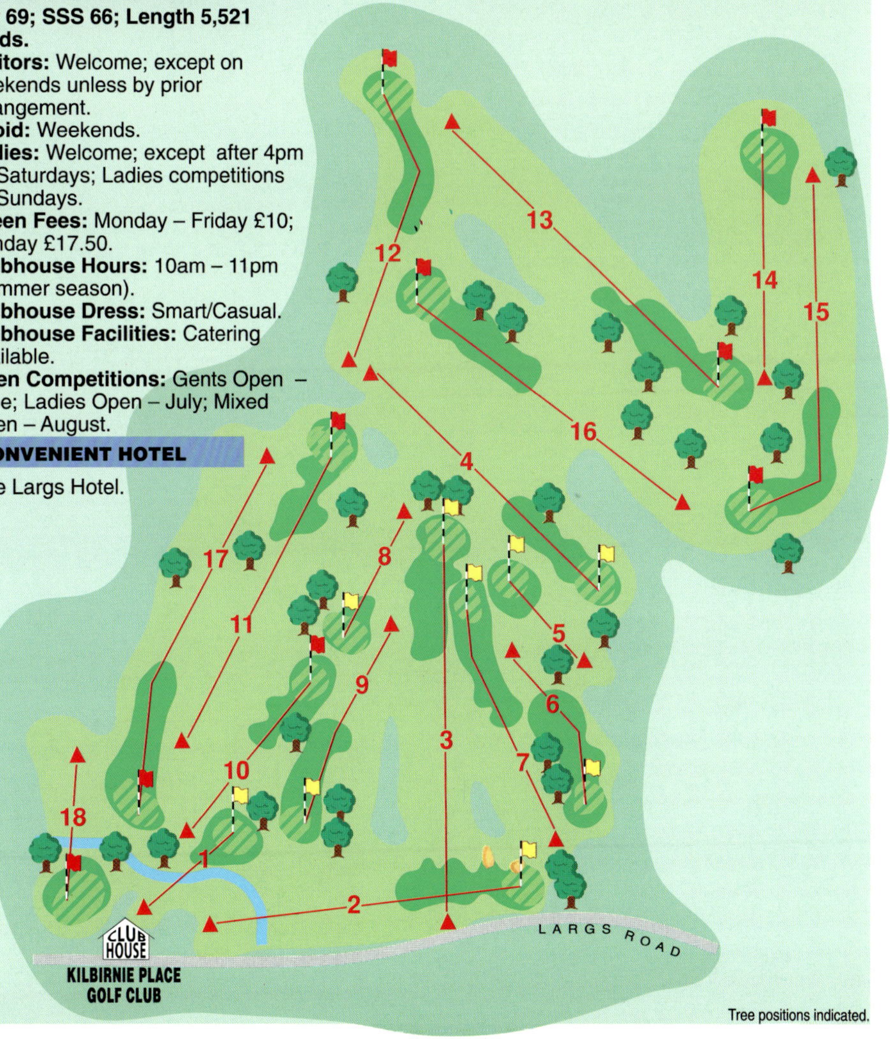

Tree positions indicated.

Kilmarnock Barassie Golf Club, 29 Hillhouse Road, Barassie, Troon. Tel: (01292) 311077.

Location: Opposite Barassie railway station.
Secretary: R L Bryce. Tel: (01292)313920.
Professional: William R Lockie. Tel: (01292) 313920.
Architect: Theodore Moone.

Links course of championship qualifying standard. Challenging even from the forward tees, burn is a feature as well as small tricky greens.

COURSE INFORMATION

Par 71; SSS 71; Length 6,473 Yards, 6,177 Metres.
Opening Hours: 8am – 11pm (summer) 8am – 6pm (winter).
Visitors: Welcome to play on Monday, Tuesday, Thursday and Friday afternoon. Prior arrangement necessary.
Avoid: No visitors allowed on Wednesday, Saturday & Sunday unless introduced by a member.
Green Fees: April 1 – Sept 30 – Men £40; Ladies £31; Juveniles £23. Friday afternoons – Men £30; Ladies £23; Juveniles £17.50. October – March – Men £28.50; Ladies £23; Juveniles £17. Friday Afternoons – Men £21.50; Ladies £17; Juveniles £13.
Juveniles: Welcome.
Clubhouse Hours: 8am – 11pm (summer); 8am – 6pm (winter).
Clubhouse Dress: Jacket & Tie in Gents Lounge and Dining Rooms.
Clubhouse Facilities: Catering available from 10am – 8pm.

CONVENIENT HOTELS

South Beach Hotel, Troon.
Ardneil Hotel, Troon.
Hospitality Inn.

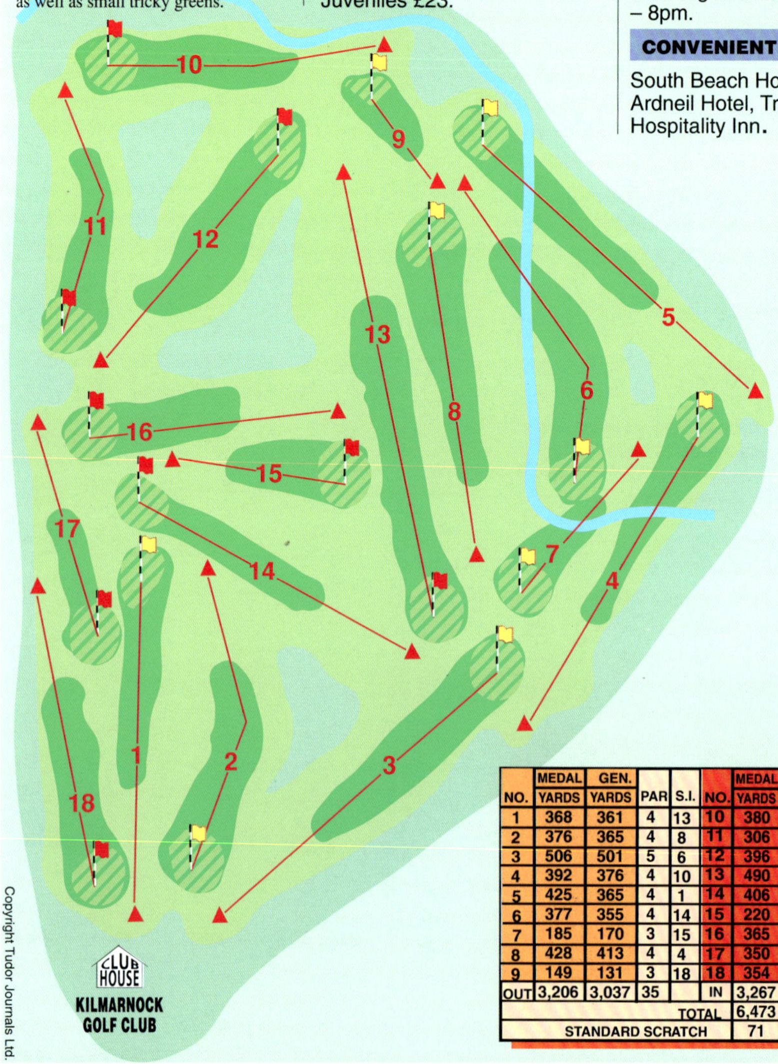

NO.	MEDAL YARDS	GEN. YARDS	PAR	S.I.	NO.	MEDAL YARDS	GEN. YARDS	PAR	S.I.
1	368	361	4	13	10	380	359	4	3
2	376	365	4	8	11	306	296	4	16
3	506	501	5	6	12	396	385	4	7
4	392	376	4	10	13	490	475	5	9
5	425	365	4	1	14	406	401	4	2
6	377	355	4	14	15	220	197	3	11
7	185	170	3	15	16	365	354	4	17
8	428	413	4	4	17	350	338	4	5
9	149	131	3	18	18	354	335	4	12
OUT	3,206	3,037	35		IN	3,267	3,140	36	
					TOTAL	6,473	6,177	71	
		STANDARD SCRATCH				71	69		

Lamlash Golf Club, Lamlash, Isle of Arran, Strathclyde.
Tel: (0770)600 296.

LOCATION: 31/2 miles south from Brodick pier on A 841.
SECRETARY: J. Henderson.

Undulating heathland course, testing par of 64. Suitable for all range of skills (beginner to low handicap). Lamlash was founded in 1889 and is the oldest course in Arran.

COURSE INFORMATION

Par 64; SSS 63; Length 4,611 Yards.
Opening hours: Daylight.
Visitors: Welcome.
Ladies: Welcome. Ladies Day Wednesday.
Green Fees: Monday – Friday £9; Saturday/Sunday £11 per day (subject to change).
Juveniles: Welcome July and August 11am – 5pm.
Clubhouse hours: 11am – 2.30pm; 8pm – 12 midnight.
Clubhouse Dress: Casual.
Clubhouse Facilities: Catering available in tearoom adjacent to 1st tee.
Open competitions: T.Graham Open 18 holes July 2; Lamlash Open 36 holes August 6/7.

CONVENIENT HOTELS

Glenisle Hotel (licensed).
Marine House Hotel (unlicensed).

NO.	MEDAL YARDS	GEN. YARDS	PAR	S.I.	NO.	MEDAL YARDS	GEN. YARDS	PAR	S.I.
1	344	330	4	5	10	276	215	4/3	4
2	189	176	3	8	11	270	225	4/3	9
3	389	370	4	1	12	231	215	3	13
4	169	112	3	14	13	191	180	3	17
5	207	170	3	16	14	213	207	3	15
6	325	311	4	3	15	269	233	4/3	2
7	294	198	4/3	6	16	102	97	3	18
8	266	210	4/3	12	17	226	181	3	11
9	354	270	4	10	18	296	290	4	7
OUT	2,537	2,147	33/31		IN	2,074	1,843	31/28	
					TOTAL	4,611	3,990	64/59	
					STANDARD SCRATCH	63			

Bunker and tree positions indicated.

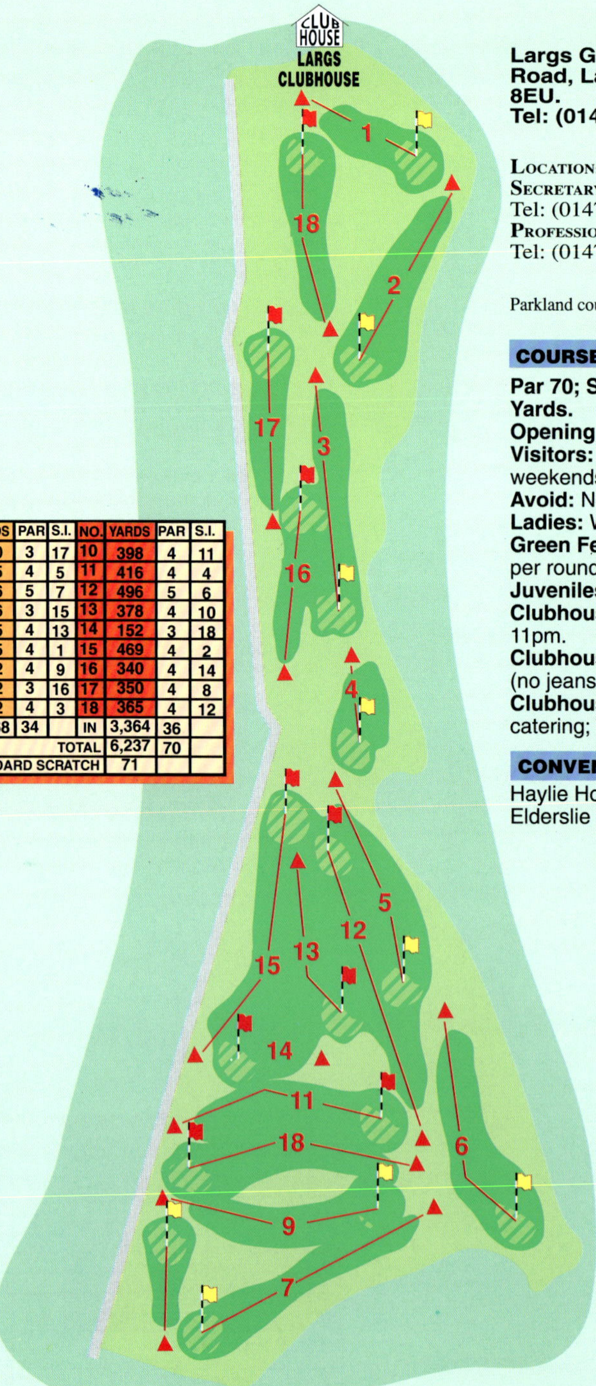

NO.	YARDS	PAR	S.I.	NO.	YARDS	PAR	S.I.
1	150	3	17	10	398	4	11
2	405	4	5	11	416	4	4
3	476	5	7	12	496	5	6
4	206	3	15	13	378	4	10
5	305	4	13	14	152	3	18
6	365	4	1	15	469	4	2
7	412	4	9	16	340	4	14
8	162	3	16	17	350	4	8
9	392	4	3	18	365	4	12
OUT	2,868	34		IN	3,364	36	
				TOTAL	6,237	70	
STANDARD SCRATCH					71		

Largs Golf Club, Irvine Road, Largs, Ayrshire. KA30 8EU.
Tel: (01475) 674681.

LOCATION: 1 mile south of Largs.
SECRETARY: B. Godfrey.
Tel: (01475) 673594.
PROFESSIONAL: R. Collinsom.
Tel: (01475) 686192.

Parkland course with scenic views.

COURSE INFORMATION

Par 70; SSS 71; Length 6,237 Yards.
Opening Hours: 8am – 11pm.
Visitors: Welcome; except at weekends.
Avoid: No weekend parties.
Ladies: Welcome.
Green Fees: £26 per day; £20 per round; Sat/Sun £26.
Juveniles: Welcome.
Clubhouse hours: 11am – 11pm.
Clubhouse Dress: Casual/smart (no jeans or trainers)
Clubhouse Facilities: Full catering; Tel (01475) 687390.

CONVENIENT HOTELS

Haylie Hotel; South Bay Hotel; Elderslie Hotel; Brisbane Hotel.

LOUDOUN GOWF

AYRSHIRE

Loudoun Gowf Golf Club,
Galston, Ayrshire,
Strathclyde.
Tel: (01563) 820551.

LOCATION: 5 miles east of Kilmarnock.
SECRETARY: T.R. Richmond.
Tel: (01563)8~~21933~~.
821993

Fairly flat parkland course with many mature trees. Takes its name from the adjacent Loudoun Castle and is constructed on what according to the old maps was "The Gowf Fields of Loudoun". Not a long course but fairly testing.

COURSE INFORMATION

Par 67; SSS 68; Length 5,844 Yards.
Opening Hours: Sunrise – Sunset.
Visitors: Welcome; weekdays only.
Avoid: First Wednesday of each month, weekends and public holidays.
Ladies: Welcome.
Green Fees: Day ticket £28; Round £16.
Juveniles: Welcome, if accompanied by an adult.
Clubhouse Hours: Noon – dusk.
Clubhouse Dress: Smart / Casual – No jeans, tracksuits or trainers.
Clubhouse Facilities: Full catering available.
Open Competitions: Loudoun Open – June; Seniors Open – August; Mixed Open – August.

CONVENIENT HOTELS

Howard Park, Kilmarnock; Loudoun Mains, Newmilns, (Chalets and caravans).

NO.	MEDAL YARDS	GEN. YARDS	PAR	S.I.	NO.	MEDAL YARDS	GEN. YARDS	PAR	S.I.
1	424	412	4	3	10	221	209	3	14
2	347	335	4	11	11	159	149	3	16
3	335	323	4	9	12	300	288	4	8
4	405	384	4	5	13	380	368	4	2
5	101	92	3	18	14	425	415	4	6
6	396	384	4	7	15	346	334	4	10
7	420	377	4	1	16	240	228	3	12
8	386	374	4	13	17	157	145	3	17
9	346	338	4	15	18	456	452	4	4
OUT	3,160	3,019	35		IN	2,684	2,588	32	
					TOTAL	5,844	5,607	67	
					STANDARD SCRATCH	68	67		

Bunker and tree positions indicated.

MOORPARK

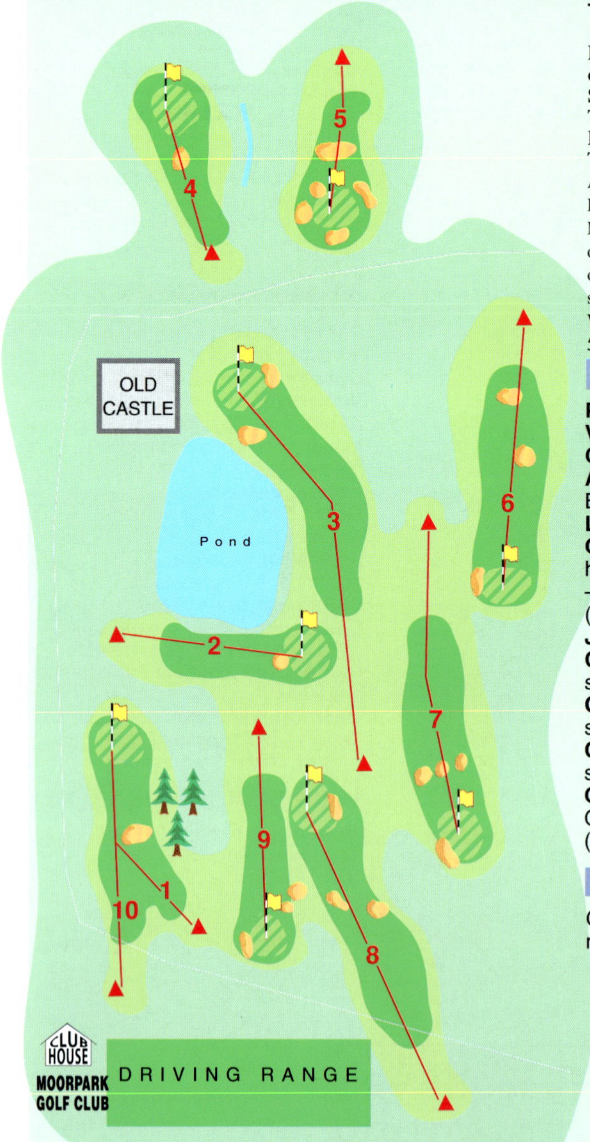

Moorpark Golf Club,
Auchenharvie Golf Complex,
Moorpark Road West,
Stevenston, Ayrshire. KA20 3HU.
Tel: (01294) 603103.

LOCATION: 30 miles west of Glasgow on A736.
SECRETARY: Iain Inglis.
Tel: (01294) 558288.
PROFESSIONAL: Bob Rodgers.
Tel: (01294) 603103.
Auchenharvie Golf Course : 9 holes, 18 tees. Driving Range. Can be quite soft from November to March. Tight small greens, shots off target frequently find the water hazard or out of bounds. Improvement work has temporarily shortened the course affecting holes 4, 5 and 6. When work is complete course will measure 5,300 yards approx. Par 67 or 68.

COURSE INFORMATION

Par 66; SSS 64; Length 4,912 Yds.
Visitors: Welcome.
Opening Hours: 8am – Dusk.
Avoid: Sat & Sun before 9am. Bookings preferred at peak times.
Ladies: Welcome.
Green Fees: Weekdays – £2.50 (9 holes), £5.00 (18 holes); Weekends – £4.30 (9 holes), £8.60 (18 holes). (1994 prices).
Juveniles: Welcome.
Clubhouse Hours: Varies on season.
Clubhouse Dress: Casual (no spikes).
Clubhouse Facilities: Hot meals, snacks, sandwiches.
Open Competitions: Moorpark G.C. Open (June); Bob Rodgers (Am – Am) Team Event (September)

CONVENIENT HOTELS

Graystones Hotel, Stevenston, 1/4 mile away (01294) 464791.

NO.	YARDS	PAR	S.I.	NO.	YARDS	PAR	S.I.
1	306	4	5	10	312	4	8
2	153	3	13	11	151	3	16
3	400	4	1	12	378	4	2
4	158	3	11	13	179	3	14
5	315	4	9	14	314	4	12
6	259	4	17	15	260	4	18
7	365	4	3	16	335	4	4
8	270	4	15	17	309	4	6
9	230	3	7	18	232	3	10
OUT	2,456	33		IN	2,470	33	
				TOTAL	4,926	66	
				STANDARD SCRATCH	64		

Bunker and tree positions indicated.

NEW CUMNOCK

AYRSHIRE

New Cumnock Golf Club,
New Cumnock,
Ayrshire, Strathclyde.
Tel: (01290) 338848.

Location: Cumnock Road.
Secretary: D.Scott.

Parkland course with out of bounds on seven holes. There are two ditches which dissect the course and also come into play at six of the holes. Although there are no bunkers on the course, there are other hazards to contend with.

COURSE INFORMATION

Par 68; SSS 65; Length 5,176 Yards.
Opening Hours: Sunrise – Sunset.
Visitors: Welcome; except Sunday before 4pm.
Avoid: Sundays before 4pm.
Laadies: Welcome.
Green Fees: £8 any time.
Juveniles: Welcome.
Clubhouse Hours: 9.30am – 4.30pm.

Clubhouse Dress: Casual.
Clubhouse Facilities: Teas, coffees, soup and filled rolls available between 9.30am & 4.30pm.

CONVENIENT HOTEL

Lochside House Hotel (next to course).

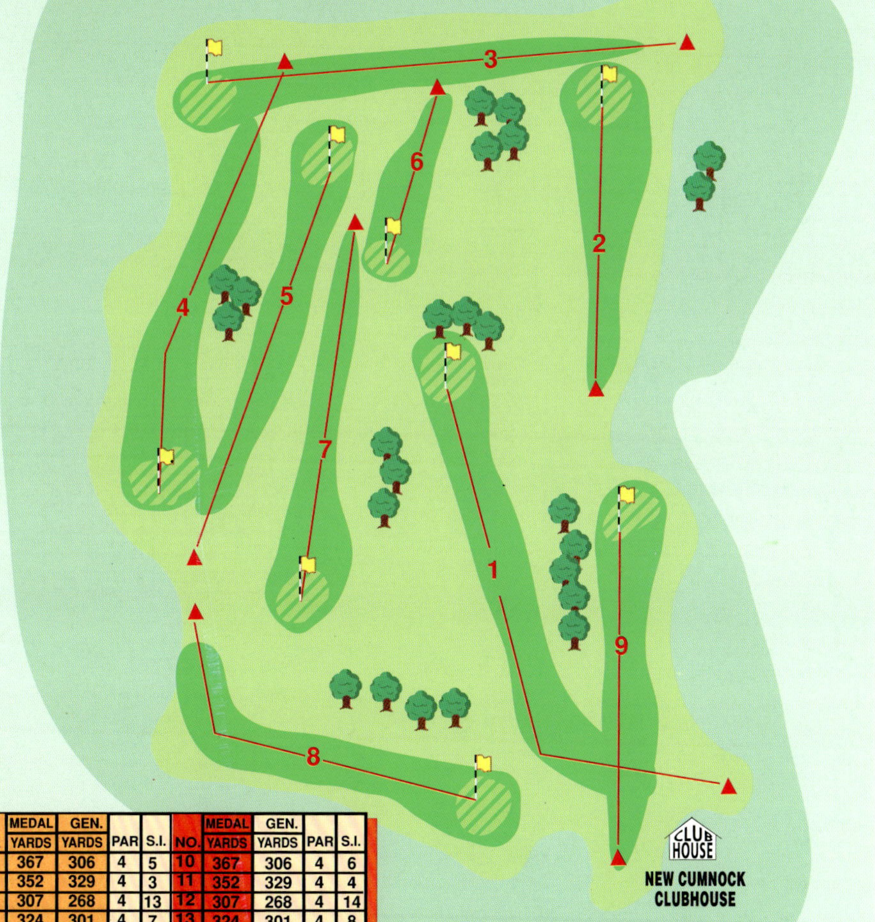

NO.	MEDAL YARDS	GEN. YARDS	PAR	S.I.	NO.	MEDAL YARDS	GEN. YARDS	PAR	S.I.
1	367	306	4	5	10	367	306	4	6
2	352	329	4	3	11	352	329	4	4
3	307	268	4	13	12	307	268	4	14
4	324	301	4	7	13	324	301	4	8
5	373	373	4	1	14	373	373	4	2
6	182	175	3	15	15	182	175	3	16
7	280	260	4	9	16	280	260	4	10
8	252	226	4	11	17	252	226	4	12
9	151	142	3	17	18	151	142	3	18
OUT	2,588	2,386	34		IN	2,588	2,386	34	
					TOTAL	5,176	4,772	68	
					STANDARD SCRATCH	65	63		

Tree positions indicated.

SHISKINE

AYRSHIRE

Shiskine Golf and Tennis Club, Shore Road, Blackwaterfoot, Isle of Arran. KA27 8EZ.
Tel: (0177086) 226.

LOCATION: Twelve miles west of the ferry terminal in Brodick.
SECRETARY: Mrs F Crawford. Braeriach, Blackwaterfoot, Isle of Arran.
ARCHITECT: James Braid and Willie Park have both been involved in the planning of the course.

Unique 12 hole links course on the south west coast of the island of Arran. The only par 5 hole on the island: wonderful views of the Mull of Kintyre.

COURSE INFORMATION

Par 42; SSS 41; Length 2,990 Yards.
Opening Hours: All day.
Avoid: No restriction times.
Visitors: Welcome.
Green Fees: £10 per round, £12 per day.
Ladies: Welcome.
Juveniles: Permitted.
Clubhouse Hours: 9.00am-9.30pm (summer).
Clubhouse Dress: Casual.
Clubhouse Facilities: Teas and Lunches (no licence).

CONVENIENT HOTEL

Kinloch Hotel, Blackwaterfoot.

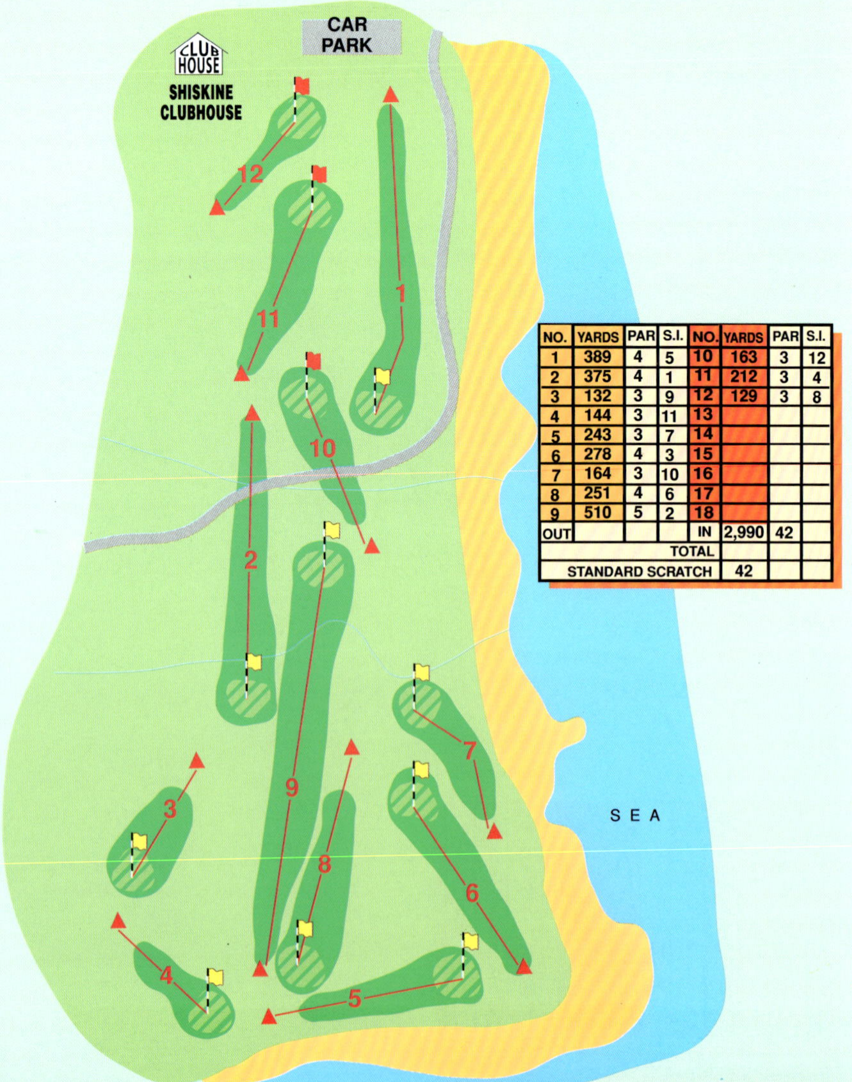

NO.	YARDS	PAR	S.I.	NO.	YARDS	PAR	S.I.
1	389	4	5	10	163	3	12
2	375	4	1	11	212	3	4
3	132	3	9	12	129	3	8
4	144	3	11	13			
5	243	3	7	14			
6	278	4	3	15			
7	164	3	10	16			
8	251	4	6	17			
9	510	5	2	18			
OUT				IN	2,990	42	
				TOTAL			
STANDARD SCRATCH					42		

Prestwick St. Cuthbert Golf Club,
East Road, Prestwick,
Ayrshire, KA9 2SX.
Tel: (01292) 477101.

Location: 1/2 mile east of Prestwick.
Secretary: J.C. Rutherford.
Tel: (01292) 477101.

Prestwick is a flat, semi-parkland course with some trees surrounding the 18 holes.

COURSE INFORMATION

Par 71; SSS 71; Length 6,470 Yards.
Visitors: Welcome; except at weekends and Bank Holidays.
Avoid: Weekends and Bank Holidays and Wednesdays if possible.
Ladies: Welcome; except after 6pm on Tuesdays and Thursdays.
Green Fees: £24 per day; £18 per round.
Juveniles: Welcome, except after 6pm on Tuesdays and Thursdays.
Clubhouse Hours: 7am – 11.30pm.
Clubhouse Dress: Neat – no jeans, track suits, training shoes or collarless shirts allowed.
Clubhouse Facilities: Full catering facilities available. Except Thursday.
Open Competitions: Rankin Smith (Ladies) May; Prestwick Boys Open July; Prestwick Open Foursomes August

CONVENIENT HOTELS

The Parkstone Hotel;
St. Nicholas Hotel.

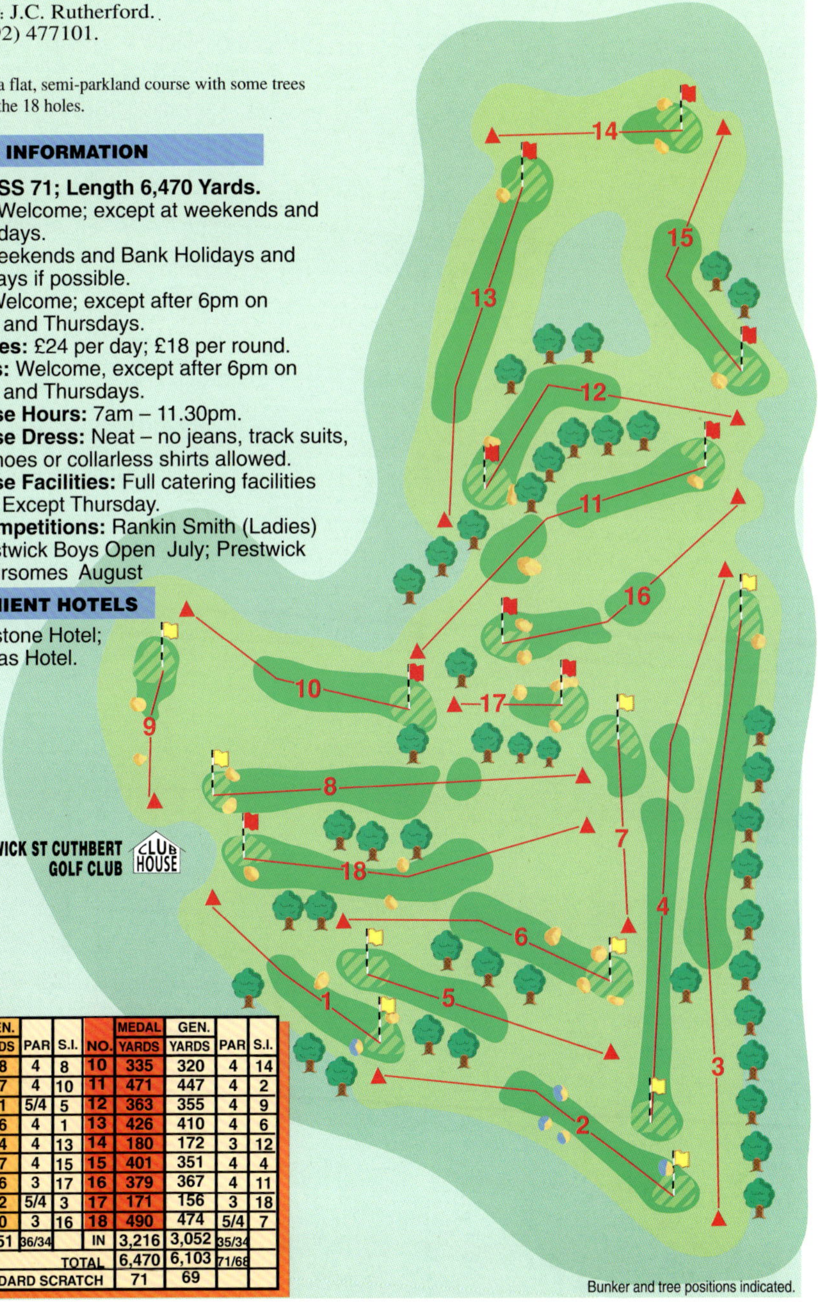

NO.	MEDAL YARDS	GEN. YARDS	PAR	S.I.	NO.	MEDAL YARDS	GEN. YARDS	PAR	S.I.
1	378	368	4	8	10	335	320	4	14
2	392	377	4	10	11	471	447	4	2
3	488	471	5/4	5	12	363	355	4	9
4	452	436	4	1	13	426	410	4	6
5	344	334	4	13	14	180	172	3	12
6	337	317	4	15	15	401	351	4	4
7	176	166	3	17	16	379	367	4	11
8	507	442	5/4	3	17	171	156	3	18
9	180	140	3	16	18	490	474	5/4	7
OUT	3,254	3,051	36/34		IN	3,216	3,052	35/34	
					TOTAL	6,470	6,103	71/68	
					STANDARD SCRATCH	71	69		

PRESTWICK ST NICHOLAS

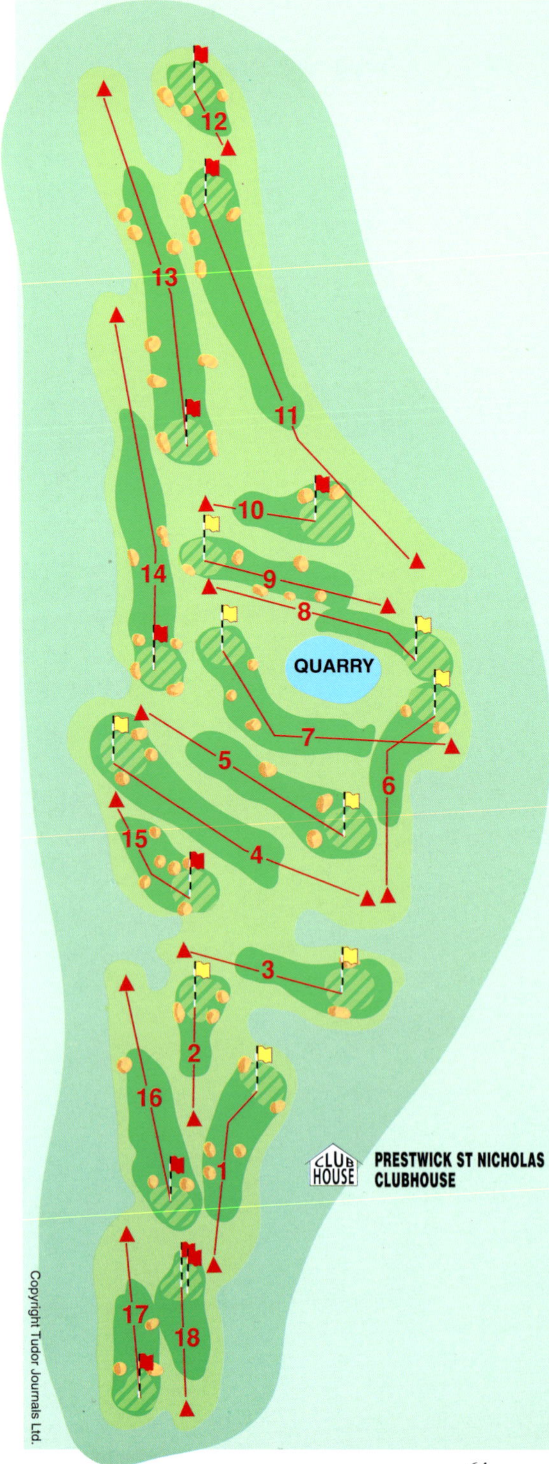

Prestwick St Nicholas Golf Club,
Grangemuir Road, Prestwick.
KA9 1SN.
Tel: (01292) 477608.

LOCATION: Prestwick.
SECRETARY: J.R. Leishman.
PROFESSIONAL: Stewart Smith.
ARCHITECT: Charles Hunter.

COURSE INFORMATION

Par 69; SSS 69; Length 5,952 Yards.
Opening hours: 9.30am (mornings), 2.30pm (afternoons).
Visitors: Welcome, weekdays only.
Avoid: Weekends and bank holidays.
Ladies: Welcome.
Green Fees: £35 per day & £20 per round.
Clubhouse hours: 9am – 10pm.
Clubhouse Dress: Neat/casual – jacket, collar and tie (no jeans allowed).
Clubhouse Facilities: Full catering facilities available.

NO.	YARDS	PAR	S.I.	NO.	YARDS	PAR	S.I.
1	342	4	7	10	165	3	15
2	172	3	17	11	498	5	2
3	281	4	13	12	139	3	18
4	420	4	3	13	456	4	8
5	406	4	9	14	412	4	6
6	326	4	11	15	276	4	10
7	454	4	1	16	379	4	4
8	360	4	5	17	301	4	16
9	338	4	12	18	227	3	14
OUT	3,099	35		IN	2,853	34	
				TOTAL	5,952	69	
				STANDARD SCRATCH	69		

Bunker positions indicated.

"If you love golf you'll love Ayrshire"

GARTFERRY HOTEL

44 Racecourse Road, Ayr KA7 2UT.

And you'll certainly love our hotel!

Our dedicated policy is to offer good value for money; with B&B from £20p.p. with evening meals from £5.95. All our rooms are ensuite with satellite TV and D/D telephones. Parties up to 20 are fully catered for both on and off the course.

For further details please contact:

Donnie MacIntyre, the proprietor Tel: (01292) 262768.

Braeval Hotel

Stay and Play "Nairn's TWO Championship Courses" and another 20 within easy reach. Golfers and parties will find a great welcome in our cosy well appointed hotel (all bedrooms en suite).

Golf Packages available with tee times and green fees arranged in advance...just arrive and play.

Crescent Road, Nairn, Scotland. IV 12 4NB.
Telephone/Fax: (01667) 452341.

Kings Arms Hotel

Our 17th century coaching inn offers an ideal base from which to golf in the Scottish Borders.

Well appointed rooms and extensive menus to suit all tastes.

"Freedom of the Fairways" golf breaks are offered from April to October (not Sat/Sun).

High Street, Melrose

For details, prices and information on The Borders' Tourist Board Golf Passes *please contact:*

Mr M. Dalgetty
Tel: (01896) 822143. Fax: (01896) 823812.

THE CARRICK LODGE HOTEL

46 Carrick Rd, Ayr, Ayrshire, Scotland, KA7 2RE. Tel: (01292) 262846. Fax: (01292) 611101.

The Carrick Lodge Hotel has eight well appointed bedrooms, all en suite and with Sky T.V.

Excellent cuisine served using local produce.

A warm atmosphere is created by our attentive staff and friendly locals

Activity breaks incorporating Golf, Sea River and Loch Fishing and Pheasant or Clay Pigeon Shooting are available. Please ask for details.

A warm welcoming atmosphere is a hallmark of the ***'Ramleh'.***

Ramleh Hotel & Fingal's Restaurant

All bedrooms have colour TV and tea/coffee makers. Fingals Restaurant is the 'place to eat' in Nairn. Local and fresh produce, traditional home style cooking, elegant and intimate surroundings - the perfect place for your golfing holiday.

Ramleh Hotel & Fingal's Restaurant, 2 Academy Street, Nairn, N12 4RJ. Telephone: (01667) 53551.
Resident Proprietors: George & Carol Woodhouse.

LOMOND HILLS HOTEL

FREUCHIE, FIFE.

FOR RESERVATIONS:
Tel: 01337-857329/857498/858180.

Scottish Tourist Board

'IN THE HEART OF FIFE'

Close to Glenrothes and many golf courses, including St. Andrews, 25 bedrooms, all with private facilities, radio, TV, direct dial telephone, centrally heated. Intimate candlelit restaurant. Freshly cooked table d'hote and a la carte including many flambe dishes. Indoor heated swimming pool and leisure centre for guests. *2 & 3 day golf breaks, including dinner.* Large car park, and function suite for lunch & tea bookings — up to 150 people.

ROYAL TROON (Old Course)

NO.	YARDS	PAR	S.I.	NO.	YARDS	PAR	S.I.
1	364	4	16	10	438	4	10
2	391	4	7	11	481	4	1
3	379	4	11	12	431	4	6
4	557	5	4	13	465	4	12
5	210	3	14	14	179	3	15
6	577	5	2	15	457	4	3
7	402	4	9	16	542	5	8
8	126	3	18	17	223	3	13
9	423	4	5	18	452	4	17
OUT	3,429	36		IN	3,668	35	
				TOTAL	7,097	71	
STANDARD SCRATCH					74		

Royal Troon Golf Club, Troon, Ayrshire. KA10 6EP.
Tel: (01292) 311555.

LOCATION: Troon, Ayrshire.
SECRETARY: J.D. Montgomerie.
PROFESSIONAL: Brian Anderson.
Tel: (01292) 313204.

Troon Golf Links is located on the west coast shore of Scotland with magnificent views of the Clyde Estuary. A taxing course with standard scratch of 74 played by low handicappers and beginners alike. Asuperb challenge from this top Scottish course.

COURSE INFORMATION

Par 71; SSS 74; Length 7,097 Yards.
Opening hours: 9am – 7pm.
Visitors: Welcome Monday, Tuesday and Thursday from 9.30am – 11am, 2.30pm – 4pm. A certificate of handicap with a maximum of 20 must be presented along with a letter of introduction from home club are conditional to play.
Avoid: No play is permitted on Wednesday, Friday, Weekends, public holidays and club competition days.
Ladies: Not permitted.
Green Fees: £85 per day – includes one round on both Old and Portland Course.
Clubhouse hours: 9am – 7pm.
Clubhouse Dress: Neat dress essential in clubhouse and on course (no jeans, trainers etc. are permitted). Ladies required to wear dresses or skirts in Dining Room.
Clubhouse Facilities: Catering included in green fees – morning coffee and choice of high tea or buffet lunch. Please advise requirements one week in advance of date of play. Caddies and bag carriers are available and should be requested in advance as they are subject to availability.

CONVENIENT HOTELS

The Marine Highland Hotel; The Piersland Hotel.

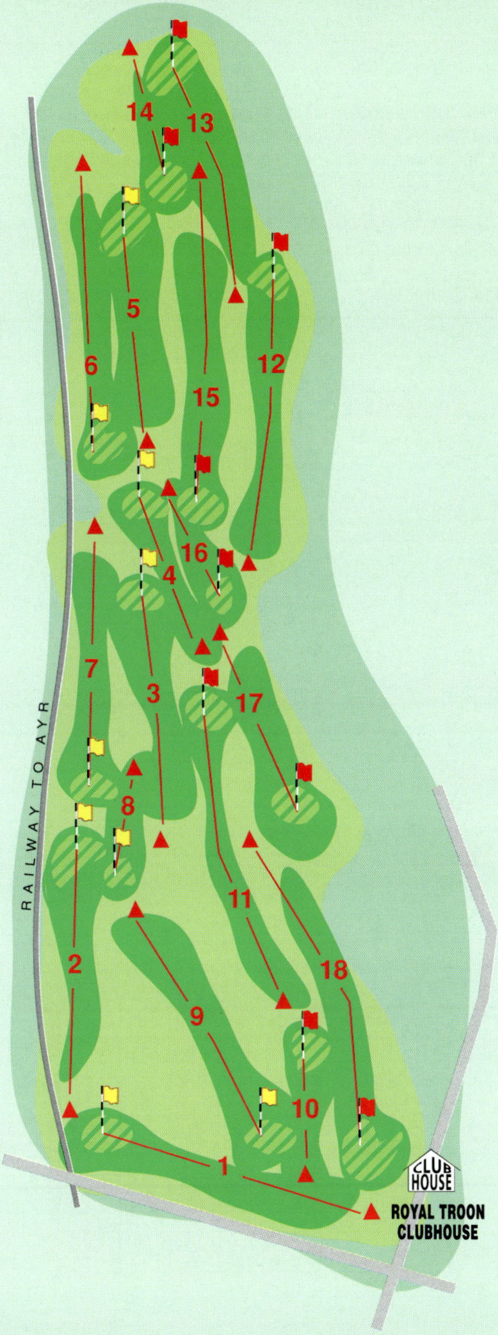

Royal Troon Golf Club, Troon, Ayrshire. KA10 6EP.
Tel: (01292) 311555.

Location: Troon, Ayrshire.
Secretary: J.D. Montgomerie.
Professional: Brian Anderson.
Tel: (01292) 313204.

Troon Golf Links is located on the west coast shore of Scotland with magnificent views of the Irish Sea. A taxing course of par 71 played by low handicappers and beginners alike.

COURSE INFORMATION

Par 71; SSS 71; Length 6,274 Yards.
Opening hours: 9am – 7pm.
Visitors: Welcome Monday, Tuesday and Thursday from 9.30am – 11am, 2.30pm – 4pm. A certificate of handicap with a maximum of 20 must be presented along with a letter of introduction from home club are conditional to play. (No visitors on weekends or after October).
Avoid: Weekends, Public holidays and club competition days.
Ladies: Welcome (not permitted on Old Course).
Green Fees: £85 per day – includes one round on both Old and Portland Course.
Clubhouse hours: 9am – 7pm.
Clubhouse Dress: Neat dress essential in clubhouse and on course (no jeans, trainers etc... are permitted). Ladies required to wear dresses or skirts.
Clubhouse Facilities: Catering included in green fees – morning coffee and choice of high tea or lunch. Please advise requirements one week in advance of date of play. Caddies and bag carriers are available and should be requested in advance as they are subject to availability.

CONVENIENT HOTELS

The Marine Highland Hotel; The Piersland Hotel.

NO.	YARDS	PAR	S.I.	NO.	YARDS	PAR	S.I.
1	462	4	9	10	154	3	16
2	427	4	5	11	494	5	6
3	352	4	13	12	485	5	2
4	194	3	7	13	353	4	12
5	349	4	15	14	214	3	10
6	409	4	1	15	498	5	4
7	368	4	11	16	155	3	18
8	147	3	17	17	311	4	8
9	420	4	3	18	497	5	14
OUT	3,128	34		IN	3,146	37	
				TOTAL	6,274	71	
STANDARD SCRATCH					71		

**Skelmorlie Golf Club,
Skelmorlie, Ayrshire.
PA17 5ES.
Tel: (01474) 520152.**

LOCATION: 30 miles west of Glasgow on A78 (via M8 / A8).
SECRETARY: Mrs Audrey Fahey. Tel: (01475) 520774.
ARCHITECT: James Braid.

18 hole, moorland (play the first five holes twice). Spectacular views over the Firth of Clyde. A friendly club that welcomes visitors.

COURSE INFORMATION

Par 64; SSS 65; Length 5,056Yards.
Visitors: Welcome.
Opening Hours: 8.30am – Dusk.
Avoid: No visitors before 4pm on Saturdays.
Ladies: Welcome.
Ladies Day: Ladies open day – second Tuesday in July.
Green Fees: Weekday round £11, weekend round £12 per round.
Juveniles: Permitted.

Clubhouse Hours: 12 noon – 11pm.
Clubhouse Dress: Smart/casual.
Clubhouse Facilities: Bar seven days per week and catering at weekends.
Open Competitions: Anaplast Open (Gents) – May. Mixed Open Foursomes – October.

CONVENIENT HOTELS

Redcliff Hotel; Heywood Hotel (both A78 approx. 2 miles).

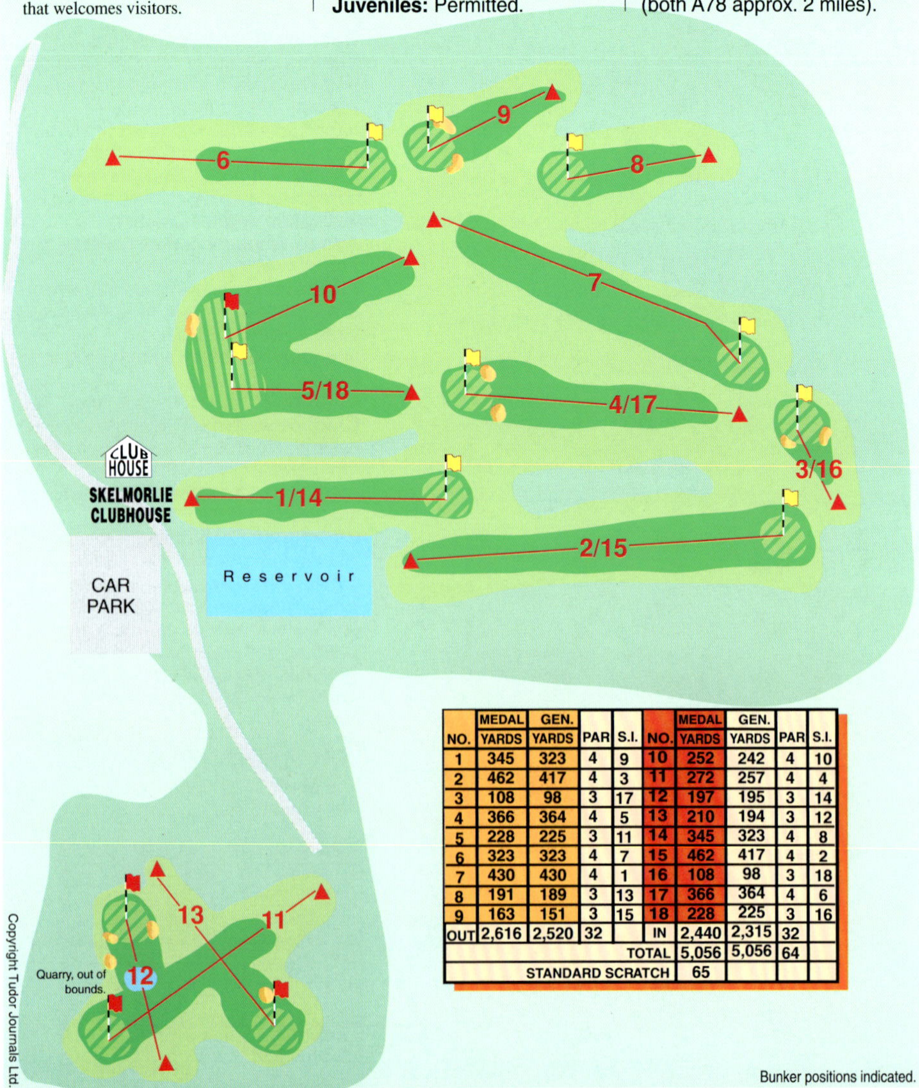

NO.	MEDAL YARDS	GEN. YARDS	PAR	S.I.	NO.	MEDAL YARDS	GEN. YARDS	PAR	S.I.
1	345	323	4	9	10	252	242	4	10
2	462	417	4	3	11	272	257	4	4
3	108	98	3	17	12	197	195	3	14
4	366	364	4	5	13	210	194	3	12
5	228	225	3	11	14	345	323	4	8
6	323	323	4	7	15	462	417	4	2
7	430	430	4	1	16	108	98	3	18
8	191	189	3	13	17	366	364	4	6
9	163	151	3	15	18	228	225	3	16
OUT	2,616	2,520	32		IN	2,440	2,315	32	
					TOTAL	5,056	5,056	64	
					STANDARD SCRATCH	65			

Bunker positions indicated.

TURNBERRY (AILSA COURSE)

AYRSHIRE

Turnberry Hotel Golf Club, Turnberry, KA26 9LT.

LOCATION: 5 miles north of Girvan on A77.
SECRETARY: Mr Tom Patterson.
PROFESSIONAL: R.S. Jamieson.
ARCHITECT: MacKenzie Ross.

Of all the great Scottish Links, the Ailsa course at the Turnberry Hotel is the most dramatic, the most spectacular and the most compellingly beautiful. Set along a rockbound coast, above the golden sweep of the sands of Turnberry Bay, the Ailsa is a fine championship course made doubly magnificent by the surrounding landscape.

COURSE INFORMATION

Par 70; SSS 72; Length 6,950 Yards.
Opening hours: First tee off time 07.30am.
Visitors: Tee off times reserved for hotel residents.
Ladies: Welcome.
Green Fees: £45 residents per round; optional round Arran course, same day.
Juveniles: Playing with adults only - if resident.
Clubhouse Hours: 7am to 10pm.
Clubhouse Dress: Informal golfing attire.
Clubhouse Facilities: Bar, carvery style restaurant – two hospitality suites for private dining.
Open competitions: 123rd British Open July 1994.

CONVENIENT HOTEL

Turnberry Hotel, Golf Courses and Spa.

NO.	MEDAL YARDS	CHAMP. YARDS	PAR	S.I.	NO.	MEDAL YARDS	CHAMP. YARDS	PAR	S.I.
1	362	350	4	9	10	430	452	4	6
2	378	428	4	13	11	157	177	3	18
3	398	462	4	5	12	391	448	4	8
4	167	167	3	17	13	379	411	4	14
5	411	441	4	3	14	400	440	4	2
6	222	222	3	15	15	168	209	3	16
7	465	528	4/5	1	16	381	409	4	10
8	427	427	4	11	17	487	500	5	4
9	413	455	4	7	18	377	431	4	12
OUT	3,238	3,480	34/35		IN	3,170	3,470	35	
					TOTAL	6,408	6,950	69/70	
					STANDARD SCRATCH	72			

Bunker positions indicated.

Father and son. Eric Thorburn.

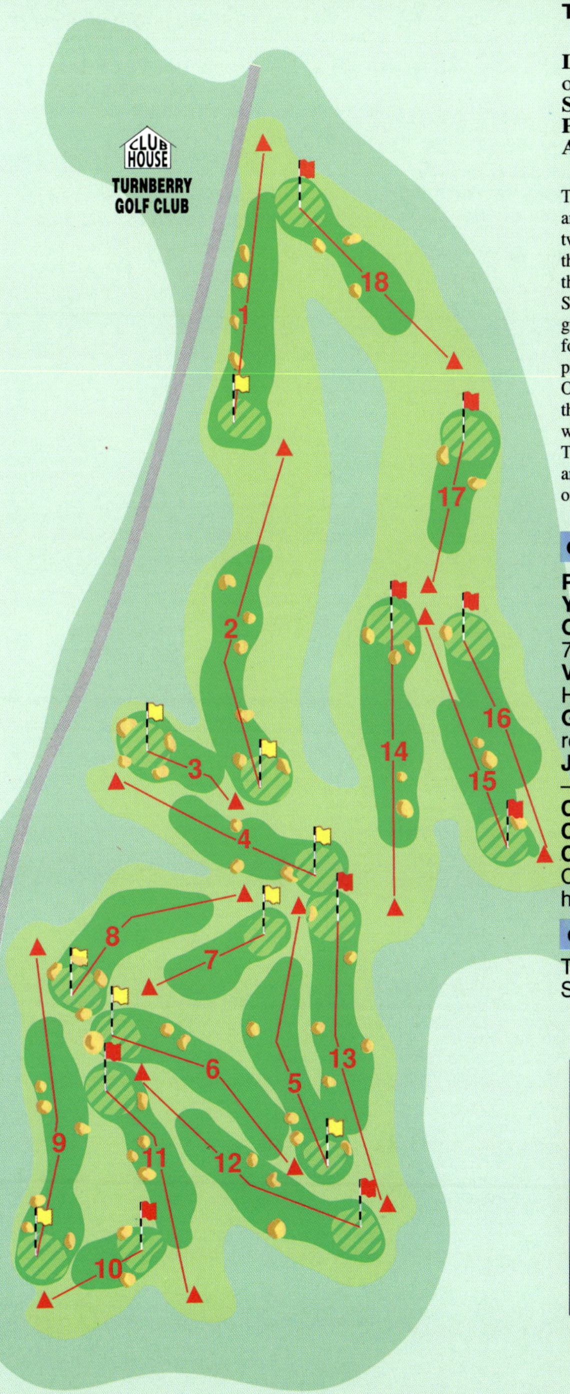

Turnberry Hotel Golf Club,
Turnberry. KA26 9LT.
Tel: (0655) 31000.

Location: 5 miles north of Girvan on A77.
Secretary: Mr Tom Patterson.
Professional: Mr R.S. Jamieson.
Architect: MacKenzie Ross.

The 16th green is one of the spots where Ailsa and Arran rub shoulders, the Arran forming a twin attraction which is often overlooked. Of the two courses, it suffered more damage in the last war, but Jimmy Alexander, Superintendent of British Transport Hotels golf courses and the man for whom the credit for the back tee on Ailsa's 9th must be given, produced the perfect compliment in his design. Occupying flatter, more sheltered land, it was the perfect foil to its distinguished neighbour when the Amateur Championship returned to Turnberry in 1983 and under new arrangement, one qualifying round was played on each course.

COURSE INFORMATION

Par 69; SSS 70; Length 6,249 Yards.
Opening hours: First Tee off time 7.30am.
Visitors: Tee off times reserved for Hotel residents. Ladies: Welcome.
Green Fees: £15 per round for residents.
Juveniles: Playing with adults only – if resident.
Clubhouse hours: 7am – 10pm.
Clubhouse Dress: Smart/Casual.
Clubhouse Facilities: Bar, Carvery style restaurant. Two hospitality suites for private dining.

CONVENIENT HOTEL

Turnberry Hotel, Golf Courses and Spa.

NO.	YARDS	PAR	S.I.	NO.	YARDS	PAR	S.I.
1	352	4	10	10	163	3	17
2	506	5	2	11	312	4	3
3	160	3	18	12	456	4	1
4	330	4	14	13	422	4	3
5	426	4	6	14	390	4	9
6	394	4	12	15	334	4	5
7	228	3	16	16	367	4	11
8	388	4	8	17	216	3	15
9	454	4	4	18	351	4	7
OUT	3,238	35		IN	3,011	34	
				TOTAL	6,249	69	
STANDARD SCRATCH					70		

Bunker positions indicated.

HOSPITALITY INN

Hospitality Inn Golf Course, 46 Annick Road, Irvine, Ayrshire, KA11 4AD.
Tel: (01294) 74272.
Fax: (01294) 77287.

LOCATION: One mile south of Irvine town centre.
MANAGER: M. Donnelly / T. Hayden Tel: (01294) 74272.

A short course with excellent quality greens. Accurate judgement of the wind is required, with the river playing a prominent part in the challenge.

COURSE INFORMATION

Par 54; Length 2,494 Yards.
Opening Hours: Sunrise – sunset.
Visitors: Welcome.
Green Fees: £3 Mon - Fri; £6 Sat & sun.
Juveniles: Welcome.
Clubhouse Hours: 8am – 12pm.
Clubhouse Dress: Smart / Casual.
Clubhouse Facilities: Full range of services provided by four star hotel.

CONVENIENT HOTELS

Hospitality Inn, on course. Many bed and breakfast houses in the area.

NO.	GEN. YARDS	PAR	S.I.	NO.	GEN. YARDS	PAR	S.I.
1	148	3	7	10	148	3	8
2	130	3	17	11	130	3	18
3	167	3	1	12	167	3	2
4	132	3	9	13	132	3	10
5	120	3	11	14	120	3	12
6	147	3	3	15	147	3	4
7	128	3	15	16	128	3	16
8	149	3	5	17	149	3	6
9	126	3	13	18	126	3	14
OUT	1,247	27		IN	1,247	27	
				TOTAL	2,494	54	
STANDARD SCRATCH							

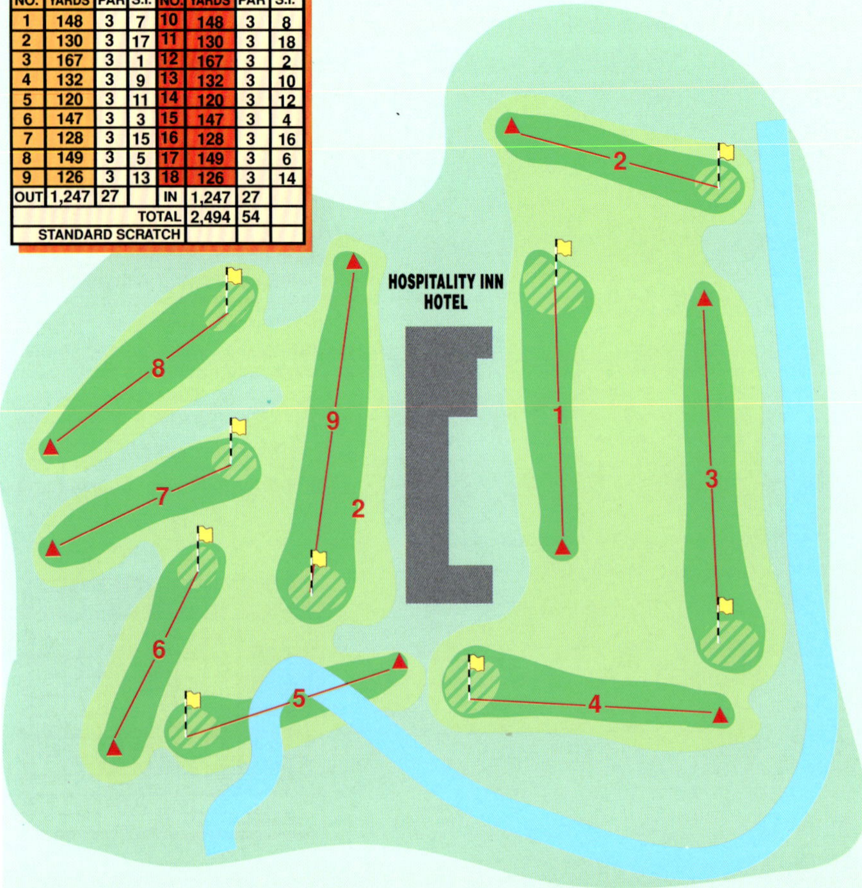

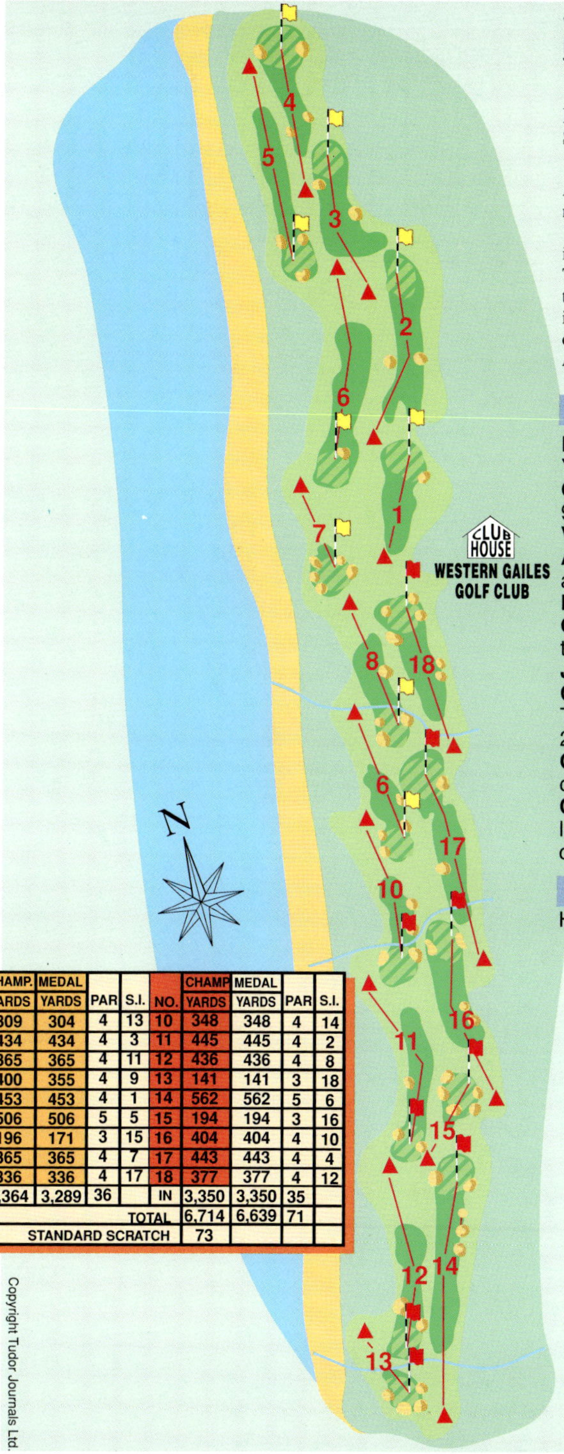

O. CHAMP. YARDS	MEDAL YARDS	PAR	S.I.	NO.	CHAMP YARDS	MEDAL YARDS	PAR	S.I.
1	309	304	4	13	10	348	348	4	14
2	434	434	4	3	11	445	445	4	2
3	365	365	4	11	12	436	436	4	8
4	400	355	4	9	13	141	141	3	18
5	453	453	4	1	14	562	562	5	6
6	506	506	5	5	15	194	194	3	16
7	196	171	3	15	16	404	404	4	10
8	365	365	4	7	17	443	443	4	4
9	336	336	4	17	18	377	377	4	12
UT	3,364	3,289	36		IN	3,350	3,350	35	
				TOTAL	6,714	6,639	71	
			STANDARD SCRATCH		73			

West Gailes Golf Club, Gailes Irvine, Ayrshire. KA11 5AE. Tel: (01294) 311649.

LOCATION: Three miles north of Troon.
SECRETARY: A.M. McBean.

A links course particularly emphasised on a marvellous stretch of holes from the 7th to the 13th. The view from the clubhouse gives an instant picture of the delights Gailes has in store. The beautiful light-coloured, fine-bladed links turf reaches out in all directions, between intruding fingers of heather and protuding sand dunes. The hills of Arran and the sharp outline of Ailsa Craig stand out from the shimmering sea.

COURSE INFORMATION

Par 71; SSS 73; Length 6,714 Yards.
Opening hours: Mar – Oct 8am – 9pm. Other months – 9am – 6.30pm.
Visitors: Welcome.
Avoid: Thursday, Saturday, Sunday and Public holidays.
Ladies: Welcome.
Green Fees: £38 per round; £50 day ticket.
Juveniles: Must be 14 or over.
Clubhouse hours: As opening hours; Tee off time for visitors 9am – 12.30; 2pm – 4pm.
Clubhouse Dress: Men; Jacket, collar and tie, Ladies; skirt.
Clubhouse Facilities: Breakfast, lunch, high tea and dinner available – contact Club Manager.

CONVENIENT HOTELS

Hospitality Inn.

Bunker positions indicated.

West Kilbride Golf Club, West Kilbride. KA23 9HT.
Tel: (01294) 823128.

LOCATION: West Kilbride.
SECRETARY: R.J. Whittingham.
Tel: (01294) 823911.
PROFESSIONAL: (01294) 823042.
ARCHITECT: Tom Morris.

Fairly flat links course on Firth of Clyde with views of Isle of Arran being the main feature.

NO.	MEDAL YARDS	GEN. YARDS	PAR	S.I.	NO.	MEDAL YARDS	GEN. YARDS	PAR	S.I.
1	335	325	4	11	10	431	369	4	2
2	346	340	4	9	11	256	256	4	18
3	482	381	5/4	7	12	174	148	3	14
4	178	164	3	13	13	419	403	4	6
5	390	380	4	1	14	316	300	4	16
6	372	347	4	5	15	406	398	4	8
7	558	483	5	15	16	357	326	4	10
8	419	386	4	3	17	442	428	4	4
9	191	170	3	17	18	380	370	4	12
OUT	3,271	2,976	36/35		IN	3,181	2,998	35	
					TOTAL	6,452	5,974	71/70	
					STANDARD SCRATCH	71	69		

COURSE INFORMATION

Par 70; SSS 71; Length 6,452 Yards.
Visitors: Week days only.
Opening hours: 8.00am – dusk.
Avoid: Saturdays and Sundays – No visitors.
Ladies: Ladies may only start between 10.30am and 12 noon & after 2.30pm on Saturdays. Also March to October,Ladies playing on weekends between 6 and 7pm only if accompanied by a gentleman member.
Green Fees: On application.
Juveniles: Welcome, but restricted.
Clubhouse Hours: Summer; Mon – Sat 7.45am – 11pm. Sun; 7.45am –10pm. Winter; 8.15am –7.30pm; Sat 10pm.
Clubhouse Dress: Casual but smart; no jeans or trainers.
Clubhouse Facilities: Morning coffee, lunches, bar meals, high teas, dinner on Saturday by prior arrangement.
Open Competitions: Open mixed foursomes 1st Sunday in August; Boys Open competition – July.

CONVENIENT HOTELS

Seamill Hydro;
Galleon Inn;
Inverclyde Hotel.

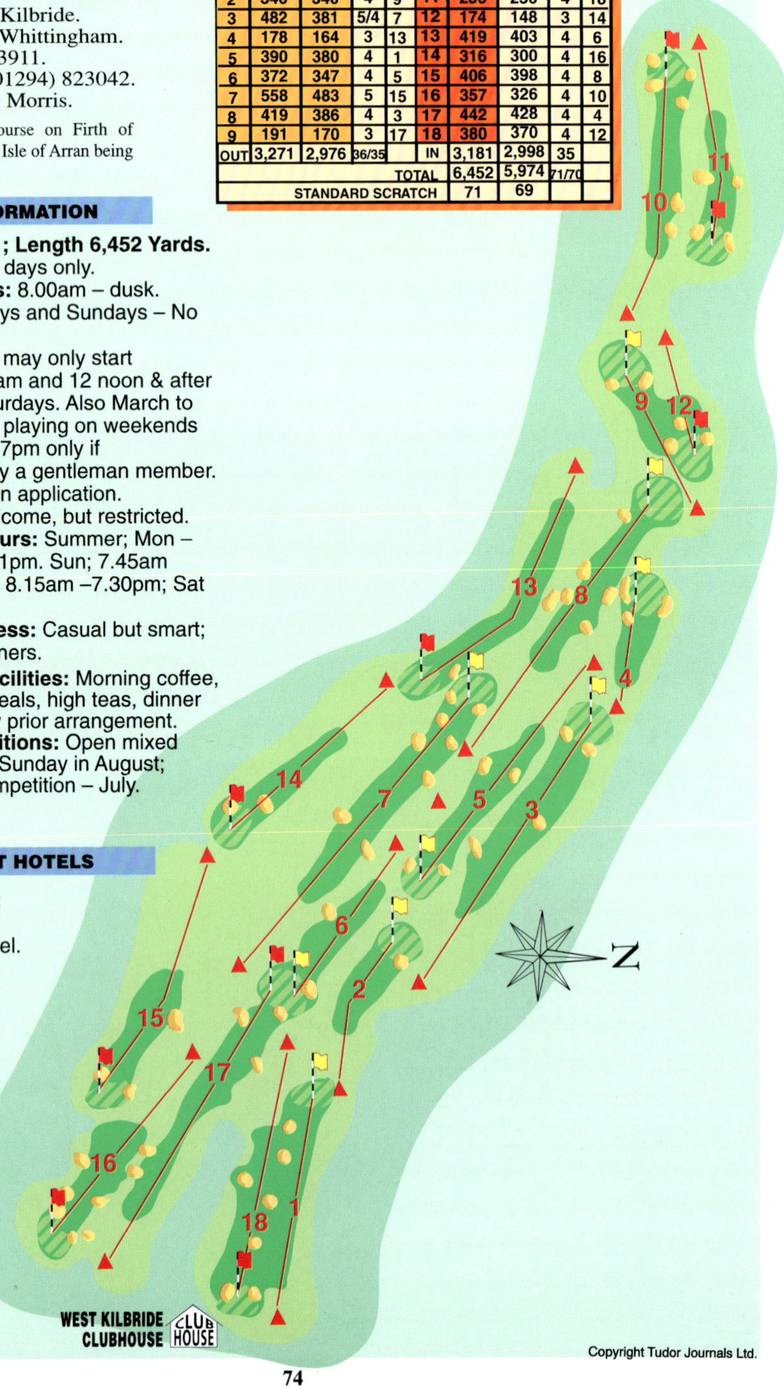

World famous St. Andrews. D. Corrance.

BORDERS

GOLF
DAYS™
SCOTLAND

Duns Golf Club, Hardens Road, Duns, Berwickshire. Tel: (01361) 882717.

LOCATION: One mile west of Duns off A6150 (signposted Longformacus).
SECRETARY: A. Campbell.
Tel: (01361) 882717.

Upland course suitable for beginners or experienced players. The course is crossed by a burn which is the main hazard. Views from the top holes south across the Tweed Valley to the Cheviot Hills.

COURSE INFORMATION

Par 68; SSS 68; Length 5,826 Yards.
Visitors: Welcome (no handicap certificate required).
Opening Hours: Daylight hours.
Avoid: Tuesdays after 3pm & weekends 8.30am – 9.30am.
Ladies: Welcome.
Green Fees: £10 per round or per day.
Juveniles: No restrictions.
Clubhouse Hours: Summer only. Mon – Thurs 7pm until 10pm; Friday – 5pm until 10pm; Saturday & Sunday 12 –2pm & 5pm – 10pm.
Clubhouse Dress: No restrictions.
Clubhouse Facilities: Limited catering – snacks in bar lounge.
Open Competitions: June and August; Others to be arranged (check with Secretary).

CONVENIENT HOTEL

Barniken House Hotel, Murray Street, Duns (Tel: (01361) 882466).

NO.	YARDS	PAR	S.I.	NO.	YARDS	PAR	S.I.
1	409	4	1	10	409	4	2
2	390	4	7	11	390	4	8
3	206	3	13	12	206	3	14
4	370	4	9	13	370	4	10
5	331	4	11	14	331	4	12
6	97	3	17	15	97	3	18
7	385	4	5	16	385	4	6
8	198	3	15	17	198	3	16
9	527	5	3	18	527	5	4
OUT	2,913	34		IN	2,913	34	
				TOTAL	5,826	68	
STANDARD SCRATCH					68		

Eyemouth Golf Club, Gunsgreen House, Eyemouth, Berwickshire. Tel: (01890) 750551.

LOCATION: Four miles north of border, off A1.
SECRETARY: M. Hope.
Tel: (01890) 759432.
PROFESSIONAL: Craig Maltman.

This is a tight, tricky seaside course on the eastern cliff tops of Eyemouth. Fast, smooth greens and panoramic views of the coast are typified by the 15th hole played from an elevated tee over a North Sea inlet to a peninsular green. It is well named; A-No-Ken (I don't know!) – which will readily come to mind on the tee.

COURSE INFORMATION

Par 66; SSS 65; Length 5,096 Yards, 4,608 Metres.
Visitors: Welcome.
Avoid: No play on June27th, August 29th. Avoid Saturday / Sunday morning and Thursday evening in the summer.
Ladies: Welcome.
Green Fees: £9 per day ticket; £3 for under 16.
Juveniles: Permitted.
Clubhouse Hours: 7am – 11pm on Tues, Wed, Fri, Sat & Sun. Lunchtimes Sat & Sun.
Clubhouse Dress: Casual.

Clubhouse Dress: Casual.

Clubhouse Facilities: No catering facilities available as yet.
Open Competitions: June, July, September.

CONVENIENT HOTELS

KIngs Hotel;
Kingsknowe Hotel;
Abbotsford.

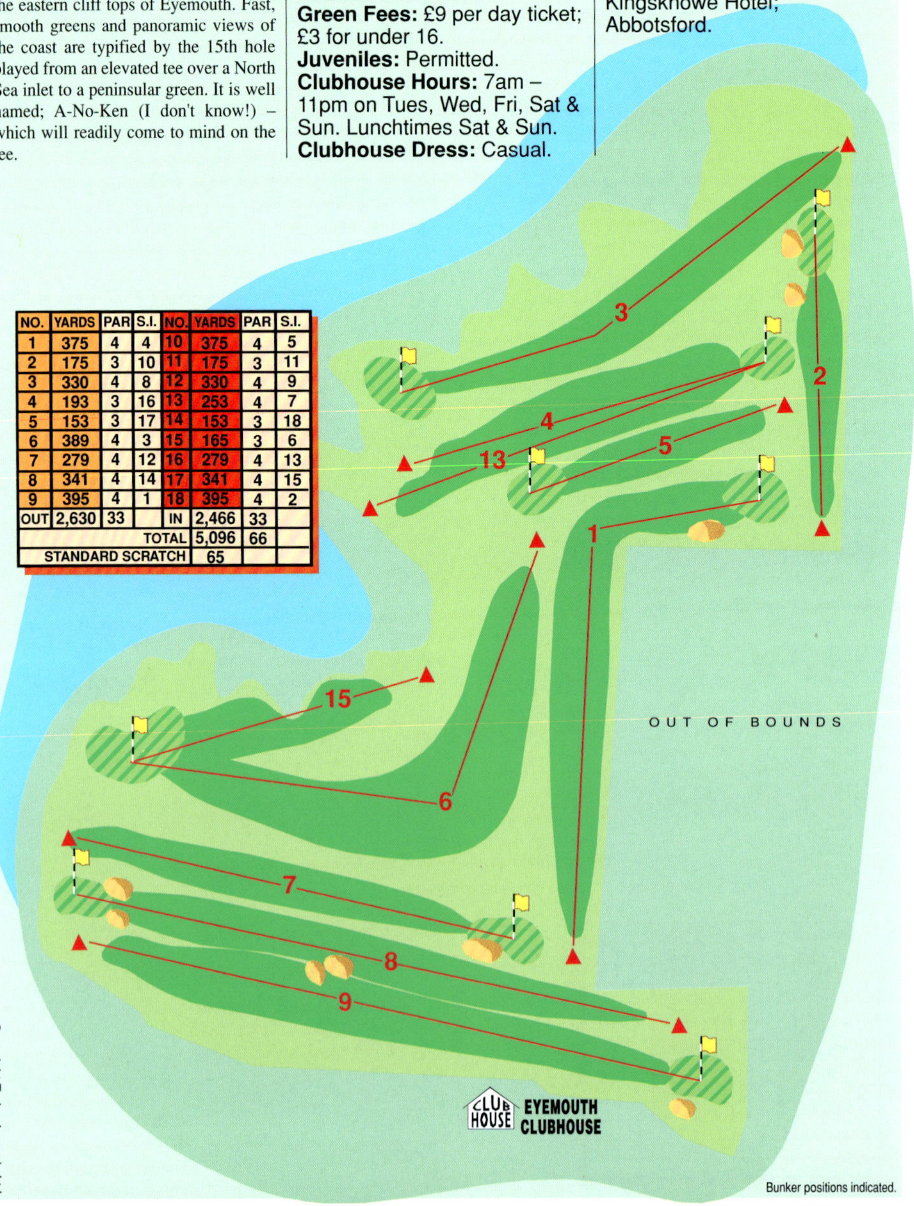

NO.	YARDS	PAR	S.I.	NO.	YARDS	PAR	S.I.
1	375	4	4	10	375	4	5
2	175	3	10	11	175	3	11
3	330	4	8	12	330	4	9
4	193	3	16	13	253	4	7
5	153	3	17	14	153	3	18
6	389	4	3	15	165	3	6
7	279	4	12	16	279	4	13
8	341	4	14	17	341	4	15
9	395	4	1	18	395	4	2
OUT	2,630	33		IN	2,466	33	
				TOTAL	5,096	66	
STANDARD SCRATCH					65		

Bunker positions indicated.

Galashiels Golf Club,
Ladhope Recreation Ground,
Galashiels.
Tel: (01896) 753724.

LOCATION: 1/4 mile north east of Galasheils on A7 to Edinburgh.
SECRETARY: R. Gass.
Tel: (01896) 55307.
ARHITECT: James Braid.

An 18 hole course overlooking Galasheils with some very panoramic views of surrounding hills. The course itself is on two levels, the first eight holes and then two holes up to the Reach, the area that all our visitors appreciate. Five holes with wonderful views finally wind down to the last three leading back to the clubhouse.

COURSE INFORMATION

Par 67; SSS 66; Length 5,185 Yards.
Opening Hours: 8am – sunset.
Visitors: Welcome; no large parties on Saturdays.
Avoid: Saturday competition days.
Ladies: Welcome; Ladies day Tuesday evening.
Green Fees: Monday – Friday £11 per round, £15 per day; Saturday/Sunday £13 per round, £18 per day.
Juveniles: Welcome.
Clubhouse Hours: Normal bar hours in evenings. Lunchtimes for parties only by arrangement.
Clubhouse Dress: Casual.
Clubhouse Facilities: Catering available by arrangement with Secretary.
Open Competitions: August and September.

CONVENIENT HOTELS

Kings Hotel – one mile;
Kingsknowe Hotel – three miles;
Abbotsford Hotel – one mile.

Bunker and tree positions indicated.

NO.	YARDS	PAR	S.I.	NO.	YARDS	PAR	S.I.
1	170	3	13	10	272	4	6
2	244	4	11	11	121	3	18
3	524	5	1	12	376	4	4
4	460	5	5	13	230	3	14
5	150	3	17	14	359	4	2
6	432	4	3	15	277	4	10
7	246	3	15	16	304	4	8
8	357	4	7	17	275	4	16
9	217	3	9	18	171	3	12
OUT	2,800	34		IN	2,385	33	
				TOTAL	5,185	67	
				STANDARD SCRATCH	66		

HAWICK

Hawick Golf Club, Vertish Hill, Hawick, Roxburghshire.
Tel: (01450) 372293.

LOCATION: 1/2 mile south of Hawick.
SECRETARY: J.H. Reilly, (10a North Bridge Street Hawick). Tel: (01450) 375594.

Hilly course with panoramic view over the Town. Testing course for the club golfer.

COURSE INFORMATION

Par 68; SSS 69; Length 5,929 Yards.
Visitors: Sundays & weekdays — by prior arrangement.
Opening Hours: 7.30am – Dusk.
Avoid: Saturdays.
Ladies: Welcome.
Ladies Day: Thursday evening for competitions.
Green Fees: £15 per round; £22 for a day ticket.
Juveniles: Welcome during daytime.
Clubhouse Hours: 11.00am – 2.30pm & 5.00pm – 11.00pm.
Clubhouse Dress: Shirts & pullovers.
Clubhouse Facilities: Catering facilities available.
Open Competitions: Hawick Open 29th August.

CONVENIENT HOTEL

Elm House Hotel, Bridge Street, Hawick.

NO.	YARDS	PAR	S.I.	NO.	YARDS	PAR	S.I.
1	195	3	11	10	382	4	10
2	350	4	9	11	390	4	2
3	388	4	3	12	292	4	14
4	325	4	13	13	198	3	8
5	338	4	15	14	388	4	6
6	445	4	1	15	437	4	4
7	449	4	7	16	292	4	18
8	144	3	17	17	276	4	16
9	430	4	5	18	210	3	12
OUT	3,064	34		IN	2,865	34	
				TOTAL	5,929	68	
STANDARD SCRATCH					69		

HIRSEL

**The Hirsel Golf Club,
Kelso Road, Coldstream,
Berwickshire. TD12 4NJ.
Tel: (01890) 882678.**

LOCATION: 1/2 mile west of Coldstream.
SECRETARY: John C. Balfour.
Tel: (01890) 883052.

Parkland course with mature and newly planted wooded areas. Divided by the River Leet which has to be played over at the 2nd, 7th and 14th holes. (Referred to in December's (1992) *Golf Monthly* as 'The Augusta of 9 holers in the Borders'. Now 18 holes.

COURSE INFORMATION

Par 70; SSS 69; Length 6,092 Yards.
Visitors: Parties of 10 players or more must pre-book.
Opening Hours: Daylight.
Avoid: Check by phone with Clubhouse; Holidays & weekends.
Ladies Day: Last Saturday in June.
Juveniles: Welcome.
Clubhouse Hours: 9.30am – 2.30pm & 5.00pm – 11.30pm (March/October).
Clubhouse Dress: Casual.
Clubhouse Facilities: Daily March/April, September/October –Tuesdays; Every day May/September.
Open Competitions: Douglas Home Trophy; Macmillan Cancer Relief Trophy.

CONVENIENT HOTELS

Tilmouth Park, Cornhill-on-Tweed; Collingwood Arms, Cornhill-on-Tweed; Crown Hotel, Market Square, Coldstream.

NO.	YARDS	PAR	S.I.	NO.	YARDS	PAR	S.I.
1	304	4	11	10	430	4	12
2	290	4	13	11	198	3	14
3	246	3	3	12	421	4	6
4	320	4	15	13	321	4	16
5	345	4	5	14	158	3	4
6	420	4	1	15	352	4	2
7	125	3	17	16	396	4	18
8	345	4	7	17	360	4	8
9	521	5	9	18	520	5	10
OUT	2,916	35		IN	3,156	35	
				TOTAL	6,072	70	
				STANDARD SCRATCH	69		

Bunker and tree positions indicated.

Innerleithan Golf Club, Leithan Water, Leithan Road, Innerleithan.
Tel: (01896) 830951.

LOCATION: Innerleithan 11/2 miles on the Heriot Road.
SECRETARY: S. Wyse.
Tel: (01896) 830071.
ARCHITECT: William Park.

Formed in 1886 Innerleithan club is located 27 miles south of Edinburgh and is situated in a picturesque valley which allows flat and easy walking. There has been maximun use of hills and burns making the course extremely challenging.

COURSE INFORMATION

Par 68; SSS 69; Length 5,984 Yards.
Opening Hours: Dawn – Dusk.
Visitors: Welcome.
Avoid: Competition days.
Ladies: Welcome. Ladies Day Tuesday evening.
Green Fees: Weekdays £10; Weekends £12.
Juveniles: Welcome; Restricted Monday – Friday evenings 5pm – 6,30pm.
Clubhouse Hours: Noon – 2.30pm; 6.30pm – closed on Monday – Friday; Saturday/Sunday 11.30am – 11pm.
Clubhouse Dress: Casual.
Clubhouse Facilities: Catering available by arrangement.

CONVENIENT HOTELS

Tweedvalley Hotel;
Traquair Arms Hotel;
Peebles Hydro Hotel.

NO.	YARDS	PAR	S.I.	NO.	YARDS	PAR	S.I.
1	175	3	15	10	175	3	16
2	347	4	13	11	347	4	14
3	474	4	1	12	474	4	2
4	375	4	7	13	375	4	8
5	100	3	17	14	100	3	18
6	200	3	11	15	200	3	12
7	422	4	3	16	422	4	4
8	526	5	5	17	526	5	6
9	373	4	9	18	373	4	10
OUT	2,992	34		IN	2,992	34	
				TOTAL	5,984	68	
STANDARD SCRATCH					69		

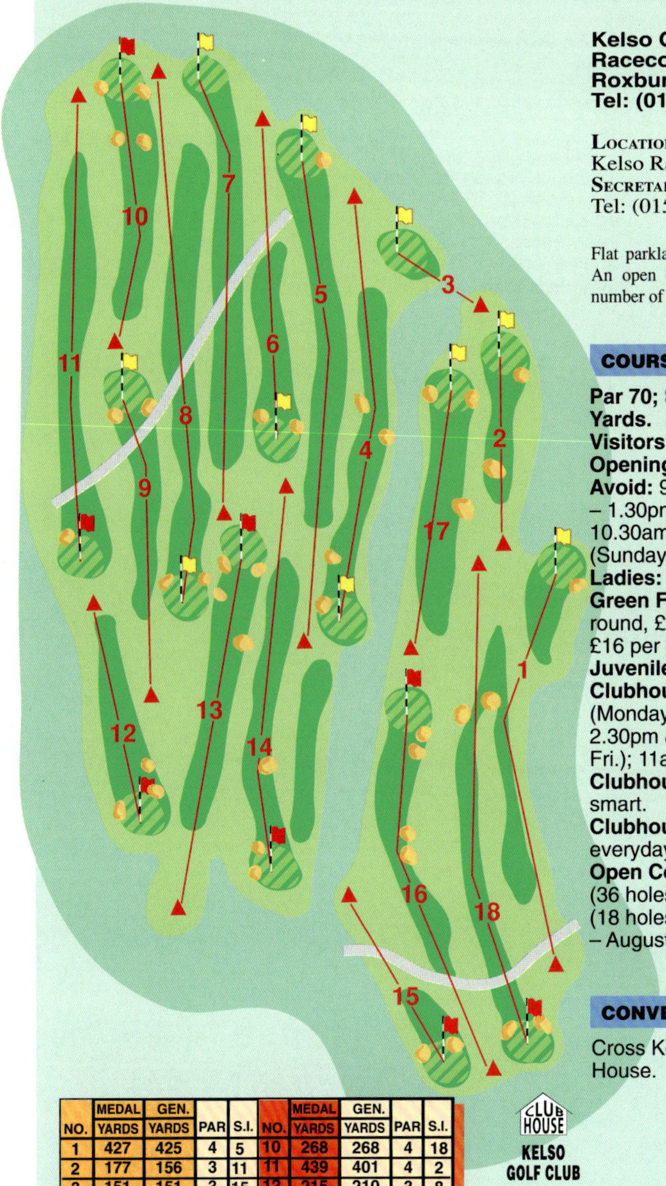

Kelso Golf Club, Berrymoss Racecourse Roads, Roxburghshire. DD5 7SL. Tel: (01573) 223009.

LOCATION: 1 mile from Kelso (inside Kelso Racecourse).
SECRETARY: J.P. Payne.
Tel: (01573) 223259.

Flat parkland course within Kelso Racecourse. An open ditch (the "Stank") is a feature on number of holes.

COURSE INFORMATION

Par 70; SSS 69; Length 6,046 Yards.
Visitors: Welcome.
Opening Hours: Dawn – Dusk.
Avoid: 9.00am – 9.30am & 1.00pm – 1.30pm (weekdays); 10.00am - 10.30am & 1.00pm – 1.30pm (Sundays).
Ladies: Welcome.
Green Fees: Weekdays – £12 per round, £20 per day; Weekends – £16 per round, £25 per day.
Juveniles: Welcome.
Clubhouse Hours: 5pm – 11pm (Monday & Tuesday), 11am – 2.30pm & 5pm – 11pm (Wed, Thurs, Fri.); 11am – 11pm Weekends.
Clubhouse Dress: Casual but smart.
Clubhouse Facilities: Catering, everyday.
Open Competitions: Scratch Open (36 holes) – May; Handicap Open (18 holes) – June; Mixed Foursomes – August.

CONVENIENT HOTELS

Cross Keys; Queen's Head; Ednam House.

NO.	MEDAL YARDS	GEN. YARDS	PAR	S.I.	NO.	MEDAL YARDS	GEN. YARDS	PAR	S.I.
1	427	425	4	5	10	268	268	4	18
2	177	156	3	11	11	439	401	4	2
3	151	151	3	15	12	215	210	3	8
4	395	342	4	9	13	369	333	4	14
5	434	358	4	3	14	350	319	4	6
6	284	256	4	17	15	176	170	3	12
7	434	384	4	1	16	330	329	4	10
8	493	463	5/4	7	17	298	295	4	16
9	315	241	4/3	13	18	491	470	5/4	4
OUT	3,110	2,776	35/33		IN	2,936	2,795	35/34	
					TOTAL	6,046	5,571	70/67	
					STANDARD SCRATCH	69	67		

Bunker positions indicated.

LANGHOLM

**Langholm Golf Club,
Langholm, Dumfriesshire.
DG13 OJR.
Tel: (013873) 80265.**

LOCATION: On the Carlisle to Edinburgh road (A7). Turn off at market place in middle of the town.
SECRETARY: W. J. Wilson.
Tel: (013873) 80673.

Langholm is a challenging 9 hole hillside course with panoramic views over the town and surrounding areas.

COURSE INFORMATION

Par 70; SSS 68; Length 5,744 Yards.
Visitors: Welcome.
Opening Hours: Dawn – Dusk.
Avoid: Saturdays 9am – 9.45am & 1pm –2pm; Sundays 9am – 10am.
Ladies: Welcome.
Green Fees: £10 – reductions with member.
Juveniles: Welcome.
Clubhouse Hours: Saturday & Sunday at competition times.
Clubhouse Dress: Casual.
Clubhouse Facilities: Catering available on request.

CONVENIENT HOTELS

Eskdale Hotel; Crown Hotel; Buck Hotel.

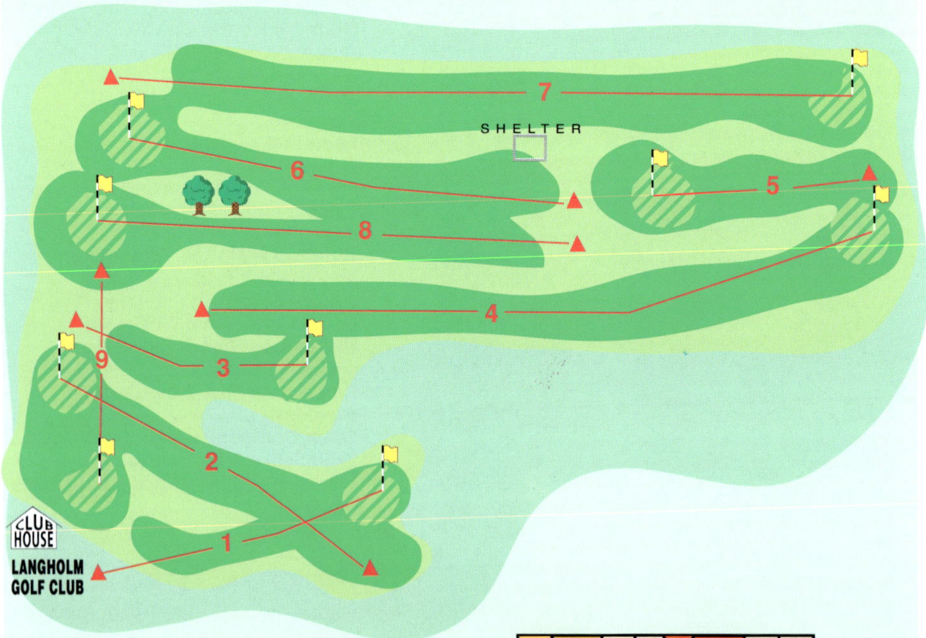

NO.	YARDS	PAR	S.I.	NO.	YARDS	PAR	S.I.
1	295	4	13	10	295	4	14
2	344	4	5	11	344	4	6
3	180	3	7	12	180	3	8
4	510	5	3	13	510	5	4
5	175	3	11	14	175	3	12
6	300	4	15	15	300	4	16
7	415	4	1	16	415	4	2
8	291	4	17	17	291	4	18
9	362	4	9	18	362	4	10
OUT	2,872	35		IN	2,872	35	
				TOTAL	5,744	70	
STANDARD SCRATCH					68		

Lauder Golf Club, 23 Browns Muir Park, Lauder, Berwickshire. TD2 6QD.
Tel: (01578) 722526.

LOCATION: Half a mile west of Lauder.
SECRETARY: Mr Dickson.
ARCHITECT: Mr W. Park Jnr.

A 9 hole course measuring 6,002 yards, it was first laid out in 1896 on a gently sloping hill. The course combines a fair test of golf with stunning views of the Laudredale district.

COURSE INFORMATION

Par 72; SSS 70; Length 6,002 Yards.
Visitors: Welcome.
Opening Hours: Sunrise – Sunset.
Avoid: Wednesday 5pm – 6pm & Sunday before 12pm.
Ladies: Welcome.
Ladies Day: Wednesday.
Green Fees: Weekdays – £7 per round; Weekends – £10 per round.
Juveniles: Welcome.
Clubhouse Hours: Varies on season.
Clubhouse Dress: Smart / Casual .
Clubhouse Facilities: Changing facilities only.

CONVENIENT HOTELS

Lauderdale Hotel; Black Bull Hotel Hotel; Eagle Hotel.

Tree positions indicated.

NO.	YARDS	PAR	S.I.	NO.	YARDS	PAR	S.I.
1	374	4		10	374	4	
2	353	4		11	353	4	
3	252	4		12	252	4	
4	351	4		13	351	4	
5	405	4		14	405	4	
6	150	3		15	150	3	
7	482	5		16	482	5	
8	368	4		17	368	4	
9	266	4		18	266	4	
OUT	3,001	36		IN	3,001	36	
				TOTAL	6,002	72	
STANDARD SCRATCH					70		

**Melrose Golf Club,
Dingleton, Melrose,
Roxburghshire.
Tel: (0189682) 2855.**

Location: South boundary of Melrose.
Secretary: W. MacRae.
Tel: (0189682) 2391.

Melrose is a very scenic course at the foot of the Eildons Hills. The fairways are tree lined with each of the holes having very different characteristics, providing a good test of golf.

COURSE INFORMATION

Par 70; SSS 68; Length 5,579 Yds
Visitors: Welcome.
Opening Hours: 8am – Dusk.
Avoid: No visitors after 4pm April – October.
Ladies: Welcome.
Ladies Day: Tuesday.
Green Fees: £15 day/round.
Juveniles: Welcome, £5, priority Wed. am (Hols).
Clubhouse Hours: Mon–Fri 5pm–11pm;Sat-Sun 11-10pm.
Clubhouse Dress: Casual.
Clubhouse Facilities: Catering available by arrangement.
Open Competitions: Every Sat and most Suns from Apr – Oct.

CONVENIENT HOTELS

The Kings Arms; The George; The Abbotsford; Bunts; George & Abbotsford The Bon Accord.

NO.	YARDS	PAR	S.I.	NO.	YARDS	PAR	S.I.
1	257	4	13	10	257	4	14
2	377	4	4	11	377	4	2
3	168	3	17	12	168	3	18
4	343	4	5	13	343	4	6
5	272	4	11	14	272	4	12
6	367	4	7	15	367	4	8
7	312	4	9	16	329	4	10
8	414	4	1	17	414	4	3
9	271	4	15	18	271	4	16
OUT	2,781	35		IN	2,798	35	
				TOTAL	5,579	70	
STANDARD SCRATCH					68		

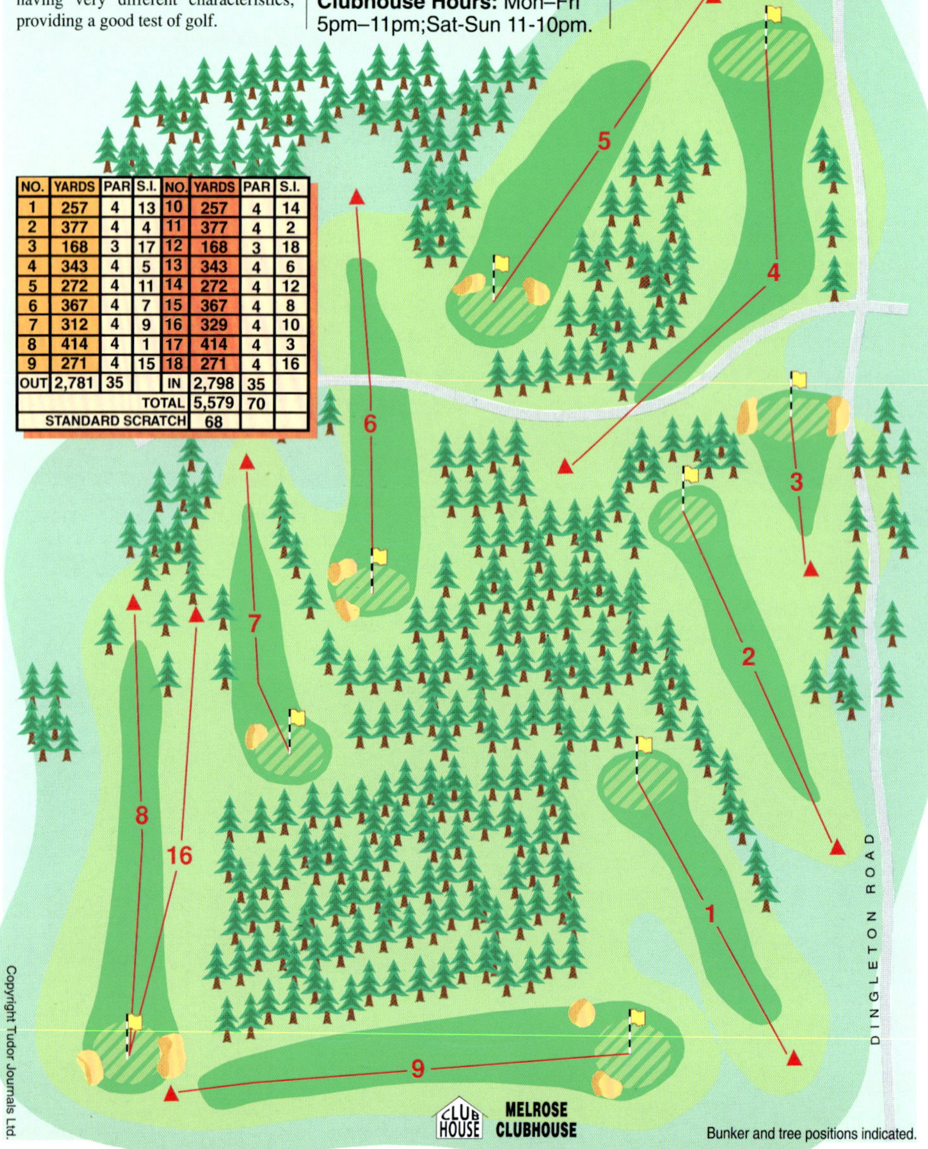

Bunker and tree positions indicated.

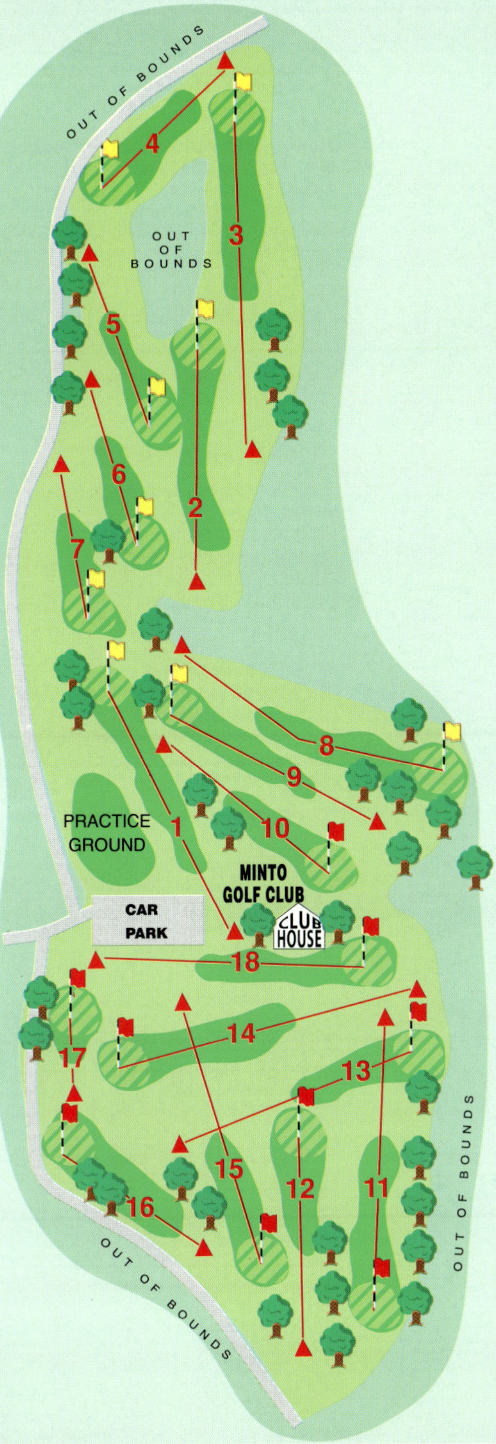

**Minto Golf Club, Denholm.
Hawick, Roxburghshire.
PD9 8SH.
Tel: (01450) 870220.**

Location: Denholm, six miles east of Hawick.
Secretary: Dr I. Todd.
Tel: (01835) 862611.

A deceptive parkland course which plays longer than its yardage. There are fine views from different parts of the course.

COURSE INFORMATION

Par 68; SSS 68; Length 5,460 Yards 4,992 Metres.
Visitors: Limited on competition days (weekends) – Telephone first.
Avoid: Competition days.
Ladies: No restrictions.
Ladies Day: None in particular.
Green Fees: £13 per round and £20 per day. Weekends – £20 per round and £27 per day.
Clubhouse Hours: Daylight.
Clubhouse Dress: Smart /casual.
Clubhouse Facilities: Thursday is Stewards day off.

CONVENIENT HOTELS

Kirklands; Mansfield House, Hawick; Queens Head, Kelso.

NO.	YARDS	PAR	S.I.	NO.	YARDS	PAR	S.I.
1	399	4	3	10	255	4	16
2	311	4	15	11	373	4	11
3	423	4	1	12	263	4	4
4	225	3	7	13	304	4	13
5	251	4	18	14	411	4	2
6	226	3	9	15	357	4	14
7	189	3	12	16	292	4	8
8	347	4	5	17	127	3	17
9	330	4	10	18	377	4	6
OUT	2,701	33		IN	2,759	35	
				TOTAL	5,460	68	
STANDARD SCRATCH					68		

Tree positions indicated.

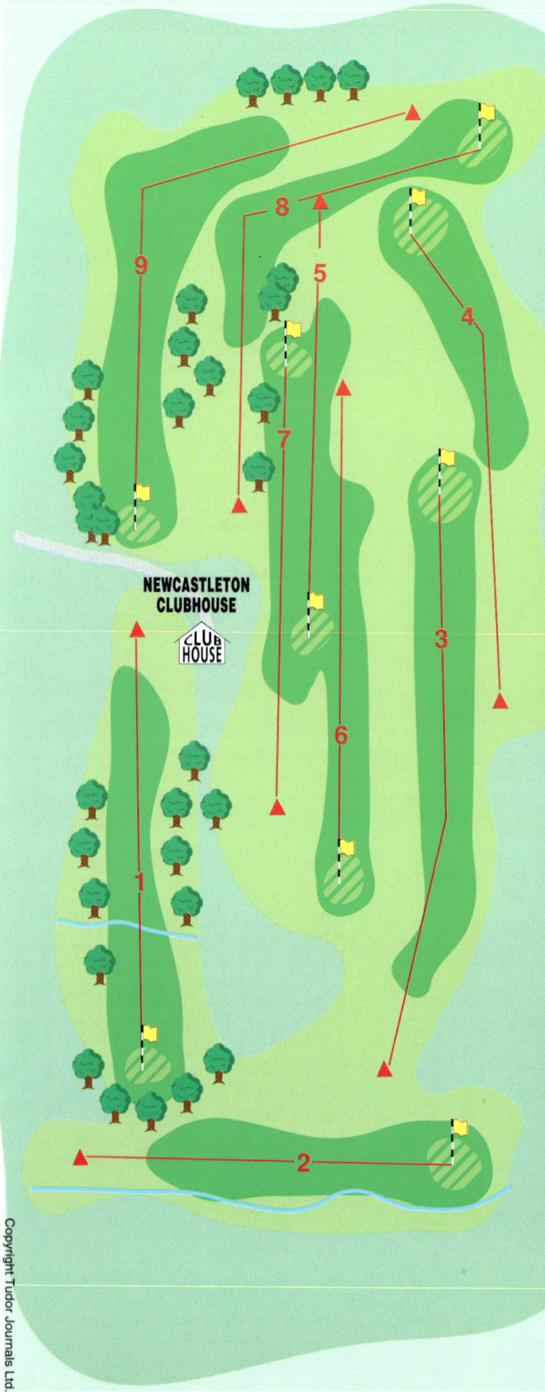

Newcastleton Golf Club, Holm Hill, Newcastleton, Roxburghshire.

LOCATION: 25 miles north of Carlisle off the A7.
SECRETARY: F.J. Ewart
Tel: (01294) 62196.
ARCHITECT: John Shade.

A hilly nine hole course with a long pedigree – it was established in 1894.

COURSE INFORMATION

Par 70; SSS 68; Length 5,748 Yards.
Visitors: Welcome.
Opening Hours: Dawn – Dusk.
Avoid: Match days.
Ladies: Welcome.
Green Fees: Weekdays – £7 ; Weekends – £8.
Juveniles: Welcome.
Clubhouse Hours: Limited
Clubhouse Dress: Inforrmal.
Clubhouse Facilities: Facilities of nearby hotels used.

CONVENIENT HOTELS

Grapes Hotel; Liddesdale Hotel; Doremouse Bistro; Copshaw Kitchen.

NO.	YARDS	PAR	S.I.	NO.	YARDS	PAR	S.I.
1	396	4	2	10	396	4	2
2	153	3	9	11	153	3	9
3	386	4	3	12	386	4	3
4	312	4	6	13	312	4	6
5	163	3	8	14	163	3	8
6	322	4	4	15	322	4	4
7	299	4	7	16	299	4	7
8	322	4	5	17	322	4	5
9	521	5	1	18	521	5	1
OUT	2,874	35		IN	2,874	35	
				TOTAL	5,748	70	
STANDARD SCRATCH					68		

Tree positions indicated.

PEEBLES

Peebles Golf Club, Kirkland Street, Peebles. EH45 8EU. Tel: (01721) 720197.

LOCATION: 23 miles south of Edinburgh.
SECRETARY: H.T. Gilmore.
Tel: (01721) 720197.

Gently sloping parkland course offering fine views of the town and Tweed Valley from the 5th fairway. Ninth hole returns to the clubhouse. Recognised as one of the best courses in the Scottish Borders, the course played host in 1993 to the Scottish Boys Team Tournament. The course transfered from municipal to private ownership in April 1991.

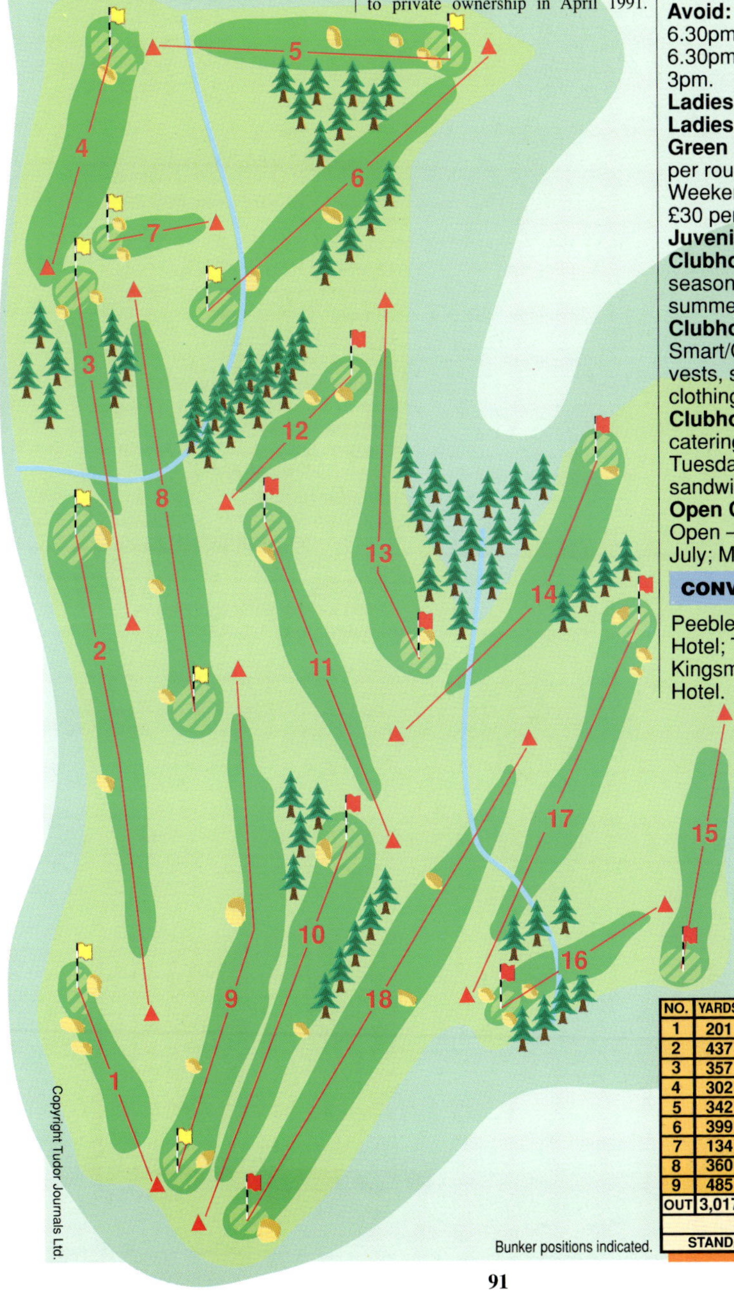

Bunker positions indicated.

COURSE INFORMATION

Par 70; SSS 69; Length 6,137 Yards.
Visitors: Welcome (subject to tee availability).
Opening Hours: 8am – sunset.
Avoid: Monday 4pm – 6.30pm, Wednesday 4pm – 6.30pm & Saturday 8am – 3pm.
Ladies: Welcome.
Ladies Day: Monday pm.
Green Fees: Weekdays – £14 per round & £22 per day; Weekends – £21 per round & £30 per day.
Juveniles: Welcome.
Clubhouse Hours: Varies on season (8am – 11pm in summer).
Clubhouse Dress: Smart/Casual – no denim, vests, spikes or waterproof clothing.
Clubhouse Facilities: Full catering all days except Tuesdays (coffee and sandwiches only).
Open Competitions: Ladies Open – June; Mens Open – July; Mens Seniors – August.

CONVENIENT HOTELS

Peebles Hotel Hydro; Park Hotel; Tontine Hotel; Kingsmuir Hotel; Green Tree Hotel.

NO.	YARDS	PAR	S.I.	NO.	YARDS	PAR	S.I.
1	201	3	9	10	369	4	5
2	437	4	1	11	329	4	12
3	357	4	7	12	169	3	17
4	302	4	15	13	306	4	14
5	342	4	13	14	377	4	2
6	399	4	3	15	426	4	8
7	134	3	18	16	195	3	16
8	360	4	11	17	409	4	4
9	485	5	6	18	540	5	10
OUT	3,017	35		IN	3,120	35	
				TOTAL	6,137	70	
	STANDARD SCRATCH				69		

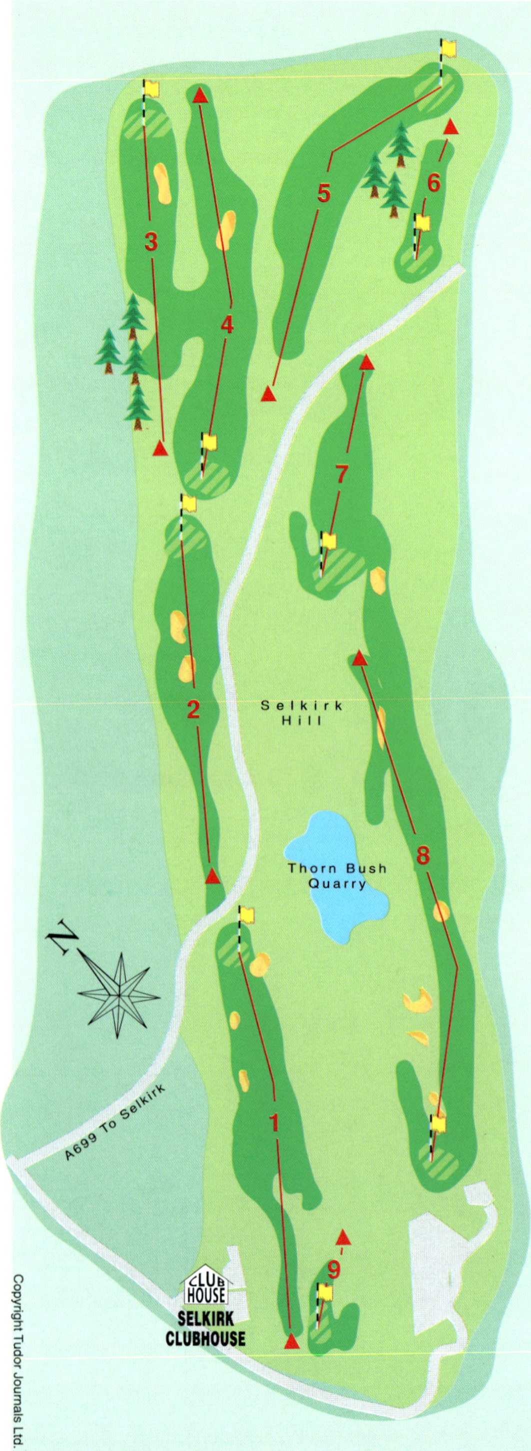

Selkirk Golf Club, Selkirk Hill, Selkirk, Selkirkshire. Tel: (01750) 20621.

LOCATION: 1 mile south of Selkirk on the A7.
SECRETARY: D.S. Wilson.
Tel: (01750) 22508.

A pleasant moorland course that goes around Selkirk Hill. A testing course for golfers of all abilities, plus superb views over the Ettrick and Yarrow valleys.

COURSE INFORMATION

Par 68; SSS 67; Length 5,620 Yards.
Visitors: Welcome.
Opening Hours: Dawn – Dusk.
Avoid: Friday evenings, Saturday & Sunday. Ladies only from 3.30pm Mondays.
Ladies: Welcome.
Ladies Day: Monday
Green Fees: £12 round; £16 day.
Juveniles: Welcome.
Clubhouse Hours: Closed Mon; Open Lunchtime & Evening during summer months..
Clubhouse Dress: Smart/Casual.
Clubhouse Facilities: Parties catered for by arrangement with secretary.
Open Competitions: Phone to check dates.

CONVENIENT HOTELS

The County Hotel; The Glen Hotel.

NO.	YARDS	PAR	S.I.	NO.	YARDS	PAR	S.I.
1	383	4		10	383	4	
2	265	4		11	265	4	
3	401	4		12	401	4	
4	379	4		13	379	4	
5	384	4		14	384	4	
6	119	3		15	119	3	
7	210	3		16	210	3	
8	518	5		17	518	5	
9	151	3		18	151	3	
OUT	2,810	34		IN	2,810	34	
				TOTAL	5,620	68	
				STANDARD SCRATCH	67		

Bunker and tree positions indicated.

ST. BOSWELLS

St Boswells Golf Club,
Braeheads, St. Boswells,
Roxburghshire. TD6 0DE.
Tel: (01835) 823527.

LOCATION: At St Boswell's Green off A68 by the River Tweed.
SECRETARY: G. Phillips.
Tel: (01835) 22359.
ARCHITECT: William Park and John Shade.

Unlike other border courses the terain is flat and presents few difficulties other than the River Tweed which is defined as a 'Lateral water hazard'. One of the many attractions of the course is its most scenic and peaceful setting, the only sounds coming from the running waters of the Tweed with accompanying bird songs.

COURSE INFORMATION

Par 66; SSS 65; Length 5,250 Yds.
Visitors: Welcome.
Opening Hours: Dawn – Dusk.
Avoid: Club competition days.
Ladies: Welcome.
Ladies Day: Tuesday evenings.
Green Fees: Weekdays £10 per round; Weekends £15 per round.
Juveniles: Welcome.
Clubhouse Dress: Casual sportswear.
Clubhouse Facilities: Tea and coffee available.
Open Competitions: Phone to check dates.

CONVENIENT HOTELS

Buccleuch Arms Hotel; Dryburgh Abbey Hotel.

NO.	YARDS	PAR	S.I.	NO.	YARDS	PAR	S.I.
1	149	3	9	10	149	3	17
2	161	3	17	11	161	3	15
3	320	4	12	12	320	4	12
4	198	3	5	13	198	3	13
5	427	4	3	14	427	4	2
6	301	4	16	15	301	4	7
7	435	4	1	16	435	4	5
8	378	4	8	17	378	4	3
9	256	4	13	18	256	4	9
OUT	2,625	33		IN	2,625	33	
				TOTAL	5,250	66	
STANDARD SCRATCH					65		

Bunker and tree positions indicated.

TORWOODLEE

Torwoodlee Golf Club, Galashiels, Selkirkshire. ID1 2NE.
Tel: (01896) 752260.

LOCATION: One mile north of Glalshiels on A7.
SECRETARY: A. Wilson.
ARCHITECT: Willie Park.

Wooded course designed by Willie Park. The River Gala runs alongside the course. The par 5 fourteenth is very challenging, with picturesque scenery making the round very enjoyable. Torwoodlee has been extended to 18 holes in 1995.

COURSE INFORMATION

Par 70; SSS 70; Length 6,061 Yards.
Visitors: Welcome.
Opening Hours: 8am – Dusk.
Avoid: Thursday afternoons & Saturdays until 5.30pm.
Ladies: Welcome.
Ladies Day: Thursday.
Green Fees: Weekdays – £12 per round & £15 per day; Weekends – £20 per round & £25 per day.
Juveniles: Welcome.
Clubhouse Hours: 8.00am – 10.30 pm.
Clubhouse Dress: Smart/Casual (no jeans).
Clubhouse Facilities: Catering available every day except Tuesdays.
Open Competitions: 3rd Saturday in August.

CONVENIENT HOTELS

Burt's Hotel, Melrose; G&A Hotel, Melrose.

NO.	YARDS	PAR	S.I.	NO.	YARDS	PAR	S.I.
1	378	4	7	10	196	3	6
2	401	4	1	11	417	4	2
3	125	3	17	12	135	3	18
4	326	4	13	13	423	4	4
5	478	5	3	14	546	5	10
6	330	4	11	15	336	4	16
7	151	3	15	16	325	4	14
8	493	5	9	17	234	3	12
9	367	4	5	18	420	4	8
OUT	3,049	36		IN	3,012	34	
				TOTAL	6,061	70	
				STANDARD SCRATCH	70		

Bunker and tree positions indicated.

GOLF
DAYS™
SCOTLAND

CLACKMANNANSHIRE

Alloa Golf Club, Schawpark, Sauchie, Clackmannanshire. Tel: (01259) 722745.

LOCATION: Sauchie.
SECRETARY: A.M. Frame.
Tel: (01259) 750100.
PROFESSIONAL: Bill Bennett.
Tel: (01259) 724476.
ARCHITECT: James Braid.

Undulating wooded parkland course with panoramic views all around. As good a test of golf as anywhere in central Scotland.

COURSE INFORMATION

Par 70; SSS 71; Length 6,230 Yards.
Opening Hours: Proshop 8.00am to 7.00pm.
Visitors: Welcome except no weekend parties.
Avoid: Sat and Sun.
Ladies: Welcome.
Ladies Day: Wed.
Green Fees: £14 per round, £22 per day; £27 Sat/Sun after 11.00am.
Juveniles: Permitted with certain restrictions.
Clubhouse Hours: 11.00am to 11.00pm.
Clubhouse Dress: Casual but smart.
Clubhouse Facilities: Full catering available.

CONVENIENT HOTELS

Claremont Lodge Hotel, Alloa; Royal Oak, Alloa.

NO.	YARDS	PAR	S.I.	NO.	YARDS	PAR	S.I.
1	333	4	15	10	318	4	16
2	478	5	3	11	350	4	10
3	325	4	17	12	428	4	2
4	168	3	13	13	313	4	18
5	508	5	7	14	422	4	8
6	321	4	9	15	173	3	14
7	155	3	11	16	401	4	6
8	393	4	1	17	474	4	4
9	467	4	5	18	203	3	12
OUT	3,148	36		IN	3,082	34	
				TOTAL	6,230	70	
STANDARD & SCRATCH					71		

Bunker positions indicated.

ALVA

Alva Golf Club, Beauclerc St, Alva, Clackmannanshire.
Tel: (0259) 760431.

Location: Back road, Alva, on A91/Stirling/St. Andrews Rd.
Secretary: A. McGuire.
Tel: (0259) 760455.

Inland wooded hillside course with fast greens. Some sloping fairways leading up to greens. Hillside burn runs between 2nd, 3rd and 5th holes.

COURSE INFORMATION

Par 66; SSS 64; Length 4,846 Yards.
Opening Hours: 7.00am Mon to Fri; 8.00am Sat/Sun.
Visitors: Welcome.
Ladies: Welcome.
Ladies Day: Thursday.
Green Fees: On application.
Juveniles: Welcome but restricted.

Clubhouse Hours: 7.00pm to 11.00pm Mon to Fri; 12.00noon to 11.00pm Sat/Sun.
Clubhouse Dress: Casual.
Clubhouse Facilities: Limited bar snacks only.

CONVENIENT HOTELS

Johnstone Arms, Alva;
The Glen Hotel, Alva.

NO.	YARDS	PAR	S.I.	NO.	YARDS	PAR	S.I.
1	301	4	7	10	301	4	8
2	281	4	11	11	281	4	12
3	171	3	13	12	171	3	14
4	130	3	15	13	130	3	16
5	397	4	1	14	397	4	2
6	298	4	9	15	298	4	10
7	89	3	17	16	89	3	18
8	377	4	3	17	377	4	4
9	379	4	5	18	379	4	6
OUT	2,423	33		IN	2,423	33	
				TOTAL	4,846	66	
				STANDARD SCRATCH	64		

Tree positions indicated.

BRAEHEAD

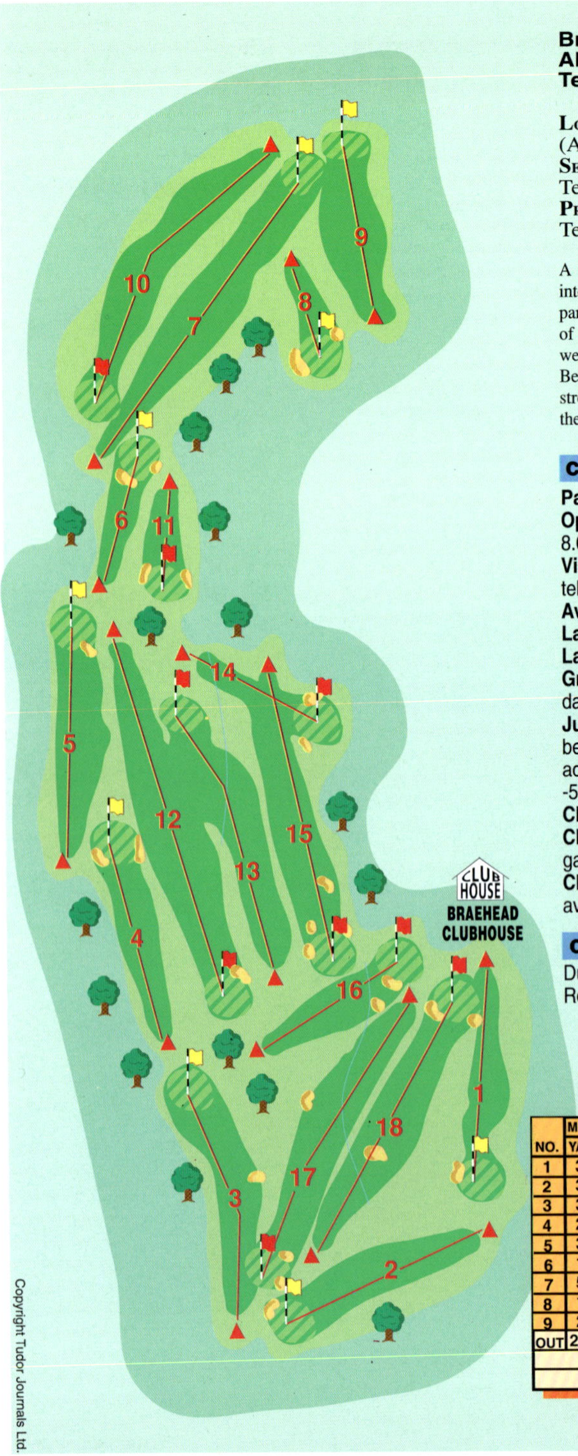

Braehead Golf Club, Cambus, Alloa, Clackmannanshire. Tel: (01259) 722078.

Location: 2 miles west of Alloa (A907).
Secretary: Paul MacMichael.
Tel: (01259) 722078.
Professional: Paul Brookes.
Tel: (01259) 722078.

A gently undulating parkland course, with an interesting variety of challenging holes. Many parts of the course afford splendid scenic views of the Forth Valley, the Ochil Hills and to the west Stirling Castle, the Wallace Monument and Ben Lomond. The course features a particularly strong finish — many members are happy to end their round, bogey, bogey!

COURSE INFORMATION

Par 70; SSS 69; Length 6,041 Yards.
Opening Hours: Start times (Summer) 8.00am to 7.00pm.
Visitors: Welcome, but advisable to telephone in advance.
Avoid: Telephone to check.
Ladies: Welcome.
Ladies Day: Wednesday.
Green Fees: Weekday £14 a round, £20 a day; weekend £20 a round, £28 a day.
Juveniles: Welcome, but start times may be restricted unless accompanied by an adult. Junior/Juvenile medal - Thurs 4.30 -5.45 pm.
Clubhouse Hours: 11.00am to 11.00pm.
Clubhouse Dress: Lounge bar — smart; games room — casual.
Clubhouse Facilities: Full catering available throughout the day.

CONVENIENT HOTELS

Dumar Hotel, Alloa;
Royal Hotel, Bridge of Allan.

NO.	MEDAL YARDS	GEN. YARDS	PAR	S.I.	NO.	MEDAL YARDS	GEN. YARDS	PAR	S.I.
1	337	337	4	13	10	477	459	5/4	1
2	331	331	4	18	11	136	128	3	15
3	361	337	4	7	12	518	518	5	8
4	294	286	4	16	13	402	402	4	2
5	342	321	4	9	14	210	183	3	10
6	159	156	3	17	15	379	379	4	4
7	505	458	5	5	16	265	214	4/3	11
8	164	142	3	14	17	468	449	4	3
9	271	271	4	12	18	422	422	4	6
OUT	2,764	2,639	35		IN	3,277	3,154	36/34	
					TOTAL	6,041	5,793	71/69	
					STANDARD SCRATCH	69	68		

Bunker and tree positions indicated.

TILLICOULTRY

CLACKMANNANSHIRE

Tillicoultry Golf Club, Alva Road, Tillicoultry FK13 6BL. Tel: (01259) 50124.

LOCATION: 9 miles east of Stirling.
SECRETARY: R. Whitehead.

Parkland course at the foot of the Ochil Hills. This course is slightly hilly at places and is a good test of accurate shot making.

COURSE INFORMATION

Par 68; SSS 66; Length 5,358 Yds.
Opening Hours: 8.00am to dusk.
Visitors: Welcome except on competition days.
Avoid: Members and guests only Wed & Fri from 4.00pm.
Ladies: No.
Ladies Day: Tues from 4.00pm.
Green Fees: £10 weekday & £15 weekends.
Juveniles: Not after 6.00pm weekdays & before 4.00pm Sat & Sun.
Clubhouse Hours: 12.00pm to 2.00pm, 7.30pm to 11.00pm.
Clubhouse Dress: No football colours.
Clubhouse Facilities: As opening hours or by arrangement.

CONVENIENT HOTEL

Castle Craig, Tillicoultry.

NO.	YARDS	PAR	S.I.	NO.	YARDS	PAR	S.I.
1	373	4	4	10	373	4	3
2	369	4	7	11	369	4	8
3	161	3	15	12	161	3	16
4	255	4	13	13	255	4	14
5	353	4	5	14	353	4	6
6	84	3	17	15	84	3	18
7	311	4	11	16	311	4	12
8	422	4	1	17	422	4	2
9	351	4	9	18	351	4	10
OUT	2,679	34		IN	2,679	34	
				TOTAL	5,358	68	
STANDARD SCRATCH					66		

Tree positions indicated.

DUNBARTONSHIRE

GOLF DAYS™ SCOTLAND

Bearsden Golf Club, Thorn Road, Bearsden, Dunbartonshire.
Tel: (0141) 942 2351.

LOCATION: Seven miles north west of Glasgow.
SECRETARY: J.R. Mercer.
Tel: (0141) 942 2381.

9 hole course with 16 greens.

COURSE INFORMATION

Par 68; SSS 69; Length 6,014 Yards.

Opening Hours: From 8.30am.
Visitors: Only with a member.
Avoid: Sat up to 5.00pm on medal days.
Ladies: Telephone for details, ladies day Thurs.
Green Fees: Tel. for details.
Juveniles: Welcome.
Clubhouse Hours: 11.00am to 11.00pm in Summer.
Clubhouse Dress: No trainers, denims, sleeveless or collarless shirts.

Clubhouse Facilities:
Restricted catering on Mon/Tues available up to 9.30pm in Summer and up to 5.30 pm in Winter.

CONVENIENT HOTELS

Burnbrae Hotel, Bearsden, (2 miles); Black Bull Thistle Hotel, Milngavie , (2½ miles); Jury's Pond Hotel, (4 miles).

NO.	YARDS	PAR	S.I.	NO.	YARDS	PAR	S.I.
1	304	4	17	10	304	4	16
2	428	4	5	11	455	4	4
3	366	4	13	12	350	4	12
4	455	4	1	13	449	4	2
5	206	3	7	14	137	3	18
6	398	4	3	15	391	4	6
7	170	3	11	16	156	3	10
8	327	4	15	17	327	4	14
9	373	4	9	18	418	4	8
OUT	3,027	34		IN	2,987	34	
				TOTAL	6,014	68	
STANDARD SCRATCH					69		

Bunker and tree positions indicated.

Cardross Golf Club, Main Road, Cardross, Dumbartonshire, G82 5LB.
Tel: (01389) 841213.

LOCATION: Five miles from Dumbarton on the Helensburgh Road.
SECRETARY: Mr P. Laing. Tel: (01389) 841754.
PROFESSIONAL: Robert Farell. Tel: (01389) 841350.
ARCHITECT: Willie Fernie originally designed the course in 1904, James Braid redesigned the course to its present layout in 1921.
A challenging undulating parkland course with a tree lined setting.

COURSE INFORMATION

Par 71; SSS 72; Length 6,469 Yards.
Visitors: Welcome, weekdays.
Opening Hours: 8am – 8pm.
Ladies: Restricted, 5pm – 6.30pm (Mon, Wed & Sat.). Saturday before 10.30am & 12noon – 2pm.
Green Fees: £20 per round, £30 per day.
Juveniles: Not allowed between 4.30pm –7pm during school holidays.
Clubhouse Hours: 8.30am – 10pm. (April – Sept) 9am –7pm. (Oct).
Clubhouse Dress: Smart but casual (no jeans, trainers).
Clubhouse Facilities: By arrangement.
Open Competitions: R.G. Wilson – May ; Cardross Open – July; Junior Open – August; Mixed fours - Aug.

CONVENIENT HOTELS

'Muirholm', Main Road, Cardross; Cardross Inn, Main Road, Cardross. (Opposite the course).

NO.	MEDAL YARDS	GEN. YARDS	PAR	S.I.	NO.	MEDAL YARDS	GEN. YARDS	PAR	S.I.
1	398	388	4	6	10	458	454	4	7
2	351	340	4	13	11	432	381	4	2
3	256	248	4	16	12	163	145	3	17
4	393	378	4	8	13	502	463	5	11
5	131	121	3	18	14	404	395	4	3
6	397	354	4	1	15	196	190	3	15
7	367	355	4	12	16	512	504	5	5
8	371	365	4	10	17	265	249	4	14
9	399	371	4	4	18	474	461	4	9
OUT	3,063		35		IN	3,406		36	
					TOTAL	6,469		71	
					STANDARD SCRATCH	71			

Clydebank Municipal, Overtoun Road, Dalmuir, Clydebank.
Tel: (0141) 952 6372.

LOCATION: Eight miles west of Glasgow.
PROFESSIONAL: R.Bowman.
Tel: (0141) 952 6372.

Well maintained municipal course with interesting features, pleasant outlook and views over River Clyde and Renfrewshire Hills.

COURSE INFORMATION

Par 67; SSS 66; Length 5,349 Yards.
Visitors: Welcome.
Ladies: Welcome.
Green Fees: Weekdays — £4.50 per round; Sun — £4.80 per round.
Juveniles: After 4.00pm Sat and Sun.
Clubhouse Hours: Sat and Sun mornings (certain periods).
Clubhouse Dress: Per Scottish Club Association rules.
Clubhouse Facilities: On request.

CONVENIENT HOTELS

Radnor Hotel;
West Highway Hotel;
Patio Hotel;
Boulevard Hotel.

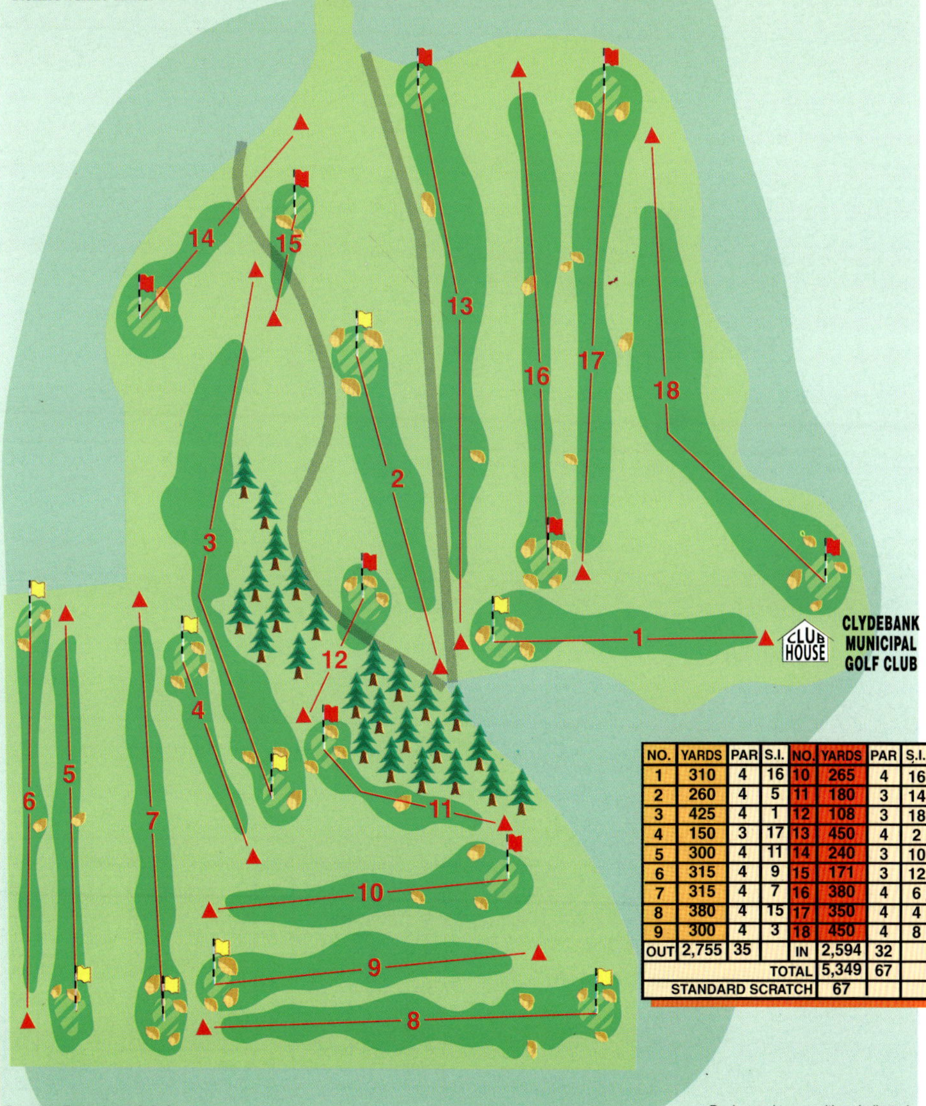

NO.	YARDS	PAR	S.I.	NO.	YARDS	PAR	S.I.
1	310	4	16	10	265	4	16
2	260	4	5	11	180	3	14
3	425	4	1	12	108	3	18
4	150	3	17	13	450	4	2
5	300	4	11	14	240	3	10
6	315	4	9	15	171	3	12
7	315	4	7	16	380	4	6
8	380	4	15	17	350	4	4
9	300	4	3	18	450	4	8
OUT	2,755	35		IN	2,594	32	
				TOTAL	5,349	67	
				STANDARD SCRATCH	67		

Bunker and tree positions indicated.

DOUGALSTON

Douglaston Golf Club,
Milngavie, Glasgow.
Tel: (0141) 956 5750.
Fax: (0141) 956 6480.

LOCATION: 7 miles North of Glasgow of A81.
SECRETARY: Grace Wilson (Club Manager).

The has tree lined fairways, lochs and flowering shrubs. The course offers golfers an idyllic setting and yet is located only 15 minutes from central Glasgow.

COURSE INFORMATION

Par 70; SSS 71; Length 6,354 Yards.
Opening Hours: 8.00am to 6.00pm.
Visitors: Mon to Fri 8am – 4.30pm.
Avoid: Weekends.
Ladies: After 3.30 pm.
Green Fees: £15 per round, £20 per day.
Juveniles: Weekdays only up until 4.30pm.
Clubhouse Hours: 11.00am to 11.00pm.

Dress for Course: Golf shoes only, no denims or collarless shirts.
Clubhouse Facilities: Catering, 11.00am to 7.00pm 7 days a week.

CONVENIENT HOTELS

Black Bull Hotel; Burnbrae Hotel; The Kirkhouse Inn.

NO.	MEDAL YARDS	GEN. YARDS	PAR	S.I.	NO.	MEDAL YARDS	GEN. YARDS	PAR	S.I.
1	443	407	4	1	10	187	158	3	16
2	348	323	4	14	11	425	406	4	2
3	187	169	3	15	12	430	390	4	5
4	500	473	5	6	13	377	369	4	10
5	326	315	4	11	14	342	301	4	12
6	163	147	3	17	15	393	371	4	4
7	383	371	4	3	16	480	446	5	13
8	367	359	4	7	17	368	357	4	8
9	478	440	5	9	18	157	144	3	18
OUT	3,195	3,004	36		IN	3,159	2,942	35	
					TOTAL	6,354	5,946	72	
					STANDARD SCRATCH	71	70		

Bunker positions indicated.

Dunbarton Golf Club,
11 Williamson Avenue
Dunbarton.
G62 7JR.
Tel: (01389) 732830.

LOCATION: 1 Mile North of Town.
SECRETARY: Roy Turnbull.
Tel: (01389) 732830.

Flat Parkland.

COURSE INFORMATION

Par 71, SSS 71, Length 6,071 Yards.
Opening Hours: 8.30am to 11.30pm.
Visitors: Public holidays and weekends.
Ladies: Mon; Wed; Fri; No Play 5–7pm.
Ladies Day: Thursday 5–7
Green Fees: £16.00.
Juveniles: Mon; Tues; Wed; Thur; Fri; 4.30 – 7.00pm.
Clubhouse Hours: 8am – 11.30pm
Clubhouse Facilites: No.

CONVENIENT HOTELS

Dalmunzie Hotel; Hotel Dumbuck.

NO.	YARDS	PAR	S.I.	NO.	YARDS	PAR	S.I.
1	337	4	7	10	422	4	4
2	376	4	3	11	510	5	8
3	332	4	11	12	155	3	18
4	158	3	17	13	334	4	10
5	355	4	9	14	310	4	16
6	257	4	15	15	307	4	14
7	256	4	5	16	489	5	2
8	186	3	13	17	386	4	6
9	408	4	1	18	339	4	12
OUT	2,765	34		IN	3,252	37	
				TOTAL	6,071	71	
STANDARD SCRATCH					71		

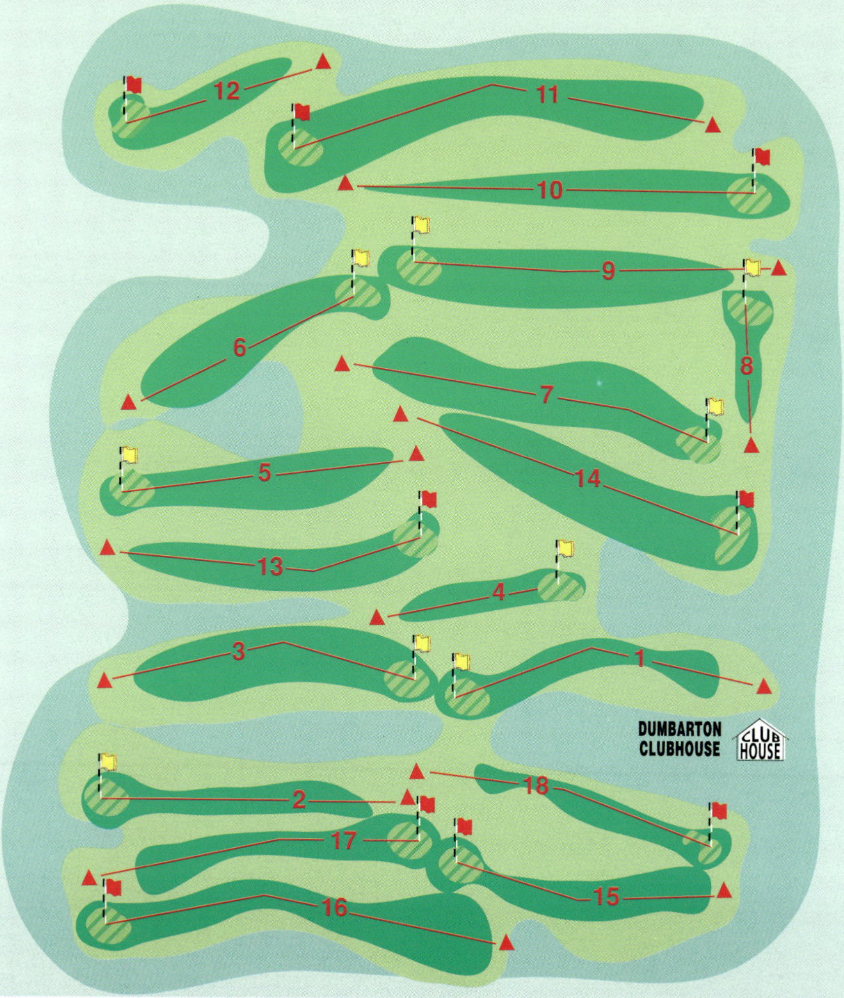

HAYSTON

DUNBARTONSHIRE

Hayston Golf Club,
Campsie Road,
Kirkintilloch. G66 1RN.
Tel: (0141) 776 1244.

LOCATION: 7 miles north of Glasgow.
SECRETARY: Mr J.V. Carmichael.
Tel: (0141)775 0723.
PROFESSIONAL: Steve Barnett.
Tel: (0141) 775 0882.
ARCHITECT: James Braid.

Tree lined parkland course.

COURSE INFORMATION

Par 69; SSS 70; Length 6,042 Yards.
Visitors: Must be introduced by a member.
Opening Hours: 8am – Dusk.
Avoid: Weekends
Ladies: Welcome.
Green Fees: £15 per round, £20 per day.
Juveniles: Restricted.
Clubhouse Hours: 8.00am – 11.00pm.

Clubhouse Dress: Lounge – collar and tie.
Clubhouse Facilities: Full catering facilities by arrangement with clubmaster.

NO.	MEDAL YARDS	GEN. YARDS	PAR	S.I.	NO.	MEDAL YARDS	GEN. YARDS	PAR	S.I.
1	420	395	4	5	10	367	340	4	12
2	502	490	5	9	11	359	353	4	6
3	289	275	4	13	12	316	251	4	16
4	118	109	3	15	13	354	341	4	4
5	340	327	4	11	14	165	158	3	14
6	434	403	4	7	15	220	208	3	8
7	437	433	4	1/19	16	489	473	5/4	2/20
8	152	142	3	17	17	384	377	4	10
9	551	519	5	3/21	18	145	138	3	18
OUT	3,243	3,093	36		IN	2,799	2,639	34/33	
					TOTAL	6,042	5,732	70/69	
					STANDARD SCRATCH	69	68		

Bunker and tree positions indicated.

HELENSBURGH

DUMBARTONSHIRE

Helensburgh Golf Club,
25 Abercromby Street,
Helensburgh. Tel: (01436) 74173.

LOCATION: 25 miles west of Glasgow.
SECRETARY: Mr D. Loch
Tel: (01436) 674173.
PROFESSIONAL: David Fotheringham.
Tel: (01436) 75505.
ARCHIRTECT: Tom Morris Snr first nine holes. In 1924 it became an 18 hole course which was redesigned by James Braid.

A moorland course which overlooks the Clyde estuary.

COURSE INFORMATION

Par 69; SSS 69; Length 6,058 Yards.
Opening Hours: Winter 8.15am to 6.30pm, Summer 7.45am to 7.00pm.
Visitors: Welcome except at weekends.
Avoid: Sat & Sun.
Ladies: Not at weekends — ladies day Tuesday.

Green Fees: £15 a round, £23 a day.
Juveniles: Restricted.
Clubhouse Hours: 9.00am to 2.30pm & 4.00pm to 11.00pm.
Clubhouse Dress: Neat dress.
Clubhouse Facilities: 11.00am to 7.00pm meals by arrangement.

CONVENIENT HOTELS

Commodore Hotel, Clyde St; Ross Lea Hotel, Rhu.

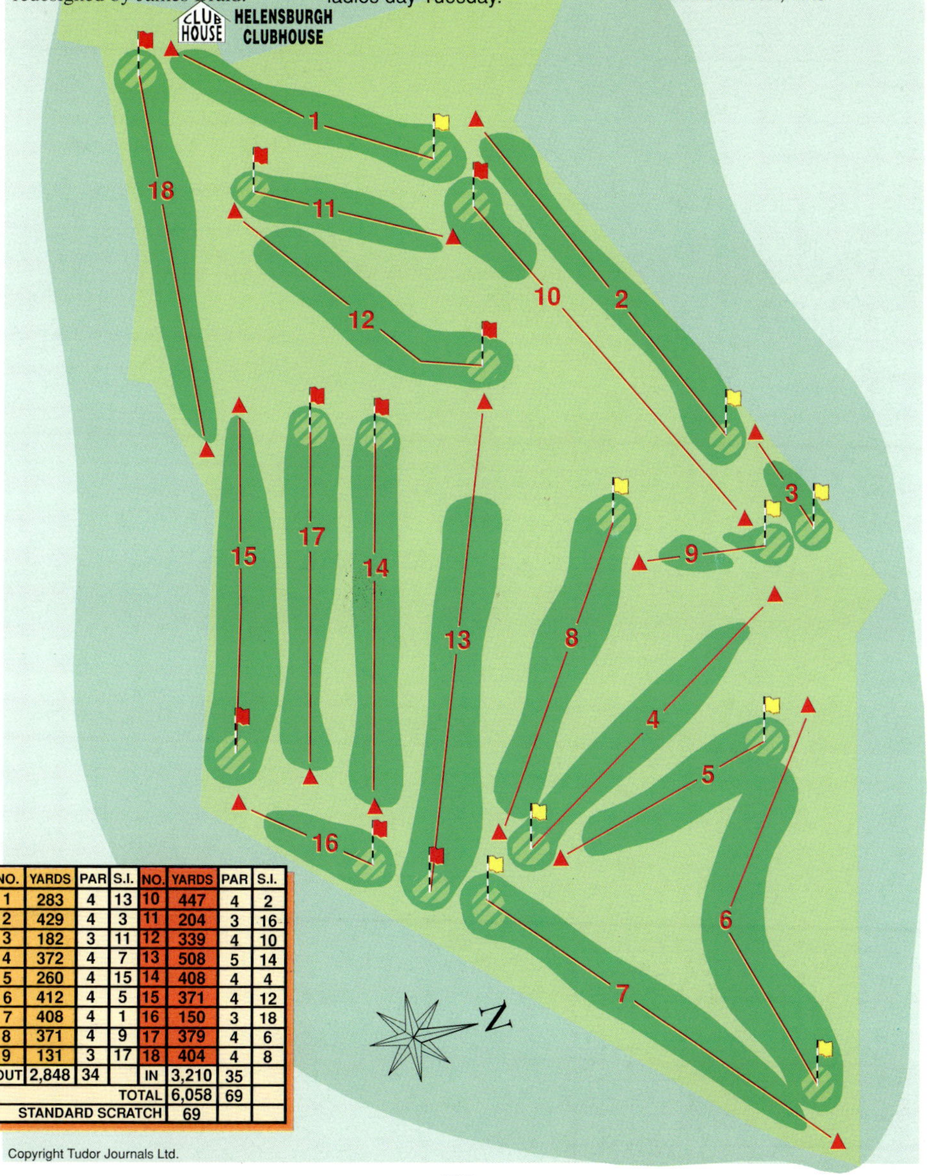

NO.	YARDS	PAR	S.I.	NO.	YARDS	PAR	S.I.
1	283	4	13	10	447	4	2
2	429	4	3	11	204	3	16
3	182	3	11	12	339	4	10
4	372	4	7	13	508	5	14
5	260	4	15	14	408	4	4
6	412	4	5	15	371	4	12
7	408	4	1	16	150	3	18
8	371	4	9	17	379	4	6
9	131	3	17	18	404	4	8
OUT	2,848	34		IN	3,210	35	
				TOTAL	6,058	69	
STANDARD SCRATCH					69		

Hilton Park Golf Club,
Auldmarroch Est.,
Stockiemuir Road,
Milngavie.
Tel: (0141) 956 5124/1215.

LOCATION: 8 miles north of Glasgow.
SECRETARY: Mrs J.A. Warnock.
Tel: (0141) 956 4657.

PROFESSIONAL: W.McCondichie.
Tel: (0141) 956 5125.
ARCHITECT: James Braid.

Tree lined rolling moorland with its 18 holes set in beautiful scenic surroundings. Hilton Course offers an interseting, challenging course and provides an enjoyable days golf.

COURSE INFORMATION

Par 70; SSS 70; Length 6,054 Yards.
Visitors: Mon-Thurs by prior arrangements.
Opening Hours: Sunrise - sunset.
Avoid: Weekends, public holidays etc.
Ladies: Restrictions on Hilton Course.
Green Fees: £20 per round, £26 per day (no weekends).
Juveniles: Strictly members only.
Clubhouse Hours: All day.
Clubhouse Dress: Smart casual until 7.00pm then collar, tie and jacket.
Clubhouse Facilities: Full catering facilities available.
Open Competitions: Seniors Open, May; Lord Fraser of Allander Tournament , Aug.

CONVENIENT HOTELS

Country Club Hotel; Kirkhouse Inn.

NO.	MEDAL YARDS	GEN. YARDS	PAR	S.I.	NO.	MEDAL YARDS	GEN. YARDS	PAR	S.I.
1	496	483	5	9	10	340	321	4	10
2	386	307	4	3	11	373	345	4	2
3	403	385	4	7	12	157	144	3	16
4	177	166	3	17	13	415	366	4	4
5	422	358	4	1	14	307	300	4	12
6	220	204	3	15	15	363	346	4	6
7	306	266	4	13	16	498	485	5	8
8	307	324	4	5	17	184	174	3	18
9	314	262	4	11	18	339	327	4	14
OUT	3,031	2,755	35		IN	2,976	2,808	35	
					TOTAL	6,007	5,563	70	
					STANDARD SCRATCH	70	67		

**Lenzie Golf Club, 19 Crosshill Road,
Lenzie. G66 5DA.
Tel: (0141) 776 1535.**

LOCATION: 6 miles from Glasgow.
SECRETARY: J.A. Chisholm.
Tel: (0141) 776 6020.
PROFESSIONAL: Jim McCallum.
Tel: (0141) 777 7748.

Challenging parkland course with many trees and ditches.

COURSE INFORMATION

Par 69; SSS 69; Length 5,984 Yards.
Visitors: By arrangement.
Opening Hours: 8.00am to dusk.
Avoid: Weekends.
Ladies: Welcome, except Tue & Thurs evenings.
Green Fees: £15 per round.
Juveniles: Permitted through the day.
Clubhouse Hours: 11am to 11pm.
Clubhouse Dress: During Summer good standard, casual.
Clubhouse Facilities: Lunches, bar lunches, high teas, dinners.

CONVENIENT HOTELS

Crowwood Hotel; Moodiesburn Hotel.

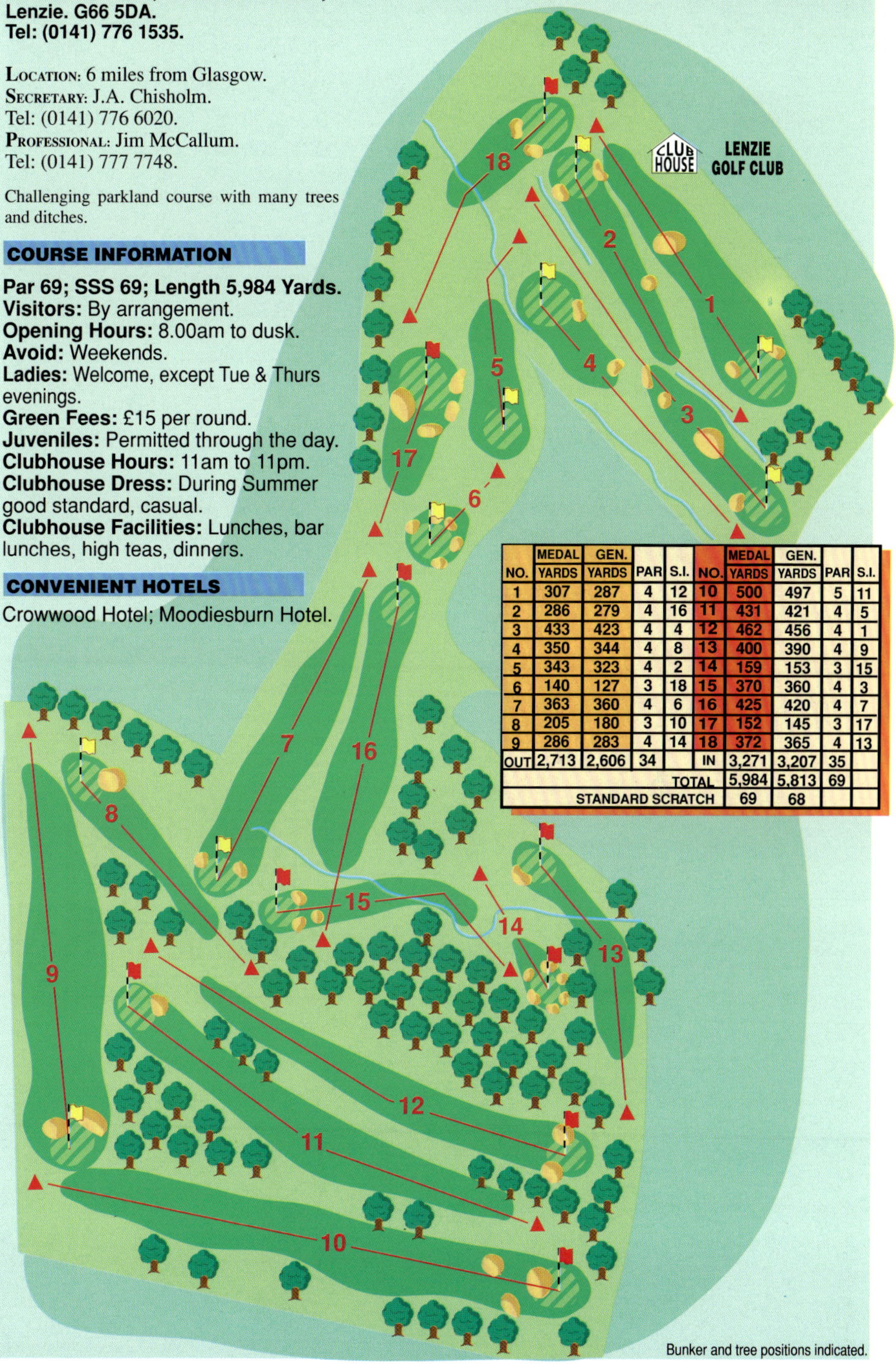

NO.	MEDAL YARDS	GEN. YARDS	PAR	S.I.	NO.	MEDAL YARDS	GEN. YARDS	PAR	S.I.
1	307	287	4	12	10	500	497	5	11
2	286	279	4	16	11	431	421	4	5
3	433	423	4	4	12	462	456	4	1
4	350	344	4	8	13	400	390	4	9
5	343	323	4	2	14	159	153	3	15
6	140	127	3	18	15	370	360	4	3
7	363	360	4	6	16	425	420	4	7
8	205	180	3	10	17	152	145	3	17
9	286	283	4	14	18	372	365	4	13
OUT	2,713	2,606	34		IN	3,271	3,207	35	
					TOTAL	5,984	5,813	69	
					STANDARD SCRATCH	69	68		

Bunker and tree positions indicated.

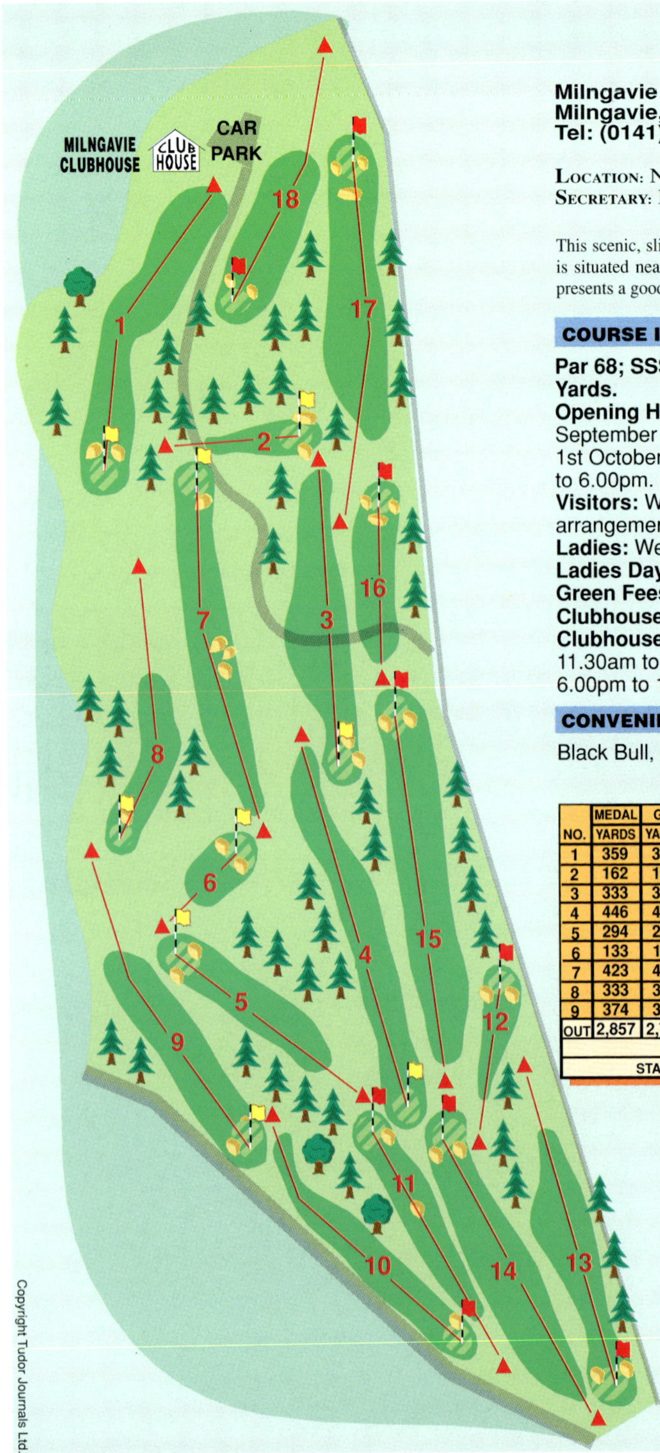

Milngavie Golf Club, Laighpark, Milngavie, G62 8EP. Tel: (0141) 956 1619.

LOCATION: North west of Glasgow.
SECRETARY: Mrs.S. Ness.

This scenic, slightly undulating moorland course is situated near the banks of Loch Lomond and presents a good challenge for any golfer.

COURSE INFORMATION

Par 68; SSS 68; Length 5,818 Yards.
Opening Hours: 1st April to 30th September — 8.00am to 11.00pm; 1st October to 31st March — 8.00am to 6.00pm.
Visitors: Welcome — prior arrangement.
Ladies: Welcome.
Ladies Day: Wednesday.
Green Fees: £15 a round, £25 a day.
Clubhouse Dress: Smart but casual.
Clubhouse Facilities: Lunch 11.30am to 2.30pm; evenings 6.00pm to 11.00pm in Summer.

CONVENIENT HOTEL

Black Bull, Milngavie.

NO.	MEDAL YARDS	GEN. YARDS	PAR	S.I.	NO.	MEDAL YARDS	GEN. YARDS	PAR	S.I.
1	359	356	4	5	10	361	352	4	6
2	162	158	3	15	11	313	299	4	12
3	333	323	4	9	12	175	170	3	16
4	446	442	4	3	13	380	376	4	1
5	294	287	4	13	14	372	339	4	10
6	133	117	3	18	15	462	460	4	8
7	423	417	4	2	16	197	193	3	17
8	333	316	4	11	17	394	390	4	4
9	374	361	4	7	18	307	296	4	14
OUT	2,857	2,777	34		IN	2,961	2,875	34	
					TOTAL	5,818	5,652	68	
STANDARD SCRATCH						68			

Bunker and tree positions indicated.

Cumbernauld Golf Club, Palacerigg Country Park, Cumbernauld G67 3HU. Tel: (01236) 734969.

Location: 2 miles south of Cumbernauld within Palacerigg Country Park off B8054.
Secretary: Jack Dunsmore.
Starters Office: (01236) 721461.
Architect: Henry Cotton.

Upland parkland course with good views North over Cumbernauld to Campsie Hills. Mostly generous wide fairways but beware of the rough. Testing 222 yards par 3 16th into prevailing wind.

COURSE INFORMATION

Par 72; SSS 71; Length 6,444 Yards.
Opening Hours: 8.00am to 8.00pm.
Visitors: Limited at weekends — avoid Sat am.
Ladies: Welcome.
Green Fees: Weekdays £7.35, Weekends £8.70.
Juveniles: Welcome.
Clubhouse Hours: 10.00am to 11.00pm.
Clubhouse Dress: Smart but casual.
Clubhouse Facilities: Meals available Wed to Sun.

CONVENIENT HOTELS

Castlecary House; Westerwood Hotel; Moddiesburn House; Crowwood Hotel.

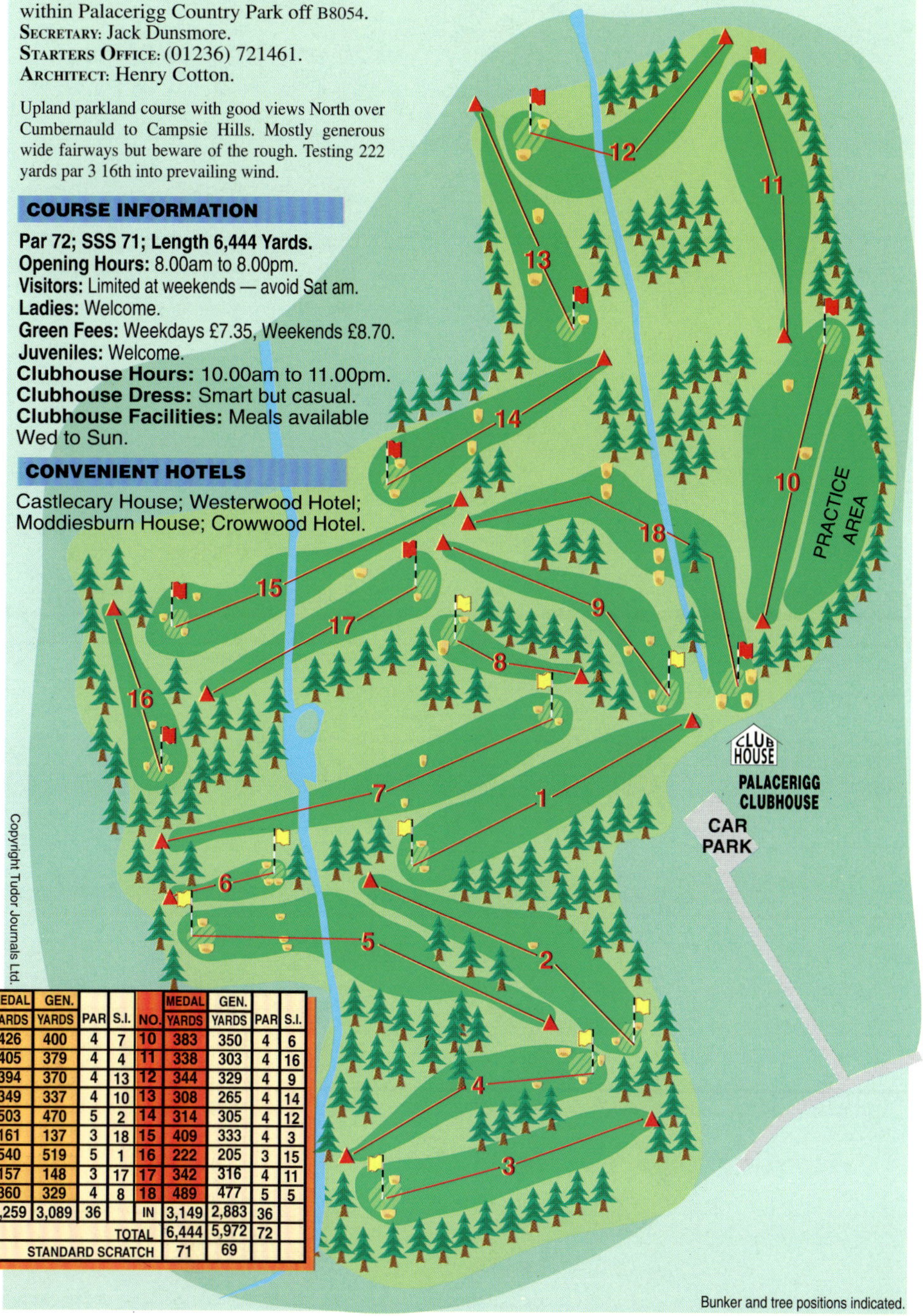

NO.	MEDAL YARDS	GEN. YARDS	PAR	S.I.	NO.	MEDAL YARDS	GEN. YARDS	PAR	S.I.
1	426	400	4	7	10	383	350	4	6
2	405	379	4	4	11	338	303	4	16
3	394	370	4	13	12	344	329	4	9
4	349	337	4	10	13	308	265	4	14
5	503	470	5	2	14	314	305	4	12
6	161	137	3	18	15	409	333	4	3
7	540	519	5	1	16	222	205	3	15
8	157	148	3	17	17	342	316	4	11
9	360	329	4	8	18	489	477	5	5
OUT	3,259	3,089	36		IN	3,149	2,883	36	
					TOTAL	6,444	5,972	72	
					STANDARD SCRATCH	71	69		

Bunker and tree positions indicated.

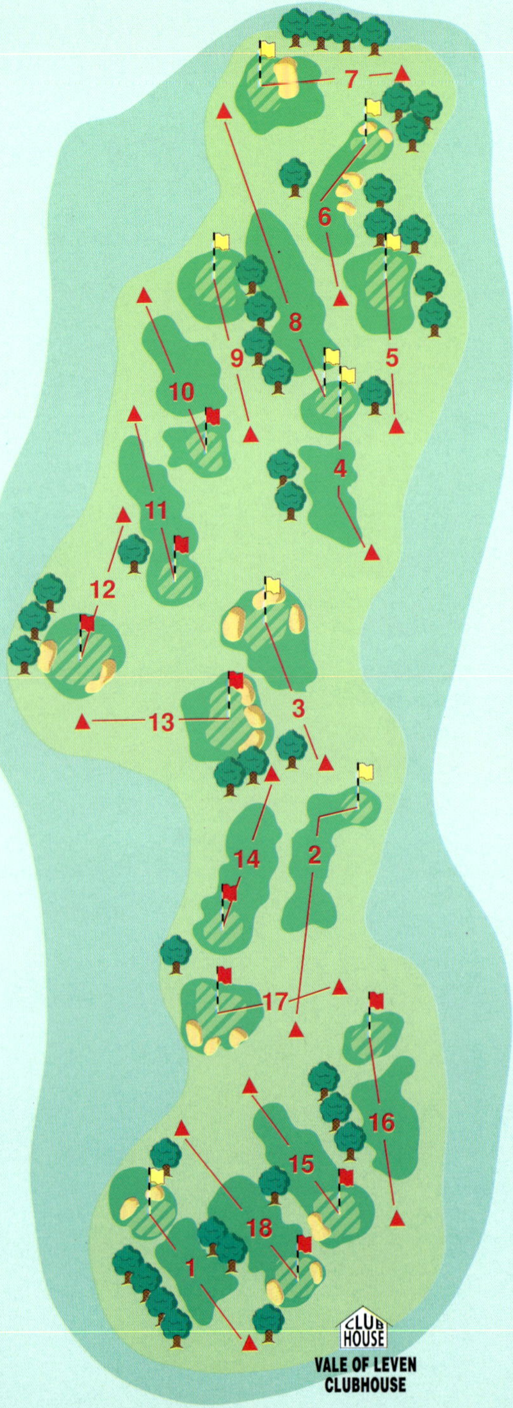

Vale of Leven Golf Club, Northfield Road, Bonhill, Alexandrla.
Tel: (01389) 52351.

LOCATION: Off A82 at Bonhill.
SECRETARY: Mr J. Stewart.
Tel: (01389) 757691.

Moorland course with scenic views of Loch Lomond and the surrounding area.

COURSE INFORMATION

Par 67; SSS 66; Length 5,162 Yards.
Opening Hours: 8.00am onwards.
Visitors: No visitors on Sat. between 1st April to 30th Sept.
Avoid: During medal competitions.
Ladies: Fri. after 5.00pm.
Ladies Day: Thursday.
Green Fees: Weekdays £12 per round, £18 per day; Weekends £16 per round, £24 per day.
Juveniles: Contact clubhouse.
Clubhouse Hours: 11.00am to 11.00pm daily.
Clubhouse Dress: No shell suits, sleeveless tops, track suits and shorts.
Clubhouse Facilities: Catering available.

CONVENIENT HOTELS

Duck Bay Marina; Tullichewan Hotel; Cameron House.

NO.	YARDS	PAR	S.I.	NO.	YARDS	PAR	S.I.
1	361	4	7	10	292	4	10
2	485	5	5	11	350	4	2
3	259	4	11	12	164	3	17
4	411	4	1	13	180	3	12
5	174	3	16	14	315	4	8
6	345	4	9	15	248	4	13
7	190	3	14	16	272	4	4
8	375	4	3	17	178	3	18
9	198	3	15	18	365	4	6
OUT	2,798	34		IN	2,364	33	
				TOTAL	5,162	67	
				STANDARD SCRATCH	66		

Bunker and tree positions indicated.

Westerwood Golf Club,
Westerwood,
St Andrews Drive,
Cumbernauld, Glasgow.
Tel: (01236) 457171.
Fax: (01236) 738478.

LOCATION: Signposted off A80 Glasgow/Stirling.
PROFESSIONAL: Steven Killen. Tel: (01236) 452772.
ARCHITECT: Seve Ballesteros and Dave Thomas.

This undulating course has impressive views in all directions. Each hole meanders through silver birches, firs, heaths and heathers, each offering different and exciting challenges to every class of golfer.

COURSE INFORMATION

Par 73; SSS 72; Length 6,429 Yds.
Visitors: All visitors welcome - course etiquette must be adhered to.
Opening Hours: 8.00am–dusk.
Ladies: Welcome.
Green Fees: Weekdays £22.50 a round, weekends £35 a round.
Juveniles: Over 14 years.
Clubhouse Hours: Breakfast from 7.00am; last meal order 9.45pm.
Clubhouse Dress: Casual but smart, no jeans.
Clubhouse Facilities: Brasserie style menu.

CONVENIENT HOTEL

Westerwood Hotel.

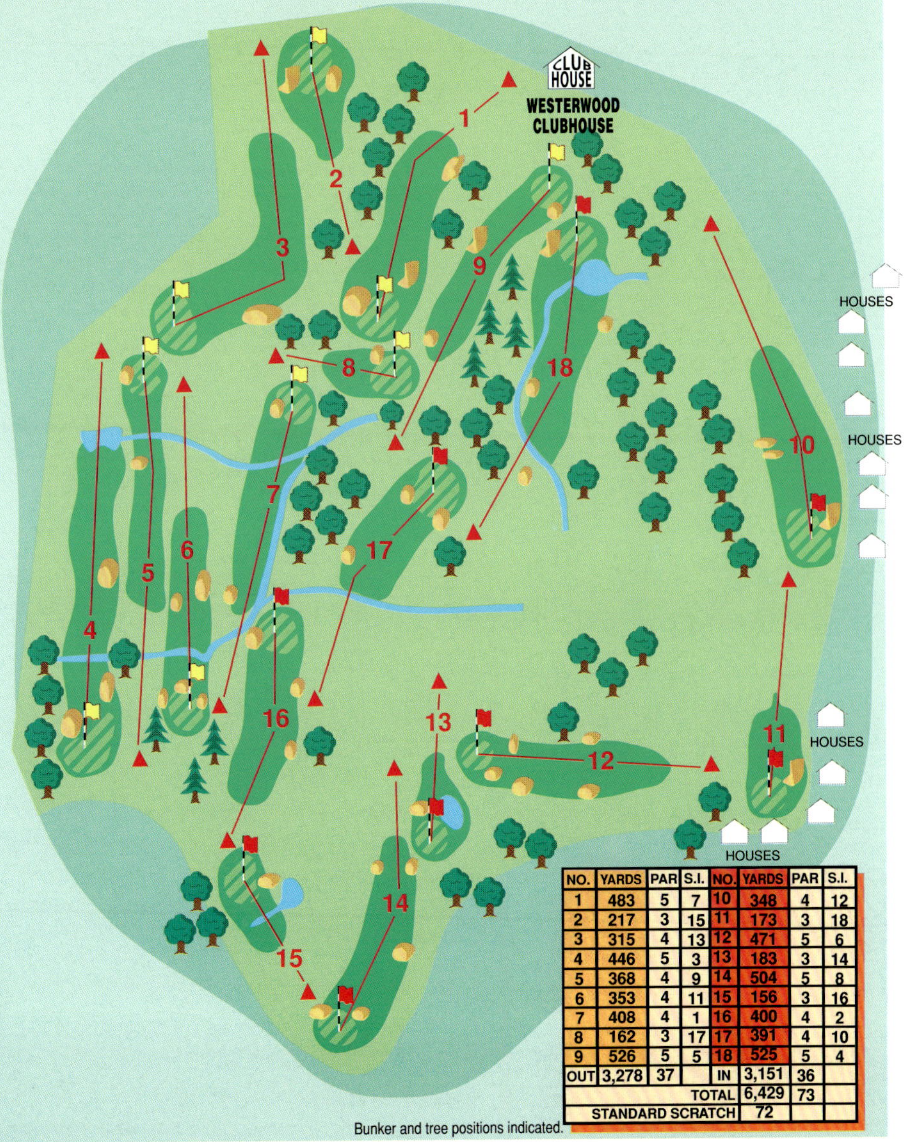

NO.	YARDS	PAR	S.I.	NO.	YARDS	PAR	S.I.
1	483	5	7	10	348	4	12
2	217	3	15	11	173	3	18
3	315	4	13	12	471	5	6
4	446	5	3	13	183	3	14
5	368	4	9	14	504	5	8
6	353	4	11	15	156	3	16
7	408	4	1	16	400	4	2
8	162	3	17	17	391	4	10
9	526	5	5	18	525	5	4
OUT	3,278	37		IN	3,151	36	
				TOTAL	6,429	73	
				STANDARD SCRATCH	72		

Bunker and tree positions indicated.

WINDYHILL

Windyhill Golf Club,
Windyhill, Bearsden,
Glasgow. G61 4QQ.
Tel: (0141) 942 2349.

LOCATION: 8 miles northwest of Glasgow.
SECRETARY: A.J. Miller.
Tel: (0141) 942 2349.
PROFESSIONAL: R. Collinson.
Tel: (0141) 942 7157.
ARCHITECT: James Braid.

Undulating, parkland / moorland course with magnificent views of the Glasgow area.

COURSE INFORMATION

Par 71; SSS 70; Length 6,254 Yards.
Visitors: Welcome.
Opening Hours: 8.30am – Dusk.
Avoid: Weekends.
Ladies: Restricted after 5pm Mondays – Wednesdays.
Green Fees: £20 (Mon -Fri)£2 w/m; £4 w/m (Sat & Sun).
Juveniles: As per ladies.
Clubhouse Hours: 8.30am – 11pm.
Clubhouse Dress: No denims, tee-shirts, training shoes etc.
Clubhouse Facilities: Every day except Thursday.
Open Competitions: Windyhill Trophy – last Sunday in August.

CONVENIENT HOTELS

Black Bull, Milngavie.

NO.	MEDAL YARDS	GEN. YARDS	PAR	S.I.	NO.	MEDAL YARDS	GEN. YARDS	PAR	S.I.
1	362	358	4	9	10	178	163	3	10
2	162	152	3	17	11	292	281	4	14
3	425	414	4	7	12	450	447	4	2
4	368	357	4	11	13	500	489	5	4
5	386	375	4	13	14	154	144	3	18
6	421	416	4	3	15	479	476	5	6
7	193	183	3	15	16	380	312	4	8
8	480	451	5/4	5	17	295	290	4	16
9	420	414	4	1	18	309	246	4/3	12
OUT	3,217	3,120	35/34		IN	3,037	2,848	36/35	
					TOTAL	6,254	5,968	71/69	
					STANDARD SCRATCH	70	69		

Bunker and tree positions indicated.

GOLF DAYS™ SCOTLAND

FIFE

LOMOND HILLS HOTEL

FREUCHIE, FIFE.

Scottish Tourist Board

'IN THE HEART OF FIFE'

Close to Glenrothes and many golf courses, including St. Andrews, 25 bedrooms, all with private facilities, radio, TV, direct dial telephone, centrally heated. Intimate candlelit restaurant. Freshly cooked table d'hote and a la carte including many flambe dishes. Indoor heated swimming pool and leisure centre for guests.

2 & 3 day golf breaks, including dinner.

Large car park, and function suite for lunch & tea bookings — up to 150 people.

FOR RESERVATIONS:

Tel: 01337-857329/857498/858180.

THE WOODSIDE HOTEL

HIGH STREET, ABERDOUR, FIFE KY3 0SW.
Tel: (01383) 860328. Fax: (01383) 860920.

NOW RE-OPEN FOLLOWING MAJOR REFURBISHMENT

You will enjoy our warm hospitality, and excellent food.
Please phone to find out how you can have FREE GOLF when you stay with us !

This fine Scottish Baronial-Style hotel is situated in Scotland's golfing heartland — only 12 miles from St. Andrews and with 25 superb courses within 25 miles. All rooms are centrally heated, have private bathroom or shower, satellite TV, telephone and tea/coffee facilities. The hotel cuisine is based on the freshest of local produce.

FREE GOLF

UNLIMITED FREE GOLF on Elie 9 hole course (accessible directly from the hotel) is included in our D, B and B rate in our unbeatable Golfing and Golf Tuition Packages. Staff with many years experience of organised itineraries personally tailored to golfers of all standards will ensure that you have a golfing holiday to remember.

THE GOLF HOTEL

Scottish Tourist Board Commended

THE GOLF HOTEL, ELIE, FIFE KY9 1EF.
TEL: 01333-330209 FAX: 01333-330381

THE CRUSOE HOTEL

Perfectly situated in this delightful harbour and surrounded by the finest golf courses in Scotland — St. Andrews, Ladybank, Leven, Elie and Crail to name a few, all within a short drive from our hotel. Come and have a relaxing golf break with us.

For further information contact:

THE CRUSOE HOTEL
THE HARBOUR, LOWER LARGO KY8 6BT.
TEL: 01333–320759. FAX: 01333–320865.

ABERDOUR

Aberdour golf Club,
Seaside Place,
Aberdour, Fife. KY3 0TX.
Tel: (01383) 860080.

LOCATION: On the shore of the River Forth. The entry to Seaside Place – from the narrow Shore Road – is via a sharp corner with parking on this private road right up to the corner.
SECRETARY: John Train.
Tel: (01383) 860080.
PROFESSIONAL: Gordon McCallum.
Tel: (01383) 860256.

The Club is located in a beautiful situation on the shore of the River Forth. It is a parkland course with some very interesting holes, for instance, every one remembers the second.

COURSE INFORMATION

Par 67; SSS 67; Length 5,460 Yards.
Opening Hours: 9am-dusk.
Visitors: Welcome but not on Sat.
Green Fees: £17 per round £28 per day Mon – Fri.
Clubhouse Hours: Closes at 11pm during the season and earlier out-of-season. Visitors are asked to vacate the premises timeously.
Clubhouse Dress: No denim, sleeveless/collarless shirts, track suits/shell suits, shorts or trainers. Similar guide-lines apply to the course.
Clubhouse Facilities: Tea, coffee, soup, sandwiches, 3 course luncheon and dinners available (limited on Tuesdays).

CONVENIENT HOTEL

The Woodside Hotel.

NO.	YARDS	PAR	S.I.	NO.	YARDS	PAR	S.I.
1	159	3	11	10	530	5	3
2	159	3	13	11	340	4	10
3	343	4	6	12	163	3	14
4	287	4	16	13	251	4	15
5	359	4	9	14	318	4	18
6	365	4	5	15	171	3	8
7	163	3	17	16	449	4	2
8	458	4	1	17	354	4	7
9	394	4	4	18	197	3	12
OUT	2,687	33		IN	2,773	34	
				TOTAL	5,460	67	
				STANDARD SCRATCH	67		

Bunker and tree positions indicated.

AUCHTERDERRAN

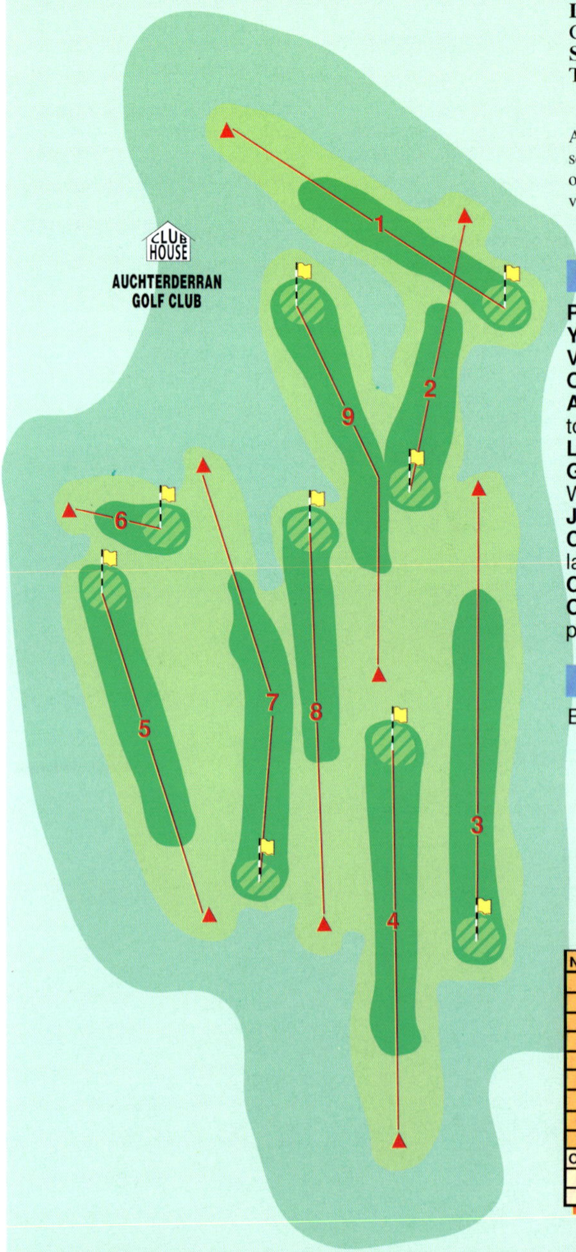

Auchterderran Golf Club, Woodend Road, Cardenden. Tel: (01592) 721579.

LOCATION: One mile north of Cardenden.
SECRETARY: William Nicholson. Tel: (01592) 722223.

An interesting nine hole course set in quiet and scenic surroundings in the former mining village of Cardenden. The course is freely open to visitors and bookings from parties are welcome.

COURSE INFORMATION

Par 66; SSS 66; Length 5,250 Yards.
Visitors: Welcome.
Opening Hours: 7am – Dusk.
Avoid: Saturday mornings & tournaments.
Ladies: Welcome.
Green Fees: Weekdays – £8; Weekends – £12.
Juveniles: Not permitted after 6pm.
Clubhouse Hours: 11am - 10 pm or later if required.
Clubhouse Dress: Casual.
Clubhouse Facilities: Catering for parties available on request.

CONVENIENT HOTEL

Bowhill Hotel, Bowhill, Cardenden.

NO.	YARDS	PAR	S.I.	NO.	YARDS	PAR	S.I.
1	201	3	15	10	201	3	16
2	316	4	7	11	316	4	8
3	432	4	1	12	432	4	2
4	341	4	3	13	341	4	4
5	248	3	13	14	248	3	14
6	117	3	17	15	117	3	18
7	287	4	11	16	287	4	12
8	338	4	5	17	338	4	6
9	345	4	9	18	345	4	10
OUT	2,625	33		IN	2,625	33	
				TOTAL	5,250	66	
STANDARD SCRATCH					66		

Balbirnie Park Golf Club, Balburnie Park, Markinch, Glenrothes, Fife. KY7 6DD.
Tel: (0592) 752006/612095.

LOCATION: 2 miles east of Glenrothes on the outskirts of Markinch.
SECRETARY: A. Bond.
Tel: (01592) 752006.

Rolling parkland course. Professional record 69, Amateur record 66. Private club established 1983.

COURSE INFORMATION

Par 71; SSS 70; Length 6,210 Yards.
Opening Hours: 7 Days.
Visitors: Welcome.
Ladies: Welcome; Ladies day Thursday.
Green Fees: Mon – Weekdays £20 round; £28 day. Weekend £28 round; £36 day.

Juveniles: Welcome.
Clubhouse Hours: Open 7 days April - Oct. 11am - 11pm open & 7 days during winter with restricted hours.
Clubhouse Dress: Smart/Casual.
Clubhouse Facilities: Snacks, lunch, high tea and full meals.

NO.	YARDS	PAR	S.I.	NO.	YARDS	PAR	S.I.
1	397	4	3	10	493	5	2
2	336	4	11	11	175	3	18
3	357	4	9	12	390	4	8
4	195	3	13	13	336	4	14
5	295	4	15	14	206	3	12
6	478	5	5	15	412	4	6
7	166	3	17	16	395	4	4
8	422	4	1	17	319	4	16
9	356	4	7	18	482	5	10
OUT	3,002	35		IN	3,208	36	
				TOTAL	6,210	71	
				STANDARD SCRATCH	70		

Bunker and tree positions indicated.

Burntisland Golf House Club, Dodhead, Burntisland, Fife. Tel: (01592) 873247.

Location: 1 mile east of Burntisland on B923.
Secretary: G. Brown. Tel: (01333) 874093.
Professional: Jacky Montgomery. Tel: (01592) 873247.
Architect: Willie Park Jnr.

Parkland course with some hills overlooking the River Forth with scenic views towards the Lothians.

COURSE INFORMATION

Par 70; SSS 69; Length 5,965 Yards.
Opening Hours: 8.00am to dusk.
Visitors: Parties limited to 24 at weekends — no four balls at weekends..
Ladies: Welcome. Ladies day Thursday.
Green Fees: Weekdays £18 round; £25 day.Weekend £25 round; £38 day.
Juveniles: Welcome.
Clubhouse Hours: 7.30am to 11.30pm.
Clubhouse Dress: Respectable — No trainers or jeans after 9.00pm.
Clubhouse Facilities: Full catering facilities.

CONVENIENT HOTELS

Inchview Hotel, Burntisland; Kingswood Hotel, Burntisland.

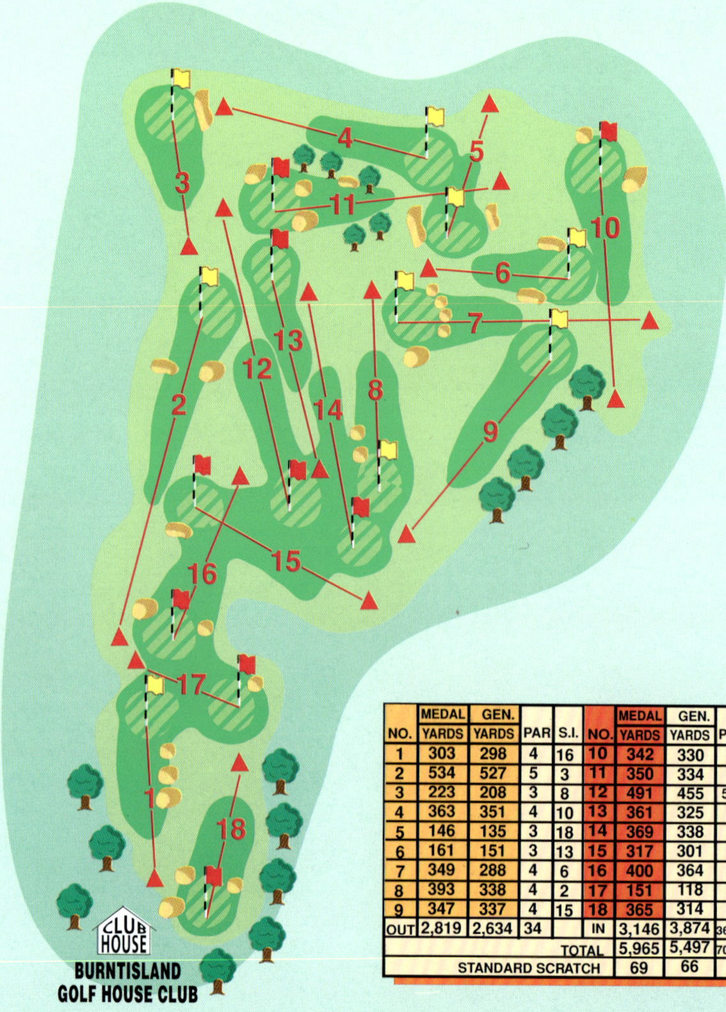

NO.	MEDAL YARDS	GEN. YARDS	PAR	S.I.	NO.	MEDAL YARDS	GEN. YARDS	PAR	S.I.
1	303	298	4	16	10	342	330	4	11
2	534	527	5	3	11	350	334	4	5
3	223	208	3	8	12	491	455	5/4	1
4	363	351	4	10	13	361	325	4	7
5	146	135	3	18	14	369	338	4	9
6	161	151	3	13	15	317	301	4	17
7	349	288	4	6	16	400	364	4	4
8	393	338	4	2	17	151	118	3	12
9	347	337	4	15	18	365	314	4	14
OUT	2,819	2,634	34		IN	3,146	3,874	36/35	
					TOTAL	5,965	5,497	70/69	
					STANDARD SCRATCH	69	66		

Bunker and tree positions indicated.

Practice makes perfect. Scottish Highland Photo Library.

COWDENBEATH MUNICIPAL

Cowdenbeath Municipal Golf Club, Cowdenbeath, Fife. KY4 8PF.
Tel: (01383) 511918.

LOCATION: 7 miles east of Dunfermline which is a major town.
SECRETARY: Jack T. Martin.
Tel: (01383) 512067.
ARCHITECT: Fife regional council (Planning Dept).

Cowenbeath, one of Fife's newest courses, is constructed on a former open cast site. Designed and constructed by Fife Regional Council. It enables golfers to test their skills on a very generous tree lined parkland course with well situated bunkers throughout this 9 hole course. Another nine holes are still at the design stage.

COURSE INFORMATION

Par 72; SSS 71; Length 6,552 Yards; 5,962 Metres.
Opening Hours: Sunrise to sunset.
Visitors: No restrictions.
Avoid: Check for club competitions at weekend.
Ladies: No restrictions.
Juveniles: Weekdays after 6pm.
Clubhouse Hours: 9am – 11pm.
Clubhouse Dress: Informal.
Clubhouse Facilities: None.
Open Competitions: 28th & 29th August.

CONVENIENT HOTELS

Struan Bank Hotel; Mosmorran Hotel; Commercial Hotel.

NO.	YARDS	PAR	S.I.	NO.	YARDS	PAR	S.I.
1	326	4	15	10	326	4	16
2	351	4	9	11	351	4	10
3	411	4	3	12	411	4	4
4	208	3	17	13	208	3	18
5	329	4	13	14	329	4	14
6	376	4	5	15	376	4	6
7	375	4	7	16	375	4	8
8	528	5	1	17	528	5	2
9	357	4	11	18	357	4	12
OUT	3,261	36		IN	3,261	36	
				TOTAL	6,552	72	
				STANDARD SCRATCH	71		

Tree positions indicated.

Crail Golfing Society,
Balcomie Clubhouse,
Fifeness, Crail.
Tel: (01333) 450278.

Location: 11 Miles South East of St. Andrews.
Secretary: Mr Horsefield. Tel: (01333) 450278.
Professional: Graeme Lennie. Tel: (01333) 450960.
Architect: Partially designed by 'Old' Tom Morris.

The Crail Golfing Society is the seventh oldest golf club in the world, and is one of even fewer possessing a complete set of minutes from its inception. The course is located at Fifeness, the most easterly point of the East Neuk of Fife and eleven miles South East of St. Andrews; it is classic links with some parkland. The course follows a magnificent coastline and every hole is within sight of the sea. It is a delightful holiday course with a SSS of 68. The clubhouse stands on a commanding position offering panoramic views of the North Sea.

COURSE INFORMATION

Par 69; SSS 68; Length 5,720 Yards.
Opening Hours: Dawn – Dusk.
Visitors: Welcome, except on some competition days.
Avoid: Up to 10am; 12noon – 2pm; 5pm – 6.30pm.
Ladies: Welcome; Ladies day Thursday.
Green Fees: Monday – Friday round £18; day £26; Saturday/Sunday round £23; Day £34. Juveniles £8 per round Monday–Friday.
Juveniles: Welcome.
Clubhouse Hours: 8am – 11pm.
Clubhouse Dress: Smart/Casual; shorts not allowed in clubhouse.
Clubhouse Facilities: Catering available daily until 8pm or by arrangement.

CONVENIENT HOTELS

Balcomie Links Hotel;
Golf Hotel;
Croma Hotel.

NO.	MEDAL YARDS	GEN. YARDS	PAR	S.I.	NO.	MEDAL YARDS	GEN. YARDS	PAR	S.I.
1	312	304	4	15	10	209	200	3	12
2	480	435	5/4	3	11	500	433	5/4	2
3	179	166	3	17	12	489	480	5	6
4	348	309	4	7	13	215	207	3	8
5	346	273	4	5	14	149	139	3	16
6	334	271	4	11	15	265	254	4	18
7	421	416	4	1	16	163	156	3	14
8	306	254	4	13	17	461	420	4	4
9	334	285	4	9	18	209	200	3	10
OUT	3,060	2,713	36		IN	2,660	2,489	33	
					TOTAL	5,720	5,202	69	
					STANDARD SCRATCH	68			

Bunker and tree positions indicated.

CUPAR

Cupar Golf Club, Hilltarvit, Cupar, Fife. KY 15 5JT. Tel: (01334) 653549.

Location: 10 miles west of St Andrews.
Secretary: C.J.H. McCulloch. Tel: (01334) 652176.

Cupar Golf Club is the oldest 9 hole Golf Club in Scotland being instituted in 1855. It is a parkland / hillside course which allows for magnificent views of the Howe of Fife and the Lomond Hills. Each hole has its own character and challenge and is maintained to a high standard of green keeping. The course will appeal to players of all handicaps.

COURSE INFORMATION

Par 68; SSS 65; Length 5,074 Yards.
Opening Hours: 09.00am for visitors.
Visitors: Welcome before 5.00pm except Sat.
Ladies: Ladies day Competition evenings on Wednesdays.
Green Fees: £10 and £12
Juveniles: Welcome.
Clubhouse Hours: Normal bar hours with extensions on Friday and Saturday evenings.
Clubhouse Dress: Informal but tidy.
Clubhouse Facilities: During bar hours full catering Facilities are available.
Open Competitions: Ladies June; Mixed July; Boys July; Mens August ; Girls August.

CONVENIENT HOTEL

Ferniecastle Hotel, Letham.

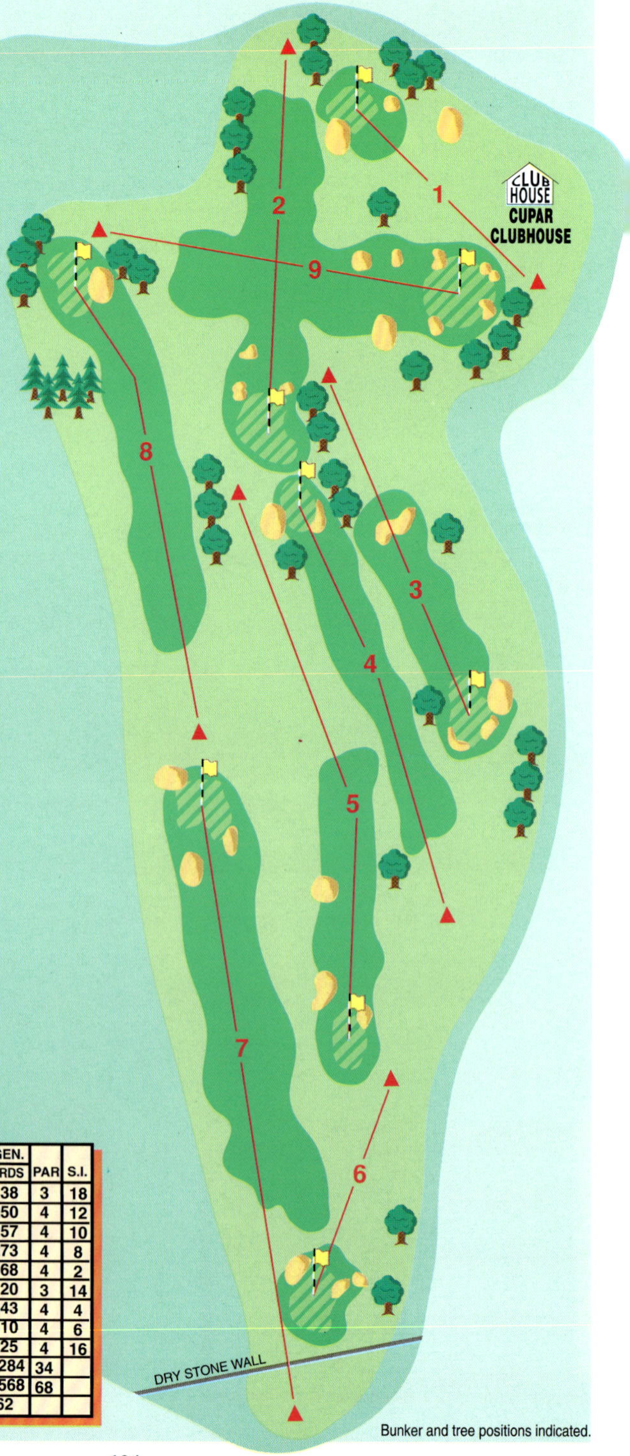

NO.	MEDAL YARDS	GEN. YARDS	PAR	S.I.	NO.	MEDAL YARDS	GEN. YARDS	PAR	S.I.
1	184	138	3	17	10	184	138	3	18
2	259	250	4	11	11	259	250	4	12
3	277	257	4	9	12	277	257	4	10
4	319	273	4	7	13	319	273	4	8
5	391	368	4	1	14	391	368	4	2
6	142	120	3	13	15	142	120	3	14
7	373	343	4	3	16	373	343	4	4
8	335	310	4	5	17	335	310	4	6
9	257	225	4	15	18	257	225	4	16
OUT	2,537	2,284	34		IN	2,537	2,284	34	
					TOTAL	5,074	4,568	68	
					STANDARD SCRATCH	65	62		

Bunker and tree positions indicated.

DUNFERMLINE

Dunfermline Golf Club, Pitfirrane, Crossford, Dunfermline. KY12 8QV. Tel: (01383) 723534.

LOCATION: 2 miles west of Dunfermline on A994.
SECRETARY: Robert De Rose. Tel: (01383) 723534.
PROFESSIONAL: S. Craig.
ARCHITECT: Stutt & Partners.

Attractive and gently undulating parkland type course, with the clubhouse being a Category 'A' listed building.

COURSE INFORMATION

Par 72; SSS 70; Length 6,243 Yards.
Opening Hours: Societies as arranged – casual visitors 10am – 12pm & 2pm – 4 pm.
Visitors: Monday to Friday only. Sunday's 10am-12noon; 2pm-4pm. No parties at weekends.
Green Fees: One round £20; Day tickets £28; No visitors at weekends.
Juveniles: Welcome.
Clubhouse Hours: Summer 8am – 11pm. (Bar 11am - 11pm).
Clubhouse Dress: Smart dress expected (no trainers, jeans or shell suits).
Clubhouse Facilities: Full catering except Monday; bar snack catering 7 days.

CONVENIENT HOTELS

Keavil House Hotel, Crossford; Pitfirrane Arms Hotel, Crossford.

NO.	MEDAL YARDS	GEN. YARDS	PAR	S.I.	NO.	MEDAL YARDS	GEN. YARDS	PAR	S.I.
1	288	277	4	18	10	402	371	4	4
2	214	176	3	11	11	315	276	4	17
3	466	460	5	1	12	348	340	4	13
4	376	356	4	5	13	165	160	3	6
5	173	158	3	16	14	383	363	4	2
6	377	360	4	3	15	498	485	5	10
7	497	458	5	7	16	163	148	3	15
8	344	327	4	14	17	507	454	5	8
9	192	170	3	9	18	535	480	5	12
OUT	2,927	2,742	35		IN	3,316	3,077	37	
					TOTAL	6,243	5,819	72	
					STANDARD SCRATCH	70	68		

**Dunnikier Park Golf Club,
Dunnikier Way, Kirkcaldy,
Fife, KY1 3LP.
Tel: (01592) 261599.**

LOCATION: Northern boundary of Kirkcaldy.
SECRETARY: R. A. Waddell.
Tel: (01592) 200627.
PROFESSIONAL: Gregor Whyte.
Tel: (01592) 642121.

Parkland course now 30 years old; tree lined fairways; flat; generous; a good test of golf.

COURSE INFORMATION

Par 72; SSS 72; Length 6,601Yards.
Opening Hours: Weekday 11am– 2.30pm 5pm–11pm. Sat. all day Sun. 11am–11pm.
Visitors: Welcome.
Winter Months: Oct – Mar. Open 7pm – 11.
Ladies: Welcome.
Green Fees: £10 Round £17 Day Weekday. £13 & £19 Weekend.

Clubhouse Hours: Mon. – Fri. 11am – 2.30pm, 5pm – 11pm. Sat. all day, Sun. 11am – 11pm.
Clubhouse dress: Sat evening – No jeans etc.
Clubhouse facilities: Full facilities available.

CONVENIENT HOTELS

Dunnikier House Hotel; Dean Park Hotel.

NO.	YARDS	PAR	S.I.	NO.	YARDS	PAR	S.I.
1	423	4	6	10	366	4	12
2	385	4	9	11	163	3	17
3	201	3	15	12	597	5	1
4	358	4	10	13	305	4	7
5	501	5	4	14	198	3	16
6	157	3	18	15	418	4	5
7	371	4	13	16	333	4	14
8	383	4	11	17	397	4	8
9	547	5	2	18	498	5	3
OUT	3,326	36		IN	3,275	36	
				TOTAL	6,601	72	
STANDARD SCRATCH					72		

Bunker and tree positions indicated.

ELIE GOLF HOUSE

Golf House Club Elie, Leven, Fife. KY9 JA5.
Tel: (01333) 330327.

LOCATION: St. Andrews 12 Miles.
SECRETARY: A. Sneddon.
Tel: (01333) 330301.
PROFESSIONAL: Robin Wilson.
Tel: (01333) 330955

18 Hole links course 6,241 yards. The course has evolved over several centuries on natural links land with the first golf club formed in 1832.

COURSE INFORMATION

Par 70; SSS 70; Length 6,241 Yards.
Opening Hours: 8.00am – sunset.
Visitors: Not before 10.00am; Not on Sundays; May – October.
Ladies: Not before 10.00am; Ladies day – Friday.
Avoid: See Above.
Green Fees: Weekday £24 per round; £32 per day; weekend £36 per round; £48 per day.
Juveniles: Not before 10.00am.
Clubhouse Hours: 8.00am – 10.30pm.
Clubhouse Dress: Smokeroom & dinning room – jacket & tie; otherwise smart casual.
Clubhouse Facilities: Lunches, snack meals.

CONVENIENT HOTELS

Golf Hotel, Elie;
The Elms, Elie.

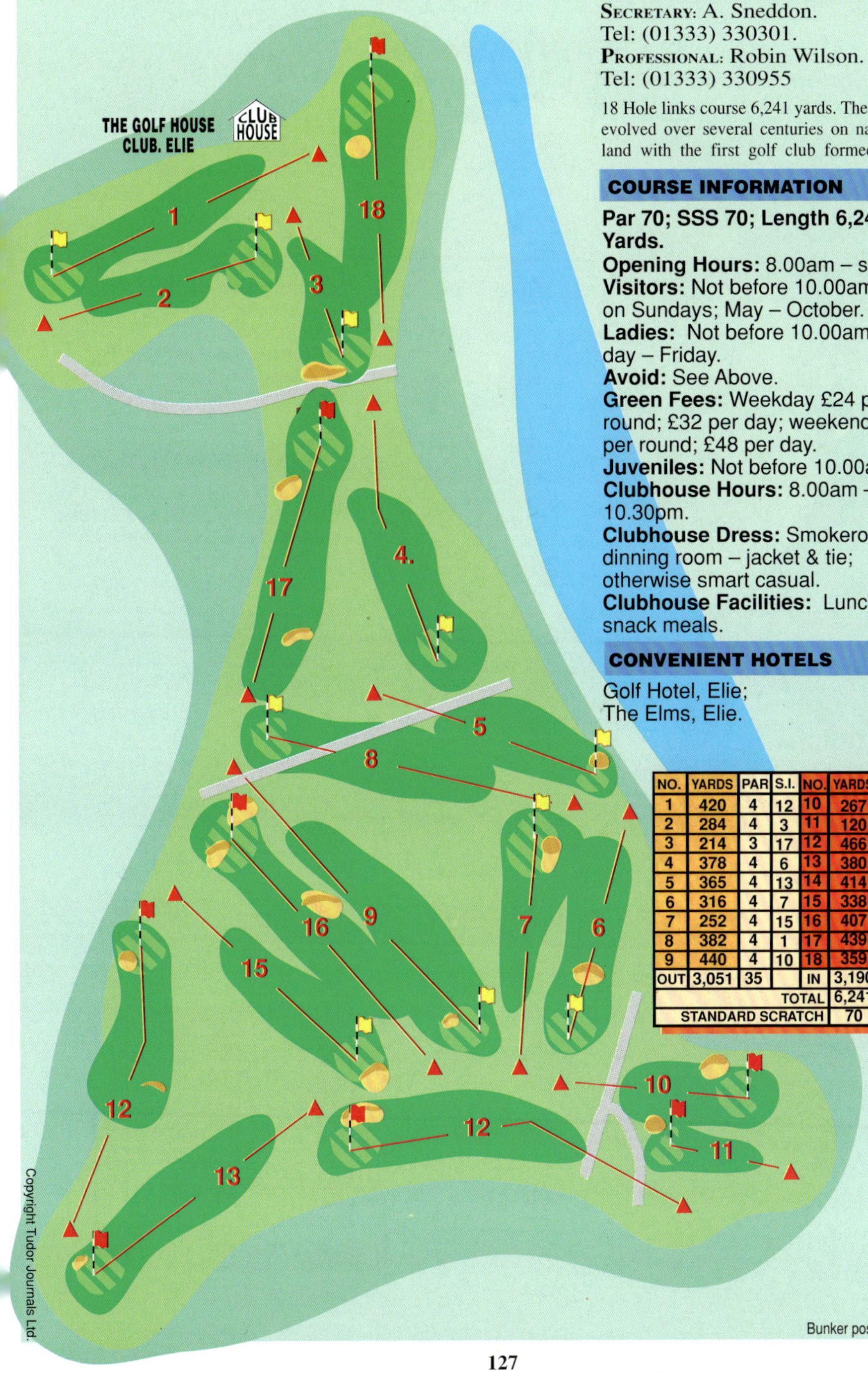

NO.	YARDS	PAR	S.I.	NO.	YARDS	PAR	S.I.
1	420	4	12	10	267	4	
2	284	4	3	11	120	3	
3	214	3	17	12	466	4	
4	378	4	6	13	380	4	
5	365	4	13	14	414	4	
6	316	4	7	15	338	4	
7	252	4	15	16	407	4	
8	382	4	1	17	439	4	
9	440	4	10	18	359	4	
OUT	3,051	35		IN	3,190	35	
				TOTAL	6,241	70	
				STANDARD SCRATCH	70		

Bunker positions indicated.

GLENROTHES

**Glenrothes Golf Club,
Golf Course Rd,
Glenrothes. KY6 2LA.
Tel: (01592) 758686/756541.**

LOCATION: Glenrothes West 35 miles North East of Edinburgh off A92.
SECRETARY: Mrs P.V. Landells. Tel: (01592) 756941.

Parkland course, pleaseant outlook to Lomond Hills and Firth of Forth. Burn comes into play on 11th, 12th, 13th and 18th holes. Wide fairways, large greens. Back nine hilly.

COURSE INFORMATION

Par 71; SSS 71; Length 6,444 Yards.

Opening Hours: 7.00am – Dusk.
Visitors: Welcome.
Ladies: As above; Ladies Day – Wednesday 17.18 – 18.18.
Green Fees: Weekday £10 per Round; £15 per Day; Weekend £11 per Round; £17 per Day.
Juveniles: Permitted.
Clubhouse Hours: 11.00am – 2.30pm; 5.00pm – 11.00pm; Summer 11.00am – 11.00pm (Weekends).
Clubhouse Dress: Smart-casual (some restrictions).
Clubhouse Facilities: Midday – 2.30pm; 5.00pm – 9.00pm.

CONVENIENT HOTELS

Rescobie, Leslie;
Balgeddie House, Glenrothes;
Balburnie House, Markinch.

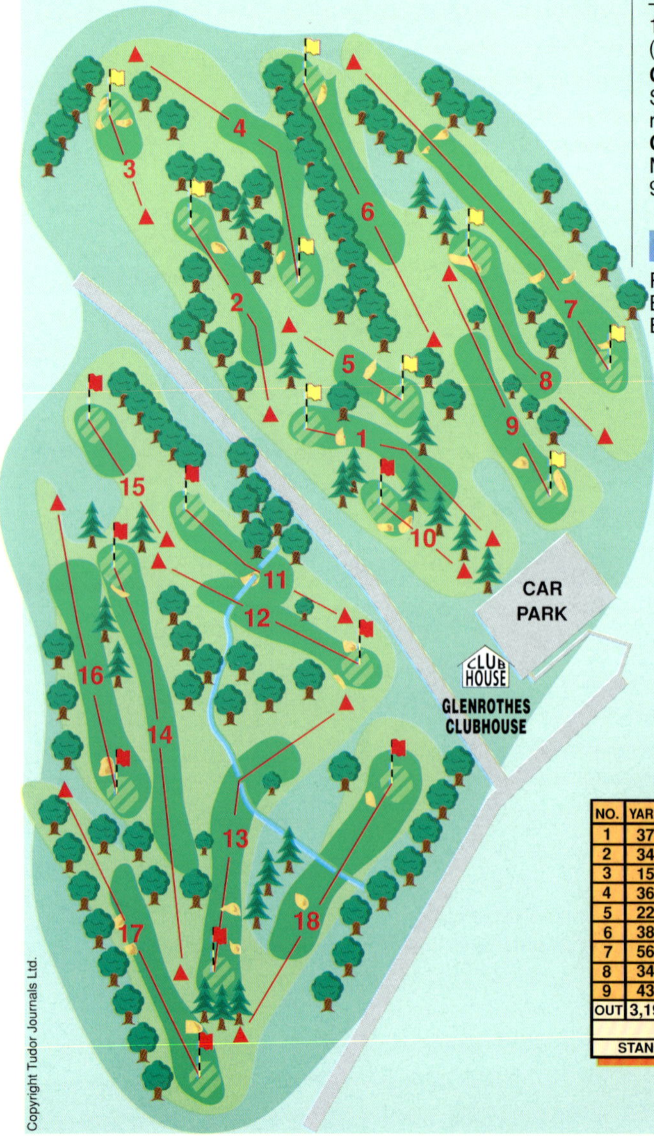

NO.	YARDS	PAR	S.I.	NO.	YARDS	PAR	S.I.
1	376	4	2	10	210	3	4
2	340	4	9	11	349	4	12
3	151	3	11	12	447	4	1
4	363	4	14	13	364	4	15
5	228	3	3	14	478	5	16
6	388	4	8	15	195	3	7
7	568	5	10	16	504	5	18
8	348	4	13	17	334	4	17
9	432	4	5	18	369	4	6
OUT	3,194	35		IN	3,250	36	
				TOTAL	6,444	71	
				STANDARD SCRATCH	71		

Bunker and tree positions indicated.

**Kinghorn Golf Club,
Macduff Cres,
Kinghorn. KY3 9RE.
Tel: (01592) 890345.**

LOCATION: 3 miles West of Kirkcaldy.
SECRETARY: J. P. Robertson.
Tel: (01592) 203397.
ARCHITECT: Tom Morris.

Clifftop links course with undulating fairways, enjoying magnificient view of River Forth, Edinburgh and the Pentland Hills. Owned by Kirkcaldy District Council.

COURSE INFORMATION

Par 65; SSS 67; Length 5,269 Yards.
Opening Hours: 7.30am – 9.00pm (or daylight hours).
Visitors: Welcome parties 12.30 Apply in Writing.
Avoid: Sat 7.30am – 9.30am, 12.00pm – 2.30pm; Thurs reserved for Kinghorn Ladies competition.
Ladies: Welcome.
Green Fees: One round £8; Day tickets £13.50; Weekend one round £10.00/£15.50.
Juveniles: Permitted before 5.00pm.
Clubhouse Hours: From 7.30pm weekdays; all day sat & sun.
Clubhouse Dress: Neat.
Clubhouse Facilities: Party catering by arrangement; full catering service at weekends.

CONVENIENT HOTEL

The Longboat , Pettycor Road, Kinghorn.

NO.	YARDS	PAR	S.I.	NO.	YARDS	PAR	S.I.
1	339	4	5	10	275	4	4
2	219	3	9	11	245	3	14
3	207	3	17	12	436	4	8
4	315	4	3	13	439	4	2
5	321	4	11	14	220	3	12
6	307	4	13	15	177	3	16
7	385	4	7	16	277	4	6
8	462	4	1	17	168	3	18
9	281	4	15	18	196	3	10
OUT	2,836	34		IN	2,433	31	
				TOTAL	5,269	65	
STANDARD SCRATCH					67		

Bunker positions indicated.

Solitude. Eric Thorburn.

LADYBANK

FIFE

**Ladybank Golf Club,
Annsmuir, Ladybank,
KY7 7RA.
Tel: (01337) 830320.**

LOCATION: 6 miles southwest of Cupar.
SECRETARY: A. M. Dick.
Tel: (01337) 830814.
PROFESSIONAL: M. J. Gray.
Tel: (01337) 830725.

Wooded heathland, flat course which is a qualifying course for British Open.

COURSE INFORMATION

Par71; SSS 72; Length 6,641 Yards.
Opening hours: 8.00am – dusk.
Visitors: No booked parties at weekend.
Ladies: Welcome.
Green Fees: Round £26; Day £35. Weekend Round £28; Day £38.
Juveniles: £10.
Clubhouse hours: 11am – dusk.

Clubhouse Dress: Informal but tidy and respectable.
Clubhouse facilities: Full catering service.
Events: Handicap June, Scratch (36) June.
Mixed August, Seniors (Gents) July.
Seniors (Ladies) September.

CONVENIENT HOTELS

Fernie Castle;
Lomond Hills Hotel.

NO.	MEDAL YARDS	GEN. YARDS	PAR	S.I.	NO.	MEDAL YARDS	GEN. YARDS	PAR	S.I.
1	374	349	4	11	10	165	150	3	18
2	548	523	5	7	11	407	402	4	4
3	391	392	4	5	12	243	237	3	14
4	166	145	3	13	13	528	509	5	10
5	344	325	4	17	14	417	359	4	2
6	372	357	4	9	15	390	378	4	12
7	543	523	5	3	16	398	370	4	8
8	159	136	3	15	17	387	348	4	16
9	401	388	4	1	18	408	380	4	6
OUT	3,298	3,138	36		IN	3,343	3,133	36	
					TOTAL	6,641	6,271	71	
					STANDARD SCRATCH	72			

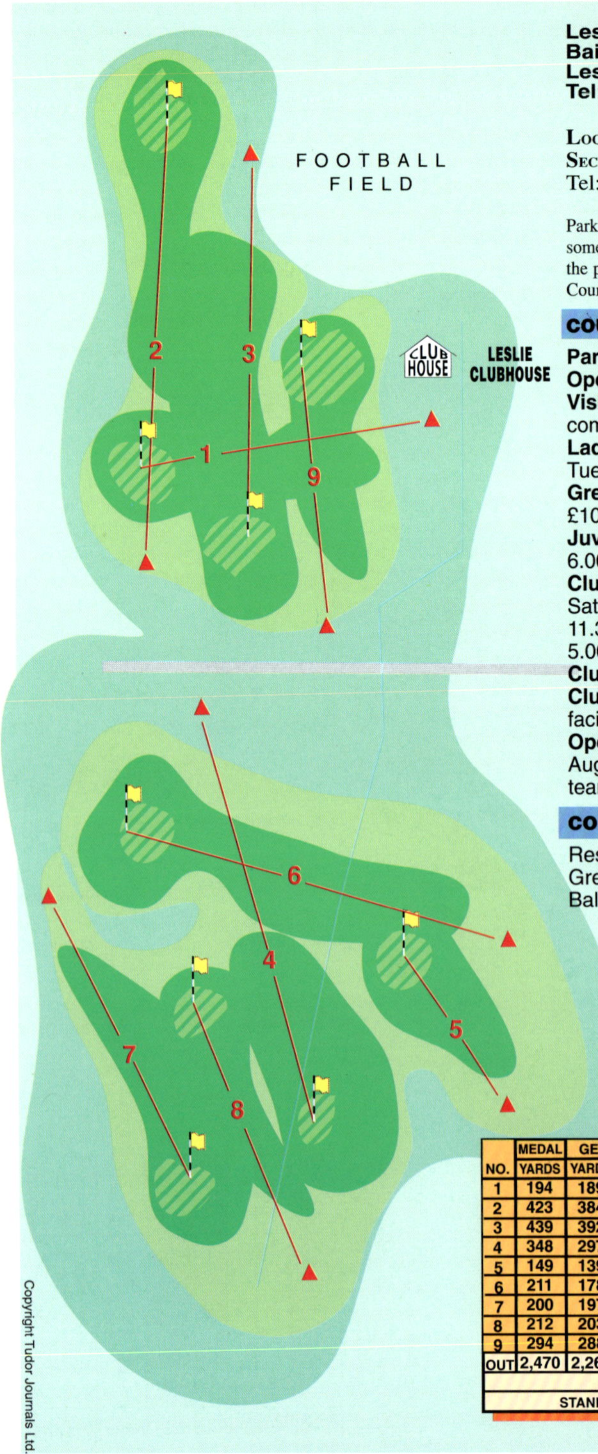

Leslie Golf Club,
Baisillie, Balsillie Laws,
Leslie, Glenrothes. KY6 3EZ.
Tel: (01592) 620040.

Location: M90 Junction 5/7, 11 Miles.
Secretary: Gordon Moore.
Tel: (01592) 620040.

Parkland course with a stream running through some fairways. A testing course where, in 1993 the par was broken for the first time since 1902. Course split in two parts by 100 yard walk.

COURSE INFORMATION

Par 62; SSS 64; Length 4,940 Yards.
Opening Hours: Sunrise – sunset.
Visitors: Welcome except during competitions.
Ladies: Welcome. Ladies day Tuesday.
Green Fees: Mon - Fri £8; Sat & Sun £10 (per round).
Juveniles: Preferrably off course by 6.00pm. Except Thursday.
Clubhouse Hours: Weekday / Sat,Sun 7.30pm – 11.00pm; Sat 11.30am – 5.00pm; Sun 12.00pm – 5.00pm.
Clubhouse Dress: Casual.
Clubhouse Facilities: Catering facilities are available on request.
Open Competitions: May (Gents); August (Ladies); Aug (Gents two man team).

CONVENIENT HOTELS

Rescobie Hotel;
Greenside Hotel;
Balgedie Hotel.

NO.	MEDAL YARDS	GEN. YARDS	PAR	S.I.	NO.	MEDAL YARDS	GEN. YARDS	PAR	S.I.
1	194	189	3	13	10	194	189	3	14
2	423	384	4	5	11	423	384	4	6
3	439	392	4	1	12	439	392	4	2
4	348	297	4	3	13	348	297	4	4
5	149	139	3	17	14	149	139	3	18
6	211	178	3	15	15	211	178	3	16
7	200	197	3	11	16	200	197	3	12
8	212	203	3	9	17	212	203	3	10
9	294	288	4	7	18	294	288	4	8
OUT	2,470	2,267	31		IN	2,470	2,267	31	
					TOTAL	4,940	4,534	62	
					STANDARD SCRATCH	64	67		

Leven Links Joint Committees, Secretary's Office, Promenade, Leven, Fife. KY8 4HS.
Tel: (01333) 421390.

Location: 1/2 Mile East of Leven, on Promenade.
Secretary: Mr. Alexander Herd.
Tel: (01333) 428859.
Fax:(01333) 428859.
Starters Box: (01333) 421390.
Professional: G.Finlayson.

Links course is used as a Qualifying course for Open Championship when played at St Andrews.

NO.	METRES	PAR	S.I.	NO.	METRES	PAR	S.I.
1	413	4	5	10	325	4	13
2	381	4	9	11	363	4	10
3	343	4	11	12	482	5	2
4	449	4	3	13	482	5	4
5	158	3	17	14	332	4	8
6	567	5	1	15	188	3	16
7	184	3	15	16	386	4	6
8	348	4	7	17	414	4	14
9	164	3	18	18	457	4	12
OUT	3,007	34		IN	3,429	37	
				TOTAL	6,436	71	
STANDARD SCRATCH					71		

COURSE INFORMATION

Par 67; SSS 71; Length 4,979 Yards.
Opening Hours: 8.00am – 8.00pm March to October.
Visitors: Not Saturdays or Friday from 12.30pm.
Ladies: Cannot play between 5.00pm and 7.00pm on Monday's and Fridays. Ladies day Tuesday.
Green Fees: Weekdays one round £18; day £26; Weekends one round £24; day £36.
Juveniles: Cannot play between 4.30pm and 7.00pm Fridays. 5.00pm –7.00pm Mon/Wed/Thurs before 10.30 and 1.00pm and 3.30 Sat/Sun.
Clubhouse Hours: 9.00am to 11.30pm.
Clubhouse Dress: Smart casual dress. (No sleeveless T-shirts, jeans or trainers).
Clubhouse Facilities: Full Catering available .

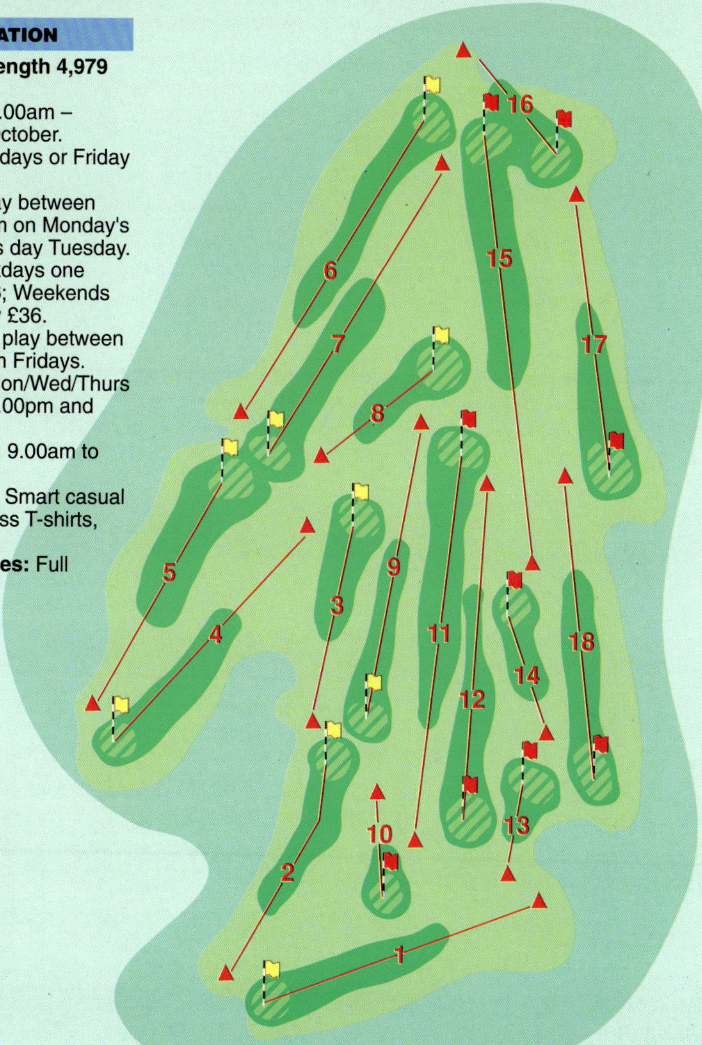

Lundin Golf Club, Golf Rd, Lundin Links, KY8 6BA. Tel: (01333) 320202.

LOCATION: 3 Miles East of Leven.
SECRETARY: A. C. McBride.
PROFESSIONAL: D. K. Webster.
Tel: (01333) 320051.
ARCHITECT: James Braid.

The course offers a mixture of true links conditions near the sea and parkland on the newer holes. There are a host of beautiful views, and although by no means an easy course, it can still be enjoyed by golfers of all levels of ability. A railway line which was closed in the mid '60s runs through the course which is an important feature providing an internal boundary which comes into play at many holes. Recently Lundin Golf Club has been honoured by the R & A as a final pre–qualifying course prior to the St. Andrews open.

COURSE INFORMATION

Par 71; SSS 71; Length 6,377 Yards.
Visitors: Mon–Fri 9.00am – 3.00pm; On Sat. visitors can only play after 2.30pm.
Avoid: Before 9.00am and after 3.00pm. No visitors on Sundays.
Ladies: Welcome.
Green Fees: Monday–Friday round £20; Day £30. Saturday £27 per round (only after 2.30pm).
Juveniles: Welcome.
Clubhouse Dress: Neat/Casual.
Clubhouse Facilities: Monday – soup and filled rolls available. Tuesday – Friday meals available.
Open Competitions: East of Scotland Strokeplay Championship June; Birkmyre Rosebowl June; Seniors Open (handicap limit–18) July.

CONVENIENT HOTELS

Old Manor Hotel; Lundin Links Hotel; Crusoe Hotel; Largo Hotel.

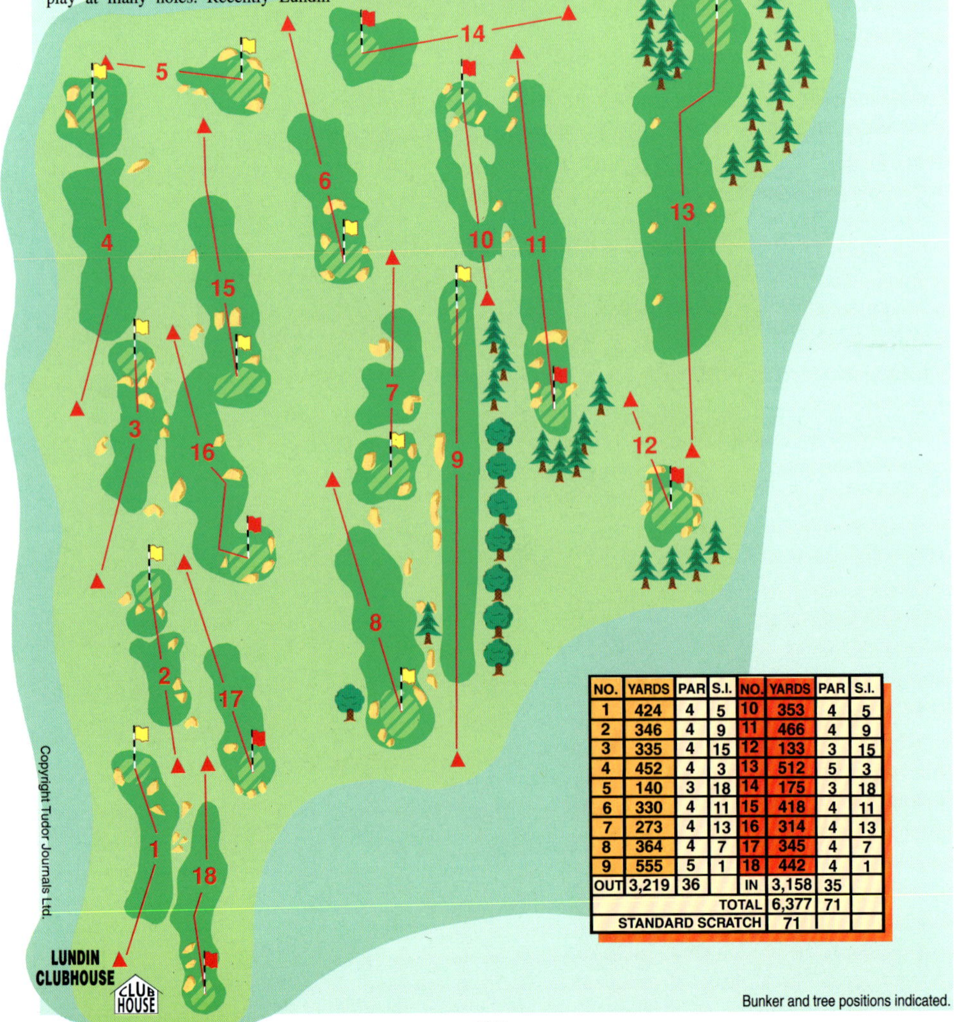

NO.	YARDS	PAR	S.I.	NO.	YARDS	PAR	S.I.
1	424	4	5	10	353	4	5
2	346	4	9	11	466	4	9
3	335	4	15	12	133	3	15
4	452	4	3	13	512	5	3
5	140	3	18	14	175	3	18
6	330	4	11	15	418	4	11
7	273	4	13	16	314	4	13
8	364	4	7	17	345	4	7
9	555	5	1	18	442	4	1
OUT	3,219	36		IN	3,158	35	
				TOTAL	6,377	71	
STANDARD SCRATCH					71		

Bunker and tree positions indicated.

PITREAVIE

FIFE

**Pitreavie Golf Club,
Queensferry Road,
Dunfermline, Fife.
Tel: (01383) 722591.**

LOCATION: 2 miles off M90, between Rosyth and Dunfermline.
SECRETARY: D. Carter.
Tel: (01383) 722591.
PROFESSIONAL: Jim Forrester.
Tel: (01383) 723151.
ARCHITECT: Dr MacKenzie.

Parkland course overlooking the Firth of Forth. A fair test of golf to novice and scratch player alike.

COURSE INFORMATION

Par 70; SSS 69; Length 6,086 Yards.
Visitors: Phone for booking.
Opening Hours: Dawn – Dusk.
Ladies: Not between 4.30pm – 6.30pm weekdays or prior to 1.00pm weekends.
Green Fees: Weekdays £16 per round, £21 per day; Weekends £27 per day.
Juveniles: Not before 4.30pm on weekdays or before 1.00pm weekends.

Clubhouse Hours: 11am – 11pm.
Clubhouse Dress: No shorts, no jeans after 7.00pm.
Clubhouse Facilities: Catering except Tuesdays.
Open Competitions: Ladies Open – June; Senior Open – June; 36 hole Open – June; Mens; 18 hole Open – August; Boys' Open – July.

CONVENIENT HOTEL

King Malcolm Hotel.

NO.	MEDAL YARDS	GEN. YARDS	PAR	S.I.	NO.	MEDAL YARDS	GEN. YARDS	PAR	S.I.
1	470	457	4	2	10	331	319	4	9
2	541	487	5	8	11	258	248	4	15
3	207	190	3	11	12	136	129	3	18
4	382	382	4	4	13	358	358	4	3
5	323	323	4	13	14	386	370	4	6
6	150	141	3	17	15	379	367	4	7
7	336	318	4	5	16	181	202	3	16
8	327	327	4	12	17	452	433	4	1
9	277	276	4	14	18	511	464	5	10
OUT	3,013	2,901	35		IN	2,992	2,890	35	
					TOTAL	6,005	5,791	70	
					STANDARD SCRATCH	69	68		

Bunker and tree positions indicated.

SALINE

Saline Golf Club, Kinedder Hill, Saline. KY12 9NF. Tel: (01383) 852 591.

LOCATION: 3 Miles NW of Dumfermline on B914 to Dollar.
SECRETARY: R. Hutchinson.
Tel: (01333) 852 591.

Hillside meadow land course, interesting challenge and offering superb views.

NO.	YARDS	PAR	S.I.	NO.	YARDS	PAR	S.I.
1	279	4	11	10	279	4	12
2	314	4	17	11	314	4	18
3	166	3	5	12	166	3	6
4	289	4	15	13	289	4	16
5	372	4	1	14	372	4	2
6	378	4	7	15	378	4	8
7	329	4	3	16	329	4	4
8	160	3	13	17	160	3	14
9	364	4	9	18	364	4	10
OUT	2,651	34		IN	2,651	34	
			TOTAL		5,302	68	
STANDARD SCRATCH					66		

COURSE INFORMATION

Par 68; SSS 66; Length 5,302 Yards.
Opening Hours: All day.
Visitors: Not on Saturdays..
Ladies: Ladies day Thursday.
Green Fees: Weekdays £8.00; Sun £10.00 for day.
Juveniles: Before 5.30pm midweek. Not untill 2.00pm. Sun not Saturday.
Clubhouse Hours: 9.00am to 11.00pm.
Clubhouse Facilities: Bar snacks 12.00pm – 3.00pm; 8.00pm – 10.00pm.
Open Competitions: Boys Open.
No other Opens.

CONVENIENT HOTEL

Pitfirrane Arms Crossfold, Dunfermline.

Tree positions indicated.

Scoonie Golf Club, North Links, Leven, Fife. KY8 4SP
Tel: (01333) 427057.

LOCATION: 2 minutes from the promenade.
SECRETARY: Stefan Kuczereta.

Links course – not very hilly so it is ideal for two rounds of golf!

COURSE INFORMATION

Par 67; SSS 66; Length 4,979 Yards.
Opening Hours: 8.00am - dusk.
Visitors: Welcome.
Ladies: Welcome.
Green Fees: Weekdays £10 round, £17 day; Weekends £12.50 round, £19 day.
Juveniles: Welcome.
Clubhouse Hours: 10.00am to 10.00pm.
Clubhouse Dress: Neat / smart.
Clubhouse Facilities: Full catering & bar facilities available .
Open Competitions: Medals; Scoonie Open May; Leven Merchants – bank hols – Aug. Seniors Open May; Scoonie boy's June.

CONVENIENT HOTEL

Caledonian Hotel.

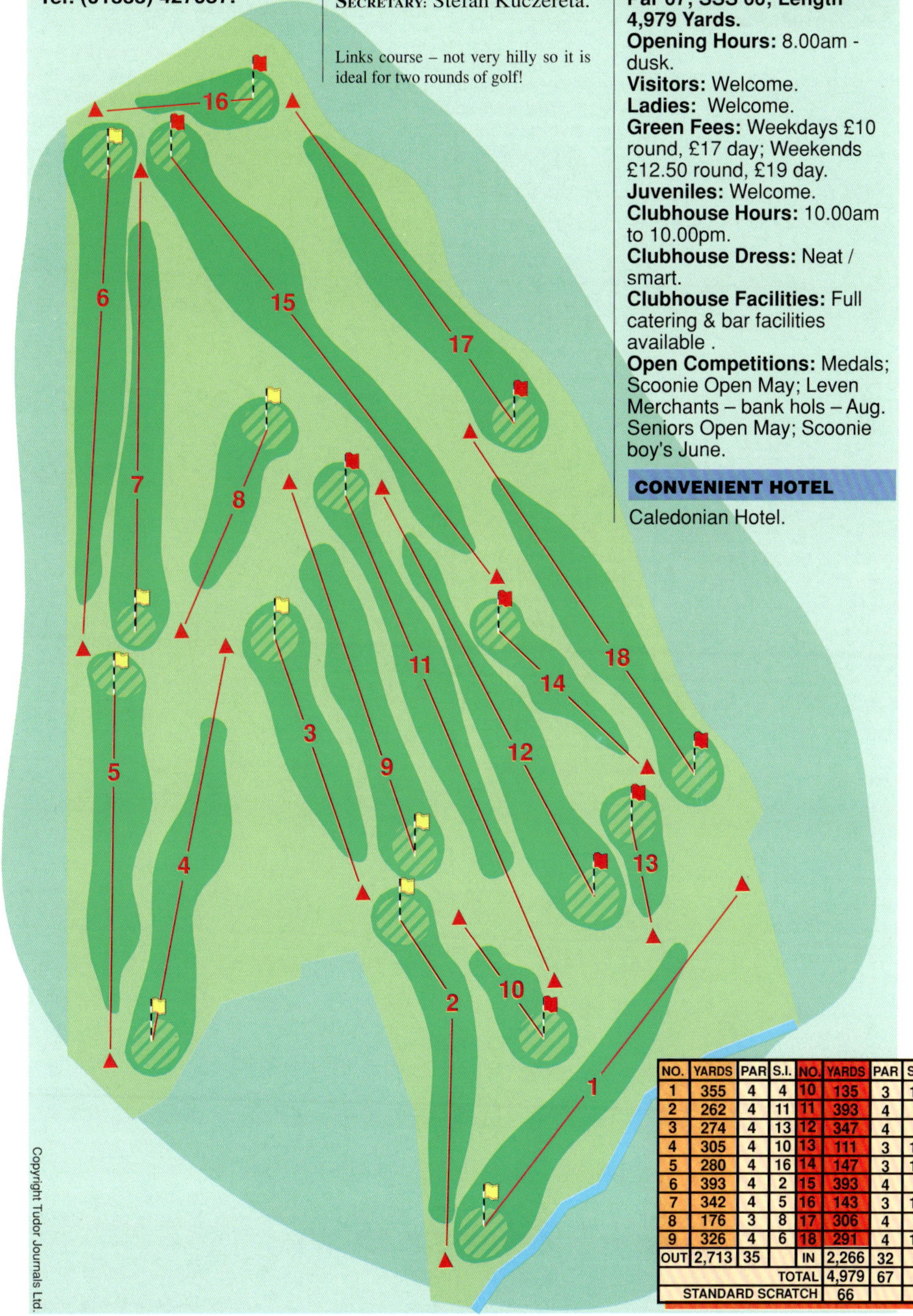

NO.	YARDS	PAR	S.I.	NO.	YARDS	PAR	S.I.
1	355	4	4	10	135	3	18
2	262	4	11	11	393	4	1
3	274	4	13	12	347	4	7
4	305	4	10	13	111	3	12
5	280	4	16	14	147	3	17
6	393	4	2	15	393	4	3
7	342	4	5	16	143	3	15
8	176	3	8	17	306	4	9
9	326	4	6	18	291	4	14
OUT	2,713	35		IN	2,266	32	
				TOTAL	4,979	67	
STANDARD SCRATCH					66		

Scotscraig Golf Club, Golf Road, Tayport, Fife. DD6 9DZ.
Tel: (01382) 552515.

LOCATION: 10 miles north of St. Andrews.
SECRETARY: K. Gourlay.
Tel: (01382) 552515.

Open qualifying course, with a links/parkland character.

COURSE INFORMATION

Par 71; SSS 72; Length 6,550 Yards.
Opening Hours: Dawn to dusk.
Visitors: Welcome 10am–11pm, 2.30pm–3.30pm by arrangement.
Ladies: Welcome.
Avoid: 11am – 2.30pm.
Green Fees: Mon – Fri £24 round; £35 day. Weekend £27 round, £40 day.
Juveniles: Welcome.
Clubhouse Hours: 9.00am to 9.00pm.
Clubhouse Facilities: Catering available except on Tuesdays.
Open Competitions: Sat 21/5/94 Open Gents; Sat 27/8/94 Mixed Foursomes; Sun1/5/94 Pro am.

NO.	YARDS	PAR	S.I.	NO.	YARDS	PAR	S.I.
1	402	4	5	10	404	4	12
2	374	4	13	11	459	4	2
3	214	3	11	12	389	4	8
4	366	4	1	13	165	3	18
5	402	4	9	14	523	5	6
6	150	3	17	15	175	3	16
7	401	4	3	16	479	5	4
8	387	4	7	17	380	4	10
9	484	5	15	18	396	4	14
OUT	3,180	35		IN	3,370	36	
				TOTAL	6,550	71	
				STANDARD SCRATCH	72		

ST. ANDREWS (Eden)

The Eden Course, St. Andrews, Fife. KY16 9SF.
Tel: (01334) 475757.
Location: St. Andrews Links.
Golf Manager: Nicky James.
Architect: H.S. Colt & redesigned byDonald Steel.

Opened for play in 1914, the Eden takes its name from the adjacent estuary and is the least typical of the St. Andrews courses. The Eden is also unique in that it lies partly on the ancient links and partly on abandoned arable land.

COURSE INFORMATION

Par 70; SSS 69; Length 6,112 Yards; 5,588 Metres.
Visitors: Telephone the information office (01334) 475757.
Green Fees: £18 Summer/£15 Winter.
Open Competitions: Eden Tournament/Strathtyrum Trophy August.

CONVENIENT HOTELS

The Old Course Hotel;
Rusacks Hotel.

NO.	YARDS	PAR	S.I.	NO.	YARDS	PAR	S.I.
1	326	4	13	10	196	3	14
2	449	4	3	11	375	4	8
3	417	4	51	12	341	4	16
4	273	4	7	13	422	4	2
5	144	3	15	14	350	4	10
6	407	4	7	15	170	3	18
7	313	4	11	16	480	5	4
8	178	3	9	17	432	4	6
9	505	5	1	18	334	4	12
OUT	3,012	35		IN	3,100	35	
				TOTAL	6,112	70	
STANDARD SCRATCH					69		

ST. ANDREWS (New Course)

FIFE

New Course, St. Andrews, Fife, KY16 9SF. Tel: (01334) 475757.

Location: St. Andrews Links.
General Manager: Nicky James. Tel: (01334) 475757.

Opened in 1896 the New Course certainly qualifies on all counts as a superb example of classic links golf.

COURSE INFORMATION

Par 71; SSS 72; Length 6,604 Yards; 6,038 Metres.
Visitors: Welcome; there are many complex rules concerning visitors to the New Course so it is advisable to telephone the Information Office.
Avoid: 8am – 9.30am & 11.30am – 12.30pm.
Green Fees: £25 Summer; £20 Winter.

CONVENIENT HOTELS

The Old Course Hotel; Rusacks Hotel.

NO.	YARDS	PAR	S.I.	NO.	YARDS	PAR	S.I.
1	336	4	7	10	46	4	6
2	367	4	13	11	347	4	14
3	511	5	3	12	518	5	4
4	369	4	9	13	157	3	18
5	180	3	17	14	386	4	8
6	445	4	5	15	394	4	12
7	356	4	11	16	431	4	2
8	481	5	1	17	229	3	16
9	225	3	15	18	408	4	10
OUT	3,270	36		IN	3,334	35	
				TOTAL	6,604	71	
				STANDARD SCRATCH	72		

= Whins

Bunker positions indicated.

ST ANDREWS (Old Course)

FIFE

St Andrews Fife. KY16 9SF.
Tel: (01334) 473393.

Location: North of the town on the A91.
Golf Manager: Nicky James.
Tel: (01334) 475757.

The most famous stretch of golfing ground in the world, St Andrews Links proudly carries the title of the Home of Golf.

It dates back to the 15th Century and the Royal and Ancient Golf Club of St Andrews was formed here in 1754. There are six courses at St Andrews. This page presents the Old Course which is characterised by its wide fairways and vast greens which may seem forgiving, but disguise a unique test of golf that has given St Andrews its formidible reputation. 24 Open Championships have been hosted here and many other professional and amateur events. Finishing at the amphitheatre 18th green is an experience in itself.

OLD COURSE

Par 72; SSS 72; Length 6,566 Yards.
Opening hours: 7am - 6pm Summer (closed Sunday).
Visitors: Welcome, all visitors will require a letter of introduction or a handicap certificate. At least 24 hours notice is required (see daily ballot). Society meetings by arrangement.
Avoid: Closed on Sundays.
Green Fees: £50 May-Nov; £40 Dec-Apr.
Juveniles: No golf facilities available.
Clubhouse Dress: Jacket and tie.
Caddies: Available.
Daily Ballot: All visitors names must be in by 2.00pm the previous day.

CONVENIENT HOTEL

The Old Course Hotel; Rusacks Hotel.

NO.	YARDS	PAR	S.I.	NO.	YARDS	PAR	S.I.
1	370	4	15	10	318	4	10
2	411	4	3	11	172	3	17
3	352	4	13	12	316	4	6
4	419	4	9	13	398	4	12
5	514	5	1	14	523	5	2
6	374	4	11	15	401	4	8
7	359	4	7	16	351	4	14
8	166	3	18	17	461	4	4
9	307	4	5	18	354	4	16
OUT	3,272	36		IN	3,294	36	
				TOTAL	6,566	72	
STANDARD SCRATCH					72		

Bunker positions indicated.

The Jubilee Course, St. Andrews, Fife, KY16 9SF.
Tel: (01334) 475757.

LOCATION: St. Andrews Links.
GENERAL MANAGER: N. James.
ARCHITECT: Designed by several architects and later redesigned by Donald Steel.

Originally laid out as a 12 hole course alongside the new course in 1896, the Jubilee was eventually extended to an 18 hole format. The course is now destined to take its place as a true equal and any golfer playing to his handicap over the Jubilee will be flushed by the warm glow of achievement.

COURSE INFORMATION

Par 72; SSS 73; Length 6,805 Yards; 6,218 Metres.
Visitors: Welcome; there are many complex rules concerning visitors to the Jubilee Course so it is advisable to telephone the Information Office; 473938.
Avoid: 8am – 9.30am & 1.30pm – 2.30pm.
Green Fees: £25 Summer; £20 Winter.

CONVENIENT HOTELS

The Old Course Hotel; Rusacks Hotel; There are many Hotels in the area.

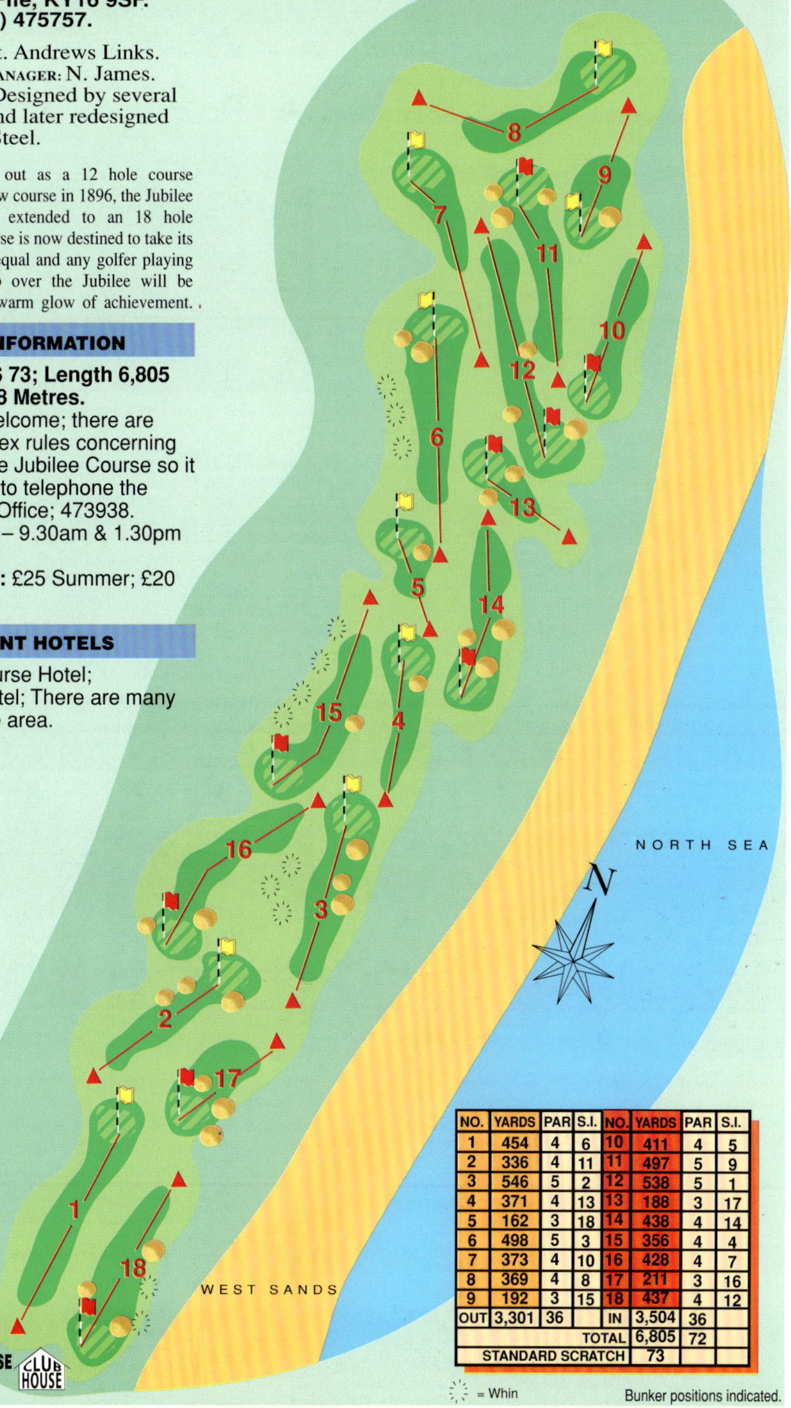

NO.	YARDS	PAR	S.I.	NO.	YARDS	PAR	S.I.
1	454	4	6	10	411	4	5
2	336	4	11	11	497	5	9
3	546	5	2	12	538	5	1
4	371	4	13	13	188	3	17
5	162	3	18	14	438	4	14
6	498	5	3	15	356	4	4
7	373	4	10	16	428	4	7
8	369	4	8	17	211	3	16
9	192	3	15	18	437	4	12
OUT	3,301	36		IN	3,504	36	
				TOTAL	6,805	72	
				STANDARD SCRATCH	73		

= Whin

Bunker positions indicated.

ST. MICHAEL'S

St. Michael's Golf Club, Leuchars, Fife. KY16 0DX. Tel: (01334) 839365.

LOCATION: 5 miles north of St. Andrews on the Dundee Rd.

SECRETARY: G.H. Jacobs.

Undulating parkland course in the heartland of the home of golf. The course is being extended to 18 holes set to open in the spring of 1996.

COURSE INFORMATION

Par 68; SSS 67; Length 5,482 Yards.

Opening Hours: Sunrise to Sunset.
Visitors: Not on Sundays; before 1pm..
Ladies: Welcome. Ladies day Tuesday.
Avoid: Sunday's before 1pm.
Green Fees: £12 per day; 5 day ticket £50.
Juveniles: Welcome; not after 4.30pm unless with an adult.
Clubhouse Hours: Normal bar hours.

Clubhouse Dress: Casual, neat.
Clubhouse Facilities: Showers / changing facilities, Catering available from steward.
Open Competitions: Sep. (H'cap 13-24); Sep (H'cap scr-12).

CONVENIENT HOTELS

Many in St. Andrew's area.

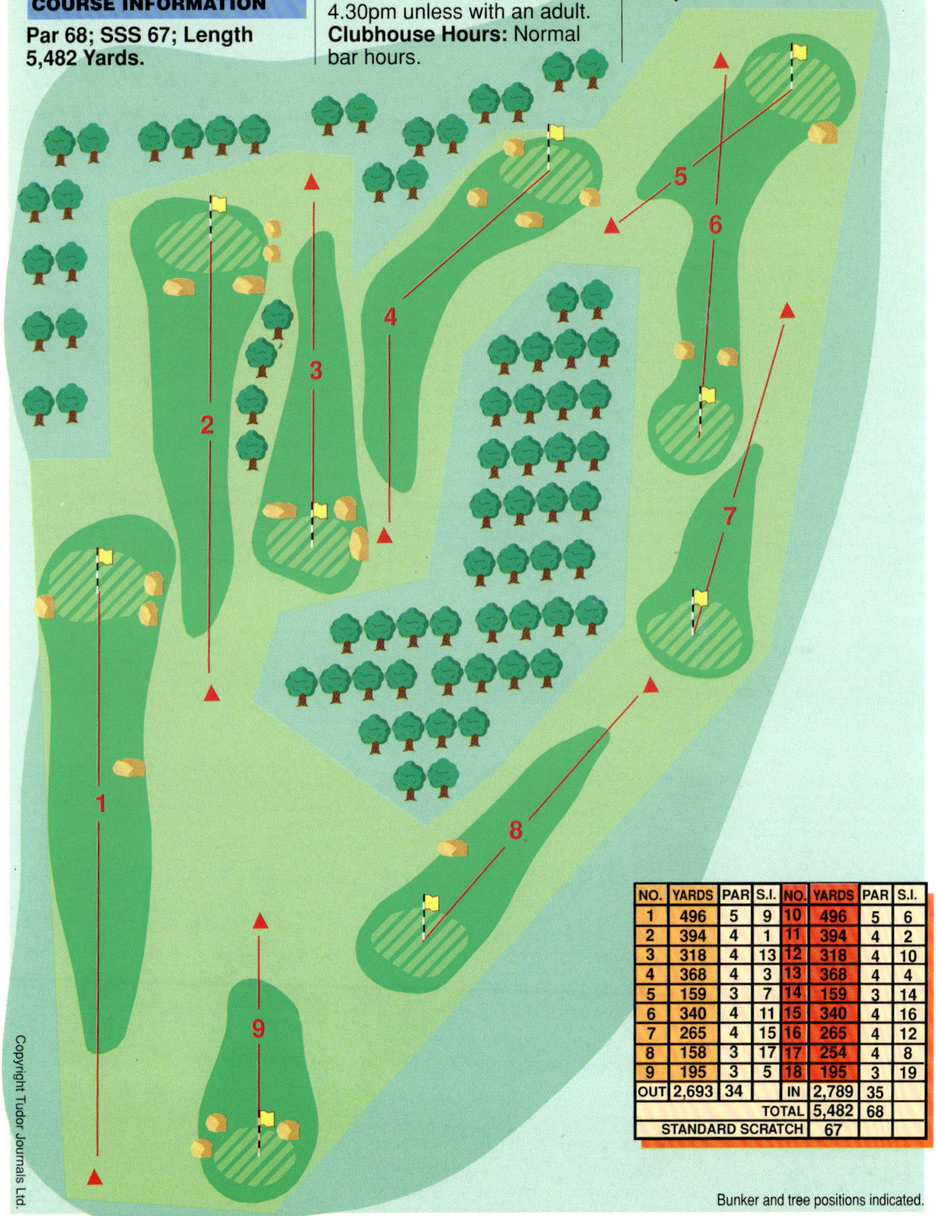

NO.	YARDS	PAR	S.I.	NO.	YARDS	PAR	S.I.
1	496	5	9	10	496	5	6
2	394	4	1	11	394	4	2
3	318	4	13	12	318	4	10
4	368	4	3	13	368	4	4
5	159	3	7	14	159	3	14
6	340	4	11	15	340	4	16
7	265	4	15	16	265	4	12
8	158	3	17	17	254	4	8
9	195	3	5	18	195	3	19
OUT	2,693	34		IN	2,789	35	
				TOTAL	5,482	68	
STANDARD SCRATCH					67		

Bunker and tree positions indicated.

Thornton Golf Club,
Station Rd, Thorton, Fife.
Tel: (01592) 771111.

LOCATION: Thorton 1 mile east of A92. Access via Station Road, Thornton Village.

ADMINISTRATOR: J. Gartshore.
Tel: (01592) 77111.

Undulating parkland course. No internal out of bounds, but out of bounds on 5 holes on periphery of course (10th, 13th, 14th, 16th, and 18th). Renowned for good greens.

COURSE INFORMATION

Par 70; SSS 69; Length 6,177 Yards.

Opening Hours: 7.00am – 7.00pm April – October.
Visitors: Weekends before 10am, and 12-2.30pm; weekdays before 9.30am.
Ladies: Welcome.
Avoid: See above. weekends – booking avisable.
Green Fees: Weekday £14 – £20; £20 Weekend £30 per day.
Juveniles: Welcome but avoid before 10.00am Weekends; avoid between 12 – 12.30pm.
Clubhouse Hours: 9am – 10pm.
Clubhouse Dress: No jeans allowed.
Clubhouse Facilities: Bar & catering 7 days , all year round.

CONVENIENT HOTELS

Crown Hotel, Thorton;
Earl David, Kirkcaldy;
Rescobie, Leslie,

NO.	YARDS	PAR	S.I.	NO.	YARDS	PAR	S.I.
1	343	4	12	10	399	4	7
2	364	4	14	11	139	3	17
3	209	3	10	12	422	4	1
4	395	4	6	13	528	5	13
5	431	4	2	14	190	3	3
6	476	5	16	15	361	4	11
7	395	4	8	16	253	4	9
8	405	4	4	17	286	4	15
9	188	3	18	18	393	4	5
OUT	3,206	35		IN	2,971	35	
				TOTAL	6,177	70	
STANDARD SCRATCH					69		

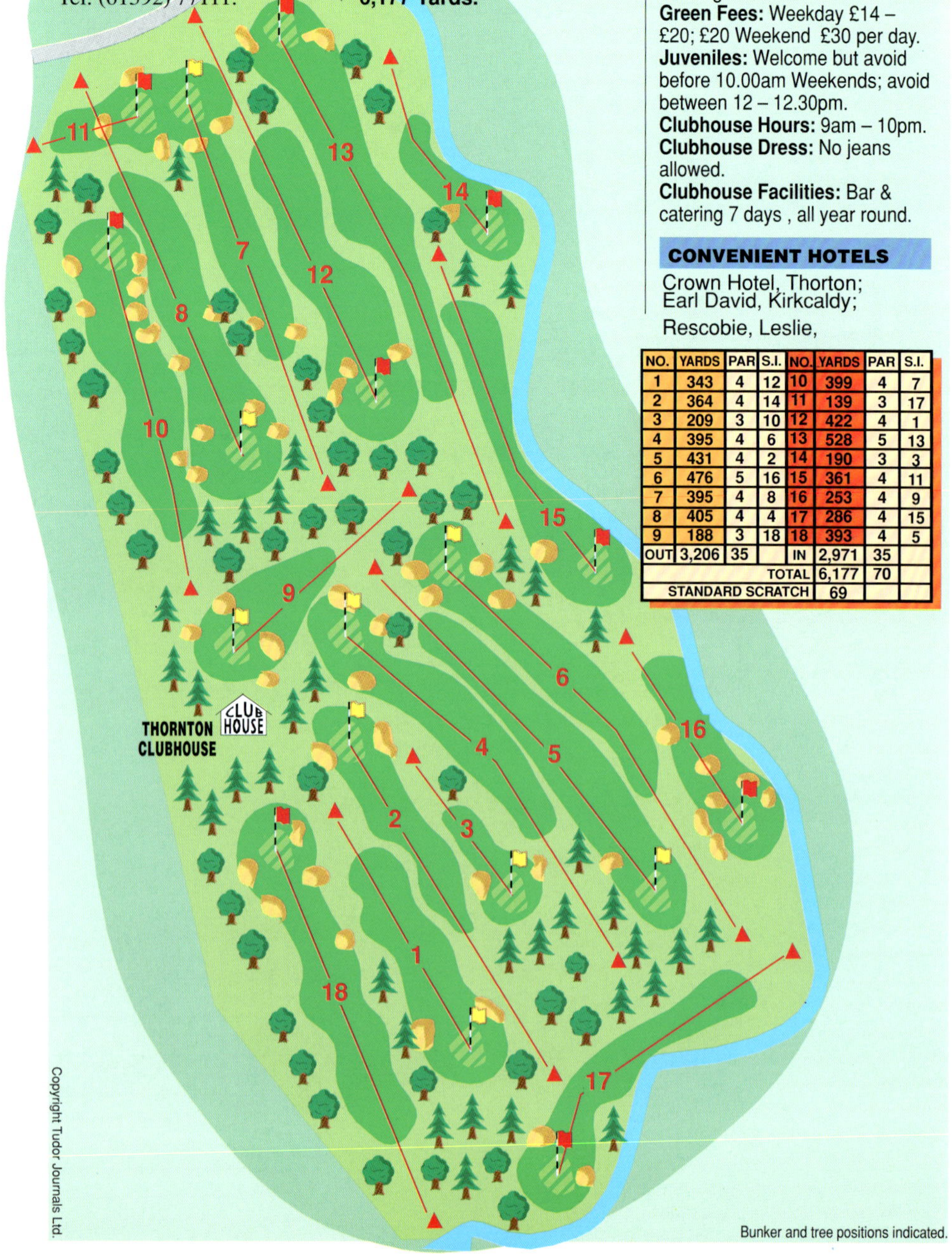

Bunker and tree positions indicated.

GOLF DAYS™ SCOTLAND

GLASGOW

BISHOPBRIGGS

GLASGOW

Bishopbriggs Golf Club,
Brackenbrae Rd, Bishopbriggs,
Glasgow. G64 2DX.
Tel: (0141) 772 1810.

LOCATION: 6 miles north of Glasgow on A803.
SECRETARY: John Magin.
Tel: (0141) 772 8938.
ARCHITECT: James Braid.

Fairly flat wooded parkland with meandering burn.

COURSE INFORMATION

Par 69; SSS 69; Length 6,041 Yards.
Visitors: With member or in authorised party.
Opening Hours: 8.30am – 11pm (October to March 6pm Mon to Wed).
Avoid: Weekends.
Ladies: No play after 5pm Tues & Thur or before 3pm Sat.
Green Fees: £20 per day.
Juveniles: No play after 5pm Tues & Thur or before 4.30pm Sat & Sun.
Clubhouse Hours: 8.30am – 11pm (October to March closes 6pm Monday to Wednesday).
Clubhouse Dress: Tailored jackets at all times; Collar and tie after 7pm.
Clubhouse Facilities: Snacks at all times & Lunch. High tea & dinners by arrangement.
Open Competitions: Mixed Open – August; Senior Open – August.

CONVENIENT HOTEL

Broadcroft Hotel, Garfield Place, Kirkintilloch.

NO.	MEDAL YARDS	GEN. YARDS	PAR	S.I.	NO.	MEDAL YARDS	GEN. YARDS	PAR	S.I.
1	370	339	4	5	10	419	407	4	8
2	135	124	3	17	11	384	372	4	10
3	295	274	4	13	12	331	325	4	12
4	367	349	4	7	13	427	407	4	2
5	417	391	4	1	14	203	176	3	16
6	206	203	3	15	15	321	308	4	14
7	337	323	4	9	16	393	373	4	4
8	414	392	4	3	17	149	127	3	18
9	507	496	5	11	18	366	336	4	6
OUT	3,048	2,891	35		IN	2,993	2,831	34	
					TOTAL	6,041	5,722	69	
					STANDARD SCRATCH	69	68		

Bunker and tree positions indicated.

CATHCART CASTLE

GLASGOW

Cathcart Castle Golf Club,
Mearns Road, Clarkston.
Tel: (0141) 638 0082.

LOCATION: 7 miles south west of Glasgow.
SECRETARY: I.G. Sutherland.
Tel: (0141) 638 9449.
PROFESSIONAL: D. Naylor.
Tel: (0141) 638 3436.

A pleasant parkland course with an interesting variety of holes.

COURSE INFORMATION

Par 68; SSS 68; Length 5,832 Yds.
Opening Hours: 8.00am to dusk.
Visitors: Must be introduced by members, parties Tues/Thur only.
Ladies: Avoid Mon, Tues & Thur after 4.30pm; Sat no start between 1.00pm and 4.00pm.
Ladies Day: Wed competition.
Green Fees: Introduced £3/£5 parties; £22 a round & £30 a day.
Juveniles: Restricted as ladies.
Clubhouse Hours: 8.30am-11.00pm.

Clubhouse Dress: Varies — collared shirt essential, no denims shorts or trainers.
Clubhouse Facilities: Bar and full range of catering.

CONVENIENT HOTEL

McDonald Hotel, Glasgow; Busby Hotel, Glasgow.

NO.	MEDAL YARDS	GEN. YARDS	PAR	S.I.	NO.	MEDAL YARDS	GEN. YARDS	PAR	S.I.
1	164	155	3	9	10	325	322	4	8
2	281	275	4	15	11	151	140	3	18
3	560	555	5	5	12	289	284	4	10
4	164	161	3	13	13	379	374	4	1
5	405	400	4	2	14	156	151	3	14
6	479	462	5	7	15	446	426	4	4
7	167	157	3	17	16	473	470	4	16
8	232	22	3	11	17	351	326	4	6
9	350	341	4	3	18	460	455	4	12
OUT	2,802	2,728	34		IN	3,030	2,948	34	
					TOTAL	5,862	5,676	68	
					STANDARD SCRATCH	68	67		

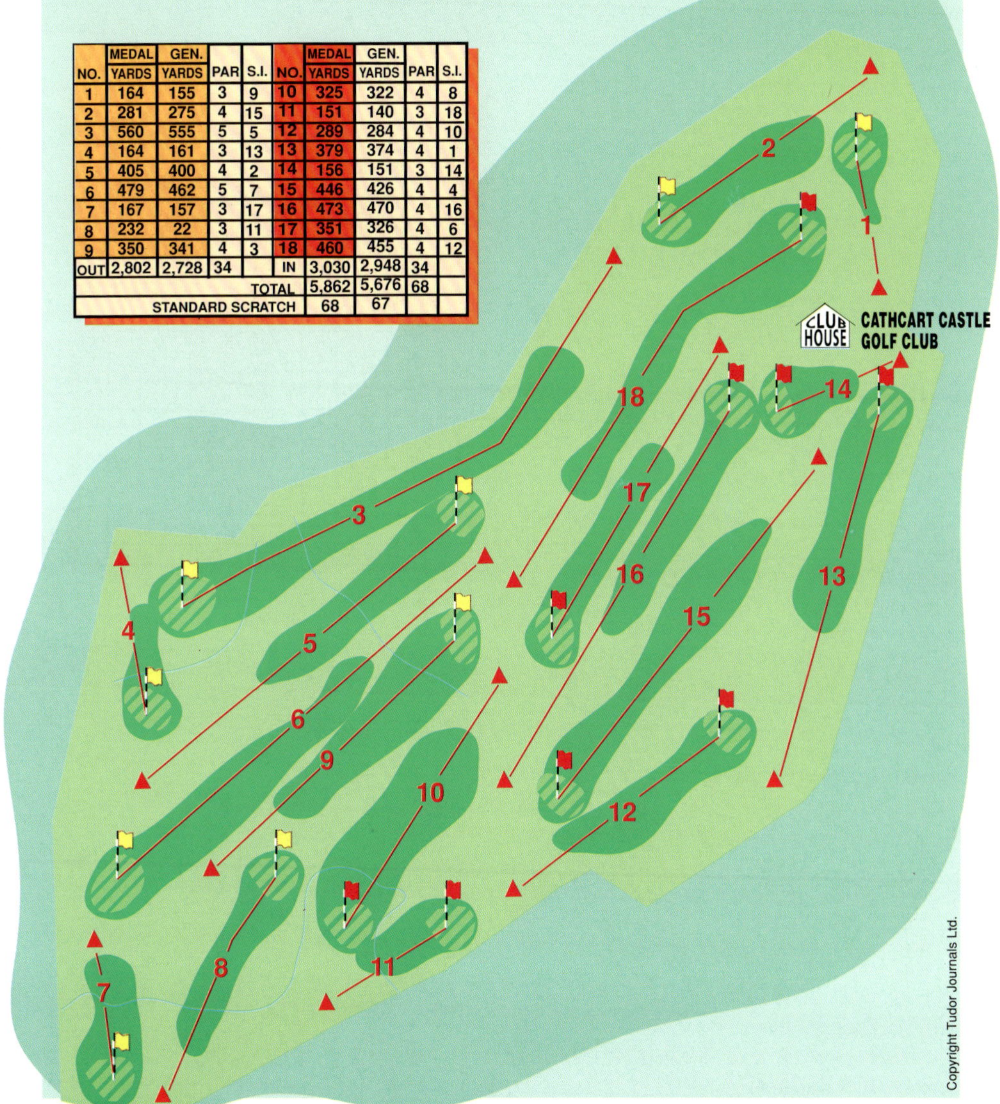

CATHKIN BRAES

Cathkin Braes Golf Club,
Cathkin Road, Rutherglen.
Glasgow G73 4SE.
Tel: (0141) 634 6605.

LOCATION: 5 miles south of Glasgow.
SECRETARY: G.L. Stevenson. Tel: (0141) 634 6605.
PROFESSIONAL: Stephen Bree. Tel: (0141) 634 0650.
ARCHITECT: James Braid.

Flat moorland turf course 600 feet above sea level.

COURSE INFORMATION

Par 71; SSS 71; Length 6,208 Yards.
Opening Hours: 8.00am to 11.00pm.
Visitors: Weekdays only.
Avoid: Tuesdays.
Ladies: Restricted Wed & Thurs evenings & weekends.
Green Fees: £20 a round, £30 a day.
Juveniles: Welcome.
Clubhouse Hours: 8.00am to 11.00pm.
Clubhouse Dress: Formal in dining room & main lounge, casual otherwise.
Clubhouse Facilities: Full catering available all week.

CONVENIENT HOTELS

Stuart & Bruce Hotel, East Kilbride; Burnside Hotel, Rutherglen.

NO.	MEDAL YARDS	GEN. YARDS	PAR	S.I.	NO.	MEDAL YARDS	GEN. YARDS	PAR	S.I.
1	378	361	4	7	10	371	335	4	8
2	276	263	4	14	11	180	155	3	15
3	299	293	4	13	12	390	380	4	4
4	424	408	4	5	13	154	142	3	17
5	116	110	3	18	14	481	439	5	2
6	504	457	5	1	15	386	367	4	12
7	369	335	4	9	16	210	205	3	16
8	363	349	4	11	17	430	386	4	6
9	458	448	5	3	18	419	396	4	10
OUT	3,187	3,024	37		IN	3,021	2,805	34	
					TOTAL	6,208	5,829	71	
					STANDARD SCRATCH	71	69		

Bunker and tree positions indicated.

CAWDER (Cawder Course)

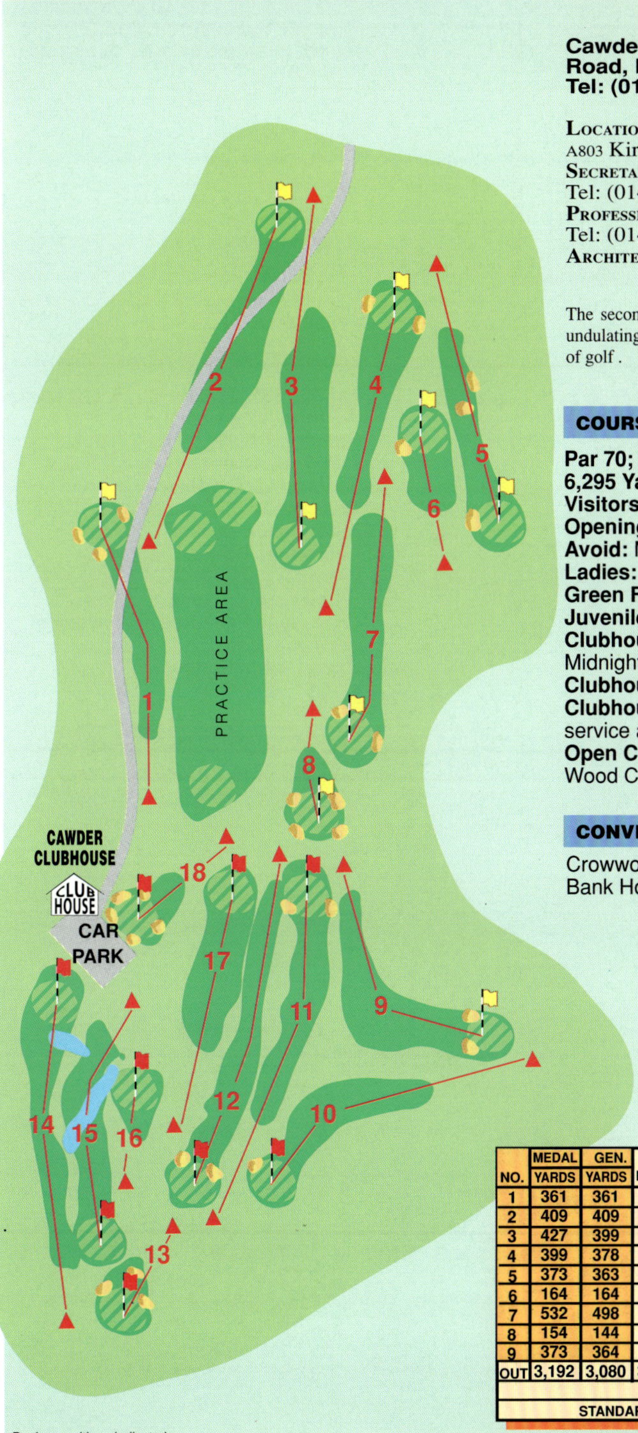

Bunker positions indicated.

**Cawder Golf Club, Cadder Road, Bishopsbriggs, Glasgow.
Tel: (0141) 772 7101.**

Location: North of Glasgow off the A803 Kirkintilloch Road
Secretary: G.T. Stoddart M.I.O.P.
Tel: (0141) 772 5167.
Professional: Ken Stevely.
Tel: (0141) 772 7102.
Architect: James Braid & Donald Steel.

The second Cawder course (called Cawder) is undulating parkland, and offers an excellent test of golf .

COURSE INFORMATION

Par 70; SSS 71; Length 6,295 Yards.
Visitors: Mid week only.
Opening Hours: 7.45am – Dusk.
Avoid: Must tee off before 4.30pm.
Ladies: Restrictions.
Green Fees: £25 per day.
Juveniles: Permitted.
Clubhouse Hours: 7.45am – Midnight.
Clubhouse Dress: Smart/Casual.
Clubhouse Facilities: Full catering service available.
Open Competitions: McKinnon Wood Cup — July.

CONVENIENT HOTEL

Crowwood House Hotel; Glazent Bank Hotel.

NO.	MEDAL YARDS	GEN. YARDS	PAR	S.I.	NO.	MEDAL YARDS	GEN. YARDS	PAR	S.I.
1	361	361	4	11	10	358	348	4	6
2	409	409	4	5	11	524	512	5	10
3	427	399	4	2	12	506	496	5	17
4	399	378	4	9	13	158	141	3	12
5	373	363	4	13	14	454	423	4	1
6	164	164	3	15	15	390	365	4	4
7	532	498	5	7	16	157	147	3	16
8	154	144	3	18	17	355	345	4	8
9	373	364	4	3	18	2041	191	3	14
OUT	3,192	3,080	35		IN	3,103	2,968	35	
					TOTAL	6,295	6,048	70	
					STANDARD SCRATCH	71	71		

CAWDER (Keir Course)

NO.	MEDAL YARDS	GEN. YARDS	PAR	S.I.	NO.	MEDAL YARDS	GEN. YARDS	PAR	S.I.
1	294	274	4	14	10	203	203	3	9
2	160	138	3	12	11	358	341	4	13
3	380	364	4	10	12	440	428	4	1
4	348	337	4	6	13	387	375	4	5
5	290	280	4	16	14	379	363	4	11
6	418	396	4	2	15	431	421	4	3
7	385	375	4	4	16	366	337	4	15
8	364	322	4	8	17	169	149	3	17
9	139	139	3	18	18	359	347	4	7
OUT	2,778	2,625	34		IN	3,092	2,964	34	
					TOTAL	5,870	5,589	68	
					STANDARD SCRATCH	68	68		

Cawder Golf Club, Cadder Road, Bishopsbriggs, Glasgow. Tel: (0141) 772 7101.

Location: North of Glasgow off the A803 Kirkintilloch Road
Secretary: G.T. Stoddart M.I.O.P.
Tel: (0141) 772 5167.
Professional: Ken Stevely.
Tel: (0141) 772 7102.
Architect: James Braid & Donald Steel.

There are two courses at Cawder; this one, the Keir is a flat parkland course, which offers a very pleasant round.

COURSE INFORMATION

Par 68; SSS 68; Length; 5,870 Yards.
Visitors: Mid week only.
Opening Hours: 7.45am – Dusk.
Avoid: Must tee off before 4.30pm.
Ladies: No restrictions.
Green Fees: £25 per day.
Juveniles: Permitted.
Clubhouse Hours: 7.45am – Midnight.
Clubhouse Dress: Smart/Casual.
Clubhouse Facilities: Full catering service available.
Open Competitions: McKinnon Wood Cup — July.

CONVENIENT HOTEL

Crowwood House Hotel; Glazent Bank Hotel.

Bunker and tree positions indicated.

COWGLEN

Cowglen Golf Club, 301 Barrhead Road, Glasgow. Tel: (0141) 632 0556.

LOCATION: South side of Glasgow.
SECRETARY: R.J.G. Jamieson. Tel: (0141) 649 9401.
PROFESSIONAL: J. McTear. Tel: (0141) 649 9401.

A testing and undulating parkland course with many interesting features which make use of the terrain and trees.

COURSE INFORMATION

Par 69; SSS 69; Length 5,976 Yards.
Visitors: Private Club. Introduced by a member or through Secretary.
Opening Hours: 8am – Dusk.
Avoid: Saturdays & competition days.
Ladies: Welcome.
Green Fees: Weekdays – £17 per round, £25 per day.
Juveniles: Restricted.

Clubhouse Hours: 8am – 11pm.
Clubhouse Dress: Smart/Casual in mixed lounge, collar and tie in smoke room.
Clubhouse Facilities: Full catering service available.

CONVENIENT HOTELS

Newlands Hotel; Tinto Firs Hotels; McDonald Hotel.

NO.	MEDAL YARDS	GEN. YARDS	PAR	S.I.	NO.	MEDAL YARDS	GEN. YARDS	PAR	S.I.
1	420	420	4	3	10	509	495	5	8
2	310	264	4	15	11	144	141	3	18
3	316	297	4	13	12	338	314	4	16
4	333	328	4	5	13	364	357	4	2
5	178	139	3	9	14	196	178	3	12
6	264	245	4	11	15	365	309	4	4
7	142	135	3	17	16	392	375	4	14
8	447	431	4	1	17	393	371	4	10
9	457	443	4	7	18	408	396	4	6
OUT	2,867	2,702	34		IN	3,109	2,936	35	
TOTAL						5,976	5,638	69	
STANDARD SCRATCH						69	67		

Bunker and tree positions indicated.

HAGGS CASTLE

GLASGOW

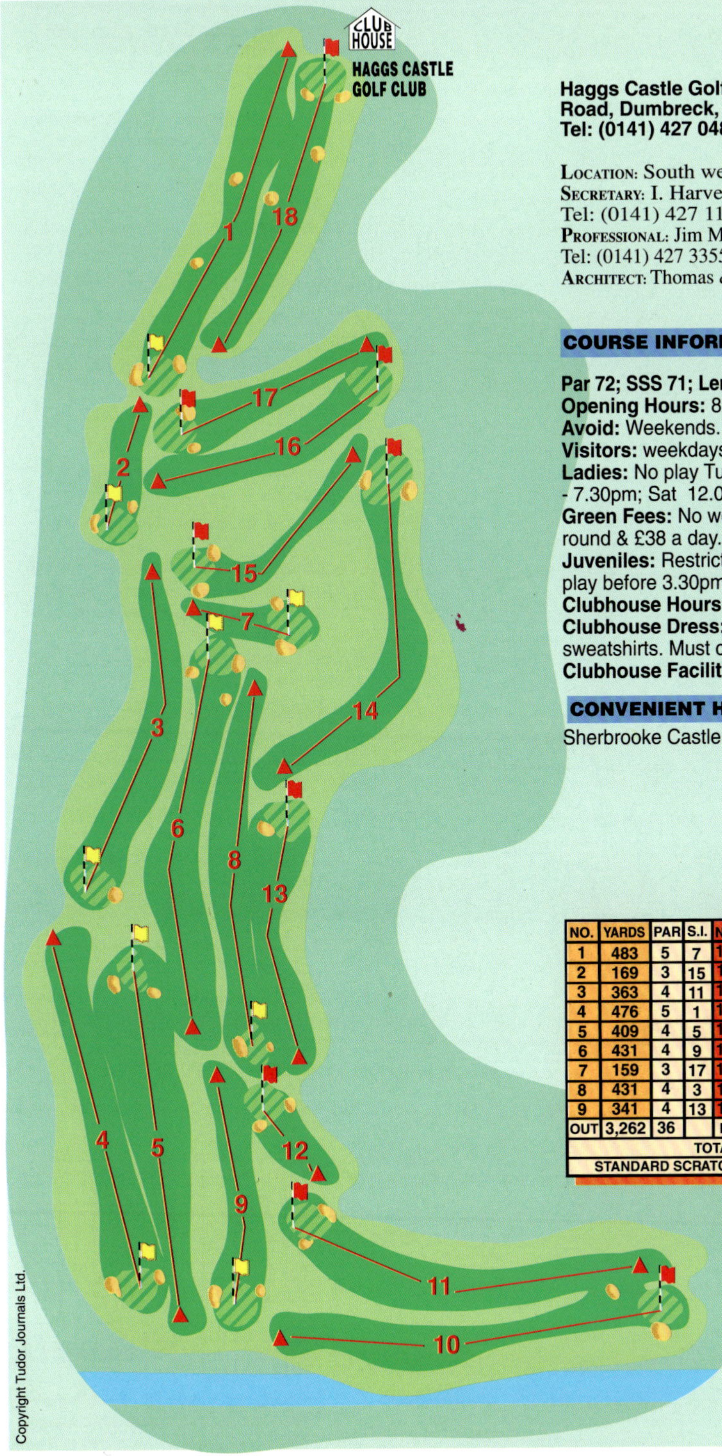

Haggs Castle Golf Club, 70 Dumbreck Road, Dumbreck, Glasgow.
Tel: (0141) 427 0480.

Location: South west Glasgow.
Secretary: I. Harvey.
Tel: (0141) 427 1157.
Professional: Jim McAlister.
Tel: (0141) 427 3355.
Architect: Thomas & Alliss.

COURSE INFORMATION

Par 72; SSS 71; Length 6,464 Yards.
Opening Hours: 8.00am -11.00pm.
Avoid: Weekends.
Visitors: weekdays by arrangement.
Ladies: No play Tues, Wed & Fri 4.30pm - 7.30pm; Sat 12.00noon - 4.00pm.
Green Fees: No weekend play — £26 a round & £38 a day.
Juveniles: Restricted as ladies plus no play before 3.30pm on Sun.
Clubhouse Hours: 8.30am -11.00pm.
Clubhouse Dress: No jeans, trainers or sweatshirts. Must change after playing
Clubhouse Facilities: Full services.

CONVENIENT HOTEL

Sherbrooke Castle Hotel.

NO.	YARDS	PAR	S.I.	NO.	YARDS	PAR	S.I.
1	483	5	7	10	383	4	4
2	169	3	15	11	372	4	10
3	363	4	11	12	172	3	18
4	476	5	1	13	323	4	16
5	409	4	5	14	425	4	2
6	431	4	9	15	340	4	6
7	159	3	17	16	363	4	12
8	431	4	3	17	348	4	14
9	341	4	13	18	476	5	8
OUT	3,262	36		IN	3,202	36	
				TOTAL	6,464	72	
				STANDARD SCRATCH	71		

Bunker positions indicated.

LINN PARK

Linn Park Golf Club, Simshill Road, Glasgow. G44.
Tel: (0141) 637 5871.

LOCATION: 3 miles south of Glasgow.
SECRETARY: Mr R. Flannagan.

The course is situated in a large park and consists of gently rolling hills with many bunkers. Quiet location and a fair test of golf.

COURSE INFORMATION

Par 63; SSS 65; Length 4,814 Yards.
Opening Hours: Summer 7am – dusk; Winter 8am – 5pm.
Visitors: No restrictions.
Avoid: No restricted times.
Ladies: No restrictions.
Green Fees: Summer weekday adults £4.30; juniors £2.00; Weekends all £4.30 ; No juniors at weekend.
Clubhouse Hours: Same as course.
Clubhouse Dress: Smart/Casual.
Clubhouse Facilities: Restrooms and refreshments.
Open Competitions: Open competition mid June.

CONVENIENT HOTEL

Numerous.

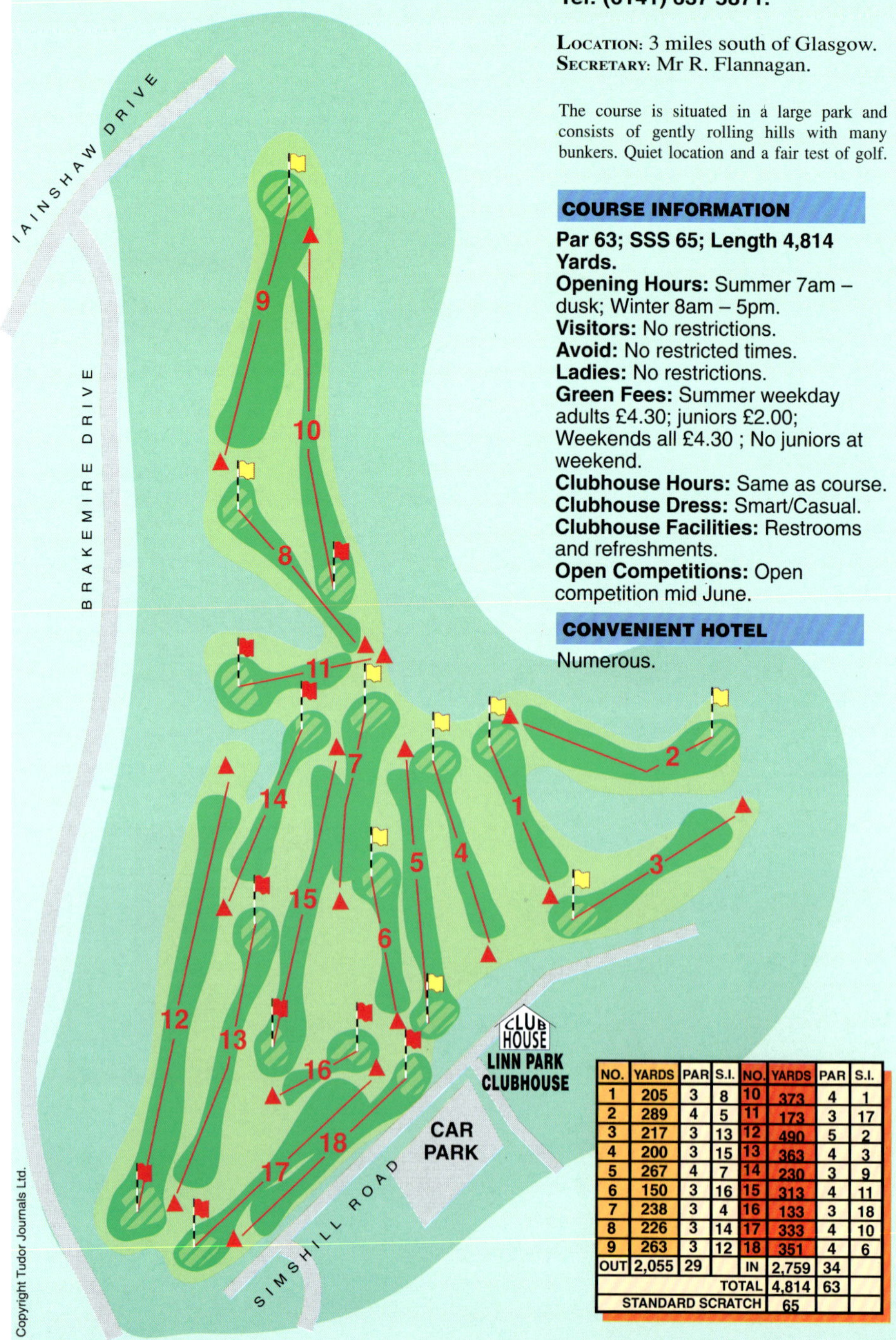

NO.	YARDS	PAR	S.I.	NO.	YARDS	PAR	S.I.
1	205	3	8	10	373	4	1
2	289	4	5	11	173	3	17
3	217	3	13	12	490	5	2
4	200	3	15	13	363	4	3
5	267	4	7	14	230	3	9
6	150	3	16	15	313	4	11
7	238	3	4	16	133	3	18
8	226	3	14	17	333	4	10
9	263	3	12	18	351	4	6
OUT	2,055	29		IN	2,759	34	
				TOTAL	4,814	63	
				STANDARD SCRATCH	65		

LITTLEHILL

Littlehill Golf Course, Auchinairn Road, Bishopsbriggs, Glasgow. G64 1UT.
Tel: (0141) 772 1916.

LOCATION: 5 miles north east of Glasgow.

Parkland course with not too much rough and few trees, providing good play for higher handicaps.

COURSE INFORMATION

Par 70; SSS 70; Length 6,199 Yards.
Opening Hours: 7am – dusk (summer) ; 8am – dusk (winter).
Avoid: No singles on Saturday or Sunday.
Ladies: Welcome.
Green Fees: Booking in advance essential. Weekdays – adults £4.30, juniors £2.10; Weekends £4.30.
Juveniles: No restrictions.
Clubhouse Hours: 7am – dusk.
Clubhouse Dress: Smart/Casual.
Clubhouse Facilities: Locker room, Golf shop & Cafe.
Open Competitions: June.

CONVENIENT HOTEL

Eagle Lodge, Bishopsbriggs.

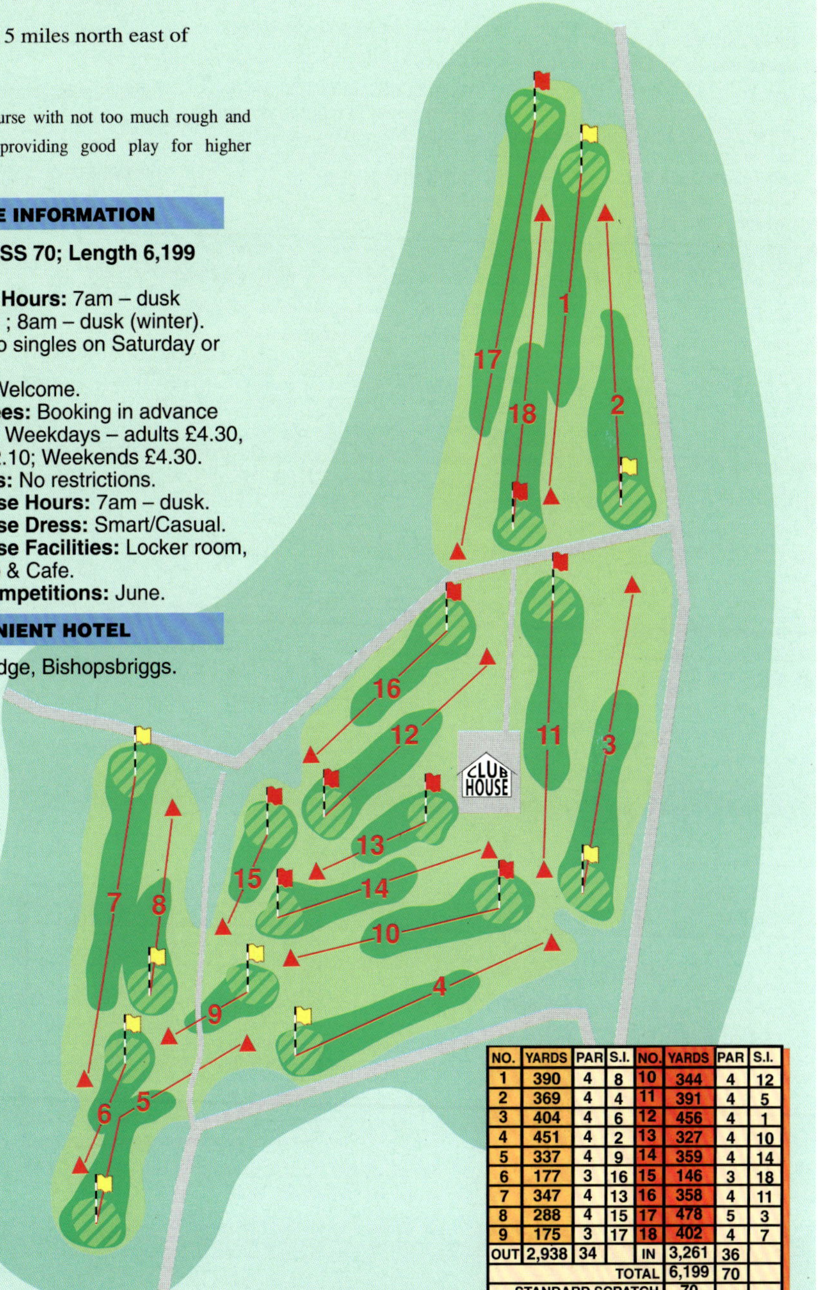

NO.	YARDS	PAR	S.I.	NO.	YARDS	PAR	S.I.
1	390	4	8	10	344	4	12
2	369	4	4	11	391	4	5
3	404	4	6	12	456	4	1
4	451	4	2	13	327	4	10
5	337	4	9	14	359	4	14
6	177	3	16	15	146	3	18
7	347	4	13	16	358	4	11
8	288	4	15	17	478	5	3
9	175	3	17	18	402	4	7
OUT	2,938	34		IN	3,261	36	
				TOTAL	6,199	70	
STANDARD SCRATCH					70		

Pollok Golf Club, 90 Barrhead Road, Pollokshaws, Glasgow. G43 1BG.
Tel: (0141) 632 1080.

LOCATION: 3 miles south west of Glasgow on B462.
SECRETARY: A. Mathison-Boyd. Tel: (0141) 632 4531.

A true parkland course with holes that are agreeably flat with subtle undulations. Each hole is sculptured between magnificent oaks and chestnuts. The quality of the greens make putting a pleasurable and satisfying experience.

COURSE INFORMATION

Par 71; SSS 70; Length 6,257 Yds.
Opening Hours: 8.30am to 10.00pm.
Visitors: By letter to Secretary Mon, Wed or Thur.
Ladies: No.
Avoid: 12.30pm to 1.30pm.
Green Fees: £26 per round & £33 per day. No weekend visitors.
Juveniles: Restricted as ladies.
Clubhouse Hours: 8.30am-10.00pm.
Clubhouse Dress: Jacket, collar and tie.
Clubhouse Facilities: Catering facilities availble. Special requirements for individual parties can be arranged.

CONVENIENT HOTELS

McDonald Hotel;
Forte Crest;
Marriot.

NO.	YARDS	PAR	S.I.	NO.	YARDS	PAR	S.I.
1	384	4	7	10	395	4	12
2	329	4	15	11	388	4	4
3	350	4	3	12	166	3	16
4	335	4	17	13	336	4	8
5	371	4	9	14	407	4	10
6	174	3	11	15	476	5	2
7	487	5	5	16	321	4	18
8	361	4	13	17	150	3	6
9	430	4	1	18	397	4	14
OUT	3,221	36		IN	3,036	35	
				TOTAL	6,257	71	
STANDARD SCRATCH					70		

Tree positions indicated.

GOLF DAYS™ SCOTLAND

LANARKSHIRE

Bellshill Golf Club, Orbiston,
Bellshill, Glasgow, ML4 2RZ.
Tel: (0698) 745124.

Location: 10 miles south of Glasgow between Bellshill and Motherwell.
Secretary: W. McLenachan.
Tel: 0698 745888.

Mature parkland course providing a good golfing challenge.

NO.	MEDAL YARDS	GEN. YARDS	PAR	S.I.	NO.	MEDAL YARDS	GEN. YARDS	PAR	S.I.
1	478	450	5	11	10	403	386	4	6
2	397	386	4	9	11	419	364	4	10
3	474	420	4	1	12	372	363	4	4
4	424	391	3	5	13	318	305	4	16
5	237	213	4	7	14	395	383	4	2
6	305	294	4	15	15	383	328	4	8
7	311	310	4	13	16	396	381	4	12
8	162	156	3	17	17	158	158	3	18
9	496	408	5	3	18	366	350	4	14
OUT	3,284	3,028	36		IN	3,210	3,018	35	
					TOTAL	6,494	6,046	71	
					STANDARD SCRATCH	72			

COURSE INFORMATION

Par 71; SSS 72; Length 6,494 Yards.
Visitors: No visiting parties Sat/Sun.
Opening Hours: 8.30am – 4.30pm.
Avoid: Saturdays.
Ladies: Welcome.
Juveniles: Permitted.
Green fees: Weekdays – £14; Weekends – £20.
Clubhouse Dress: No denims or training shoes.
Clubhouse Facilities: Full catering facilities available.

CONVENIENT HOTEL

Hattonrigg Hotel, Bellshill.

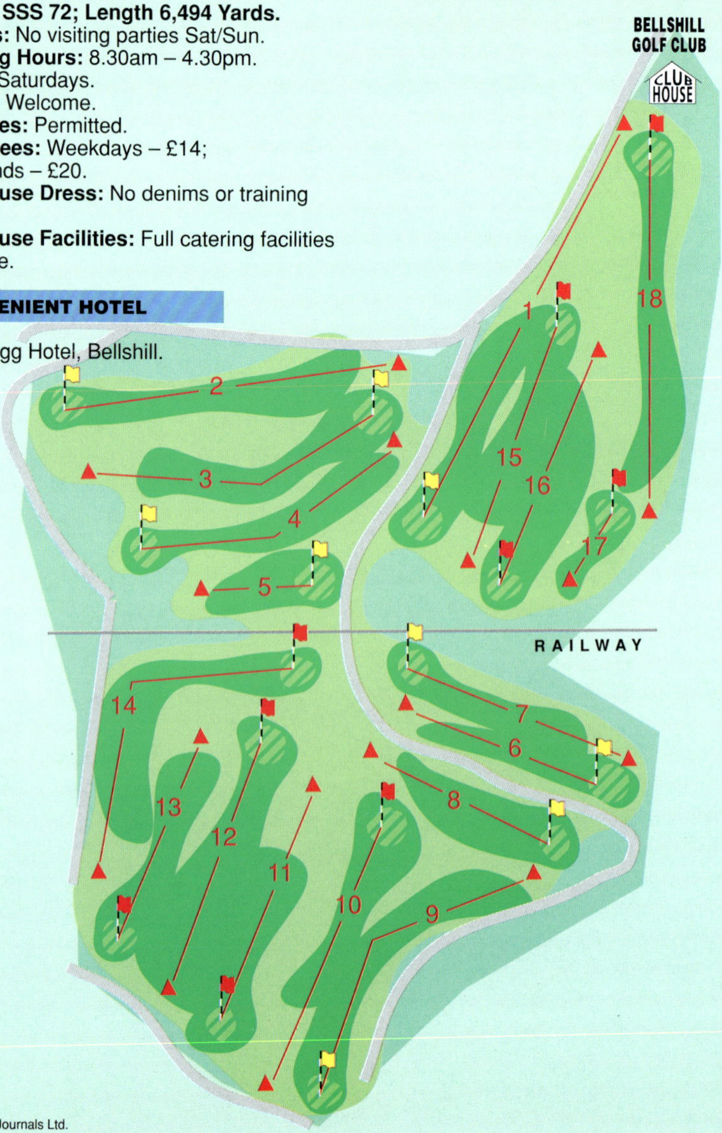

Biggar Golf Club, The Park, Broughton Road, Biggar. ML12 6AH.
Tel: (01899) 20319.

LOCATION: Biggar 1/2 mile, 20 miles south of Edinburgh on A702.
SECRETARY: W.S. Turnbull.
Tel: (01899) 20566.
ARCHITECT: Wilie Park Jnr.

A flat scenic parkland in rolling border country. There are many amenities also in the Park grounds including an all weather tennis court, boating pond, childrens play area, caravan park and fishing in the nearby River Clyde and Tweed.

COURSE INFORMATION

Par 67; SSS 66; Length 5,406Yards; 4,920 Metres.
Opening Hours: 8am – Dusk.
Visitors: Welcome; booking essential.
Avoid: Saturday before 9.30am; 12 noon - 1.30pm and after 5.00pm.
Ladies: Welcome.
Green Fees: Monday - Friday £11.00; Saturday/Sunday £14. Reductions for Juveniles and Senior Citizens.
Juveniles: Welcome.
Clubhouse Hours: 8.00am - 12 midnight.

Clubhouse Dress: Smart/Casual - no jeans allowed.
Clubhouse Facilities: All day bar and catering facilities available. Visitors must leave before 8.30pm on Saturdays.
Open Competitions: Mixed Open September.

CONVENIENT HOTELS

Various hotels in the area. Contact Tourist Information Office, High Street, Biggar, Lanarkshire for details.

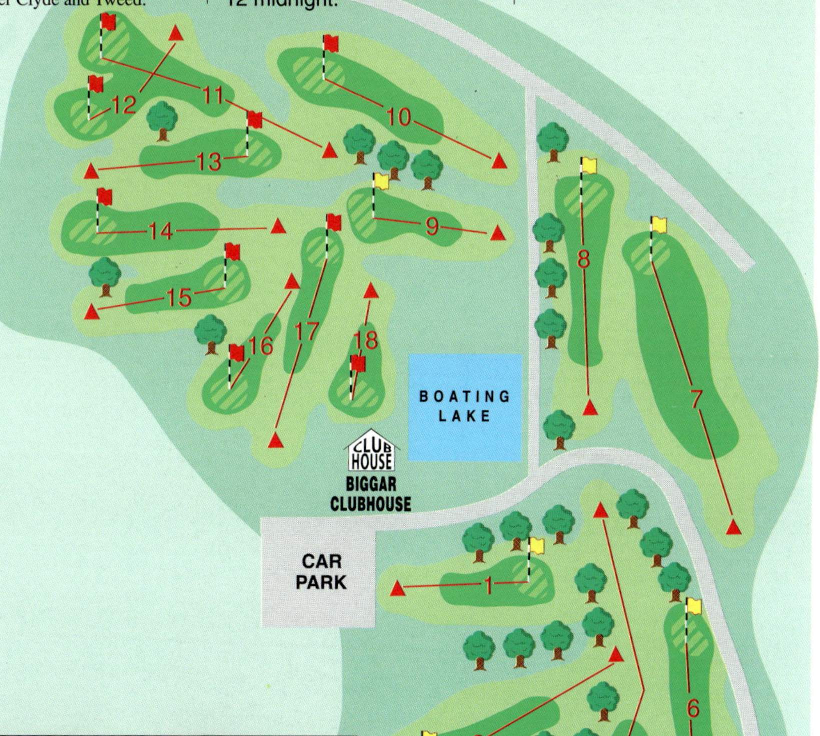

NO.	MEDAL YARDS	GEN. YARDS	PAR	S.I.	NO.	MEDAL YARDS	GEN. YARDS	PAR	S.I.
1	254	254	4	11	10	408	378	4	4
2	407	386	4	3	11	407	387	4	2
3	294	294	4	9	12	201	197	3	14
4	412	412	4	1	13	353	347	4	6
5	159	159	3	15	14	363	357	4	8
6	317	300	4	7	15	333	333	4	12
7	360	340	4	5	16	346	310	4	10
8	200	183	3	13	17	252	252	4	18
9	130	130	3	17	18	210	210	3	16
OUT	2,533	2,458	33		IN	2,873	2,771	34	
					TOTAL	5,406	5,229	67	
					STANDARD SCRATCH	66	65		

Tree positions indicated.

Blairbeth Golf Club, Burnside, Rutherglen, Glasgow.
Tel: (041) 634 3355.

LOCATION: 1 mile south of Rutherglen.
SECRETARY: F.T. Henderson.
Tel: (041) 632 0604.

Hilly parkland course.

COURSE INFORMATION

Par 70; SSS 67; Length 5,481 Yards.
Opening Hours: 8am - midnight.
Visitors: Visiting parties by prior arrangement or introduction by member.
Avoid: No parties permitted at weekends.
Ladies: Welcome, restricted playing times.

Green Fees: Weekdays £14 or £21 including catering.
Juveniles: Permitted.
Clubhouse Hours: 8am - Midnight.
Clubhouse Dress: Casual.
Clubhouse Facilities: Catering facilities available.
Open Competitions: Jackson Cup.

CONVENIENT HOTEL

Kings Park Hotel.

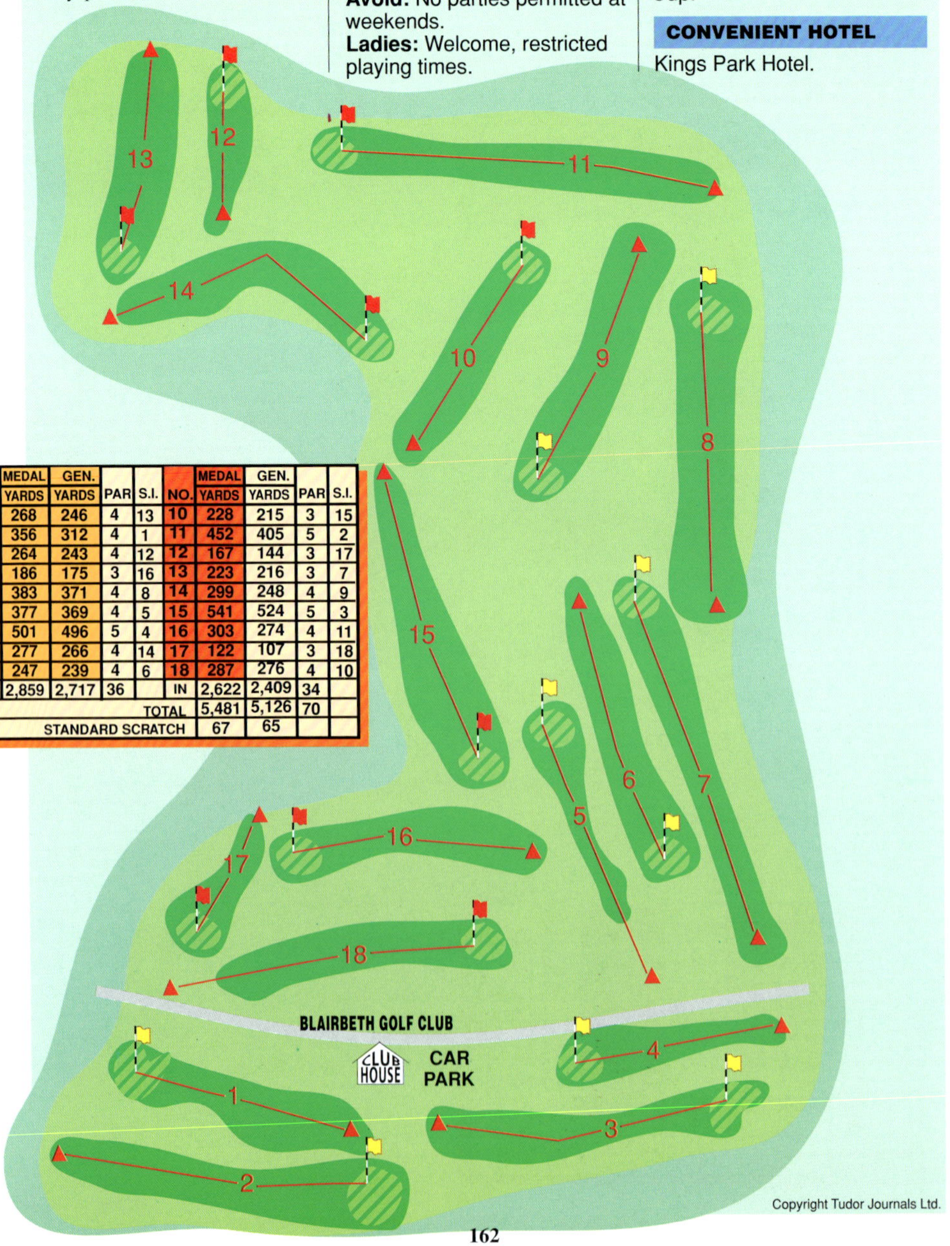

NO.	MEDAL YARDS	GEN. YARDS	PAR	S.I.	NO.	MEDAL YARDS	GEN. YARDS	PAR	S.I.
1	268	246	4	13	10	228	215	3	15
2	356	312	4	1	11	452	405	5	2
3	264	243	4	12	12	167	144	3	17
4	186	175	3	16	13	223	216	3	7
5	383	371	4	8	14	299	248	4	9
6	377	369	4	5	15	541	524	5	3
7	501	496	5	4	16	303	274	4	11
8	277	266	4	14	17	122	107	3	18
9	247	239	4	6	18	287	276	4	10
OUT	2,859	2,717	36		IN	2,622	2,409	34	
					TOTAL	5,481	5,126	70	
					STANDARD SCRATCH	67	65		

BOTHWELL CASTLE

LANARKSHIRE

Bothwell Castle Golf Club,
Blantyre Road, Bothwell, G71.
Tel: (0698) 853 177.

Location: 3 miles north of Hamilton.
Secretary: A.D.C Watson.
Tel: (0698) 852 052.
Architect: Loudon & Inglis.

Parkland course in Bothwell Castle; surrounded by mature trees.

COURSE INFORMATION

Par 71; SSS 70; Length 6,243 Yards.
Opening Hours: Visitors 10am - 11am; 2pm - 3pm.
Visitors: Welcome weekdays only.
Ladies: Welcome; ladies day 5th June.
Green Fees: £18 per round; £25 per day.
Clubhouse Hours: 8am - 11pm, Bar 11am - 11pm.
Clubhouse Dress: Smart/casual - no jeans.
Clubhouse Facilities: Snacks, lunch and dinners available.
Open Competitions: Mixed 5th September.

CONVENIENT HOTELS

Silver Trees Hotel;
Bothwell Bridge Hotel.

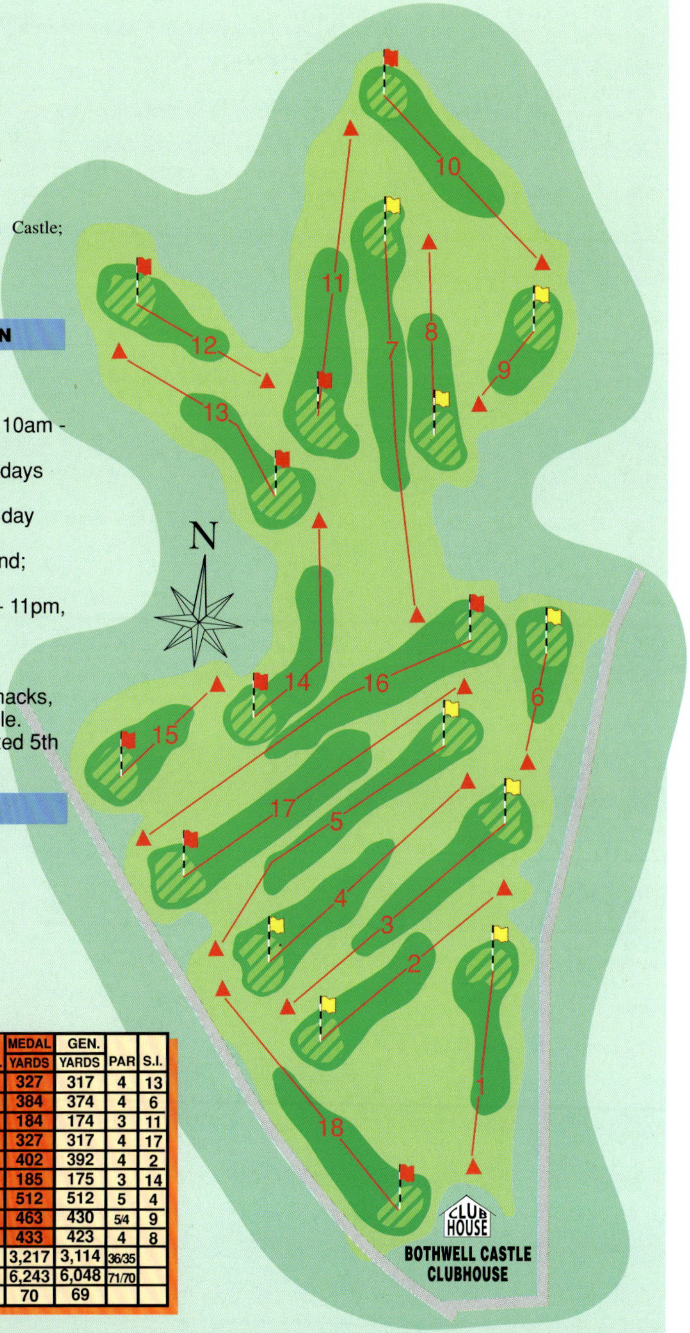

NO.	MEDAL YARDS	GEN. YARDS	PAR	S.I.	NO.	MEDAL YARDS	GEN. YARDS	PAR	S.I.
1	341	331	4	10	10	327	317	4	13
2	333	323	4	16	11	384	374	4	6
3	397	397	4	3	12	184	174	3	11
4	398	392	4	8	13	327	317	4	17
5	423	397	4	1	14	402	392	4	2
6	159	149	3	15	15	185	175	3	14
7	482	472	5	5	16	512	512	5	4
8	314	304	4	18	17	463	430	5/4	9
9	179	169	3	12	18	433	423	4	8
OUT	3,026	2,934	35		IN	3,217	3,114	36/35	
					TOTAL	6,243	6,048	71/70	
					STANDARD SCRATCH	70	69		

Cambuslang Golf Club,
Westburn Drive,
Cambuslang. G72 7AN.
Tel: (0141) 641 3130.

LOCATION: 3/4mile from Cambuslang station.
SECRETARY: Mr W. Lilly. Tel: (0141) 641 3130.

Nine hole parkland course.

COURSE INFORMATION

Par 66; SSS 64; Length 6,072 Yards.
Visitors: Introduced.
Opening Hours: 8.30am – Dusk.
Avoid: Saturday, Sunday & Tuesday.
Ladies: Off the course by 6pm except Tuesday & Friday.
Green Fees: £10 per day.
Juveniles: Same as ladies.
Clubhouse Hours: 11am – 2pm & 4pm – 10pm.
Clubhouse Dress: Smart / Casual.
Clubhouse Facilities: All day during opening hours.

CONVENIENT HOTEL

Cambus Court, Central Avenue, Cambuslang.

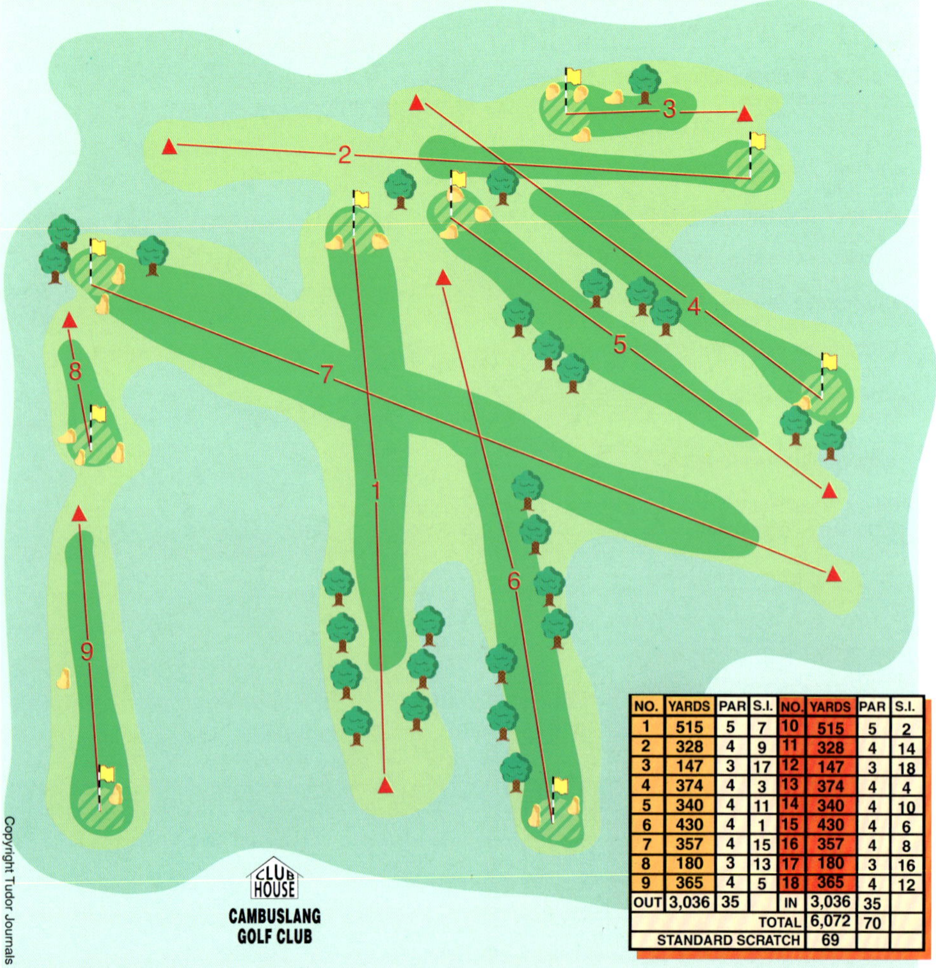

NO.	YARDS	PAR	S.I.	NO.	YARDS	PAR	S.I.
1	515	5	7	10	515	5	2
2	328	4	9	11	328	4	14
3	147	3	17	12	147	3	18
4	374	4	3	13	374	4	4
5	340	4	11	14	340	4	10
6	430	4	1	15	430	4	6
7	357	4	15	16	357	4	8
8	180	3	13	17	180	3	16
9	365	4	5	18	365	4	12
OUT	3,036	35		IN	3,036	35	
				TOTAL	6,072	70	
				STANDARD SCRATCH	69		

Bunker and tree positions indicated.

CARLUKE

Carluke Golf Club,
Maudslie Road,
Hallcraig, Carluke,
Glasgow.
Tel: (01555) 771070.

LOCATION: 20 miles from Glasgow.
SECRETARY: J.H. Muir.
Tel: (01555) 770620.

Interesting parkland course with scenic views of over the Clyde Valley. An enjoyable course for all classes of golfer.

COURSE INFORMATION

Par 70; SSS 68; Length 5,805 Yards.
Visitors: Welcome.
Opening Hours: Daylight hours.
Avoid: After 4pm Monday – Friday & public holidays.
Ladies: No restrictions.
Ladies Day: Tuesday evenings.
Green Fees: £15 per round & £20 per day.
Juveniles: Permitted.
Clubhouse Hours: All day Opening.
Clubhouse Dress: Smart Casual – no football colours, shorts etc.
Clubhouse Facilities: Full catering available – all day until 9pm.
Open Competitions: Men's H'cap – August; Men's Senior – June; Mixed Foursomes – June & July; Ladies – May.

CONVENIENT HOTEL

The Popinjay Hotel,
Rosebank, Lanarkshire.

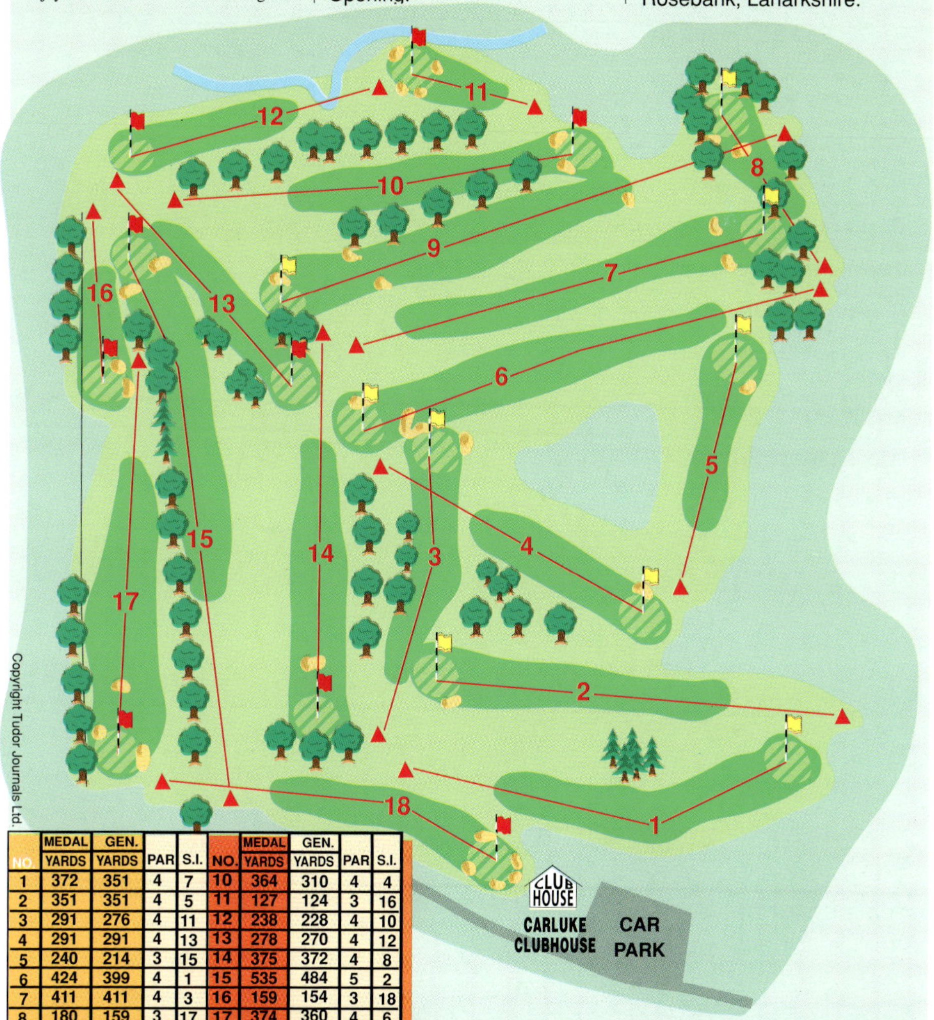

NO.	MEDAL YARDS	GEN. YARDS	PAR	S.I.	NO.	MEDAL YARDS	GEN. YARDS	PAR	S.I.
1	372	351	4	7	10	364	310	4	4
2	351	351	4	5	11	127	124	3	16
3	291	276	4	11	12	238	228	4	10
4	291	291	4	13	13	278	270	4	12
5	240	214	3	15	14	375	372	4	8
6	424	399	4	1	15	535	484	5	2
7	411	411	4	3	16	159	154	3	18
8	180	159	3	17	17	374	360	4	6
9	482	478	5	9	18	319	312	4	14
OUT	3,042	2,930	35		IN	2,769	2,614	35	
					TOTAL	5,811	5,544	70	
					STANDARD SCRATCH	68	67		

Bunker and tree positions indicated.

Carnwath Golf Club, Main Street,
Carnwath.
Tel: (0555) 840251.

LOCATION: Lanark 7 miles.
SECRETARY: Billy Bruce.
Tel: (0498) 425249.

Fairly short but testing golf course with small well protected greens, hilly in part. Sandy sub soil means course is normally dry underfoot, good views of surrounding countryside.

COURSE INFORMATION

Par 70; SSS 69; Length 5,953 Yards.
Visitors: Welcome on Sunday. On Sunday would advise phoning clubhouse.
Opening Hours: 8.00am.
Avoid: Saturday after 3.30pm on weekdays and Sundays.
Ladies: Welcome.
Green Fees: Day ticket only £18 midweek £22 Sundays.
Juveniles: Welcome but restricted.
Clubhouse Hours: 11.00am - 9.00pm for visitors.
Clubhouse Dress: No trainers, no shorts, no denims/shell suits.
Clubhouse Facilities: Full meals, snacks.

CONVENIENT HOTEL

Tinto Hotel at Symington.

NO.	MEDAL YARDS	GEN. YARDS	PAR	S.I.	NO.	MEDAL YARDS	GEN. YARDS	PAR	S.I.
1	193	165	3	15	10	164	149	3	18
2	234	230	3	5	11	270	256	4	6
3	335	315	4	11	12	321	302	4	14
4	174	161	3	17	13	365	356	4	4
5	371	353	4	3	14	264	248	4	12
6	397	380	4	9	15	311	296	4	10
7	499	475	5	7	16	295	276	4	16
8	430	416	4	1	17	455	445	4	2
9	375	359	4	13	18	500	450	5/4	8
OUT	3,008	2,854	34		IN	2,945	2,778	36/35	
					TOTAL	5,953	5,632	70/69	
					STANDARD SCRATCH	69	67		

Bunker and tree positions indicated.

CROW WOOD

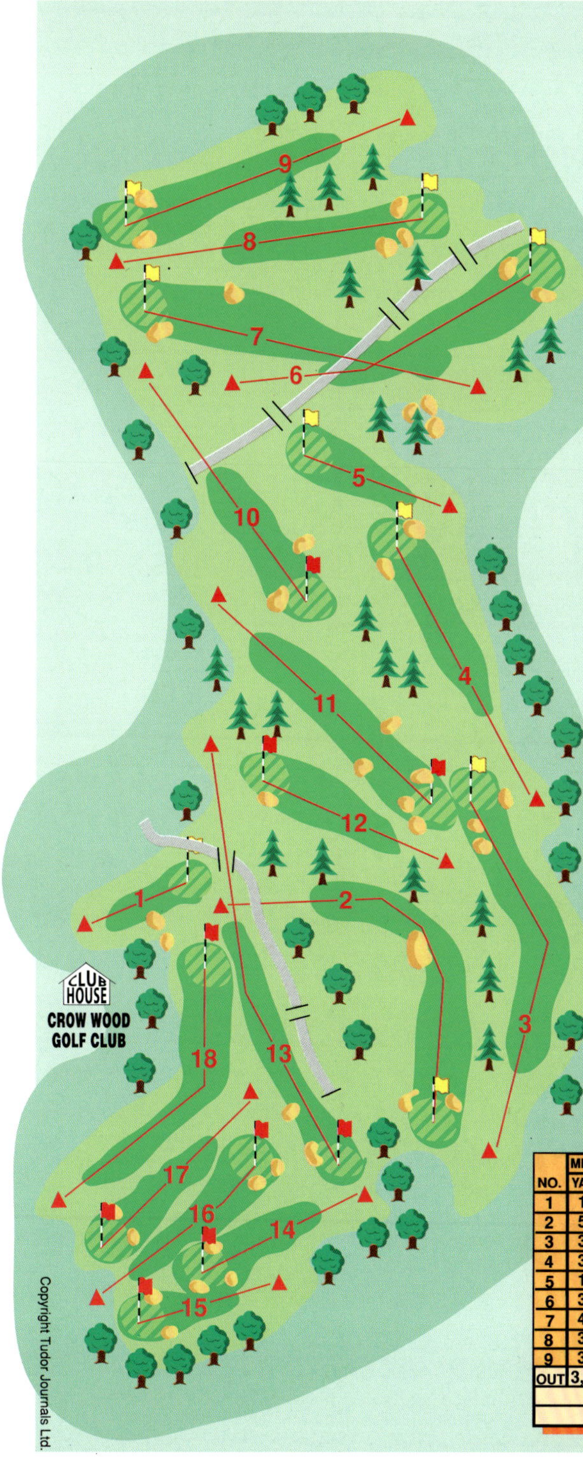

Crow Wood Golf Club, Muirhead, Glasgow. G69 9JF.
Tel: (0141) 7792011.

Location: 5 Miles North East of Glasgow on A80 to Stirling.
Secretary: Ian McInnes.
Tel: (0141) 7794954.
Architect: James Braid (1925).

Crow Wood is a magnificently appointed 18 hole parkland course, where rolling fairways enjoy the scenic backdrop of the Campsie Fells. A course calculated to provide golfing success to the willing student or master golfer's needs. The nutured greens and fairways of Crow Wood stand just such examination. With the course being a SSS70 and yet another triumph in layout for that most eminent of golf club designers James Braid. Guaranteed to provide a stern test no matter the level of your game.

COURSE INFORMATION

Par 71; SSS 70; Length 6,272 Yards.
Opening Hours: 8am – dusk.
Visitors: Mid–week only by prior arrangement with secretary.
Ladies: Welcome. Ladies day – Wednesday. Priority from 5.15 – 6.15pm.
Green Fees: £16 one round; £24 two rounds.
Juveniles: Permitted; Pay adult rates.
Clubhouse Hours: 8am – 11pm.
Clubhouse Dress: Smart/Casual.
Clubhouse Facilities: Catering available from 11am – 9pm.
Open Competitions: Open mixed, July; Seniors (over 55), August; Garnkirk Trophy (scratch Competition, Max Handicap 4).

CONVENIENT HOTELS

Crow Wood Hotel;
Garfield House Hotel;
Moodiesburn House Hotel.

NO.	MEDAL YARDS	GEN. YARDS	PAR	S.I.	NO.	MEDAL YARDS	GEN. YARDS	PAR	S.I.
1	146	130	3	17	10	291	267	4	16
2	538	530	5	4	11	402	381	4	3
3	362	350	4	9	12	277	252	4	18
4	354	336	4	13	13	453	411	4	1
5	197	157	3	11	14	349	305	4	12
6	378	364	4	6	15	167	142	3	14
7	421	415	4	2	16	336	316	4	10
8	372	364	4	15	17	386	369	4	5
9	333	318	4	8	18	517	495	5	7
OUT	3,093	2,937	35		IN	3,178	2,938	36	
					TOTAL	6,272	5,875	71	
	STANDARD SCRATCH					70			

Bunker and tree positions indicated.

Douglas Water Golf Club,
Douglas Water, Lanark.
Tel: (055 588) 361.

LOCATION: 7 miles South West of Lanark.
SECRETARY: R. McMillan.

Compact course with undulating fairways and small greens.

COURSE INFORMATION

Par 72; SSS 69; Length 2,945 Yards; 2,452 Metres.
Visitors: Restricted on Saturdays for competitions.
Opening Hours: 7.00am - 10.00pm.
Avoid: Monday between 6.00pm - 7.00pm.
Ladies: Welcome, Monday 6.00pm - 7.00pm.
Green Fees: Weekday £5.00, weekends £7.00.
Juveniles: During school holidays off the course before 6.00pm.
Clubhouse Hours: 7.00am - 10.00pm.
Clubhouse Dress: Informal.
Clubhouse Facilities: Snacks during week - filled rolls, tea and coffee. Saturday and Sunday and bank holidays.

NO.	YARDS	PAR	S.I.	NO.	YARDS	PAR	S.I.
1	279	4	7	10	279	4	8
2	304	4	13	11	304	4	14
3	256	4	11	12	256	4	12
4	201	3	15	13	201	3	16
5	488	5	3	14	488	5	4
6	564	5	1	15	564	5	2
7	313	4	9	16	313	4	10
8	385	4	5	17	385	4	6
9	155	3	17	18	155	3	18
OUT	2,945	36		IN	2,945	36	
				TOTAL	5,890	72	
STANDARD SCRATCH					69		

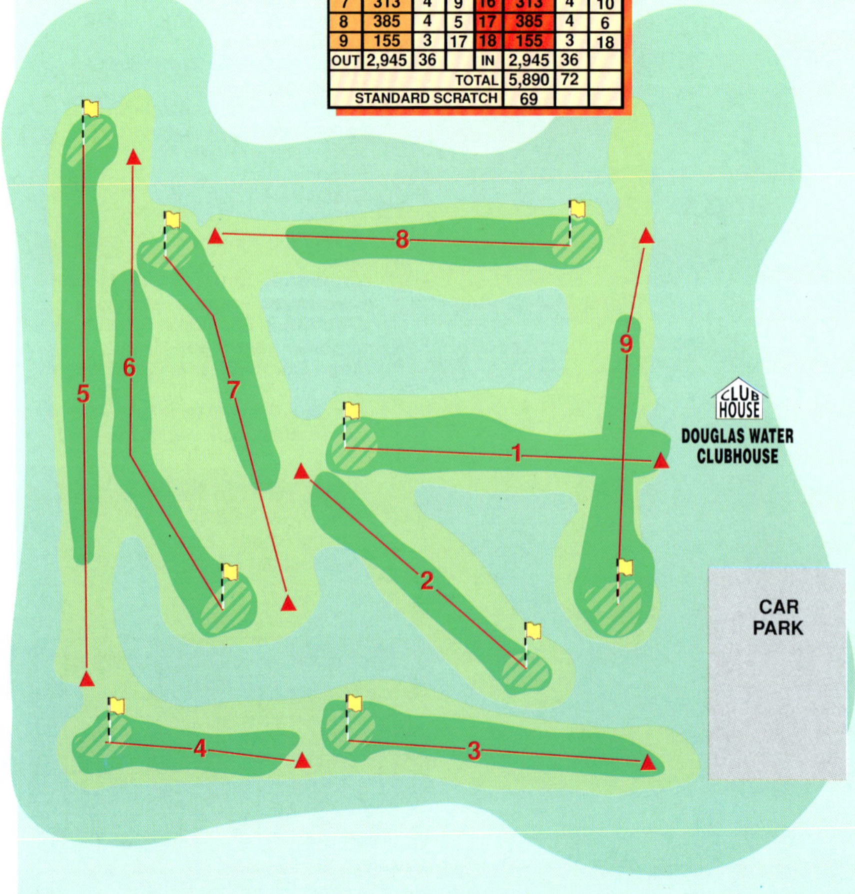

EAST KILBRIDE

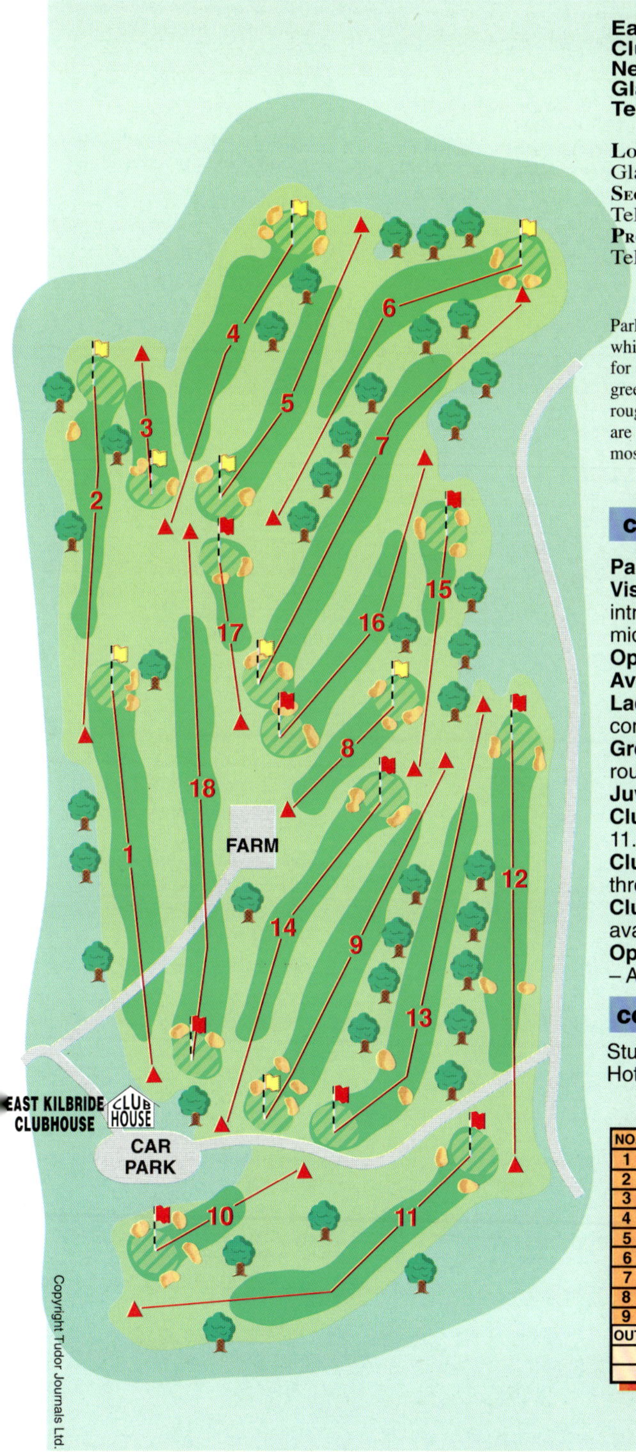

East kilbride Golf Club,Chapelside Road, Nerston, East Kilbride, Glasgow. G74 4PF.
Tel: (013552) 47728.

LOCATION: 10 miles south east of Glasgow.
SECRETARY: William Gray.
Tel: (013552) 47728.
PROFESSIONAL: Alistair Taylor.
Tel: (013552) 22192.

Parkland course with variable topography which with its length presents a real challenge for any standard of golfer. The course has large greens and strategically placed bunkers. Any rough areas which are liable to come into play are well maintained and are not too punitive to most golfers

COURSE INFORMATION

Par 71; SSS 71; Length 6,419 Yards.
Visitors: Welcome but must be introduced by member (parties mid-week).
Opening Hours: 8am – 11.00pm.
Avoid: Saturday & Sunday mornings.
Ladies: No play during gents competitions.
Green Fees: Mon - Fri £18 per round; £25 per day.
Juveniles: Introduced by member.
Clubhouse Hours: 8.00am – 11.00pm.
Clubhouse Dress: Casual but smart throughout.
Clubhouse Facilities: Catering available mid-day to 8.00pm.
Open Competitions: Seniors Open – August.

CONVENIENT HOTELS

Stuart Hotel; Bruce Hotel; Westpoint Hotel; Crutherland House Hotel.

NO.	YARDS	PAR	S.I.	NO.	YARDS	PAR	S.I.
1	412	4	3	10	193	3	16
2	404	4	11	11	427	4	4
3	132	3	15	12	443	4	10
4	355	4	7	13	493	4	2
5	333	4	13	14	390	4	12
6	402	4	9	15	259	3	14
7	527	5	1	16	329	4	6
8	185	3	17	17	179	3	18
9	401	4	5	18	555	5	8
OUT	3,151	35		IN	3,268	34	
				TOTAL	6,419	68	
STANDARD SCRATCH					71		

Bunker and tree positions indicated.

HOLLANDBUSH

LANARKSHIRE

Hollandbush Golf Club,
Acretop Head,
Lesmahagow,
Lanarkshire.
Tel: (01555) 893646.

LOCATION: Nine miles south of Hamilton.
SECRETARY: Mr J. Hamilton.
Tel: (01555) 893484.
PROFESSIONAL: J. Rae.
Tel: (01555) 893646.

A meadowland course situated on the edge of the moorland.

COURSE INFORMATION

Par 70; SSS 69; Length 6,133 Yards.
Opening Hours: 8am – Dusk.
Visitors: Welcome.
Avoid: Competition Days.
Ladies: Welcome.
Ladies day: Thursday.
Green Fees: Weekdays – £12 per day £8 per round & weekends – £15 per day £10 per round.

Clubhouse Hours: 8.00am – 8.00pm.
Clubhouse Dress: Smart /Casual.
Juveniles: Permitted.
Clubhouse Facilities: Catering available (except Tuesday).

NO.	MEDAL YARDS	GEN. YARDS	PAR	S.I.	NO.	MEDAL YARDS	GEN. YARDS	PAR	S.I.
1	515	485	5	3	10	212	199	3	16
2	311	297	4	13	11	349	332	4	8
3	299	291	4	15	12	356	345	4	6
4	442	430	4	1	13	176	165	3	18
5	340	328	4	11	14	262	253	4	14
6	171	166	3	17	15	263	252	4	10
7	516	477	5	5	16	476	441	5/4	4
8	335	314	4	9	17	259	250	4	12
9	414	403	4	7	18	437	429	4	2
OUT	3,343	3,191	37		IN	2,790	2,666	35	
					TOTAL	6,133	5,857	72/71	
					STANDARD SCRATCH	70	69		

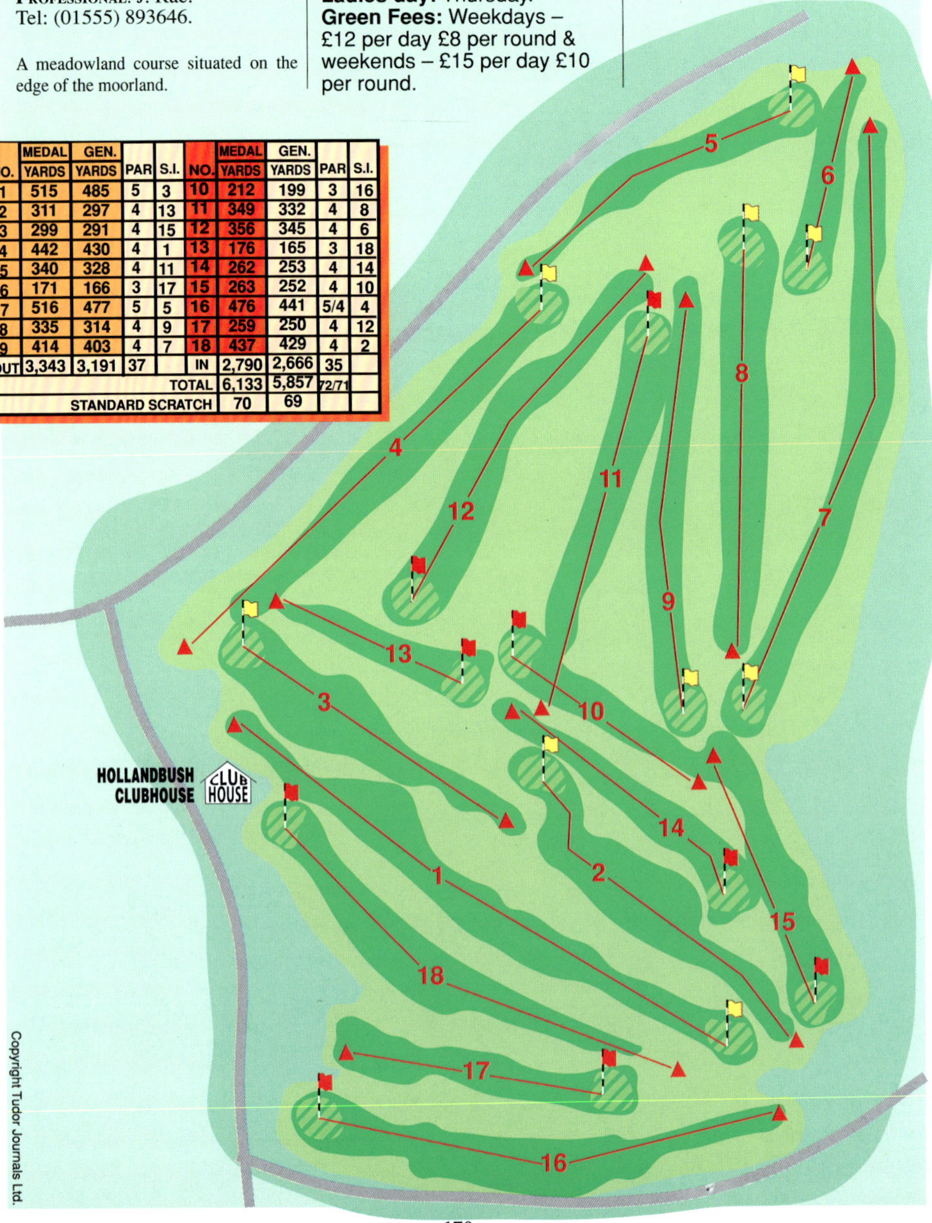

Kirkhill Golf Club, Greenlees Road, Cambuslang, Glasgow. G72 8YN.
Tel: (0141) 641 3083.

Location: South side of Glasgow.
Secretary: Mr H.G. Marshall.
Tel: (0141) 641 8499.
Architect: James Braid.

Kirkhill as the name might suggest is fairly hilly but not excessively so. It is a parkland course and with many small greens, presents a good test. There are some holes of particular interest, for example, the par 3 7th hole is played from a high tee to a green much lower, the par 4 10th hole because of its difficulty (which is also applicable to the par 3 16th hole) has a gully and burn in front of the green calling for an accurate tee shot.

COURSE INFORMATION

Par 69; SSS 69; Length 5,862 Yards, 5,364 Metres.
Visitors: Welcome.
Opening Hours: 8am – 8pm.
Avoid: Weekends
Ladies: Phone to check.
Ladies Day: Thursday.
Green Fees: £12 per round; £20 per day.
Juveniles: Phone to check.
Clubhouse Hours: 8am – 11pm.
Clubhouse Dress: Smart / Casual – no collarless shirts or denims.
Clubhouse Facilities: 7days per week from 10am.
Open Competitions: Phone for enquiries.

CONVENIENT HOTELS

Stewart Hotel; Bruce Hotel (both in East Kilbride).

NO.	YARDS	PAR	S.I.	NO.	YARDS	PAR	S.I.
1	445	4	3	10	351	4	12
2	256	4	11	11	418	4	2
3	158	3	17	12	339	4	14
4	289	4	7	13	318	4	9
5	153	3	13	14	392	4	6
6	485	5	1	15	380	4	15
7	190	3	16	16	154	3	18
8	408	4	5	17	476	5	4
9	205	3	10	18	445	4	8
OUT	2,589	33		IN	3,273	36	
				TOTAL	5,862	69	
STANDARD SCRATCH					69		

Bunker and tree positions indicated.

Lanark Golf Club, The Moor, Lanark, Lanarkshire.
Tel: (0555) 663219.

LOCATION: 30 miles south of Glasgow, off A74.
SECRETARY: G.H. Cuthill.
Tel: (0555) 663219.
PROFESSIONAL: Ron Wallace.
Tel: (0555) 661456.

Tough moorland course, especially when the prevailing wind blows. The regional qualifier for the "Open" is to be played at Lanark from 1992–1997 inclusive.

COURSE INFORMATION

Par 70; SSS 71; Length 6,423 Yards.
Opening hours: 8.00am to dusk.
Visitors: Welcome Monday-Friday before 4pm. No visitors at weekends. Handicap certificate preferred.
Avoid: No parties on a Friday.
Ladies: Welcome on Friday.
Green Fees: Weekdays £18 per round; £28 per day.
Juveniles: Nine hole course available; £1.75.

Clubhouse hours: Vary.
Clubhouse Dress: No denims, trainers, tracksuits or shell suits. Smart dress at all times.
Clubhouse Facilities: Catering available from 11.30am-9.00pm most days.

CONVENIENT HOTELS

Clydesdale Hotel - Lanark;
Cartland Bridge - Lanark.

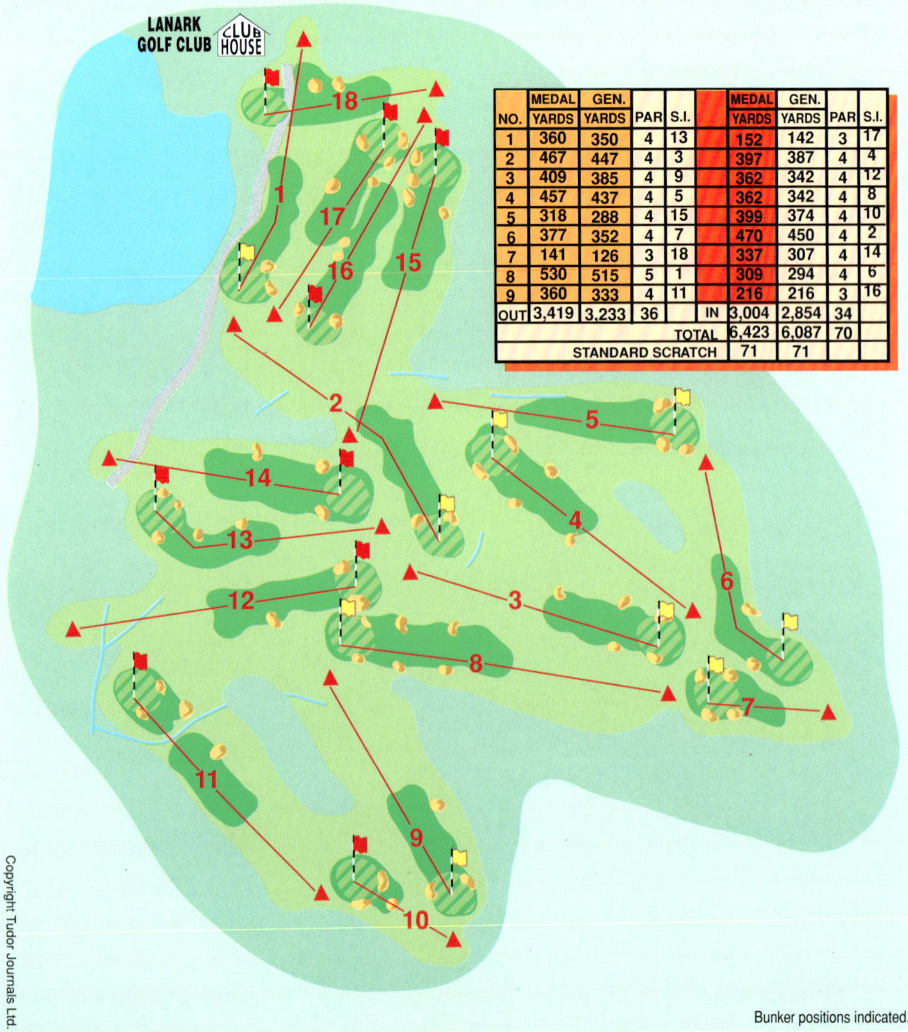

NO.	MEDAL YARDS	GEN. YARDS	PAR	S.I.		MEDAL YARDS	GEN. YARDS	PAR	S.I.
1	360	350	4	13		152	142	3	17
2	467	447	4	3		397	387	4	4
3	409	385	4	9		362	342	4	12
4	457	437	4	5		362	342	4	8
5	318	288	4	15		399	374	4	10
6	377	352	4	7		470	450	4	2
7	141	126	3	18		337	307	4	14
8	530	515	5	1		309	294	4	6
9	360	333	4	11		216	216	3	16
OUT	3,419	3,233	36		IN	3,004	2,854	34	
					TOTAL	6,423	6,087	70	
					STANDARD SCRATCH	71	71		

Bunker positions indicated.

Leadhills Golf Club, Leadhills, Biggar, MU2 6XR.

Location: 6 miles off A74 at Abington.
Secretary: G. Shaw.

Short but testing. Course which claims the title of the highest in Great Britain at 1,500 feet above sea level.

COURSE INFORMATION

Par 64; SSS 62; Length 2,031 Yards.
Visitors: Welcome.
Opening Hours: Daylight hours.
Ladies: Welcome.
Green Fees: £4.00 per day.
Juveniles: Welcome.
Clubhouse Dress: Casual.

CONVENIENT HOTEL

Hopetown Arms Hotel; Leadhills (200 metres).

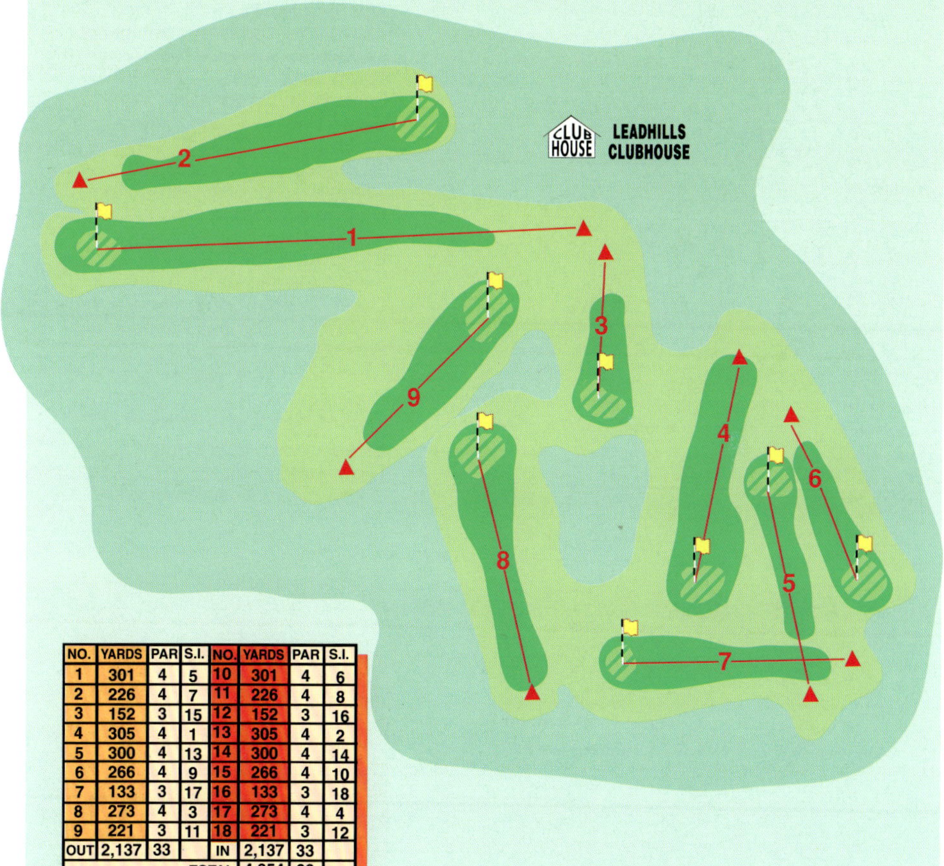

NO.	YARDS	PAR	S.I.	NO.	YARDS	PAR	S.I.
1	301	4	5	10	301	4	6
2	226	4	7	11	226	4	8
3	152	3	15	12	152	3	16
4	305	4	1	13	305	4	2
5	300	4	13	14	300	4	14
6	266	4	9	15	266	4	10
7	133	3	17	16	133	3	18
8	273	4	3	17	273	4	4
9	221	3	11	18	221	3	12
OUT	2,137	33		IN	2,137	33	
				TOTAL	4,354	66	
STANDARD SCRATCH					64		

MOUNT ELLEN

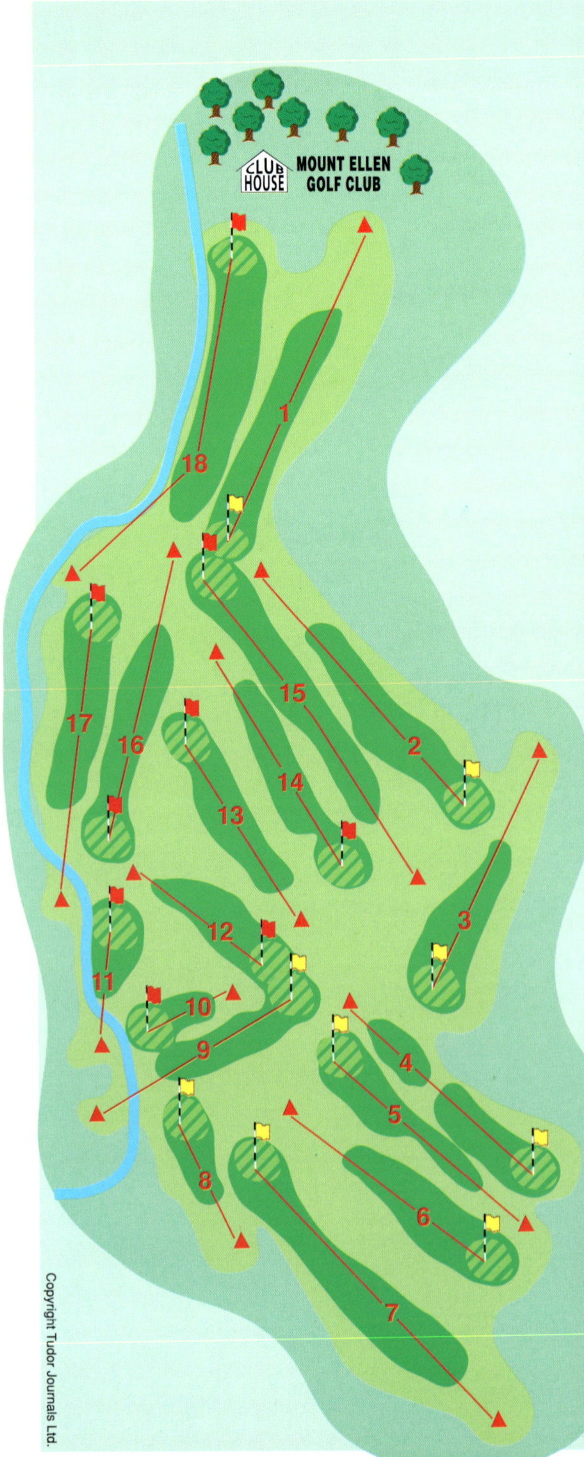

Mount Ellen Golf Club,
Gartcosh, Glasgow. G69 9EY.
Tel: (0236) 872277.

LOCATION: 8 miles north east of Glasgow.
SECRETARY: W.J. Dickson.
PROFESSIONAL: G. Reilly.
Tel: (0236) 872632.

Small and tricky. Best greens in Lanarkshire. Well bunkered. A good test of your golf.

COURSE INFORMATION

Par 68; SSS 68; Length 5,525 Yards.
Visitors: Welcome.
Opening Hours: 8am – Dusk.
Avoid: Weekends (not permitted).
Ladies: Tuesdays & Thursdays no play between 5pm – 7pm.
Ladies Day: Wednesday.
Green Fees: £12 per round & £20 per day.
Juveniles: Same as ladies.
Clubhouse Hours: 8am – 11pm.
Clubhouse Dress: Smart / Casual – no jeans or trainers.
Clubhouse Facilities: Full catering – excellent service.
Open Competitions: Two Pro-Am's – one in May & one in September; Senior Open – early June; Mount Ellen G.C. Open – July.

CONVENIENT HOTELS

Moodiesburn House Hotel;
Crow-wood Hotel.

NO.	YARDS	PAR	S.I.	NO.	YARDS	PAR	S.I.
1	355	4	4	10	156	3	18
2	331	4	6	11	166	3	16
3	282	4	12	12	233	3	15
4	285	4	14	13	300	4	8
5	328	4	7	14	405	4	2
6	308	4	9	15	434	4	5
7	461	4	1	16	292	4	11
8	191	3	17	17	307	4	10
9	265	4	13	18	426	4	3
OUT	2,806	35		IN	2,719	33	
				TOTAL	5,525	68	
STANDARD SCRATCH					68		

Tree positions indicated.

SHOTTS

LANARKSHIRE

**Shotts Golf club, Blairhead,
Benhar Road, Shotts, ML7 5BJ.
Tel: (0501) 820431.**

Location: Between Glasgow & Edinburgh on B7057. M8 1 1/2 miles.
Secretary: J. McDermott.
Tel: (0501) 820431.
Professional: Jim Forrester.
Tel: (0501) 826658.
Architect: James Braid.

Undulating moorland with holes offering variety. Difficult tree line on 8 fairways.

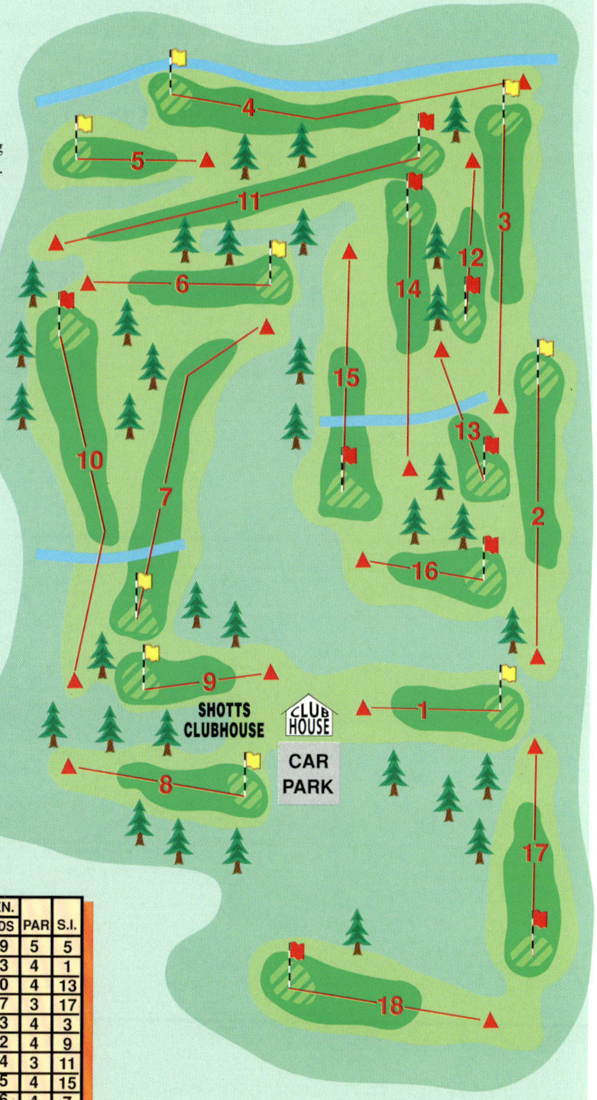

COURSE INFORMATION

Par 70; SSS 70; Length 6,125 Yards.
Visitors: No visitors on Saturday before 3.45pm.
Opening Hours: 7.30am - sunset.
Avoid: Saturday and Sunday.
Ladies: Welcome on Tuesday.
Green Fees: £14 per day, weekend £16.
Juveniles: Welcome.
Clubhouse Hours: 11am.
Clubhouse Dress: Neat, no denims allowed.
Clubhouse Facilities: Full all day.
Open Competitions: September.

CONVENIENT HOTELS

Newhouse Travel Inn (6 miles);
Station Hotel Shotts (1 miles).

NO.	MEDAL YARDS	GEN. YARDS	PAR	S.I.	NO.	MEDAL YARDS	GEN. YARDS	PAR	S.I.
1	328	318	4	14	10	478	449	5	5
2	302	290	4	16	11	457	433	4	1
3	444	364	4	2	12	348	340	4	13
4	409	387	4	4	13	152	137	3	17
5	136	119	3	18	14	416	403	4	3
6	368	344	4	10	15	331	302	4	9
7	352	342	4	6	16	222	204	3	11
8	385	361	4	8	17	298	265	4	15
9	322	304	4	12	18	381	376	4	7
OUT	3,046	2,829	35		IN	3,079	2,909	35	
					TOTAL	6,125	2,829	70	
					STANDARD SCRATCH	70			

Tree positions indicated.

STRATHAVEN

Strathaven Golf Club,
Glasgow Road, Strathaven,
Lanarkshire, ML10 6NL.
Tel: (01357) 20421.

Location: Outskirts of Strathaven, off Glasgow Road.
Secretary: A.W.Wallace.
Tel: (01357) 20421.
Professional: Mr M McCrorie.
Tel: (0357) 21812.

Parkland, tree lined, undulating. 600 feet above sea level.

COURSE INFORMATION

Par 71; SSS 70; Length 6,204 Yards.
Visitors: Monday to Friday.
Avoid: 12.00pm - 1.00pm.
Ladies: As above.
Ladies Day: Thursdays.
Green Fees: Weekdays £17.50 single round. £25.00 day ticket.
Juveniles: Accompanied by adult only.

Clubhouse Hours: 7.45am to 11.30pm.
Clubhouse Dress: Casual but no denim jeans.
Clubhouse Facilities: Available - 12noon - 9.30pm.

CONVENIENT HOTELS

Strathavon Hotel;
Springvale Hotel.

NO.	MEDAL YARDS	GEN. YARDS	PAR	S.I.	NO.	MEDAL YARDS	GEN. YARDS	PAR	S.I.
1	365	357	4	5	10	487	425	5/5	10
2	204	193	3	9	11	410	399	4	4
3	482	457	5/4	13	12	338	328	4	16
4	159	147	3	15	13	323	316	4	6
5	335	323	4	2	14	298	287	4	18
6	348	39	4	7	15	137	128	3	12
7	375	365	4	11	16	446	435	4	1
8	507	496	5	17	17	356	346	4	14
9	226	215	3	3	18	408	397	4	8
OUT	3,001	2,892	35/34		IN	3,203	3,061	36/35	
					TOTAL	6,204	5,953	71/73	
					STANDARD SCRATCH	70	69		

Tree positions indicated.

Strathclyde Park Golf Club, Mote Hill, Hamilton, Lanarkshire.
To book golf course Tel: (01698) 266155.

LOCATION: Hamilton/Motherwell exit junction when heading North, 2nd exit at 1st roundabout – 2nd exit at 2nd roundabout pass ice rink.
SECRETARY: Kevin Will.
Tel: (01324) 557968.
PROFESSIONAL: W. Walker.
Tel: (01698) 285511.

Wooded Parkland 9 holes where golfers can enjoy the views of the race course and Strathclyde Park Loch.

COURSE INFORMATION

Par 72; SSS 70; Length 6,350 Yards.
Opening Hours: Summer 7am - 9pm Winter 8am - 2pm.
Avoid: Team matches, Horse racing nights. Medals March - September every 2nd week.
Ladies: Welcome.
Green Fees: £2.20 per 9 holes (adult). £1.10 Junior, 65p OAP.
Clubhouse Hours: Late opens 9.30am – 9.00pm bar opens 11am – 10pm.
Clubhouse Dress: Casual.
Clubhouse Facilities: Hot and cold snacks bar meals served all day in cafe or bar.
Open Competitions: End of March to end of September.

CONVENIENT HOTEL

Travel Lodge.

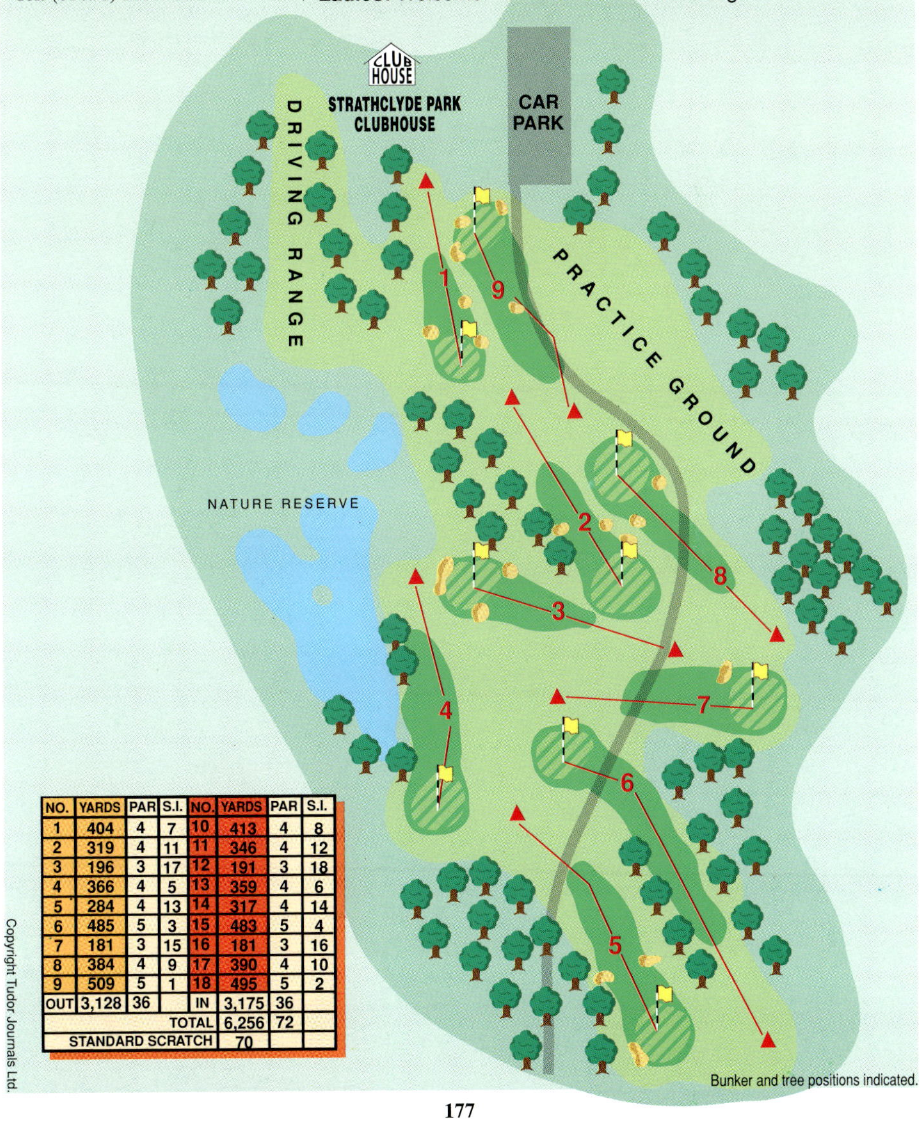

NO.	YARDS	PAR	S.I.	NO.	YARDS	PAR	S.I.
1	404	4	7	10	413	4	8
2	319	4	11	11	346	4	12
3	196	3	17	12	191	3	18
4	366	4	5	13	359	4	6
5	284	4	13	14	317	4	14
6	485	5	3	15	483	5	4
7	181	3	15	16	181	3	16
8	384	4	9	17	390	4	10
9	509	5	1	18	495	5	2
OUT	3,128	36		IN	3,175	36	
				TOTAL	6,256	72	
STANDARD SCRATCH					70		

Bunker and tree positions indicated.

WISHAW

Wishaw Golf Club, 55 Cleland Road, Wishaw, Lanarkshire, ML2 7PH.
Tel: (0698) 372869.

LOCATION: 2 miles from A74 Motherwell junction.
SECRETARY: Mr J.A. Mitchell.
Tel: (0698) 372869.
PROFESSIONAL: Mr J. Campbell.
Tel: (0698) 358274.
ARCHITECT: James Braid.

Parkland course which proves deceptively difficult. Bunkers around every green except the 10th, the greens themselves being difficult to hit and hold. Four extremely difficult par 3 holes, with out of bounds on three. The finishing five holes are our a good test of the best golfers and can easily destroy a good score.

COURSE INFORMATION

Par 69; SSS 69; Length 6,073 yards.
Visitors: Welcome.
Opening Hours: 8.00am.
Avoid: Saturday, midweek after 10.00am & Sunday before 10.00am.
Ladies: As above.
Ladies Day: Tuesday.
Green Fees: £12 per round, £20 per day, £25 Sunday.
Juveniles: Permitted.
Clubhouse Hours: All day untill 11.00pm.
Clubhouse Dress: Informal, no track suits or T-shirts.
Clubhouse Facilities: 11.00am – 9.00pm.

CONVENIENT HOTELS

Moorings Hotel;
Hamilton Road;
Motherwell.

Bunker and tree positions indicated.

NO.	MEDAL YARDS	GEN. YARDS	PAR	S.I.	NO.	MEDAL YARDS	GEN. YARDS	PAR	S.I.
1	386	359	4	9	10	297	278	4	12
2	346	332	4	11	11	182	163	3	16
3	392	385	4	4	12	399	393	4	7
4	483	469	5	1	13	287	277	4	14
5	395	383	4	5	14	455	441	4	2
6	136	157	3	15	15	388	372	4	10
7	304	276	4	13	16	447	429	4	3
8	160	148	3	18	17	186	179	3	17
9	390	379	4	8	18	414	401	4	6
OUT	3,018	2,888	35		IN	3,055	2,933	34	
					TOTAL	6,073	5,821	69	
					STANDARD SCRATCH	69	69		

GOLF DAYS™ SCOTLAND

LOTHIAN

Baberton Golf Club, Juniper Green, Edinburgh, Midlothian. EH14 5DU.
Tel: (0131) 453 3361.

LOCATION: 5 miles west of Edinburgh off the A70.
SECRETARY: E.W. Horberry. Tel: (0131) 453 4911.
PROFESSIONAL: K. Kelly Tel: (0131) 453 3555.
ARCHITECT: James Braid.

Founded in 1893 this most attractive parkland course was originally 9 holes, later extended to 18 holes, to a James Braid plan.

COURSE INFORMATION

Par 69; SSS 70; Length 6,098 Yards.
Opening Hours: Visitors 9.30am to 4pm.
Visitors: Welcome by prior arrangement.
Avoid: After 4pm weekdays and weekends.
Ladies: Visitors 9.30am to 4pm; Ladies day Thursday.
Green Fees: £18 per round; £28 per day.
Juveniles: Not permitted.

Clubhouse Hours: Bar 11am to 10.30pm.
Clubhouse Dress: No jeans or trainers; Jackets required after 7pm.
Clubhouse Facilities: Lunch 12 noon to 2pm; Evening meals by arrangement; snacks available

CONVENIENT HOTELS

Braid Hills Hotel; Royal Scot Hotel

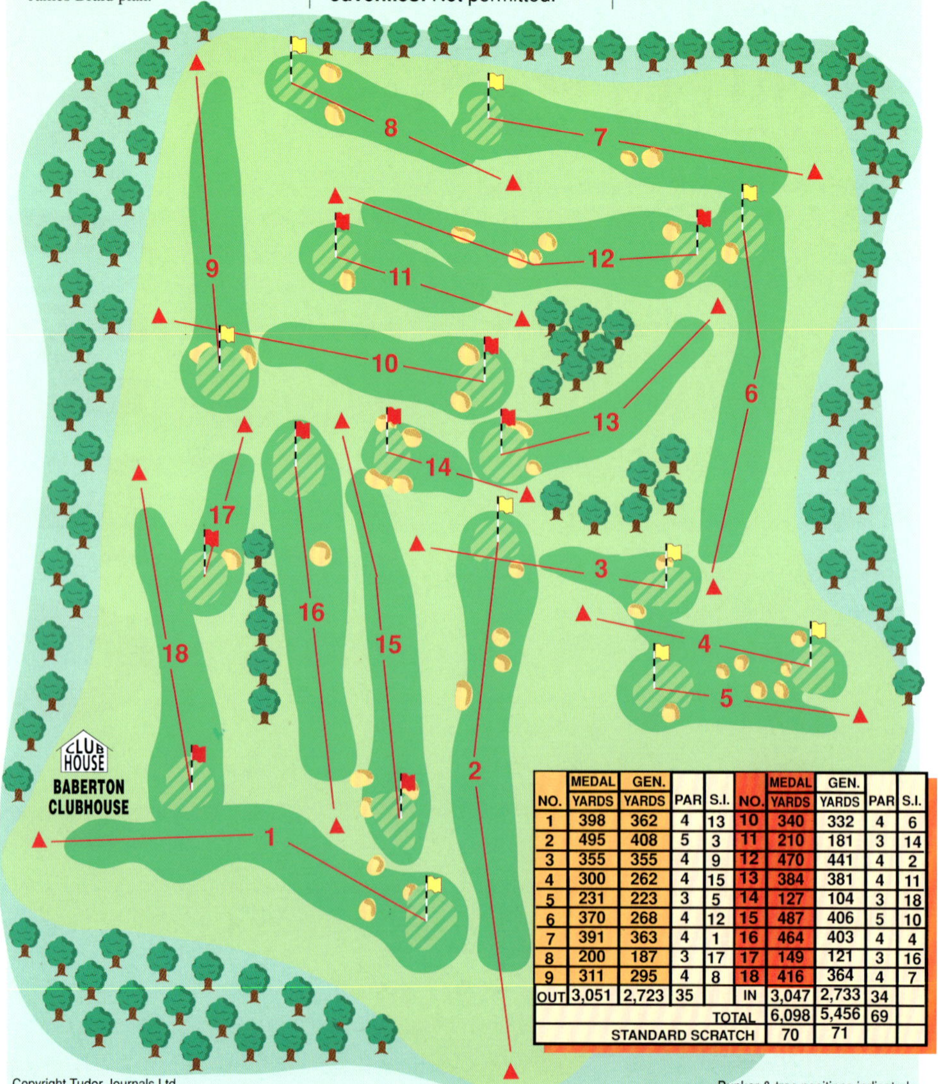

NO.	MEDAL YARDS	GEN. YARDS	PAR	S.I.	NO.	MEDAL YARDS	GEN. YARDS	PAR	S.I.
1	398	362	4	13	10	340	332	4	6
2	495	408	5	3	11	210	181	3	14
3	355	355	4	9	12	470	441	4	2
4	300	262	4	15	13	384	381	4	11
5	231	223	3	5	14	127	104	3	18
6	370	268	4	12	15	487	406	5	10
7	391	363	4	1	16	464	403	4	4
8	200	187	3	17	17	149	121	3	16
9	311	295	4	8	18	416	364	4	7
OUT	3,051	2,723	35		IN	3,047	2,733	34	
					TOTAL	6,098	5,456	69	
					STANDARD SCRATCH	70	71		

Bunker & tree positions indicated.

BRUNTSFIELD LINKS

LOTHIAN

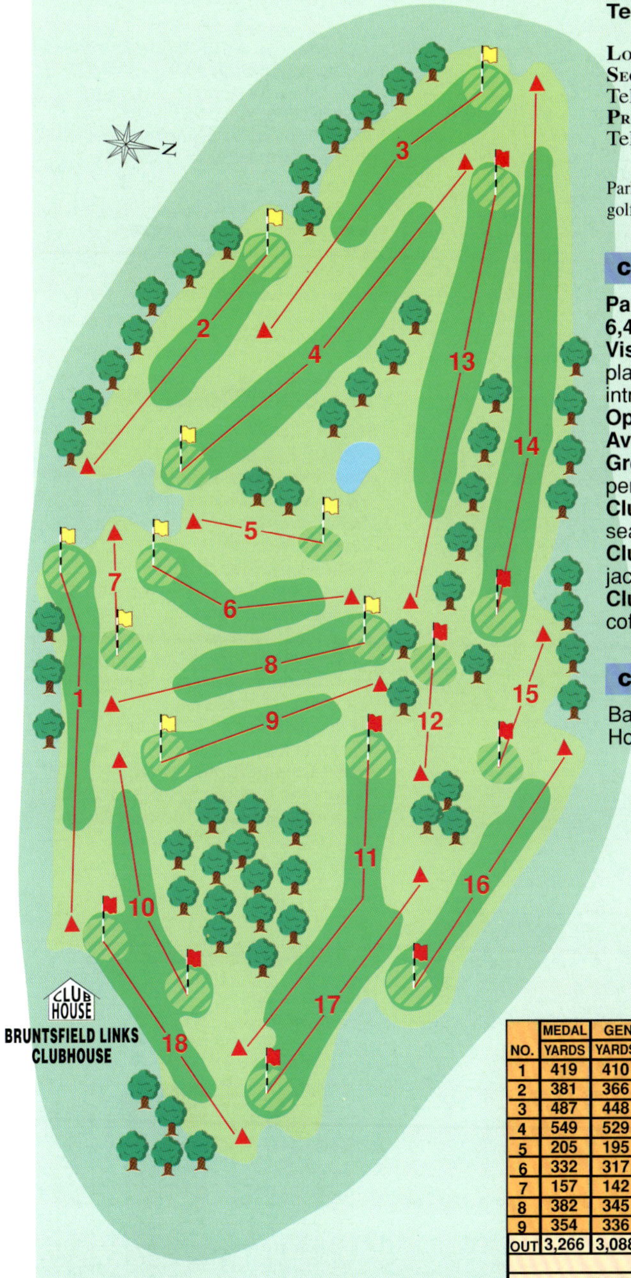

Bruntsfield Links Golfing Society, 32 Barnton Avenue, Davidson's Mains, Edinburgh, EH4 6JH.
Tel: (0131) 336 2006.

Location: 3 miles west of Edinburgh.
Secretary: Cdr. D.M. Sandford.
Tel: (0131) 336 1479.
Professional: B. MacKenzie.
Tel: (0131) 336 4050.

Parkland course which offers an interesting golfing challenge.

COURSE INFORMATION

Par 71; SSS 71; Length 6,407 Yards.
Visitors: Welcome on weekdays, playing with a member or suitably introduced.
Opening Hours: 8am – Dusk.
Avoid: Weekends (members only).
Green Fees: £30 per round & £40 per day.
Clubhouse Hours: Varies on season.
Clubhouse Dress: Conventional jacket and tie.
Clubhouse Facilities: Morning coffee & lunches.

CONVENIENT HOTELS

Barnton Hotel; Capital Moat House Hotel; Holiday Inn.

NO.	MEDAL YARDS	GEN. YARDS	PAR	S.I.	NO.	MEDAL YARDS	GEN. YARDS	PAR	S.I.
1	419	410	4	5	10	339	325	4	10
2	381	366	4	11	11	415	392	4	3
3	487	448	5/4	9	12	168	158	3	16
4	549	529	5	1	13	455	445	4	2
5	205	195	3	13	14	493	479	5	8
6	332	317	4	7	15	170	160	3	17
7	157	142	3	18	16	373	355	4	12
8	382	345	4	15	17	381	370	4	6
9	354	336	4	4	18	347	337	4	14
OUT	3,266	3,088	36/35		IN	3,141	3,021	35	
					TOTAL	6,407	6,109	71/70	
					STANDARD SCRATCH	71	70		

Tree positions indicated.

Tree positions indicated.

Bathgate Golf Club, Edinburgh Road, Bathgate, West Lothian. Tel: (01506) 652232.

Location: 15 Miles west of Edinburgh on the A89.
Secretary: W. Gray.
Tel: (01506) 630505.
Professional: Sandy Strachan.
Tel: (01506) 630553.

A parkland course generally fairly flat, situated near the town centre and the railway station with frequent train services between Bathgate and Edinburgh. This is the course where the late Eric Brown and Bernard Gallacher, both Ryder Cup Captains and players learnt to play golf.

COURSE INFORMATION

Par 71; SSS 70; Length 6,328 Yards; 5831 Metres.
Opening Hours: Daylight.
Visitors: Welcome.
Avoid: Weekends; Telephone first.
Ladies: Welcome;
Ladies Day: Tuesday.
Green Fees: Monday – Friday £15 per round, £22 per day.
Juveniles: Welcome with adult.
Clubhouse Hours: 11am – 11pm.
Clubhouse Dress: Casual/Neat. No jeans or sleeveless shirts.
Clubhouse Facilities: Catering available from 8.30am – 8.30pm.
Open Competitions: Mixed foursomes June; Seniors Open June; Handicap Open July; Scratch Open August.; Ladies Open August; Boys Open July.

CONVENIENT HOTELS

The Fairways;
The Kaim Park.

NO.	YARDS	PAR	S.I.	NO.	YARDS	PAR	S.I.
1	478	5	3	10	406	4	8
2	457	4	5	11	176	3	16
3	336	4	11	12	507	5	2
4	220	3	15	13	224	3	14
5	489	5	1	14	433	4	6
6	336	4	13	15	519	5	4
7	383	4	7	16	330	4	12
8	153	3	17	17	148	3	18
9	356	4	9	18	377	4	10
OUT	3,208	36		IN	3,120	35	
				TOTAL	6,328	71	
				STANDARD SCRATCH	70		

BROOMIEKNOWE

Broomieknowe, 36 Golf Course Road, Bonnyrigg, Mid Lothian. H19 2HZ.
Tel: (0131) 6639317.

LOCATION: 6 Miles South of Edinburgh off A6094.
SECRETARY: Mr White.
Tel: (0131) 6639317.
PROFESSIONAL: M. Patchett.
Tel: (0131) 6602035.

The course is situated in a large park. It consists of gently rolling hills with many bunkers. Quiet.

COURSE INFORMATION

Par 68; SSS 68; Length 5,754 Yards.
Opening Hours: Dawn to Dusk.
Visitors: No parties at weekends.
Avoid: Competition days – phone to check.
Ladies: No restrictions on weekdays – weekends phone.

Green Fees: Weekday £17/rd; £25/day. Weekend £25 no day tickets.
Juveniles: Permitted – before 5pm weekday – weekend / phone.
Clubhouse Hours: 11am – 2.30pm & 5pm – 11pm; Weekends 11am – 11pm.
Clubhouse Dress: Smart / Casual – no denims or trainers.
Clubhouse Facilities: Bar – catering Tues – Sunday. Parties catered for by arrangement.
Open Competitions: Handicap May; Open Scots August; Ladies/Juniors July; Open Mixed August.

CONVENIENT HOTELS

Dalhousie Castle, Bonnyrigg; 1 mile County Hotel, Dalkeith, High Street;
Motel Derry, Eskbank, Dalkeith.

NO.	YARDS	PAR	S.I.	NO.	YARDS	PAR	S.I.
1	316	4	15	10	417	4	3
2	347	4	10	11	183	3	11
3	369	4	4	12	441	4	1
4	294	4	17	13	430	4	7
5	384	4	8	14	408	4	5
6	188	3	6	15	153	3	18
7	342	4	13	16	297	4	16
8	381	4	2	17	309	4	9
9	177	3	12	18	318	4	14
OUT	2,798	34		IN	2,956	34	
				TOTAL	5,754	68	
STANDARD SCRATCH					68		

DALMAHOY (East Course)

Dalmahoy Hotel Country Club Resort, Kirknewton, Midlothian, EH27 8EB.
Tel: (0131) 333 4105.

Location: 7 miles west of Edinburgh on the A71.
Secretary: Miss J. Wilson.
Professional: Mr B. Anderson.
Architect: J. Braid.

Host to many major tournaments, the two 18 hole courses at Dalmahoy are set in wooded countryside with numerous lakes and streams. The West course features two spectacular crossings of the Gogan Burn and is popular with players at every level. While the internationally renouned East course presents a greater challenge and hosted the Solheim Cup during 1992.

COURSE INFORMATION

Par 72; SSS 72; Length 6,677 Yards.
Opening Hours: 7.30am.

Visitors: No visitors Sat. or Sun. (members and guests only).
Avoid: Saturdays & Sundays.
Ladies: Encouraged.
Green Fees: £39 Weekday; Resident £25 Weekday.
Juveniles: Restricted, must be members guest.
Clubhouse Hours: 7am -10.30pm.

Clubhouse Dress: Casual.
Cluhouse Facilities: Full catering with Bistro restaurant and club bar; full leisure facilities.

CONVENIENT HOTELS

Dalmahoy Hotel Country Club Resort.

EAST COURSE

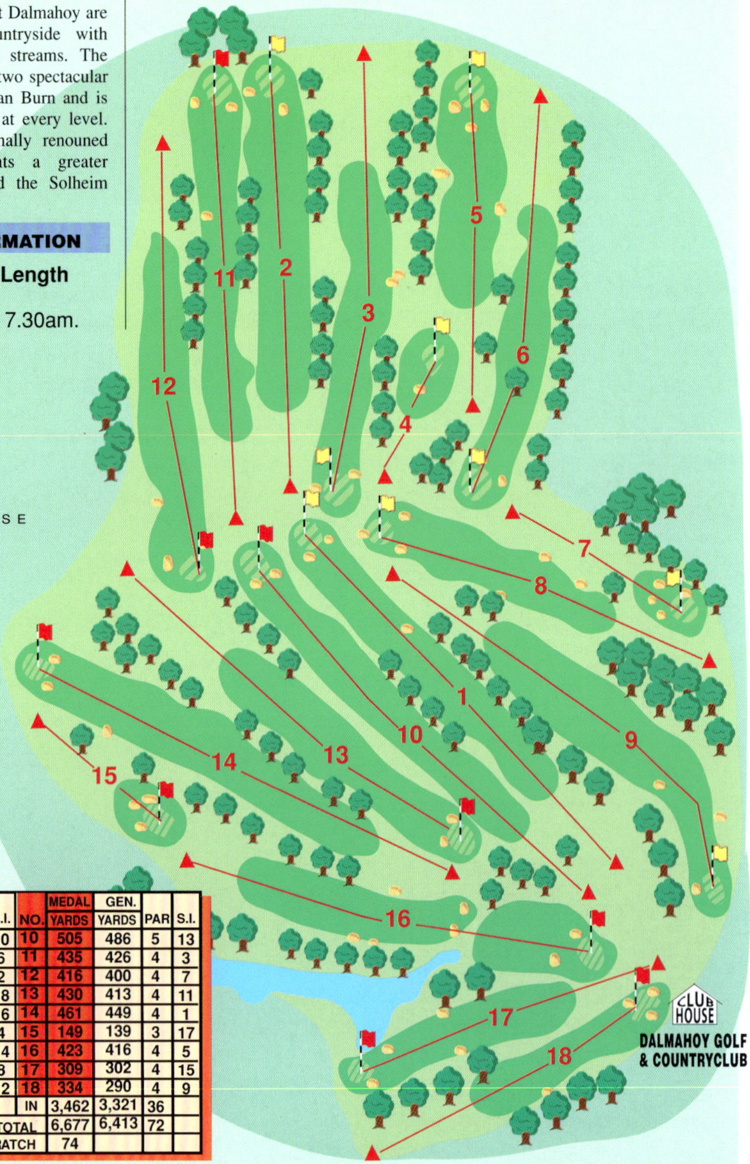

NO.	MEDAL YARDS	GEN. YARDS	PAR	S.I.	NO.	MEDAL YARDS	GEN. YARDS	PAR	S.I.
1	495	478	5	10	10	505	486	5	13
2	406	381	4	6	11	435	426	4	3
3	431	416	4	2	12	416	400	4	7
4	145	138	3	18	13	430	413	4	11
5	306	301	4	16	14	461	449	4	1
6	390	385	4	4	15	149	139	3	17
7	206	175	3	14	16	423	416	4	5
8	356	347	4	8	17	309	302	4	15
9	480	471	5	12	18	334	290	4	9
OUT	3,215	3,092	36		IN	3,462	3,321	36	
					TOTAL	6,677	6,413	72	
					STANDARD SCRATCH	74			

Bunker & tree positions indicated.

DALMAHOY (West Course)

Dalmahoy Hotel Country Club Resort, Kirknewton, Midlothian. EH27 8EB. Tel: (0131) 333 4105.

Location: 7 miles west of Edinburgh on the A71.
Secretary: Miss J. Wilson.
Professional: Mr B. Anderson.
Architect: James Braid.

Host to many major tournaments, the two 18 hole courses at Dalmahoy are set in wooded countryside with numerous lakes and streams. The West course features two spectacular crossings of the Gogan Burn and is popular with players at every level. While the internationally renouned East course presents a greater challenge and hosted the Solheim Cup during 1992.

COURSE INFORMATION

Par 68; SSS 66; Length 5,185 Yards.
Opening Hours: 7.30am.
Visitors: Welcome.
Avoid: Saturdays & Sundays.
Ladies: Welcome.
Green Fees: £27 Weekday; Resident £18 Weekday.
Juveniles: Restricted, must be members guest.
Clubhouse Hours: 7.30am -10.30pm.
Clubhouse Dress: Casual.
Cluhouse Facilities: Full catering with Bistro restaurant and club bar; full leisure facilities.

CONVENIENT HOTELS

Dalmahoy Hotel Country Club Resort.

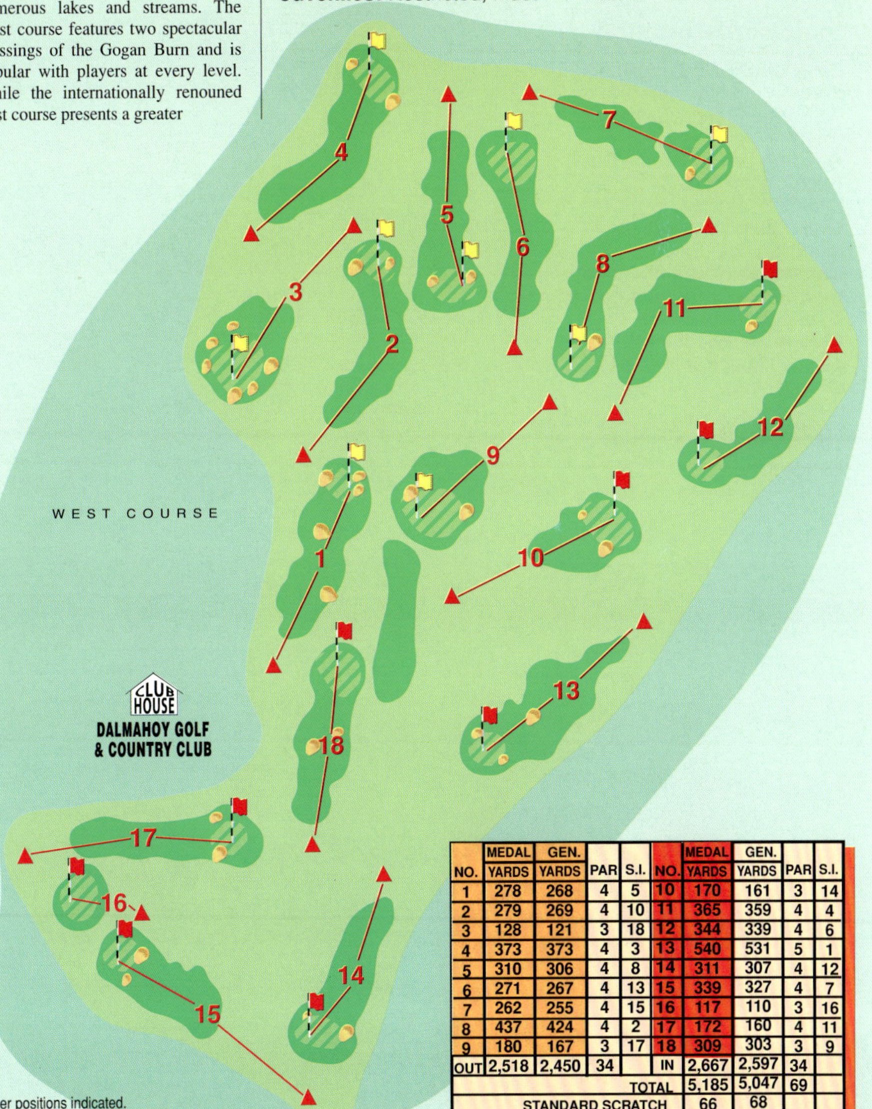

NO.	MEDAL YARDS	GEN. YARDS	PAR	S.I.	NO.	MEDAL YARDS	GEN. YARDS	PAR	S.I.
1	278	268	4	5	10	170	161	3	14
2	279	269	4	10	11	365	359	4	4
3	128	121	3	18	12	344	339	4	6
4	373	373	4	3	13	540	531	5	1
5	310	306	4	8	14	311	307	4	12
6	271	267	4	13	15	339	327	4	7
7	262	255	4	15	16	117	110	3	16
8	437	424	4	2	17	172	160	4	11
9	180	167	3	17	18	309	303	3	9
OUT	2,518	2,450	34		IN	2,667	2,597	34	
					TOTAL	5,185	5,047	69	
STANDARD SCRATCH						66	68		

Bunker positions indicated.

Duddingston Golf Club Ltd,
Duddingston Road West,
Edinburgh. E15 3QD.
Tel: (0131) 6611005

NO.	YARDS	PAR	S.I.	NO.	YARDS	PAR	S.I.
1	491	5	8	10	185	3	12
2	171	3	11	11	438	4	1
3	408	4	6	12	378	4	7
4	450	4	2	13	428	4	3
5	338	4	17	14	148	3	18
6	202	3	15	15	317	4	16
7	381	4	4	16	386	4	5
8	530	5	10	17	503	5	9
9	321	4	13	18	345	4	14
OUT	3,292	36		IN	3,128	35	
				TOTAL	6,420	71	
	STANDARD SCRATCH				72		

LOCATION: 3 miles southeast of Edinburgh off A1.
SECRETARY: John C. Small
Tel: (0131) 6617688.
PROFESSIONAL: Alistair McLean.
Tel: (0131) 6614301.

Undulating parkland course with burn coming into play on many holes.

COURSE INFORMATION

Par 71; SSS 72; Length 6,420 Yards.
Visitors: Weekdays only (phone to book).
Opening Hours: 8am – Dusk.
Avoid: Weekends.
Ladies: Welcome.
Green Fees: Weekdays – £22 per round; £30 per day.
Clubhouse Hours: 9am – 11pm.
Clubhouse Dress: Smart/Casual – no denims or trainers.
Clubhouse Facilities: Bar; Meals 12 – 2.00pm. Parties catered by arrangement.

CONVENIENT HOTEL

Kings Manor.

Bunker & tree positions indicated.

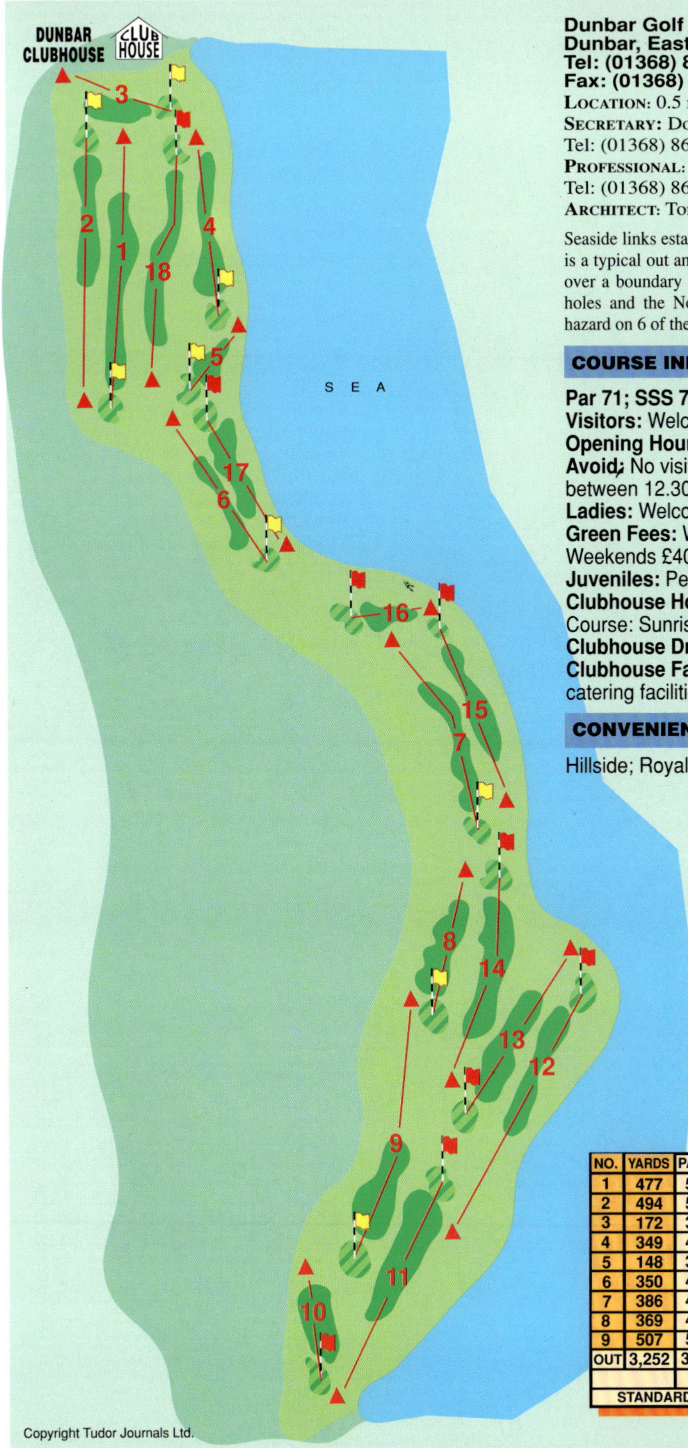

Dunbar Golf Club, East Links,
Dunbar, East Lothian.
Tel: (01368) 862317.
Fax: (01368) 865202.

LOCATION: 0.5 miles east of Dunbar.
SECRETARY: Don Thompson.
Tel: (01368) 862317.
PROFESSIONAL: Derek Small.
Tel: (01368) 862086.
ARCHITECT: Tom Morris.

Seaside links established in 1856. The course is a typical out and back links, out of bounds over a boundary wall, comes into play on 8 holes and the North Sea is a lateral water hazard on 6 of the inward holes.

COURSE INFORMATION

Par 71; SSS 71; Length 6,426 Yards.
Visitors: Welcome; not on Thursdays.
Opening Hours: Sunrise – Sunset.
Avoid: No visitors before 9.30 and between 12.30 and 2pm.
Ladies: Welcome.
Green Fees: Weekdays £28 per day; Weekends £40 per day.
Juveniles: Permitted with an adult.
Clubhouse Hours: Bar: 11am to 10pm; Course: Sunrise – Sunset.
Clubhouse Dress: Jacket after 7.30pm.
Clubhouse Faclilities: Full catering facilities.

CONVENIENT HOTELS

Hillside; Royal Mackintosh; Craigengelt.

NO.	YARDS	PAR	S.I.	NO.	YARDS	PAR	S.I.
1	477	5	8	10	202	3	9
2	494	5	3	11	417	4	6
3	172	3	16	12	459	4	1
4	349	4	13	13	378	4	10
5	148	3	17	14	433	4	4
6	350	4	11	15	343	4	12
7	386	4	5	16	166	3	18
8	369	4	14	17	339	4	15
9	507	5	2	18	437	4	7
OUT	3,252	37		IN	3,174	34	
				TOTAL	6,426	71	
STANDARD SCRATCH					71		

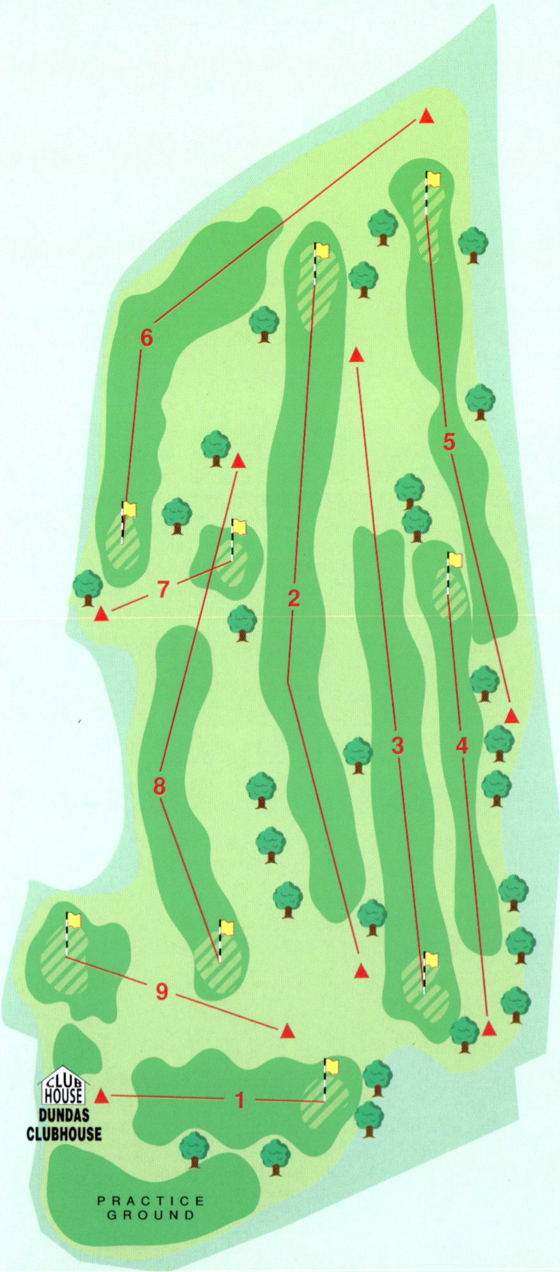

Dundas Park Golf Club,
Hope Cottage
Loch Road,
South Queensferry. EH30 9LS
Tel: (0131) 3311416.

LOCATION: Dundas estate, South of Queensferry on the A8000.
SECRETARY: Keith D. Love.
Tel: (0131) 3311416

Gently undulating parkland course, with superb views and excellent fairways resulting from years of careful attention. There are beautiful and cleverly placed trees.

COURSE INFORMATION

Par 70; SSS 69; Length 6,024 Yards.
Opening Hours: Sunrise – Sunset.
Visitors: On application to secretary.
Avoid: Competition days.
Ladies: On application to secretary.
Green Fees: £8 per day ticket.
Juveniles: Members only.
No Clubhouse.

COURSE INFORMATION

Forth Bridges Moat House; Hawes Inn; South Queensferry.

NO.	YARDS	PAR	S.I.	NO.	YARDS	PAR	S.I.
1	254	4	13	10	254	4	14
2	496	5	3	11	496	5	4
3	418	4	1	12	418	4	2
4	302	4	11	13	302	4	12
5	392	4	5	14	392	4	6
6	402	4	9	15	402	4	10
7	156	3	15	16	156	3	16
8	393	4	7	17	393	4	8
9	199	3	17	18	199	3	18
OUT	3,012	35		IN	3,012	35	
				TOTAL	6,024	70	
				STANDARD SCRATCH	69		

Tree positions indicated.

Gifford Golf Club, Gifford, East Lothian.
Tel: (01620) 810591.

LOCATION: 4.5 miles south of Haddington.
SECRETARY: D. A. Fantom.
Tel: (01620) 810267.
ARCHITECTS: W. Wood (Royal Epsom 1904).

9 hole parkland course undulating and wooded, bisected by a burn.

COURSE INFORMATION

Par 71; SSS 70; Length 6,243 Yards.

Opening Hours: Dawn to dusk.
Visitors: Course closed from 4pm, Tuesday & Wednesday, and Saturday & Sunday noon.
Avoid: Course closed all day 1st Sunday of the month April to October.
Ladies: Welcome.
Green Fees: £10 per day ticket, weekdays; £10 - 9 or 18 holes, weekends.
Juveniles: Welcome.
Green Fees: £3 per day, weekdays. Full price weekends.
Clubhouse Hours: Changing rooms only.
Clubhouse Dress: Neat.
Clubhouse Facilities: No catering or bar available.
Open Competitions: Mixed Open May; Ladies Open August .

CONVENIENT HOTELS

Tweeddale Arms Hotel (01620) 810240; Goblin Ha' Hotel (01620) 810244.

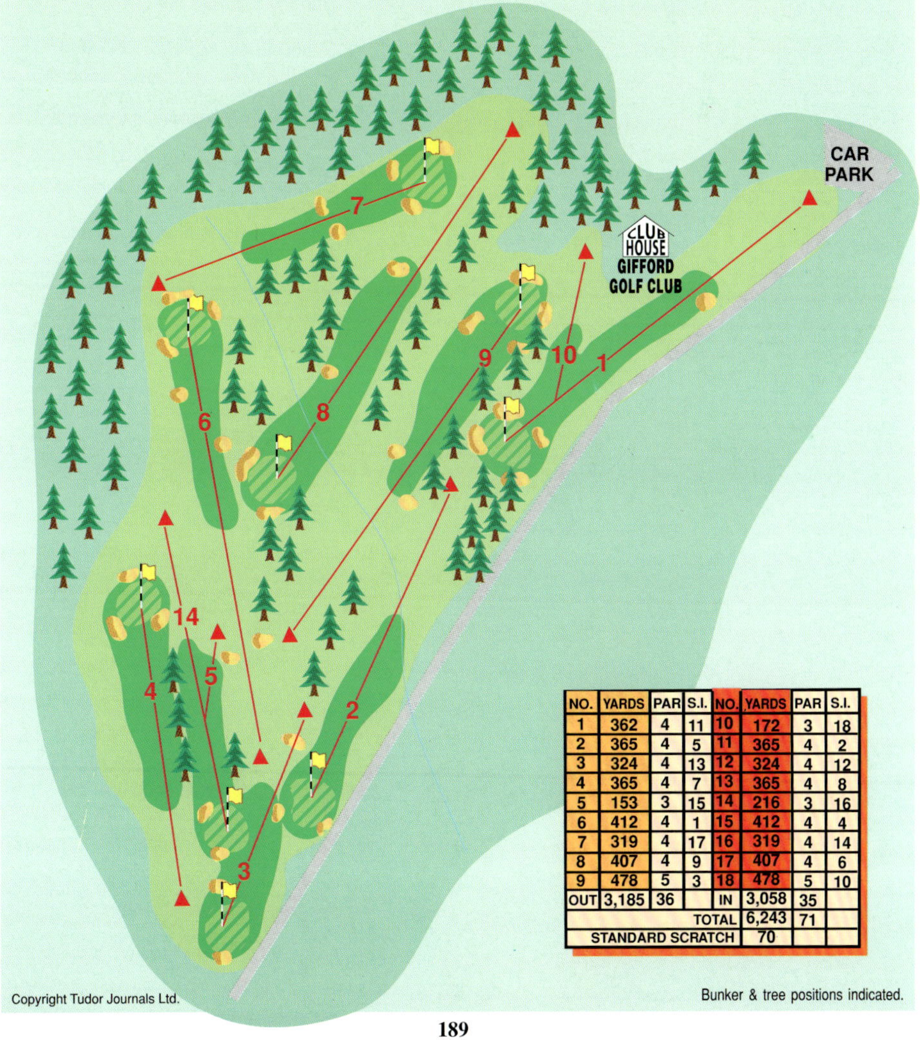

NO.	YARDS	PAR	S.I.	NO.	YARDS	PAR	S.I.
1	362	4	11	10	172	3	18
2	365	4	5	11	365	4	2
3	324	4	13	12	324	4	12
4	365	4	7	13	365	4	8
5	153	3	15	14	216	3	16
6	412	4	1	15	412	4	4
7	319	4	17	16	319	4	14
8	407	4	9	17	407	4	6
9	478	5	3	18	478	5	10
OUT	3,185	36		IN	3,058	35	
				TOTAL	6,243	71	
STANDARD SCRATCH					70		

Bunker & tree positions indicated.

Glen Golf Club, East Links, North Berwick, East Lothian. Tel: (01620) 892726.

LOCATION: Edinburgh 23 miles; 1.5 miles east off the A198.
SECRETARY: D.R. Montgomery. Tel: (01620) 895288.
ARCHITECT: H. MacKenzie Ross.

A fine seaside links with panoramic views out to the Firth of Forth and to the Islands. The course is a fair test under any conditions. The 13th hole surrounded by the shore on two sides will linger in the memory of every golfer.

COURSE INFORMATION

Par 69; SSS 69; Length 5,723 Yards.
Opening hours: Daylight Hours.
Visitors: Welcome.
Avoid: Saturday before 2.30pm; Sunday before 9.30am.
Ladies: Welcome.
Green Fees: Monday – Friday £14 per round; £21 per day. Weekend: £18 per round, £26 per day.
Juveniles: Welcome. 1/2 price Monday – Friday.
Clubhouse hours: 11am – 11pm.
Clubhouse Dress: Informal; No shellsuits.
Clubhouse Facilities: Catering available everyday – bar meals, lunches, high tea.
Open Competitions: Gents' Open; Open Mixed foursomes (RNLI) July; Ladies Open.

CONVENIENT HOTELS

The Brentwood Hotel;
The Nether Abbey Hotel.

NO.	YARDS	PAR	S.I.	NO.	YARDS	PAR	S.I.
1	328	4	10	10	341	4	7
2	358	4	4	11	300	4	15
3	302	4	16	12	409	4	2
4	175	3	17	13	133	3	18
5	362	4	1	14	336	4	5
6	432	5	8	15	399	4	9
7	366	4	14	16	186	3	13
8	350	4	6	17	395	4	3
9	254	3	12	18	297	4	11
OUT	2,927	35		IN	2,796	34	
				TOTAL	5,723	69	
STANDARD SCRATCH					69		

Bunker positions indicated.

GOGARBURN

**Gogarburn Golf Club,
Hanley Lodge,
Roddinglaw Road,
Newbridge, EH28 8NN.
Tel: (0131) 3334718.**

LOCATION: 6 miles west of Edinburgh on south side of main Edinburgh to Glasgow road.
SECRETARY: W.D. Leary.
Tel: (0131) 3334110.

A short course in a beautifully secluded setting amongst fine mature trees. A test of accuracy rather than long hitting. For club competitions and for handicap purposes we play nine holes twice, the 6th, 7th and 8th being omitted.

COURSE INFORMATION

12 Holes
Par 43; Length 3,021 Yards.
Opening Hours: 8am – dusk
Visitors: Welcome at all times before 5pm.
Ladies: Welcome.
Green Fees: £7 per round; £12 day ticket.
Juveniles: Restricted.
Clubhouse Hours: 11am – 10pm.
Clubhouse Dress: Informal.
Clubhouse Facilities: Licenced bar and catering.
Open Competitions: Gogarburn Open; Ladies 3rd Sunday in June; Men, 2nd Sunday in August.

CONVENIENT HOTELS

Norton House, Maybury Hotel, Barnton Hotel.

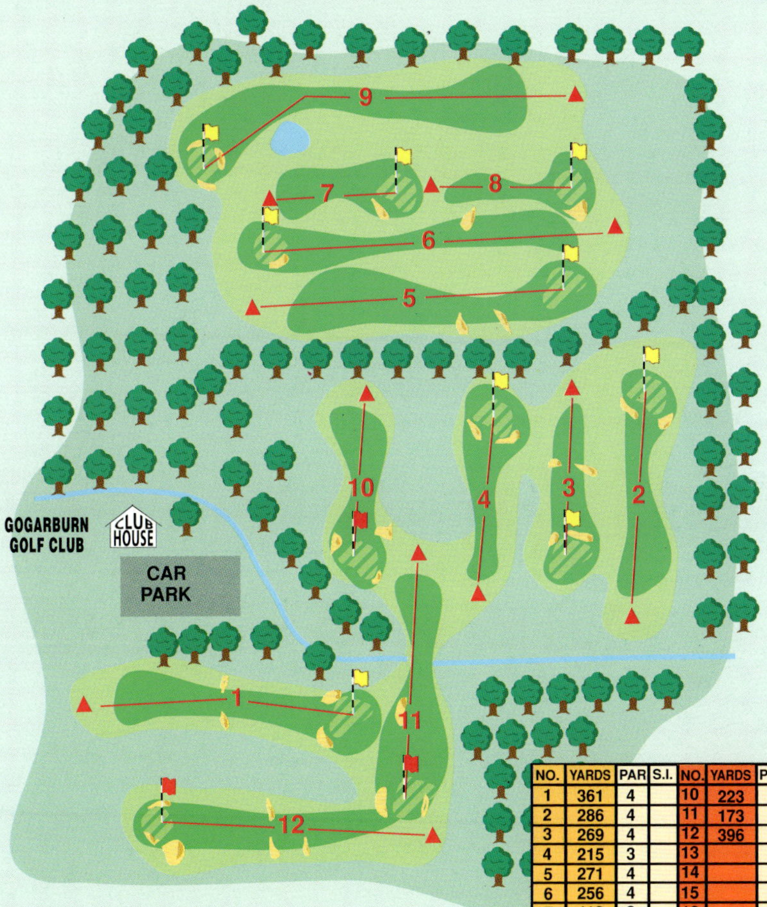

NO.	YARDS	PAR	S.I.	NO.	YARDS	PAR	S.I.
1	361	4		10	223	3	
2	286	4		11	173	3	
3	269	4		12	396	4	
4	215	3		13			
5	271	4		14			
6	256	4		15			
7	112	3		16			
8	118	3		17			
9	341	4		18			
OUT	2,129			IN	2,129		
				TOTAL	4,258	43	
				STANDARD SCRATCH			

Bunker & tree positions indicated.

Gullane Golf Club, Gullane, East Lothian, EH31 2BB. Tel: (01620) 842255.

LOCATION: 18 miles east of Edinburgh on A198 Edinburgh / North Berwick road.
SECRETARY: A.J.B. Taylor.
Tel: (01620) 842255. Fax: (01620) 842327.
PROFESSIONAL: J.M. Hume.
Tel: (01620) 843111.

COURSE INFORMATION

Par 71; SSS 71; Length 6,466 Yards.
Visitors: Welcome (reservations taken by phone).
Ladies: Welcome.
Green Fees: Weekdays – £37 per round & £53 per day, Weekends – £47 per round; Weekly charges – All courses for five days £116, all courses for seven days £167; Courses one & two (Weekdays) – £44 per day & (Weekends) – £56 per day. Courses one & three – £54 per day. Booking fee – £10 per player.
Clubhouse Facilities: Catering arranged with Clubmaster.

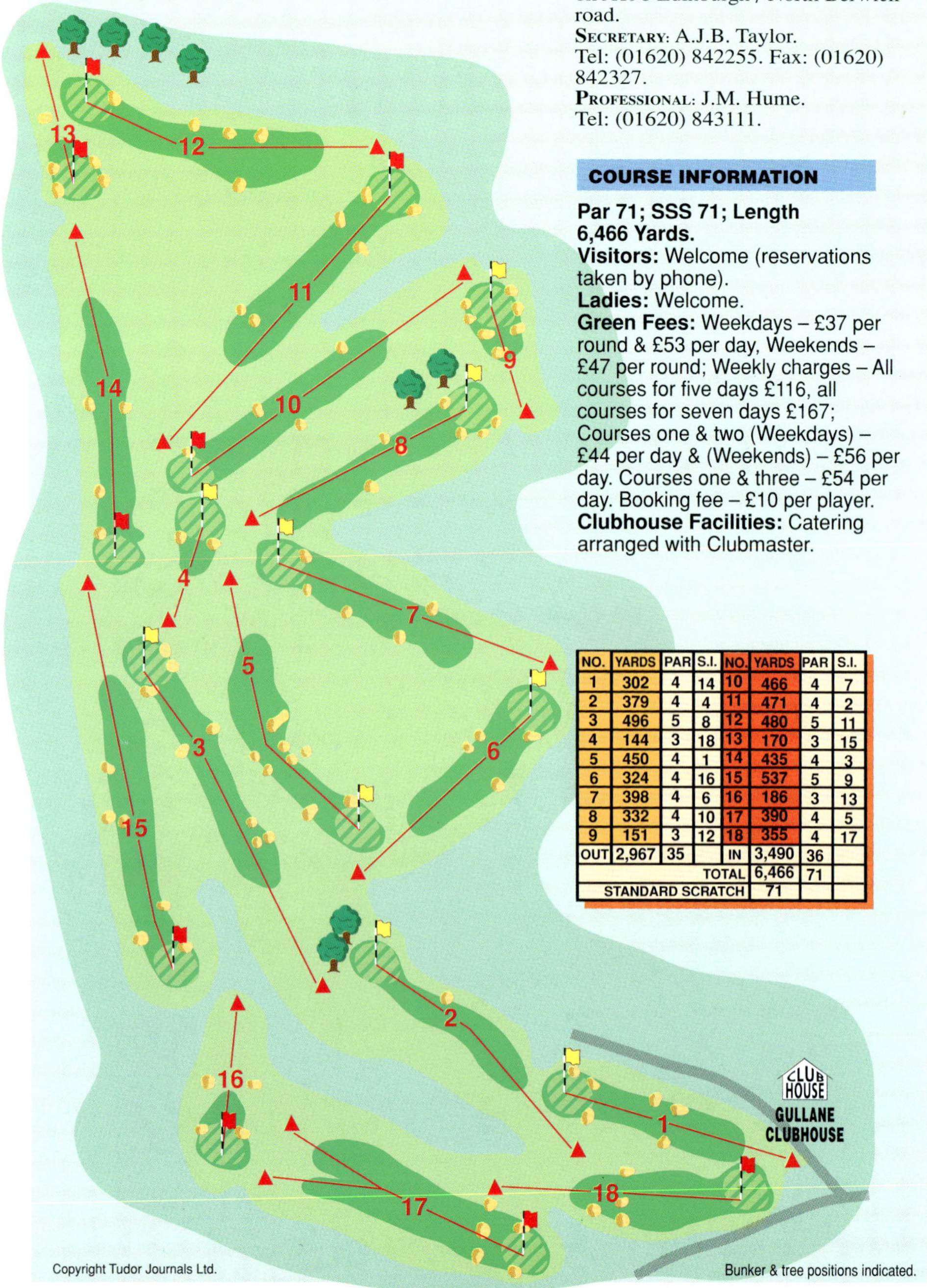

NO.	YARDS	PAR	S.I.	NO.	YARDS	PAR	S.I.
1	302	4	14	10	466	4	7
2	379	4	4	11	471	4	2
3	496	5	8	12	480	5	11
4	144	3	18	13	170	3	15
5	450	4	1	14	435	4	3
6	324	4	16	15	537	5	9
7	398	4	6	16	186	3	13
8	332	4	10	17	390	4	5
9	151	3	12	18	355	4	17
OUT	2,967	35		IN	3,490	36	
				TOTAL	6,466	71	
STANDARD SCRATCH					71		

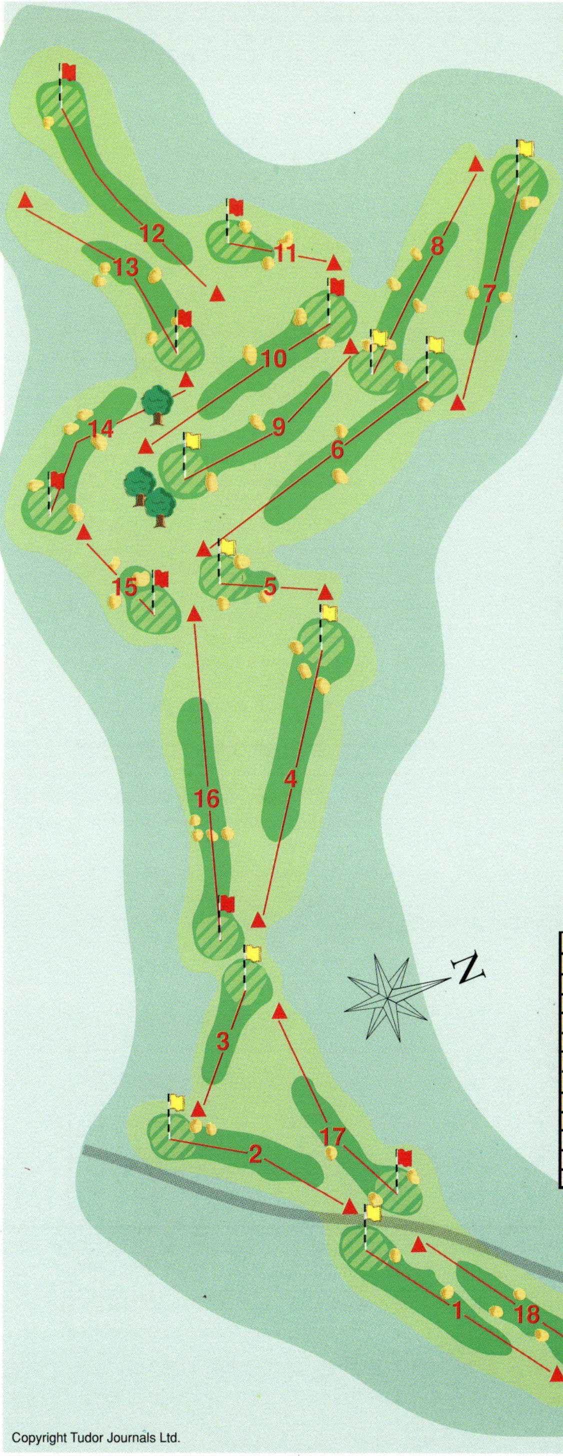

Gullane Golf Club, Gullane, East Lothian, EH31 2BB. Tel: (01620) 842255.

LOCATION: 18 miles East of Edinburgh on A198 Edinburgh / North Berwick road.
SECRETARY: A.J.B. Taylor.
Tel: (01620) 842255.
Fax: (01620) 842327.
PROFESSIONAL: J.M. Hume.
Tel: (01620) 843111.

COURSE INFORMATION

Par 71; SSS 70; Length 6,244 Yards.
Visitors: Welcome (reservations taken by phone). **Ladies:** Welcome.
Green Fees: Weekdays – £17 per round & £25 per day, Weekends – £21 per round & £32 per day; Weekly charges – All courses for five days £116, all courses for seven days £167; Courses One & Two (Weekdays) – £44 per day & (Weekends) – £56 per day. Courses Two & Three – £21 per day (Weekdays) & £27 per day (Weekends). Booking fee – £10 per player.
Clubhouse Dress: Smart / Casual.
Clubhouse Facilities: Catering by arrangement with Clubmaster.

NO.	YARDS	PAR	S.I.	NO.	YARDS	PAR	S.I.
1	366	4	9	10	381	4	6
2	334	4	7	11	215	3	16
3	237	4	13	12	408	4	10
4	425	4	1	13	400	4	2
5	171	3	17	14	336	4	12
6	498	5	5	15	175	3	18
7	358	4	15	16	527	5	4
8	393	4	3	17	361	4	8
9	354	4	11	18	305	4	14
OUT	3,136	36		IN	3,108	35	
				TOTAL	6,244	71	
STANDARD SCRATCH					70		

Bunker & tree positions indicated.

GULLANE (No. 3 Course)

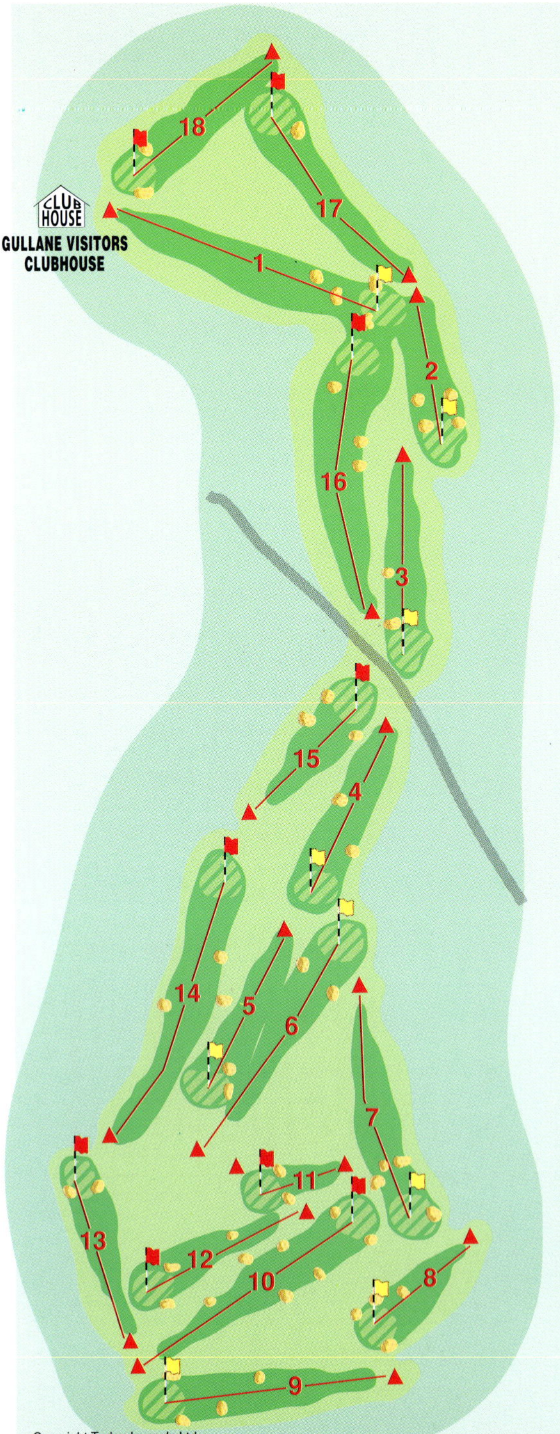

Gullane Golf Club, Gullane, East Lothian. EH31 2BB. Tel: (01620) 842255.

Location: 18 miles east of Edinburgh on the A198 Edinburgh to North Berwick road.
Secretary: A.J.B. Taylor.
Tel: (01620) 842255. Fax: (01620) 842327.
Professional: J.M. Hume.
Tel: (01620) 843111.

COURSE INFORMATION

Par 66; SSS 65; Length 5,166 Yards.
Visitors: Welcome (reservations taken by phone).
Ladies: Welcome.
Green Fees: Weekdays – £10.50 per round & £16 per day; Weekends £12.50 per round & £19 per day; Weekly charges – All courses for five days £116 & £167 for seven days; course Three £38 for five days & £59 for seven days. Courses One & Three, weekdays £41 per day; Courses Two & Three – £21 per day.
Juveniles: Welcome.
Clubhouse Hours: Varies on season.
Clubhouse Dress: Casual (no spikes).
Clubhouse Facilities: Catering by arrangement with Clubmaster.

NO.	YARDS	PAR	S.I.	NO.	YARDS	PAR	S.I.
1	345	4	3	10	450	4	4
2	144	3	17	11	135	3	18
3	293	4	5	12	371	4	8
4	250	4	13	13	186	3	14
5	314	4	7	14	426	4	2
6	342	4	1	15	169	3	12
7	311	4	11	16	379	4	6
8	165	3	15	17	328	4	10
9	327	4	9	18	231	3	16
OUT	2,491	34		IN	2,491	32	
				TOTAL	5,166	66	
STANDARD SCRATCH					65		

Bunker positions indicated.

HADDINGTON

Haddington Golf Club, Amisfield Park, Haddington, East Lothian.
Tel: (0162 082) 3267.

LOCATION: 17 miles east of Edinburgh on the A1, 3/4 mile east of Haddington.
SECRETARY: Tom Speirs. Tel: (0162 082) 3627.
PROFESSIONAL: J. Sandilands. Tel: (0162 082) 2727.

Haddington is a typical inland course partially tree lined, undulating meadowland and, bounded on the north side by the River Tyne.

COURSE INFORMATION

Par 71; SSS 70; Length 6,280 Yards.
Opening Hours: 8am – 7.30pm.
Visitors: Welcome.
Avoid: Saturday/Sunday 8am – 10am; 12pm – 2pm; Wednesday 4.00 5.30pm. 5pm – 6.15pm.
Ladies: Welcome.
Green Fees: Monday – Friday round £11, day £15; weekends; round £15; day£19.
Juveniles: Welcome.
Clubhouse Hours: 10am – 11pm (1st April to 30th September); 1st October to 31st March weekends only.
Clubhouse Dress: Neat – no collarless shirts or jeans.
Clubhouse Facilities: Catering and bar facilities available.

CONVENIENT HOTELS

The George Hotel;
The Maitlandfield House;
Brown's Hotel.

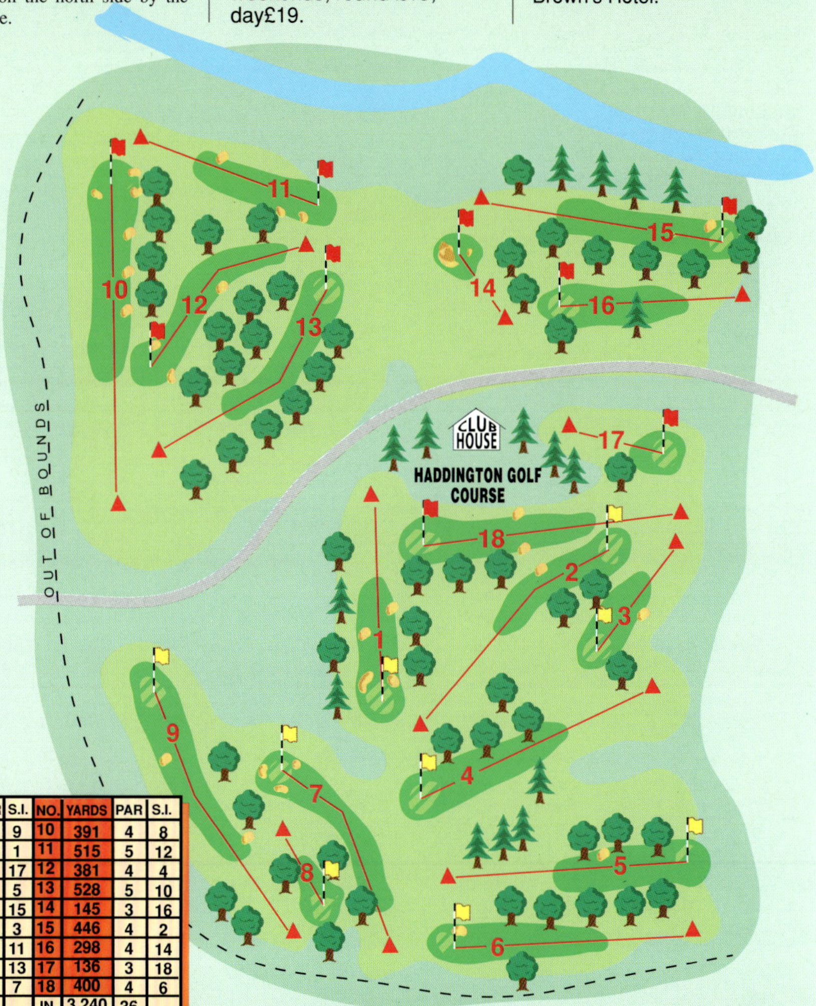

NO.	YARDS	PAR	S.I.	NO.	YARDS	PAR	S.I.
1	352	4	9	10	391	4	8
2	461	4	1	11	515	5	12
3	281	4	17	12	381	4	4
4	364	4	5	13	528	5	10
5	347	4	15	14	145	3	16
6	382	4	3	15	446	4	2
7	351	4	11	16	298	4	14
8	149	3	13	17	136	3	18
9	353	4	7	18	400	4	6
QUT	3,040	35		IN	3,240	36	
				TOTAL	6,280	71	
STANDARD SCRATCH					70		

Bunker & tree positions indicated.

HARBURN

LOTHIAN

Harburn Golf Club, Harburn, West Calder, West Lothian. EH55 8RS. Tel: (01506) 871526.

LOCATION: 2 miles south of West Calder.
SECRETARY: Frank Vinter.
Tel: (01506) 871131.
PROFESSIONAL: T. Stangoe.
Tel: (01506) 871582.

COURSE INFORMATION

Par 69; SSS 69; Length 5,921 Yards.
Opening Hours: 8am – 11.00pm (usual bar hours).
Visitors: Min: 12; Max: 30.
Avoid: Wednesdays and two weekends per month.
Ladies: Welcome.
Green Fees: Weekday round: £15; Day: £20; Weekend: £21; Day: £30.
Juveniles: Permitted.
Clubhouse Hours: 8am – 11pm.
Clubhouse Dress: Informal.
Clubhouse Facilities: Yes.

CONVENIENT HOTEL

Livingston Hilton;
Harburn House.

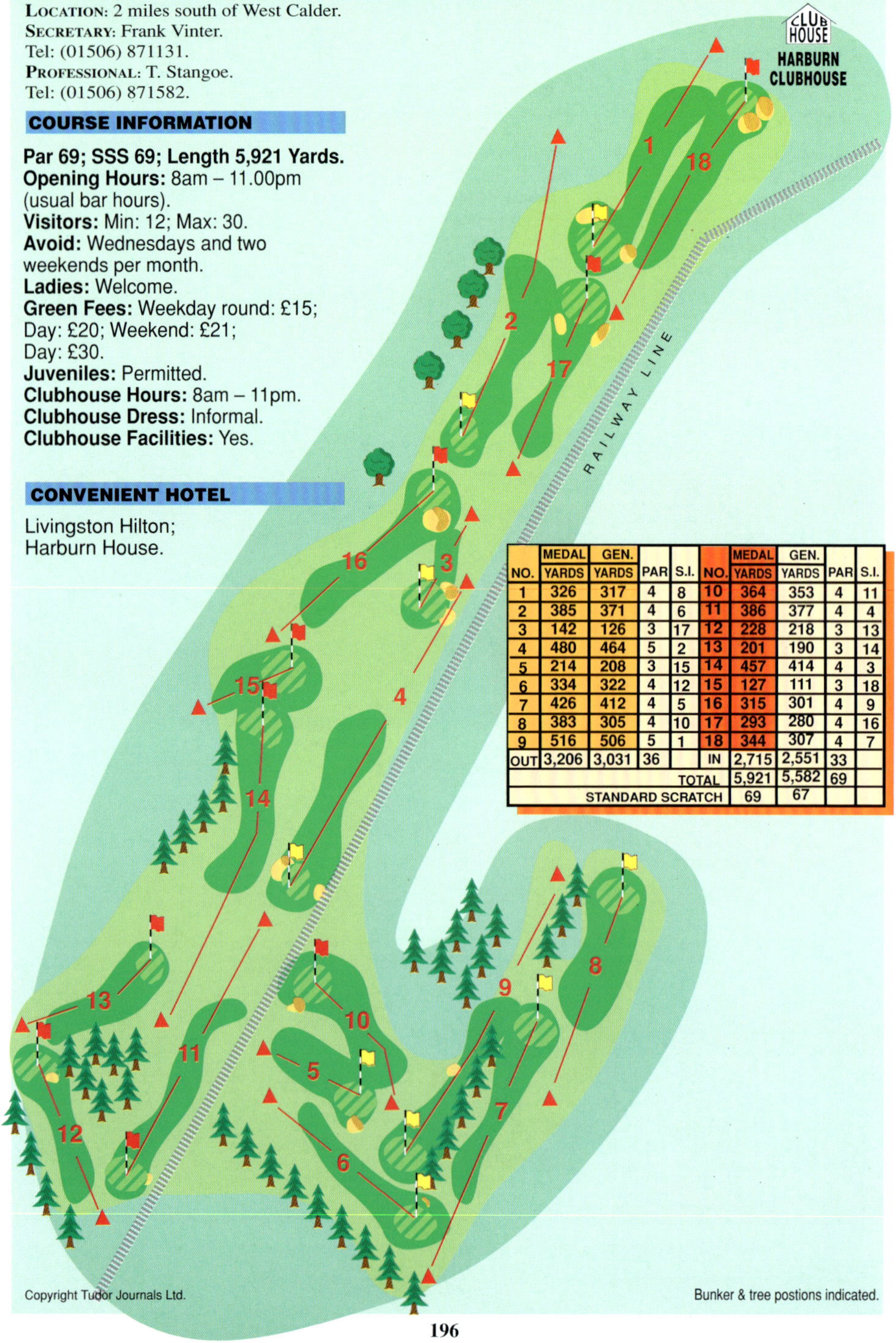

NO.	MEDAL YARDS	GEN. YARDS	PAR	S.I.	NO.	MEDAL YARDS	GEN. YARDS	PAR	S.I.
1	326	317	4	8	10	364	353	4	11
2	385	371	4	6	11	386	377	4	4
3	142	126	3	17	12	228	218	3	13
4	480	464	5	2	13	201	190	3	14
5	214	208	3	15	14	457	414	4	3
6	334	322	4	12	15	127	111	3	18
7	426	412	4	5	16	315	301	4	9
8	383	305	4	10	17	293	280	4	16
9	516	506	5	1	18	344	307	4	7
OUT	3,206	3,031	36		IN	2,715	2,551	33	
					TOTAL	5,921	5,582	69	
					STANDARD SCRATCH	69	67		

Bunker & tree postions indicated.

The Honourable Company of Edinburgh Golfers, Muirfield, Gullane, East Lothian.
Tel: (0620) 842123. Fax: (0620) 842977.

LOCATION: On the Duncur Road, the last road on the left leaving Gullane for North Berwick.
SECRETARY: Group Captain J.A.Prideaux.
Tel: (0620) 842123.

Muirfield is a championship links and has a formidable reputation as befits one of the top Scottish courses. A golfing experience that should not be missed, Muirfield offers the top challenge of golf on one of the world's most famous courses.

COURSE INFORMATION

Par 70; SSS 73; Length 6,062 Yards.
Visitors: Only on Tues, & Thurs with prior approval.
Ladies: Must be accompanied by a male golfer.
Green Fees: £50 per round; £70 per day.
Clubhouse Dress: Jacket, collar and tie.
Clubhouse facilities: Lunch for golfers.

CONVENIENT HOTEL

Greywalls Hotel, Gullane.

NO.	YARDS	PAR	S.I.	NO.	YARDS	PAR	S.I.
1	340	4	13	10	340	4	14
2	318	4	9	11	318	4	10
3	187	3	17	12	187	3	18
4	455	5	3	13	455	5	4
5	376	4	5	14	376	4	6
6	318	4	11	15	318	4	12
7	197	3	15	16	197	3	16
8	368	4	1	17	368	4	2
9	482	5	7	18	182	5	8
OUT	3,031	36		IN	3,031	36	
				TOTAL	6,062	72	
STANDARD SCRATCH					73		

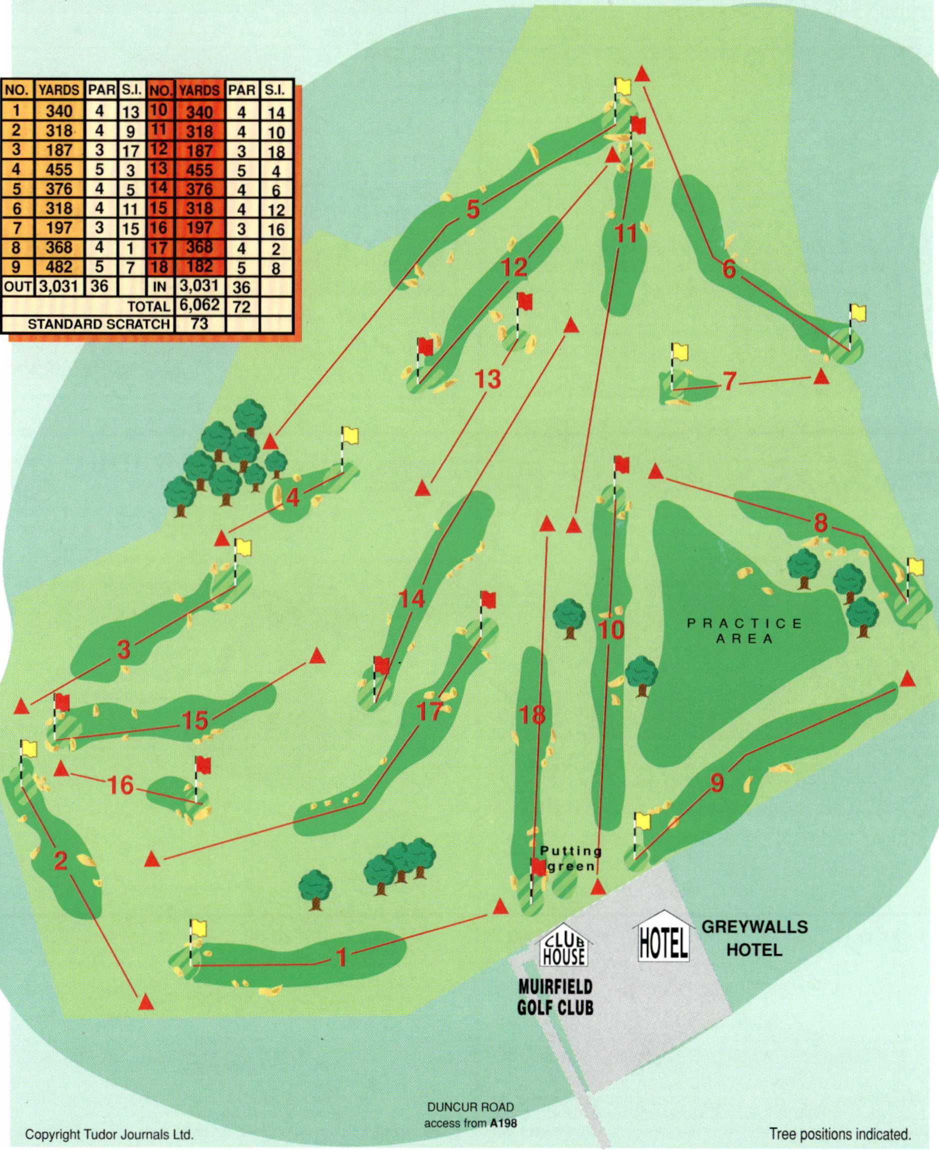

Tree positions indicated.

KINGSKNOWE

Kingsknowe Golf Club,
326 Lanark Road,
Edinburgh
Midlothian.
Tel: (0131) 441 1144

LOCATION: Southwest of Edinburgh on A70.
SECRETARY: R. Wallace.
Tel: (0131) 441 1145.
ARCHITECT: Alex Herd.

A well kept undulating parkland course.

COURSE INFORMATION

Par 69; SSS 69; Length 5,979 Yards.
Opening Hours: 8am – Sunset.
Visitors: Welcome, Telephone in advance.
Avoid: Peak times.
Ladies: Welcome.
Green Fees: Monday – Friday £16 per round; £20 per day; Weekends £25 per round.
Juveniles: Welcome; subject to certain times of the day.
Clubhouse Hours: 8am – 10.30pm.
Clubhouse Dress: Smart/Casual; No jeans, collarless shirts or trainers allowed.
Clubhouse Facilities: Catering within opening hours. Lunches, bar snacks and evening meals available except on Tuesday. Telephone booking or written application required for visiting parties.
Open Competitions: Open Mixed Foursomes – last Saturday in July.

CONVENIENT HOTELS

Post House – Edinburgh, three miles; Orwell Lodge – 1.5 miles.

NO.	YARDS	PAR	S.I.	NO.	YARDS	PAR	S.I.
1	168	3	14	10	392	4	4
2	303	4	13	11	149	3	18
3	488	5	11	12	316	4	10
4	364	4	7	13	422	4	2
5	432	4	1	14	307	4	17
6	326	4	9	15	230	3	12
7	345	4	16	16	460	4	3
8	416	4	4	17	335	4	8
9	223	3	6	18	303	4	15
OUT	3,065	35		IN	2,914	34	
				TOTAL	5,979	69	
				STANDARD SCRATCH	69		

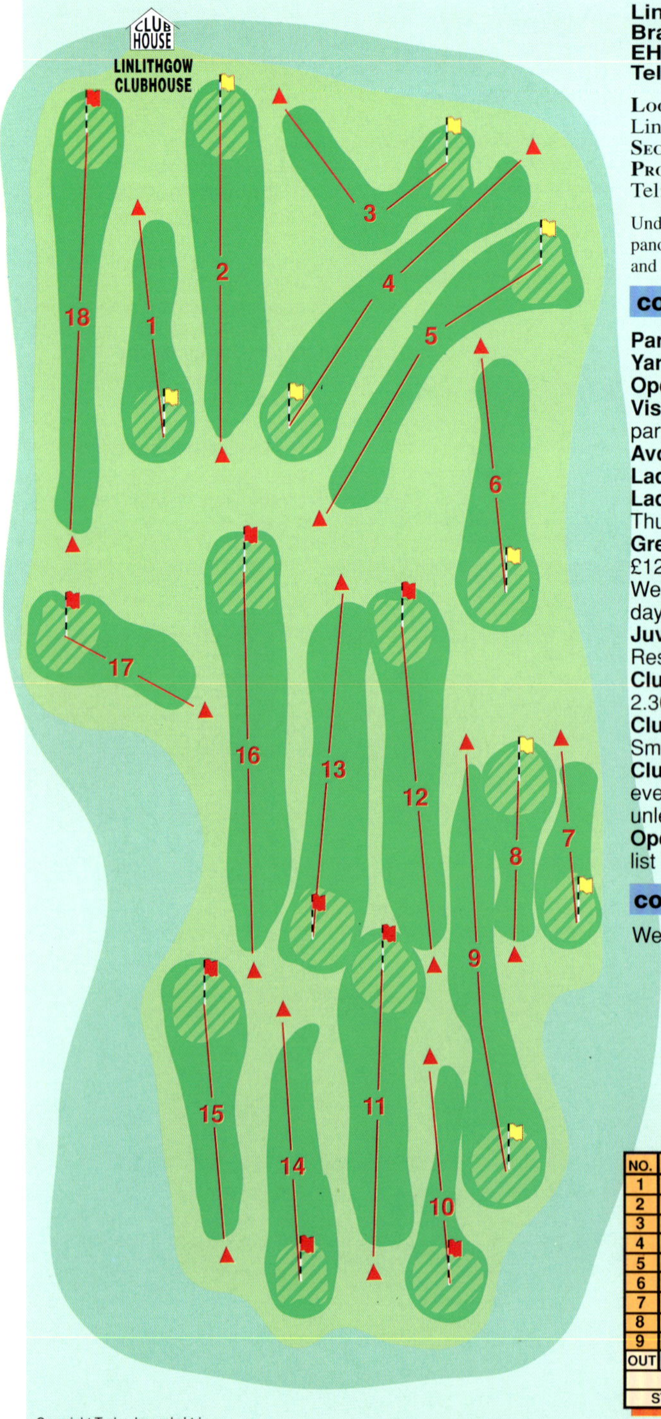

Linlithgow Golf Club, Braehead, Linlithgow EH49 6QF. Tel: (01506) 842585.

LOCATION: South West of Linlithgow.
SECRETARY: Mr T. Thomson.
PROFESSIONAL: D. Smith.
Tel: (01506) 844356.

Undulating parkland course with panoramic views of the Forth Valley, and beyond.

COURSE INFORMATION

Par 70; SSS 68: Length 5,365 Yards.
Opening Hours: 7am – Dusk.
Visitors: Welcome; No visiting parties on Saturdays.
Avoid: Saturdays.
Ladies: Welcome.
Ladies Day: Tuesday and Thursday.
Green Fees: Monday – Friday £12 per round, £18 day ticket. Weekends; £18 per round; £25 day ticket.
Juveniles: Welcome; Restricted.
Clubhouse Hours: 11am – 2.30pm; 5pm – 11pm.
Clubhouse Dress: Smart/Casual wear.
Clubhouse Facilities: Catering every day except Tuesday, unless by prior arrangement.
Open Competitions: Fixture list on request.

CONVENIENT HOTEL

West Port Hotel, Linlithgow.

NO.	YARDS	PAR	S.I.	NO.	YARDS	PAR	S.I.
1	312	4	14	10	220	3	9
2	384	4	6	11	311	4	13
3	279	4	10	12	435	5	7
4	376	4	4	13	475	5	3
5	282	4	12	14	267	4	15
6	250	4	8	15	246	4	11
7	168	3	18	16	406	4	1
8	169	3	16	17	154	3	17
9	417	4	2	18	399	4	5
OUT	2,637	34		IN	2,913	36	
				TOTAL	5,365	70	
				STANDARD SCRATCH	68		

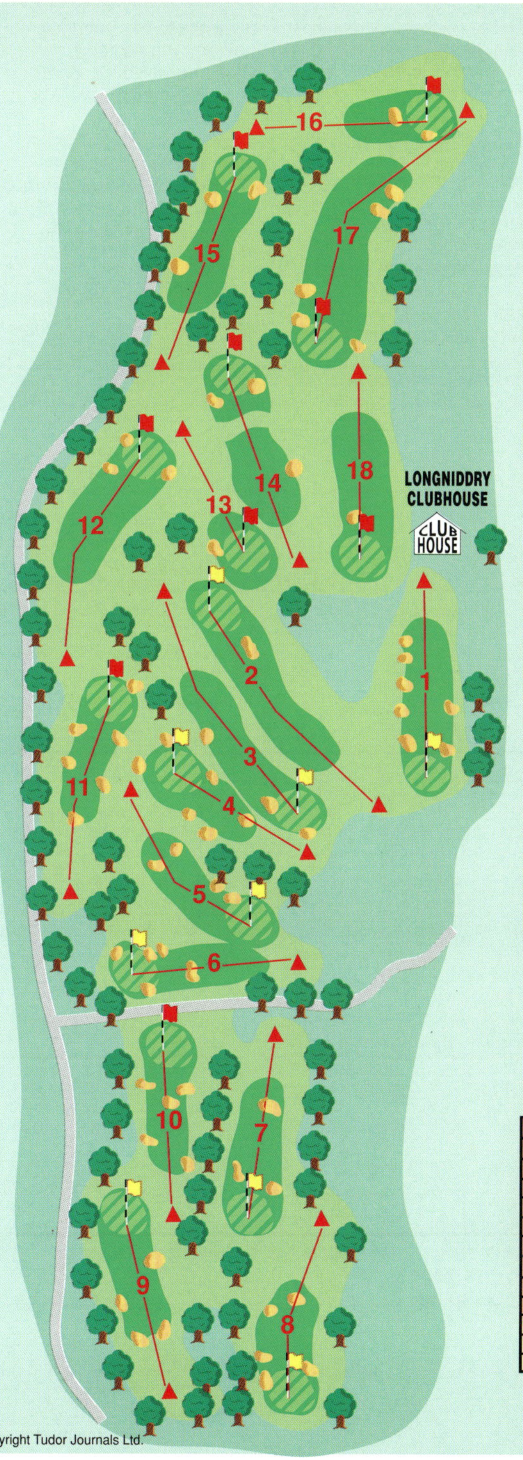

Longniddry Golf Club, Links Road, Longniddry, East Lothian.
Tel: (01875) 852141; Fax: 853371

LOCATION: 13 miles east of Edinburgh, off A1.
SECRETARY: Neil Robertson.
Tel: (01875) 852141.
PROFESSIONAL: W.J. Gray.
Tel: (01875) 852228.
ARCHITECT: Harry Colt.

Partially parkland and links. Undulating, no par 5's, but difficult 4's demanding accuracy. Unusually the SSS is higher than the par.

COURSE INFORMATION

Par 68; SSS 70; Length 6,219 Yards.
Visitors: Welcome, handicap certificate required.
Opening Hours: 9am–4pm visitors except competition days..
Avoid: Competition days; public holidays.
Ladies: Welcome-with handicap certificates.
Green Fees: £25 round; £35 day.
Juveniles: Welcome but restricted.
Clubhouse Hours: Open 8am.
Clubhouse Dress: Jacket & Tie required in the dining room after 5pm and at weekends. Mens' Bar relaxed.
Clubhouse Facilities: Catering 7 days, but restricted on Fridays.

CONVENIENT HOTELS

Green Craigs, Aberdlady; Kilspindie House Hotel, Kilspindie.

NO.	YARDS	PAR	S.I.	NO.	YARDS	PAR	S.I.
1	398	4	7	10	364	4	10
2	416	4	11	11	333	4	14
3	461	4	3	12	381	4	2
4	199	3	17	13	174	3	15
5	314	4	9	14	403	4	8
6	168	3	16	15	425	4	4
7	430	4	1	16	145	3	18
8	367	4	13	17	434	4	6
9	374	4	5	18	433	4	12
OUT	3,127	34		IN	3,092	34	
				TOTAL	6,219	68	
STANDARD SCRATCH					70		

Bunker & tree positions indicated.

LUFFNESS

Luffness New Golf Club,
Aberlady,
East Lothian. EH32 0QA.
Tel: (01620) 843 114.
Fax: (01620) 842 933.

LOCATION: Gullane 1 mile on the (A198), Longriddry 4 Miles.
SECRETARY: Ian Tedford.
Tel: (01620) 843 336.
ARCHITECT: Tom Morris.

Luffness today is famous for it's high quality of greens, still acknowledged by all, including those professionals who play the qualifying rounds at Luffness when the open Championship is held at Muirfield. The course is flat apart from undulations associated with seaside courses. The fairways are well kept, and the bunkers are placed fairly to punish the errant shot. All in all Luffness provides a first class test of golf in an enviroment of considerable scenic beauty.

COURSE INFORMATION

Par 69; SSS 69; Length 6,122 Yards.
Opening Hours: 8am–6pm (Winter); 8am–10pm (Summer).
Visitors: Introduction by member or arrangement through own club necessary.
Avoid: Weekends and public holidays.
Ladies: Welcome with Gentlemen after 10am weekdays only (except Thurs).
Juveniles: 14+ handicap holders with adult..
Clubhouse Hours: 8am – 10pm (Summer) 8am – 6pm (Winter)
Clubhouse Dress: Jacket and tie required.
Clubhouse facilities: Formal dining room Tuesday – Friday; Sandwiches available on Monday only.

CONVENIENT HOTELS

Golf Hotel, Gullane; Marine Hotel, North Berwick.

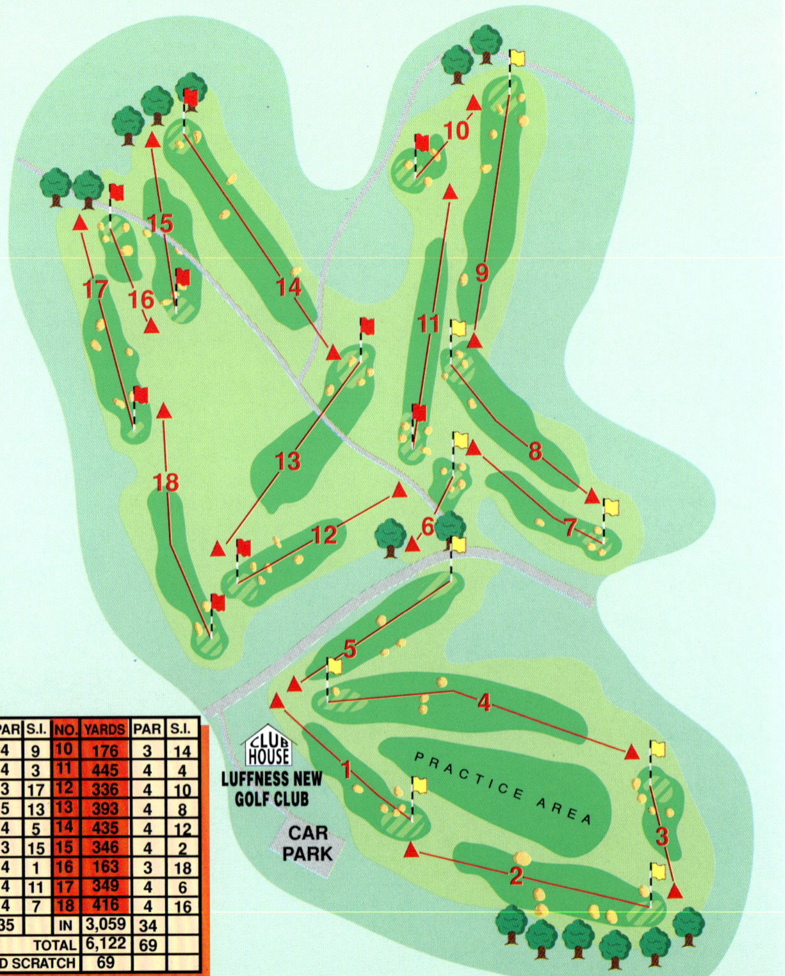

NO.	YARDS	PAR	S.I.	NO.	YARDS	PAR	S.I.
1	332	4	9	10	176	3	14
2	420	4	3	11	445	4	4
3	196	3	17	12	336	4	10
4	531	5	13	13	393	4	8
5	326	4	5	14	435	4	12
6	155	3	15	15	346	4	2
7	293	4	1	16	163	3	18
8	383	4	11	17	349	4	6
9	427	4	7	18	416	4	16
OUT	3,063	35		IN	3,059	34	
				TOTAL	6,122	69	
STANDARD SCRATCH					69		

Bunker & tree positions indicated.

Merchants Of Edinburgh Golf Club, 10 Craighill Gardens, Morningside, Edinburgh. EH10 5PY.
Tel: (0131) 4471219.

LOCATION: SW of Edinburgh.
SECRETARY: A. M. Montgomery.
Tel: (0131) 4471219.
PROFESSIONAL: Neil Colquhoun.
Tel: (0131) 4478709.

Short course, a mixture of hill and parkland. Several hidden holes. Affords fine views of surrounding countryside and the city.

COURSE INFORMATION

Par 65; SSS 64; Length 4,889 Yards.
Opening Hours: 8am onwards.
Visitors: Welcome; Weekdays only, before 4pm.
Avoid: Weekends and after 4pm.
Ladies: Welcome.
Green Fees: £15 Day, £15 Round.
Juveniles: Only with members.
Clubhouse Hours: 11am – 2pm; 4pm – 10.30pm (bar hours).
Clubhouse Dress: Smart/Casual.
Clubhouse Facilities: By arrangement with Clubmaster.

CONVENIENT HOTEL

Braid Hills Hotel.

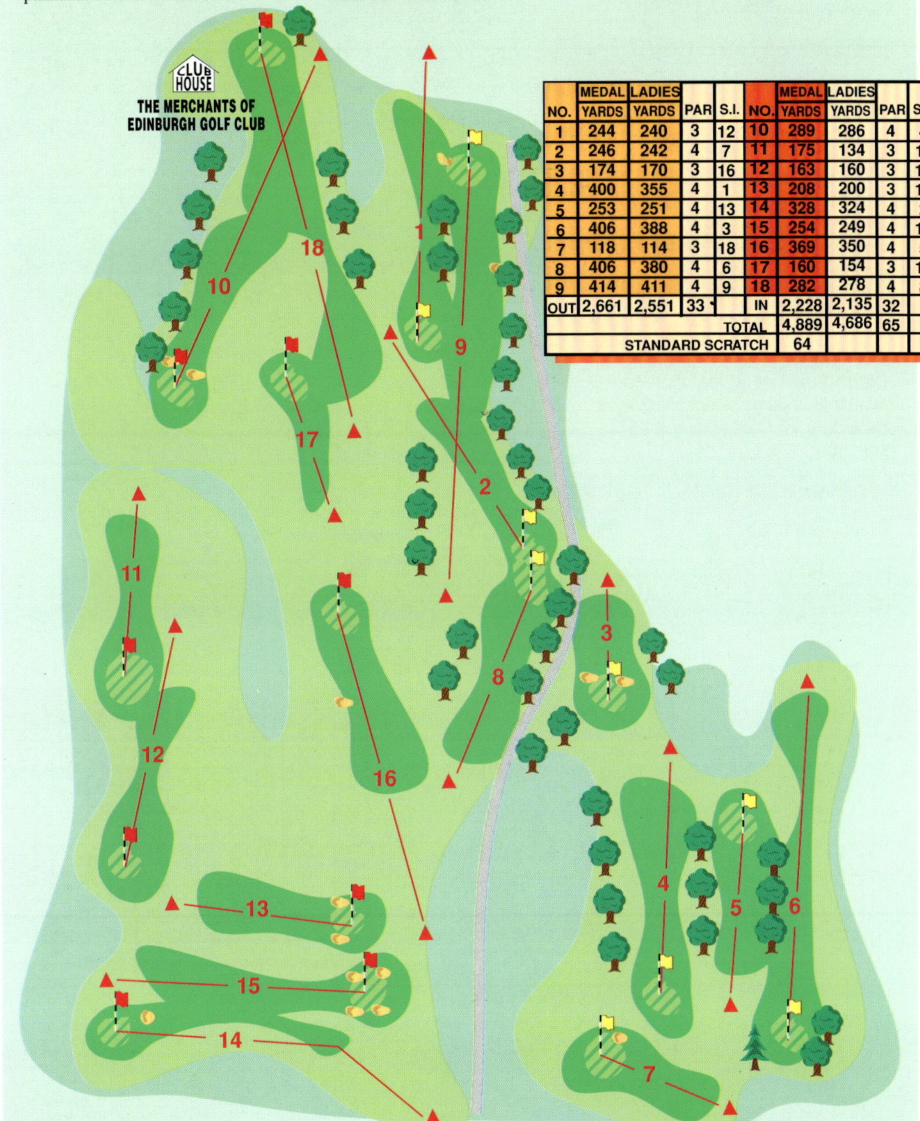

NO.	MEDAL YARDS	LADIES YARDS	PAR	S.I.	NO.	MEDAL YARDS	LADIES YARDS	PAR	S.I.
1	244	240	3	12	10	289	286	4	4
2	246	242	4	7	11	175	134	3	11
3	174	170	3	16	12	163	160	3	17
4	400	355	4	1	13	208	200	3	14
5	253	251	4	13	14	328	324	4	2
6	406	388	4	3	15	254	249	4	15
7	118	114	3	18	16	369	350	4	5
8	406	380	4	6	17	160	154	3	10
9	414	411	4	9	18	282	278	4	8
OUT	2,661	2,551	33		IN	2,228	2,135	32	
					TOTAL	4,889	4,686	65	
					STANDARD SCRATCH	64			

Bunker & tree positions indicated.

Mortonhall Golf Club, 231 Braid Road, Edinburgh, Mid Lothian. Tel: (0131) 447 2411.

LOCATION: 3 Miles south of Edinburgh off the A702.
SECRETARY: Mrs C. D. Morrison.
Tel: (0131) 447 6974.
PROFESSIONAL: D.B. Horn.
Tel: (0131) 447 5185.
ARCHITECT: F.W. Hawtree.

Mortonhall is a scenic moorland course with fine views of Edinburgh City.

COURSE INFORMATION

Par 72; SSS 71; Length 6,557 Yards.
Visitors: Introduction by member or handicap certificate required.
Opening Hours: 8am – dusk.
Avoid: Weekends.
Ladies: Welcome.
Green Fees: Monday – Friday: £25/round; £28 two rounds Saturday & Sunday: £33/ round; £38/day.
Juveniles: Welcome but restricted.
Clubhouse Hours: 8am – 11.30pm.
Clubhouse Dress: Neat – Jacket & tie required.
Clubhouse Faclilities: Catering available; lunch (except Monday & Saturday); Snacks available at any time.

CONVENIENT HOTEL

Braid Hills Hotel.

NO.	MEDAL YARDS	GEN. YARDS	PAR	S.I.	NO.	MEDAL YARDS	GEN. YARDS	PAR	S.I.
1	362	333	4	7	10	150	132	3	16
2	465	436	4	1	11	394	375	4	6
3	175	175	3	13	12	505	487	5	8
4	543	530	5	3	13	429	417	4	2
5	390	375	4	11	14	391	376	4	14
6	335	321	4	17	15	517	504	5	4
7	165	148	3	15	16	339	328	4	12
8	516	501	5	5	17	150	150	3	18
9	341	330	4	9	18	390	377	4	10
OUT	3,292	3,149	36		IN	3,265	3,146	36	
					TOTAL	6,557	6,295	72	
					STANDARD SCRATCH	71	70		

Bunker & tree positions indicated.

Murrayfield Golf Club,
43 Murrayfield Road,
Edinburgh. EH12 6EU.
Tel: (0131) 337 3478.

Location: Two miles west of Edinburgh.
Secretary: Mrs M.K. Hermiston.
Tel: (0131) 337 3478.
Professional: J. Fisher.
Tel: (0131) 337 3479.

Murrayfield is a tree lined parkland course situated on the east side of Corstorphine Hill.

COURSE INFORMATION

Par 70; SSS 69; Length 5,727 Yards.
Visitors: Welcome with a member or by prior arrangement.
Opening Hours: 8am – Sunset.
Avoid: Weekends. Visitors with members only.
Ladies: Welcome.
Ladies Day: Thursday.
Green Fees: £22 per round, £28 per day.
Juveniles: Welcome only if with a juvenile member.

Clubhouse Hours: 8.00am – 7.30pm (Winter); 8am – 10.30pm (Summer).
Clubhouse Dress: Neat dress essential – jacket & tie.
Clubhouse Facilities: Catering available – lunch each day except Monday. High tea & dinner by prior arrangement – snacks available in casual bar each day.

CONVENIENT HOTELS

Ellersly House Hotel; Murrayfield Hotel.

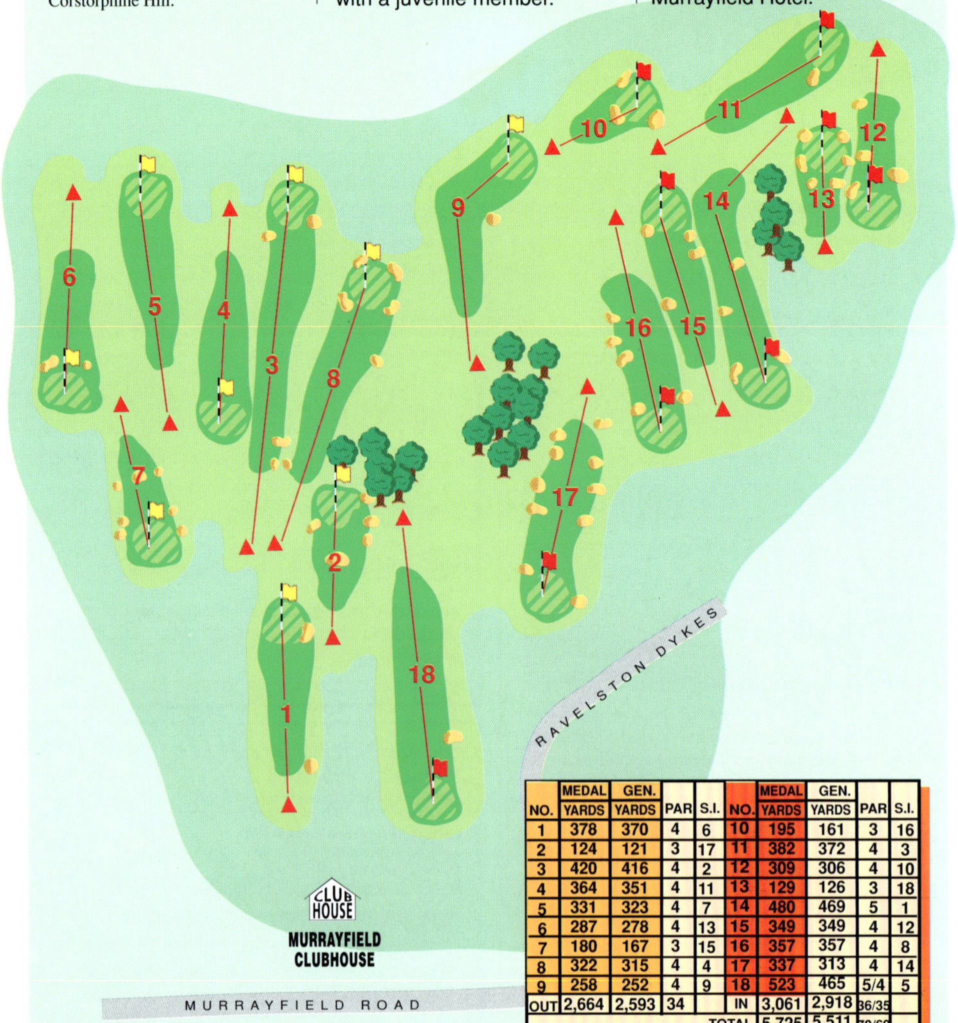

NO.	MEDAL YARDS	GEN. YARDS	PAR	S.I.	NO.	MEDAL YARDS	GEN. YARDS	PAR	S.I.
1	378	370	4	6	10	195	161	3	16
2	124	121	3	17	11	382	372	4	3
3	420	416	4	2	12	309	306	4	10
4	364	351	4	11	13	129	126	3	18
5	331	323	4	7	14	480	469	5	1
6	287	278	4	13	15	349	349	4	12
7	180	167	3	15	16	357	357	4	8
8	322	315	4	4	17	337	313	4	14
9	258	252	4	9	18	523	465	5/4	5
OUT	2,664	2,593	34		IN	3,061	2,918	36/35	
					TOTAL	5,725	5,511	70/69	
					STANDARD SCRATCH	68	67		

Bunker & tree positions indicated.

**Musselburgh Golf Club,
Monktonhall,
Musselburgh. EH21 6SA.
Tel: (0131) 665 2005.**

LOCATION: At the A1 end of the Edinburgh City by-pass (A720) on the B6415 to Musselburgh.
SECRETARY: S. Sullivan.
Tel: (0131) 665 2005.
PROFESSIONAL: Frazer Mann.
Tel: (0131) 665 7055.
ARCHITECT: James Braid.

Undulating parkland with trees and rivers.

COURSE INFORMATION

Par 71; SSS 73; Length 6,614 Yards.

Visitors: Welcome.
Opening Hours: Dawn – Dusk.
Avoid: Before 9.30am Weekdays & 10am Weekends; Competition days.
Ladies: Welcome.
Green Fees: Weekdays – £17 per round, £25 per day; Weekends – £21 per day, £30 per day.
Juveniles: No restrictions.
Clubhouse Hours: Summer ,8am – 1130pm; Winter closes at 5.30pm on Monday, Tuesday & Thursday.
Clubhouse Dress: Smart/Casual – no denims, shorts or tee shirts.

Clubhouse Facilities: Closed on Tuesdays.
Open Competitions: Ladies Open – July; Open Mixed Foursomes – May; Handicap Open – August; Scratch Open – August; Boys' Open – July.

CONVENIENT HOTELS

Granada Lodge Hotel, Musselburgh.
Ravelston House Hotel, Musselburgh.
Kings Manor Hotel, Edinburgh .
Woodside Hotel, Musselburgh.

NO.	MEDAL YARDS	GEN. YARDS	PAR	S.I.	NO.	MEDAL YARDS	GEN. YARDS	PAR	S.I.
1	375	361	4	11	10	442	389	4	4
2	425	387	4	9	11	185	176	3	16
3	144	129	3	17	12	486	441	5/4	2
4	529	488	5	1	13	377	360	4	12
5	388	371	4	13	14	414	375	4	7
6	136	142	3	15	15	401	376	4	14
7	478	442	5/4	3	16	150	150	3	18
8	396	384	4	8	17	408	408	4	5
9	409	393	4	6	18	471	396	4	10
OUT	3,280	3,097	36/35		IN	3,334	3,071	35/34	
					TOTAL	6,614	6,168	71/69	
					STANDARD SCRATCH	73	70		

Bunker & tree positions indicated.

NIDDRY CASTLE

Niddry Castle Golf Club,
Winchburgh,
West Lothian.
Tel: (01506) 891097.

LOCATION: Winchburgh, between Kirkliston and Linlithgow on the B9080.
SECRETARY: M. Walker.

Undulating with trees, very tight 9 holes. A test of accuracy rather than length, requiring a well thought out approach to score well.

COURSE INFORMATION

Par 70; SSS 67; Length 5,514 Yards.
Opening Hours: Sunrise to Sunset.
Visitors: Phone Clubhouse for booking.
Avoid: Saturday until after 3pm.
Ladies: Welcome.
Green Fees: £7.50 Weekday; £10 Weekends.
Juveniles: Welcome.
Clubhouse Hours: 8am–dusk, Summer 9am–2pm, Winter.
Clubhouse Dress: Smart/Casual.
Clubhouse Facilities: Very limited catering facilities.

CONVENIENT HOTELS

Tally Ho, Winchburgh,
Newliston Arms, Kirkliston.

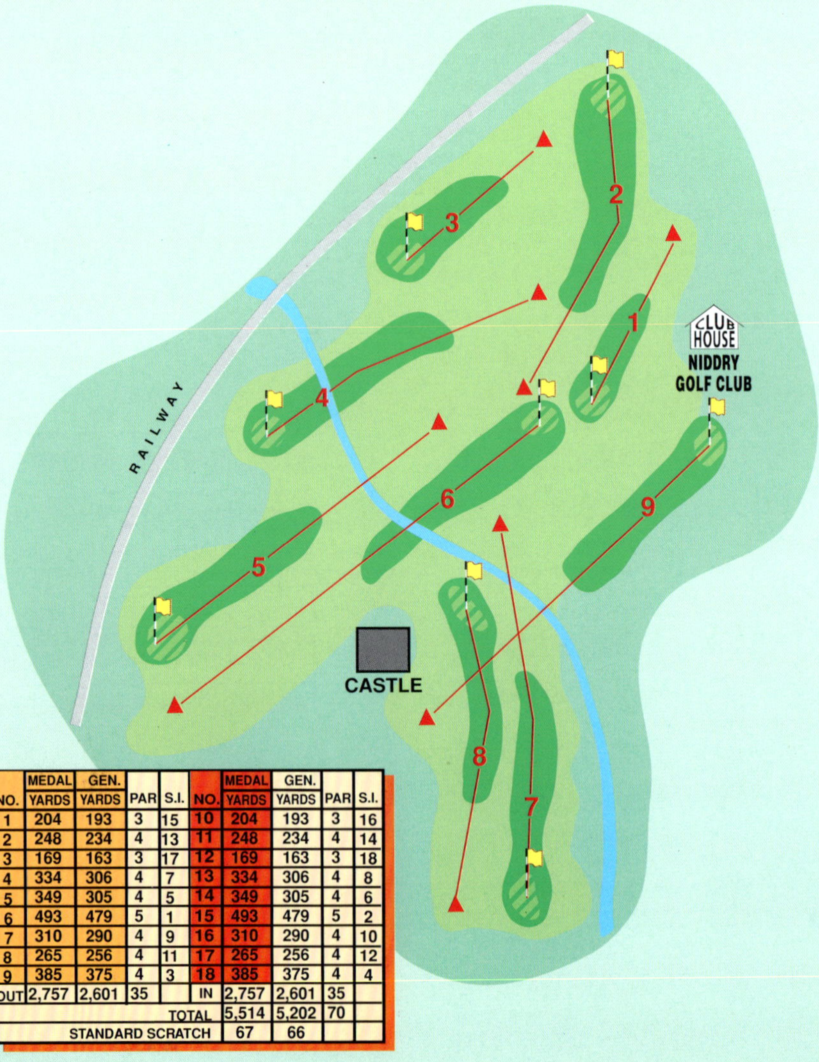

NO.	MEDAL YARDS	GEN. YARDS	PAR	S.I.	NO.	MEDAL YARDS	GEN. YARDS	PAR	S.I.
1	204	193	3	15	10	204	193	3	16
2	248	234	4	13	11	248	234	4	14
3	169	163	3	17	12	169	163	3	18
4	334	306	4	7	13	334	306	4	8
5	349	305	4	5	14	349	305	4	6
6	493	479	5	1	15	493	479	5	2
7	310	290	4	9	16	310	290	4	10
8	265	256	4	11	17	265	256	4	12
9	385	375	4	3	18	385	375	4	4
OUT	2,757	2,601	35		IN	2,757	2,601	35	
					TOTAL	5,514	5,202	70	
					STANDARD SCRATCH	67	66		

**North Berwick Golf Club,
West Links, Beach Road, North Berwick, East Lothian.
Tel: (01620) 895040**

LOCATION: 24 miles east of Edinburgh.
SECRETARY: W. Gray.
PROFESSIONAL: David Huish.
Tel: (01620) 3233.

Seaside links course.

COURSE INFORMATION

Par 71; SSS 71; Length 6,420 Yards.
Visitors: Welcome.
Avoid: Members Competition days.
Ladies: Welcome; Ladies day first Wednesday of each month.
Green Fees: Weekdays; March - October Round £25; Day £35. Saturday/Sunday Round £35; Day £45.
Juveniles: Welcome.
Clubhouse Hours: 7.30am to 10.30pm (summer) Bar 11am - 11pm.
Clubhouse Dress: Smart/Casual
Clubhouse Facilities: Catering available all week.
Open Competitions: North Berwick Handicap Mixed Foursomes September.

CONVENIENT HOTELS

Blenheim Hotel; Point Gary Hotel; Fairways Hotel - Beach Road.

NO.	YARDS	PAR	S.I.	NO.	YARDS	PAR	S.I.
1	328	4	9	10	176	3	18
2	431	4	11	11	550	5	2
3	464	4	1	12	389	4	8
4	175	3	15	13	365	4	12
5	373	4	5	14	376	4	6
6	162	3	17	15	192	3	14
7	354	4	3	16	381	4	4
8	495	5	13	17	425	4	10
9	510	5	7	18	274	4	16
OUT	3,292	36		IN	3,128	35	
				TOTAL	6,420	71	
STANDARD SCRATCH					71		

PORTOBELLO

Portobello Golf Club,
Stanely Street,
Edinburgh, Mid Lothian.
Tel: (0131) 669 4361.

LOCATION: 4 miles east of Edinburgh.
SECRETARY: Alastair Cook. Tel: (0131) 669 5271.

A flat links type municipal course with narrow greens and many sand bunkers. A large number of young staked trees and patches of light rough seperate the fairways.

COURSE INFORMATION

Par 64; SSS 64; Length 4,800 Yards.
Opening Hours: Dawn – Dusk, (7am – 10pm in summer).
Visitors: Welcome.
Avoid: Competition days.
Ladies: Welcome.
Green Fees: £3 (9 Holes).
Juveniles: Welcome.

CONVENIENT HOTEL

King's Manor, Milton Road, Edinburgh (approx 1.5 miles).

NO.	YARDS	PAR	S.I.	NO.	YARDS	PAR	S.I.
1	405	4	1	10	405	4	2
2	95	3	17	11	95	3	18
3	330	4	3	12	330	4	4
4	183	3	13	13	183	3	14
5	290	4	9	14	290	4	10
6	325	4	7	15	325	4	8
7	170	3	15	16	170	3	16
8	365	4	5	17	365	4	6
9	217	3	11	18	217	3	12
OUT	2,400	32		IN	2,400	32	
				TOTAL	4,800	64	
STANDARD SCRATCH					64		

Bunker & tree positions indicated.

PRESTONFIELD

LOTHIAN

Prestonfield Golf Club,
6 Priestfield Road North,
Edinburgh.
Tel: (0131) 667 1273.

LOCATION: 2 miles south east of Edinburgh, off the A68 Dalkeith Rd.
SECRETARY: Mr Elder.
Tel: (0131) 667 9665 or (0131) 667 1273.
PROFESSIONAL: Brian M. Commins.
Tel: (0131) 667 8597.
ARCHITECT: James Braid.

Parkland situated near the heart of Edinburgh and next to the Royal Park of Holyrood. A good test of golf with some fine par 4's. A friendly reception always awaits our visitors.

COURSE INFORMATION

Par 70; SSS 70; Length 5,731 Metres.
Opening Hours: 8am Clubhouse; Bar 11am.
Visitors: Welcome – Not between 12 noon–1.30pm Saturday and not before 11.30am Sunday.
Avoid: Between 12–1.30pm Saturday; Before 11.30am Sunday
Ladies: Welcome.
Green Fees: £17 per round; £25 per day (Weekdays); £25 per round; £30 per day (Weekends).
Juveniles: Some restrictions.
Clubhouse Hours: 8am–10.30pm.
Clubhouse Dress: Smart/Casual.
Clubhouse Facilities: Full catering available.

NO.	METRES	PAR	S.I.	NO.	METRES	PAR	S.I.
1	270	4	11	10	322	4	12
2	141	3	15	11	406	4	2
3	525	5	1	12	399	4	6
4	415	4	3	13	141	3	18
5	166	3	13	14	327	4	10
6	349	4	7	15	342	4	8
7	471	5	9	16	240	4	16
8	400	4	5	17	402	4	4
9	134	3	17	18	281	4	14
OUT	2,871	35		IN	2,860	35	
				TOTAL	5,731	70	
STANDARD SCRATCH					70		

Bunker & tree positions indicated.

RAVELSTON

Ravelston Golf Club, 24 Ravelston Dykes Road, Edinburgh.
Tel: (0131) 315 2486.

LOCATION: Off Queensferry Road (A90), Forth Road Bridge Road.
SECRETARY: F. Philip.
Tel: (0131) 315 2486.
ARCHITECT: James Braid.

Situated on the north-east slope of the Corstorphine Hill, the club enjoys a panoramic view of the kingdom of Fife, the Firth of Forth, North Berwick Law, Arthur's Seat and a comprehensive vista of Edinburgh. Founded in 1912, the development of the course was interrupted by two World Wars. Over the 80 odd years of the club's existence, the general sequence of holes has been varied only once, with the development of the 7th hole, appropriately named after the designer and builder Arbuckle, being the only real change.

COURSE INFORMATION

Par 65; SSS 65; Length 5,200 Yards.
Opening Hours: 9am – Sunset.
Visitors: Welcome.
Avoid: No visitors permitted at weekends.
Green Fees: £15.
Juveniles: Welcome.
Clubhouse Hours: 9am–Sunset.
Clubhouse Dress: Casual.
Clubhouse Facilities: Light snacks, tea, coffee and soft drinks available. There is no bar on the premises.

CONVENIENT HOTELS

Ellersley House, Holiday Inn, Garden Court.

NO.	MEDAL YARDS	GEN. YARDS	PAR	S.I.	NO.	MEDAL YARDS	GEN. YARDS	PAR	S.I.
1	341	337	4	3	10	341	337	4	4
2	237	234	3	9	11	237	234	3	10
3	310	305	4	14	12	310	305	4	13
4	346	336	4	11	13	346	336	4	12
5	125	120	3	18	14	125	120	3	17
6	398	395	4	1	15	398	395	4	2
7	329	319	4	8	16	329	319	4	7
8	394	390	4	6	17	394	390	4	5
9	120	115	3	15	18	120	115	3	16
OUT	2,600	2,551	33		IN	2,600	2,551	33	
					TOTAL	5,200	5,012	66	
					STANDARD SCRATCH	65	65		

Bunker & tree positions indicated.

ROYAL MUSSELBURGH

Bunker & tree positions indicated.

Royal Musselburgh Golf Club, Prestongrange House, PrestonPans. EH32 9RP.

Location: 8 miles southeast of Edinburgh on the A198, North Berwick Road.
Secretary: T. H. Hardie. Tel: (01875) 810276.
Professional: John Henderson. Tel: (01875) 810139.
Architect: Jimmy Braid.

Very interesting parkland course fairly undulating (no steep hills) tree surrounds contained in own estate very interesting. Fairly well sheltered views of Edinburgh and Firth of Forth.

COURSE INFORMATION

Par 70; SSS 70; Length 6,237 Yards.
Visitors: Applications to Secretary.
Opening hours: 8.00am to Dusk.
Avoid: Friday afternoons.
Ladies Open Day: First Thursday in May.
Fees: Weekday £18 per round £30 per day Weekend £30 per round.
Juveniles: Consult with professional.
Clubhouse Hours: 11.00am to 11.00pm.
Clubhouse Dress: No trainers, jeans, tee-shirts, shell suits, track suits.
Clubhouse facilities: 9.30 onwards every day.
Open Competitions: Willie Park Open Amateur first Saturday in August.

CONVENIENT HOTELS

Golf Inn Gullane, Marine North Berwick.

NO.	YARDS	PAR	S.I.	NO.	YARDS	PAR	S.I.
1	349	4		10	356	4	
2	295	4		11	370	4	
3	368	4		12	362	4	
4	365	4		13	452	4	
5	329	4		14	149	3	
6	176	3		15	440	4	
7	391	4		16	176	3	
8	420	4		17	352	4	
9	477	5		18	410	4	
OUT	3,170	36		IN	3,067	34	
				TOTAL	6,237	70	
				STANDARD SCRATCH	70		

NO.	MEDAL YARDS	GEN. YARDS	PAR	S.I.	NO.	MEDAL YARDS	GEN. YARDS	PAR	S.I.
1	122	114	3	15	10	165	164	3	6
2	293	266	4	5	11	250	222	4	18
3	314	300	4	3	12	116	111	3	16
4	190	178	3	1	13	312	242	4	8
5	112	103	3	11	14	173	171	3	4
6	436	415	5	7	15	454	407	5	12
7	300	296	4	13	16	153	142	3	10
8	274	262	4	9	17	282	276	4	14
9	257	224	4	17	18	449	385	4	2
OUT	2,298	2,158	34		IN	2,354	2,120	33	
					TOTAL	4,652	4,278	67	
					STANDARD SCRATCH	66	69		

Torphin Hill Golf Club,
Torphin Road,
Edinburgh, Midlothian.
EH13 0PG.
Tel: (0131) 441 1100.

LOCATION: South West boundary of Edinburgh.
SECRETARY: E.H. Marchant.

Torphin Hill Golf Club allows a good test of golf with staggering views of Edinburgh and the Pentlands. One hill hole, the play on a plateau, offers great scenery.

COURSE INFORMATION

Par 67; SSS 66; Length 4,652 Yards.
Opening hours: 7.30am – Sunset.
Visitors: Welcome. Weekend parties not permitted.
Avoid: Competition days.
Ladies: Welcome.
Green Fees: Monday – Friday £12; Weekends £20.
Juveniles: Welcome.
Clubhouse Hours: Summer 11am – 11.30pm; Weekends 11am – 11.30pm; Sundays 11am – 11pm.
Clubhouse Dress: Neat.
Clubhouse Facilities: Catering available everyday except Tuesdays.
Open Competitions: Numerous, contact club for information.

Tree positions indicated.

West Linton, Peeblesshire, EH46 7HN.
Tel: (01968) 660463.

LOCATION: North West of Peebles on the A702.
SECRETARY: G. Scott.
Tel: (01968) 675843.
PROFESSIONAL: R. Forrest.
Tel: (01968) 660256.

Scenic moorland course with views of Pentland and Moorfoot Hills. A real challenge of golf.

COURSE INFORMATION

Par 69; SSS 70; Length 6,132 Yards.
Opening Hours: Daylight Hours.
Visitors: Not Before 1pm Saturday and Sunday.
Avoid: Medal Days.
Green Fees: Weekday £15; Day Ticket £22; Weekend round £25.
Clubhouse Hours: 8am — 11pm.
Clubhouse Dress: Informal.
Clubhouse Facilities: Except Tuesdays.

CONVENIENT HOTELS

Linton Hotel; Raemartin Hotel; Gordon Arms.

NO.	YARDS	PAR	S.I.	NO.	YARDS	PAR	S.I.
1	307	4	14	10	348	4	10
2	143	3	18	11	469	4	4
3	353	4	7	12	203	3	17
4	525	5	3	13	295	4	13
5	470	4	5	14	376	4	2
6	360	4	9	15	503	5	8
7	330	4	11	16	415	4	6
8	447	4	1	17	196	3	15
9	162	3	16	18	230	3	12
OUT	3,097	35		IN	3,035	34	
				TOTAL	6,132	69	
STANDARD SCRATCH					70		

Tree positions indicated.

WEST LOTHIAN

West Lothian Golf Club, Airngrath Hill, By Linlithgow, West Lothian.
Tel: (01506) 826030.

NO.	YARDS	PAR	S.I.	NO.	YARDS	PAR	S.I.
1	434	4	5	10	361	4	6
2	396	4	9	11	317	4	12
3	458	4	1	12	375	4	2
4	373	4	14	13	336	4	13
5	159	3	18	14	161	3	16
6	363	4	11	15	513	5	8
7	506	5	4	16	423	4	3
8	369	4	7	17	505	5	10
9	151	3	15	18	140	3	17
OUT	3,209	35		IN	3,131	36	
				TOTAL	6,340	71	
STANDARD SCRATCH					71		

LOCATION: 1 mile south of Linthigow, towards Bo'ness.
SECRETARY: Mr A. O'Neil.
Tel: (01506) 826030.

COURSE INFORMATION

Par 71; SSS 71; Length 6,340 Yards.
Visitors: By arrangement with the starter or outing convenor.
Avoid: No play after 4pm midweek.
Ladies: Welcome.
Green Fees: Daily ticket Monday – Friday £18, Weekend £24, Round ticket Monday – Friday £12, Weekend £16.
Juveniles: Welcome, but restricted.
Clubhouse Hours: 11am – 11pm.
Clubhouse Dress: Collared shirt at all times; No shorts in clubhouse.
Clubhouse Facilities: Catering available by arrangement. Filled rolls normally available.
Open Competitions: Gents Open September; Mixed Open August.

CONVENIENT HOTEL

Earl O'Murray Hotel, Bonsyde, Linlithgow

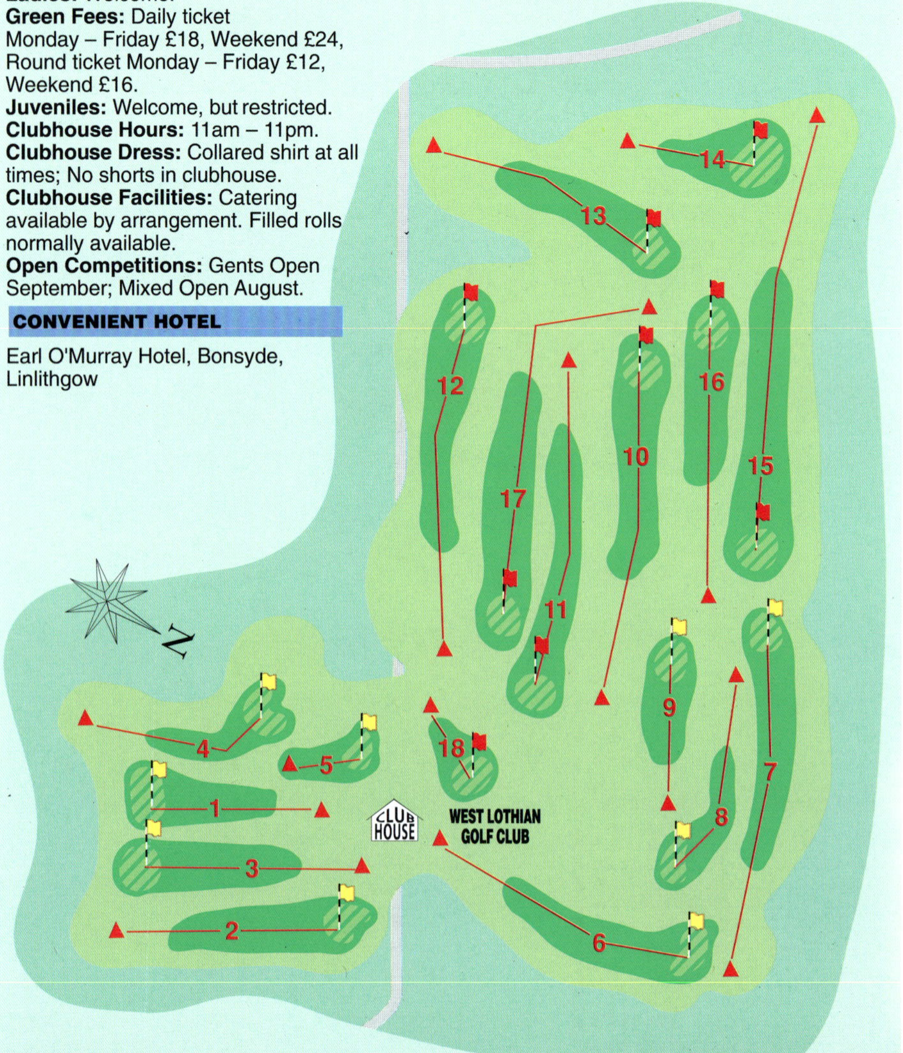

NO.	YARDS	PAR	S.I.	NO.	YARDS	PAR	S.I.
1	238	3	11	10	212	3	14
2	369	4	3	11	183	3	17
3	287	4	8	12	303	4	6
4	140	3	18	13	368	4	2
5	307	4	5	14	202	3	16
6	322	4	10	15	234	3	12
7	438	4	1	16	311	4	7
8	250	3	13	17	490	5	4
9	236	3	15	18	265	4	9
OUT	2,587	32		IN	2,568	33	
				TOTAL	5,155	65	
STANDARD SCRATCH					65		

Winterfield Golf Club, St Magarets, North Road, Dunbar, East Lothian. EH42 1AU. Tel: (01368) 862280.

Location: West side of Dunbar.
Secretary: Mr M. O'Donnell.
Tel: (01368) 862564.
Professional: Kevin Phillips.
Tel: (01368) 863562.

COURSE INFORMATION

Par 65; SSS 65; Length 5,155 Yards.
Visitors: Welcome.
Opening Hours: 7am – Dusk (summer), 9pm – Dusk (winter).
Ladies: No.
Green Fees: Mon - Fri £10.50/round; £12.60/day Sat & Sun £12.60/round; £19/day.
Juveniles: £5/round; £6/weekday; no concession at weekends.
Clubhouse Dress: Smart/casual.
Clubhouse Facilities: Normal bar/catering.
Open Competitions: Two ball — May; Belhanen Trophy — June; Craig-en-Gelt — July; Mixed foursomes — August; St, Margarets Rosebowl — September.

CONVENIENT HOTELS

Bayswell, Bayswell Park; Craig-en-Gelt, Marine Road (both five minutes walk from the course); Springfield Guest House, Edinburgh Road (two minutes walk from the course).

Bunker positions indicated.

NORTH

GOLF
DAYS™
SCOTLAND

Abernethy Golf Club, Nethy Bridge, Inverness.
Tel: (01479) 821305.

Location: Aviemore 10 miles, Grantown 5 miles.
Secretary: Mrs E. Knight.
Tel: (01479) 873558.

Delightful nine hole course close to pine woods and with superb views to the vally of River Spey. The course is ideal for the holiday golfer and although of no great length it can present a real chalenge to the experience player.

COURSE INFORMATION

Par 66; SSS 66; Length 5,102 Yards.
Opening Hours: All year (weather permitting).
Visitors: Welcome.
Ladies: Welcome.
Green Fees: Mon – Fri £9; Sat & Sun £12.
Clubhouse Hours: 9am – 6pm (April – Oct.).
Clubhouse Dress: Informal.
Clubhouse Facilities: Catering facilities available.

Open Competitions: Mens Open Tournament August; Ladies Open July; Open Mixed Foursomes July & September.

CONVENIENT HOTELS:

The Nethbridge Hotel; The Mountview Hotel; The Heatherbrae Hotel.

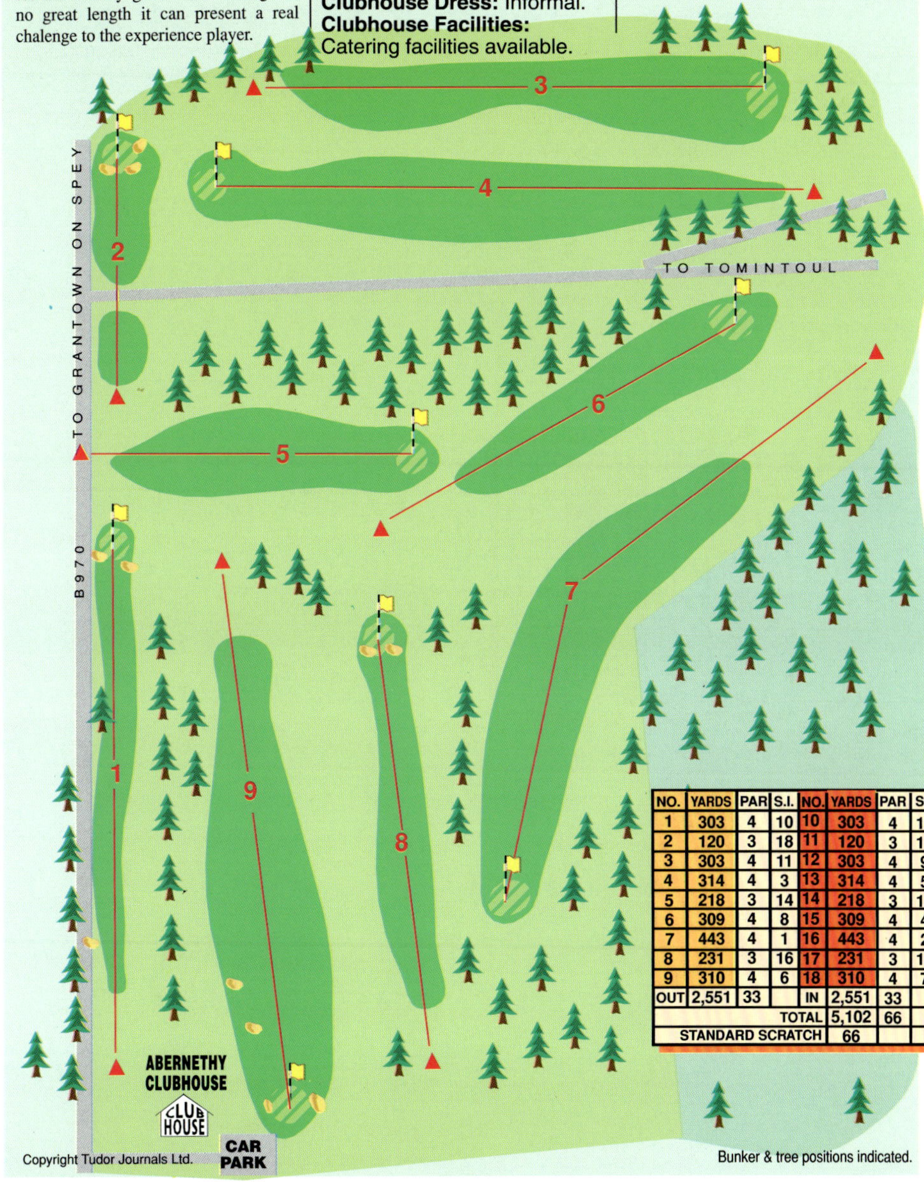

NO.	YARDS	PAR	S.I.	NO.	YARDS	PAR	S.I.
1	303	4	10	10	303	4	12
2	120	3	18	11	120	3	17
3	303	4	11	12	303	4	9
4	314	4	3	13	314	4	5
5	218	3	14	14	218	3	13
6	309	4	8	15	309	4	4
7	443	4	1	16	443	4	2
8	231	3	16	17	231	3	15
9	310	4	6	18	310	4	7
OUT	2,551	33		IN	2,551	33	
				TOTAL	5,102	66	
STANDARD SCRATCH					66		

Alness Golf Club, Ardross Road, Alness, Ross & Cromarty.
Tel: (01349) 883877.

LOCATION: Approx. 26 miles North of Inverness and 3 miles off the A9.
SECRETARY: Mrs Jean Whitelaw.
Tel: Evening (01349) 883579
Day (01349) 883579.

Beautifully situated 9 hole inland course with views out over the Cromarty Firth with the Averon River running down one side and views over the hills in the background. Very interesting and tricky course.

COURSE INFORMATION

Par 66; SSS 64; Length 2,473 Yards.
Opening Hours: Daylight hours.
Visitors: Welcome. Except when Club competition are in progress.
Avoid: Club Competition days.
Ladies: Welcome but as above.
Ladies Day: Monday night; tee reserved from 5pm – 7pm.
Green Fees: £9 per day at all times; SC & Jun 50%.
Juveniles: Permitted, but restricted.

Clubhouse Hours: Summertime - licening hours; Wintertime - restricted hours.
Clubhouse Dress: Informal but resonably smart.
Clubhouse Facilities: Snacks can be arranged as required for parties, etc.
Open Competitions: Mixed; Junior Open August: Ladies Open last Saturday in June.

CONVENIENT HOTELS

Morven House Hotel; Station Hotel; Commercial Hotel, Alness.

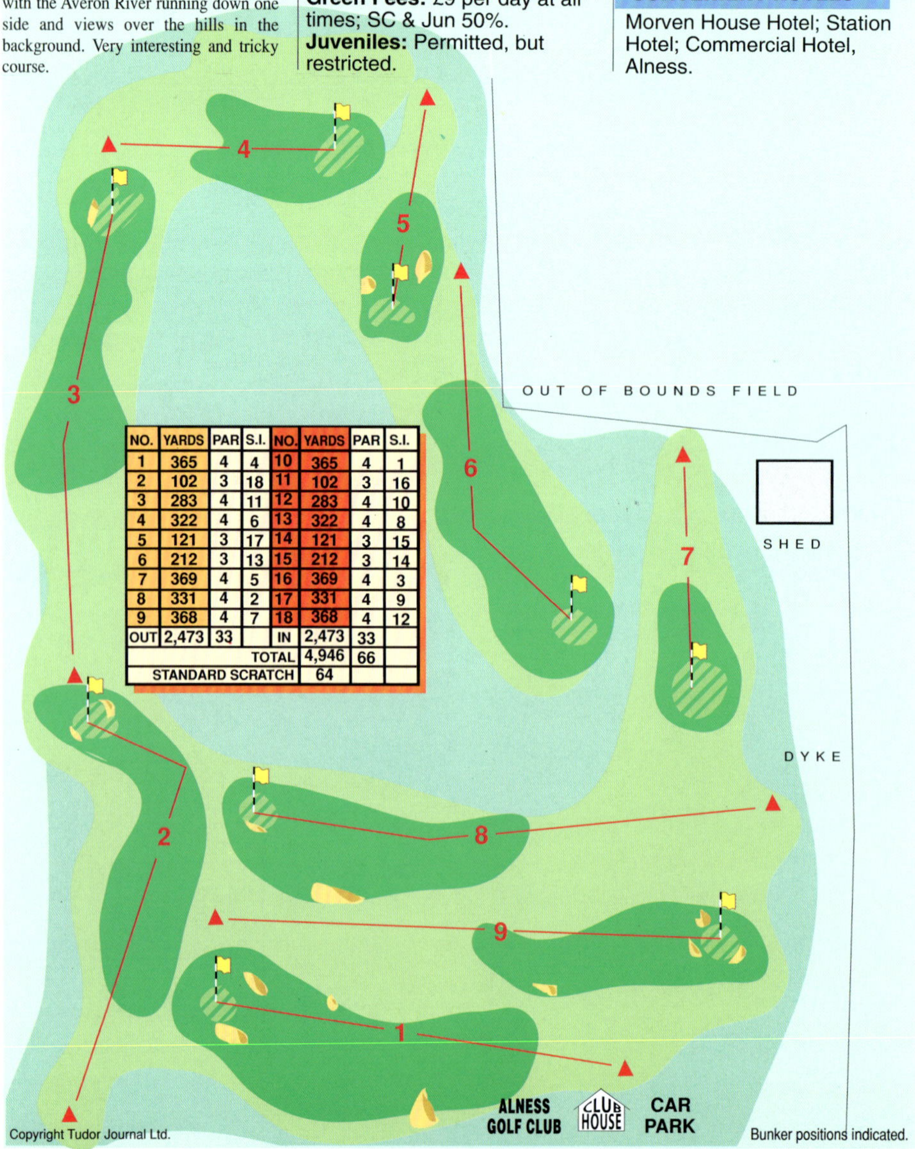

NO.	YARDS	PAR	S.I.	NO.	YARDS	PAR	S.I.
1	365	4	4	10	365	4	1
2	102	3	18	11	102	3	16
3	283	4	11	12	283	4	10
4	322	4	6	13	322	4	8
5	121	3	17	14	121	3	15
6	212	3	13	15	212	3	14
7	369	4	5	16	369	4	3
8	331	4	2	17	331	4	9
9	368	4	7	18	368	4	12
OUT	2,473	33		IN	2,473	33	
				TOTAL	4,946	66	
				STANDARD SCRATCH	64		

Bunker positions indicated.

Askernish Golf Club, Lochboisdale, South Vist, Scotland.

Location: 5 miles north west of Lochboisdale.
Secretary: A.L. MacDonald.
Tel: (01878) 700541.
Architect: Tom Morris

Designed by Tom Morris in 1891, 9 holes 18 tee off's. Sands course beside Atlantic Ocean. Spectacular scenery of South Vist and other Western Islands at every hole. One of the few remaining traditional/natural courses in existence.

COURSE INFORMATION

Par 67, SSS 67, Length 5,042 Yards.
Visitors: Welcome.
Opening Hours: All hours Sunrise-Sunset.
Ladies: Welcome.
Fees: £3.50 round; £5 per day.
Juveniles: Permitted.
Clubhouse Hours: All hours sunrise-sunset.
Open Competitions: August.

CONVENIENT HOTELS

Borrodale Hotel; Lochboisdale Hotel; Grianaig Guest House.

NO.	YARDS	PAR	S.I.	NO.	YARDS	PAR	S.I.
1	347	4	4	10	397	4	3
2	170	3	16	11	123	3	17
3	200	3	14	12	205	4	13
4	415	4	2	13	520	5	1
5	261	4	11	14	267	4	12
6	199	3	15	15	116	3	18
7	353	4	7	16	276	4	10
8	358	4	5	17	335	4	6
9	250	4	8	18	250	4	9
OUT	2,553	33		IN	2,489	35	
				TOTAL	5,042	68	
				STANDARD SCRATCH	67		

Bunker positions indicated.

GOLF BREAKS
at
THE BOAT HOTEL
Boat of Garten
AA ★★★ RAC

Situated overlooking the beautiful but challenging Boat of Garten Golf Course – the 'Gleneagles' of the Highlands – the Boat Hotel offers you superb value 'Tee Break' holidays with golf on any of 6 local courses. Special rates for Golf Societies and all golf reserved in advance.

The Boat Hotel is family owned and run with all rooms en-suite, TV/radio, direct dial phone, hairdryer, tea/coffee facilities. Excellent food using the best of local produce complimented by a wide choice of wines.

BOAT HOTEL
Contact: **Suzanne Wilson, Golf Desk, Boat of Garten, Inverness-shire. PH24 3BH.**
Tel: 01479 831258 Fax: 01479 831414.

GOLF IN SCOTLAND
Ireland and England

We plan and arrange golfing holidays for individuals and groups to Scotland Ireland, and England.

◆

Our comprehensive service offers Custom Tours, Package Tours and Guided Tours on Legendary Courses and Hidden Gems.

◆

For further information and brochures contact:

The Scottish Golf & Travel Service

12 Rutland Square,
Edinburgh EH1 2BB.
SCOTLAND

Tel: 1 800 847 8064
Fax: 1 800 546 3510

CRAIGARD HOUSE HOTEL
Overlooking Boat of Garten golf course
Kinchurdy Road, Boat of Garten, Inverness-shire PH24 3BP
Tel: 0479 831206 Fax: 0479 831423

An elegantly restored Victorian Shooting Lodge that offers traditional Highland Hospitality, excellent Scottish Cuisine and Fine Wines together with over 80 Malt Whiskys in Braids Bar.
Many top quality 18-hole courses within easy access, including the championship courses at Nairn and Royal Dornoch as well as the beautiful yet heartbreaking Boat of Garten which abutts our grounds.

All inclusive Golf Packages available; Starting Times arranged; Secure club storeroom; Transport can be arranged to and from courses.

The style and comfort of Country House living.

Stay and play some of the Highlands courses. Strathpeffer, Fortrose & Rosemarkie, Nairn, Tain, Inverness, Royal Dornoch and our local course Muir of Ord.
Relax in homely comfort with us and enjoy the seclusion of our 60 acre estate, the "Lairds" house awaits your arrival, your sure to want to come back, golf break packages available, golfing parties very welcome.

ORD HOUSE
Muir of Ord, Ross-shire,
Scotland, IV6 7UH.
Tel/Fax: (01463) 870492.

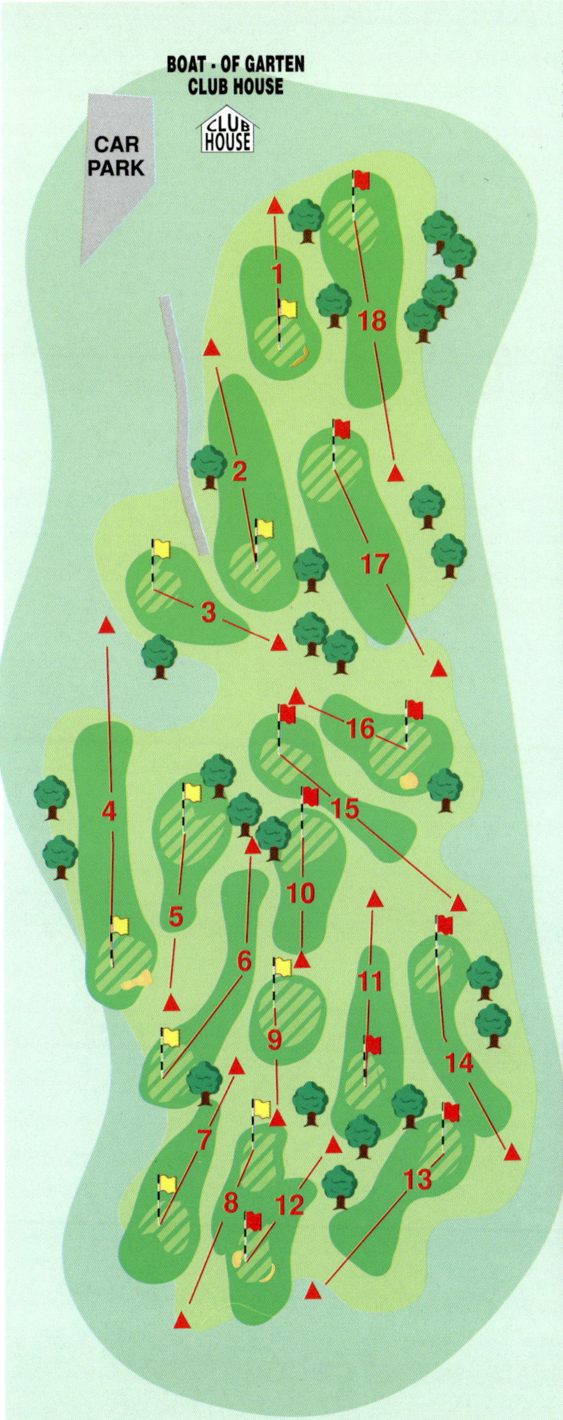

Boat-Of-Garten Golf Club,
Boat-Of-Garten,
Inverness-shire, PH24 3BQ.
Tel: (0147983) 1282.

Location: 25 miles South of Inverness.
Secretary: Paddy Smith.
Architect: James Braid.

A difficult course with birch tree lined fairways over looking Cairngorm Mountains.

COURSE INFORMATION

Par 69; SSS 69; Length 5,837 Yards.
Opening Hours: 7.30am onwards.
Visitors: Visitors can play from 9.30-5.30.
Ladies: Welcome.
Fees: £18 weekdays, £23 weekends.
Juveniles: Must be accompanied by an adult.
Clubhouse Hours: 9.30 – 11pm.
Clubhouse Dress: Casual.
Open Competitions: 36 open - August.

CONVENIENT HOTEL

Boat Hotel, Craigard Hotel.

NO.	YARDS	PAR	S.I.	NO.	YARDS	PAR	S.I.
1	188	3	15	10	271	4	16
2	360	4	7	11	379	4	4
3	163	3	13	12	349	4	10
4	485	5	3	13	432	4	2
5	333	4	11	14	323	4	8
6	403	4	1	15	307	4	14
7	386	4	5	16	168	3	18
8	355	4	9	17	344	4	12
9	154	3	17	18	437	4	6
OUT	2,827	34		IN	3,010	35	
				TOTAL	5,837	69	
STANDARD SCRATCH					69		

Bunker & tree positions indicated.

Bonar-Bridge / Ardgay Golf Club, Bonar-Bridge, Sutherland.
LOCATION: 1/2 miles north of Bonar-Bridge on A9.
SECRETARY: Mr Turner & Mr F. Mussard.
Tel: (01549) 421248 & (01863) 766375.

A short but attractive heathland course giving magnaificent views of Migaale and surrounding hills.

Par 66; SSS 63; Length 4,626 Yards.
Opening Hours: Daylight hours.
Visitors: Welcome.
Avoid: Major open competitions (4 or 5 weekends per season).
Ladies: Welcome; ladies day Thursday morning.
Green Fees: £8 day; £40 week.
Juveniles: Welcome.

Clubhouse Hours: 10am - 8pm (May - September)
Clubhouse Dress: Informal.
Clubhouse Facilities: "Changing rooms only, No catering."

Dun Roarnin Hotel; Lady Ross Hotel, Ardgay; Bridge Hotel.

NO.	YARDS	PAR	S.I.	NO.	YARDS	PAR	S.I.
1	339	4	9	10	339	4	4
2	297	4	15	11	297	4	14
3	278	4	5	12	278	4	6
4	190	3	13	13	190	3	12
5	302	4	3	14	302	4	2
6	174	3	7	15	174	3	8
7	285	4	1	16	285	4	10
8	137	3	17	17	137	3	16
9	311	4	11	18	311	4	18
OUT	2,313	33		IN	2,313	33	
				TOTAL	4,626	66	
STANDARD SCRATCH					63		

BRORA

NORTH

**Brora Golf Club, Golf Road,
Brora, Sutherland.
KW9 6QS. Tel: (01408) 621417.**

LOCATION: 54 miles North of Inverness.
SECRETARY: J. Frazer.
Tel: (01408) 621417.

Brora presents all the attributes of the Scottish seaside links, there is bent and gorse - often in full bloom for golf week - Juniper and Thyme in profusion. The layout is classic: an easy opening hole, a short hole facing each cardinal point of the compass, a hole you can't reach in two shots and the last green under the clubhouse window. The course will ensure that you can use every club in the bag, and that you will have to adapt and manufacture according to whether the course is running fast or slow. The greens are renowned for their texture. The ball runs true on the seaside fescue. While pin placements are generous there are lovely swingly borrows on virtually every green.

COURSE INFORMATION

Par 69; SSS 69; Length 6,110 Yards.
Opening Hours: All day.
Visitors: Welcome.
Avoid: Club competitions days and Sunday afternoon.
Ladies: Welcome any day; Ladies day Thursday evening.
Green Fees: £16 per day; £70 per week.
Juveniles: Welcome.
Clubhouse Hours: All day from Easter-October otherwise evenings and weekends only.
Clubhouse Dress: No denim, sleeveless/collarless shirts, track suits/shell suits, shorts or trainers. Similar guide-lines apply to the course.
Clubhouse Facilities: Full catering and bar facilities available.

CONVENIENT HOTELS

The Royal Marine Hotel;
The Links Hotel;
The Bayview Hotel.

	MEDAL	GEN.				MEDAL	GEN.		
NO.	METRES	METRES	PAR	S.I.	NO.	METRES	METRES	PAR	S.I.
1	297	280	4	13	10	435	425	4	6
2	344	334	4	9	11	412	412	4	8
3	447	447	4	1	12	362	314	4	10
4	325	313	4	15	13	125	108	3	18
5	428	400	4	3	14	334	305	4	16
6	174	164	3	7	15	430	399	4	2
7	350	340	4	11	16	345	335	4	12
8	501	501	5	5	17	438	438	4	4
9	162	149	3	17	18	201	190	3	14
OUT	3,028	2,928	35		IN	3,082	2,926	34	
					TOTAL	6,110	5,854	69	
					STANDARD SCRATCH	69	68		

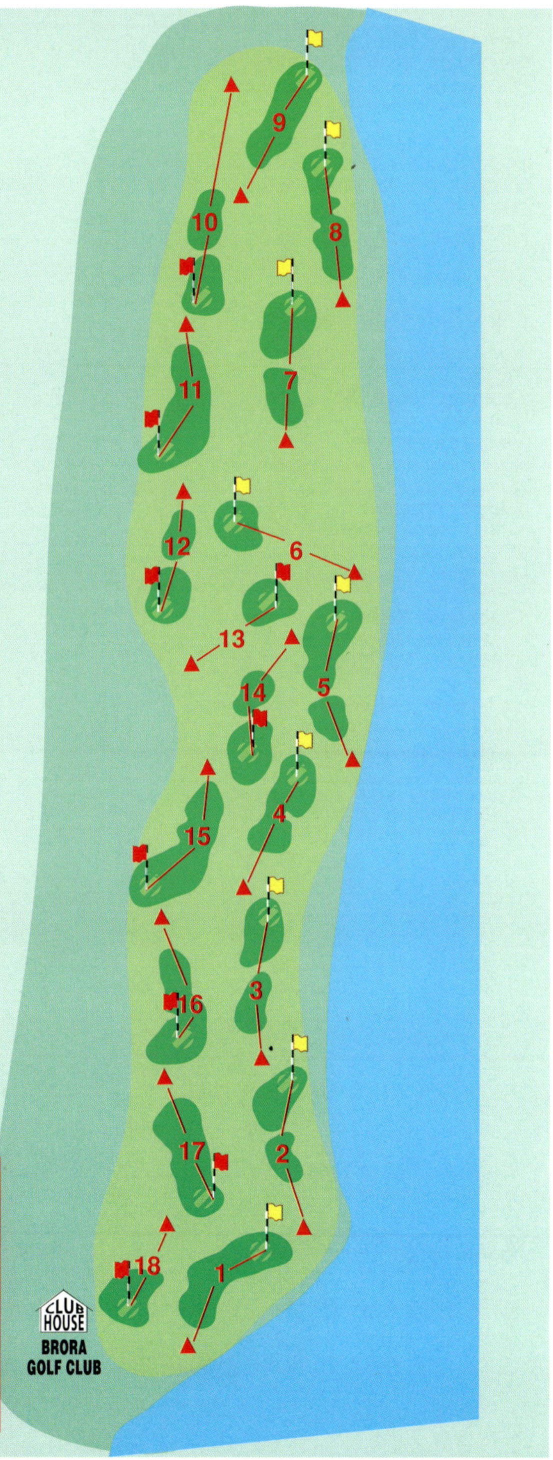

CARRBRIDGE

NORTH

**Carrbridge Golf Club,
Carrbridge, Inverness-shire.
PA23 3AU.
Tel: (01479) 841623.**

Location: 8 miles north of Aviemore.
27 miles south of Inverness.
Secretary: Mrs A.T. Baird.
Tel: (01479) 841506.

Part parkland, part heathland with magnificent views of Cairngorms. Challenging small course with friendly atmosphere.

NO.	YARDS	PAR	S.I.	NO.	YARDS	PAR	S.I.
1	480	5/4	7	10	480	5/4	6
2	334	4	5	11	334	4	4
3	342	4	11	12	342	4	10
4	331	4/3	3	13	331	4/3	2
5	258	4/3	13	14	258	4/3	12
6	270	4/3	17	15	270	4/3	16
7	262	4	9	16	262	4	8
8	174	3	15	17	174	3	14
9	231	3	1	18	269	3	18
OUT	2,682	35/31		IN	2,720	35/31	
				TOTAL	5,402	71/63	
STANDARD SCRATCH					68		

COURSE INFORMATION

Par 71; SSS 68; Length 5,402 Yards.
Opening Hours: 9am – 8pm Summer.
Visitors: Welcome.
Avoid: Sunday (mornings); Wednesday after 5pm.
Ladies: Welcome.
Green Fees: Mon – Fri £10 (£11 high season;Sat & Sun £12
Juveniles: Accompanied by adult weekends.
Clubhouse Hours: 9am – 8pm.
Clubhouse Dress: Informal.
Clubhouse Facilities: Light snacks coffee tea etc.
Open competitions: August, September, June, May.

CONVENIENT HOTELS

Dalrachney Lodge, Carrbridge Hotel, Struan House Hotel, Cairn Hotel.

Durness Golf Club, Balnakeil, Durness, Sutherland, IV27 4PG.

LOCATION: 1 mile west of Durness.
SECRETARY: Mrs L. Mackey. Tel: (01971) 511364.
ARCHITECTS: F.R.M. Keith L J Ross, I Morrison.

The course comprises 9 greens with 18 tees allowed substantial variation in the layout of the second 9 holes. Generally undulating terrain incorporating water haxards. The last hole is 155 yards across an inlet of the sea to a well guarded green on an opposite cliff edge.

COURSE INFORMATION

Par 70; SSS 69; Length 5,555 Yards, 5050 Metres.
Visitors: Welcome.
Avoid: Sunday mornings.
Ladies: Welcome.
Green Fees: £9; £36 per week.
Clubhouse Hours: Sunrise – Sunset.
Clubhouse Dress: Informal.
Clubhouse Facilities: Snacks available June – September 12noon - 5pm.

Open Competitions: Ladies Open August; Mens Open August.

CONVENIENT HOTELS

The Cape Wrath Hotel; The Parkhill Hotel; The Far North Hotel; Sango Sands Caravan & CampingPark.

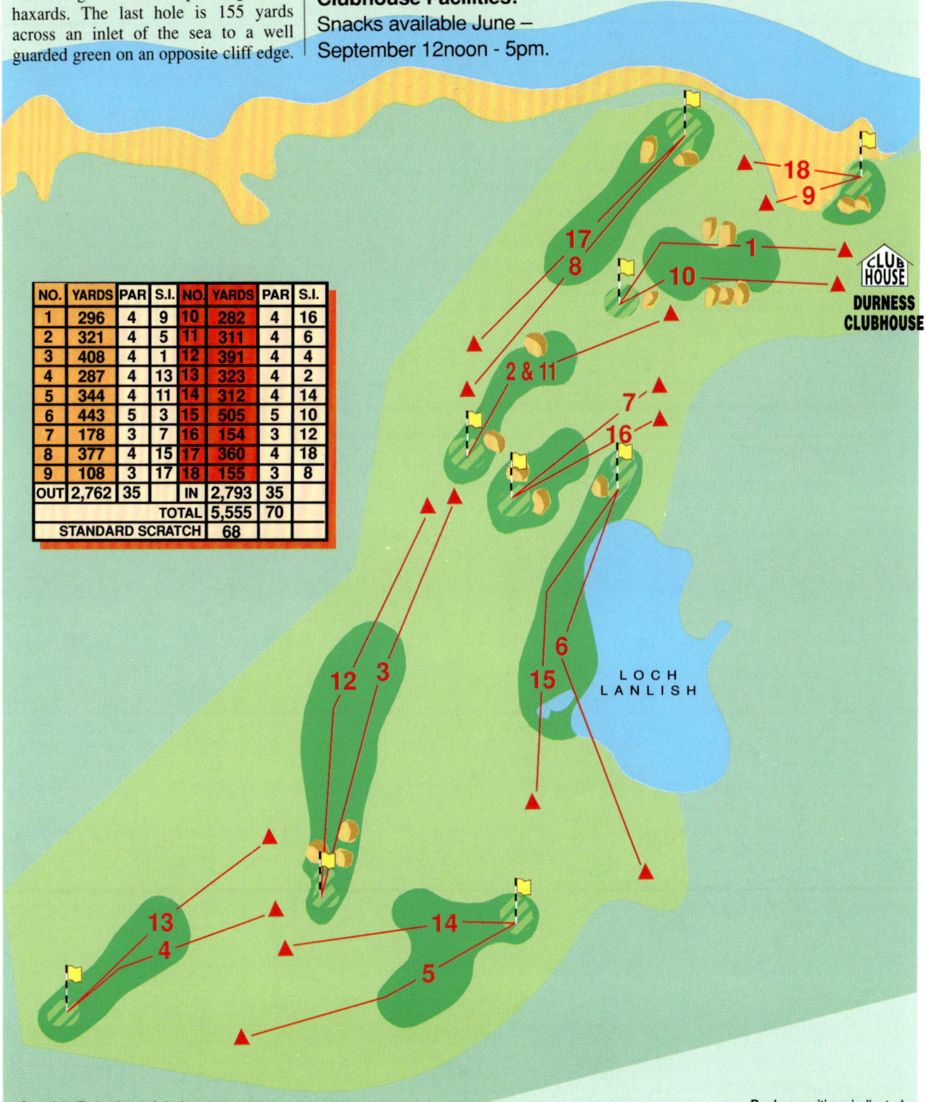

NO.	YARDS	PAR	S.I.	NO.	YARDS	PAR	S.I.
1	296	4	9	10	282	4	16
2	321	4	5	11	311	4	6
3	408	4	1	12	391	4	4
4	287	4	13	13	323	4	2
5	344	4	11	14	312	4	14
6	443	5	3	15	505	5	10
7	178	3	7	16	154	3	12
8	377	4	15	17	360	4	18
9	108	3	17	18	155	3	8
OUT	2,762	35		IN	2,793	35	
				TOTAL	5,555	70	
				STANDARD SCRATCH	68		

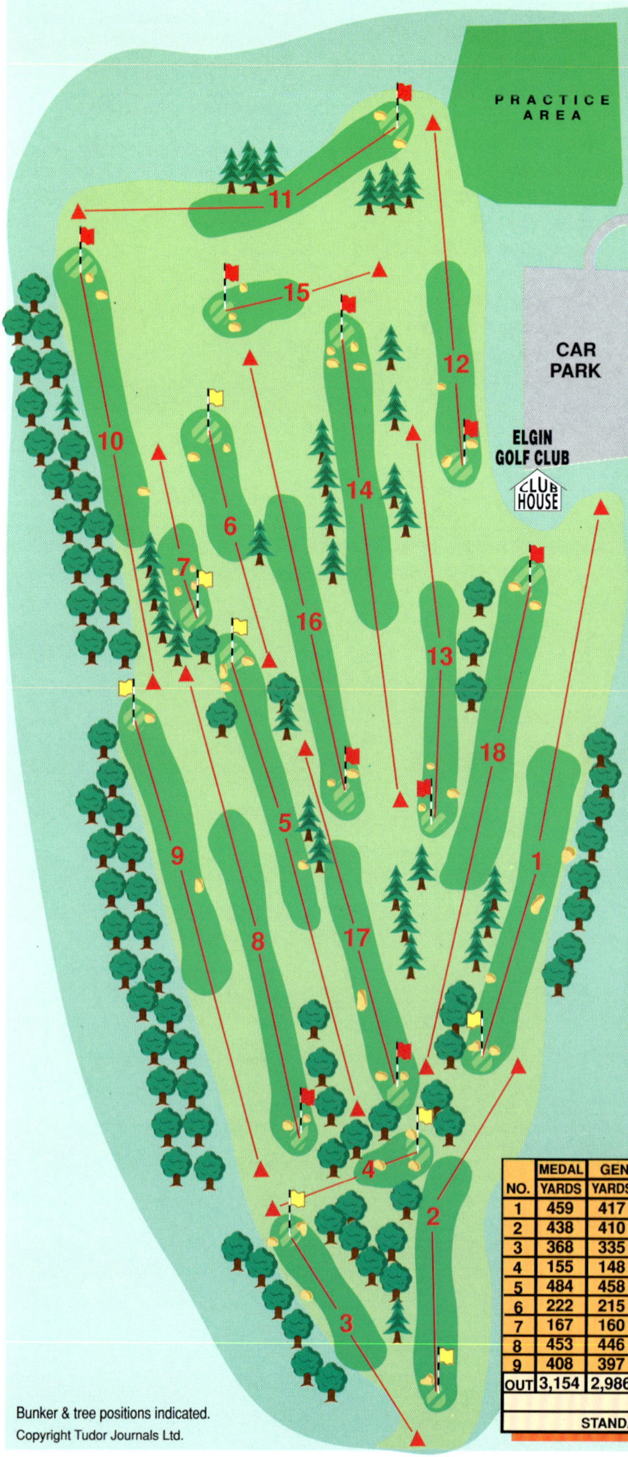

Bunker & tree positions indicated.

Elgin Golf Club,
Hardhillock,
Birnie Road, Elgin,
IV30 3SX.
Tel: (01343) 542338.

LOCATION: 1 mile south of Elgin.
SECRETARY: David Black.
PROFESSIONAL: Mr Ian P Rodger.
Tel: (01343) 542884

Mature inland course. Undualting parkland that was established in 1906. Rated in the top five courses in the North and is one of the finest examples of an inland course in the North.

COURSE INFORMATION

Par 69; SSS 71; Length 6,401 Yards.
Opening Hours: 8am – 7.30 pm.
Visitors: By prior arrangement advisable.
Avoid: Prior to 10.30 at weekends.
Ladies: Welcome.
Ladies Day: Tuesday.
Fees: Weekdays £18 & £24, weekends £24 and £30.
Clubhouse Hours: 8 am – 7.30 pm.
Clubhouse Dress: Smart Casual (no jeans / shellsuits / t-shirts).
Clubhouse Facilities: Daily catering & Bar.
Open Competitions: May (Mixed), May (36 Hour Mens), Sep, June (36 hole mens), July (5 day open).

CONVENIENT HOTELS

The Laichmoray,
The Mansion House,
St Leonards, The Braelossie.

NO.	MEDAL YARDS	GEN. YARDS	PAR	S.I.	NO.	MEDAL YARDS	GEN. YARDS	PAR	S.I.
1	459	417	4	4	10	428	421	4	3
2	438	410	4	6	11	375	368	4	12
3	368	335	4	11	12	278	271	4	18
4	155	148	3	13	13	325	297	4	14
5	484	458	5	17	14	462	439	4	2
6	222	215	3	1	15	188	181	3	8
7	167	160	3	15	16	417	410	4	10
8	453	446	4	9	17	334	327	4	16
9	408	397	4	7	18	440	409	4	5
OUT	3,154	2,986	34		IN	3,247	3,123	35	
					TOTAL	6,401	6,109	69	
					STANDARD SCRATCH	71	69		

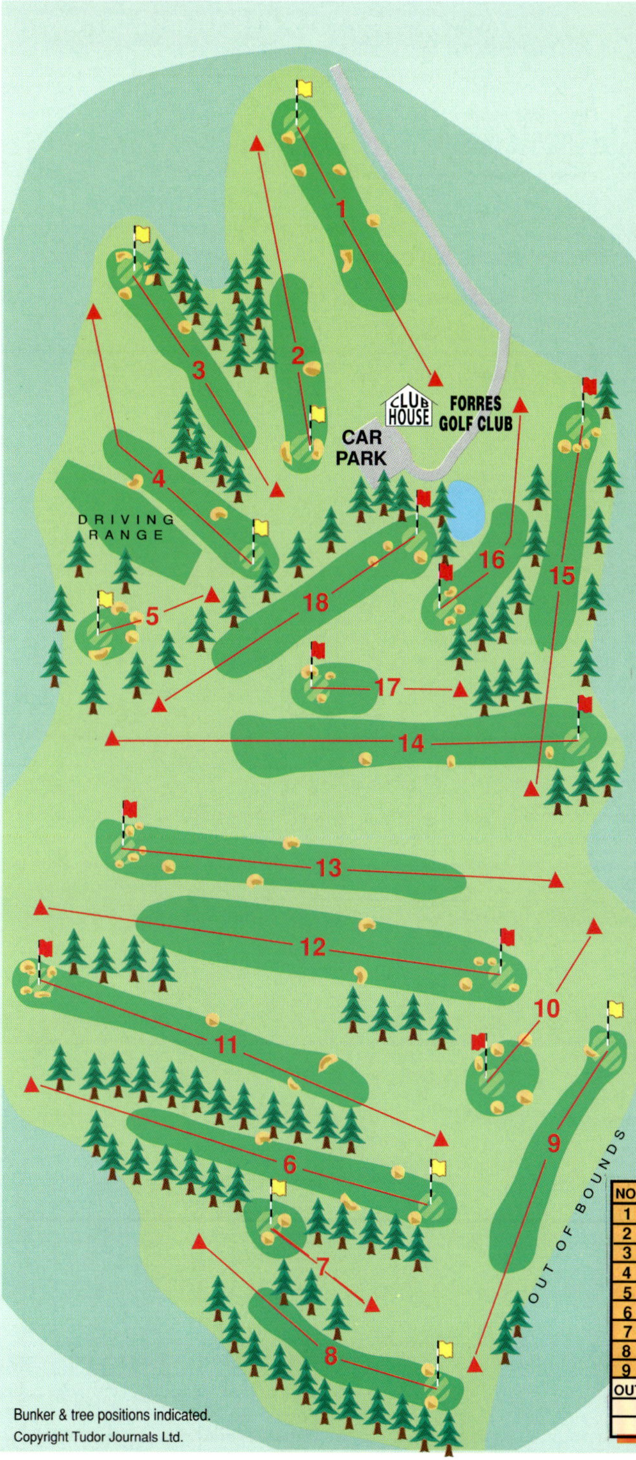

Bunker & tree positions indicated.

Forres Golf Club,
Muityshade, Forres,
Morayshire, IV36 0RD.
Tel: (01309) 672949.

Location: 1 mile south of Forres.
Secretary: Mr Harpeur.
Tel: (01309) 672949.
Professional: Sandy Aird.
Tel: (01309) 672250.
Architect: Willie Park of Musselburgh.

Gently rolling parkland course with several tree lined holes. Forres is also a very scenic course with views to the hills to the west and south as well as to Findhorn Bay and the hills to the north beyond the Moray Frith.

COURSE INFORMATION

Par 70; SSS 69; Length 6,236 Yards.
Opening Hours: Dawn to dusk.
Visitors: Difficult at weekends – contact secretary.
Ladies: Welcome.
Ladies Day: Tuesday.
Fees: £14 Mon – Fri; £20 Sat & Sun; 5 day adult ticket £45.
Juveniles: Welcome.
Clubhouse Hours: 7am – 11pm.
Clubhouse Dress: Smart Casual.
Clubhouse Facilities: Full bar and catering all day.
Open competitions: May; June; July; August.

CONVENIENT HOTELS

Ramnee Park; Parkmount House; Carisbrooke

NO.	METRES	PAR	S.I.	NO.	METRES	PAR	S.I.
1	306	4	16	10	248	3	13
2	337	4	2	11	45	4	7
3	323	4	14	12	430	4	1
4	379	4	6	13	398	4	3
5	142	3	18	14	427	4	9
6	505	5	10	15	383	4	5
7	189	3	12	16	322	4	15
8	348	4	8	17	159	3	17
9	482	5	4	18	370	4	11
OUT	3,011	36		IN	3,192	34	
				TOTAL	6,236	70	
				STANDARD SCRATCH	70		

FORT AUGUSTUS

Fort Angustus Golf Club,
Markethill, Fort Angustus.
PH 32 4AU.
Tel: (01320) 366660.

LOCATION: West end of Fort Angustus.
SECRETARY: H. Frazer. Tel: (01320) 366309.

Generally regarded as one of the most scenically beautiful in the country, with Caledonian pines bordering the Caledonian Canal, birch woods to the west and heather clad hills to the south. With 18 tees set at varying distances and aspects to the greens the course offers a fine test of golf.

COURSE INFORMATION

Par 67; SSS 67; Length 5,454 Yards.
Opening Hours: Daylight.
Ladies: Welcome.
Ladies Day: Tuesday.
Green Fees: £10 per day (no other tariff).
Juveniles: Permitted (half price).
Clubhouse Hours: 9am – 5pm.
Clubhouse Dress: Unrestricted.
Clubhouse Facilities: Bar/Lounge.
Open Competitions: July.

CONVENIENT HOTELS

Lovat Arms Hotel,
Tel (01320) 366206.

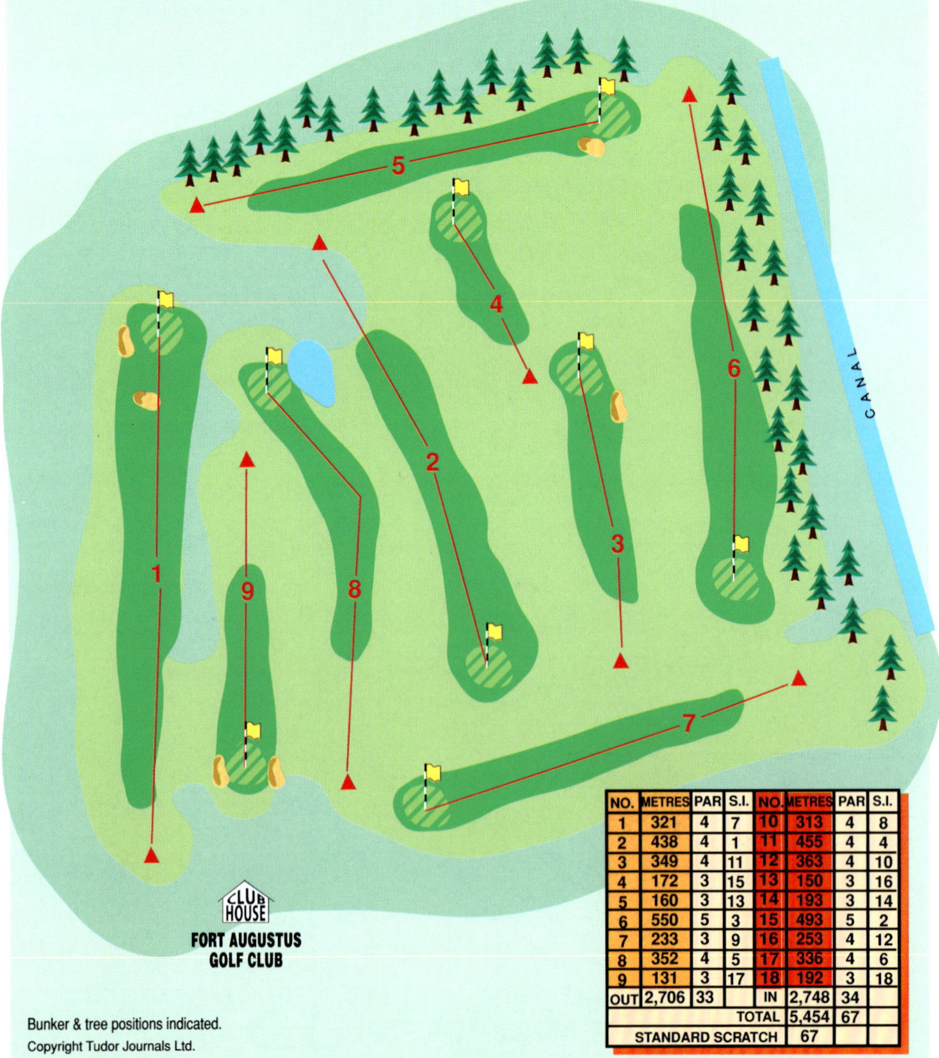

NO.	METRES	PAR	S.I.	NO.	METRES	PAR	S.I.
1	321	4	7	10	313	4	8
2	438	4	1	11	455	4	4
3	349	4	11	12	363	4	10
4	172	3	15	13	150	3	16
5	160	3	13	14	193	3	14
6	550	5	3	15	493	5	2
7	233	3	9	16	253	4	12
8	352	4	5	17	336	4	6
9	131	3	17	18	192	3	18
OUT	2,706	33		IN	2,748	34	
				TOTAL	5,454	67	
STANDARD SCRATCH					67		

Bunker & tree positions indicated.

FORTROSE & ROSEMARKIE

NORTH

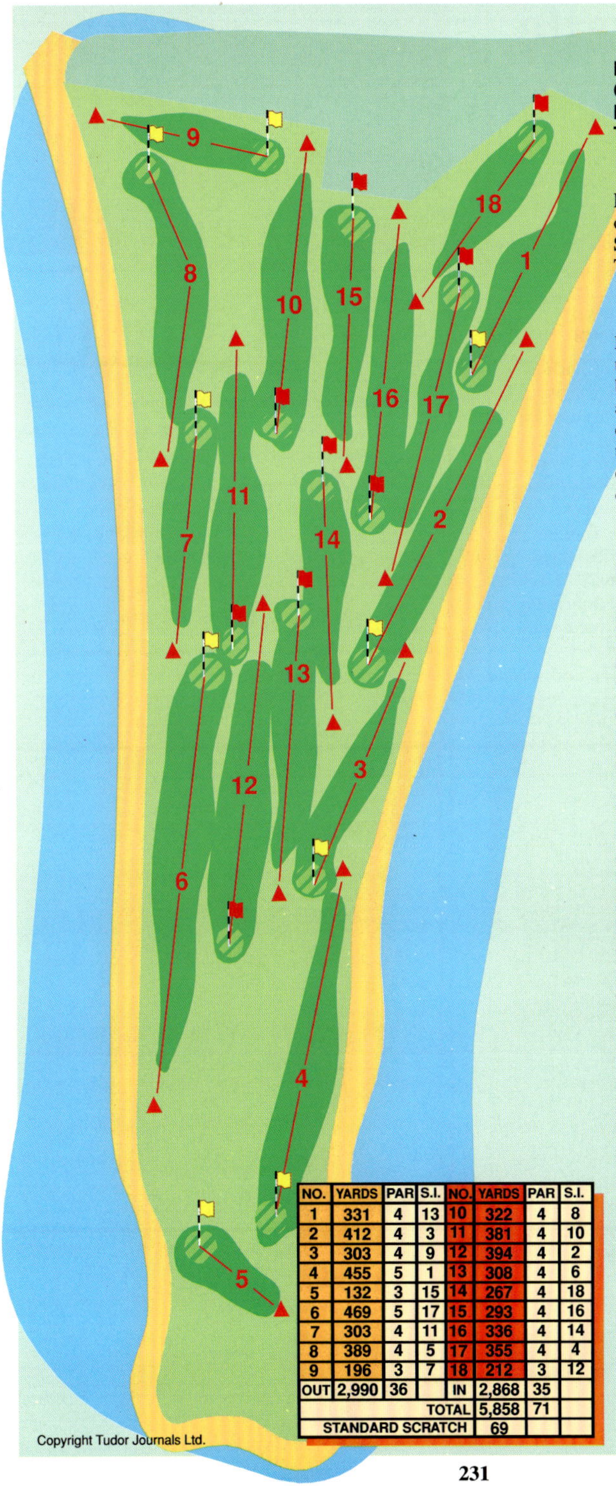

Fortrose & Rosemarkie Golf Club, Ness Road East, Fortrose, IV10 8SE.
Tel: (01381) 620529.

LOCATION: Black Isle, 12 miles north of Inverness.
SECRETARY: Margaret Collier.
Tel: (01381) 620529.

Fortrose and Rosemarkie golf course is unique as it is bordered on three sides by the sea. A links course which may appear relatively simple but the contours of the fairways and greens plus the prevailing winds have proved the course to be a real challenge to all levels of golfers.

COURSE INFORMATION

Par 71; SSS 69; Length 5,858 Yards.
Opening Hours: Daylight hours.
Visitors: Welcome, one player in each group should have a handicap.
Avoid: Members priority. 9 – 10.15am; 1 – 2.15pm; 4.45 – 6.30pm.
Ladies: Welcome; avoid the above times. Ladies day Tues.
Green Fees: Monday-Friday £15 per round. Saturday/Sunday £21 per round.
Juveniles: Welcome but restricted Saturday/Sunday 8.45 –10am & 12noon 12 – 2pm. Monday-Friday 4.45pm – 6.30pm.
Clubhouse Hours: 11am – 10pm (Winter); 11am – 11pm (Summer).
Clubhouse Dress: Shirt with collar and long slacks.
Clubhouse Facilities: Snacks available and meals by arrangement.
Open Competitions: Gents Open F/some April; Open Mixed F/somes May; Ladies Open June; Gents Open July; Juniors Open July (am).

NO.	YARDS	PAR	S.I.	NO.	YARDS	PAR	S.I.
1	331	4	13	10	322	4	8
2	412	4	3	11	381	4	10
3	303	4	9	12	394	4	2
4	455	5	1	13	308	4	6
5	132	3	15	14	267	4	18
6	469	5	17	15	293	4	16
7	303	4	11	16	336	4	14
8	389	4	5	17	355	4	4
9	196	3	7	18	212	3	12
OUT	2,990	36		IN	2,868	35	
				TOTAL	5,858	71	
				STANDARD SCRATCH	69		

CONVENIENT HOTELS

The Royal Fortrose.

Dornoch Castle

DORNOCH, SUTHERLAND. IV25 3SD
Tel: (01862) 810216. Fax: (01862) 810981

Play GOLF on the famous Royal Dornoch Championship Course, and stay at the charming Dornoch Castle. Your room looks out over lovely sheltered formal gardens or the magnificent Dornoch Firth. All have private facilities: those in the new wing have modern decor, while those in the Castle enjoy the highest level of traditional atmosphere and elegance. Beaches and golf courses are within walking distance. Superb food ("Taste of Scotland" recommended) in one of the finest Restaurants of the area with a cellar to match will make your visit an experience not to be forgotten.

alton burn hotel

Situated close to Nairn's Championship Courses, The Alton Burn offers true golfing hospitality under the personal supervision of the resident owners. Special rates for golf breaks with all tee off times arranged for your convenience. Putting green and practice area within the hotels secluded grounds and overlooking the Moray Firth.

Nairn, Scotland.
Tel: Nairn 01667 453325/452051

The Stotfield Hotel

A wedge shot away from Koray Golf Club. Superior rooms with magnificent sea views. Spacious Wedgewood dining rooms. Traditional Sunday lunch served. Sunlounge a la carte restaurant. Bourbon Street American style bar and grill. Newly refurnished function room. Conference suite. Firth lounge bar - sizzler steaks a speciality. Attractive golfing packages at Moray's premier golf hotel. Reductions for residents.

AA ★★★

Stotfield Road, Lossiemouth, IV31 6QS
Tel: (01343) 812011. Fax (01343) 814820

GOLF BROCHURES

**When thinking of producing a golf related brochure, be it for a club or a hotel, or a holiday plan, you should consult the experts.
For a quotation to embrace the full service from concept, through the best golf photography, to copy writing, design and printing.**

Tudor Journals Limited

97 Botanic Avenue, Belfast, BT7 1JN. Telephone: (01232) 320088. Fax: (01232) 323163.

Staple Inn Buildings North, 335 High Holborn, London, WC1V 7PJ.

Gairloch Golf Club,
Gairloch, IV21 2BE.
Tel: (01445) 712407.

Location: 60 miles west of Dingwall.
Secretary: A. Shinkins. Tel: (01445) 781346.

A seaside links course of 9 holes with spectacular views of the local area and islands.

COURSE INFORMATION

Par 62; SSS 63; Length 4,562 Yards.
Opening Hours: Dawn – Dusk.
Visitors: Welcome.
Avoid: No restricted times.
Ladies: Welcome.
Green Fees: £15 per day; £12 per round; Senior citizens & juniors £7 per day.
Juveniles: With adult no restrictions. Unaccompanied after 2pm.
Clubhouse Hours: 9am-8pm (Easter-September).
Clubhouse Facilities: Light refreshments available.
Open Competitions: Gairloch Bank of Scotland Open, July; Tomatin Distillery Mixed Open, August.

CONVENIENT HOTELS

Gairloch Hotel; Gairloch Sands Hotel; Myrtle Bank Hotel; Millcroft Hotel.

NO.	MEDAL YARDS	GEN. YARDS	PAR	S.I.	NO.	MEDAL YARDS	GEN. YARDS	PAR	S.I.
1	312	309	4	6	10	312	309	4	5
2	185	182	3	11	11	185	182	3	10
3	198	166	3	9	12	198	166	4	12
4	248	209	3	7	13	248	209	4	8
5	411	261	4	3	14	411	261	5	4
6	196	189	3	14	15	196	189	4	15
7	94	91	3	18	16	94	91	4	13
8	521	476	5	1	17	521	476	4	2
9	116	114	3	17	18	116	114	4	16
OUT	2,281	1,997	31		IN	2,281	1,997	36	
					TOTAL	4,562	3,994	72	
					STANDARD & SCRATCH	63	62		

Garmouth & Kingston Golf Club, Garmouth, Fochabers, Morayshire. Tel: (01343) 87388.

LOCATION: North east of Elgin.
SECRETARY: A. Robertson.
Tel: (01343) 87231.

Situated on the west bank of the River Spey, between the twin villages of Garmouth and Kingston. A delightful golf course which offers its own challenge to all standards of golfers. Being flat by nature it is particulary suited to the elderly and family golfers. A modern clubhouse and its facilities are available for use by visitors.

COURSE INFORMATION

Par 67; SSS 67; Length 5,460 Yards.
Opening Hours: All hours.
Visitors: Only when club competitions are not held.
Avoid: After 5pm Tuesday evenings.
Fees: £11 round; £17 day Mon – Fri. £16 & £22 weekends.
Juveniles: Welcome.
Ladies: Welcome.
Ladies Day: Tuesday evenings.
Clubhouse Hours: 7am – 11.30pm.
Clubhouse Dress: No restriction.
Clubhouse Facilities: From 1st May to 30th Sept or by prior arrangement.
Open Competitions: April; May; July; August.

CONVENIENT HOTELS

Garmouth Hotel, Garmouth;
Gordon Arms Hotel, Fochabers.

NO.	YARDS	PAR	S.I.	NO.	YARDS	PAR	S.I.
1	368	4	8	10	384	4	6
2	373	4	13	11	239	3	9
3	417	4	1	12	269	4	18
4	419	4	7	13	126	3	16
5	420	4	3	14	386	4	11
6	106	3	17	15	406	4	2
7	332	4	10	16	217	3	12
8	338	4	5	17	503	5	4
9	166	3	15	18	147	3	14
OUT	2,939	34		IN	2,677	33	
				TOTAL	5,616	37	
STANDARD SCRATCH					67		

Bunker & tree positions indicated.

Golspie Golf Club,
Ferry Road,
Golspie, Sutherland.
Tel: (01408) 633266.

LOCATION: 11 miles North of Dornoch.
SECRETARY: Mrs Marie MacLeod.

Fairly Flat course. Seaside links wooded with heather and the Lochy Pond providing the hazards.

COURSE INFORMATION

Par 68; SSS 68; Length 5,836 Yards.
Visitors: Welcome.
Opening Hours: Open every day.
Avoid: All competition days.
Ladies Day: Tuesday night.
Fees: £15 per day.
Juveniles: Yes.
Clubhouse Hours: All day during season (April – September).
Clubhouse Dress: Casual.
Clubhouse Facilities: Hot meals, snacks, changing room, golf shop, trolley hire.
Open Competitions: July, July, August, August.

CONVENIENT HOTELS

Golf Links Hotel, Golspie;
Stags Head Hotel, Golspie.

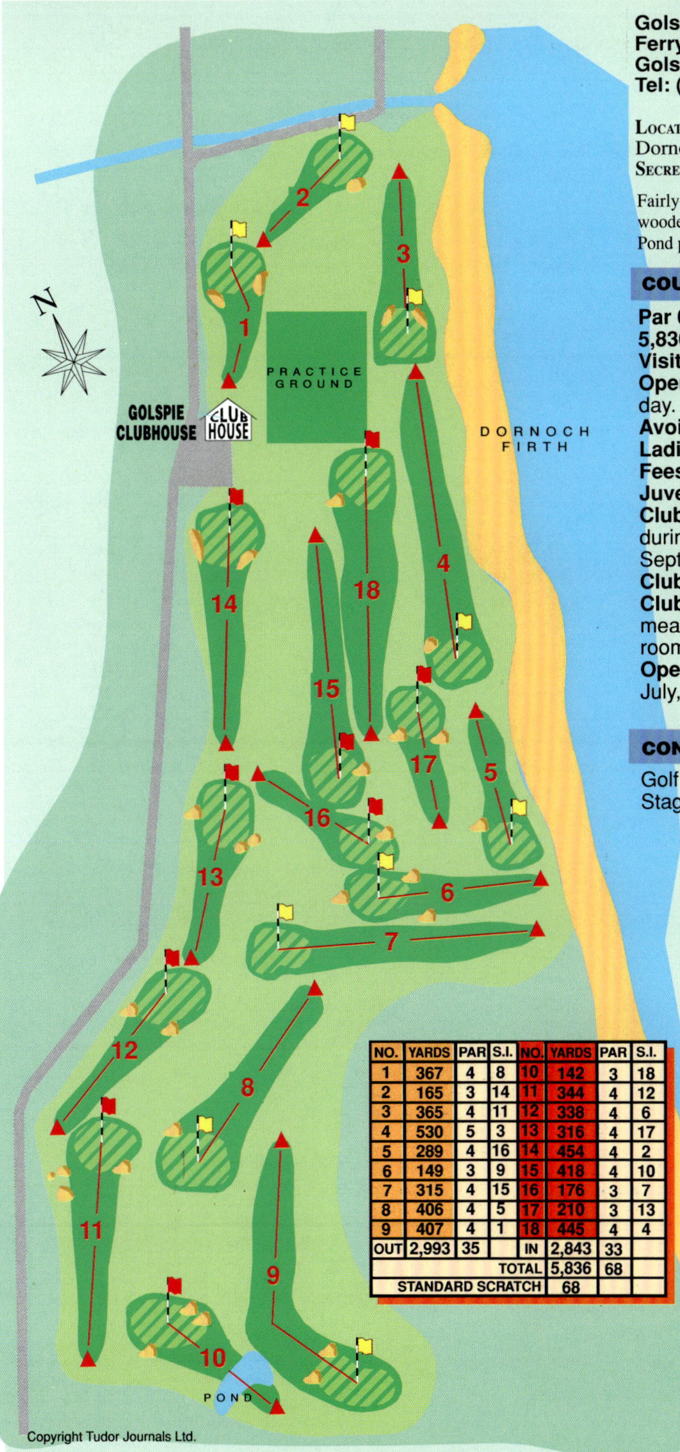

NO.	YARDS	PAR	S.I.	NO.	YARDS	PAR	S.I.
1	367	4	8	10	142	3	18
2	165	3	14	11	344	4	12
3	365	4	11	12	338	4	6
4	530	5	3	13	316	4	17
5	289	4	16	14	454	4	2
6	149	3	9	15	418	4	10
7	315	4	15	16	176	3	7
8	406	4	5	17	210	3	13
9	407	4	1	18	445	4	4
OUT	2,993	35		IN	2,843	33	
				TOTAL	5,836	68	
STANDARD SCRATCH					68		

Bunker positions indicated.

Grantown Golf Club,
Grantown-on-Spey,
Morayshire.
Tel: (01479) 872079.

LOCATION: East side of Grantown.
SECRETARY: D. Elms.
Tel: (01479) 872715.
PROFESSIONAL: Bill Mitchell.
Tel: (01479) 872398.
ARCHITECT: Willie Park / James Braid.

An easy, generous course on relatively flat ground for the first six holes, however the middle six bring you back to reality with the ninth being a hole to savour. The last six in undulating moorland with tight shots required on holes 13 and 15.

COURSE INFORMATION

Par 70, SSS 68, Length 5,745 Yards.
Visitors: Members have priority 8-10am Sat and Sun.
Opening Hours: 8am-Dusk.
Ladies: Welcome.
Fees: £13 per day Mon-Fri; £18 Sat & Sun per day.
Juveniles: Permitted, U16 half above price.
Clubhouse Hours: 9.30-11pm.
Clubhouse Dress: Casual.
Clubhouse Facilities: 9.30-5.30pm or later by arrangement.
Open Competitions: Not yet fixed.

CONVENIENT HOTELS

Dunvegan 872301, Garth 872836; Strathspey Hotel 872002.

NO.	YARDS	PAR	S.I.	NO.	YARDS	PAR	S.I.
1	295	4	15	10	366	4	8
2	441	4	2	11	192	3	13
3	414	4	6	12	412	4	1
4	328	4	14	13	296	4	16
5	362	4	9	14	377	4	4
6	479	5	5	15	267	4	12
7	379	4	3	16	137	3	18
8	158	3	17	17	277	4	7
9	274	4	11	18	291	4	10
OUT	3,130	36		IN	2,615	34	
				TOTAL	5,745	70	
STANDARD SCRATCH					68		

Bunker & tree positions indicated.

Hopeman Golf Club, Hopeman, Morayshire.
Tel: (01343) 830578.

LOCATION: 7 miles north of Elgin on B9012.
SECRETARY: W H Dunbar.
Tel: (01343) 830687.

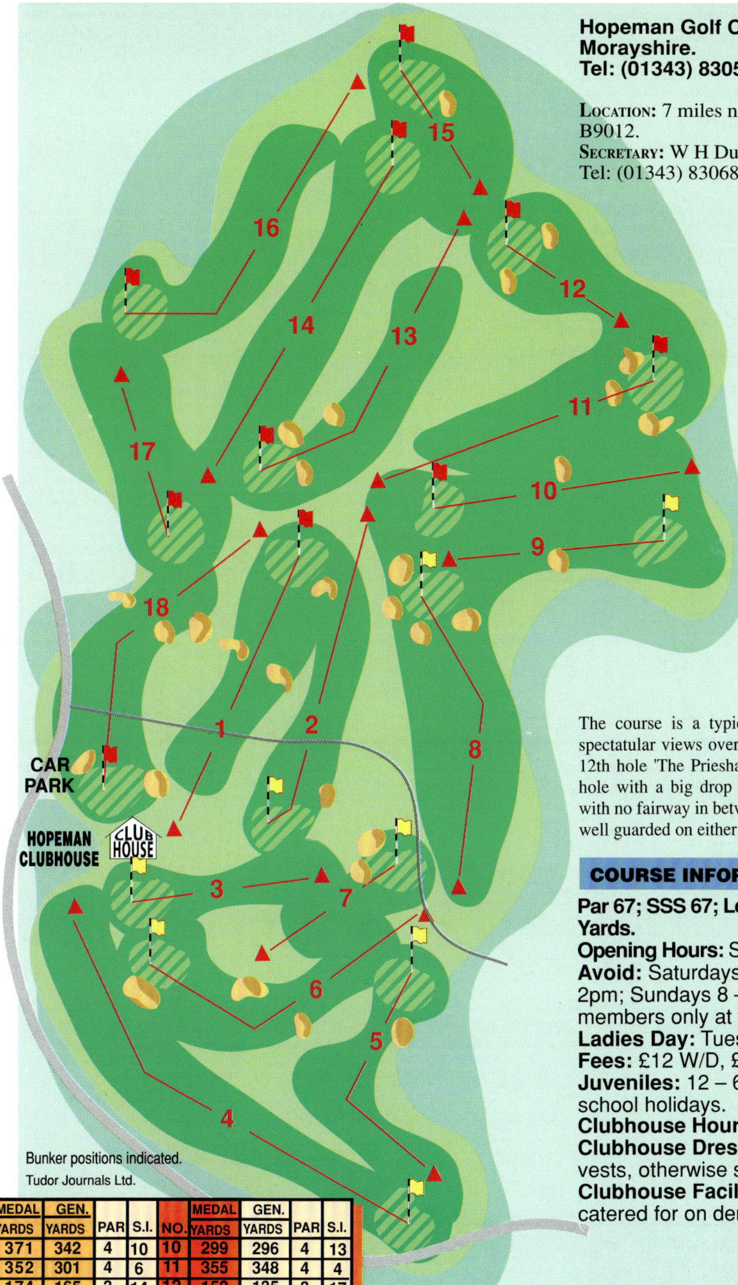

Bunker positions indicated.
Tudor Journals Ltd.

NO.	MEDAL YARDS	GEN. YARDS	PAR	S.I.	NO.	MEDAL YARDS	GEN. YARDS	PAR	S.I.
1	371	342	4	10	10	299	296	4	13
2	352	301	4	6	11	355	348	4	4
3	174	165	3	14	12	152	135	3	17
4	471	460	4	3	13	344	339	4	8
5	342	334	4	9	14	383	371	4	5
6	371	361	4	1	15	106	91	3	18
7	198	179	3	16	16	384	354	4	2
8	346	341	4	11	17	194	194	3	15
9	302	271	4	12	18	387	383	4	7
OUT	2,927	2,754	34		IN	2,604	2,511	33	
					TOTAL	5,531	5,265	67	
					STANDARD SCRATCH	67	67		

The course is a typical links course with spectatular views over the Moray Firth. The 12th hole 'The Prieshach' is the best known hole with a big drop from the tee to green with no fairway in between. The fairways are well guarded on either side by grass bunkers.

COURSE INFORMATION

Par 67; SSS 67; Length 5,531 Yards.
Opening Hours: Sunrise – Sunset.
Avoid: Saturdays 8 – 10am, 12 – 2pm; Sundays 8 – 9.30am, members only at these times.
Ladies Day: Tuesday evenings.
Fees: £12 W/D, £17 W/E.
Juveniles: 12 – 6pm during school holidays.
Clubhouse Hours: 8am – 11pm.
Clubhouse Dress: No sleeveless vests, otherwise suitable attire.
Clubhouse Facilities: Societies catered for on demand.

CONVENIENT HOTELS

Hopeman Lodge provides rental accomodation in the main house and in chalets adjacent on to the course. Station Hotel & Clashack Lodge Hotel in Hopeman.

Isle of Skye Golf Club,
Sconser, Isle of Skye,
IV 48 8TD.
Tel: (01478) 650351.

Location: Between Broadford and Portree.
Secretary: A. MacKenzie.
Tel: (01478) 650351.

COURSE INFORMATION

Par 66; SSS 64, Length 4,796 Yards.
Visitors: Welcome.
Opening Hours: Anytime.
Avoid: Saturday morning.
Ladies: Welcome.
Fees: £8 day; Sat & Sun £10 day.
Open Competitions: BT open July.

CONVENIENT HOTELS

Sligachan Hotel.

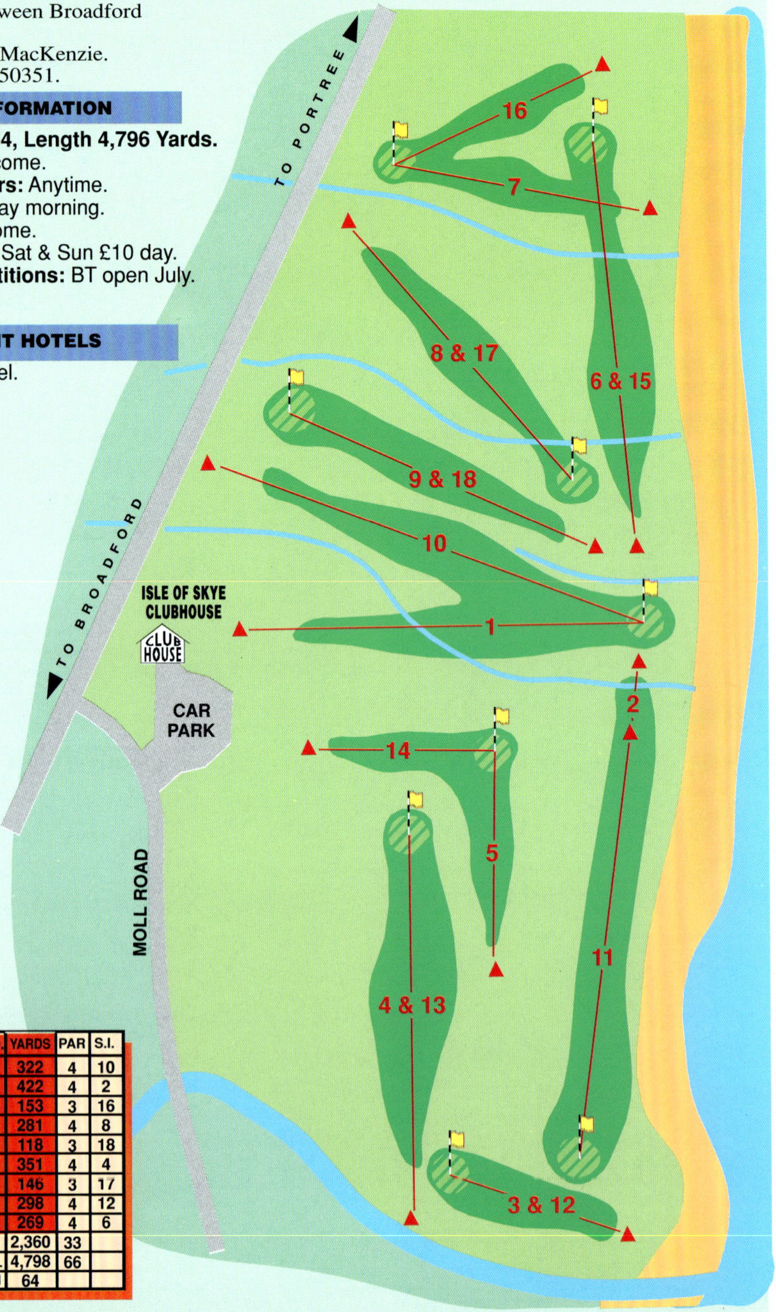

NO.	YARDS	PAR	S.I.	NO.	YARDS	PAR	S.I.
1	322	4	9	10	322	4	10
2	452	4	1	11	422	4	2
3	153	3	15	12	153	3	16
4	281	4	7	13	281	4	8
5	160	3	13	14	118	3	18
6	351	4	3	15	351	4	4
7	152	3	14	16	146	3	17
8	298	4	11	17	298	4	12
9	269	4	5	18	269	4	6
OUT	2,438	33		IN	2,360	33	
				TOTAL	4,798	66	
STANDARD SCRATCH					64		

KINGUSSIE

NORTH

Kingussie Golf Club,
Gynack Road, Kingussie,
Inverness-shire.
Tel: (01504) 661374.

Location: Half a mile from Kingussie.
Secretary: N.D. MacWilliam.
Tel: (01504) 661600.

A very scenic course which provides a good test of golf.

COURSE INFORMATION

Par 67; SSS 66; Length 5,555 Yards.
Opening Hours: Daylight.
Visitors: Welcome.
Avoid: Various days and weekends.
Ladies: Welcome.
Green Fees: Weekdays – £12 per round, £15 per day; Weekends – £14 per round, £18 per day.

Juveniles: Permitted.
Clubhouse Hours: 11am – 11pm.
Clubhouse Dress: Smart.
Clubhouse Facilities: Catering available.

CONVENIENT HOTELS

Numerous in the area.

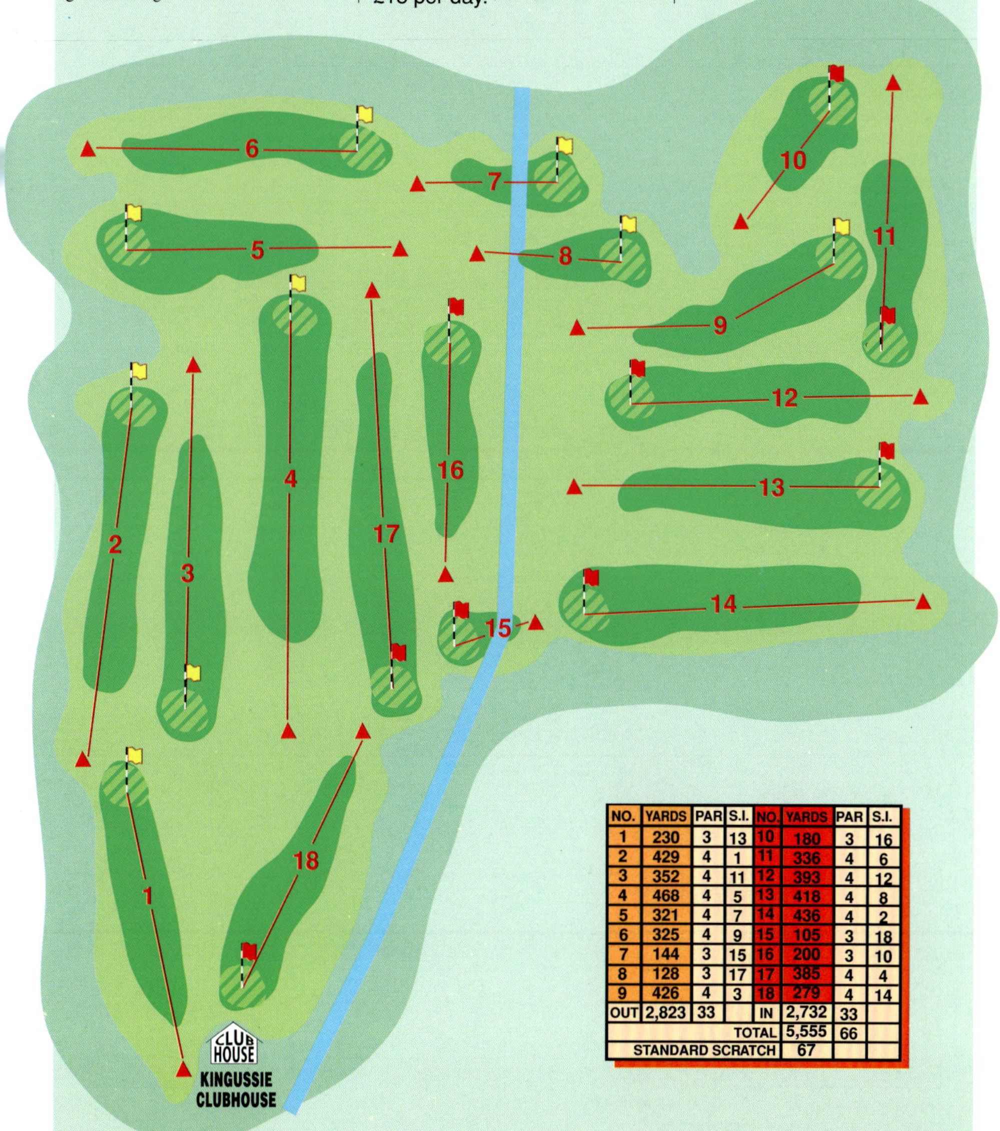

NO.	YARDS	PAR	S.I.	NO.	YARDS	PAR	S.I.
1	230	3	13	10	180	3	16
2	429	4	1	11	336	4	6
3	352	4	11	12	393	4	12
4	468	4	5	13	418	4	8
5	321	4	7	14	436	4	2
6	325	4	9	15	105	3	18
7	144	3	15	16	200	3	10
8	128	3	17	17	385	4	4
9	426	4	3	18	279	4	14
OUT	2,823	33		IN	2,732	33	
				TOTAL	5,555	66	
STANDARD SCRATCH					67		

Lochcarron Golf Club,
Lochcarron,
Strathcarron.

Location: Half a mile east of Lochcarron Village.
Secretary: G.B. Weighill.
Tel: (01520) 722257.

Seaside links and parkland course with very interesting 2nd hole. A short course but great accuracy required. Attractive location and views.

COURSE INFORMATION

Par 62; SSS 60; Length 3,578 Yards.
Visitors: Welcome.
Opening Hours: Daylight.
Avoid: Saturday 2-5pm.
Ladies: Welcome.
Fees: £5 per round, £8 per day, £18 per week.
Juveniles: Permitted.
Clubhouse Hours: None.
Clubhouse Dress: N/A.
Open Competitions: July.

CONVENIENT HOTEL

Lochcarron Hotel.

NO.	YARDS	PAR	S.I.	NO.	YARDS	PAR	S.I.
1	201		13	10	201	3	14
2	209		3	11	209	4	4
3	284		5	12	284	4	6
4	225		11	13	225	4	12
5	158		15	14	158	3	16
6	144		17	15	144	3	10
7	178		7	16	178	3	8
8	125		1	17	125	3	2
9	265		9	18	265	4	10
OUT	1,789			IN	1,789	31	
				TOTAL	3,578	62	
STANDARD SCRATCH					60		

Bunker position indicated.

Moray Golf Club, Storfield Road, Lossiemouth, Morayshire.
Tel: (01343) 812018.

Location: 6 miles north of Elgin.
Secretary: J Hamilton.
Tel: (01343) 812018.
Professional: A. Thomson.
Tel: (01343) 813330.

Both old and new courses Moray are typical links courses. A delight to play and a sure test of accuracy.

COURSE INFORMATION

Par 69; SSS 69; Length 6,005 Yards.
Opening Hours: Sunrise – sunset.
Visitors: Welcome – handicap certificates requested.
Avoid: Not before 10pm.
Ladies: Welcome.
Ladies Day: Mon & Wed.
Fees: On request.
Juveniles: Welcome.
Clubhouse Hours: 11am – 11pm.
Clubhouse Dress: Casual, no sleeveless T shirts.
Clubhouse Facilities: Catering available.
Open Competitions: Moray Open; Boyd Anderson & Tantalus.

CONVENIENT HOTELS

Stotfield Hotel;
Lavenock Bank Hotel; Skerrybrae Hotel; Huntly House Hotel.

NO.	MEDAL YARDS	GEN. YARDS	PAR	S.I.	NO.	MEDAL YARDS	GEN. YARDS	PAR	S.I.
1	361	354	4	10	10	323	318	4	9
2	322	265	4	14	11	158	147	3	17
3	420	415	4	2	12	445	433	4	4
4	141	130	3	16	13	347	342	4	11
5	362	355	4	5	14	503	500	5	1
6	103	96	3	18	15	404	390	4	6
7	426	416	4	7	16	319	314	4	13
8	411	404	4	3	17	177	170	3	15
9	364	350	4	12	18	419	406	4	8
OUT	2,910	2,785	34		IN	3,095	3,020	35	
					TOTAL	6,005	5,805	69	
					STANDARD SCRATCH	69	68		

MORAY (OLD COURSE)

NO.	MEDAL METRES	GEN. METRES	PAR	S.I.	NO.	MEDAL METRES	GEN. METRES	PAR	S.I.
1	333	321	4	11	10	314	254	4	14
2	493	482	5	3	11	415	398	4	2
3	400	391	4	8	12	402	390	4	10
4	203	201	3	13	13	422	397	4	4
5	419	408	4	6	14	417	408	4	7
6	141	134	3	17	15	190	149	3	18
7	439	428	4	9	16	359	348	4	12
8	460	438	4	1	17	497	457	5	5
9	316	284	4	15	18	423	414	4	16
OUT	3,204	3,087	35		IN	3,439	3,215	36	
					TOTAL	6,643	6,302	71	
					STANDARD SCRATCH	73	73		

Moray Golf Club, Storfield Road, Lossiemouth, Morayshire.
Tel: (01343) 812018.

LOCATION: 6 miles north of Elgin.
SECRETARY: J. Hamilton.
Tel: (01343) 812018.
PROFESSIONAL: A. Thomson.
Tel: (01343) 813330.

Both old and new Moray are typical links courses. A delight to play and a sure test of accuracy and golf.

COURSE INFORMATION

Par 71; SSS 73; Length 6,643 Yards.
Opening Hours: Sunrise – Sunset.
Visitors: Welcome handicap certificates requested.
Avoid: Not before 10am.
Ladies: Welcome.
Ladies Day: Mon & Wed.
Fees: On Request.
Juveniles: Welcome.
Clubhouse Hours: 11am – 11pm.
Clubhouse Dress: Casual no sleeveless T shirts.
Clubhouse Facilities: Catering available.
Open Competitions: Moray Open Boyd Anderson & Tantalus.

CONVENIENT HOTELS

Statfield Hotel; Lavenock Bank Hotel; Skerrybrae Hotel; Huntly House Hotel.

THE MUIR OF ORD

The Muir of Ord Golf Club, Great North Road, Muir of Ord, IV6 7SX.
Tel: (01463) 870825.

LOCATION: 15 miles north of Invernness on A862 or A9/A832.
SECRETARY: Mr Brown.
Tel: (01463) 870825.
PROFESSIONAL: Mr Graham Vivers.
Tel: (01463) 871311.
ADMINISTRATOR: Mr D. Noale.
Tel: (01463) 870825.
ARCHITECT: Partly laid out by Mr James Braid.

The course was partly laid out by James Braid. Although in yardage terms it could be considered quite short, the gorse and heather lined fairways and tightly bunkered small greens make it a fine test for those shooting birdies, or an enjoyable easily walked day out on holiday. The course is split on one side by a road and the other by a railway line.

COURSE INFORMATION

Par 67; SSS 66; Length 5,202 Yards.
Visitors: Prohibited before 11am Saturday & Sunday.
Ladies: Welcome.
Ladies Day: Mondays 1.45pm – 3.00pm and 4.45pm – 6.30pm.
Green Fees: Weekends £12 day; Weekends £15 day.
Juveniles: Tee reserved Wednesdays 5.00pm – 5.45pm.
Clubhouse Hours: (Summer) all day – 9.00am – 11.00pm.
Clubhouse Dress: Casual.
Clubhouse Facilities: Catering available.
Open Competitions: Mens Open – April; Open Mixed Pairs – May; Mens 36 hole Open – May; Ladies Open – June.

CONVENIENT HOTELS

Numerous choice in the area.

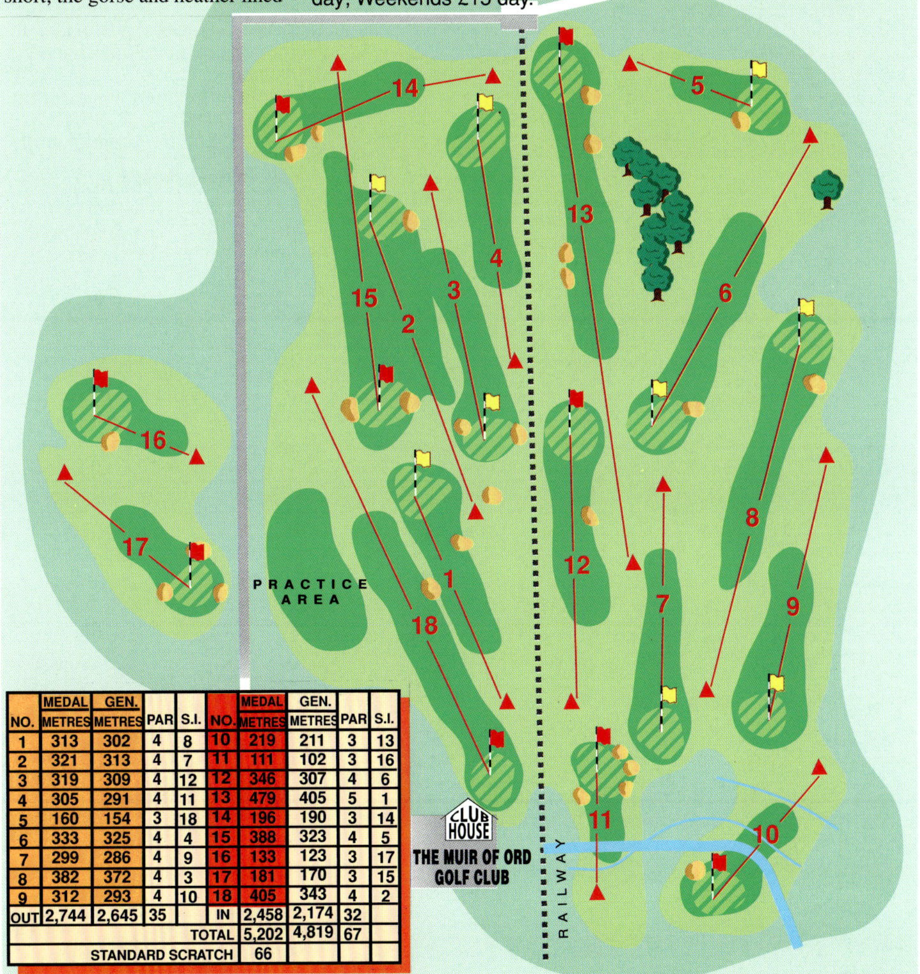

NO.	MEDAL METRES	GEN. METRES	PAR	S.I.	NO.	MEDAL METRES	GEN. METRES	PAR	S.I.
1	313	302	4	8	10	219	211	3	13
2	321	313	4	7	11	111	102	3	16
3	319	309	4	12	12	346	307	4	6
4	305	291	4	11	13	479	405	5	1
5	160	154	3	18	14	196	190	3	14
6	333	325	4	4	15	388	323	4	5
7	299	286	4	9	16	133	123	3	17
8	382	372	4	3	17	181	170	3	15
9	312	293	4	10	18	405	343	4	2
OUT	2,744	2,645	35		IN	2,458	2,174	32	
					TOTAL	5,202	4,819	67	
					STANDARD SCRATCH	66			

Bunker & tree positions indicated.

Nairn Golf Club, Seabank Road, Nairn, Nairnshire. IV12 4HB. Tel: (01667) 453208. Fax: (01667) 456328.

LOCATION: Nairn West Shore.
SECRETARY: Jim Somerville.
Tel: (01667) 452103.
PROFESSIONAL: Robin Fyfe.
Tel: (01667) 452787.
ARCHITECT'S NAME: A Simpson, Old Tom Morris, James Braid.

Nairn is very much a traditional Scottish links wih the opening holes stretching out along the shoreline. At the 10th comes the turn round and the head for home. It is a fine test of golf for amateur and professional alike and with the abundant heather, the great sea of gorse and the distant mountains providing a spectacular backdrop. This is a genuine championship course and with the "Blue Riband" of Amateur Golf the Amatuer Championship in 1994.

COURSE INFORMATION

Par 72; SSS 72, Length 6,722 Yards.
Visitors: Avoid (8-10.30am) and (12.30 - 2.30pm) at weekends.
Opening hours: 8.00am - 6.00am.
Ladies Day: Tuesdays (9.00-10.00am).
Juveniles: With senior handicap.
Clubhouse hours: 9.00-6.00pm (Winter) – 9.00 - 11.00pm (Summer).
Clubhouse Dress: Tie and jacket in dining room after 7pm - no jeans permitted.
Clubhouse facilities: full catering available (Telephone A. Belford (01667) 452103 for arrangement).

CONVENIENT HOTELS

Golf View (452301), Windsor (453108), Newton (453144), Ramleh (453551), Altonburn (453325), Links (453321).

NO.	YARDS	PAR	S.I.	NO.	YARDS	PAR	S.I.
1	400	4	13	10	540	5	5
2	499	5	4	11	161	3	18
3	400	4	10	12	445	4	2
4	145	3	17	13	435	4	7
5	378	4	1	14	221	3	15
6	183	3	12	15	309	4	11
7	551	5	6	16	422	4	3
8	359	4	9	17	361	4	14
9	359	4	16	18	554	5	8
OUT	3,274	36		IN	3,448	36	
				TOTAL	6,722	72	
STANDARD SCRATCH					72		

Bunker & tree positions indicated.

NAIRN DUNBAR

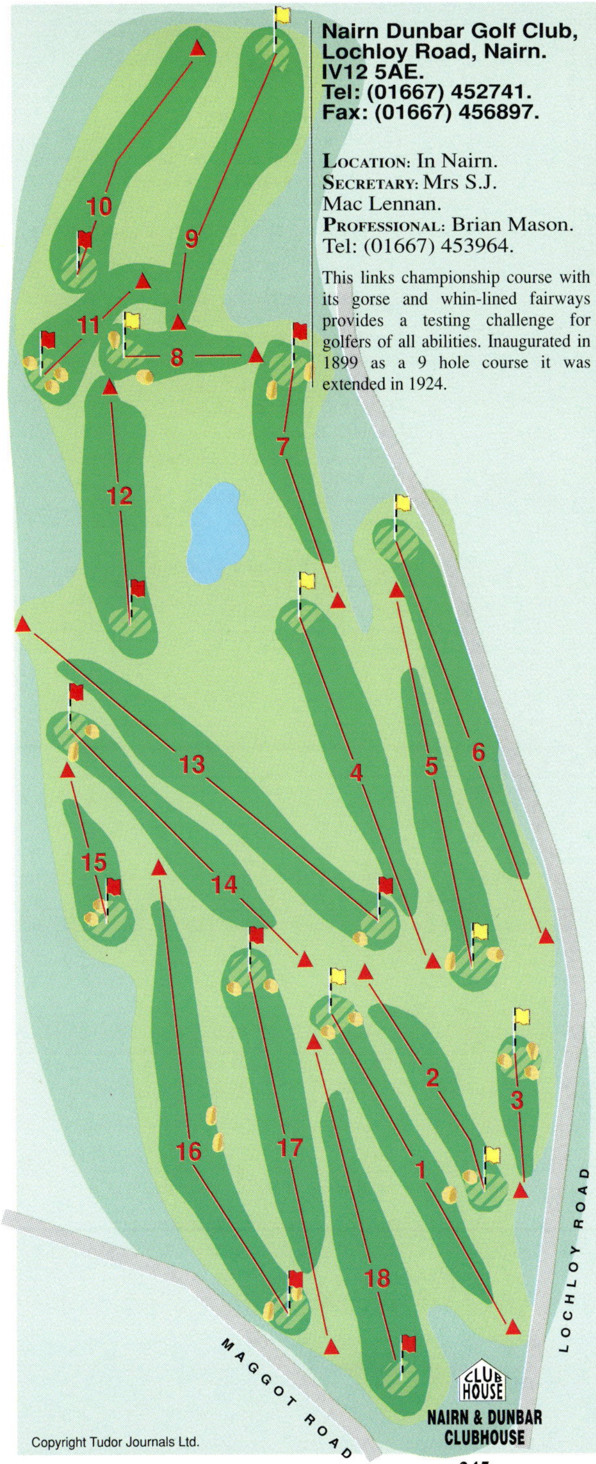

Nairn Dunbar Golf Club, Lochloy Road, Nairn. IV12 5AE. Tel: (01667) 452741. Fax: (01667) 456897.

LOCATION: In Nairn.
SECRETARY: Mrs S.J. Mac Lennan.
PROFESSIONAL: Brian Mason. Tel: (01667) 453964.

This links championship course with its gorse and whin-lined fairways provides a testing challenge for golfers of all abilities. Inaugurated in 1899 as a 9 hole course it was extended in 1924.

COURSE INFORMATION

Par 72; SSS 72; Length 6,712 Yards.
Opening Hours: 8am – 7pm.
Visitors: Welcome.
Avoid: 8am – 9.30am, 12.30pm – 1.30pm, 4.30pm – 7.30pm.
Ladies: Welcome.
Green Fees: Monday–Friday Round £18.50; Day £25; Saturday/Sunday Round £25; Day £30.
Juveniles: Welcome but restricted between 8am – 10am; 12noon – 2pm and 5pm – 7pm.
Clubhouse Hours: 11am – 11pm.
Clubhouse Dress: Smart/Casual no jeans.
Clubhouse Facilities: Catering facilities available.

CONVENIENT HOTELS

The Windsor Hotel.
The Links Hotel.
The Golf View Hotel.

NO.	YARDS	PAR	S.I.	NO.	YARDS	PAR	S.I.
1	418	4	5	10	414	4	2
2	333	4	15	11	126	3	18
3	189	3	13	12	381	4	9
4	448	4	8	13	529	5	6
5	453	4	1	14	346	4	14
6	419	4	7	15	161	3	16
7	395	4	3	16	503	5	11
8	155	3	17	17	442	4	4
9	501	5	10	18	499	5	12
OUT	3,311	35		IN	3,401	37	
				TOTAL	6,712	72	
STANDARD SCRATCH					72		

Bunker positions indicated.

NO.	YARDS	PAR	S.I.	NO.	YARDS	PAR	S.I.
1	350	4	9	10	220	3	16
2	484	5	12	11	302	4	5
3	348	4	2	12	481	5	15
4	153	3	17	13	142	3	8
5	259	4	6	14	218	3	10
6	322	4	11	15	286	4	7
7	145	3	1	16	284	4	14
8	268	4	18	17	309	4	4
9	516	5	3	18	319	4	13
OUT	2,845	36		IN	2,561	34	
				TOTAL	5,406	70	
STANDARD SCRATCH						68	

Orkney Golf Club, Grainbank, Kirkwall, Orkney.
Tel: (01856) 2457.

Location: One mile west of Kirkwall.
Secretary: L. Howard.
Tel: (01856) 874165.

Parkland course with beautiful views over town and North Isles.

COURSE INFORMATION

Par 70, SSS 67, Length 5,411 Yards.
Visitors: Welcome.
Avoid: Competition days.
Opening Hours: All hours.
Ladies: Welcome.
Fees: £10 per day; £35 per week; £50 per fortnight
Juveniles: Welcome.
Clubhouse Hours: All hours 11am - 11pm.
Clubhouse Dress: Optional
Clubhouse Facilities: Catering Facilities available.
Open Competitions: July (36 holes).

Reay Golf Club, Reay, by Thurso, Caithness.
Tel: (01847) 811288.

Location: 12 miles from Thurso.
Secretary: Miss Patricia Peebles.
Tel: (01847) 81537.

Being the most northerly links on the British mainland the course is a natural seaside linls overlooking Sandside Bay and the Pentland Firth. The length of the course is 5,884 yards with the opening hole being a tricky 240 yard par 3 - the downfall of amny a good medal round. Thereafter things can only get easier with the nexy few holes being varied and interesting - attempt the short cuts but beware the penalties.

COURSE INFORMATION

Par 69; SSS 68; Length 5,884 Yards.
Opening Hours: 8am-dusk.
Visitors: Welcome.
Avoid: Saturday mornings May – September; Competitions.
Ladies: Welcome.
Green Fees: £10.
Juveniles: Welcome.
Clubhouse Hours: 12 noon – 2pm weekdays (June – Sept), 8pm – 11pm every evening.
Clubhouse Dress: Neat.
Clubhouse Facilities: Bar snacks and lunches available from June – September.
Open Competition: Mens Open – June; Ladies Open – July; Mixed Open – August.

CONVENIENT HOTELS

The Forss House Hotel, Forrs; The Melvich Hotel, Melvich.

NO.	YARDS	PAR	S.I.	NO.	YARDS	PAR	S.I.
1	238	3	9	10	360	4	6
2	431	4	5	11	414	4	2
3	370	4	11	12	349	4	10
4	584	5	1	13	309	4	12
5	145	3	17	14	479	5	4
6	492	5	3	15	138	3	18
7	198	3	13	16	309	4	16
8	400	4	7	17	334	4	8
9	174	3	15	18	160	3	14
OUT	3,032	34		IN	2,852	35	
				TOTAL	5,884	69	
				STANDARD SCRATCH	68		

Royal Dornoch Golf Club, Golf Road, Dornoch, Sutherland, IV25 3LW.
Tel: (01862) 810219.

LOCATION: 51 miles north of Inverness.
SECRETARY: J.S. Duncan.
PROFESSIONAL: W.E. Skinner.
ARCHITECT: Tom Morris, J. Sutherland, D. Ross & G.Duncan.

One of the great natural links courses in the world. In the words of Herbert Warren Wim "A thoroughly modern old links with that rare equipoise of charm and charater that only great courses possess". There is plenty of room off the tee but where to place your drive depends on the wind and the pin positions. If you think out your shot will be rewarded.

COURSE INFORMATION

Par 70; SSS 73; Length 6,514 Yards.
Opening Hours: 7am – 11pm.
Visitors: Welcome.
Avoid: Major competitions.
Ladies: Welcome.
Green Fees: On request.
Juveniles: Welcome (with handicap).
Clubhouse Hours: 7am – 11pm.
Clubhouse Dress: Smart/Casual.
Clubhouse Facilities: Catering facilities available throughout the day.
Open Competitions: Carnegie Shield – second week in August.

CONVENIENT HOTELS

The Royal Golf Hotel; The Castle Hotel; The Marine Hotel.

NO.	MEDAL YARDS	GEN. YARDS	PAR	S.I.	NO.	MEDAL YARDS	GEN. YARDS	PAR	S.I.
1	331	300	4	7	10	147	142	3	16
2	177	167	3	15	11	446	434	4	4
3	414	398	4	11	12	507	489	5	12
4	427	403	4	3	13	166	148	3	18
5	354	317	4	9	14	445	439	4	2
6	163	163	3	17	15	319	298	4	10
7	463	423	4	1	16	402	395	4	6
8	396	386	4	5	17	405	390	4	8
9	496	447	5	13	18	456	446	4	14
OUT	3,221	3,004	35		IN	3,293	3,181	35	
					TOTAL	6,514	6,185	70	
					STANDARD SCRATCH	73			

Bunker positions indicated.

NO.	YARDS	PAR	S.I.	NO.	YARDS	PAR	S.I.
1	355	4	8	10	386	4	9
2	153	3	18	11	175	3	45
3	368	4	3	12	358	4	13
4	337	4	12	13	362	4	7
5	371	4	6	14	156	3	16
6	142	3	17	15	368	4	2
7	388	4	1	16	323	4	14
8	333	4	10	17	457	4	4
9	381	4	5	18	363	4	11
OUT	2,828	34		IN	2,948	34	
				TOTAL	5,776	68	
STANDARD SCRATCH					70		

Shetland Golf Club, P.O. Box 18, Lerwick, Shetland
Tel: (01595) 840369.

LOCATION: 31/2 miles north of Lerwick.
SECRETARY: Mr D. Bently.
Tel: (01595) 840369.
ARCHITECT: Frazer Middleton.

All the holes can be seen from the clubhouse. The course is set in a valley with a burn running down the middle which comes into play in five holes. There are water hazards at a further three holes. The ground is generally soft, so there is never much run on the ball so it always plays longer than the 5776 yards.

COURSE INFORMATION

Par 68; SSS 70; Length 5,776 Yards.
Visitors: Welcome; except Tuesday nights and certain competitions.
Avoid: Certain competitions (phone in advance) and Tuesday nights.
Ladies: Welcome; except certain competitions
Ladies Day: Tuesday night.
Green Fees: £8 per day.
Juveniles: Permitted.
Clubhouse hours: 7.30pm – 11pm. Mon – Frid; All day Sat & sun.
Clubhouse Dress: Informal.
Clubhouse Facilities: Limited.
Open Competitions: Seniors Open & Mixed Open August; Ladies Open & Junior Open June.

Spean Bridge Golf Club,
Spean Bridge,
Ivernesshire, PH34 4EU.

LOCATION: 9 miles north of Fort William on A92.
SECRETARY: John MacLennan.
Tel: (01397) 712340.

Rural setting 9 hole course set on a hillside with good views of the Ben Nevis range mountains.

COURSE INFORMATION

Par 66; SSS 62; Length 2,230 Yards.
Opening Hours: All day.
Visitors: Welcome.
Avoid: Tuesday after five.
Ladies: Welcome.
Green Fees: £7 per day.
Juveniles: Welcome
Clubhouse Dress: No restrictions.
Clubhouse Facilities: None.

CONVENIENT HOTELS

Spean Bridge Hotel.
Numerous guest houses in the area.

NO.	YARDS	PAR	S.I.	NO.	YARDS	PAR	S.I.
1	119	3		10	119	3	
2	256	4		11	256	4	
3	270	4		12	270	4	
4	250	4		13	250	4	
5	272	4		14	272	4	
6	305	4		15	305	4	
7	287	4		16	287	4	
8	266	4		17	266	4	
9	178	3		18	178	3	
OUT	2,203	33		IN	2,203	33	
				TOTAL	4,406	66	
				STANDARD SCRATCH	62		

Tree positions indicated.

STORNAWAY

NORTH

Stornoway Golf Club, Lady Lever Park, Stornoway, Outer Hebrides.
Tel: (01851) 762240.

LOCATION: In the grounds of Lewis Castle 1/2 mile from town centre, Isle of Lewis.
SECRETARY: G. Davies.
Tel: (01851) 702971.

Stornoway presents an intriguing course playing harder that its 5178 yards sss 66 implies. On the inward half, the 551 yard par 5 hole aptly named the "Dardanelles" is reputedly one of the most difficult par 5's in Europe, and the course is worth playing just for the challenge of it.

NO.	YARDS	PAR	S.I.	NO.	YARDS	PAR	S.I.
1	353	4	15	10	182	3	14
2	483	5	3	11	551	5	1
3	174	3	13	12	295	4	8
4	346	4	9	13	266	4	10
5	312	4	1	14	309	4	3
6	280	4	11	15	143	3	18
7	273	4	7	16	362	4	5
8	267	4	18	17	230	3	16
9	143	3	5	18	209	3	12
OUT	2,631	35		IN	2,547	33	
				TOTAL	5,178	68	
STANDARD SCRATCH							

COURSE INFORMATION

Par 68; SSS 66; Length 5,119 Yards.
Visitors: Welcome; except on Sundays.
Avoid: Sundays.
Ladies: Welcome.
Green Fees: £10 per day; £30 per week; £50 per fortnight.
Juveniles: Welcome.
Clubhouse Hours: Monday – Friday 4pm – 11pm; Saturday 11am – 11pm during winter. In season clubhouse is open 7am – 11pm; and the bar is open from 11am – 2pm; 4pm – 11pm.
Clubhouse Dress: Smart/Casual.
Clubhouse Facilities: Snack meals are available during bar opening hours and coffee is available throughout the day from the shop. Toilets and showers are available to visitors.

CONVENIENT HOTEL

The Caria Hotel Group.

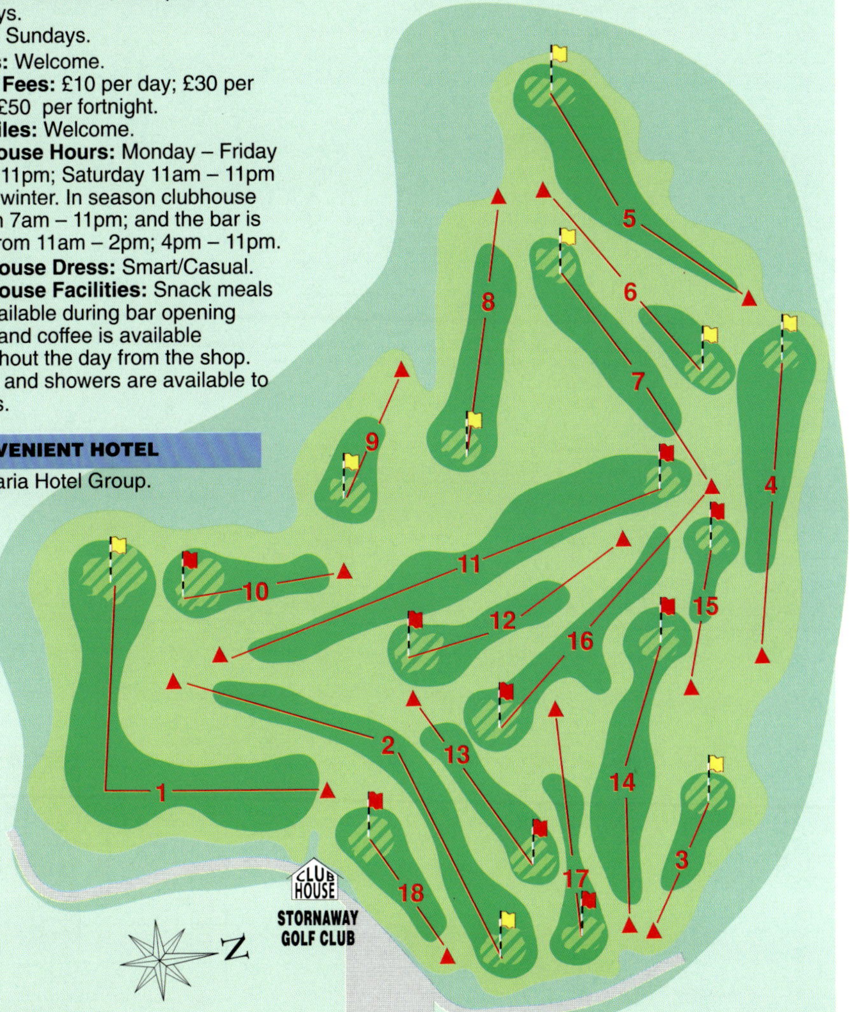

STRATHPEFFER

Strathpeffer Spa Golf Club, Strathpeffer. IV14 9AS.
Tel: (01997) 21219.

LOCATION: 1/4 mile north of Strathpepper Square (Signposted).
SECRETARY: N. Roxburgh. Tel: (01997) 421396.
ARCHITECT: Willie Park.

Upland course; panoramic views of mountains and moorlands; no bunkers, but plenty of natural hazards — burns, ponds, broom, whin, etc., Course is short, but very testing. Two par 3 holes across water.

COURSE INFORMATION

Par 65; SSS 65; Length 4,792 Yards.
Opening Hours: Daylight hours.
Visitors: Welcome; check weekends and Competition days Tues/Fri.
Avoid: Club competition times; Sundays before 10.30am.
Ladies: Welcome; see above.
Ladies Day: Friday 4pm – 7.30pm; Members only.
Green Fees: Weekdays £10 per round; £15 per day; Weekends £12 per round; £18 per day.
Juveniles: Welcome; restricted as above.
Clubhouse Hours: 8am – 12pm.
Clubhouse Dress: Casual, but respectable.
Clubhouse Facilities: Snacks all day, lunch 12 – 2.30pm; High teas - booking only.
Open Competitions: Junior Open Sept., Ladies May; Open Mixed Foursomes June 18 hole Wall-on May & Sept.

CONVENIENT HOTELS

Brunstane Lodge; Strathpeffer; Holly Lodge Hotel; Strathpeffer; Craigdarroch Lodge Hotel, Contin, Strathpeffer.

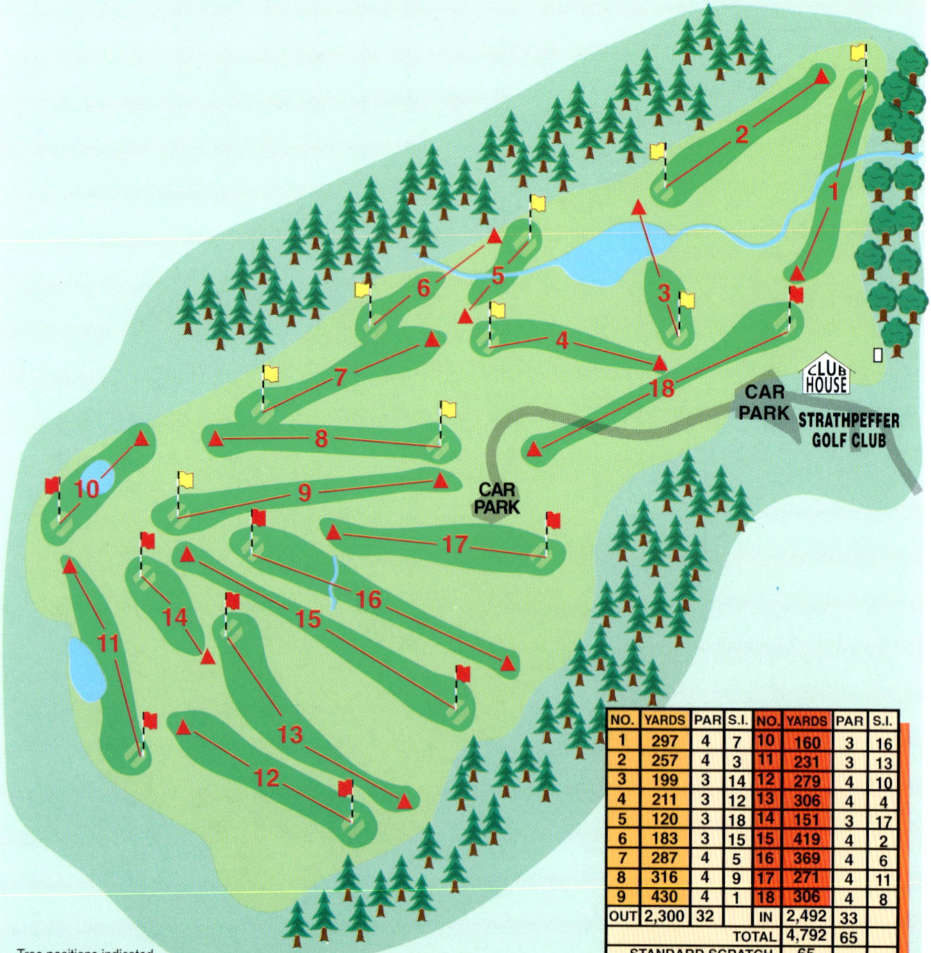

NO.	YARDS	PAR	S.I.	NO.	YARDS	PAR	S.I.
1	297	4	7	10	160	3	16
2	257	4	3	11	231	3	13
3	199	3	14	12	279	4	10
4	211	3	12	13	306	4	4
5	120	3	18	14	151	3	17
6	183	3	15	15	419	4	2
7	287	4	5	16	369	4	6
8	316	4	9	17	271	4	11
9	430	4	1	18	306	4	8
OUT	2,300	32		IN	2,492	33	
				TOTAL	4,792	65	
				STANDARD SCRATCH	65		

Tree positions indicated.

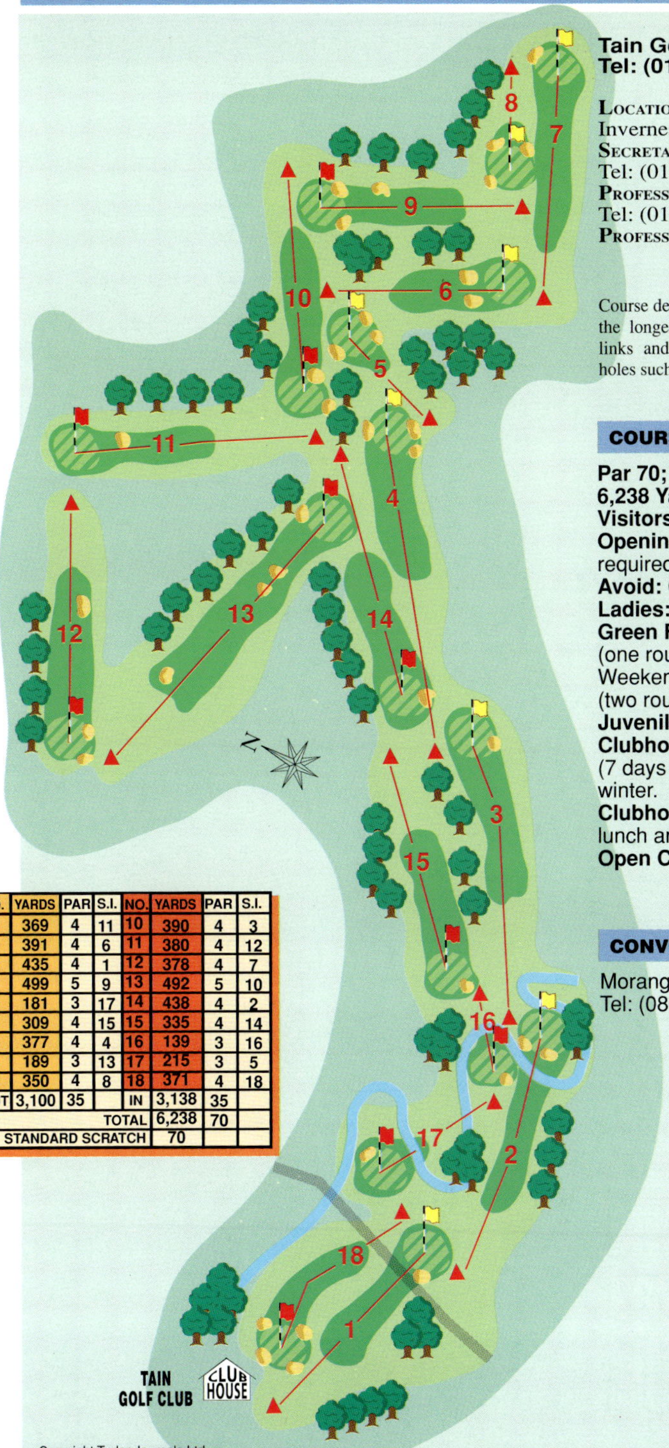

NO.	YARDS	PAR	S.I.	NO.	YARDS	PAR	S.I.
1	369	4	11	10	390	4	3
2	391	4	6	11	380	4	12
3	435	4	1	12	378	4	7
4	499	5	9	13	492	5	10
5	181	3	17	14	438	4	2
6	309	4	15	15	335	4	14
7	377	4	4	16	139	3	16
8	189	3	13	17	215	3	5
9	350	4	8	18	371	4	18
OUT	3,100	35		IN	3,138	35	
				TOTAL	6,238	70	
				STANDARD SCRATCH	70		

Bunker & tree positions indicated.

Tain Golf Club, Tain, IV19 1PA.
Tel: (01862) 892314.

Location: 35 miles North of Inverness.
Secretary: Mrs K. Ross
Tel: (01862) 892314.
Professional: D & J Geekie.
Tel: (01294) 893313.
Professional: Tom Morris.

Course designed in 1890 by Tom Morris. It is the longest course in Rosshire and is part links and part inland with several testing holes such as the Alps 11th hole.

COURSE INFORMATION

Par 70; SSS 70; Length 6,238 Yards.
Visitors: Welcome.
Opening Hours: Whenever required.
Avoid: Competition days.
Ladies: Welcome.
Green Fees: Weekdays – £12 (one round), £18 (two rounds); Weekends – £18 (one round), £24 (two rounds).
Juveniles: Welcome.
Clubhouse Hours: 11am – 11pm (7 days in summer) restricted in winter.
Clubhouse Facilities: Full bar, lunch and evening meals menu.
Open Competitions: Numerous.

CONVENIENT HOTELS

Morangie House Hotel, Tain,
Tel: (0862) 892281.

TARBAT

Tarbat Golf Club,
Portmahomack,
IV20 1YA.
Tel: (01862 87) 236.

LOCATION: 9 Miles South East of Tain (Follow B9165 from A9).

SECRETARY: D Wilson.
Tel: (01349) 852131.
Fax: (01349) 853715.

A testing links course situated overlooking the Dornoch Firth, with 3/4 tight greens. A challenging course for low handicappers.

COURSE INFORMATION

Par 66; SSS 65; Length 2,568 Yards.
Opening Hours: Sunrise – Sunset.
Visitors: Welcome; except Saturday morning.
Avoid: Saturday morning.
Ladies: Welcome; except Saturday morning.
Ladies Day: Wednesday.
Green Fees: Weekdays £5 per day; £20 per week; Weekend £6 per day
Juveniles: Accompanied by an adult.
Clubhouse hours: Sunrise – Sunset.
Clubhouse Dress: Casual.
Clubhouse Facilities: Coffee and tea.
Open Competitions: August.

CONVENIENT HOTELS

Castle Hotel, Tel: 87263;
Oyster Catcher, Tel: 87560;
Caledonian Hotel, Tel: 87345.

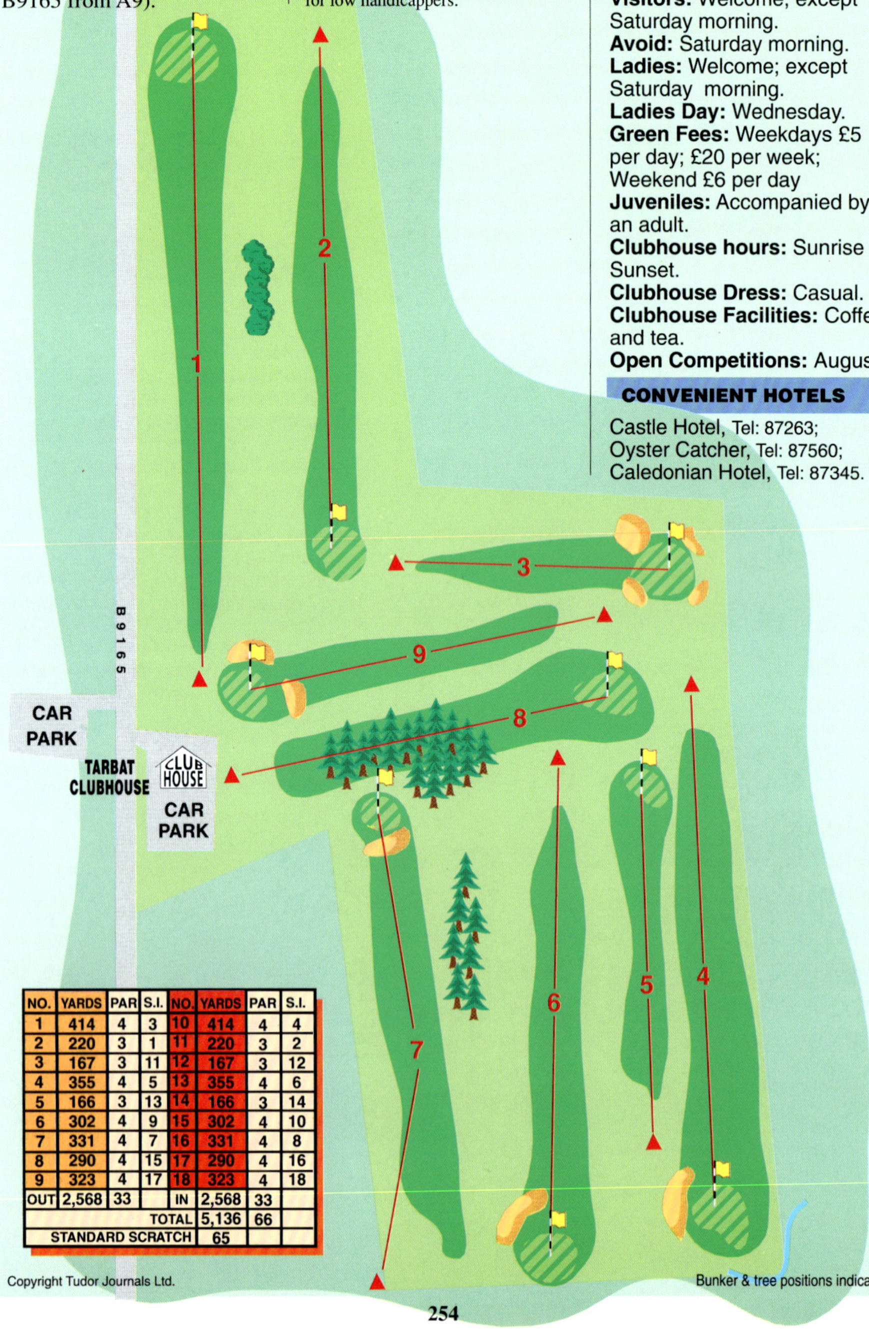

NO.	YARDS	PAR	S.I.	NO.	YARDS	PAR	S.I.
1	414	4	3	10	414	4	4
2	220	3	1	11	220	3	2
3	167	3	11	12	167	3	12
4	355	4	5	13	355	4	6
5	166	3	13	14	166	3	14
6	302	4	9	15	302	4	10
7	331	4	7	16	331	4	8
8	290	4	15	17	290	4	16
9	323	4	17	18	323	4	18
OUT	2,568	33		IN	2,568	33	
				TOTAL	5,136	66	
STANDARD SCRATCH					65		

Bunker & tree positions indicated.

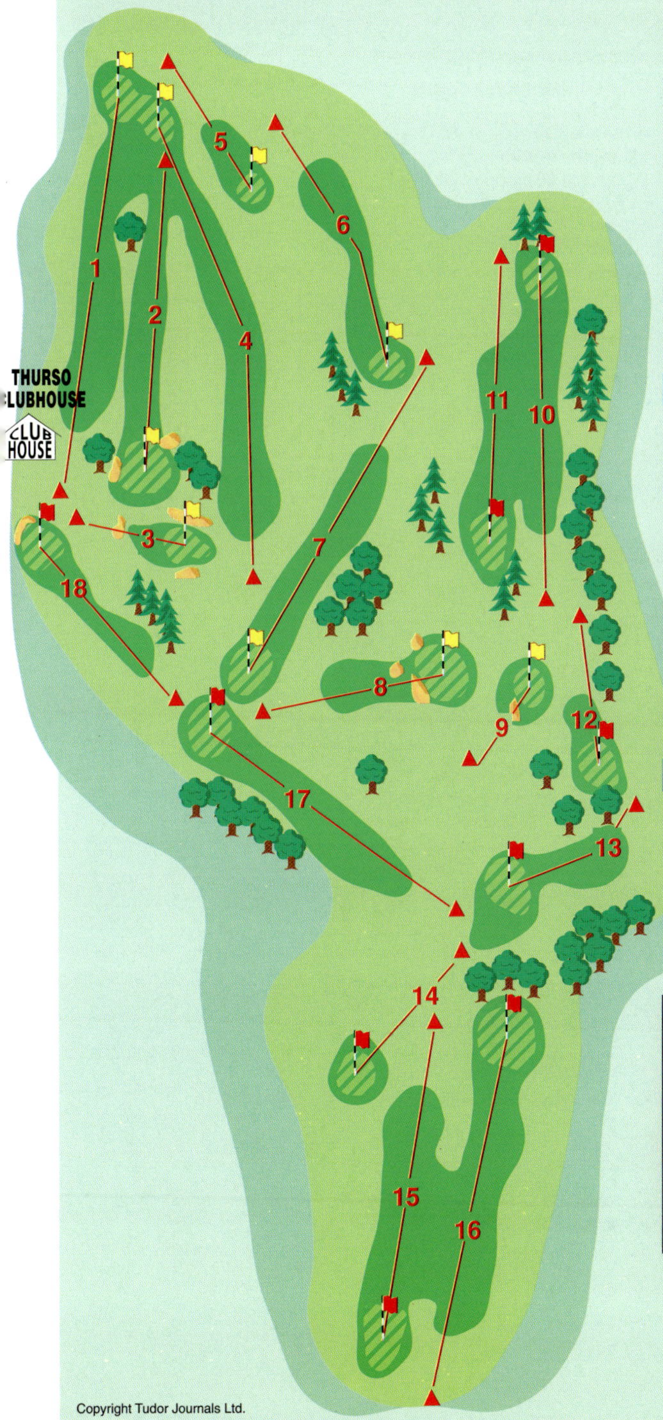

Thurso Golf Club,
Newlands of Geise, Thurso.
Tel: (01847) 893807.

LOCATION: One and a half miles west of Thurso on B874.
SECRETARY: Mrs Wendy Meiklejohn.
Tel: (01847) 895024.

Course offers magnificent panaromic views of Dunnet Head and the Orkney Islands. Recent extensive drainage and fairway contouring have greatly improved the course. Clubhouse renowned for its friendly atmosphere and the welcome given to visitors.

COURSE INFORMATION

Par 69; SSS 69; Length 5,818 Yards.
Visitors: Welcome.
Opening Hours: All day.
Avoid: Tuesday 4.30 – 6.00pm, Thursday 4.30 – 6.00 pm.
Ladies: No restrictions.
Ladies Day: Tuesday.
Fees: £10 (£5 with a member).
Juveniles: Permitted.
Clubhouse Hours: 9am – 11pm summer season.
Clubhouse Dress: Casual.
Clubhouse Facilities: As above hours.

CONVENIENT HOTELS

Royal Pentland; Central; St Clair; Station; Weigh Inn, Thurso.

NO.	YARDS	PAR	S.I.	NO.	YARDS	PAR	S.I.
1	406	4	3	10	410	4	4
2	373	4	7	11	365	4	8
3	186	3	12	12	219	3	9
4	514	5	1	13	274	4	11
5	189	3	14	14	148	3	18
6	353	4	10	15	354	4	13
7	492	5	5	16	429	4	2
8	270	4	17	17	372	4	6
9	158	3	15	18	306	4	16
OUT	2,941	35		IN	2,941	34	
				TOTAL	5,818	69	
STANDARD SCRATCH					69		

Bunker & tree positions indicated.

TORVEAN

Torvean Golf Club,
Glenurquhart Road,
Inverness-Shire.
Tel: (01463) 711434.

LOCATION: West Side of Inverness on A82 Towards Fortwilliam.
SECRETARY: Mrs K.M. Gray. Tel: (01463) 225651.
ARCHITECT: William Hamilton.

A municipal Golf course set approximately one mile from Inverness town centre. A parkland course which was extended 1989 to include a challenging 565 yards par 5. Continually being improved with the planting of trees and the recent installation of a new green on the 18th, Torvean is a fair test of golf for any player.

COURSE INFORMATION

Par 69; SSS 68; Length 5,784 Yards.
Opening hours: 8am – 9pm Summer months.
Visitors: Welcome; booking preferred at weekends.
Ladies: Welcome.
Ladies Day: Sunday.
Green Fees: Weekdays £8.60 round £11.50 day; Weekends £10 round £13 day.
Juveniles: Welcome.
Clubhouse Hours: 11am – 11pm; 7 days, April – October.
Clubhouse Dress: Casual.
Clubhouse Facilities: Light catering available.

CONVENIENT HOTEL

Loch Ness House Hotel. (Opposite Clubhouse)

NO.	YARDS	PAR	S.I.	NO.	YARDS	PAR	S.I.
1	194	3	8	10	286	4	15
2	358	4	4	11	526	5	9
3	273	4	16	12	400	4	5
4	270	4	18	13	410	4	3
5	565	5	2	14	338	4	11
6	277	4	12	15	174	3	17
7	157	3	14	16	471	4	1
8	277	4	6	17	164	3	13
9	220	3	10	18	424	4	7
OUT	2,591	34		IN	3,193	35	
				TOTAL	5,784	69	
STANDARD SCRATCH					68		

Tree positions indicated.

Whalsay Golf Club, Skaw Taing,
Whalsay, Shetland Isles.
Tel: (01806) 6481.

LOCATION: Isle of Whalsay in Shetland, 12 miles from Lerwick.
SECRETARY: H.A. Sandison, C. Hutchinson.
Tel: (01806) 6450 or 6481.

The most northerly golf course in the British Isles on a heathland with cliff coastline. Offers a challenging test in golf skills while allowing the player to enjoy the magnificent scenery. Good tees and greens – best in Summer and Autumn.

COURSE INFORMATION

Par 70; SSS 70; Length 6,009 Yards.
Opening Hours: All day.
Visitors: Welcome.
Ladies: Welcome.
Green Fees: £5 per day & £20 per week.
Juveniles: Permitted.
Clubhouse Hours: All day.
Clubhouse Dress: Casual.
Clubhouse Facilities: No catering. Changing rooms. Refreshments can be arranged by members.
Open Competitions: Whalsay Open – June.

CONVENIENT HOTELS

Lingaveg Guest House;
Tel: (01806) 6489.

NO.	YARDS	PAR	S.I.	NO.	YARDS	PAR	S.I.
1	401	4	10	10	381	4	4
2	399	4	4	11	398	4	12
3	150	3	17	12	529	5	1
4	311	4	6	13	202	3	14
5	140	3	18	14	342	4	8
6	337	4	9	15	346	4	13
7	165	3	15	16	510	5	3
8	482	5	2	17	175	3	16
9	355	4	11	18	386	4	7
OUT	2,740	34		IN	3,269	36	
				TOTAL	6,009	70	
				STANDARD SCRATCH	70		

Wick Golf Club, Reiss, Wick, Caithness. KW1 4RW. Tel: (01955) 2726.

LOCATION: 3 miles north of Wick off the A9.
SECRETARY: Mr J.S. Bain. 5 Miller Ave, Wick. Tel: (01955) 3278.
ARCHITECT: Sutherland.

Typical links course. Challenging to all standards of golfers. Panoramic view of Sinclair Bay. Well worth a visit. One of the oldest courses in the north of Scotland. Established 1870.

COURSE INFORMATION

Par 69; SSS 69; Length 5,976 Yards.
Opening Hours: All day.
Visitors: Welcome, no restrictions.
Avoid: Wednesdays mens competitions.
Ladies: Welcome.
Green Fees: £10 after 5 pm; £15 Day ticket.
Juveniles: Welcome.
Clubhouse Hours: Evenings Sat from 11am - Sunday 12pm.
Clubhouse Dress: Casual.
Clubhouse Facilities: New clubhouse facility. Showers, catering etc.

CONVENIENT HOTELS

Mackay's Hotel, Wick;
Mercury, Wick.

NO.	MEDAL YARDS	GEN. YARDS	PAR	S.I.	NO.	MEDAL YARDS	GEN. YARDS	PAR	S.I.
1	286	279	4	15	10	403	389	4	3
2	353	328	4	8	11	171	164	3	12
3	352	332	4	6	12	416	364	4	2
4	203	192	3	11	13	390	368	4	5
5	423	407	4	1	14	149	144	3	18
6	375	335	4	13	15	291	283	4	14
7	389	371	4	4	16	188	149	3	9
8	507	440	5	10	17	549	534	5	16
9	152	140	3	17	18	379	296	4	7
OUT	3,040	2,824	35		IN	2,936	2,691	34	
					TOTAL	5,976	5,515	69	
					STANDARD SCRATCH	69	72		

Bunker positions indicated.

Banchory Golf Club, Kinneskie, Banchory, Kincardineshire. B31 3TA. Tel: (01330) 822365.

Location: South West of Banchory centre.
Secretary: W.N. Donaldson. Tel: (01330) 822365.
Pro Shop: Tel: (01330) 822447.

Attractive parkland course on the banks of the River Dee. Easy walking course with the 11th and 12th holes the most challenging. Excellent lounge, dining and locker room facilities and a well stocked professionl shop.

COURSE INFORMATION

Par 67; SSS 66; Length 5,245 Yds.
Opening Hours: Summer 7am to 7.30pm; Winter 8.30pm to dusk.
Visitors: Welcome except Thurs & weekends.
Avoid: Members times 9.30am & 12.30pm to 2.00pm.
Ladies: Welcome — Ladies day Thurs.
Green Fees: Weekdays £19, weekends £21.
Juveniles: Must be with an adult.
Clubhouse Hours: Summer 7.00am to 11.00pm, Winter 8.30am to 10.00pm.
Clubhouse Dress: Smart/Casual.
Clubhouse Facilities: Full catering facilities.

CONVENIENT HOTELS

Bunett Arms Hotel;
Tor-na-Coill Hotel;
Banchory Lodge.

NO.	YARDS	PAR	S.I.	NO.	YARDS	PAR	S.I.
1	315	4	12	10	353	4	7
2	224	3	5	11	183	3	9
3	125	3	17	12	416	4	1
4	444	4	2	13	326	4	14
5	288	4	13	14	88	3	16
6	485	5	3	15	213	3	8
7	188	3	10	16	321	4	11
8	266	4	15	17	137	3	18
9	396	4	6	18	477	5	4
OUT	2,731	34		IN	2,514	33	
				TOTAL	5,245	67	
STANDARD SCRATCH					66		

Bunker and tree positions indicated.

BRAEMAR

**Braemar Golf Club,
Cluniebank Road, Braemar,
AB3 5XX.
Tel: (01339) 741618.**

Location: 1.2 miles from Braemar.
Secretary: John Pennett.
Tel: (01224) 704471.
Architect: Joe Anderson.

Braemar is the highest 18 hole course in the British Isles at 1,200 ft above sea level and has the reputation of having the finest greens in the area. The course is reasonably flatened the River Clune comes into play on several of the holes. The second hole is among the best in Scotland and is the subject of a famous painting by Willlie Forbes.

COURSE INFORMATION

Par 65; SSS 64; Length 4,916 Yards.
Opening Hours: Daylight hours.
Visitors: Welcome.
Ladies: Welcome
Green Fees: Weekdays – £11 per round, £15 per day; w/e – £15 per round, £20 per day.
Juveniles: Welcome.

Clubhouse Hours: Mon to Sat 11.00am to midnight; Sun 11.00am to 11.00pm.
Clubhouse Dress: No shorts or hats.
Clubhouse Facilities: Meals seven days a week.

CONVENIENT HOTELS

Moorfield Hotel, Braemar; Fife Arms Hotel, Braemar; Invercauld Arms Hotel.

NO.	MEDAL YARDS	GEN. YARDS	PAR	S.I.	NO.	MEDAL YARDS	GEN. YARDS	PAR	S.I.
1	356	337	4	7	10	409	409	4	3
2	369	369	4	2	11	277	206	4/4	12
3	185	144	3	9	12	334	334	4	6
4	403	369	4	5	13	173	158	3	14
5	231	231	3	4	14	310	310	4	10
6	103	103	3	18	15	421	397	4	1
7	207	207	3	11	16	261	261	4	15
8	253	253	4	13	17	245	245	3	8
9	257	257	4	16	18	122	122	3	17
OUT	2,364	2,270	32		IN	2,552	2,442	33	
					TOTAL	4,916	4,712	65	
					STANDARD SCRATCH	64	63		

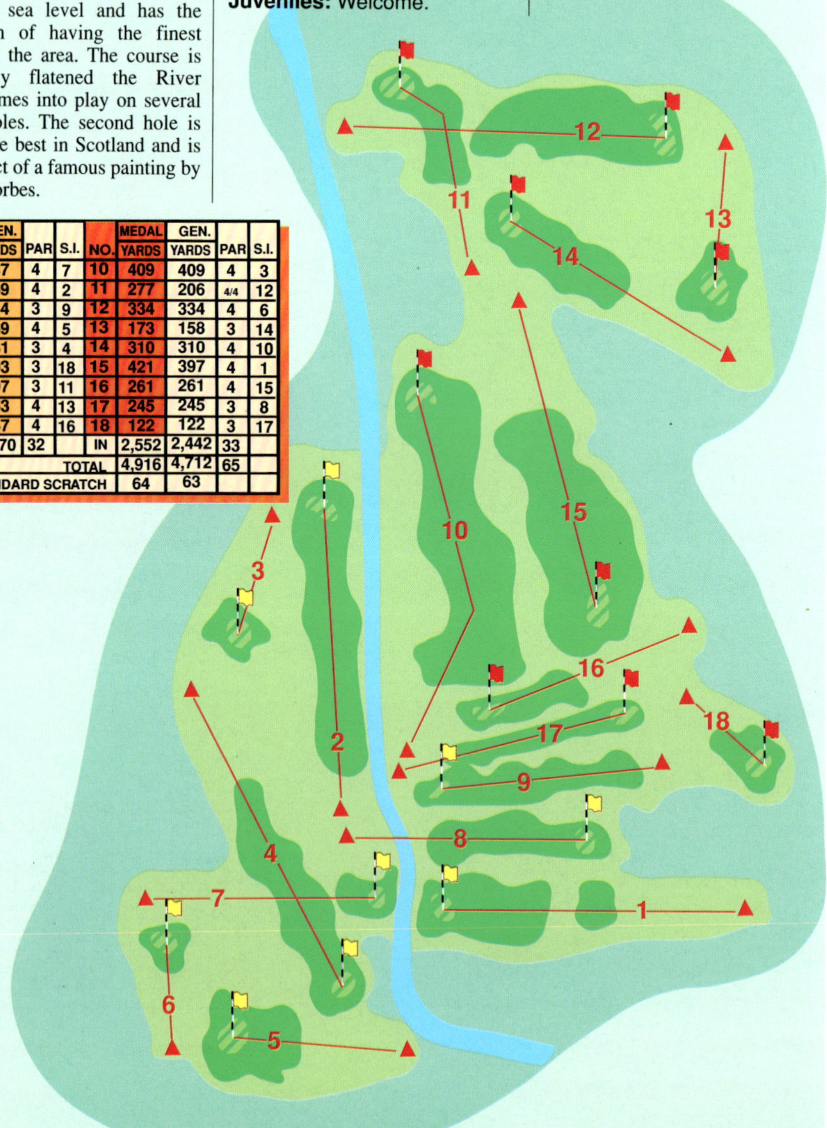

Bunker and tree positions indicated.

Buckpool Golf Club, Barhill Road, Buckie, Banffshire. AB56 1DU.

Location: West end of Buckpool, 1/2 mile off A98.
Secretary: Tel: (01528) 34322.

Links course with superb views over the Moray Firth. There are no steep gradients, but interest is maintained by glorious masses of whin & broom which line the fairways, while the greens, particularly the last plateau one, have subtle slopes & borrows which set fascinating problems.

COURSE INFORMATION

Par 70; SSS 70; Length 6,257 Yards.
Opening Hours: Sunrise to sunset.
Visitors: Welcome — parties by arrangement.
Avoid: No parties before 9.30am Sat & Sun.
Ladies: Welcome.
Green Fees: Weekdays £8 a round, £10 a day; weekends £12 a round, £18 a day.
Juveniles: Permitted.
Clubhouse Hours: 9.00am onwards.
Clubhouse Dress: Informal.
Clubhouse Facilities: Catering available daily during peak season.

CONVENIENT HOTEL

Marine Hotel, Marine Place, Buckie.

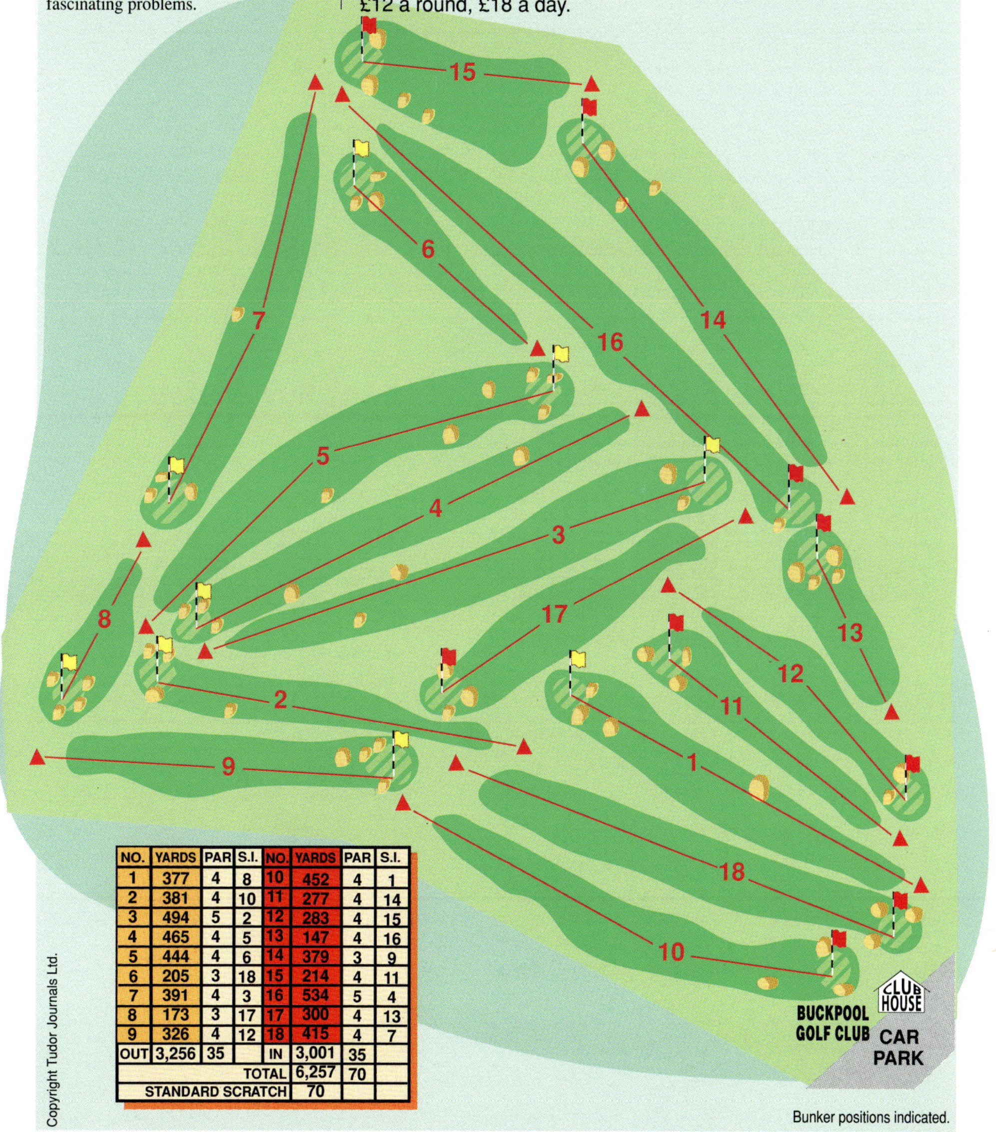

NO.	YARDS	PAR	S.I.	NO.	YARDS	PAR	S.I.
1	377	4	8	10	452	4	1
2	381	4	10	11	277	4	14
3	494	5	2	12	283	4	15
4	465	4	5	13	147	4	16
5	444	4	6	14	379	3	9
6	205	3	18	15	214	4	11
7	391	4	3	16	534	5	4
8	173	3	17	17	300	4	13
9	326	4	12	18	415	4	7
OUT	3,256	35		IN	3,001	35	
				TOTAL	6,257	70	
				STANDARD SCRATCH	70		

Bunker positions indicated.

CRUDEN BAY

Cruden Bay Golf Club, Cruden Bay, Aberdeenshire AB42 7NN.

LOCATION: 221/2 miles north east of Aberdeen.
PROFESSIONAL & CLUB ADMINISTRATOR: Robbie Stewart. Tel: (01779) 812285.
ARCHITECT: Tom Morris.

Ranked in the top forty courses in Britain, Cruden Bay presents a real challenge for the serious golfer whereas the holiday player will appreciate the magnificent views over the bay to Slains Castle. Those wishing a relaxing 9 holes will find the short but tricky St. Olaf course ideal. These traditional links have been described as eccentric, that may be, what is beyond doubt is that Cruden Bay provides an excellent golfing experience.

COURSE INFORMATION

Par 70; SSS 71; Length 6,370 Yards.
Opening Hours: 8.00am till dark.
Visitors: Welcome except weekends and competition days before 3.30pm.
Ladies: Welcome except weekends and competition days.
Ladies Day: Tuesday.
Green Fees: Weekdays £20; weekends £28.
Juveniles: Not allowed on 18 hole course without a handicap.
Clubhouse Hours: 11.00am to 11.00pm.
Clubhouse Dress: Smart/casual.
Clubhouse Facilities: Full bar and catering facilities, bookings required for high tea and evening meals.

CONVENIENT HOTELS

Kilmarnoch Arms Hotel;
Red House Hotel;
St. Olaf Hotel.

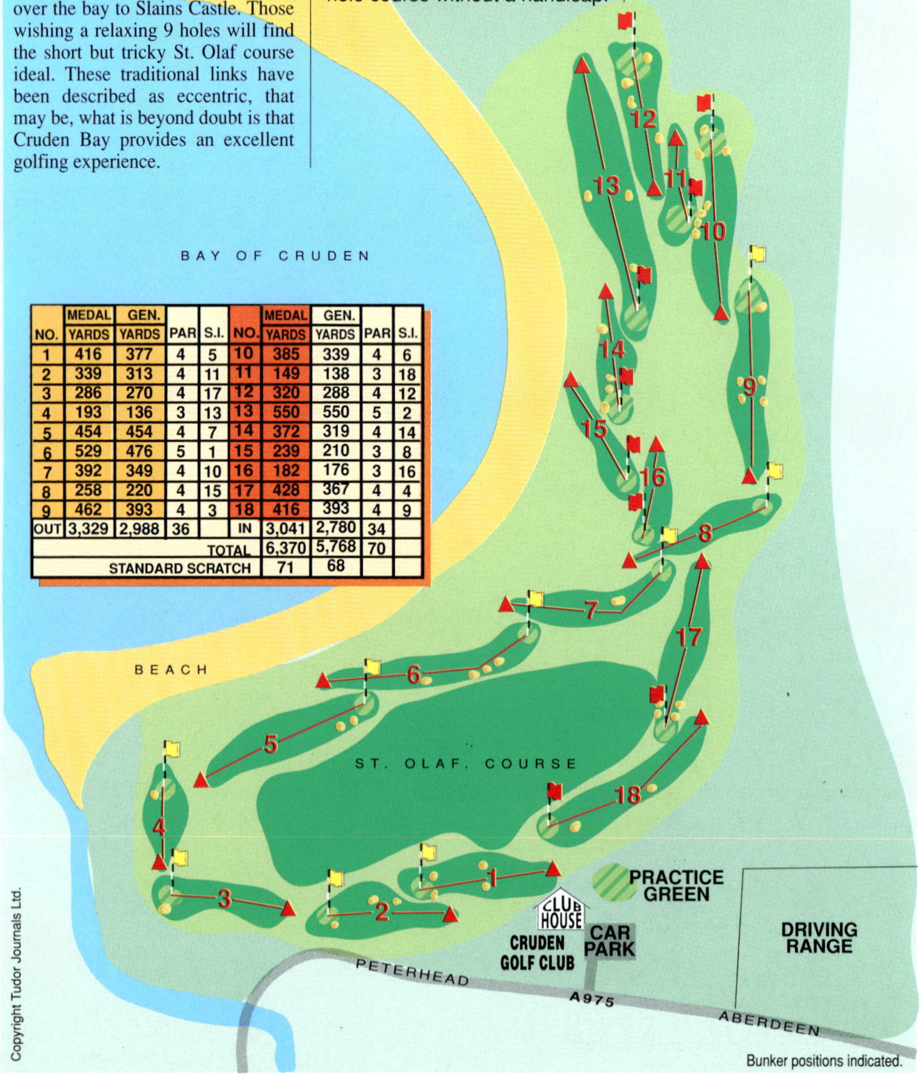

NO.	MEDAL YARDS	GEN. YARDS	PAR	S.I.	NO.	MEDAL YARDS	GEN. YARDS	PAR	S.I.
1	416	377	4	5	10	385	339	4	6
2	339	313	4	11	11	149	138	3	18
3	286	270	4	17	12	320	288	4	12
4	193	136	3	13	13	550	550	5	2
5	454	454	4	7	14	372	319	4	14
6	529	476	5	1	15	239	210	3	8
7	392	349	4	10	16	182	176	3	16
8	258	220	4	15	17	428	367	4	4
9	462	393	4	3	18	416	393	4	9
OUT	3,329	2,988	36		IN	3,041	2,780	34	
					TOTAL	6,370	5,768	70	
					STANDARD SCRATCH	71	68		

Cullen Golf Club, The LInks, Cullen, Buckie Banffshire.
Tel: (01542) 840685.

LOCATION: Off A98 midway between Aberdeen and Inverness.
SECRETARY: L.I.G. Findlay.
Tel: (01542) 840174.

Traditional seaside Scottish Links course with elevated section, natural rock landscaping and sandy beach coming into play at several holes; on elevated section of course panoramic sea coast and rural views; several tricky par 3 holes and hidden holes prove an adequate test for any golfer. Putting green and practice net area available.

NO.	YARDS	PAR	S.I.	NO.	YARDS	PAR	S.I.
1	344	4	7	10	309	4	2
2	130	3	10	11	245	3	15
3	236	3	18	12	182	3	6
4	129	3	12	13	149	3	17
5	360	4	1	14	207	3	9
6	172	3	8	15	510	5	3
7	231	3	14	16	348	4	5
8	275	4	4	17	262	4	16
9	194	3	11	18	327	4	13
OUT	2,071	30		IN	2,539	33	
				TOTAL	4,610	63	
STANDARD SCRATCH					62		

COURSE INFORMATION

Par 63; SSS 62; Length 4,610 Yds.
Opening Hours: Dawn – Dusk.
Visitors: Welcome — slight restrictions on Wed. & Sat. due to Medal Competitions.
Avoid: Weekends & society bookings.
Ladies: Welcome — ladies day Tues.
Green Fees: Daily ticket: weekdays £10, weekends £13.
Juveniles: Permitted — certain restrictions on tee times during Summer period.
Clubhouse Hours: 11.00am to 11.00pm (normal licensing hours).
Clubhouse Dress: Casual golf club dress acceptable.
Clubhouse Facilities: Full licensed clubhouse with full catering facilities April to October. Other times by arrangement with club steward.

CONVENIENT HOTELS

Seafield Arms Hotel;
Cullen Bay Hotel;
Royal Oak Hotel;
Bayview Hotel.
Grant Arms Hotel;
Waverley Hotel;
Three Kings Inn.

Bunker positions indicated.

Deeside Golf Club, Bieldside, Aberdeen.
Tel: (01224) 869457.

LOCATION: 4 miles West of Aberdeen.
SECRETARY: A.G. Macdonald.
Tel: (01224) 869457.
PROFESSIONAL: F.J. Coutts.
Tel: (01224) 861041.

18 hole parkland course adjoining the River Dee. An attractive course with mature trees throughout.

COURSE INFORMATION

Par 71; SSS 69; Length 5,971 Yards.
Opening Hours: 8.00am – Sunset.
Visitors: Welcome except before 4.00pm on Sat. & competition dates.
Ladies: Welcome restrictions as above.
Green Fees: Weekdays £20 a round; weekends £25.
Juveniles: Must be accompanied by an adult.
Clubhouse Hours: 8.00am to 10.30pm (summer).
Clubhouse Dress: Jacket — no denims or shell suits.
Clubhouse Facilities: As required.

CONVENIENT HOTELS

Bieldside Hotel;
Cults Hotel.

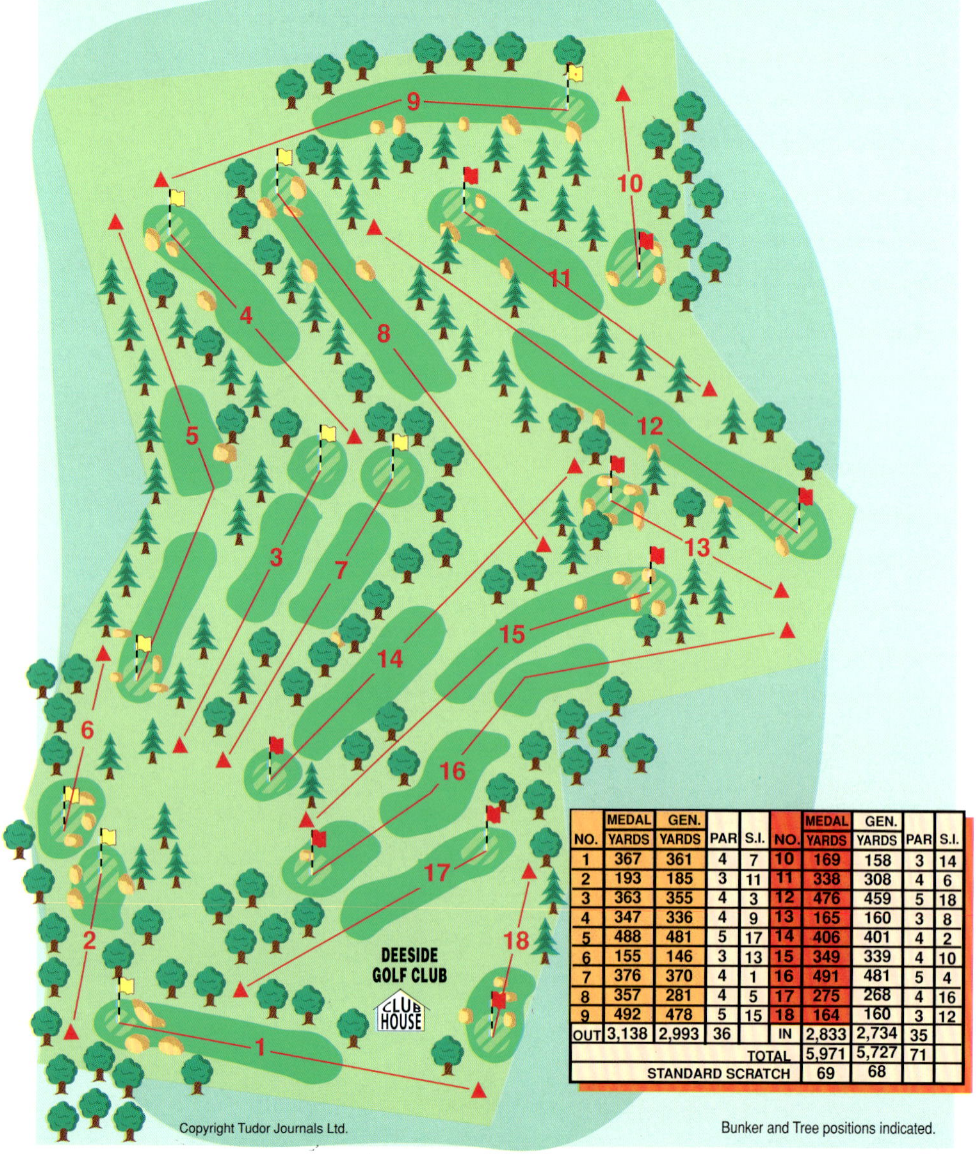

NO.	MEDAL YARDS	GEN. YARDS	PAR	S.I.	NO.	MEDAL YARDS	GEN. YARDS	PAR	S.I.
1	367	361	4	7	10	169	158	3	14
2	193	185	3	11	11	338	308	4	6
3	363	355	4	3	12	476	459	5	18
4	347	336	4	9	13	165	160	3	8
5	488	481	5	17	14	406	401	4	2
6	155	146	3	13	15	349	339	4	10
7	376	370	4	1	16	491	481	5	4
8	357	281	4	5	17	275	268	4	16
9	492	478	5	15	18	164	160	3	12
OUT	3,138	2,993	36		IN	2,833	2,734	35	
					TOTAL	5,971	5,727	71	
					STANDARD SCRATCH	69	68		

Bunker and Tree positions indicated.

DUFF HOUSE ROYAL

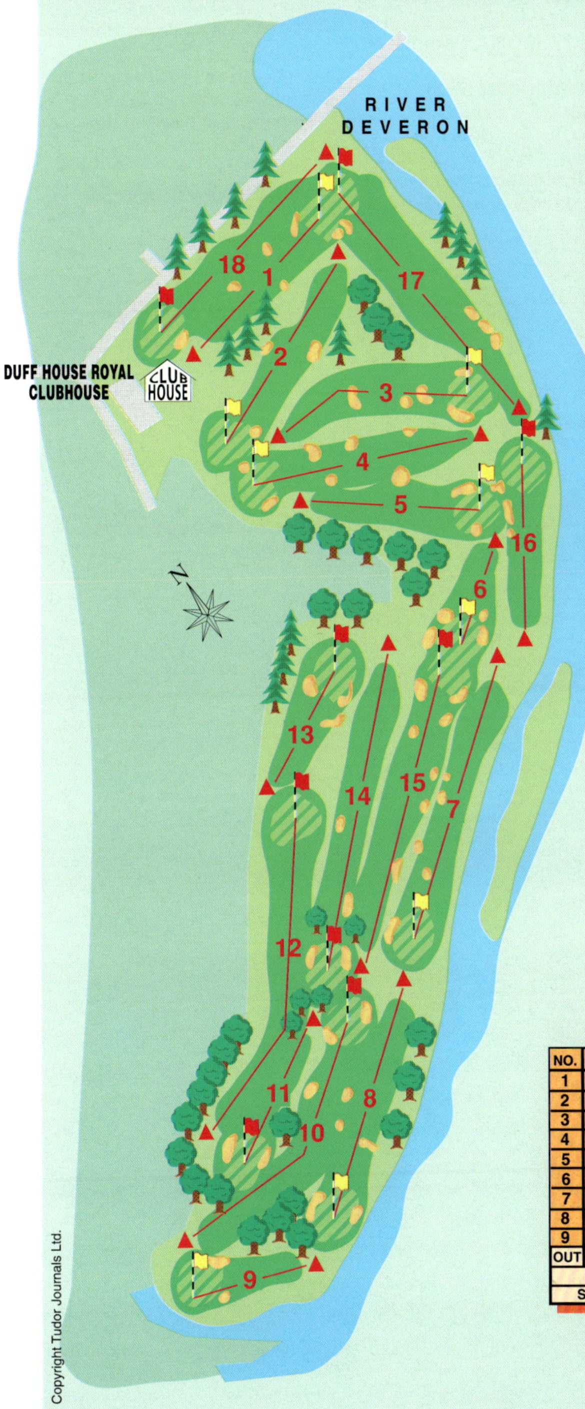

Duff House Royal Golf Club,
The Barnyards, Banff. AB4 3SX.
Tel: (01261) 812062.

Location: Moray Firth Coast.
Secretary: R. Walker.
Tel: (01261) 812062.
Professional: Bob Strachan.
Architect: Dr. McKenzie.

A pleasant parkland course, a feature being the large two–tier greens. Fairways are lush turf and generally flat but still prove to be an excellent test of golf.

COURSE INFORMATION

Par 68; SSS 69; Length 6,161 Yards.
Visitors: Welcome but some restrictions during monthly medal competitions.
Ladies: Welcome — restrictions as listed above.
Green Fees: Weekdays £13 a round, £17 a day; weekends £19 a round, £25 a day.
Juveniles: Permitted.
Clubhouse Hours: Bar hours in Summer till 11.00pm, Winter till 10.30pm.
Clubhouse Dress: Informal.
Clubhouse Facilities: Full catering.

CONVENIENT HOTELS

Banff Springs Hotel; County Hotel; Fife Lodge, Banff;

NO.	YARDS	PAR	S.I.	NO.	YARDS	PAR	S.I.
1	314	4	13	10	403	4	9
2	366	4	8	11	214	3	15
3	392	4	3	12	498	5	2
4	367	4	10	13	175	3	17
5	330	4	12	14	434	4	7
6	139	3	18	15	468	4	5
7	460	4	1	16	242	3	14
8	381	4	6	17	462	4	4
9	172	3	16	18	344	4	11
OUT	2,921	34		IN	3,240	34	
				TOTAL	6,161	68	
STANDARD SCRATCH					69		

Bunker and tree positions indicated.

Dufftown Golf Club, Dufftown, Banffshire. Tel & Fax: (01340) 820325.

LOCATION: 1 mile from Dufftown on Tomintoul Road.
SECRETARY: D.M. Smith.
Tel: (01340) 820033.

A scenic course with superb views, the highest part of the course above 1,000 feet. The 10th hole is very impressive with all its 462 yards being open to view from its high plateau tee.

COURSE INFORMATION

Par 67; SSS 67; Length 5,308 Yards.
Opening Hours: Sunrise to sunset.
Visitors: Welcome.
Ladies: Welcome — ladies day Tuesday.
Green Fees: £10 a round, £12 a day any day.
Juveniles: Welcome.

Clubhouse Hours: 11.00am to 11.00pm Mon to Fri; 11.00am to 11.45pm Sat/Sun.
Clubhouse Dress: Smart.
Clubhouse Facilities: Snacks may be available daily, bar lunches and evening meals by prior arrangement.

CONVENIENT HOTELS

Craigellachie Hotel.

NO.	YARDS	PAR	S.I.	NO.	YARDS	PAR	S.I.
1	288	4	6	10	462	4	1
2	285	4	10	11	290	4	9
3	333	4	12	12	222	3	17
4	367	4	2	13	359	4	3
5	143	3	14	14	397	4	5
6	345	4	4	15	200	3	11
7	103	3	18	16	325	4	13
8	276	4	8	17	411	4	7
9	305	4	16	18	197	3	15
OUT	2,445	34		IN	2,863	33	
				TOTAL	5,308	67	
				STANDARD SCRATCH	67		

FRASERBURGH

Fraserburgh Golf Club, Philorth,
Fraserburgh. AB4 5TL.
Tel: (01346) 518287.

LOCATION: 1 mile East of Fraserburgh.
SECRETARY: J. Grant.
Tel: (01346) 518287 or the office on (01346) 516616.

Recognised as one of the best traditional links course in Scotland. Providing continuous subtle changes at each hole to experienced and novice players alike. New 9 hole course par 35 opening in 1995.

COURSE INFORMATION

Par 70; SSS 70; Length 6,279 Yds.
Opening Hours: Daylight hours.
Visitors: Welcome.
Avoid: Some weekends.
Ladies: Welcome — ladies day Mon/Wed.
Green Fees: Weekdays £11, weekends £15.
Juveniles: Welcome.
Clubhouse Hours: Casual but neat.
Clubhouse Dress: Casual golf club dress acceptable.
Clubhouse Facilities: Showers, visitors room, bar seven days. Catering — Tues to Sun inclusive.

CONVENIENT HOTELS

Royal, Alexandra Station;
Tufted Duck, St. Comb;
Waterside Inn, Peterhead.

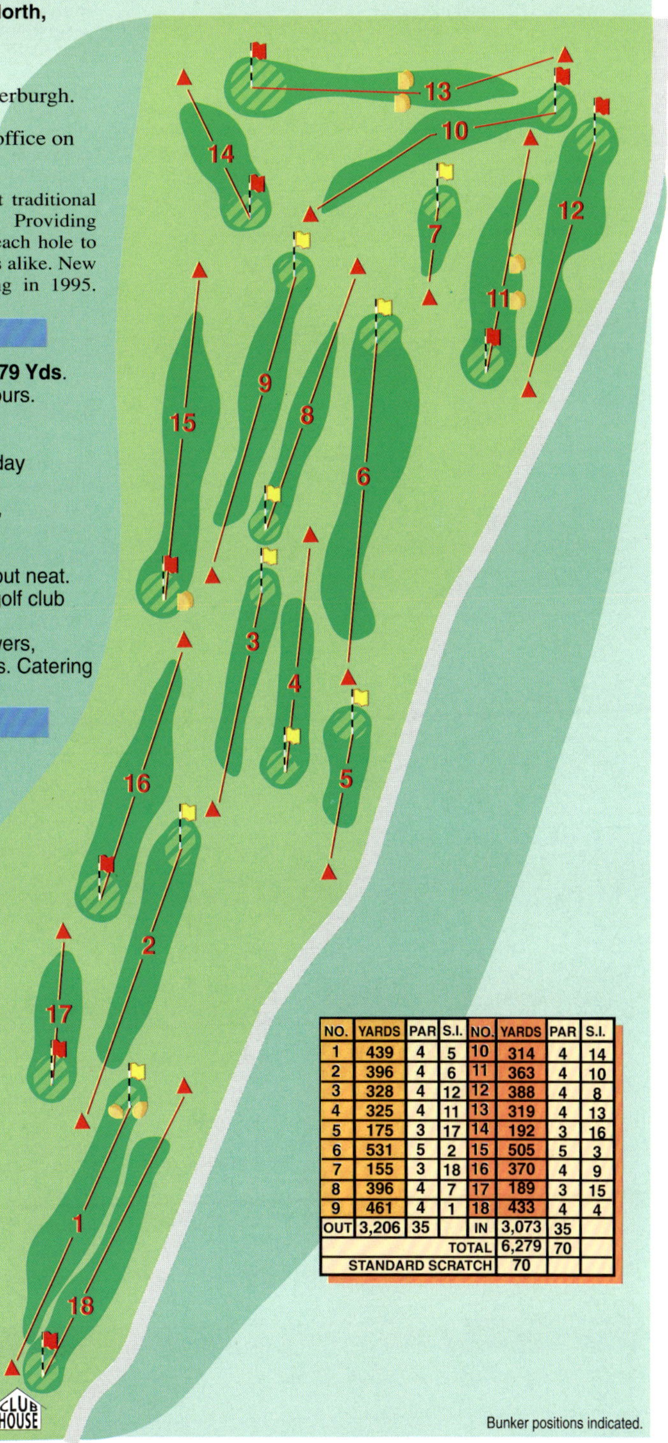

NO.	YARDS	PAR	S.I.	NO.	YARDS	PAR	S.I.
1	439	4	5	10	314	4	14
2	396	4	6	11	363	4	10
3	328	4	12	12	388	4	8
4	325	4	11	13	319	4	13
5	175	3	17	14	192	3	16
6	531	5	2	15	505	5	3
7	155	3	18	16	370	4	9
8	396	4	7	17	189	3	15
9	461	4	1	18	433	4	4
OUT	3,206	35		IN	3,073	35	
				TOTAL	6,279	70	
STANDARD SCRATCH					70		

Bunker positions indicated.

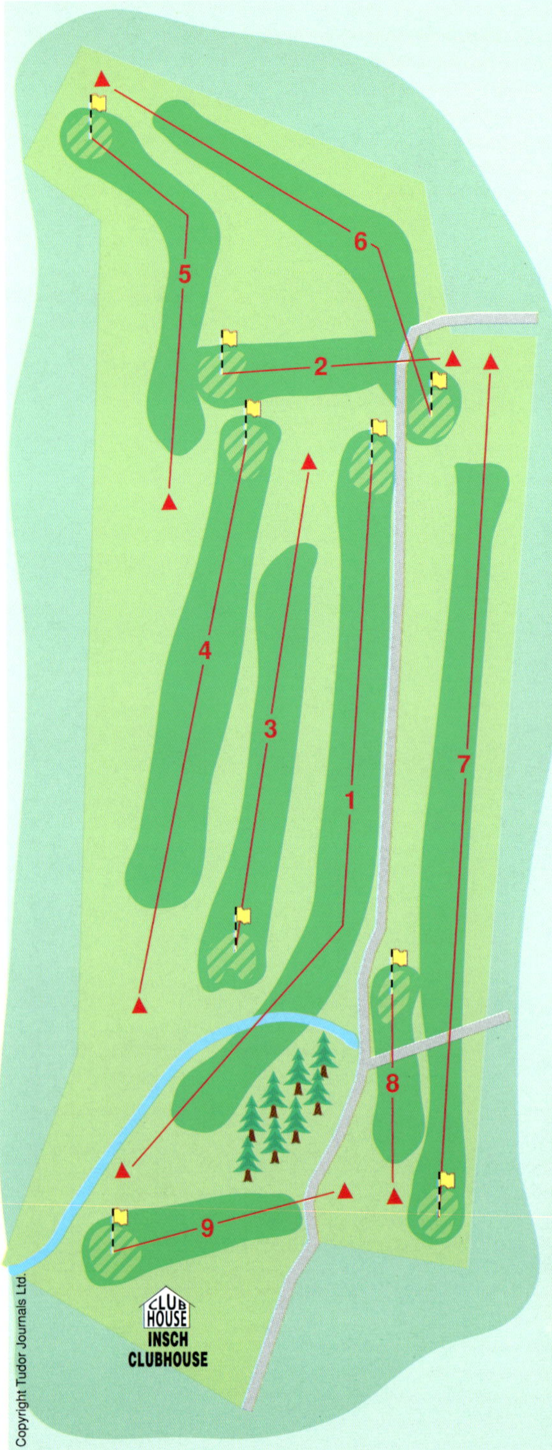

Insch Golf Club, Golf Terrace, Insch, Aberdeenshire.
Tel: (01464) 820363.

LOCATION: 28 miles north west of Aberdeen off the Inverness Road (A96).
SECRETARY: Brian Leith.
Tel: (01464) 820144.

The Insch course has 9 holes with all the usual hazards, such as the bunker to the left of the 6th green or the stream just within driving distance of the 8th tee. Quite a challenging course with an 18 hole length of 5,838 yards (SSS 67) par 70, it comes right up to professional standards. Extension to 18 holes commences 1995.

COURSE INFORMATION

Par 70; SSS 67; Length 5,838 Yds.
Opening Hours: Sunrise to sunset.
Visitors: Mon from 4.30pm; Tues from 5.00pm; Wed from 4.0pm.
Ladies: Welcome — ladies day Mon from 4.30pm.
Green Fees: £10 weekdays, £12 weekends.
Juveniles: After 6.00pm except if accompanied by by a senior member.
Clubhouse Dress: Optional.
Clubhouse Facilities: Bar open on Mon, Tues, Thur and Fri evenings. Sat/Sun open all day. Catering available on request.

CONVENIENT HOTELS

Commercial Hotel;
Station Hotel.

NO.	YARDS	PAR	S.I.	NO.	YARDS	PAR	S.I.
1	529	5	4	10	529	5	4
2	127	3	18	11	127	3	18
3	380	4	8	12	380	4	8
4	357	4	6	13	357	4	6
5	321	4	10	14	321	4	10
6	294	4	12	15	294	4	12
7	497	5	2	16	497	5	2
8	136	3	16	17	136	3	16
9	175	3	14	18	175	3	14
OUT	2,816	35		IN	2,816	35	
				TOTAL	5,838	70	
				STANDARD SCRATCH	67		

INVERALLOCHY

Inverallochy Golf Club, Inverallochy, Nr. Fraserburgh, Aberdeenshire.

LOCATION: 31/2 miles off the A92, Nr. Fraserburgh.
SECRETARY: R. Mutch.
Tel: (01346) 582000.

The course is on the North East coastline, with 4 holes bordering the North Sea. Normal links weather conditions can make very difficult golf on windy days. The course is constantly being improved as membership grows. No bunkers but plenty of links rough and out of bounds at 8 holes.

COURSE INFORMATION

Par 65; SSS 65; Length 5,137 Yds.
Opening Hours: Sunrise to sunset.
Visitors: Welcome.
Ladies: Welcome.
Green Fees: £8 weekdays, £10 weekends.
Juveniles: Welcome.
Clubhouse Hours: Evenings, weekend.
Clubhouse Facilities: Limited catering at weekends.

CONVENIENT HOTELS

Station Hotel, Fraserburgh.
Tel: (01346) 513343.

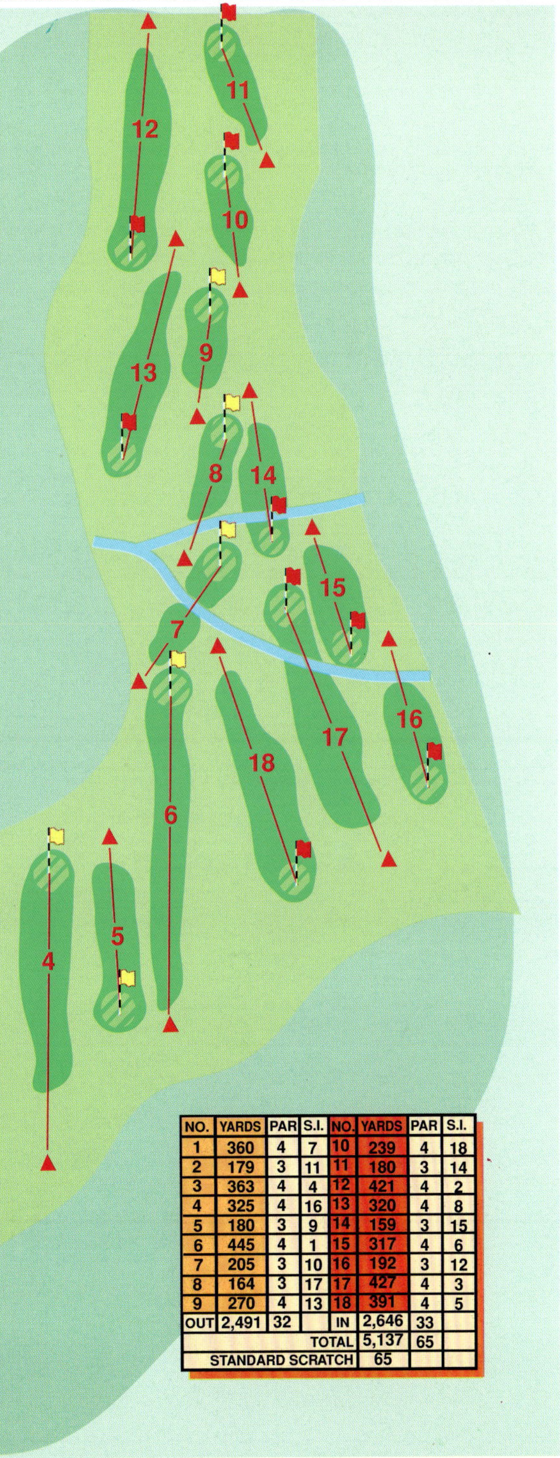

NO.	YARDS	PAR	S.I.	NO.	YARDS	PAR	S.I.
1	360	4	7	10	239	4	18
2	179	3	11	11	180	3	14
3	363	4	4	12	421	4	2
4	325	4	16	13	320	4	8
5	180	3	9	14	159	3	15
6	445	4	1	15	317	4	6
7	205	3	10	16	192	3	12
8	164	3	17	17	427	4	3
9	270	4	13	18	391	4	5
OUT	2,491	32		IN	2,646	33	
				TOTAL	5,137	65	
				STANDARD SCRATCH	65		

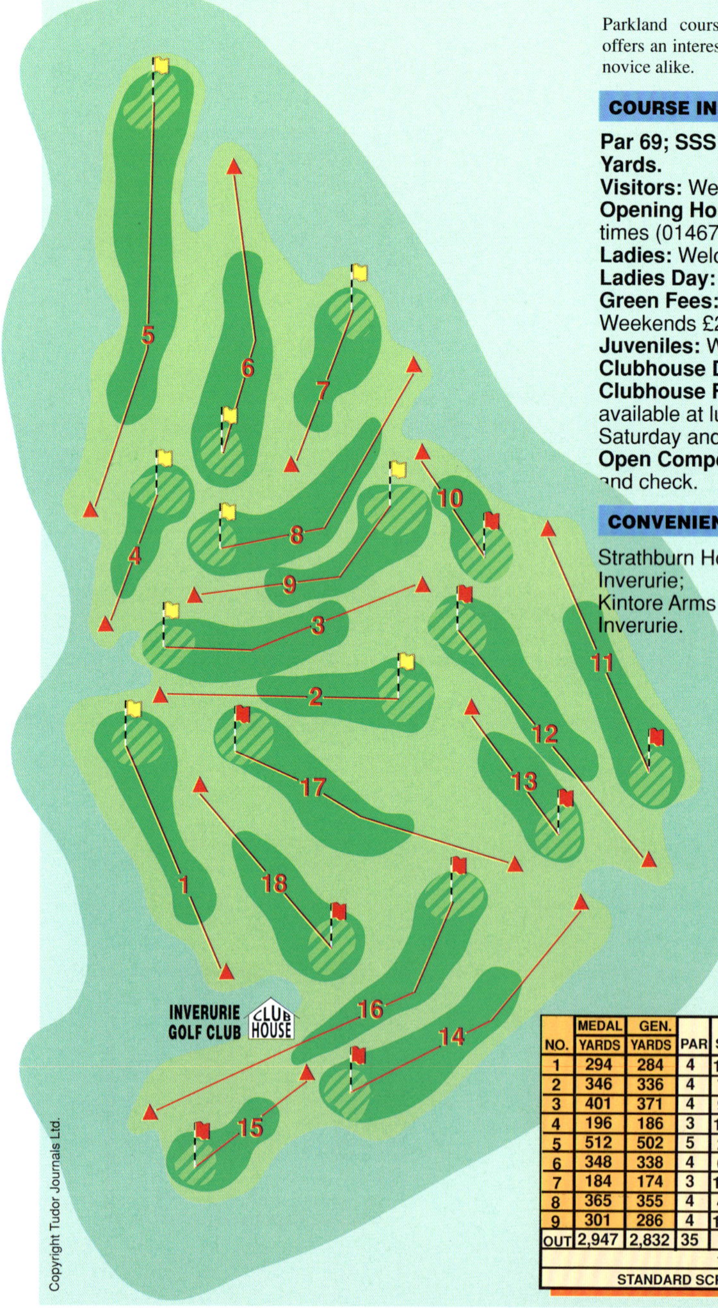

Inverurie Golf Club, Blackhall Road, Inverurie, Aberdeenshire. Tel: (01467) 620207.

LOCATION: 16 miles west of Aberdeen.
SECRETARY: Bill Cameron.

Parkland course, partially wooded, which offers an interesting test of golf to expert and novice alike.

COURSE INFORMATION

Par 69; SSS 68; Length 5,711 Yards.
Visitors: Welcome.
Opening Hours: Phone for available times (01467) 620193).
Ladies: Welcome.
Ladies Day: Tuesday.
Green Fees: Weekdays £14 Weekends £21.
Juveniles: Welcome.
Clubhouse Dress: Smart / Casual.
Clubhouse Facilities: Catering available at lunchtimes and all day Saturday and Sunday.
Open Competitions: Please phone and check.

CONVENIENT HOTELS

Strathburn Hotel, Burghmuir Drive, Inverurie;
Kintore Arms Hotel, HIgh Street, Inverurie.

NO.	MEDAL YARDS	GEN. YARDS	PAR	S.I.	NO.	MEDAL YARDS	GEN. YARDS	PAR	S.I.
1	294	284	4	17	10	128	123	3	18
2	346	336	4	7	11	304	304	4	12
3	401	371	4	9	12	322	316	4	10
4	196	186	3	11	13	257	247	4	14
5	512	502	5	2	14	369	354	4	3
6	348	338	4	6	15	183	163	3	16
7	184	174	3	13	16	444	440	4	1
8	365	355	4	4	17	407	364	4	5
9	301	286	4	15	18	350	340	4	8
OUT	2,947	2,832	35		IN	2,764	2,651	34	
					TOTAL	5,711	5,483	69	
					STANDARD SCRATCH	68	67		

Keith Golf Club, Fife Park, Keith, Banffshire AB55 3DF.
Tel: (01542) 882469.

SECRETARY: A. Stronach.
Tel: (01542) 882831.

Open course giving panoramic views to the player, a challenge to the lower handicap player, in particular the par 3 3rd hole and the par 3 7th hole. Excellent greens giving satisfaction to all players. Hospitality second to none, a friendly welcome awaits all who visit the course.

COURSE INFORMATION

Par 69; SSS 68; Length 5,614 Yds.
Visitors: Welcome (ring prior to visit).
Ladies: Welcome.
Green Fees: Midweek £8 round £10 day; Sat & Sun £10 Round £15 day; Jnrs £2 day.
Juveniles: Mon & Fri — 4.30pm to 6.00pm — tee reserved for jnrs only.
Clubhouse Hours: 8.00am to 11.00pm.
Clubhouse Dress: Casual.
Clubhouse Facilities: Full facilities.

CONVENIENT HOTELS

Ugie Hotel.

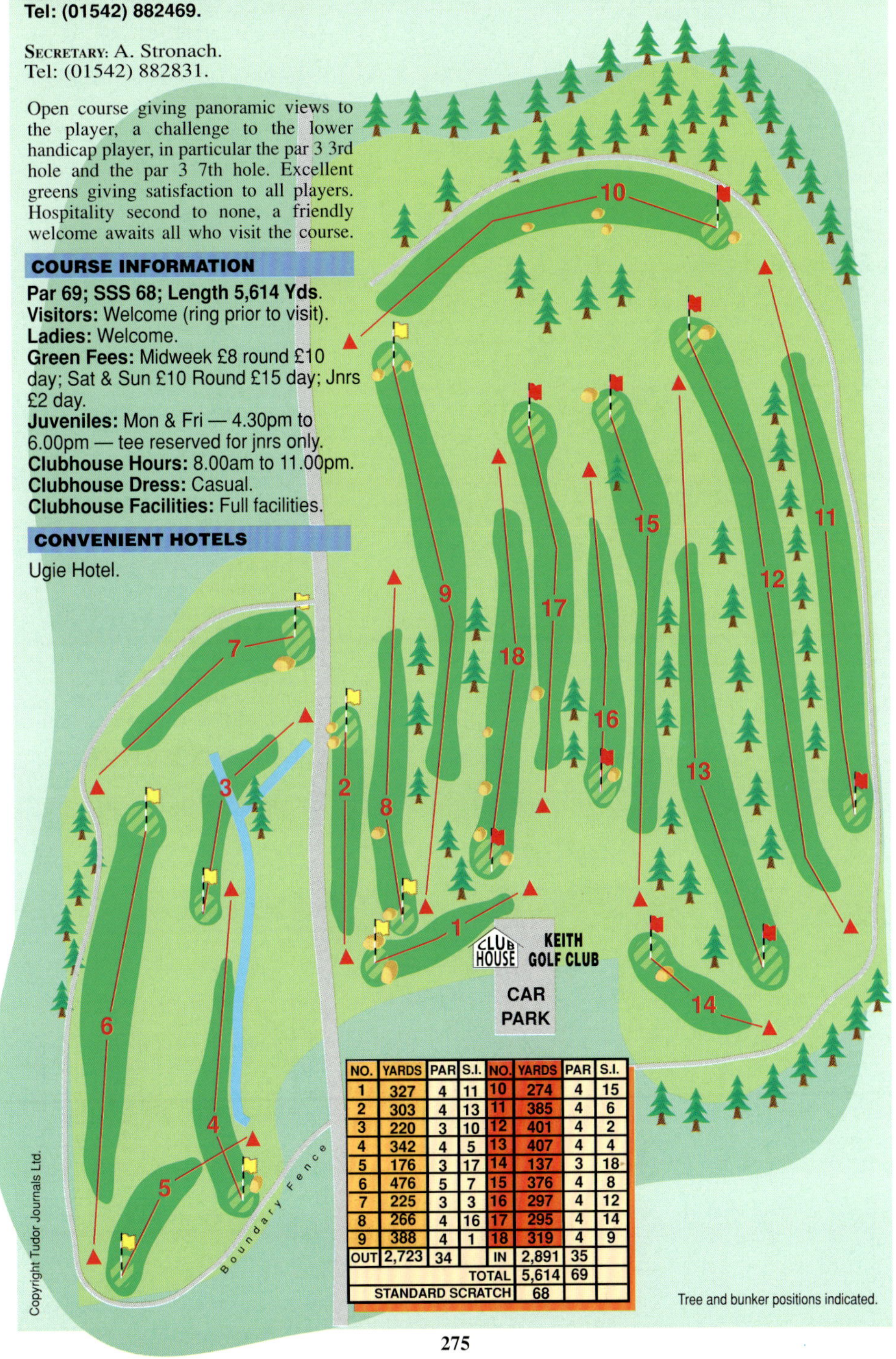

NO.	YARDS	PAR	S.I.	NO.	YARDS	PAR	S.I.
1	327	4	11	10	274	4	15
2	303	4	13	11	385	4	6
3	220	3	10	12	401	4	2
4	342	4	5	13	407	4	4
5	176	3	17	14	137	3	18
6	476	5	7	15	376	4	8
7	225	3	3	16	297	4	12
8	266	4	16	17	295	4	14
9	388	4	1	18	319	4	9
OUT	2,723	34		IN	2,891	35	
				TOTAL	5,614	69	
STANDARD SCRATCH					68		

Tree and bunker positions indicated.

Kemnay Golf Club, Kemnay, Aberdeenshire. Tel: (01467) 42225; Golf shop Tel: (01467) 642225; Office Tel: (01467) 643746.

LOCATION: 15 miles from Aberdeen. Tel: (01467) 643047.

There are one or two changes which have occured recently, the major one being that we have now completed our new eighteen hole layout, details of which are shown on the enclosed card.

COURSE INFORMATION

Par 70; SSS 68; Length 5,903 Yards.
Opening Hours: Daylight hours.
Visitors: Welcome.
Avoid: Tues. evenings & competitions.
Ladies: Welcome — Thur. evenings.
Green Fees: Weekdays £12 per round, £17 per day; £14 per round, £20 per day weekends. (Juveniles half price).
Juveniles: Must be accompanied by an adult on evenings and Sun. (£4 per round).
Clubhouse Hours: Open all day during Summer Season.
Clubhouse Dress: Informal.
Clubhouse Facilities: Meals, snacks available each day during summer Season.

CONVENIENT HOTELS

Parkhill Lodge;
Kemnay & Burnett Arms.

NO.	YARDS	PAR	S.I.	NO.	YARDS	PAR	S.I.
1	352	4	11	10	308	4	8
2	282	4	17	11	326	4	16
3	340	4	12	12	208	3	3
4	180	3	15	13	498	5	2
5	374	4	9	14	403	4	10
6	386	4	4	15	420	4	7
7	348	4	6	16	356	4	5
8	160	3	14	17	170	3	18
9	488	5	1	18	304	4	13
OUT	2,910	35		IN	2,993	35	
				TOTAL	5,903	70	
STANDARD SCRATCH					68		

Bunker and tree positions indicated.

NO.	YARDS	PAR	S.I.	NO.	YARDS	PAR	S.I.
1	292	4	15	10	319	4	6
2	333	4	13	11	165	3	16
3	379	4	9	12	203	3	14
4	478	5	3	13	260	4	10
5	378	4	11	14	259	4	12
6	391	4	7	15	147	3	18
7	201	3	17	16	311	4	8
8	402	4	5	17	452	4	2
9	581	5	1	18	435	4	4
OUT	3,435	37		IN	2,551	33	
				TOTAL	5,986	70	
STANDARD SCRATCH					69		

McDonald Golf Club, Allon, Aberdeenshire.
Tel: (01358) 720576.

Location: 15 miles north of Aberdeen.
Secretary: G. Ironside.
Tel: (01358) 720576.
Professional: R. Urquhart.
Tel: (01358) 722891.

Outward half is approximately 12 years old and has matured to give a good test of golf – beware of hooking and the water which comes into play on many of the holes. The inward half is of a mature parkland nature with plenty of trees to encourage straight shots.

COURSE INFORMATION

Par 70; SSS 69; Length 5,986 Yards.
Opening Hours: Dawn – Dusk (tee bookable from 7am – 7pm).
Visitors: Welcome.
Avoid: Wednesdays.
Ladies: Welcome.
Ladies Day: Tuesdays.
Green Fees: Weekdays £14, £16 on Saturday & £20 on Sunday.
Juveniles: No under 12's after 5pm.
Clubhouse Hours: 11am to 11.30pm.
Clubhouse Dress: Informal.
Clubhouse Facilities: Limited catering available.

CONVENIENT HOTELS

Buchan Hotel,Tel: (01358) 720208;
Mercury Hotel, Tel (01358) 720666;
New Inn Hotel, Tel (01358) 720425;
Station Hotel, Tel: (01358) 720209.

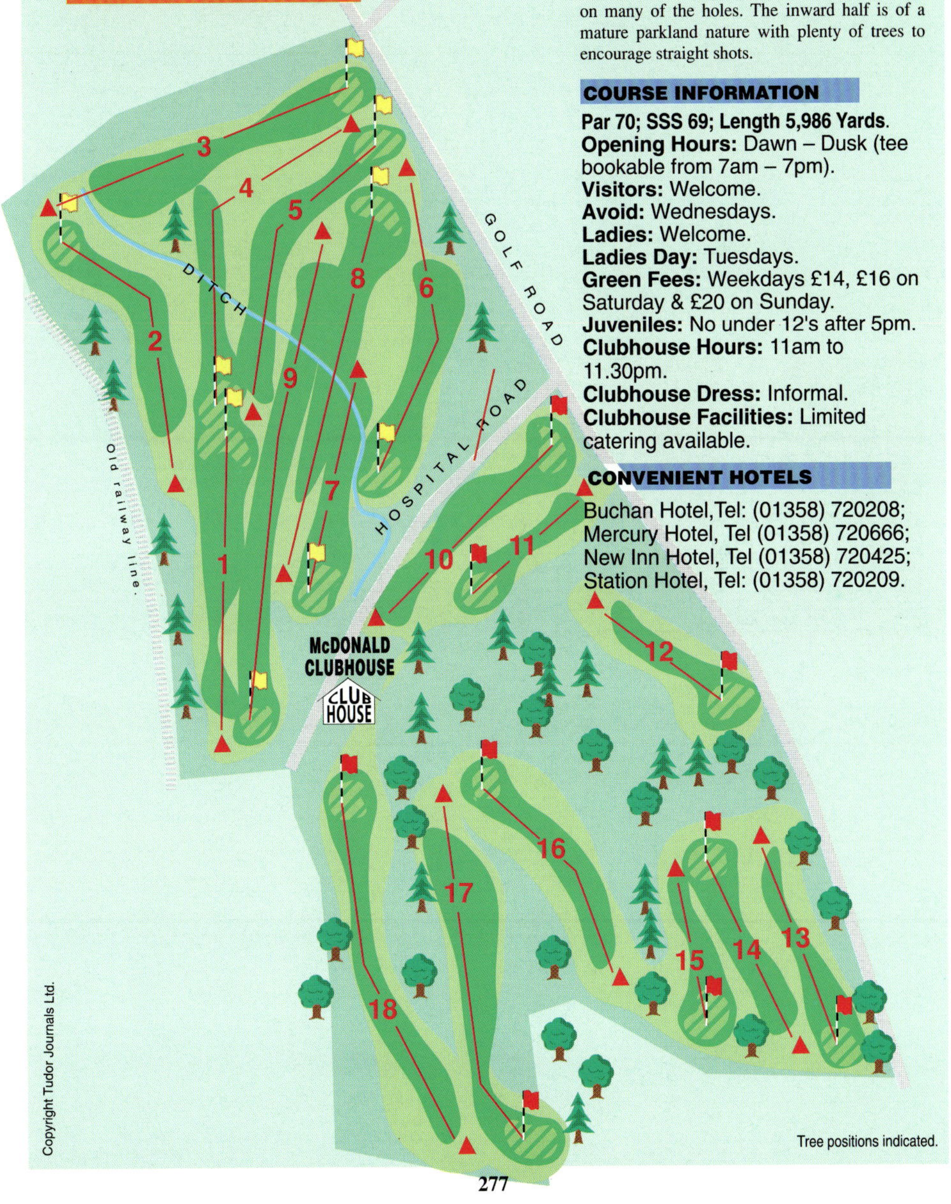

Tree positions indicated.

MURCAR

Murcar Golf Club, Bridge of Don, Aberdeenshire. AB23 8BD. Tel: (01224) 704345.

LOCATION: 5 miles North East of Aberdeen.
SECRETARY: R Matthews
Tel: (01224) 704354.
PROFESSIONAL: A White.
Tel: (01224) 704370.

Typical links course with a bracing sea breeze and a fairly challenging layout.

COURSE INFORMATION

Par 71; SSS 71; Length 6,241Yds.
Opening Hours: 8.30am – 10.00pm.
Visitors: Welcome – avoid Sat & Sun am & Wed pm.
Ladies: Welcome.
Green Fees: Weekdays £18 round; £25 weekends round.
Juveniles: Must be accompanied by an adult.

Clubhouse Hours: 8.00am to 10.00pm.
Clubhouse Dress: No denim type jeans, trainer type shoes or shorts.
Clubhouse Facilities: Mon till 2.00pm catering Snacks only Tuesday.

CONVENIENT HOTELS

The Mill of Mundurno
Travel Inn.

NO.	MEDAL YARDS	GEN. YARDS	PAR	S.I.	NO.	MEDAL YARDS	GEN. YARDS	PAR	S.I.
1	322	300	4	13	10	395	385	4	1
2	367	340	4	9	11	338	312	4	10
3	401	380	4	4	12	152	144	3	16
4	489	423	4	7	13	383	365	4	3
5	162	152	3	17	14	476	442	5	12
6	439	421	4	2	15	351	332	4	8
7	423	411	4	6	16	160	139	3	18
8	383	362	4	11	17	359	307	4	5
9	312	280	4	15	18	329	314	4	14
OUT	3,298	3,069	36		IN	2,943	2,740	35	
					TOTAL	6,241	5,809	71	
					STANDARD SCRATCH	70	68		

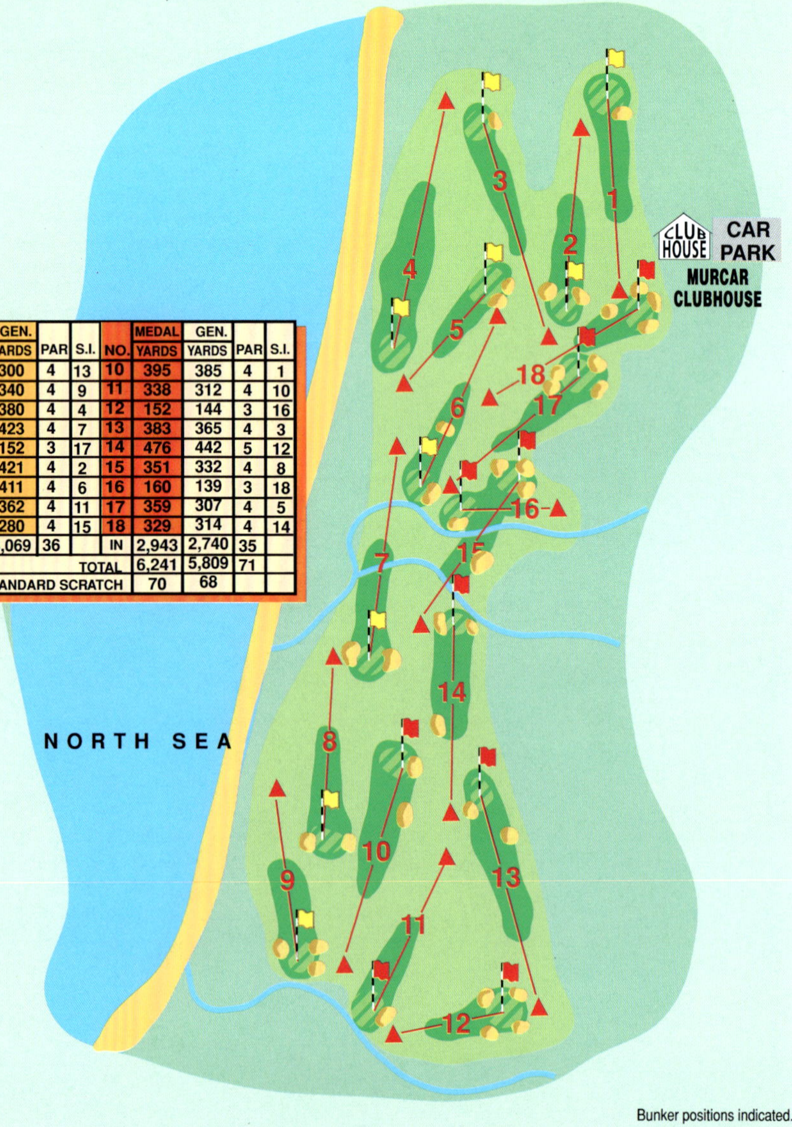

Bunker positions indicated.

NO.	MEDAL YARDS	GEN. YARDS	PAR	S.I.	NO.	MEDAL YARDS	GEN. YARDS	PAR	S.I.
1	390	370	4	4	10	337	299	4	15
2	543	500	5	8	11	381	367	4	9
3	313	313	4	18	12	428	412	4	1
4	378	354	4	2	13	399	384	4	7
5	320	320	4	14	14	362	343	4	11
6	170	170	3	16	15	210	197	3	3
7	405	380	4	12	16	504	487	5	13
8	493	493	5	10	17	432	422	4	5
9	181	143	3	6	18	359	359	4	17
OUT	3,193	3,043	36		IN	3,412	3,270	36	
					TOTAL	6,605	6,313	72	
					STANDARD SCRATCH	73			

Newmachar Golf Club, Newmachar, Aberdeenshire AB2 0UU. Tel: (01651) 863002.

Location: 12 miles north of Aberdeen on A947.
Secretary: George McIntosh. Tel: (01651) 863002.
Professional: Glenn Taylor. Tel: (01651) 862127.
Architect: Dave Thomas.

Newmachar Golf Club consists of many lakes and streams with tees attractively grounded by fine stands of bracken and pine. Some 15,000 new trees have been planted to enhance the appearance still further.

COURSE INFORMATION

Par 72; SSS 73; Length 6,605 Yards.
Opening Hours: 7.30am to 7.00pm.
Visitors: Welcome — advance booking essential.
Avoid: Sat & Sun mornings.
Ladies: Welcome — ladies day Thur.
Green Fees: Weekdays £20 a round, £30 per day; weekends £30 a round, £45 per day.
Juveniles: Permitted.
Clubhouse Hours: 11.00am to 11.00pm.
Clubhouse Dress: Smart but casual.
Clubhouse Facilities: Full catering, bar & changing facilities available.

CONVENIENT HOTELS

Dyce Skean Dhu, Dunavon Hotel, Victoria St. Dyce.

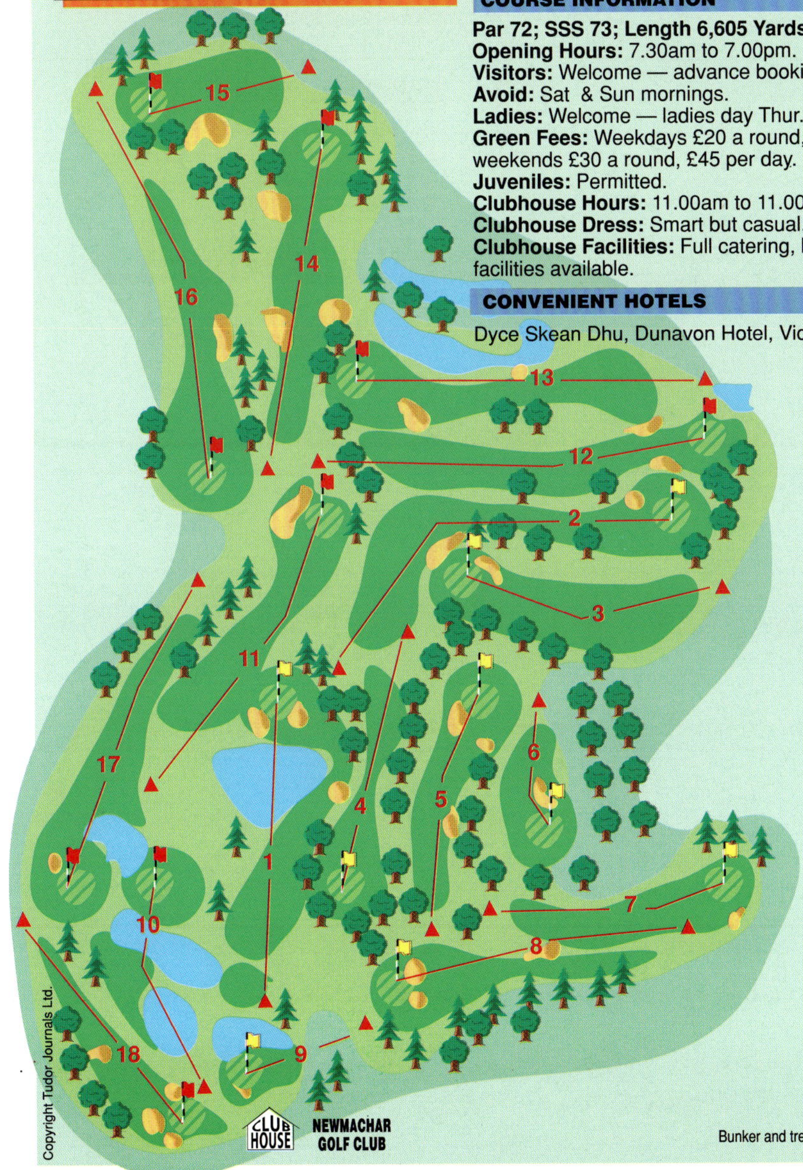

Bunker and tree positions indicated.

OLDMELDRUM

Oldmeldrum Golf Club, Kirkrae, Oldmeldrum, Aberdeenshire.
Tel: (01651) 872648.

LOCATION: 17 miles north west of Aberdeen.
SECRETARY: Douglas Petrie.
Tel: (01651) 872383.

Undulating parkland course with water features and tree lined fairways. Some testing par 4's especially on windy days. Tight 1st and 18th holes with out of bounds on both sides of a shared fairway.

COURSE INFORMATION

Par 70; SSS 69; Length 5,988 Yards.
Opening Hours: Sunrise to sunset.
Visitors: Welcome, telephone club shop for tee times (01651) 873555.
Avoid: Weekdays 4,30pm – 6.30pm, weekends 12.00noon – 2.00pm.
Ladies: Welcome.
Green Fees: Weekdays £12 a day; weekends £18 a day.
Juveniles: After 5.00pm during school holidays. Must play with an adult.
Clubhouse Hours: 11.00am to 11.00pm 7 days a week.
Clubhouse Dress: Casual.
Clubhouse Facilities: Catering — Full service 7 days a week.

CONVENIENT HOTELS

Oldmeldrum.

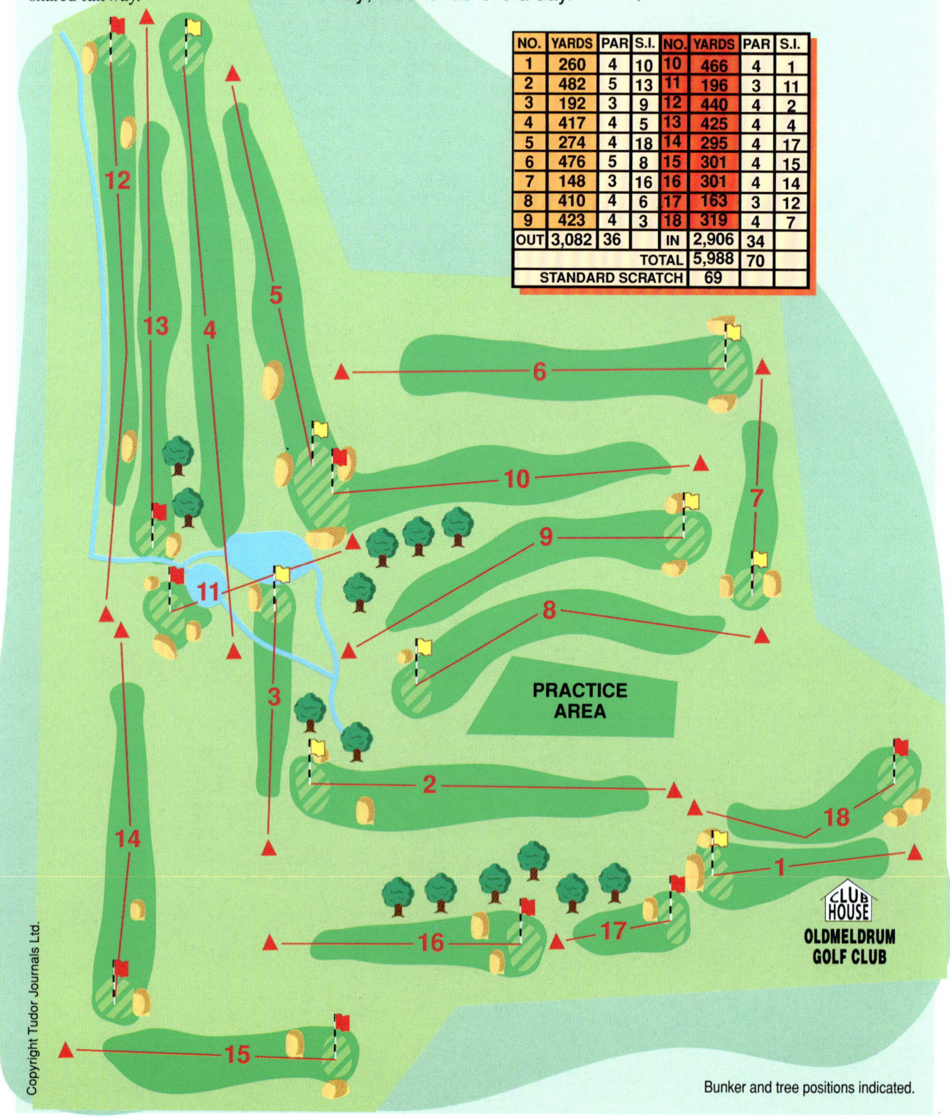

NO.	YARDS	PAR	S.I.	NO.	YARDS	PAR	S.I.
1	260	4	10	10	466	4	1
2	482	5	13	11	196	3	11
3	192	3	9	12	440	4	2
4	417	4	5	13	425	4	4
5	274	4	18	14	295	4	17
6	476	5	8	15	301	4	15
7	148	3	16	16	301	4	14
8	410	4	6	17	163	3	12
9	423	4	3	18	319	4	7
OUT	3,082	36		IN	2,906	34	
				TOTAL	5,988	70	
STANDARD SCRATCH					69		

Bunker and tree positions indicated.

Peterculter Golf Club, Oldtown, Burnside Road, Peterculter, Aberdeen AB1 0LN.
Tel & fax: (01224) 734994.

LOCATION: 8 miles west of Aberdeen off the A93.
SECRETARY: R.C. Burnett.
Tel: (01224) 734994.
PROFESSIONAL: Dean Vannet.
Tel: (01224) 734994.
ARCHITECT: Cattanach & Robertson.

A very scenic, undulating inland course which presents a good challenge to the keen golfer.

COURSE INFORMATION

Par 68; SSS 69; Length 5,947 Yds.
Opening Hours: Daylight hours.
Visitors: Welcome.
Avoid: Members only from 4.00pm to 6.30pm Mon to Fri.
Ladies: Welcome — ladies day Tues.
Green Fees: Weekdays £16 a day, £11 after 2.30pm; weekends £21 a day, £15 after 4.00pm.
Juveniles: Welcome — over 7 years.
Clubhouse Hours: April - October 11.00am to 11.00pm, November - March limited opening.
Clubhouse Dress: Smart but casual.
Clubhouse Facilities: Full time 4 star chef, fully licensed.
Open Competitions: Seniors Open-Aug, Gents Open Foursomes-Sept, Mixed Open Foursomes-Sept.

CONVENIENT HOTELS

Ardoe House;
Maryculter House Hotel;
Inverey House;
Banchory Lodge;
Marcliffe at Pitfodels.

NO.	MEDAL YARDS	GEN. YARDS	PAR	S.I.	NO.	MEDAL YARDS	GEN. YARDS	PAR	S.I.
1	344	328	4	10	10	324	310	4	15
2	173	161	3	16	11	338	295	4	13
3	445	431	4	2	12	435	421	4	1
4	360	350	4	4	13	382	370	4	3
5	150	139	3	14	14	136	124	3	17
6	516	503	5	12	15	325	240	4/3	9
7	156	141	3	18	16	392	352	4	7
8	408	395	4	6	17	538	528	5	5
9	179	180	3	8	18	346	333	4	11
OUT	2,731	2,628	33		IN	3,216	2,973	36/35	
					TOTAL	5,947	5,601	69/68	
					STANDARD SCRATCH	69	68		

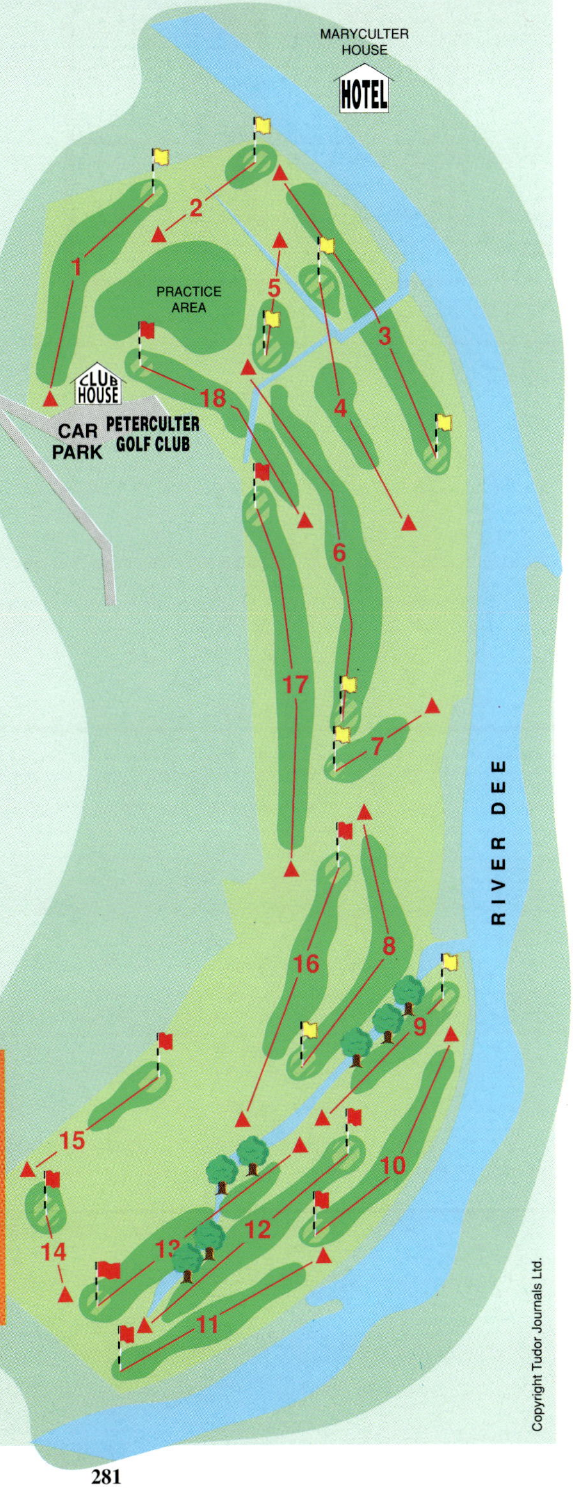

Tree positions indicated.

NO.	MEDAL YARDS	GEN. YARDS	PAR	S.I.	NO.	MEDAL YARDS	GEN. YARDS	PAR	S.I.
1	384	372	4	14	10	237	225	3	7
2	498	488	5	6	11	334	323	4	15
3	418	406	4	12	12	188	164	3	17
4	485	474	5	8	13	538	524	5	5
5	135	126	3	18	14	371	361	4	13
6	382	368	4	3	15	399	385	4	4
7	431	419	4	10	16	367	358	4	11
8	178	164	3	16	17	418	411	4	2
9	438	424	4	1	18	506	493	5	9
OUT	3,349	3,239	36		IN	3,358	3,244	36	
					TOTAL	6,707	6,483	72	
					STANDARD SCRATCH	72	71		

Portlethen Golf Club, Badentoy Road, Portlethen, Aberdeen. AB4 4YA.
Tel: (01224) 782575.

LOCATION: 5 miles south of Aberdeen off the A92.
SECRETARY: Alan Joss.
Tel: (01224) 781090.
PROFESSIONAL: Muriel Thomson.
Tel: (01224) 782571.

A demanding course of mixed character, open parkland in places, tree lined in others. Water comes into play on no less than 8 holes in the form of ponds and streams.
Forward visitor tees are being built to facilitate the need for a shorter course for visitors.

COURSE INFORMATION

Par 72; SSS 72; Length 6,707 Yards.
Visitors: None after 4pm unless with a member.
Opening Hours: 7am – sunset.
Avoid: Saturdays.
Ladies: Welcome.
Ladies Day: Saturday mornings.
Green Fees: Weekdays – £10 per round, £15 per day; Weekends – £15 per round.
Juveniles: Permitted.
Clubhouse Hours: 9am – 11pm.
Clubhouse Dress: Smart in lounge, but otherwise no restrictions.
Clubhouse Facilities: Open 9am – 9pm every day. Catering and bar facilities.
Open Competitions: Mens' Open – Last saturday in August.

CONVENIENT HOTEL

Hillside House Hotel.

Bunker and tree positions indicated.

ROYAL ABERDEEN

Royal Aberdeen Golf Club, Balgownie, Links Road, Bridge of Don. Tel: (01224) 702571.

LOCATION: 2 miles from Aberdeen off A92/Ellon Road.
SECRETARY: G.F. Webster.
PROFESSIONAL: Ronnie MacAskill.
Tel: (01224) 702221.
ARCHITECT: R. Simpson & J. Braid.

Traditional old links set amongst wonderful sand dunes. The Club was established in 1780 and the course in 1888. An excellent balance of long and short par 4's, testing par 3's and 2 par 5's that play differently every day — wind conditions play a big part in the negotiation of Balgownie Links.

COURSE INFORMATION

Par 70; SSS 71; Length 6,372 Yards.
Opening Hours: 8.00am till 11.00pm.
Visitors: Welcome, except Sat & Sun after 3.30pm.
Avoid: 8.00am to 9.30am; 4.30pm to 6.30pm.
Ladies: Welcome, restricted in Main Lounge, Dining Room only.
Ladies Day: Tues, Thurs 9.00am to 11.00am.
Green Fees: £35 a round, £45 a day or round weekend.
Juveniles: Some restrictions — 1/2 green fees.
Clubhouse Hours: 8.00am to 11.00pm.
Clubhouse Dress: Jacket, tie in Main Lounge & Dining Room; casual (no jeans or trainers) in Old Bar.
Clubhouse Facilities: Full catering, Main Lounge, Old Bar.

CONVENIENT HOTELS

Udny Arms, Newburgh;
Marcliffe at Pitfodels;
Quality Inn.

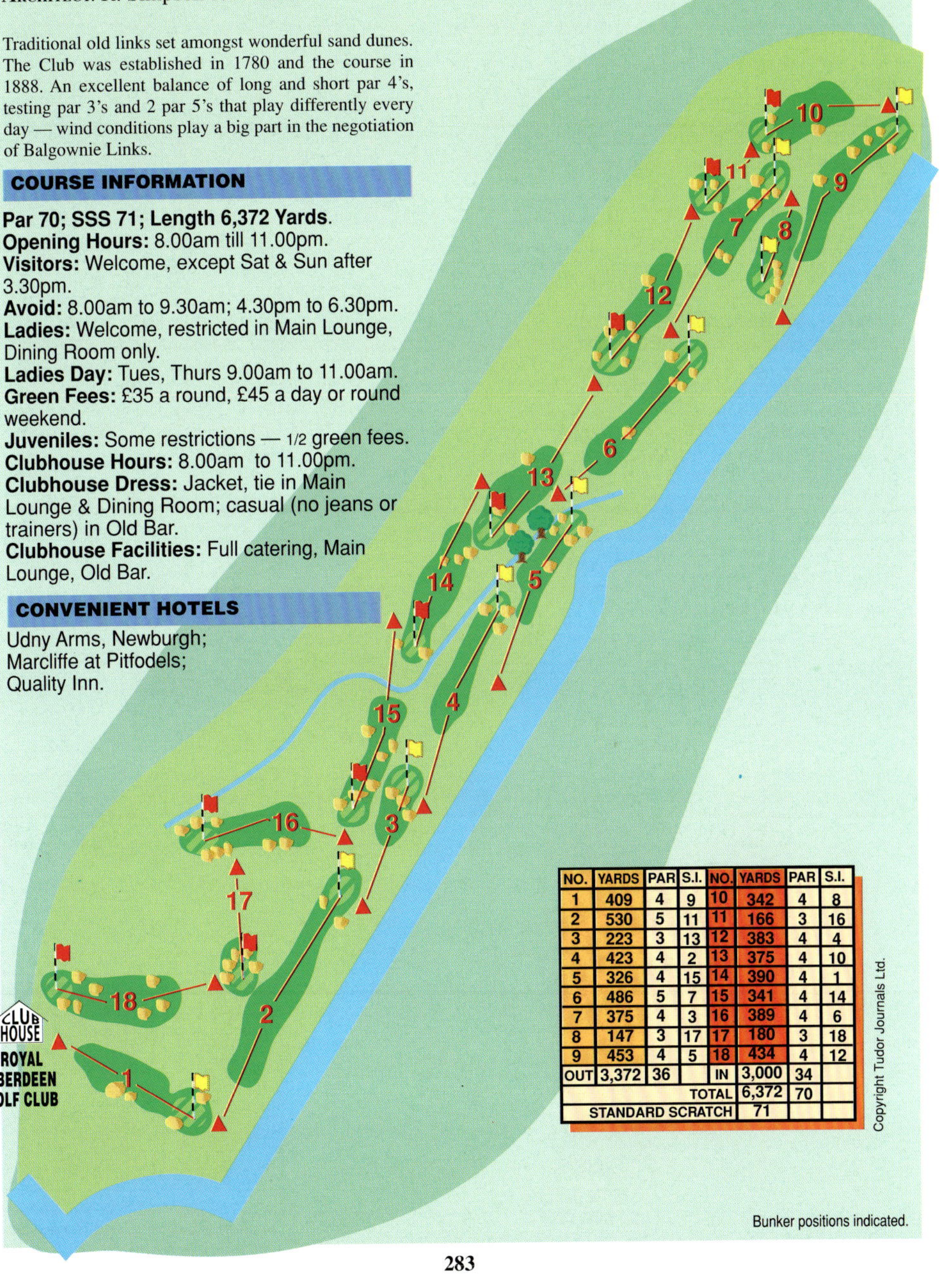

NO.	YARDS	PAR	S.I.	NO.	YARDS	PAR	S.I.
1	409	4	9	10	342	4	8
2	530	5	11	11	166	3	16
3	223	3	13	12	383	4	4
4	423	4	2	13	375	4	10
5	326	4	15	14	390	4	1
6	486	5	7	15	341	4	14
7	375	4	3	16	389	4	6
8	147	3	17	17	180	3	18
9	453	4	5	18	434	4	12
OUT	3,372	36		IN	3,000	34	
				TOTAL	6,372	70	
STANDARD SCRATCH					71		

Bunker positions indicated.

ROYAL TARLAIR

Royal Tarlair Golf Club, Buchan Street, Macduff AB4 1TA.
Tel: (01261) 32548/32897.

LOCATION: 45 miles North of Aberdeen.
SECRETARY: Mrs T. Watt.
Tel: (01261) 833739.

Royal Tarlair is a seaside course but not a links course. Magnificent view of Moray Firth and the main characteristic of the course is the famous 13th hole called "Cliuet".

COURSE INFORMATION

Par 74; SSS 68; Length 5,214 Yds.
Opening Hours: All day in Summer — from 1st April to 30th September.
Visitors: Welcome anytime - book at weekends.
Ladies: Welcome — ladies day Mon & Wed evenings.
Green Fees: Weekdays £10 a round, £15 a day; weekends £12.50 a round, £19 a day.
Juveniles: Permitted with adult, restricted to after 6.30pm.
Clubhouse Hours: Mon to Fri 11.00am to 2.30pm, 5.00pm to 11.00pm; Sat & Sun 11.00am to 11.00pm.
Clubhouse Dress: Informal.
Clubhouse Facilities: Full catering available.

CONVENIENT HOTELS

Highland Haven, Macduff.

NO.	YARDS	PAR	S.I.	NO.	YARDS	PAR	S.I.
1	265	4	13	10	308	4	10
2	355	5	5	11	334	4	6
3	106	3	17	12	321	4	8
4	409	5	3	13	129	3	18
5	278	4	9	14	270	4	14
6	308	4	7	15	284	4	12
7	161	3	15	16	351	5	4
8	476	5	1	17	215	4	16
9	277	4	11	18	367	5	2
OUT	2,635	37		IN	2,579	37	
				TOTAL	5,214	74	
				STANDARD SCRATCH	68		

Bunker positions indicated.

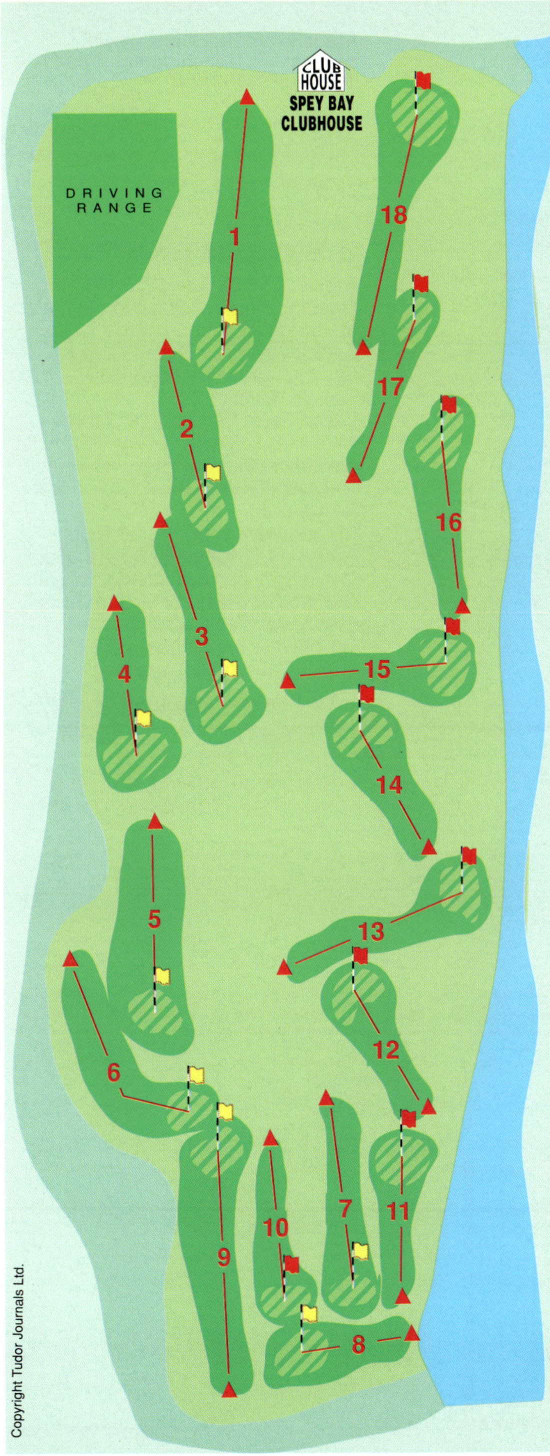

Spey Bay Golf Club, Spey Bay Hotel, Spey Bay, Fochabers. IV32 7PJ. Tel: (01343) 820424.

Location: 5 miles off A96 at Fochabers.
Hotel Manager: Tel: (01343) 820404.

Spey Bay Golf Course is an 18 hole links course of 5,682 yards, Par 70 created in 1905. It has a good reputation for all year round golf and is popular with local golfers and visitors. Adjacent to the golf course is the Spey Bay Driving Range. 16 covered bays are available to practice your golf in comfort.

COURSE INFORMATION

Par 70; SSS 69; Length 5,682 Yds.
Opening Hours: 8.00am -11.00pm.
Visitors: Welcome, avoid Sun 8.30am - 9.30am & 12.15pm - 2.15pm.
Ladies: Welcome .
Ladies day: 5.30pm - 6.30pm Tues.
Green Fees: Mon- Fri £10 round £15 day; Sat & Sun £13 round £18 day. Jnrs half price. Special Package deals for groups - book in advance.
Juveniles: Welcome.
Clubhouse Hours: Hotel licensed 11.00am - 11.00pm.
Clubhouse Facilities: Lunch 12.00pm - 2.00pm; supper 5.30pm - 8.30.

CONVENIENT HOTEL

Spey Bay Hotel.

NO.	YARDS	PAR	S.I.	NO.	YARDS	PAR	S.I.
1	427	4	5	10	385	4	4
2	351	4	9	11	297	4	15
3	374	4	11	12	318	4	6
4	195	3	16	13	299	4	10
5	393	4	1	14	300	4	14
6	312	4	12	15	150	3	17
7	383	4	7	16	517	5	3
8	138	3	18	17	339	4	13
9	476	5	2	18	410	4	8
OUT	3,049	35		IN	3,015	36	
				TOTAL	5,682	71	
STANDARD SCRATCH					70		

Stonehaven Golf Club, Cowie, Stonehaven, Kincardshire. AB3 2RH. Tel: (01569) 762124.

LOCATION: 1 mile north of Stonehaven.
SECRETARY: R.O. Blair.

Inland type course situated partially on cliff tops and positioned north of town with outstanding views.

COURSE INFORMATION

Par 66; SSS 65; Length 5,103 Yards.
Opening Hours: 8.00am to dusk.
Visitors: Welcome.
Avoid: Sat up to 4.00pm.
Ladies: Welcome — ladies day Tues & Thurs.
Green Fees: Weekdays £13 a day; weekends £18 a day — day ticket only.
Juveniles: Permitted aged ten years and over and must be a club member (of any club).
Clubhouse Hours: Mon to Thurs 8.00am to 11.00pm; Fri & Sat 8.00am to midnight; Sun 8.00am to 11.00pm.
Clubhouse Dress: Smart but Casual.
Clubhouse Facilities: Full catering inc. bar snacks and bar lunches. Dinners must be pre-arranged.

CONVENIENT HOTELS

Commodore Hotel (01569-62936);
County Hotel (01569-64386);
Royal Hotel (01569-62979).

NO.	MEDAL YARDS	GEN. YARDS	PAR	S.I.	NO.	MEDAL YARDS	GEN. YARDS	PAR	S.I.
1	305	300	4	15	10	329	294	4	6
2	203	198	3	7	11	272	257	4	16
3	331	326	4	9	12	416	396	4	1
4	364	359	4	3	13	252	247	4/3	14
5	376	376	4	5	14	169	149	3	18
6	190	171	3	13	15	161	156	3	12
7	170	165	3	11	16	482	447	5/4	4
8	159	132	3	17	17	315	268	4	8
9	398	391	4	2	18	211	172	3	10
OUT	2,496	2,418	32		IN	2,607	2,386	34/32	
					TOTAL	5,103	4,804	66/64	
					STANDARD SCRATCH	65	64		

Bunker and tree positions indicated.

STRATHLENE

NO.	YARDS	PAR	S.I.	NO.	YARDS	PAR	S.I.
1	347	4	9	10	318	4	13
2	344	4	11	11	368	4	10
3	369	4	7	12	385	4	3
4	210	3	15	13	147	3	17
5	305	4	6	14	515	5	12
6	350	4	4	15	396	4	5
7	178	3	18	16	272	4	14
8	440	4	2	17	379	4	8
9	425	4	1	18	188	3	16
OUT	2,968	34		IN	2,968	35	
				TOTAL	5,936	69	
STANDARD SCRATCH					69		

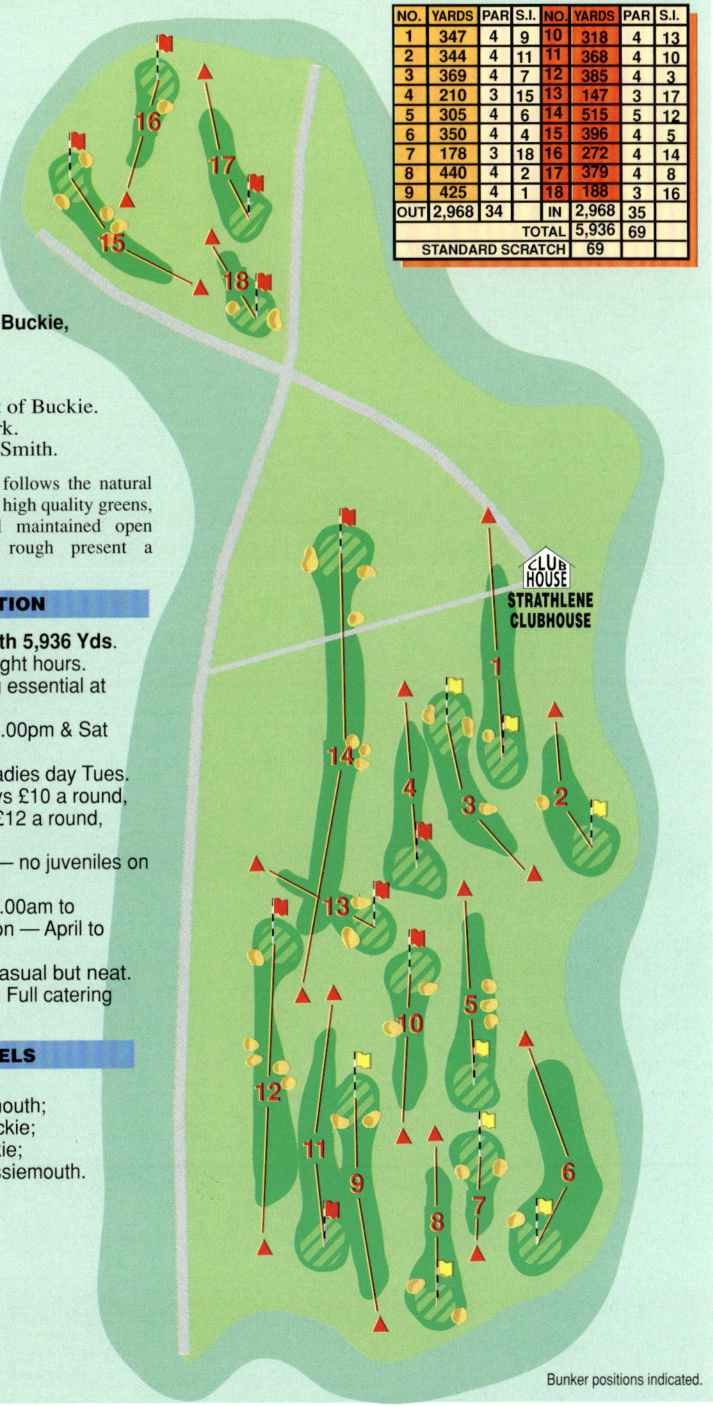

Strathlene Golf Club, Buckie,
Banffshire. AB5 2DJ.
Tel: (01542) 31798.

LOCATION: 1/2 mile East of Buckie.
SECRETARY: G.M.L. Clark.
ARCHITECT: George G. Smith.

A coastal course which follows the natural contours of the land. The high quality greens, complemented by well maintained open fairways and natural rough present a challenge to every golfer.

COURSE INFORMATION

Par 69; SSS 69; Length 5,936 Yds.
Opening Hours: Daylight hours.
Visitors: Prior booking essential at weekends.
Avoid: Fri 3.30pm to 6.00pm & Sat 12.00pm to 2.00pm.
Ladies: Welcome — ladies day Tues.
Green Fees: Weekdays £10 a round, £14 a day; weekends £12 a round, £18 a day.
Juveniles: Permitted — no juveniles on 1st tee after 6.30pm.
Clubhouse Hours: 11.00am to 11.00pm — high season — April to September.
Clubhouse Dress: Casual but neat.
Clubhouse Facilities: Full catering available.

CONVENIENT HOTELS

Marine Hotel, Buckie;
Garmouth Hotel, Garmouth;
St. Andrews Hotel, Buckie;
Mill House Hotel, Buckie;
Skerry Brae Hotel, Lossiemouth.

TARLAND

Tarland Golf Club, Tarland, Aberdeenshire. AB3 4YN.
Tel: (013398) 81413.

LOCATION: 30 miles west of Aberdeen and 5 miles north of Aboyne.
SECRETARY: J.H. Honeyman.
Tel: (013398) 81413.
ARCHITECT: Tom Morris.

Easy walking, difficult upland course. Panoraminc long distance views to Lochnager. Not normally busy Mon to Fri, no reservations at weekends.

COURSE INFORMATION

Par 67; SSS 68; Length 5,888 Yards.
Opening Hours: Sunrise to sunset.
Visitors: Welcome.
Avoid: Check by telephone call prior to play.
Ladies: Welcome.
Green Fees: Under review at time of going to press.
Juveniles: Mon to Sat welcome, must be accompanied by a playing adult on Sun.

Clubhouse Hours: 9.00am to midnight (7 days).
Clubhouse Dress: Casual.
Clubhouse Facilities: Morning tea/coffee. Bar lunches/suppers. Licensed 11.00am to midnight.

CONVENIENT HOTELS

Crossroads Hotel (approx. 5 miles); Birse Lodge, Aboyne (approx. 5 miles).

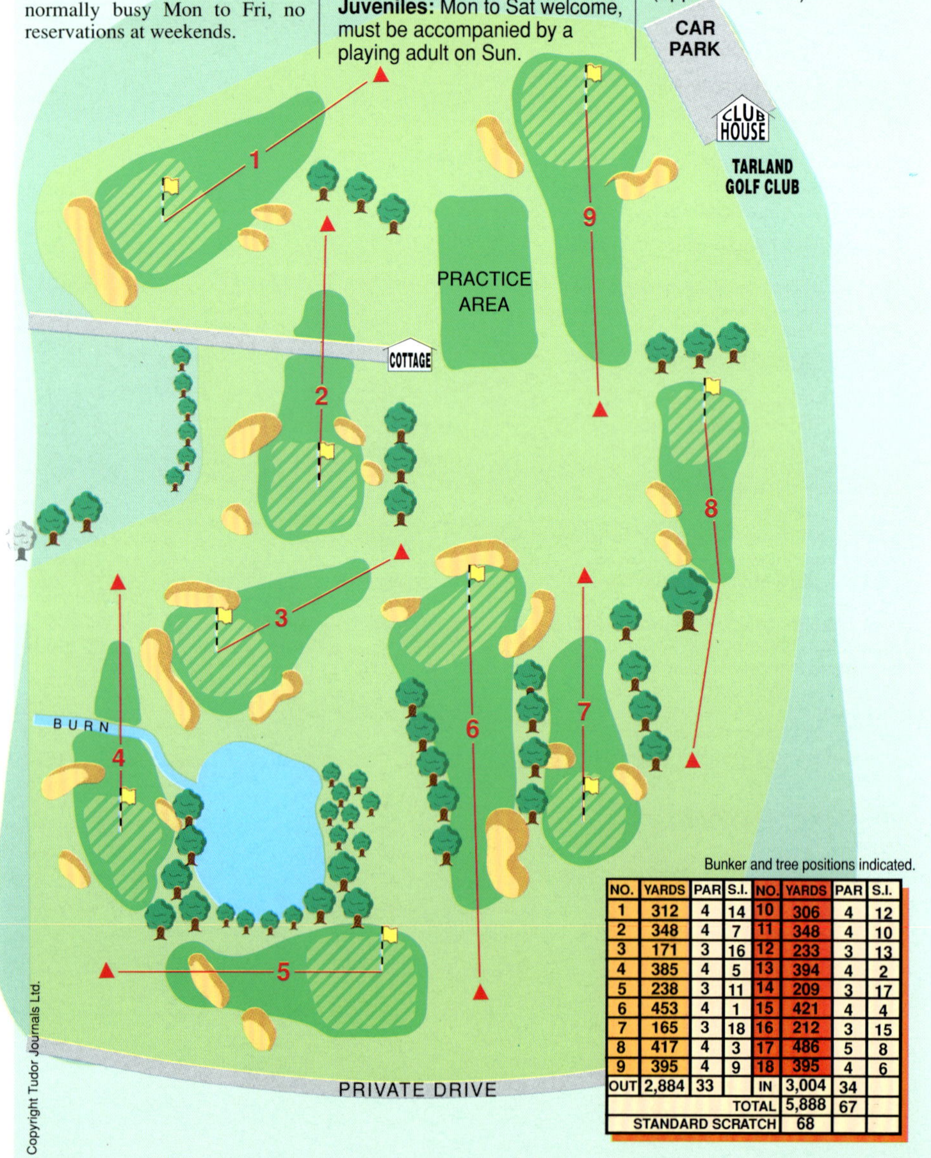

Bunker and tree positions indicated.

NO.	YARDS	PAR	S.I.	NO.	YARDS	PAR	S.I.
1	312	4	14	10	306	4	12
2	348	4	7	11	348	4	10
3	171	3	16	12	233	3	13
4	385	4	5	13	394	4	2
5	238	3	11	14	209	3	17
6	453	4	1	15	421	4	4
7	165	3	18	16	212	3	15
8	417	4	3	17	486	5	8
9	395	4	9	18	395	4	6
OUT	2,884	33		IN	3,004	34	
				TOTAL	5,888	67	
STANDARD SCRATCH					68		

Torphins Golf Club, Torphins, Aberdeenshire AB31 4JU.
Tel: (01339) 882115.

LOCATION: 6 miles from Banchory and 1/2 mile west of Torphins via Wester Beltie.
SECRETARY: Mrs S. Mortimer.
Tel: (01339) 882563.

A nine hole village course with lots of character. Hilly in parts with beautiful views of the highlands. Quite short but demanding, friendly and welcoming to visitors.

COURSE INFORMATION

Par 64; SSS 63; Length 4,684 Yds.
Opening Hours: Sunrise to sunset.
Visitors: Welcome.
Avoid: Closed one day of each weekend for competitions. Members night Tues. after 5.00pm.
Ladies: Welcome.
Green Fees: Weekdays £10; weekends £12; £6 after 6.30pm anyday.
Juveniles: Must be accompanied by an adult at weekends & after 4.30pm weekdays.

Clubhouse Hours: Part time.
Clubhouse Dress: Casual.
Clubhouse Facilities: Light refreshments.

CONVENIENT HOTEL

Learney Arms Hotel, Torphins.

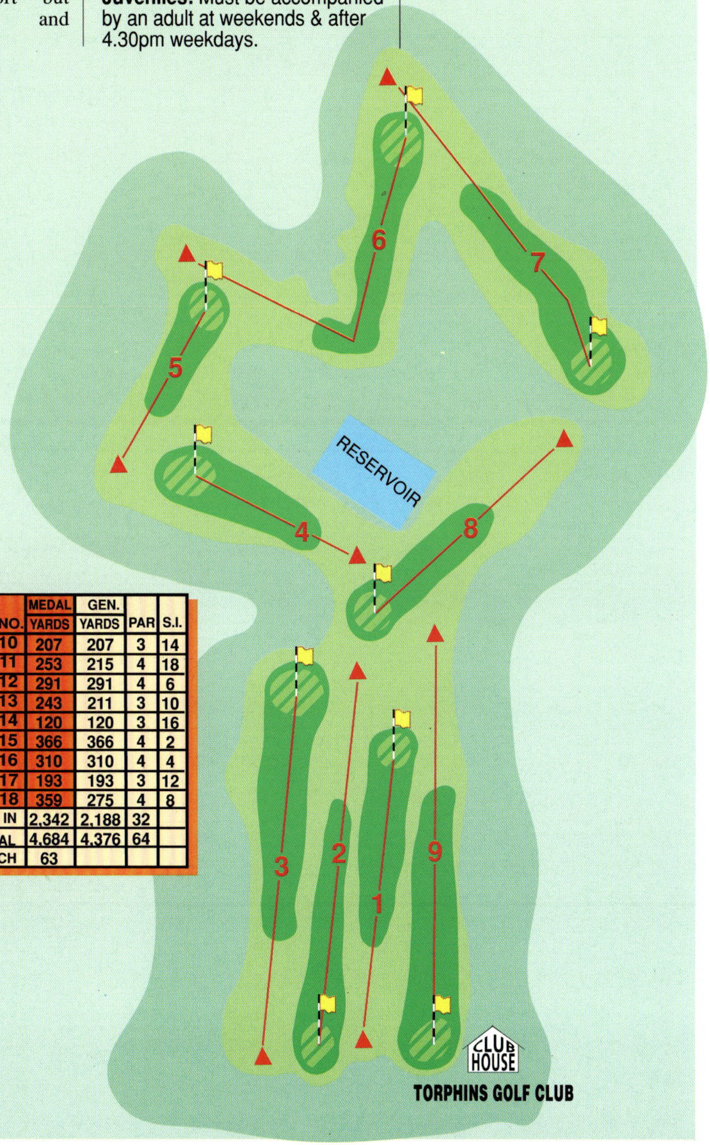

NO.	MEDAL YARDS	GEN. YARDS	PAR	S.I.	NO.	MEDAL YARDS	GEN. YARDS	PAR	S.I.
1	207	207	3	13	10	207	207	3	14
2	253	215	4	17	11	253	215	4	18
3	291	291	4	5	12	291	291	4	6
4	243	211	3	9	13	243	211	3	10
5	120	120	3	15	14	120	120	3	16
6	366	366	4	1	15	366	366	4	2
7	310	310	4	3	16	310	310	4	4
8	193	193	3	11	17	193	193	3	12
9	359	275	4	7	18	359	275	4	8
OUT	2,342	2,188	32		IN	2,342	2,188	32	
					TOTAL	4,684	4,376	64	
					STANDARD SCRATCH	63			

Turriff Golf Club, Rosehall, Turriff, Aberdeenshire. AB53 7HB.
Tel: (01888) 562982.

LOCATION: Turriff.
SECRETARY: J.G. Littlejohn.
Tel: (01888) 562982.
PROFESSIONAL: Robin Smith.
Tel: (01888) 563025.
ARCHITECT: G.M. Fraser.

Picturesque course alongside the River Deveron with some testing holes. Inland course with many trees planted throughout. Four holes uphill with the rest fairly flat. Gives a fair test of golf and can be enjoyed by most average golfers.

COURSE INFORMATION

Par 69; SSS 68; Length 6,145 Yds.
Opening Hours: 7.00am to 7.00pm.
Visitors: Welcome, not before 10.00am at the weekend and certain times on Wed.
Avoid: To avoid disappointment prior booking with professional up to 4 days in advance is required.
Ladies: Welcome — ladies day Tues.
Green Fees: Weekdays £13 a round, £16 a day; weekends £17 a round, £22 a day.
Clubhouse Hours: 11.00am to 11.00pm.
Clubhouse Dress: Casual, but smart.
Clubhouse Facilities: Catering all day apart from Wed, prior reservation appreciated.

CONVENIENT HOTELS

Union Hotel, Turriff;
Banff Springs Hotel, Banff.

NO.	YARDS	PAR	S.I.	NO.	YARDS	PAR	S.I.
1	330	4	15	10	163	3	16
2	354	4	5	11	349	4	8
3	337	4	9	12	461	4	2
4	141	3	17	13	296	4	14
5	384	4	1	14	419	4	4
6	475	5	7	15	212	3	12
7	446	4	3	16	307	4	6
8	344	4	13	17	122	3	18
9	354	4	11	18	383	4	10
OUT	3,165	36		IN	2,712	33	
				TOTAL	5,877	69	
STANDARD SCRATCH					68		

Bunker and tree positions indicated.

Balgonie

BALGONIE COUNTRY HOUSE

Situated at the heart of Royal Deeside and overlooking the challenging Ballater Golf Course.

This fine Edwardian Country House ensures a memorable visit.

Country House of the year 1993. AA Inspectors House of the year 1994.

AA***

Braemar Place, Ballater, Royal Deeside AB35 5RQ. Tel/Fax: (01397) 55482.

THE TASTE OF SCOTLAND

UDNY ARMS HOTEL

Genuine hospitality and exceptional award-winning cuisine are the hallmarks of this friendly hotel, run by the Craig family and their convival staff. Locals and guests mingle together in the lively bar, while a choice of restaurants attracts lovers of good food – the fresh seafood, in particular, is superb.

The bedrooms are comfortable and homely, many enjoying views across Newburgh's golf course to the coast. Golfers have the pick of three championship courses within a 10-minute drive, Royal Aberdeen, Cruden Bay & Murcar, while walkers can explore Newburgh's huge dunes and deserted beaches.

NEWBURGH, ELLON, ABERDEENSHIRE, AB41 0BL.
TEL: 01358-789444. FAX: 01358 789012.

The Burnett Arms Hotel

Situated in the centre of beautiful Royal Deeside "The Burnett" is within three minutes walk of Banchory Golf Course, with 20 other courses within a 45 minute drive. Family owned and run, all rooms have TV. & Satellite, DD' phone, Hairdryer, Tea/coffee and en suite facilites.

With Westhill Hotel, Westhill and The Queen's Hotel, Dundee we can offer three centres holidays and golf.

For further information / reservations
Tel: (01330) 824944. Fax: (01330) 825553.

PERTH & KINROSS

GOLF DAYS™ SCOTLAND

ABERFELDY

Aberfeldy Golf Club,
Taybridge Road, Aberfeldy.
PH15 2BH.
Tel: (01887) 820535.

LOCATION: 10 miles from Ballinluig off A9.

Flat riverside course founded in 1895.

COURSE INFORMATION

Par 68; SSS 67; Length 5,466 Yards.
Opening Hours: Daylight hours.
Visitors: Welcome.
Avoid: Tuesday & Wednesday evenings.
Ladies: Welcome, avoid Tuesday and Wednesday evenings.
Fees: 18 holes £13; £20 day ticket 7 days a week.
Juveniles: Welcome.
Clubhouse hours: 9am – 11.15pm.
Clubhouse Facilities: All meals available.

CONVENIENT HOTELS

Breadalbane; Crown; Palace; Weem; Moness & Balnearn.

NO.	YARDS	PAR	S.I.	NO.	YARDS	PAR	S.I.
1	231	3	15	10	231	3	16
2	335	4	7	11	335	4	8
3	266	4	11	12	266	4	12
4	310	4	9	13	310	4	10
5	259	3	13	14	259	3	14
6	510	5	1	15	510	5	2
7	340	4	5	16	340	4	6
8	374	4	3	17	374	4	4
9	108	3	17	18	108	3	18
OUT	2,733	34		IN	2,733	34	
				TOTAL	5,466	68	
STANDARD SCRATCH					67		

AUCHTERARDER

PERTH/KINROSS

Auchterarder Golf Club, Ochil Road, Auchterarder. PH3 1LS.
Tel: (0764) 662804.

LOCATION: 1 mile southwest of Auchterarder.
SECRETARY: W.M. Campbell.
Tel: (0764) 662804.
PROFESSIONAL: G.Baxter.
Tel: (0764) 663711.

Easy walking heathland course with scenic views to Glendevon. Part woodland.

COURSE INFORMATION

Par 69; SSS 68; Length 5,778 Yards.
Opening Hours: 7.00pm – Dusk.
Visitors: Welcome; Sundays (Max. 24people).

Avoid: Wednesdays.
Ladies: Welcome; Ladies Day; Tuesday.
Green Fees: Monday–Friday £18; Saturday/Sunday; £26.
Juveniles: Welcome; half price.
Clubhouse Hours: Mon-Sat 11am–11pm; Sun 12.30 –11pm.
Clubhouse Dress: Smart/Casual.
Clubhouse Facilities: Full catering facilities available except Thursdays.
Open Competitions: Mens Open 15 August; Ladies 29 May; Seniors 1st Sept; Mixed 10 July; Juniors 31 July.

CONVENIENT HOTEL

Cairn Lodge Golf Inn.

NO.	YARDS	PAR	S.I.	NO.	YARDS	PAR	S.I.
1	380	4	3	10	359	4	9
2	303	4	16	11	339	4	6
3	343	4	10	12	167	3	15
4	142	3	17	13	289	4	18
5	406	4	7	14	211	3	14
6	476	5	1	15	513	5	4
7	363	4	5	16	219	3	8
8	157	3	13	17	445	4	2
9	478	5	11	18	188	3	12
OUT	3,048	36		IN	2,730	33	
				TOTAL	5,778	69	
				STANDARD SCRATCH	68		

BISHOPSHIRE

NO.	YARDS	PAR	S.I.	NO.	YARDS	PAR	S.I.
1	238	4		10	238	4	
2	180	3		11	180	3	
3	156	3		12	120	3	
4	447	4		13	447	4	
5	269	4		14	269	4	
6	187	3		15	187	3	
7	365	4		16	365	4	
8	226	3		17	226	3	
9	282	4		18	282	4	
OUT	2,151	32		IN	2,314	32	
				TOTAL	4,664	64	
STANDARD SCRATCH					64		

Bishopshire Golf Club, Kinnesswood, Kinross–shire.

LOCATION: 3 miles east of Kinross off M90.
SECRETARY: J. Proudfoot.
Tel: (01592) 780203.
ARCHITECTS: Willie Park.

Hilly course overlooking Loch Leven.

COURSE INFORMATION

Par 64, SSS 64, Length 4,664 Yards.
Opening Hours: Sunrise to sunset.
Visitors: Welcome.
Avoid: Fri (competitions) 5.30pm onwards.
Ladies: Welcome.
Green Fees: W/days £5; W/ends £6.
Juveniles: Welcome.

CONVENIENT HOTEL

Lomond Hotel.

Tree positions indicated.

BLAIR ATHOLL

NO.	MEDAL YARDS	GEN. YARDS	PAR	S.I.	NO.	MEDAL YARDS	GEN. YARDS	PAR	S.I.
1	438	433	4	2	10	438	433	4	4
2	339	305	4	11	11	339	305	4	10
3	278	274	4	9	12	278	274	4	12
4	96	91	3	17	13	96	91	3	18
5	347	342	4	7	14	347	342	4	6
6	245	240	3	13	15	245	240	3	14
7	340	335	4	5	16	340	335	4	8
8	264	259	4	15	17	264	259	4	16
9	508	503	5	1	18	508	503	5	3
OUT	2,855	2,810	35		IN	2,855	2,810	35	
					TOTAL	5,710	5,620	70	
					STANDARD SCRATCH	69	70		

Blair Atholl Golf Club, Blair Atholl, Perthshire PH18 5TG.
Tel: (01796) 481407.

Location: 35 miles North of Perth off A9.
Secretary: J.A. McGregor.
Tel: (01796) 481274.

Flat nine hole parkland course.

COURSE INFORMATION

Par 70, SSS 69, Length 5,710 Yards.
Opening Hours: 7.00am to dusk.
Visitors: Welcome.
Avoid: Sundays 9.00am & 1.00pm. Wed after 6.00pm.
Ladies: Welcome.
Ladies Day: Tues from 1.00pm.
Green Fees: Weekdays £11; weekends £14.
Clubhouse Hours: 11.00am to 11.00pm.
Clubhouse Dress: Formal.
Clubhouse Facilities: Snacks, lunches & bar.
Club Competitions: Wednesday pm & Sunday.

CONVENIENT HOTELS

Tilt Hotel, Blair Atholl; Atholl Arms Hotel, Blair Atholl.

COMRIE

Comrie Golf Club, Comrie, Perthshire.
Tel: (01764) 670055

LOCATION: 7 miles west of Crieff.
SECRETARY: D.G. MCGlashan.
Tel: (01764) 670544.

The course was established in 1891 and is now one of the best 9-hole courses in Scotland. It is slightly hilly, but a great test of skill. The views from the course are magnificent.

NO.	MEDAL YARDS	GEN. YARDS	PAR	S.I.	NO.	MEDAL YARDS	GEN. YARDS	PAR	S.I.
1	340	300	4	11	10	340	300	4	12
2	261	252	4	13	11	261	252	4	14
3	175	174	3	15	12	175	174	3	16
4	408	349	4	5	13	408	349	4	6
5	173	158	3	17	14	173	158	3	18
6	492	453	5	1	15	492	453	5	2
7	372	358	4	7	16	372	358	4	8
8	361	336	4	9	17	361	336	4	10
9	438	397	4	3	18	438	397	4	4
OUT	3,020	2,777	35		IN	3,020	2,777	35	
					TOTAL	6,040	5,554	70	
					STANDARD SCRATCH	69			

COURSE INFORMATION

Par 70; SSS 69; Length 6,040 Yards.
Opening Hours: Sunrise – Setset.
Visitors: Welcome except Mondays and Tuesdays from 4.30pm.
Avoid: Mondays and Tuesdays from 4.30pm.
Ladies: Welcome.
Green Fees: Mon – Fri £10; £12 Sat & Sun.
Clubhouse facilities: Light snacks and soft drinks during Summer months and at weekends.

CONVENIENT HOTELS

Royal Hotel, Comrie;
Comrie Hotel, Comrie.

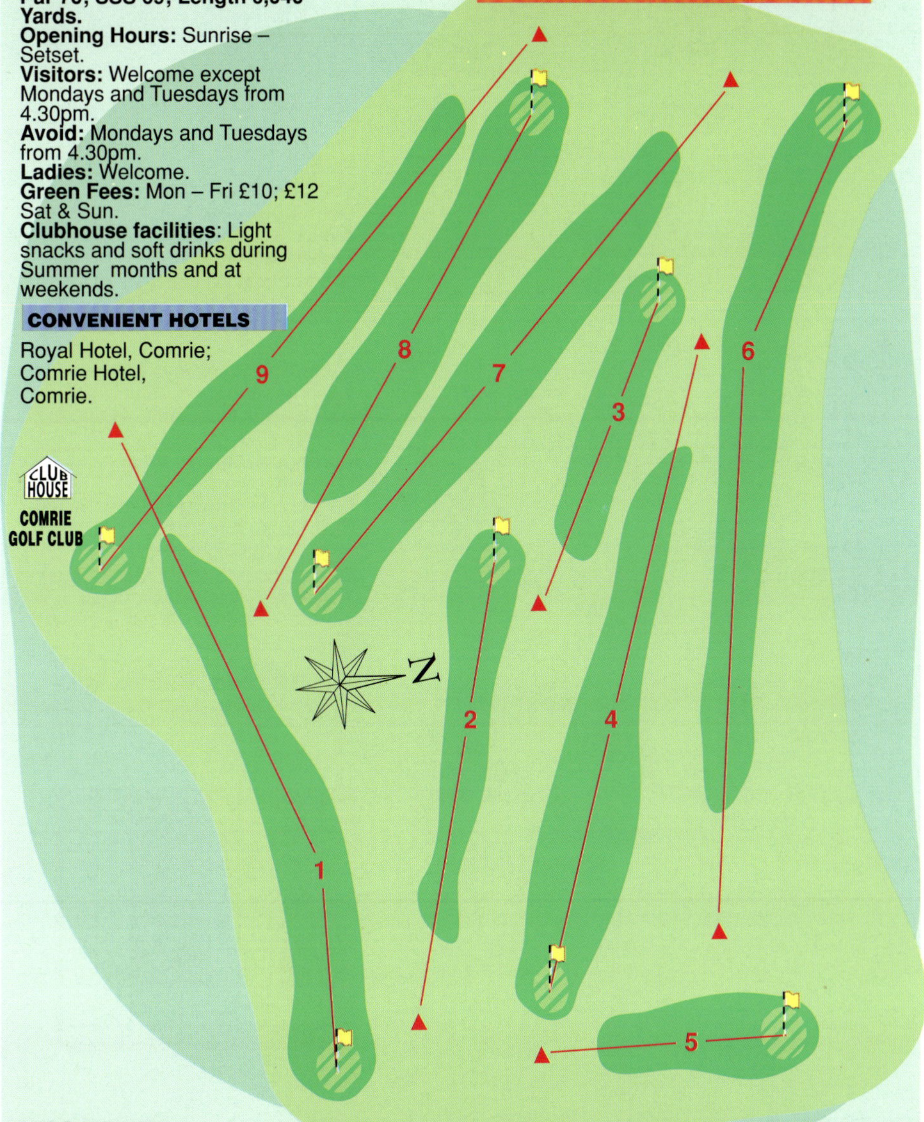

CRAIGIE HILL

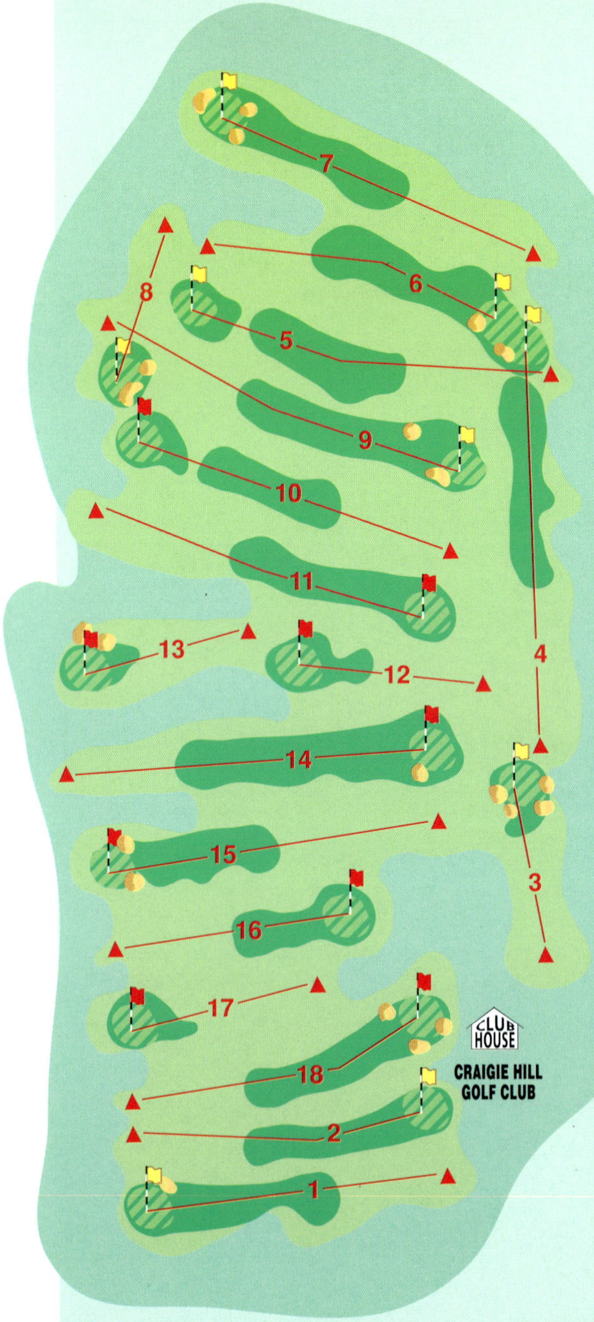

Craigie Hill Golf Club,
Cherrybank, Perth. PH2 ONE.
Tel: (01738) 620829.

LOCATION: West boundary of Perth.
SECRETARY: Mr Allen.
Tel: (01738) 620829.
PROFESSIONAL: Frank Smith.
Tel: (01738) 622644.
ARCHITECT: Willie Fernie and Joe Anderson.

Hilly course with scenic views, at west end of town. Easily accessable from A9 and M90.

COURSE INFORMATION

Par 66; SSS 66; Length 5,379 Yards.
Visitors: Welcome.
Opening Hours: 8am – Dusk.
Avoid: Saturdays.
Ladies: Welcome.
Green Fees: Weekdays £10 per round, £15 per day; Sundays £20 per day; Juniors (Mon–Fri.) £3 per round.
Juveniles: Weekdays 9.30am – 12pm & 2.30pm – 4.30pm. Tee reservations Mon. 4pm – 4.30pm; Sunday 5.30pm – 6.30pm.
Clubhouse Hours: 11am – 11.30pm.
Clubhouse Dress: Smart / Casual.
Clubhouse Facilities: Bar lunches, high teas & dinners.
Open Competitions: Mens' Open – July; Boys' Open – July; Open mixed foursomes – June; Seniors' Open – September.

CONVENIENT HOTEL

Lovat Hotel, Glasgow Road, Perth.

NO.	YARDS	PAR	S.I.	NO.	YARDS	PAR	S.I.
1	391	4	9	10	344	4	10
2	384	4	5	11	393	4	4
3	146	3	15	12	212	3	8
4	327	4	7	13	187	3	16
5	380	4	1	14	356	4	2
6	310	4	13	15	330	4	12
7	362	4	3	16	233	3	14
8	135	3	18	17	199	3	17
9	328	4	11	18	362	4	6
OUT	2,763	34		IN	2,616	32	
				TOTAL	5,379	66	
STANDARD SCRATCH					66		

Bunker positions indicated.

CRIEFF (DORNOCK COURSE)

PERTH/KINROSS

Crieff Golf Club, Perth Road, Crieff, Perthshire. PH7 3LR. Tel: (01764) 652909/652397.

LOCATION: Perth 27km, Edinburgh 83km, Glasgow 109km.

SECRETARY: L.J. Rundle. Tel: (01764) 652397.

SENIOR PROFESSIONAL: J.M.Stark.

CLUB PROFESSIONAL: D.J.W. Murchie.

Creiff has two parkland courses – Ferntower and Dornock. There excellent views over Strathearn valley from both courses. Advance booking strongly advised, but last minute enquirers may be fortunate.

COURSE INFORMATION

Par: 71; SSS 77; Length 2,386 Yards 2,182 Metres.

Opening Hours: Sunrise – Sunset.

Visitors: Welcome. Handicap certificates normally required.

Avoid: Restrictions vary, enquire when booking.

Ladies: Welcome.

Juveniles: Welcome, but there are some restrictions.

Green Fees: Mon – Fri £7 per round/£11 2 rounds; Weekends £11 per round/ £14 2 rounds.

Clubhouse Dress: Smart/Casual.

Clubhouse Facilities: All facilities are available, changing rooms, showers and catering.

CONVENIENT HOTELS

Crieff Hydro; Murraypark Hotel; Arduthie Hotel.

NO.	YARDS	PAR	S.I.	NO.	YARDS	PAR	S.I.
1	325	4	9	10	325	4	10
2	196	3	13	11	196	3	14
3	331	4	7	12	331	4	8
4	205	3	3	13	205	3	2
5	163	3	17	14	163	3	18
6	256	4	11	15	256	4	12
7	365	4	5	16	365	4	6
8	162	3	15	17	162	3	16
9	383	4	1	18	383	4	4
OUT	2,386	32		IN	2,386	32	
				TOTAL	4,772	64	
STANDARD SCRATCH					63		

Bunker & tree positions indicated.

DALMUNZIE

Dalmunzie Golf Course,Spittal of Glenshee, Blairgrowie. Tel: (01250) 855226.

LOCATION: 18 miles north of Blairgrowie on A93. At Spittal of Glenshee.
SECRETARY: S. Stewart.

Small well kept hilly course set in beautiful scenery — claimed to be the highest in Britain.

COURSE INFORMATION

Par 60, SSS 60, Length 4,070 Yards.
Opening Hours: Daylight hours.
Visitors: Welcome.
Avoid: 10.30 to 12.00pm Monday.
Ladies: Welcome.
Green Fees: 9 holes £5.00; day £8.50 all week.
Juveniles: Welcome.
Clubhouse Facilites: For drinks etc, go to Dalmunzie Hotel.

CONVENIENT HOTEL

Dalmunzie Hotel.

NO.	YARDS	PAR	S.I.	NO.	YARDS	PAR	S.I.
1	248	3	5	10	248	3	6
2	146	3	15	11	146	3	16
3	267	4	13	12	267	4	14
4	122	3	17	13	122	3	18
5	164	3	3	14	164	3	4
6	455	4	1	15	455	4	2
7	115	3	9	16	115	3	10
8	173	3	11	17	173	3	12
9	345	4	7	18	345	4	8
OUT	2,035	30		IN	2,035	30	
				TOTAL	4,070	60	
				STANDARD SCRATCH	60		

Bunker positions indicated.

DUNKELD & BIRNHAM

Dunkeld & Birnam Golf Club,
Fungarth, Dunkeld.
Tel: (01350) 727524.

LOCATION: Dunkeld, 1 mile off A923.
SECRETARY: Mrs W. Sinclair.
Tel: (01350) 727 564.

Heathland course with panoramic views a testing 9 holes.

COURSE INFORMATION

Par 68; SSS 66; Length 5,240 Yards.
Visitors: Welcome.
Opening Hours: Sunrise - sunset.
Avoid: Some restricted times.
Ladies: Welcome.
Ladies Day: Sat Afternoon.
Green fees: Mon – Fri R £11 D £13; W/e R £16 D £22.
Juveniles: Juniors allowed but some restrictions.

Clubhouse: 11.00am - 11.00pm.
Clubhouse dress: No Jeans.
Clubhouse Facilities: Meals available and snacks.
Competitions: Gents June Ladies July. Open mixed August. Gents Senior Sept.

COURSE INFORMATION

Stakis Dunkeld House Resort Hotel; Royal Dunkeld Hotel.

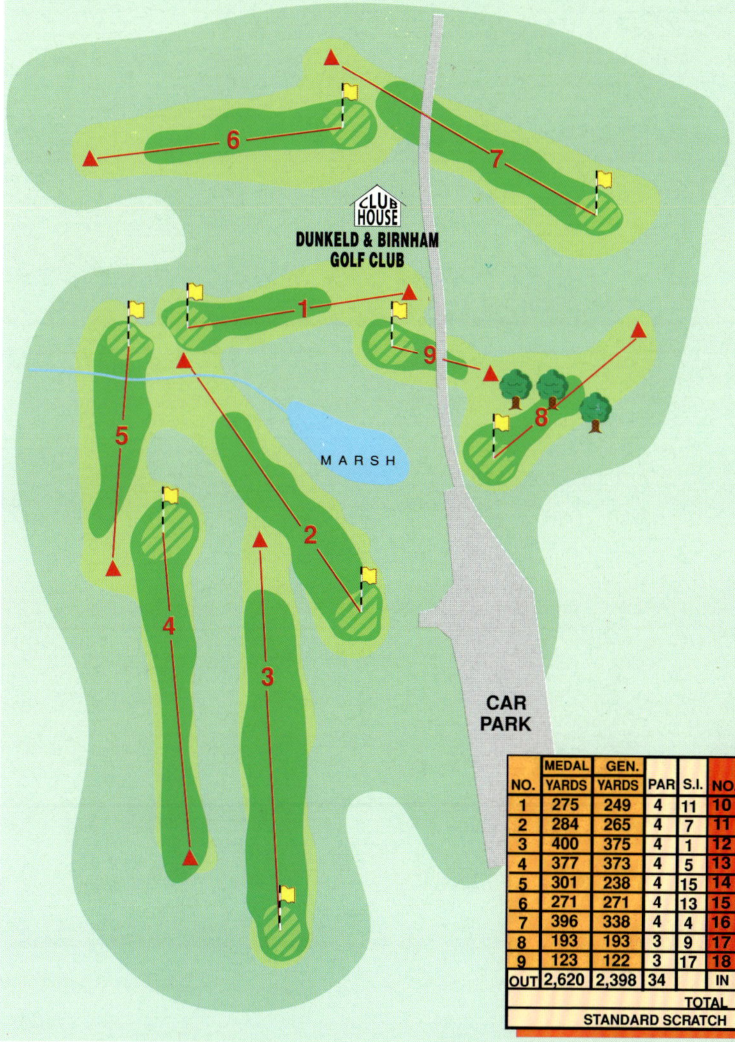

NO.	MEDAL YARDS	GEN. YARDS	PAR	S.I.	NO.	MEDAL YARDS	GEN. YARDS	PAR	S.I.
1	275	249	4	11	10	275	249	4	12
2	284	265	4	7	11	284	265	4	8
3	400	375	4	1	12	400	375	4	2
4	377	373	4	5	13	377	373	4	6
5	301	238	4	15	14	301	238	4	16
6	271	271	4	13	15	271	271	4	14
7	396	338	4	4	16	396	338	4	3
8	193	193	3	9	17	193	193	3	10
9	123	122	3	17	18	123	122	3	18
OUT	2,620	2,398	34		IN	2,620	2.398	34	
					TOTAL	5,240	4,848	68	
					STANDARD SCRATCH	66	65		

The sheltered green.

Scottish Highland Photo Library.

GLENEAGLES (King's Course) PERTH / KINROSS

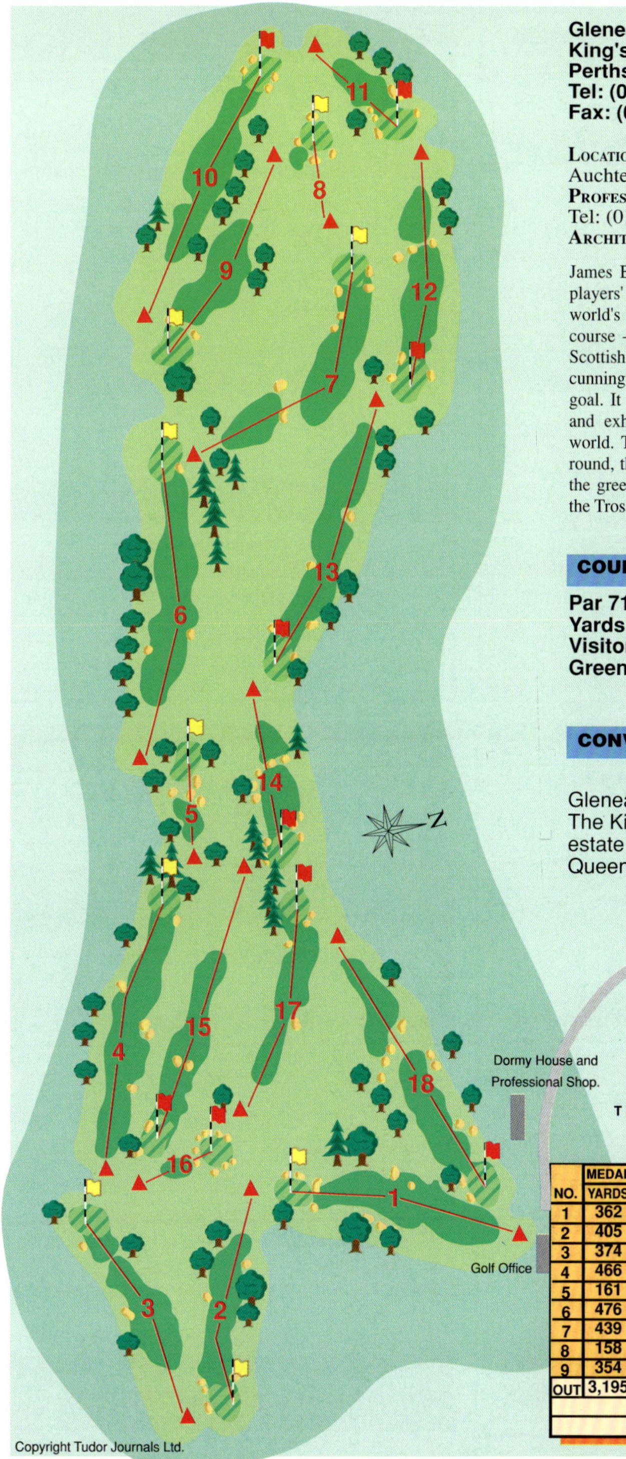

Gleneagles Hotel Golf Office,
King's Course, Auchterarder,
Perthshire, PH3 1NF.
Tel: (01704) 663543.
Fax: (01764) 664440.

Location: Just off the A9 beside Auchterarder.
Professional: Greg Schofield. Tel: (01764) 665543.
Architect: James Braid.

James Braid's plan was to test even the best players' shot making skills all the way. The world's greatest golfers when they play this course – as they do every July in the Bell's Scottish Open – almost universally admire the cunning and craft with which he acheived that goal. It is certainly one of the most beautiful and exhilarating places to play golf in the world. The sweeping views from the tees all round, the rock faced mountains to the North, the green hills to the South, and the peaks of the Trossachs on the Western horizon.

COURSE INFORMATION

Par 71; SSS 71; Length 6,471 Yards.
Visitors: Resident members only.
Green Fees: Prices on request.

CONVENIENT HOTELS

Gleneagles Hotel on the course. The King's Course is on the Hotel's estate which also includes the Queen's and Monarch's courses.

NO.	MEDAL YARDS	GEN. YARDS	PAR	S.I.	NO.	MEDAL YARDS	GEN. YARDS	PAR	S.I.
1	362	352	4	6	10	447	429	5	1
2	405	386	4	14	11	230	221	3	10
3	374	360	4	9	12	395	352	4	13
4	466	443	4	2	13	448	423	4	7
5	161	149	3	16	14	260	249	4	15
6	476	455	5	8	15	459	438	4	3
7	439	430	4	4	16	135	128	3	18
8	158	155	3	17	17	377	367	4	11
9	354	335	4	12	18	525	453	5	5
OUT	3,195	3,065	35		IN	3,,276	3,060	36	
					TOTAL	6,471	6,125	71	
	STANDARD SCRATCH					71	69		

GLENEAGLES (QUEEN'S COURSE)

Gleneagles Hotel Golf Office, Queen's Course, Auchterarder, Perthshire, PH 1NF.
Tel: (01764) 663543.
Fax: (01764) 664440.

LOCATION: Just off the A9 beside Auchterarder.
SECRETARY: Greg Schofield.
Tel: (01764) 665543.
ARCHITECT: James Braid.

The Queen's course is an excellent test of golf coupled with breathtaking views of the Scottish scenery. It is heavily wooded with a variety of dog-leg holes and the Loch-an-Eerie to negotiate.

COURSE INFORMATION

Par 68; SSS 69; Length 5,192 Yards.

Visitors: Residents and members only.

Green Fees: On request.

CONVENIENT HOTELS

Gleneagles Hotel on the course. The Queen's course is on the hotel's estate which also includes the Kings and Monarchs courses.

At 3,192 yards long, the challenge of the first nine can be deceptive, with even some of the best players finding it a test to make par into a fresh south westerly breeze. The homeward nine offer great satisfaction as a fortunate player can swoop home in a flurry of birdies.

NO.	MEDAL YARDS	GEN. YARDS	PAR	S.I.	NO.	MEDAL YARDS	GEN. YARDS	PAR	S.I.
1	409	387	4	5	10	421	403	4	4
2	146	130	3	17	11	318	309	4	13
3	421	411	4	1	12	433	407	4	3
4	355	351	4	10	13	140	132	3	18
5	177	163	3	15	14	215	177	3	9
6	437	407	4	6	15	252	251	4	16
7	491	476	5	8	16	378	369	4	11
8	337	310	4	12	17	204	183	3	14
9	419	415	4	2	18	412	379	4	7
OUT	3,192	3,050	35		IN	2,773	2,610	33	
					TOTAL	3,192	3,050	68	
					STANDARD SCRATCH	69	67		

Bunker and tree positions indicated.

GLENEAGLES (MONARCH COURSE)

The Gleneagles Hotel Golf Courses, Gleneagles Monarch Course, Auchterarder, Perthshire, PH3 1NF.
Tel: (0764) 663543. Fax: (0764) 664440.

LOCATION: Just off the A9, beside Auchterarder.
PROFESSIONAL: Greg Schofield. Tel: (0764) 663543.
ARCHITECT: Jack Nicklaus.

From the back tees, the Monarch measures 7,081 yards – the longest inland course in Scotland. However the tees are graded at each hole in five stages, including a challenging 6,551 yards from the white markers down to the 5,065 from the red. Designed by Jack Nicklaus, the Monarch course offers superb views and even better golf.

COURSE INFORMATION

Par 72; SSS 74; Length 7,081Yards.
Visitors: Resident and members only.
Green Fees: On request.

CONVENIENT HOTELS

The Gleneagles Hotel, on the course.

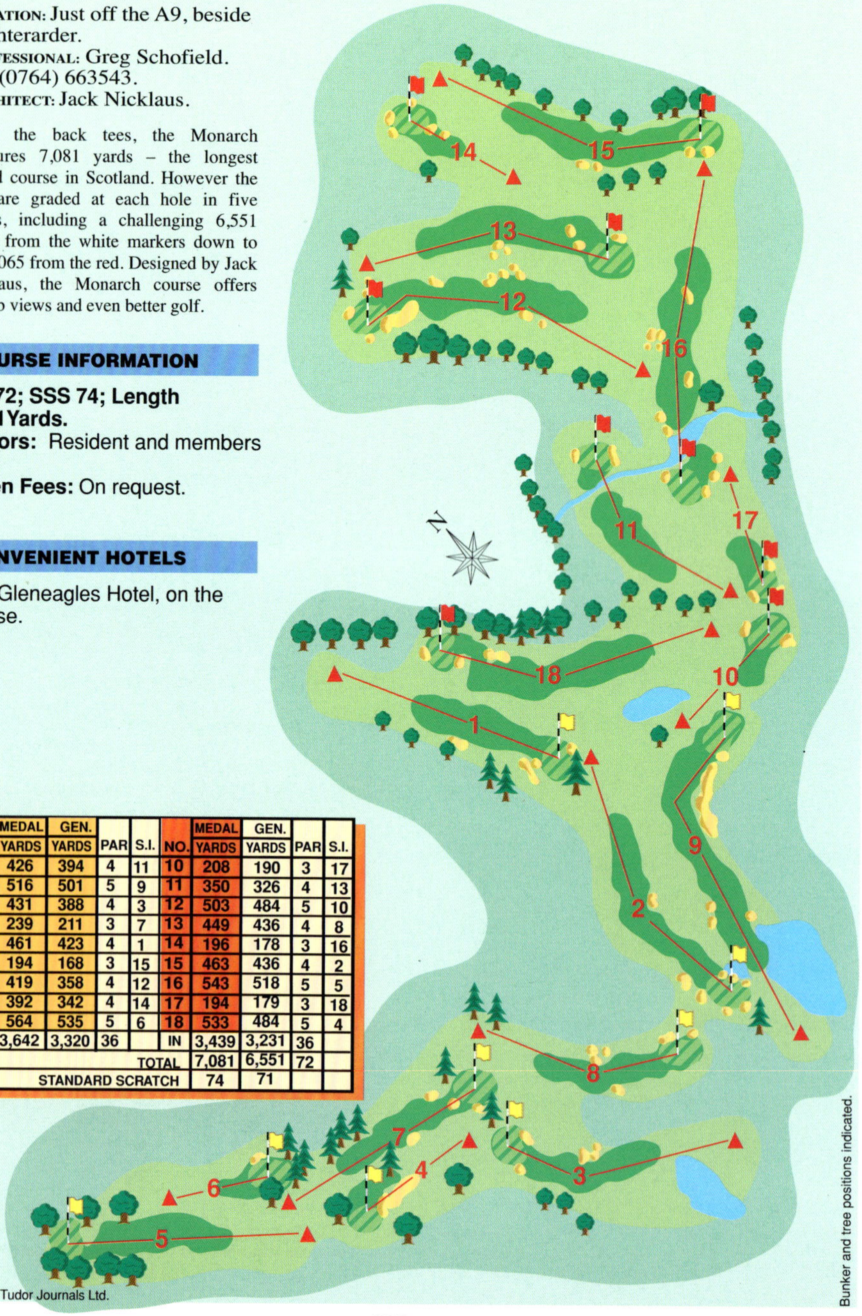

NO.	MEDAL YARDS	GEN. YARDS	PAR	S.I.	NO.	MEDAL YARDS	GEN. YARDS	PAR	S.I.
1	426	394	4	11	10	208	190	3	17
2	516	501	5	9	11	350	326	4	13
3	431	388	4	3	12	503	484	5	10
4	239	211	3	7	13	449	436	4	8
5	461	423	4	1	14	196	178	3	16
6	194	168	3	15	15	463	436	4	2
7	419	358	4	12	16	543	518	5	5
8	392	342	4	14	17	194	179	3	18
9	564	535	5	6	18	533	484	5	4
OUT	3,642	3,320	36		IN	3,439	3,231	36	
					TOTAL	7,081	6,551	72	
					STANDARD SCRATCH	74	71		

Bunker and tree positions indicated.

KILLIN

Killin Golf Club, Killin, Perthshire
Tel: (01567) 820312.

LOCATION: West end of Loch Tay.
SECRETARY: A. Chisholm.
CLUBMASTER: G. Hibbert.
ARCHITECT: John Duncan.

Challenging parkland type course situated amongst Perthshire Highlands. Modern changing facilities complement a well maintained and attractive course.

COURSE INFORMATION

Par 66; SSS 65; Length 5,066 Yards.
Opening Hours: 8.30am – Dusk.
Visitors: Welcome.
Avoid: Gents Medals, generally Monday night.
Ladies: Welcome; Medals Tuesday or Thursday evening.
Green Fees: £10 per Round; £13 per day. No weekend pass available.
Juveniles: Welcome £6 with an adult.
Clubhouse hours: 8.30am – Dusk.
Clubhouse Dress: Casual/smart.
Open Competitions: Gents Open 1st Saturday in August; Mixed Open – Last Saturday in May; Ladies Open – 1st Saturday in June.

NO.	MEDAL YARDS	GEN. YARDS	PAR	S.I.	NO.	MEDAL YARDS	GEN. YARDS	PAR	S.I.
1	288	264	4	9	10	288	264	4	10
2	207	196	3	11	11	207	196	3	4
3	208	200	3	12	12	208	200	3	15
4	394	359	4	3	13	394	359	4	2
5	100	95	3	14	14	100	95	3	16
6	326	280	4	7	15	326	280	4	8
7	340	305	4	5	16	340	305	4	6
8	156	148	3	17	17	156	148	3	18
9	514	491	5	1	18	514	491	5	13
OUT	2,533	2,338	33		IN	2,533	2,338	33	
					TOTAL	5,066	4,676	66	
					STANDARD SCRATCH	65	63		

Bunker positions indicated.

King James VI Golf Club,
Moncreiffe Island, Perth.
Tel: (0738) 25170.

LOCATION: Island in River Tay, Perth.
SECRETARY: Mrs Dorothy Barraclough.
Tel: (0738) 32460.
PROFESSIONAL: Mr Tony Coles.
Tel: (0738) 32460.
ARCHITECT: Tom Morris.

An excellent 18-hole parkland course right in the centre of Perth. Club formed in 1858 and moved to Moncreiffe Island in 1897. One of only two golf courses situated on an island in a river.

COURSE INFORMATION

Par 68; SSS 68; Length 5,664 Yards.
Opening hours: 8am to Sunset.
Visitors: Welcome.
Avoid: Saturdays & before 10am on Sundays.
Ladies: Welcome.
Green Fees: Weekday Round £13; Day £20; Sunday (day) £27; Afternoon Round £15.
Juveniles: Welcome; Not between 4.30pm and 7pm and not before 2pm weekends.
Clubhouse Hours: 7.45am – 11pm.
Clubhouse dress: Casual but smart.
Clubhouse Facilities: Full bar menu available all day.
Open Competitions: Ladies – June; Gents 36 Hole 11 – July; Gents 18 Hole – August Open Week – September; Mixed Open – Setpember.

CONVENIENT HOTELS

Salutation Hotel, Perth; Sunbank House Hotel, Perth.

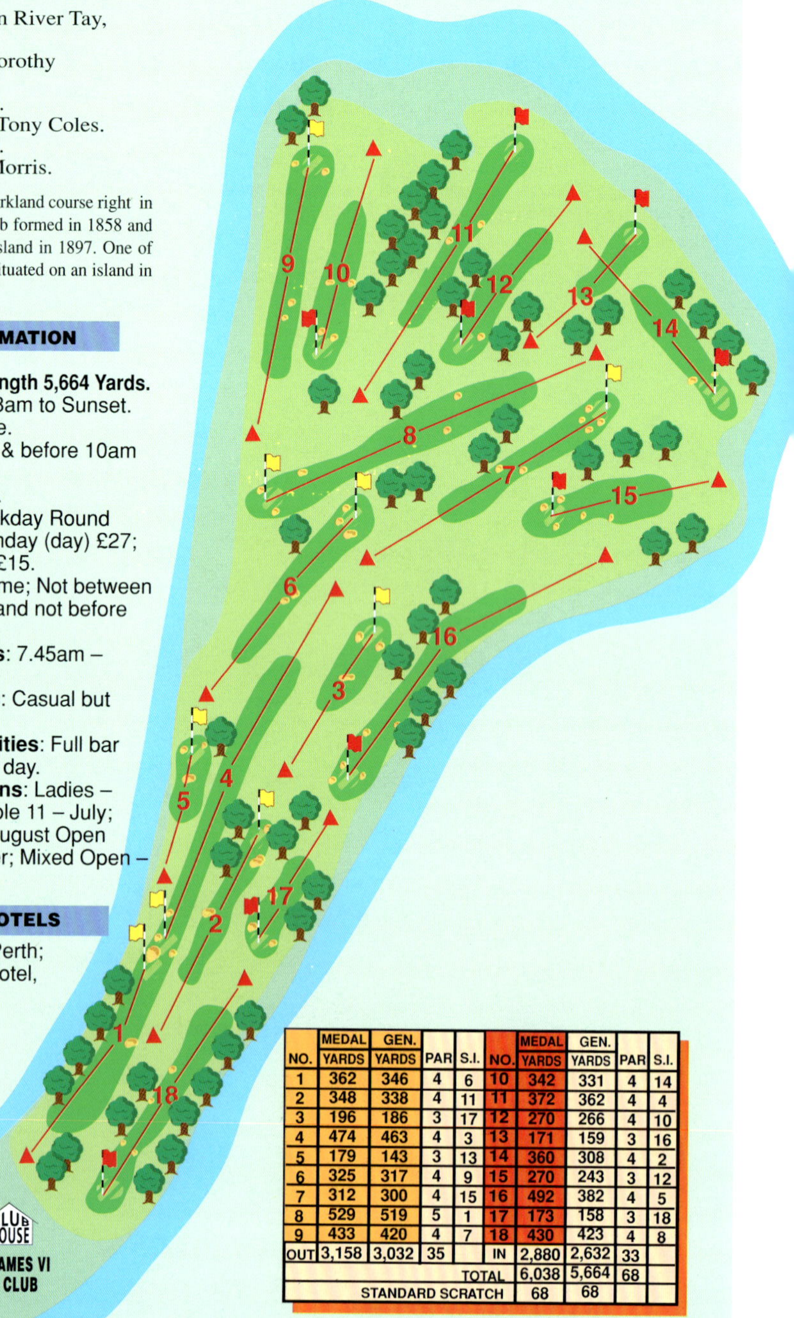

NO.	MEDAL YARDS	GEN. YARDS	PAR	S.I.	NO.	MEDAL YARDS	GEN. YARDS	PAR	S.I.
1	362	346	4	6	10	342	331	4	14
2	348	338	4	11	11	372	362	4	4
3	196	186	3	17	12	270	266	4	10
4	474	463	4	3	13	171	159	3	16
5	179	143	3	13	14	360	308	4	2
6	325	317	4	9	15	270	243	3	12
7	312	300	4	15	16	492	382	4	5
8	529	519	5	1	17	173	158	3	18
9	433	420	4	7	18	430	423	4	8
OUT	3,158	3,032	35		IN	2,880	2,632	33	
					TOTAL	6,038	5,664	68	
					STANDARD SCRATCH	68	68		

Bunker and tree positions indicated.

THE GREEN HOTEL (Blue Course) PERTH/KINROSS

**Green Hotel Golf Courses,
2 The Muirs, Kinross,
KY13 7AS
Tel: (01577) 863467.
Fax: (01577) 863180.**

Location: 17 miles south of Perth, 25 miles north of Edinburgh off M90 Junction 6.
Secretary: Mrs M. Smith.
Tel: (01577) 863407.
Professional: Stewart Geraghty.
Tel: (01577) 865125.
Architect: Sir David Montgomery.

One of two inland park courses in beautiful scenery. Mature woodland course providing a good golfing challenge.

NO.	YARDS	PAR	S.I.	NO.	YARDS	PAR	S.I.
1	199	3	12	10	355	4	9
2	406	4	14	11	501	5	15
3	492	5	10	12	379	4	1
4	173	3	8	13	350	4	3
5	305	4	16	14	179	3	11
6	372	4	18	15	550	5	13
7	343	4	4	16	399	4	5
8	435	4	2	17	166	3	17
9	402	4	6	18	450	4	7
OUT	3,127	35		IN	3,329	36	
				TOTAL	6,456	71	
STANDARD SCRATCH					71		

COURSE INFORMATION

Par: 71; SSS 71; Length 6,456 Yards, 5,905 Metres.
Opening Hours: 8am – Sunset.
Visitors: Welcome.
Ladies: Welcome.
Juveniles: Welcome.
Green Fees: Weekday round £14, Per Day £20; Weekend Round £20, £30 Per Day.
Clubhouse Hours: 8am – 11pm.
Clubhouse Facilities: Full catering facilities available.
Clubhouse Dress: Casual/Smart.
Open Competitions: Kinross June.

CONVENIENT HOTELS

Green Hotel, Kinross.
Reduced rates for hotel residents (playing golf).

Bunker and tree positions indicated.

THE GREEN HOTEL (Red Course) PERTH/KINROSS

Green Hotel Golf Courses,
2 the Muirs, Kinross,
KY13 7AS.
Tel: (01577) 863467.
Fax: (01577) 863180.

Location: 17 miles south of Perth, 25 miles north of Edinburgh off M90 Junction 6.
Secretary: Mrs M. Smith.
Tel: (01577) 863407.
Professional: Stewart Geraghty.
Tel: (01577) 865125.
Architect: Sir David Montgomery.

Two inland park courses in beautiful scenery offering a stimulating challenge to both the holiday golfer and low handicap player.

COURSE INFORMATION

Par 72; SSS 70; Length 6,257 Yards, 5,719 Metres.
Opening Hours: 8 am – Sunset.
Visitors: Welcome.
Ladies: Welcome.
Green Fees: Weekday round £14, £20 per day; Weekend round £20, £30 per day.
Juveniles: Welcome.
Clubhouse Hours: 8am – 11pm.
Clubhouse Dress: Casual/Smart.
Clubhouse Facilities: Full catering facilities available.
Open Competitions: Kinross, June.

CONVENIENT HOTELS

Green Hotel, Kinross. Reduced rates for hotel residents (playing golf).

NO.	YARDS	PAR	S.I.	NO.	YARDS	PAR	S.I.
1	336	4	8	10	372	4	3
2	311	4	18	11	200	3	13
3	203	3	10	12	513	5	9
4	487	5	6	13	191	3	5
5	510	5	16	14	395	4	7
6	269	4	4	15	375	4	1
7	337	4	14	16	162	3	17
8	483	5	12	17	338	4	15
9	444	4	2	18	331	4	11
OUT	3,380	38		IN	2,877	34	
				TOTAL	6,257	72	
STANDARD SCRATCH					70		

Bunker and tree positions indicated.

Milnathort Golf Club,
South Street, Milnathort,
Kinross-Shire
Tel: (01577) 864069

LOCATION: 1 mile north of Kinross. M90 junction 6 (north) or junction 7 (south).

Undulating inland course with lush fairways and excellent greens, most of the year. Strategically placed copses of trees require accurate tee shots. The course is being made more interesting by the addition of different tees and greens for each hole.

COURSE INFORMATION

Par 71; SSS 69; Length 5,969 yards.
Opening hours: Daylight hours.
Visitors: Welcome.
Avoid: Phone at weekends.
Ladies: Welcome.
Ladies Day: Monday/Wednesday.
Green Fees: £12 day ticket weekdays; £17 day ticket weekends.
Juveniles: Welcome. Only with members when busy.
Clubhouse hours: 9am/dusk Weekdays & Sundays, 8am/dusk Saturday.
Clubhouse Dress: Informal/Smart.
Clubhouse Facilities: Changing rooms (Showers), snacks available most of the day, meals by arrangements.

CONVENIENT HOTELS

Thistle, New Road, Milnathort, Jolly Beggars, New Road, Milnathort.

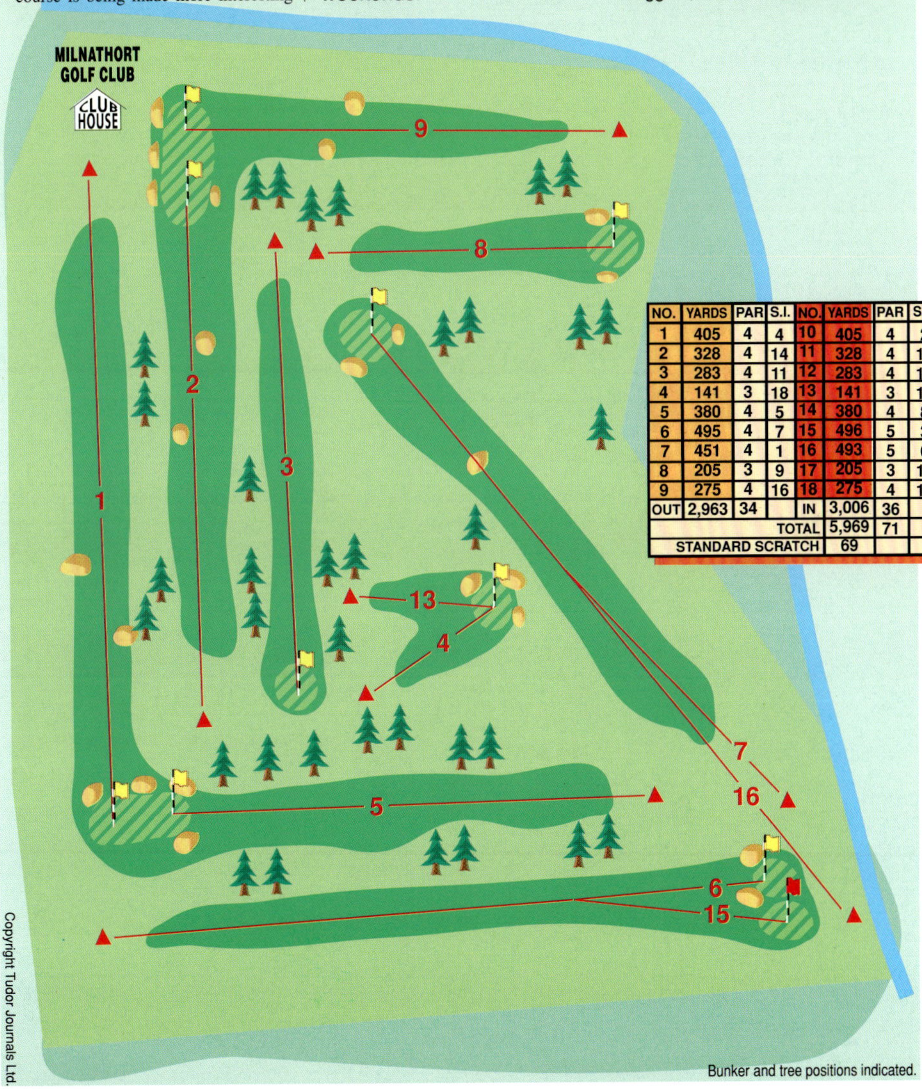

NO.	YARDS	PAR	S.I.	NO.	YARDS	PAR	S.I.
1	405	4	4	10	405	4	2
2	328	4	14	11	328	4	13
3	283	4	11	12	283	4	10
4	141	3	18	13	141	3	17
5	380	4	5	14	380	4	8
6	495	4	7	15	496	5	3
7	451	4	1	16	493	5	6
8	205	3	9	17	205	3	12
9	275	4	16	18	275	4	15
OUT	2,963	34		IN	3,006	36	
				TOTAL	5,969	71	
				STANDARD SCRATCH	69		

MUCKHART

**Muckhart Golf Club,
Muckhart, By Dollar,
Clackmannanshire.
Tel: (025 981) 423.**

Location: A91, 3 miles east of Dollar. Turn right for Rumbling bridge.
Manager: J. Muston.
Tel: (0259) 781 423.
Professional: K. Salmoni.
Tel: (02959) 781 493.

A typical traditional Scottish village course. Each tee has a different view with the Ochill Hills to the north and the Forth Valley to the south.

COURSE INFORMATION

Par 72; SSS 70; Length 6,034 Yards.
Opening Hours: 8am –Dusk.
Visitors: Welcome.
Avoid: Before 10am and between 12–3pm on weekends and Bank holidays.
Ladies: Welcome; Ladies day Tuesday.
Green Fees: Monday–Friday £12; Saturday/Sunday £18.
Juveniles: Welcome; Not permitted unaccompanied before 4pm at weekend.
Clubhouse Hours: Daylight hours.
Clubhouse Dress: Smart.
Clubhouse Facilities: Catering available all day every day.
Open Competitions: Mens Open – August; Ladies – July; Mixed – Aug.

CONVENIENT HOTELS

Gartwhinzean Hotel, Powmill; Castle Campbell, Dollar.

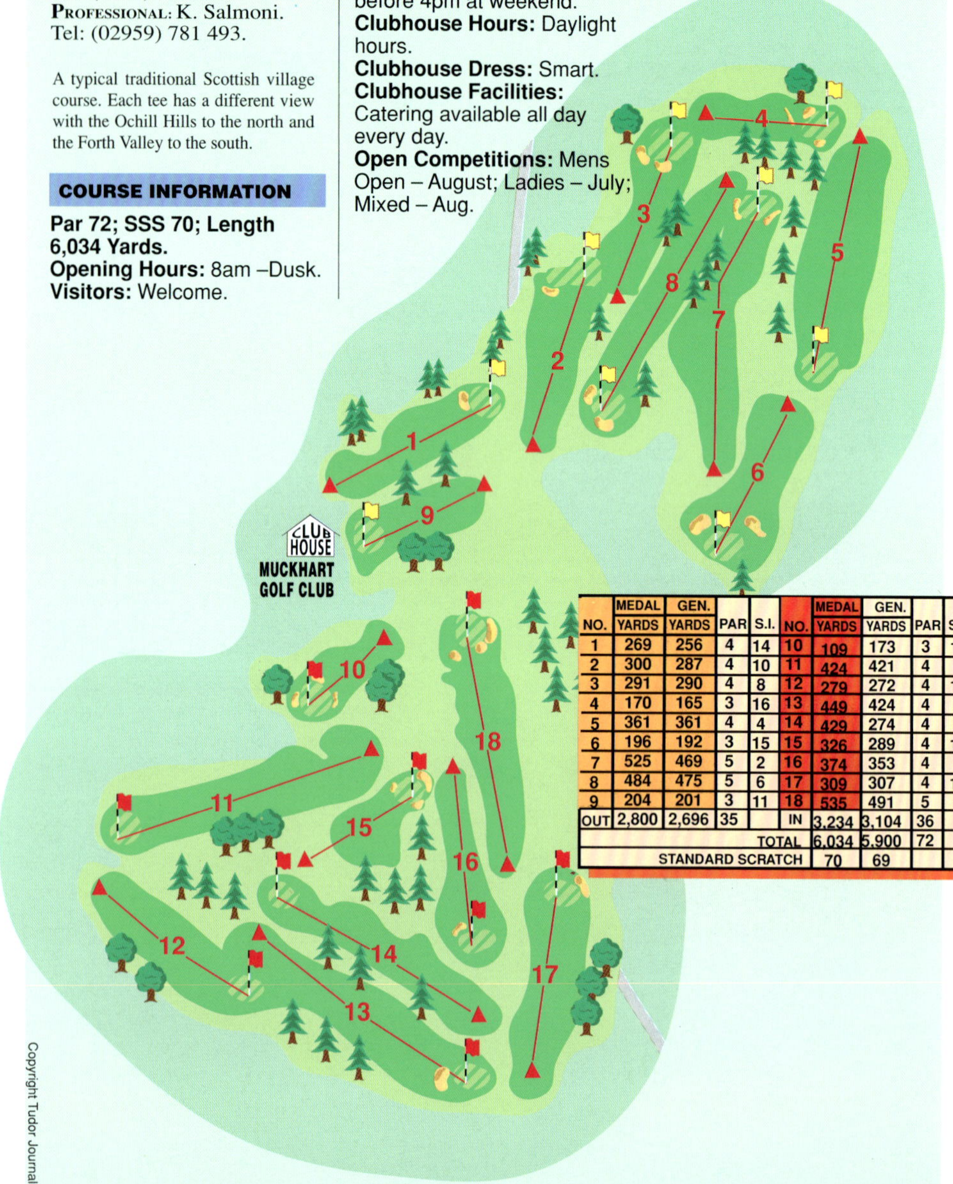

NO.	MEDAL YARDS	GEN. YARDS	PAR	S.I.	NO.	MEDAL YARDS	GEN. YARDS	PAR	S.I.
1	269	256	4	14	10	109	173	3	18
2	300	287	4	10	11	424	421	4	1
3	291	290	4	8	12	279	272	4	13
4	170	165	3	16	13	449	424	4	7
5	361	361	4	4	14	429	274	4	3
6	196	192	3	15	15	326	289	4	12
7	525	469	5	2	16	374	353	4	9
8	484	475	5	6	17	309	307	4	17
9	204	201	3	11	18	535	491	5	5
OUT	2,800	2,696	35		IN	3,234	3,104	36	
					TOTAL	6,034	5,900	72	
					STANDARD SCRATCH	70	69		

Bunker and tree positions indicated.

MURRAYSHALL

Murrayshall Golf Club,
Murrayshall, New Scone, Perth.
PH2 7PH.
Tel: (01738) 551171.

LOCATION: 3 miles north of Perth off A94.
PROFESSIONAL: George Finlayson.
Tel: (01738) 552784.
ARCHITECT: J. Hamilton Stutt.

Murrayshall is an undulating parkland course set in beautiful countryside. Each hole offers a different challenge to the golfer and features include water hazards, white sanded bunkers and stone bridges. Many of the fairways are tree-lined.

COURSE INFORMATION

Par 73; SSS 71; Length 6,446 Yards, 5,877 Metres.
Opening hours: 8am till dusk - weekends, 8.30am till dusk weekdays.
Visitors: Welcome.
Avoid: 8am - 9.30am Weekends.
Ladies: Welcome.
Green Fees: Weekdays £20 per round, £30 per day, Weekends £25 per round, £40 per day.
Juveniles: Welcome.
Clubhouse Hours: 8.30am - 11pm
Clubhouse Dress: Smart/Casual (No Denims/T.Shirts/Trainers,etc.)
Clubhouse Facilities: Catering all day.
Open Competition: Gents Open July.

CONVENIENT HOTEL

Murrayshall Country House Hotel (Adjacent)

NO.	MEDAL YARDS	GEN. YARDS	PAR	S.I.	NO.	MEDAL YARDS	GEN. YARDS	PAR	S.I.
1	400	373	4	3	10	309	299	4	13
2	490	460	5	9	11	354	332	4	11
3	478	456	5	5	12	494	479	5	8
4	167	129	3	18	13	416	395	4	1
5	367	331	4	12	14	179	162	3	15
6	317	302	4	14	15	512	490	5	4
7	379	366	4	2	16	217	196	3	10
8	198	170	3	16	17	472	455	5	6
9	498	478	5	7	18	199	170	3	17
OUT	3,294	3,065	37		IN	3,152	2,970	36	
					TOTAL	6,446	6,043	73	
					STANDARD SCRATCH	71	69		

Bunker and tree positions indicated.

MUTHILL

Muthill Golf Club, Peat Road, Muthill. PH5 2AD.
Tel: (01764) 81523.

LOCATION: 3 miles south of Crieff on A822.
SECRETARY: W.H. Gordon
Tel: (01764) 653319.

Undulating parkland course, not too steep with panoramic views of surrounding hills.

COURSE INFORMATION

Par 66; SSS 63; Length 2,350 Yards.
Opening Hours: Sunrise – Sunset.
Visitors: Welcome.
Avoid: Evenings when club competitions are played, Wednesday evenings.
Ladies: Welcome.
Ladies Day: Thursday evenings.
Green Fees: Monday – Friday £8 per day; Saturday &Sunday £12.
Juveniles: Must be accompanied by playing adults; Restricted in week-day evenings and from 1.30p.m. weekends.
Clubhouse Dress: Neat / casual.
Clubhouse Facilities: No bar or catering facilities available.
Open Competitions: Ladies Open September; Mixed Open September.

CONVENIENT HOTEL

Drummond Arms Hotel – Muthill.

NO.	YARDS	PAR	S.I.	NO.	YARDS	PAR	S.I.
1	224	4	11	10	224	4	12
2	186	3	17	11	186	3	18
3	286	4	7	12	286	4	8
4	274	4	9	13	274	4	10
5	144	3	15	14	144	3	16
6	395	4	1	15	395	4	2
7	322	4	5	16	322	4	6
8	332	4	3	17	332	4	4
9	205	3	13	18	205	3	14
OUT	2,350	33		IN	2,350	33	
				TOTAL	4,700	66	
STANDARD SCRATCH					63		

Tree positions indicated.

STRATHTAY

NO.	MEDAL YARDS	GEN. YARDS	PAR	S.I.	NO.	MEDAL YARDS	GEN. YARDS	PAR	S.I.
1	286	240	4	7	10	286	240	4	7
2	218	202	3	12	11	218	202	3	12
3	212	212	3	17	12	212	212	3	17
4	155	145	3	5	13	155	145	3	5
5	256	236	4	11	14	256	236	4	11
6	370	319	4	6	15	370	319	4	6
7	144	111	3	13	16	144	111	3	13
8	288	272	4	1	17	288	272	4	1
9	114	109	3	9	18	114	109	3	9
OUT	2,043	1,846	31		IN	2,043	1,846	31	
					TOTAL	4,086	3,692	62	
					STANDARD SCRATCH	63	63		

Strathtay Golf Club, Strathtay, By Pitlochry, Perthshire.

LOCATION: 4 miles east Ballinluig (on A9). Across River Tay from Grandtully on A827.
SECRETARY: Tom Lind.
Tel: (01350) 727797.

Very scenic course, hilly and tree-fringed with beautiful views east and west along the Tay Valley.

COURSE INFORMATION

Par 62, SSS 63, Length 4,086 Yards.
Opening Hours: 9.00am – Dusk.
Visitors: Welcome. See Tuesday.
Avoid: Sun afternoon 12.00noon to 4.00pm May–Sept.
Ladies: Welcome.
Ladies Day: Mon evenings May to Oct.
Mixed Foursomes: Tues. May – Sept. 6.30pm.
Green Fees: Weekdays £8; weekends £10.
Juveniles: Only with adults.
Clubhouse Facilities: By arrangement.

CONVENIENT HOTELS

Grandtully Hotel;
Bendarroch House.

Tree positions indicated.

Taymouth Castle Golf Course,
Kenmore, Perthshire.
PH15 2NT.
Tel: (01887) 830228.
Fax: (01887) 830765.

LOCATION: 5 miles west of Aberfeldy.
PROFESSIONAL: Alex Marshall.
ARCHITECT: James Braid.

One of Scotland's most picturesque and enjoyable parkland courses. Set within Taymouth Castle Estate with the magnificent castle as a backdrop. Taymouth is not hilly and has many fine features. The course is surrounded by beautiful mature broad-leaf trees, the fairways are wide, and the rough forgiving. This is a course where the scenery plays an additional role in challenging the golfer.

COURSE INFORMATION

Par 69; SSS 69; Length 6,066 Yards.
Visitors: Welcome.
Opening Hours: 8am – 6pm.
Avoid: weekends before 3pm.
Ladies: No restrictions.
Green Fees: Weekdays – £16 per round & £26 per day; Weekends – £20 per round & £36 per day.
Juveniles: No restrictions.
Clubhouse Hours: 8am – 9pm.
Clubhouse Dress: Tidy but informal.
Clubhouse Facilities: Restaurant, bar, changing rooms and shop.

CONVENIENT HOTELS

Kenmore Hotel (1mile) Tel: (01887) 830205; Farlayer House Hotel (5miles) Tel: (01887) 820332.

NO.	MEDAL YARDS	GEN. YARDS	PAR	S.I.	NO.	MEDAL YARDS	GEN. YARDS	PAR	S.I.
1	296	261	4	14	10	182	173	3	17
2	306	304	4	9	11	452	414	4	4
3	420	379	4/5	3	12	444	437	4/5	2
4	170	152	3	16	13	298	290	4	11
5	543	518	5	1	14	190	183	3	15
6	365	351	4	7	15	410	382	4	6
7	283	245	4	13	16	174	142	3	18
8	383	364	4	12	17	330	326	4	8
9	377	375	4	5	18	443	438	4/5	10
OUT	3,143	2,949	36/37		IN	2,923	2,785	33/35	
					TOTAL	6,066	5,734	69/72	
					STANDARD SCRATCH	69	67		

Bunker and tree positioned indicated.

GOLF DAYS™ SCOTLAND

RENFREWSHIRE

Barshaw Municipal Golf Course, Barshaw Park, Paisley.
Tel: (0141) 889 2908.

LOCATION: 1 mile east of Paisley Cross, off A737.
SECRETARY: W. Collins
Tel: (0141) 884 2533.

A course that offers plenty of variety over both flat and hilly countryside.

COURSE INFORMATION

Par 68; SSS 67; Length 5,703 Yards.
Visitors: Welcome.
Opening Hours: Dawn – Dusk.
Avoid: No restricted times.
Ladies: Welcome.
Green Fees: £6 per adult, £3 per O.A.P., Junior & Unemployed per round 7 days a week.
Juveniles: Welcome.
Clubhouse Hours: 7a.m. — 9p.m.
Clubhouse Dress: Casual.
Clubhouse Facilities: Snack bar at the rear of Clubhouse.

CONVENIENT HOTEL

'Brabloch', Gallowhill, Paisley.

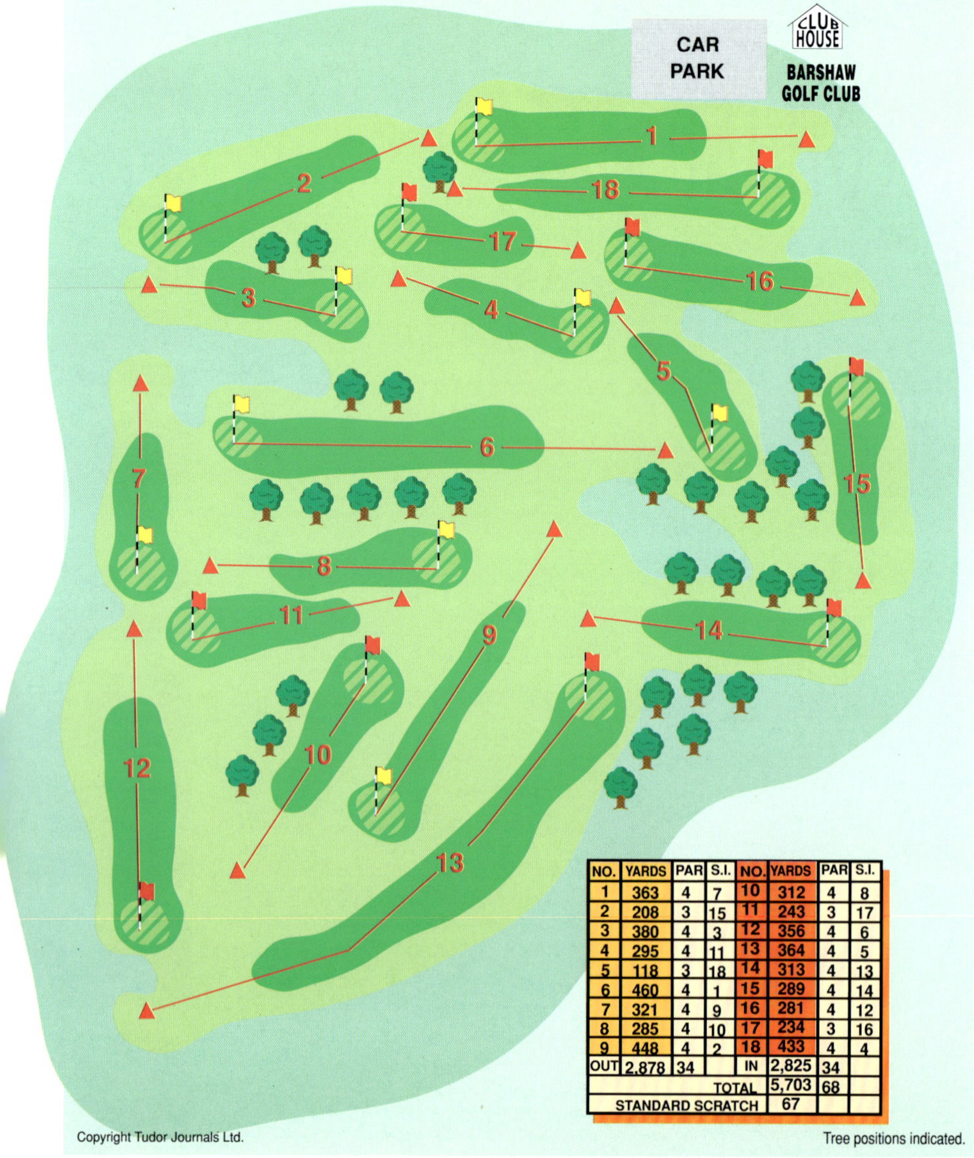

NO.	YARDS	PAR	S.I.	NO.	YARDS	PAR	S.I.
1	363	4	7	10	312	4	8
2	208	3	15	11	243	3	17
3	380	4	3	12	356	4	6
4	295	4	11	13	364	4	5
5	118	3	18	14	313	4	13
6	460	4	1	15	289	4	14
7	321	4	9	16	281	4	12
8	285	4	10	17	234	3	16
9	448	4	2	18	433	4	4
OUT	2,878	34		IN	2,825	34	
				TOTAL	5,703	68	
				STANDARD SCRATCH	67		

Tree positions indicated.

BONNYTON

Bonnyton Golf Club, Eaglesham, Glasgow, G76 0QA.
Tel: (01355) 302781.

LOCATION: South west of Eaglesham.
PROFESSIONAL: Kendal McWade. Tel: (01355) 302256.

A typical moorland course that offers a good test of the game.

COURSE INFORMATION

Par 72; SSS 71; Length 6,255 Yards.
Opening Hours: Sunrise - Sunset.
Visitors: Welcome except at weekends.
Avoid: Weekends.
Ladies: Welcome.
Green Fees: £27 per day.
Juveniles: Welcome.
Clubhouse Hours: 8am until Dusk.
Clubhouse Dress: Neat but casual.
Clubhouse Facilities: Full catering and bar facilities available.

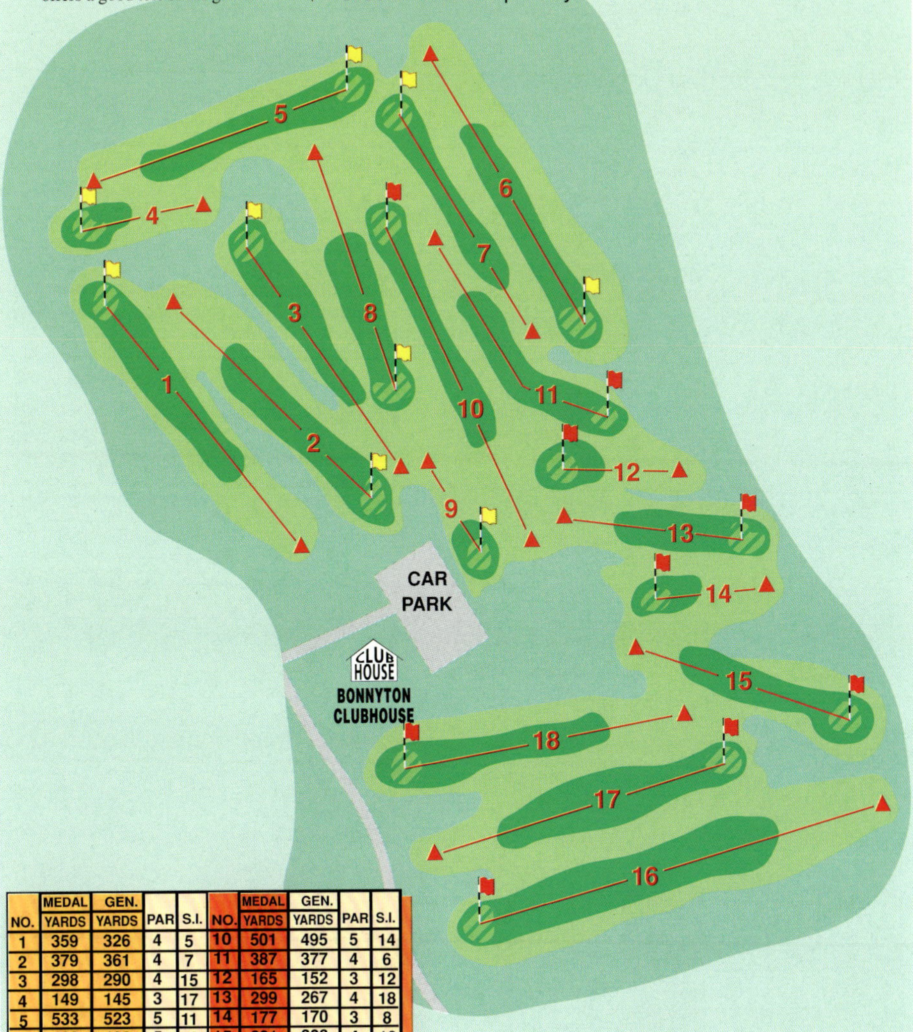

NO.	MEDAL YARDS	GEN. YARDS	PAR	S.I.	NO.	MEDAL YARDS	GEN. YARDS	PAR	S.I.
1	359	326	4	5	10	501	495	5	14
2	379	361	4	7	11	387	377	4	6
3	298	290	4	15	12	165	152	3	12
4	149	145	3	17	13	299	267	4	18
5	533	523	5	11	14	177	170	3	8
6	492	480	5	13	15	321	303	4	16
7	394	388	4	3	16	482	439	5	2
8	407	397	4	1	17	374	374	4	10
9	167	167	3	9	18	371	359	4	4
OUT	3,178	3,077	36		IN	3,077	2,936	36	
					TOTAL	6,255	6,013	72	
					STANDARD SCRATCH	71	70		

Caldwell Golf Club, Caldwell, Uplawmoor, Renfrewshire
Tel: (01505) 850329.

LOCATION: 5 miles south west of Barrhead on the A736 Glasgow to Irvine road
SECRETARY: H.I.F. Harper Tel: (01505) 850366.
PROFESSIONAL: S. Forbes Tel: (01505) 850616.

This pleasant parkland course straddles both Renfrewshire and Ayrshire where the burns, that form county boundaries, make difficult hazards for most of the holes on the outward half.

COURSE INFORMATION

Par 70; SSS 70; Length 6,228 Yards.
Opening Hours: 8.30 am - 7.00 pm.
Visitors: Welcome except weekends.
Avoid: Weekends and after 4pm during the week.
Ladies: Welcome, Ladies day Wednesday.
Green Fees: £16 per round; £24 per day.
Juveniles: Welcome.
Clubhouse Hours: 8.00pm - 11.00pm.
Clubhouse Dress: No jeans, trainers, tee shirts etc...
Clubhouse Facilities: Full facilities except Thursdays, soup & rolls only.

CONVENIENT HOTELS

The Green Acres Hotel; Dalmenny Hotel; Uplawmoor Hotel.

NO.	MEDAL YARDS	GEN. YARDS	PAR	S.I.	NO.	MEDAL YARDS	GEN. YARDS	PAR	S.I.
1	395	393	4	7	10	311	274	4	18
2	422	406	4	1	11	391	378	4	4
3	160	153	3	17	12	345	308	4	12
4	304	298	4	15	13	360	354	4	10
5	516	448	5/4	5	14	212	206	3	16
6	382	345	4	9	15	131	114	3	14
7	422	339	4	3	16	395	389	4	2
8	331	324	4	11	17	547	501	5	6
9	196	184	3	13	18	406	384	4	8
OUT	3,130	2,890	35/34		IN	3,098	2,926	35	
TOTAL						6,228	5,816	70/69	
STANDARD SCRATCH						70			

Bunker and tree positions indicated.

Cochrane Castle,
Craigston, Johnstone.
PA5 OHF.
Tel: (01505) 320146.

LOCATION: 10 miles west of Glasgow half a mile off A737

SECRETARY: J.C. Cowan.
Tel: (01505) 812283.

PROFESSIONAL: Stuart Campbell.
Tel: (01505) 3284465.

Parkland course, fairly hilly, with five par threes and three par fives. Varied layout requiring a variety of shots. There are a large number of trees throughout the course.

COURSE INFORMATION

Par 71; SSS 71; Length 6,226 Yards.
Visitors: Welcome.
Opening Hours: All day, every day.
Avoid: Saturday & Sunday.
Ladies: Before 3pm Saturday & before 12 noon on Sundays.
Green Fees: £17 per round & £25 per day.
Juveniles: Permitted (restricted hours).

Clubhouse Hours: All day until 11pm.
Clubhouse Dress: Casual – Jacket and tie in dining room.
Clubhouse Facilities: Not available on Monday.

CONVENIENT HOTEL

Lynnhurst; Bird in Hand.

NO.	MEDAL YARDS	GEN. YARDS	PAR	S.I.	NO.	MEDAL YARDS	GEN. YARDS	PAR	S.I.
1	166	156	3	15	10	346	338	4	8
2	332	325	4	11	11	361	352	4	14
3	454	415	4	5	12	394	363	4	4
4	428	420	4	7	13	348	340	4	10
5	500	476	5	3	14	167	147	3	18
6	156	147	3	17	15	423	418	4	6
7	331	321	4	9	16	486	480	5	2
8	554	554	5	1	17	164	158	3	16
9	211	203	3	13	18	405	399	4	12
OUT	3,132	3,017	35		IN	3,094	2,995	35	
					TOTAL	6,226	6,012	71	
					STANDARD SCRATCH	71	69		

Bunker & tree positions indicated.

EASTWOOD

RENFREWSHIRE

Eastwood Golf Club,
Muirshield, Loganswell,
Newton Mearns,
Glasgow. G77 6RX.
Tel. (01355) 500261.

LOCATION: 9 miles south west of Glasgow.
SECRETARY: V.E. Jones.
Tel: (01355) 500280 (am).
PROFESSIONAL:
A.McGuiness.
Tel: (01355) 500285.

Hilly Moorland.

COURSE INFORMATION

Par 68; SSS 69; Length 5,864 Yards.
Visitors: By prior application to secretary.
Opening Hours: All day.
Ladies: By application.
Green Fees: One round £20 – Day Ticket £30.
Juveniles: As above.

Clubhouse Hours: 8am – 11pm.
Clubhouse Dress: Formal and casual.
Clubhouse Facilities: Catering.

CONVENIENT HOTEL

MacDonald Hotel, Giffnock.

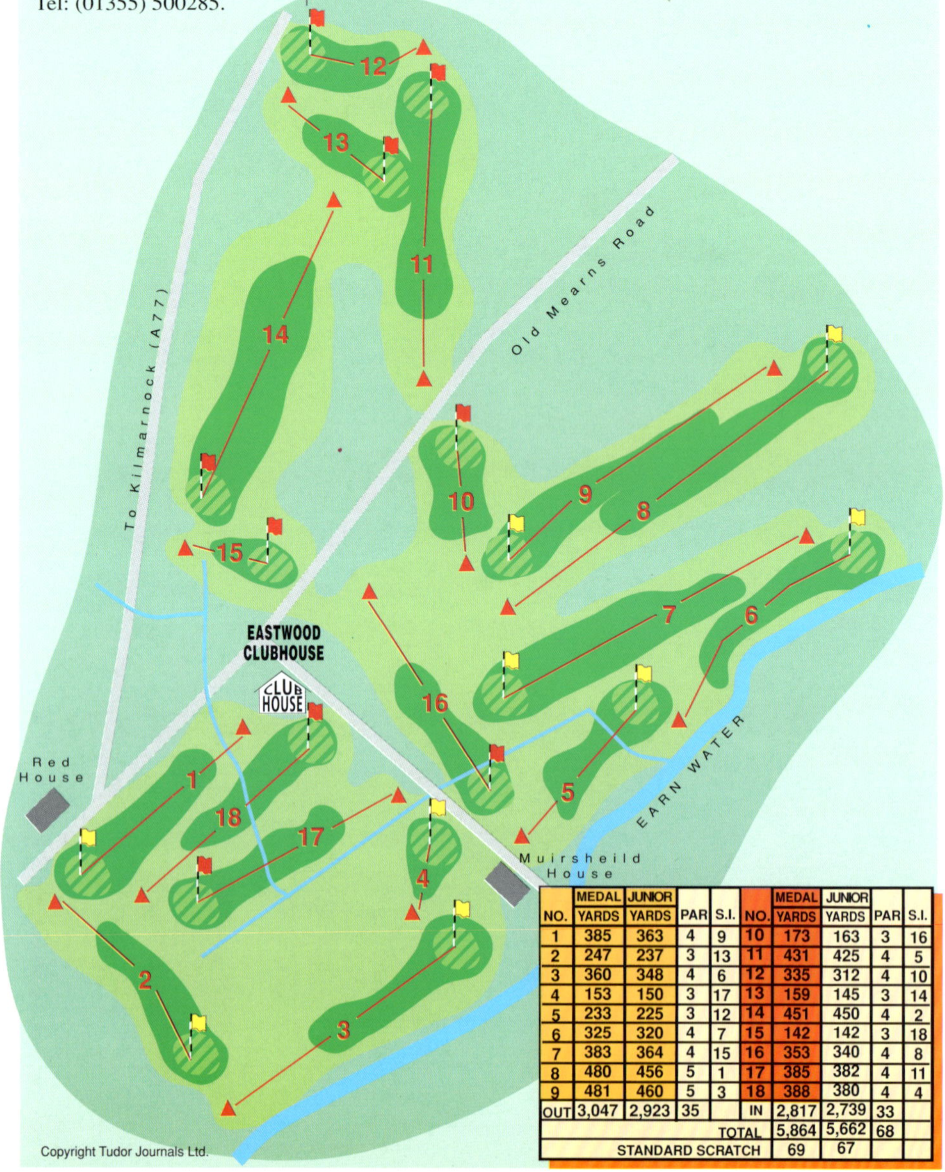

NO.	MEDAL YARDS	JUNIOR YARDS	PAR	S.I.	NO.	MEDAL YARDS	JUNIOR YARDS	PAR	S.I.
1	385	363	4	9	10	173	163	3	16
2	247	237	3	13	11	431	425	4	5
3	360	348	4	6	12	335	312	4	10
4	153	150	3	17	13	159	145	3	14
5	233	225	3	12	14	451	450	4	2
6	325	320	4	7	15	142	142	3	18
7	383	364	4	15	16	353	340	4	8
8	480	456	5	1	17	385	382	4	11
9	481	460	5	3	18	388	380	4	4
OUT	3,047	2,923	35		IN	2,817	2,739	33	
					TOTAL	5,864	5,662	68	
					STANDARD SCRATCH	69	67		

Erskine Golf Club, Golf Road, Bishopton, Renfrewshire. PA7 5PH. Tel: (01505) 862302.

LOCATION: 1 1/2 miles west of Erskine Bridge on B815.
SECRETARY: T.A McKillop. Tel: (01505) 862302.
PROFESSIONAL: Peter Thompson. Tel: (01505) 862108.

Pleasant parkland course on the south side of the River Clyde offering scenic views of the north of the river towards Cowal and the Loch Lomond hills.

COURSE INFORMATION

Par 71; SSS 70; Length 6,241 Yards, 6,086 Metres.
Visitors: Welcome mid week before 4.30pm.
Opening Hours: 7.30am – Dusk.
Avoid: Weekends and evenings.
Ladies: Restricted Tuesday, Thursday evenings & Saturdays.
Ladies Day: Wednesday.
Green Fees: £22 per round & £35 per day.
Juveniles: Some restrictions as visitors.
Clubhouse Hours: 7.30am onwards.
Clubhouse Dress: Smoke room – Jacket and tie; Mixed lounge – Smart/Casual.
Clubhouse Facilities: 10am onwards

CONVENIENT HOTELS

Forte Post Hotel, Erskine; Bishopton Hotel.

NO.	MEDAL YARDS	GEN. YARDS	PAR	S.I.	NO.	MEDAL YARDS	GEN. YARDS	PAR	S.I.
1	328	322	4	10	10	371	358	4	7
2	367	361	4	4	11	181	176	3	14
3	321	316	4	13	12	435	427	4	1
4	308	295	4	17	13	314	304	4	16
5	320	311	4	8	14	346	336	4	11
6	133	124	3	15	15	412	409	4	6
7	432	422	4	2	16	467	457	4	9
8	365	352	4	12	17	398	385	4	3
9	484	478	5	5	18	259	253	4	18
OUT	3,058	2,981	36		IN	3,183	3,105	35	
					TOTAL	6,241	6,086	71	
					STANDARD SCRATCH	70	69		

Bunker positions indicated.

Gleddoch Golf Club,
Langbank. PA14 6YE.
Tel: (01475) 540304.

LOCATION: 11 miles from Glasgow International Airport.
SECRETARY: Mr D Tierney.
PROFESSIONAL: K Campbell. Tel: (01475) 540704.

Lovely scenic views of the River Clyde Estuary, very near the M8 motorway with access to all areas.

COURSE INFORMATION

Par 72; SSS 71; Length 6,375 Yards.
Opening Hours: 8.00am – Dusk.
Visitors: Welcome.
Avoid: Medal Times.
Ladies: Welcome avoid medal times.
Green Fees: £25 per day.
Juveniles: Welcome.
Clubhouse Hours: Open 8am.
Clubhouse Dress: No jeans, Trainers, etc.
Clubhouse Facilities: Full catering and bar facilities available**.**

CONVENIENT HOTEL

Gleddoch House Hotel.

NO.	MEDAL YARDS	GEN. YARDS	PAR	S.I.	NO.	MEDAL YARDS	GEN. YARDS	PAR	S.I.
1	319	309	4	11	10	314	304	4	10
2	181	160	4	15	11	524	464	5/4	4
3	517	435	5/4	1	12	172	107	3	13
4	389	379	4	9	13	496	395	5/4	2
5	476	429	5/4	7	14	185	165	3	14
6	408	398	4	3	15	372	354	4	16
7	145	122	4	17	16	396	379	4	8
8	270	265	3	18	17	423	409	4	6
9	377	313	4	5	18	393	354	4	12
OUT	3,082	2,805	36/34		IN	3,275	2,931	36/34	
					TOTAL	6,375	5,736	72/68	
					STANDARD SCRATCH	71	67		

Bunker & tree positions indicated.

Gourock Golf Club, Cowal View, Gourock.
Tel: (01475) 631001.

LOCATION: 3 miles west of Greenock on A78.
SECRETARY: M.J. Walker. Tel: (01475) 631001.
PROFESSIONAL: Anthony Green. Tel: (01475) 636834.
ARCHITECT: Henry Cotton after James Braid.

Mooland/parkland course – testing in wind with spectacular views over Firth of Clyde.

COURSE INFORMATION

Par 73; SSS 71; Length 6,492 Yards.
Visitors: Welcome (letter or phone call preferred).
Opening Hours: 9.00am – Dusk.
Avoid: Saturdays.
Ladies: Limited hours.
Green Fees: £16 per round, £22 per day; Sun £20 per round. No golfing on a Saturday.
Juveniles: Permitted.
Clubhouse Hours: 9.00am – 11.00pm.
Clubhouse Dress: Good casual (no jeans).
Clubhouse Facilities: Bar snacks most days – Full catering available provided notice is given.
Open Competitions: May, July (Men's); May (Seniors); July (Ladies).

CONVENIENT HOTEL

Gantock Hotel (Stakis).

NO.	MEDAL YARDS	GEN. YARDS	PAR	S.I.	NO.	MEDAL YARDS	GEN. YARDS	PAR	S.I.
1	476	388	5	5	10	280	260	4	16
2	332	282	4	13	11	505	410	5	2
3	368	343	4	1	12	465	382	4	10
4	146	138	3	17	13	481	459	5	4
5	340	330	4	11	14	333	326	4	12
6	365	338	4	9	15	382	299	4	6
7	167	165	3	15	16	316	248	4	14
8	502	448	5	3	17	159	140	3	18
9	460	329	4	7	18	415	369	4	8
OUT	3,156	2,761	36		IN	3,336	2,893	37	
					TOTAL	6,492	5,654	73	
					STANDARD SCRATCH	71	71		

Tree positions indicated.

Greenock Golf Club,
Forsyth Street, Greenock,
Renfrewshire.
Tel: (01475) 720793.

LOCATION: One mile south west of Greenock on the A8.
SECRETARY: E.J. Black.
Tel: (01475) 720793.
PROFESSIONAL: Graham Ross.
Tel: (01475) 787236.

Moorland course with some hills offering a good test of golf for most golfers.

COURSE INFORMATION

Par 68; SSS 69; Length 5888 Yards.
Opening Hours: From 8.00am.
Visitors: Welcome except on Saturdays.
Avoid: Saturdays.
Ladies: Welcome, tee off before 5.00pm.
Green Fees: £15 per day, £20 weekends.
Juveniles: Welcome, but restricted.
Clubhouse Hours: 8am until 11.30pm
Clubhouse Dress: Smart but casual.
Clubhouse Facilities: Catering from 2.00pm - 9.00pm.

CONVENIENT HOTEL

Tontine, Arogowan Square Greenock.

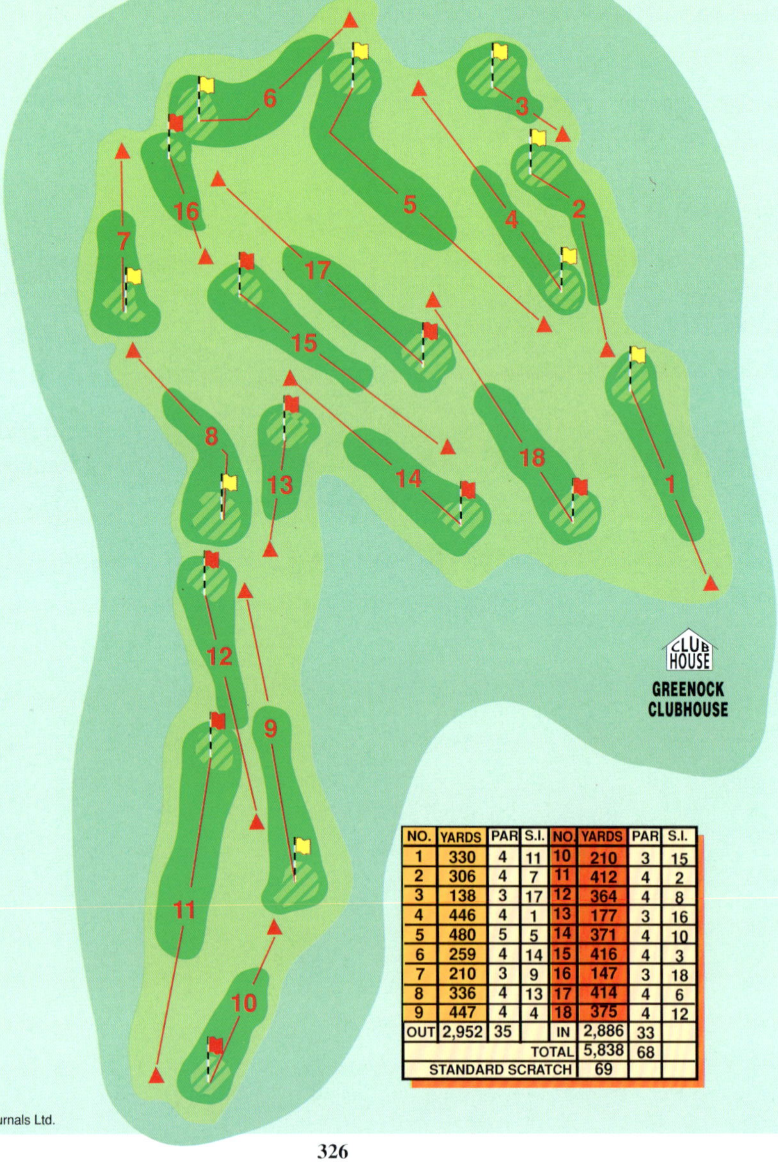

NO.	YARDS	PAR	S.I.	NO.	YARDS	PAR	S.I.
1	330	4	11	10	210	3	15
2	306	4	7	11	412	4	2
3	138	3	17	12	364	4	8
4	446	4	1	13	177	3	16
5	480	5	5	14	371	4	10
6	259	4	14	15	416	4	3
7	210	3	9	16	147	3	18
8	336	4	13	17	414	4	6
9	447	4	4	18	375	4	12
OUT	2,952	35		IN	2,886	33	
				TOTAL	5,838	68	
STANDARD SCRATCH					69		

Kilmacolm Golf Club,
Kilmacolm, Renfrewshire.
Tel: (050 587) 2139.

LOCATION: 10 miles west of Paisley.
SECRETARY: R.F. McDonald.
PROFESSIONAL: David Stewart. Tel: (050 587) 2695.
ARCHITECT: Willie Campbell.

Kilmacolm Golf Course is situated on a plateau some 400ft above sea level and lies either side of the Houston Road. Maximum use is made of the natural hills and hollows making this one of the most attractive of inland courses. One of the particular attractions is the fact that very few of the holes run in a similar direction. While length at Kilmacolm is not a factor, the course demands accurate driving and well judged second shots. A programme of tree planting in the early 70's has enhanced the character and charm of the older trees, rhododendrons and heather.

COURSE INFORMATION

Par 69; SSS 68; Length; 5964 Yards.

Opening Hours: 8.30am to 11.00pm (Summer); 8.30am to 7.30pm (Winter).
Visitors: Welcome weekdays only. Must be accompanied by a member.
Avoid: Weekends.
Ladies: Welcome, restricted times.
Green Fees: Round £20; £25 per day.
Juveniles: Welcome.
Clubhouse Hours: See opening hours.
Clubhouse Dress: Smart/Casual. Jacket and tie required in lounge.
Clubhouse Facilities: Catering facilities available.

CONVENIENT HOTEL

Gryffe Arms, Bridge of Weir.

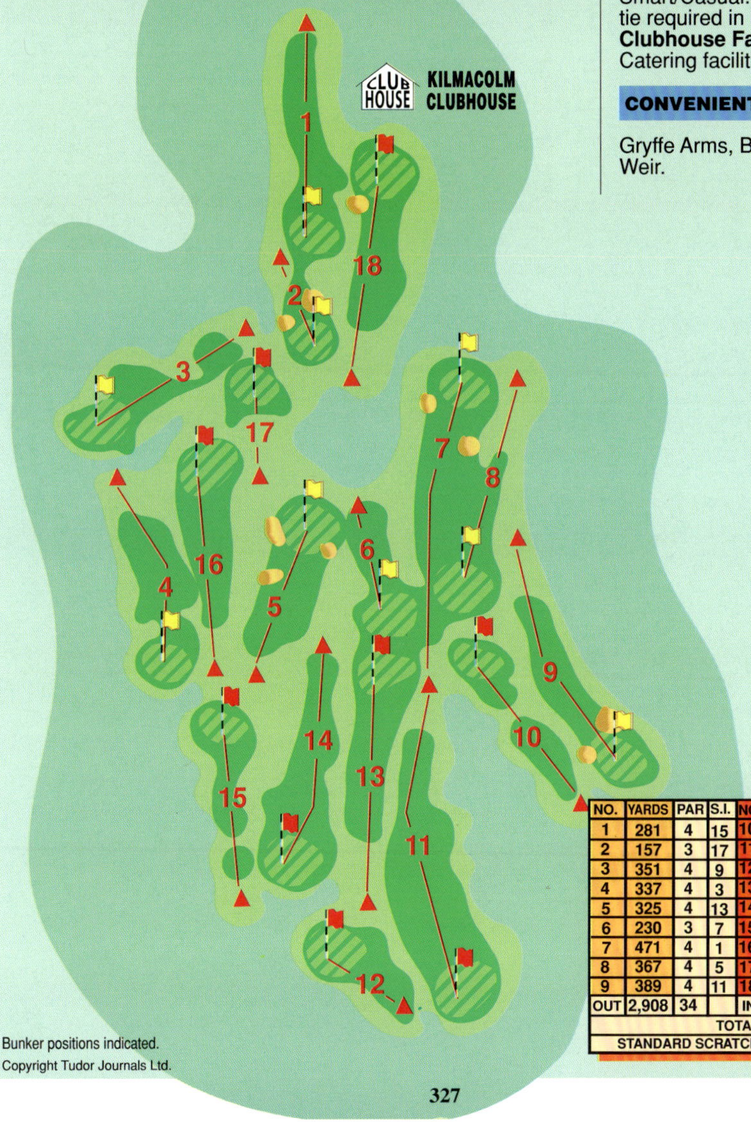

NO.	YARDS	PAR	S.I.	NO.	YARDS	PAR	S.I.
1	281	4	15	10	325	4	12
2	157	3	17	11	506	5	4
3	351	4	9	12	162	3	16
4	337	4	3	13	429	4	2
5	325	4	13	14	400	4	8
6	230	3	7	15	333	4	14
7	471	4	1	16	351	4	6
8	367	4	5	17	140	3	18
9	389	4	11	18	410	4	10
OUT	2,908	34		IN	3,056	35	
				TOTAL	5,964	69	
STANDARD SCRATCH					68		

Bunker positions indicated.

Lochwinnoch Golf Club,
Burnfoot Road,
Lochwinnoch,
Renfrewshire.
Tel: (01505) 842153.

Location: Nine miles south of Paisley.
Secretary: Mrs E. McBride.
Professional: G Reilly.
Tel: (01505) 843029.

COURSE INFORMATION

Par 71; SSS 71; Length 6,243 Yards.
Opening Hours: Sunrise — sunset.
Visitors: Welcome.
Avoid: Friday afternoons, Saturday & Sunday.
Ladies: Welcome.
Green Fees: £20 per day.
Juveniles: Welcome.
Clubhouse Hours: 11am — 11.00pm (Summer); 12.30am — 6.00pm (Winter).
Clubhouse Dress: Smart/Casual - No jeans or trainers.
Clubhouse facilities: Lunches 11.00am — 2.30pm, except Mon. & Fri.

CONVENIENT HOTELS

Lynnhurst Hotel, Johnstone;
Bowfield Country Club, Howwood.

NO.	MEDAL YARDS	GEN. YARDS	PAR	S.I.	NO.	MEDAL YARDS	GEN. YARDS	PAR	S.I.
1	446	433	4	3	10	399	355	4	1
2	484	484	5	9	11	442	442	4	10
3	216	216	3	15	12	352	352	4	11
4	446	389	4	7	13	125	123	3	18
5	445	445	4	5	14	377	293	4	4
6	317	253	4	12	15	236	236	4	8
7	489	437	5/4	2	16	275	275	4	14
8	146	146	3	17	17	505	417	5/4	6
9	348	348	4	13	18	195	195	3	16
OUT	3,337	3,151	36/35		IN	2,906	2,688	35/34	
					TOTAL	6,243	5,839	71/69	
					STANDARD SCRATCH	71	68		

Bunker & tree positions indicated.

The Old Course Ranfurly Golf Club Ltd, Ranfurly Place, Bridge of Weir, PA11 3DE.
Tel: (01505) 613612.

LOCATION: 15 miles west of Glasgow – 5 miles west of Glasgow airport (off M8).
SECRETARY: Mr R. Mitchell.
Tel: (01505) 613214.

Well kept and prepared heathland type course of a difficult nature with a number of blind driving holes.

COURSE INFORMATION

Par 70; SSS 69; Length 6,089 Yards.
Visitors: Private Club – No visitors unless accompanied by a member.
Opening Hours: Times vary (contact club for information).
Avoid: Weekends.
Ladies: Contact Secretary.
Green Fees: £3 with member.
Juveniles: With adults.

Clubhouse Hours: Times vary.
Clubhouse Dress: Smart, casual for course & collar and tie for dining room.
Clubhouse Facilities: Contact Clubmaster.

CONVENIENT HOTELS

Gryffe Arms, Bridge of Weir. Ther also many hotels situated within Paisley (six miles away) and around Glasgow airport.

NO.	MEDAL YARDS	GEN. YARDS	PAR	S.I.	NO.	MEDAL YARDS	GEN. YARDS	PAR	S.I.
1	454	443	4	5	10	382	353	4	10
2	355	328	4	11	11	482	482	5	2
3	364	364	4	9	12	415	404	4	6
4	506	499	5	3	13	121	112	3	18
5	166	174	3	15	14	389	381	4	4
6	502	472	5/4	7	15	321	314	4	14
7	224	206	3	13	16	201	194	3	8
8	301	293	4	17	17	338	333	4	12
9	426	421	4	1	18	142	139	3	16
OUT	3,298	3,200	36		IN	2,791	2,712	34	
					TOTAL	6,089	5,912	70/69	
					STANDARD SCRATCH	69	68		

Bunker & tree positions indicated.

Fore! D. Corrance.

Paisley Golf Club,
Braehead, Paisley.
PA2 8TZ.
Tel: (0141) 884 2292.

LOCATION: Braehead, Paisley.
SECRETARY: W.J. Cunningham.
Tel: (0141) 884 3903.
PROFESSIONAL: Grant Gilmour.
Tel: (0141) 884 4114.

An exposed moorland course which provides plenty of variety throughout the holes.

COURSE INFORMATION

Par 71; SSS 72; Length; 6424 Yards.
Opening Hours: 9.00am to sunset.
Visitors: Societies only (by arrangement).
Avoid: Avoid after 4pm, weekends & Public Holidays.
Ladies: Societies only (by arrangement).

Green Fees: £20 per round, £25 per day.
Clubhouse Hours: Open from 9.00am.
Clubhouse Dress: Smart/Casual. No jeans, Trainers, etc...
Clubhouse Facilities: Bar snacks, lunches, High Tea & Dinner by arrangement.

NO.	MEDAL YARDS	GEN. YARDS	PAR	S.I.	NO.	MEDAL YARDS	GEN. YARDS	PAR	S.I.
1	398	383	4	5	10	413	372	4	1
2	373	341	4	10	11	322	322	4	13
3	499	499	5	3	12	509	487	5	11
4	389	389	4	2	13	170	170	3	15
5	398	398	4	8	14	376	346	4	7
6	352	341	4	18	15	200	200	3	9
7	338	338	4	14	16	539	457	5/4	4
8	183	178	3	16	17	162	162	3	17
9	402	397	4	12	18	443	435	4	6
OUT	3,332	3,264	36		IN	3,134	2,951	33/35	
					TOTAL	6,466	6,215	71/70	
					STANDARD SCRATCH	72	72		

Bunker & tree positions indicated.

PORT GLASGOW

Port Glasgow Golf Club, Devol Road, Port Glasgow. PA14 5XE. Tel: (01475) 704181.

Location: M8 west of Glasgow, 1 mile south of town centre, near industrial estate.
Secretary: Mr N.L. Mitchell. Tel: (01475) 706273.

Moorland course at the top of Port Glasgow with panoramic views over the River Clyde.

COURSE INFORMATION

Par 68; SSS 68; Length 5,712 Yards.
Opening Hours: 8am – Dusk.
Visitors: Not on Saturdays; Sundays only introduced; Weekdays before 4pm.
Avoid: No restricted times.
Ladies: As above.
Green Fees: Round £12; Day £18.
Juveniles: Not permitted.
Clubhouse Hours: Variable.
Clubhouse Dress: Casual but no denims, trainers, track or shellsuits, sleeveless shirts.
Clubhouse Facilities: Bar & restaurant.
Open Competitions: I. McDougall (Greensome); J. Baxter (Open Handicap); D. Gourdie (Open Handicap).

CONVENIENT HOTELS

Clune Brae Hotel, Port Glasgow;
Star Hotel, Port Glasgow.

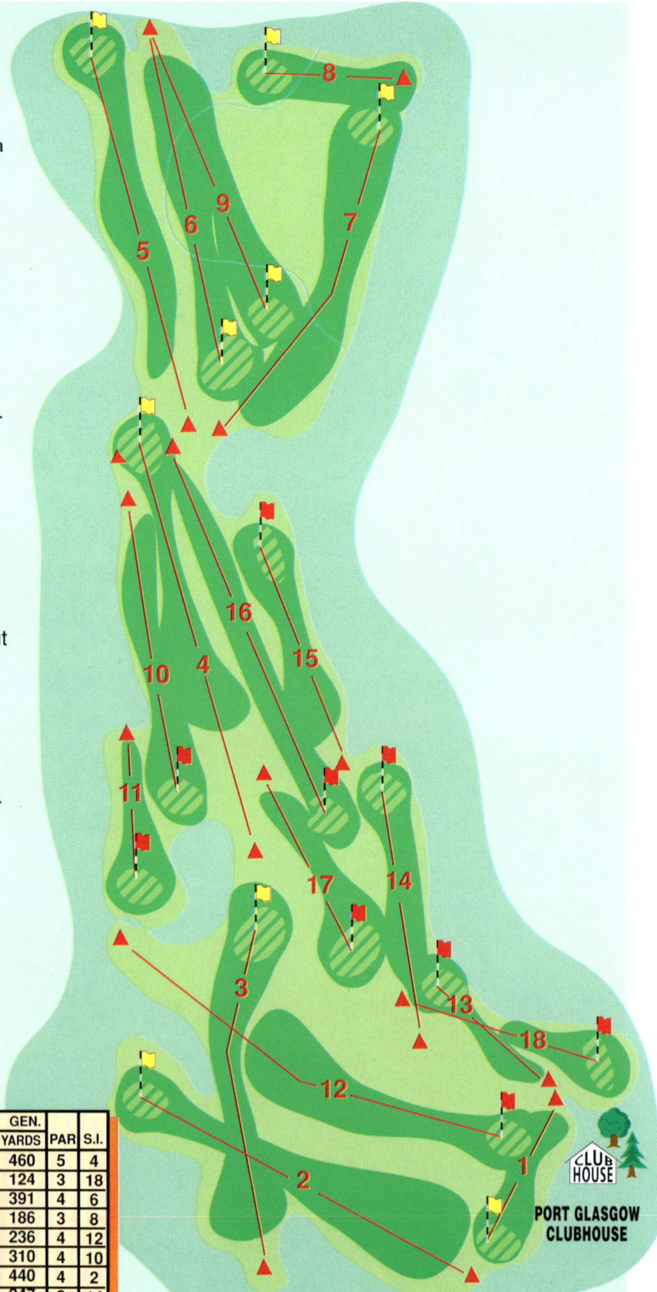

NO.	MEDAL YARDS	GEN. YARDS	PAR	S.I.	NO.	MEDAL YARDS	GEN. YARDS	PAR	S.I.
1	165	165	3	17	10	490	460	5	4
2	352	342	4	3	11	132	124	3	18
3	306	306	4	13	12	391	391	4	6
4	505	505	5	1	13	186	186	3	8
5	427	427	4	5	14	278	236	4	12
6	285	375	4	9	15	316	310	4	10
7	347	347	4	11	16	445	440	4	2
8	156	150	3	15	17	247	247	3	14
9	381	371	4	7	18	213	210	3	16
OUT	3,024	2,988	35		IN	2,688	2,604	33	
					TOTAL	5,712	5,592	68	
					STANDARD SCRATCH	68	66		

Tree positions indicated.

RANFURLY CASTLE

RENFREWSHIRE

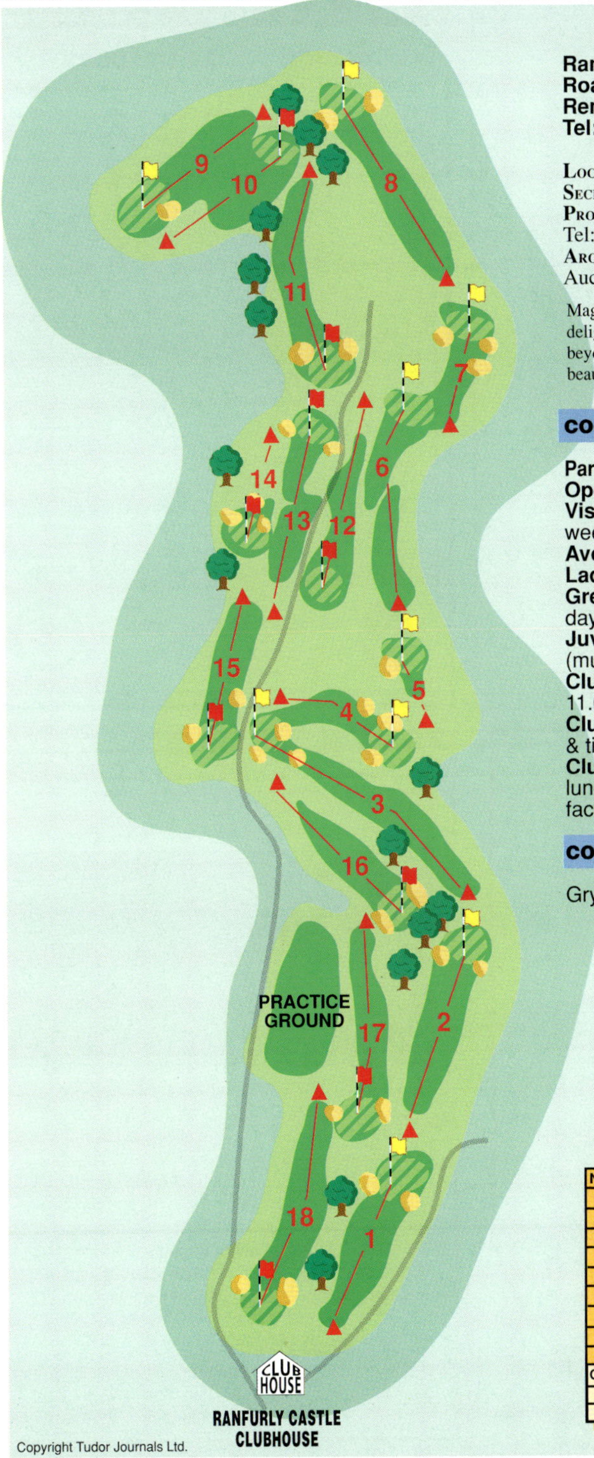

Ranfurly Castle Golf Club, Golf Road, Bridge of Weir, Renfrewshire.
Tel: (01505) 612609.

LOCATION: 7 miles west of Paisley.
SECRETARY: J. Walker.
PROFESSIONAL: Tom Eckford.
Tel: (01505) 614795.
ARCHITECT: Andrew Kirkcaldy & Willie Auchterlonie.

Magnificent moorland course in 240 acres, with delightful views of the valley of the Clyde and beyond. A severe test of golf with very fast and beautifully kept greens.

COURSE INFORMATION

Par 70; SSS 71; Length; 6,284 Yards.
Opening Hours: 8.30 am - 11.00 pm.
Visitors: Welcome, except weekends.
Avoid: Weekends.
Ladies: Welcome, weekdays only.
Green Fees: £22 per round; £30 per day.
Juveniles: Welcome, weekdays only (must be over 10).
Clubhouse Hours: 8.00am - 11.00pm.
Clubhouse Dress: Jacket collar & tie.
Clubhouse Facilities: Snack lunches available, Full catering facilities by request.

CONVENIENT HOTEL

Gryffe Arms Hotel, Bridge of Weir.

NO.	YARDS	PAR	S.I.	NO.	YARDS	PAR	S.I.
1	319	4	13	10	294	4	18
2	396	4	3	11	441	4	2
3	490	5	9	12	381	4	10
4	269	4	17	13	370	4	6
5	139	3	15	14	185	3	12
6	403	4	5	15	389	4	4
7	184	3	11	16	347	4	14
8	461	4	1	17	411	4	16
9	383	4	7	18	422	4	8
OUT	3,044	35		IN	3,240	35	
				TOTAL	6,284	70	
STANDARD SCRATCH					71		

Bunker & tree positions indicated.

GOLF DAYS™ SCOTLAND

SOUTH

Castle Douglas Golf Club,
Abercromby Road, Castle Douglas.
Tel: (01556) 2801.

LOCATION: Castle Douglas.
SECRETARY: A.D.Millar.
Tel: (01556) 502099.

Attractive 9 hole parkland course on the edge of town, apart from one hill gently undulating.

COURSE INFORMATION

Par 68; SSS 66; Length 5,408 Yards.
Opening Hours: 8am – Dusk.
Visitors: Welcome, except during open competitions, Tues and Thurs evening.
Ladies: Welcome.
Green Fees: £12 Weekdays, £15 Weekends.
Juveniles: Welcome.
Clubhouse Hours: 12 noon onwards during summer months.
Clubhouse Dress: Neat.
Clubhouse Facilities: Restaurant and bar facilities available.

CONVENIENT HOTELS

Imperial Hotel, Castle Douglas;
Douglas Arms Hotel, Castle Douglas;
Kings Arms Hotel, Castle Douglas.

NO.	YARDS	PAR	S.I.	NO.	YARDS	PAR	S.I.
1	101	3	17	10	101	3	18
2	261	4	13	11	261	4	14
3	367	4	5	12	367	4	6
4	314	4	9	13	314	4	10
5	296	4	11	14	296	4	12
6	443	4	3	15	443	4	2
7	173	3	15	16	173	3	16
8	438	4	1	17	438	4	4
9	311	4	7	18	311	4	8
OUT	2,704	34		IN	2,704	34	
				TOTAL	5,408	68	
STANDARD SCRATCH					66		

**Colvend Golf Club,
Sandyhills, Nr Dalbeattie,
Kirkcudbrightshire.
Tel: (0155 663) 398.**

LOCATION: 6 miles south of Dalbeattie on A710 Solway coast road.
SECRETARY: J.B. Henderson. Tel: (01556) 610878.
ARCHITECT: Dave Thomas.

Nine challenging holes over a picturesque course situated on the Solway Coast with superb views over the Galloway Hills and the Solway Firth.

COURSE INFORMATION

Par 66; SSS 62; Length 2,322 Yards.
Opening Hours: Dawn–Dusk.
Visitors: Welcome.
Avoid: Course closures include: April – September every Tuesday at 2pm; Thursdays at 5.30pm; and some Sundays for member's competitions.
Ladies: Welcome.
Green Fees: Adults £12; Juveniles: £6 (pay full fee on Saturday/Sunday).
Juveniles: Welcome.
Clubhouse Hours: 11am – 11pm April to October.
Clubhouse Dress: Casual.
Clubhouse Facilities: Snacks all day, lunch and dinner served. Full changing and bar facilities.

CONVENIENT HOTELS

Clonyard House Hotel;
Barons Craig Hotel;
Mabie House, Dumfries.

NO.	MEDAL YARDS	GEN. YARDS	PAR	S.I.	NO.	MEDAL YARDS	GEN. YARDS	PAR	S.I.
1	257	251	4	7	10	257	251	4	8
2	113	111	3	17	11	113	111	3	18
3	356	326	4	1	12	356	326	4	2
4	176	174	3	15	13	176	174	3	16
5	303	293	4	9	14	303	293	4	10
6	333	324	4	3	15	333	324	4	4
7	325	325	4	5	16	325	325	4	6
8	186	173	3	13	17	186	173	3	14
9	273	263	4	11	18	273	263	4	12
OUT	2,322	2,240	33		IN	2,322	2,240	33	
					TOTAL	4,644	4,480	66	
					STANDARD SCRATCH	63	62		

CRICHTON ROYAL

Crichton Royal Golf Club,
Dumfries, Dumfriesshire.
Tel: (0387) 55301 ext. 2122.

LOCATION: 1 mile from Dumfries on Bankend Road.
SECRETARY: A.B. McKay.

Challenging parkland tree-lined nine hole course.

COURSE INFORMATION

Par 70; SSS 69; Length 5,952 Yds.

Opening Hours: Variable.
Visitors: Welcome, depending on club competitions.
Avoid: Tuesday — Gents competition.
Ladies: Welcome — Ladies day day Thursday.
Green Fees: £12 weekdays, £15 Weekends.
Juveniles: Restricted.
Clubhouse Hours: Variable — weekdays open lunchtime /evenings; weekends open all day.

Clubhouse Dress: Informal.
Clubhouse Facilities: Lunches and evening meals available.

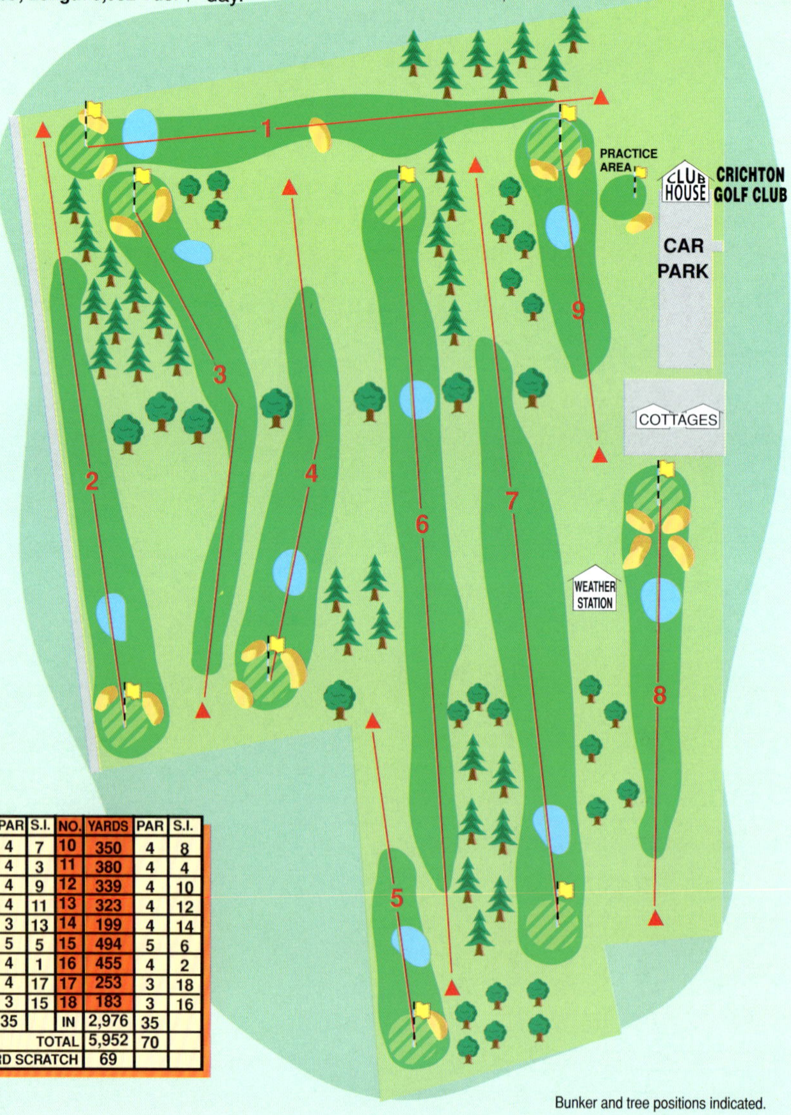

NO.	YARDS	PAR	S.I.	NO.	YARDS	PAR	S.I.
1	350	4	7	10	350	4	8
2	380	4	3	11	380	4	4
3	339	4	9	12	339	4	10
4	323	4	11	13	323	4	12
5	199	3	13	14	199	4	14
6	494	5	5	15	494	5	6
7	455	4	1	16	455	4	2
8	253	4	17	17	253	3	18
9	183	3	15	18	183	3	16
OUT	2,976	35		IN	2,976	35	
				TOTAL	5,952	70	
STANDARD SCRATCH					69		

Bunker and tree positions indicated.

Dumfries & County Golf Club, Nunfield, Edinburgh Road, Dumfries.
Tel: (01387) 253585.

LOCATION: 1 mile north east of Dumfries on A701.
SECRETARY: E.C. Pringle.
Tel: (01387) 253585.
PROFESSIONAL: Gordon Gray.
Tel: (01387) 268918.

Dumfries & County Golf Club, founded in 1912, is an undulating parkland course with mature trees. The course has two loops of nine holes, the ninth and eighteenth both finishing at the clubhouse. Each hole is different with rolling, undulating fairways and seven plateau greens. Its main features are the par 5 seventh, with a blind, tight second shot, and the par 3 fourteenth — "The Wee Yin".

COURSE INFORMATION

Par 69; SSS 68; Length 5,928 Yards.
Opening Hours: 8.00am–8.00pm (depending on daylight).
Visitors: Welcome — not before 9.30am weekdays & 10.00am Sundays. Not on Saturday & Sundays.
Avoid: 11.30am to 2.00pm & 4.00pm to 6.30pm.
Ladies: Welcome — Ladies day Tuesday.
Green Fees: Weekdays — £22, Weekends — £26.
Juveniles: Must be accompanied by an adult.
Clubhouse Hours: 11.00am – 2.00pm & 4.00pm – 11.00pm.
Clubhouse Dress: No jeans, trainers, T-shirts or shorts.
Clubhouse Facilities: Catering available.
Open Competitions: Mixed Open – May; Mens Open – May; Junior Open – June; Mens Open – June; Ladies Open – June; Mens Open – Aug.

CONVENIENT HOTELS

Mabie House, Dumfries;
Cairndale Hotel, Dumfries;
Station Hotel, Dumfries;
Moreig Hotel. Dumfries;
Waverley Hotel, Dumfries.

NO.	MEDAL YARDS	GEN. YARDS	PAR	S.I.	NO.	MEDAL YARDS	GEN. YARDS	PAR	S.I.
1	291	273	4	11	10	278	266	4	14
2	395	380	4	5	11	332	317	4	12
3	329	267	4	15	12	428	403	4	8
4	327	313	4	9	13	450	413	4	2
5	374	274	4	3	14	90	90	3	18
6	178	164	3	17	15	371	352	4	6
7	519	496	5	7	16	201	179	3	16
8	433	416	4	1	17	381	370	4	4
9	172	165	3	13	18	379	282	4	10
OUT	3,018	2,748	35		IN	2,910	2,672	34	
					TOTAL	5,928	5,420	69	
					STANDARD SCRATCH	68	72		

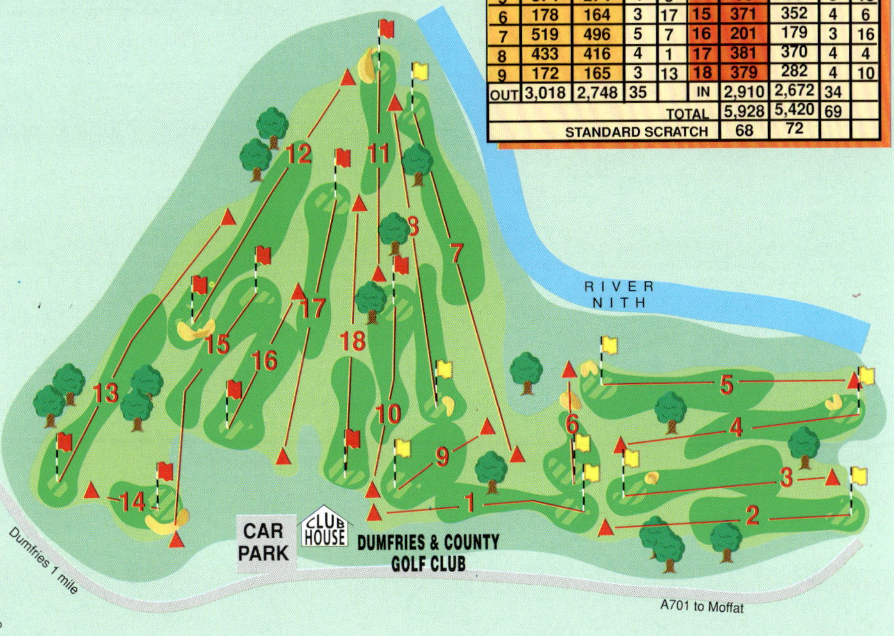

Bunker and tree positions indicated.

Dumfries & Galloway Golf Club, Laurieston Avenue, Dumfries.
Tel: (01387) 253582.

Location: One mile west of the town centre on the A75.
Secretary: Mr J. Donnowho. Tel: (01387) 263848.
Professional: Mr Joe Fergusson. Tel: (01387) 256902.
Architect: Mr Willie Fernie.

A fine private parkland course with undulating fairways.

COURSE INFORMATION

Par 68; SSS 68; Length 5,803 Yards.
Visitors: Welcome.
Opening Hours: 8.30am – 7.00pm.
Avoid: Before 10am and competition days.
Ladies: Welcome.
Ladies Day: Tuesday.
Green Fees: £20 weekdays & £24 weekends.
Juveniles: Must be accompanied by an adult .

Clubhouse Hours: 11.30am – 2.00pm & 4.00pm – 10.30pm.
Clubhouse Dress: No jeans, shellsuits, tracksuits, football tops, sleeveless vests or trainers.
Clubhouse Facilities: Catering daily except Mondays.
Open Competitions: Gents May (over 60), June (scratch), July (over 45), September. Ladies April, August (scratch), September Mixed

NO.	YARDS	PAR	S.I.	NO.	YARDS	PAR	S.I.
1	337	4	9	10	432	4	2
2	497	5	7	11	355	4	4
3	439	4	3	12	192	3	16
4	146	3	15	13	326	4	8
5	565	5	1	14	163	3	17
6	321	4	11	15	234	3	13
7	413	4	5	16	357	4	6
8	207	3	14	17	352	4	10
9	125	3	18	18	342	4	12
OUT	3,050	35		IN	2,753	33	
				TOTAL	5,803	68	
STANDARD SCRATCH					68		

Bunker and tree positions indicated.

IMPERIAL HOTEL

AA ** ** RAC

Ideally situated in the centre of Dumfries and Galloway the Imperial Hotel is a perfect base for your holiday, where golfers of all abilities have a splendid choice available, all within easy reach. We will be happy to arrange your golf from championship links at the renowned 'Southerness' to the testing nine hole courses. You will find the green fees to be very reasonable.

The hotel's golf photo's indicate the propietor, and many of his customers have more than a passing interest. Dinner, bed and breakfast from £33 per person in a room with en-suite facilities, colour T.V, Tea/Coffee maker, Telephone and Late Bar.

A Brochure and Golf Fact Sheet are available.

Castle Douglas, Kirkcudbrightshire.

Tel: 01556-502086. Fax: 01556- 503009.

SELKIRK ARMS HOTEL

High Street, Kirkcudbright, Dumfries & Galloway.

AA ** ** RAC

16 bedrooms all en suite, TV, telephone and tea and coffee facilities. Excellent restaurant serving prime Galloway beef and locally caught fish. Your ideal base for golf in the South of Scotland with "Southerness" just a short drive, and Kirkcudbright on the doorstep. Relax and enjoy your golf break please telephone or fax for further details. Parties welcome with reductions.

FOR RESERVATIONS:

Tel: (01557) 330402. Fax: (01557) 331639.

Lagganmore Golf Club

PORTPATRICK *(near Stranraer)*

This is a brand new, 18 hole golfing experience. The original 9 hole course was opened in 1991 and is maturing nicely. The course layout is interesting and contains some testing holes most notably the Par 5, 7th which has a blind water hazard. The back nine holes were completed for Spring 1995. This golfing complex contains a 9 bay flood lit driving range with a bar, tearoom, and dining area.

Five chalets & two self catering cottages. B&B £25 per person per night including FREE GOLF.

Tel: (01776) 810 499 / 810 262.

KIRKCUDBRIGHT

Kirkcudbright Golf Club,
Stirling Crescent,
Kirkcudbright, DG6 4EZ.
Tel: (01557) 30314.

LOCATION: Kirkcudbright Town.
SECRETARY: J. H. Sommerville.
Tel: (01557) 30314.
ARCHITECT: Edward M. Shamash.

The course is situated on rising hill ground above the town affording the visitor incomparable views of the Solway, Dee Valley and Galloway Hills. Parkland in nature, the fairways are shaped by the natural ground configuration. The judicious use of burns introduces water hazards around the turn. Following the centenary year in 1994, the course — extended to 18 holes in 1976 — continues to develop and improve.

COURSE INFORMATION

Par 66; SSS 67; Length 5,598 Yards.
Opening Hours: Dawn – Dusk.
Visitors: Welcome.
Avoid: Tuesday and Wednesday which are competition days.
Ladies: Welcome. Ladies day Tuesday.
Green Fees: £20 per day; £15 per round.
Juveniles: Welcome.
Clubhouse Hours: 9,30am - 2.30pm; 7.30pm - 11.00pm.
Clubhouse Dress: Casual/Smart; no jeans or sleeveless shirts.
Clubhouse Facilities: Catering available — morning coffee, snacks, lunch, evening meal everyday.

Open Competitions: Numerous competitions — telephone Secretary for details.

CONVENIENT HOTELS

The Royal; The Commercial; The Selkirk; Arden House; Gordon House.

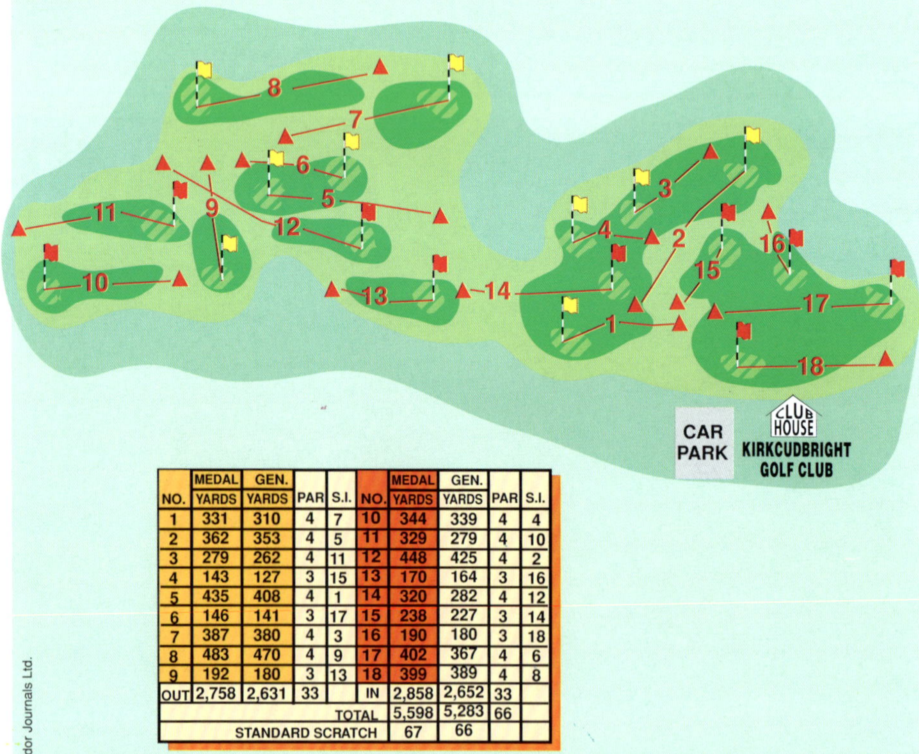

NO.	MEDAL YARDS	GEN. YARDS	PAR	S.I.	NO.	MEDAL YARDS	GEN. YARDS	PAR	S.I.
1	331	310	4	7	10	344	339	4	4
2	362	353	4	5	11	329	279	4	10
3	279	262	4	11	12	448	425	4	2
4	143	127	3	15	13	170	164	3	16
5	435	408	4	1	14	320	282	4	12
6	146	141	3	17	15	238	227	3	14
7	387	380	4	3	16	190	180	3	18
8	483	470	4	9	17	402	367	4	6
9	192	180	3	13	18	399	389	4	8
OUT	2,758	2,631	33		IN	2,858	2,652	33	
					TOTAL	5,598	5,283	66	
					STANDARD SCRATCH	67	66		

Lagganmore Golf Club,
Portpatrick, Wigtownshire.
Tel: (01776) 810 499 / 810 262.

LOCATION: Not far from the picturesque fishing village of Portpatrick.
PROPRIETORS: Mr J. Henderson. Mr &Mrs E. J. Hornby.
Tel: (01776) 810 499/810 262.
ARCHITECT: Nigel Williams.

18 holes course set amidst natural hazards, the seventh par five hailed as the best in Wigtownshire.

COURSE INFORMATION

Par 70; Length 5,970 Yards.
Opening Hours: Dawn – dusk.
Visitors: Golf parties Welcome.
Tel: (01776) 810449/810262.
Green Fees: £10 per round £15 per day.
Juveniles: Welcome.
Clubhouse: Licensed.
Clubhouse Facilities: Catering.

NO.	YARDS	PAR	S.I.	NO.	YARDS	PAR	S.I.
1	317	4		10	426	4	
2	326	4		11	481	5	
3	388	4		12	429	4	
4	372	4		13	145	3	
5	190	3		14	388	4	
6	350	4		15	172	3	
7	493	5		16	350	4	
8	390	4		17	351	4	
9	153	3		18	319	4	
OUT	2,909	35		IN	3,061	35	
				TOTAL	5,970	70	
STANDARD SCRATCH							

Bunker and tree positions indicated.

LOCHMABEN

Lochmaben Golf Club,
Castlehill Gate,
Lochmaben, Dumfriesshire.
Tel: (01387) 810552.

Location: 4 miles west of Lockerbie on A709 — 8 miles from Dumfries.
Secretary: J.M. Dickie.
Tel: (01387) 810713.
Architect: James Braid.

A beautiful parkland course in a picturesque setting. The second green is on the site of the former Lochmaben Castle and moat.

COURSE INFORMATION

Par 67; SSS 66; Length 4,863 Metres.
Opening Hours: 8am-dusk.
Visitors: Welcome Mon–Fri up to 5.00pm — avoid club comp on Sun.
Ladies: Welcome — Ladies day Thur.
Green Fees: £12 per round £15 per day Mon – Fri; £15 per round £20 per day Weekends.
Juveniles: Welcome.
Juveniles: Welcome.
Clubhouse Hours: 11.00am–2.00pm & 5.00pm–11.00pm.
Clubhouse Dress: Informal.
Clubhouse Facilities: Catering.

CONVENIENT HOTELS

Balcastle Hotel, Lochmaben; The Queens Hotel, Lockerbie.

NO.	METRES	PAR	S.I.	NO.	METRES	PAR	S.I.
1	287	4		10	137	3	
2	172	3		11	360	4	
3	174	3		12	471	5	
4	284	4		13	400	4	
5	328	4		14	289	4	
6	369	4		15	119	3	
7	282	4		16	389	4	
8	106	3		17	300	4	
9	275	4		18	121	3	
OUT	2,277	33		IN	2,586	34	
				TOTAL	4,863	67	
STANDARD SCRATCH					66		

Lockerbie Golf Club, Corrie Road, Lockerbie, Dumfriesshire.
Tel: (01576) 203363.

LOCATION: 1/2 mile from Lockerbie on Corrie Road.
SECRETARY: J. Thomson.
Tel: (01576) 202462.
ARCHITECT: J. Braid.

Parkland course with beautiful views and fairways set between young plantations it contains the only pond holes in south west Scotland. A very fair test of golf, suitable for all standards.

COURSE INFORMATION

Par 68; SSS 66; Length 5,418 Yds.
Opening Hours: 8.00am–11.00pm.
Visitors: Welcome — restricted times on Sun.
Avoid: Pre-booking advised, Tel. (0576) 202462.
Ladies: Welcome — ladies day, Tuesday
Green Fees: £16 Mon-Fri; £20 Sat; £16 Sun.
Juveniles: Welcome.
Clubhouse Hours: 11.00am-11.00pm.

Clubhouse Dress: Reasonable standard.
Clubhouse Facilities: Catering available all day.

CONVENIENT HOTELS

Queens Hoptel;
Kings Arms Hotel;
MabieHouse, Dumfries;
Ravenshill Hotel;
Lockerbie Manor Hotel;
Townhead Hotel.

NO.	MEDAL YARDS	GEN. YARDS	PAR	S.I.	NO.	MEDAL YARDS	GEN. YARDS	PAR	S.I.
1	341	336	4	5	10	361	355	4	10
2	189	184	3	16	11	128	123	3	18
3	206	201	3	13	12	400	395	5	1
4	370	365	4	9	13	330	325	4	11
5	413	408	4	2	14	415	410	4	3
6	121	116	3	15	15	258	253	4	17
7	341	336	4	7	16	328	323	4	8
8	355	350	4	12	17	308	303	4	6
9	363	358	4	4	18	191	186	3	14
OUT	2,699	2,654	33		IN	2,719	2,673	35	
					TOTAL	5,418	5,279	68	
					STANDARD SCRATCH	66			

Tree positions indicated.

The Moffat Golf Club, Coatshill, Moffat, DG10 9SB. Tel: (01683) 20020.

LOCATION: Leave A4 at Beattock, follow A701 for 1 mile into Moffat (course signposted).
SECRETARY: T.A. Rankin. Tel: (01683) 20020.
ARCHITECT: Ben Sayers.

Moorland and scenic this 18 hole course offers a spectacular panorama.

COURSE INFORMATION

Par 69; SSS 67; Length 5,218 Yds.

Opening Hours: From 8.00am.
Visitors: Welcome except avoid Wed.
Avoid: Course closures include: April – September every Wednesday from 12noon; Thursdays at 5.30pm; and some Saturdays and Sundays for members' competitions.
Ladies: Welcome (ladies day Tues) except avoid Wed.
Green Fees: Weekday £17; Weekend £25 (day tickets only).
Juveniles: Weekdays — permitted; weekends — only with an adult.

Clubhouse Hours: 8.00am to 11.00pm.
Clubhouse Dress: "Reasonable" dress required, no specific requirements.
Clubhouse Facilities: All day, but enquire at clubhouse (Tel: 01683 20020).

CONVENIENT HOTELS

Annandale Hotel; Auchen Castle Hotel; Balmoral Hotel; Beechwood Country House; Buccleuch Arms Hotel; Moffat House Hotel.

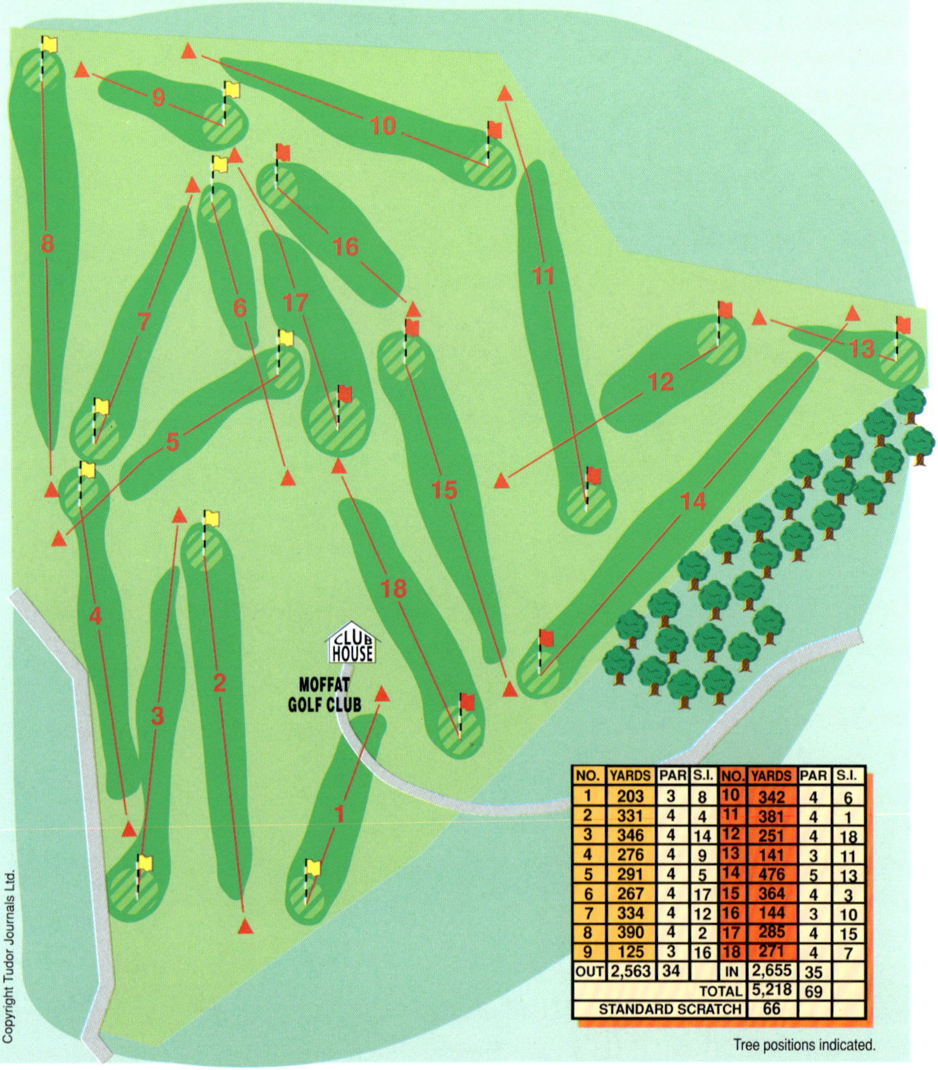

NO.	YARDS	PAR	S.I.	NO.	YARDS	PAR	S.I.
1	203	3	8	10	342	4	6
2	331	4	4	11	381	4	1
3	346	4	14	12	251	4	18
4	276	4	9	13	141	3	11
5	291	4	5	14	476	5	13
6	267	4	17	15	364	4	3
7	334	4	12	16	144	3	10
8	390	4	2	17	285	4	15
9	125	3	16	18	271	4	7
OUT	2,563	34		IN	2,655	35	
				TOTAL	5,218	69	
STANDARD SCRATCH					66		

Tree positions indicated.

NEW GALLOWAY

New Galloway Golf Club, New Galloway, Dumfriesshire.
Tel: (0164 42) 737.

LOCATION: South end of New Galloway on A762.
SECRETARY: A.R. Brown.
Tel: (0164 43) 455.

A superb nine hole course with excellent tees & first class greens. The views over Loch Ken and indeed in every direction must rank amongst the most beautiful in the country. The clubhouse has recently been refurbished and now has every amenity.

COURSE INFORMATION

Par 68; SSS 65; Length 2,503 Yards.
Opening Hours: Dawn–Dusk.
Visitors: Welcome.
Ladies: Welcome.
Green Fees: Adults £10; Juveniles: £5 (under 18's only).
Juveniles: Welcome.
Clubhouse Hours: Bar 12.00pm to 2.00pm.
Clubhouse Dress: Casual/neat.
Clubhouse Facilities: Bar — open May to Sept.

CONVENIENT HOTELS

Leamington Hotel, New Galloway; Kenmure Arms Hotel, New Galloway; Crosskeys Hotel, New Galloway; Kenbridge Hotel, New Galloway; Cairn Edwards (B&B), New Galloway; Kilmar (B&B), Balmaclellan.

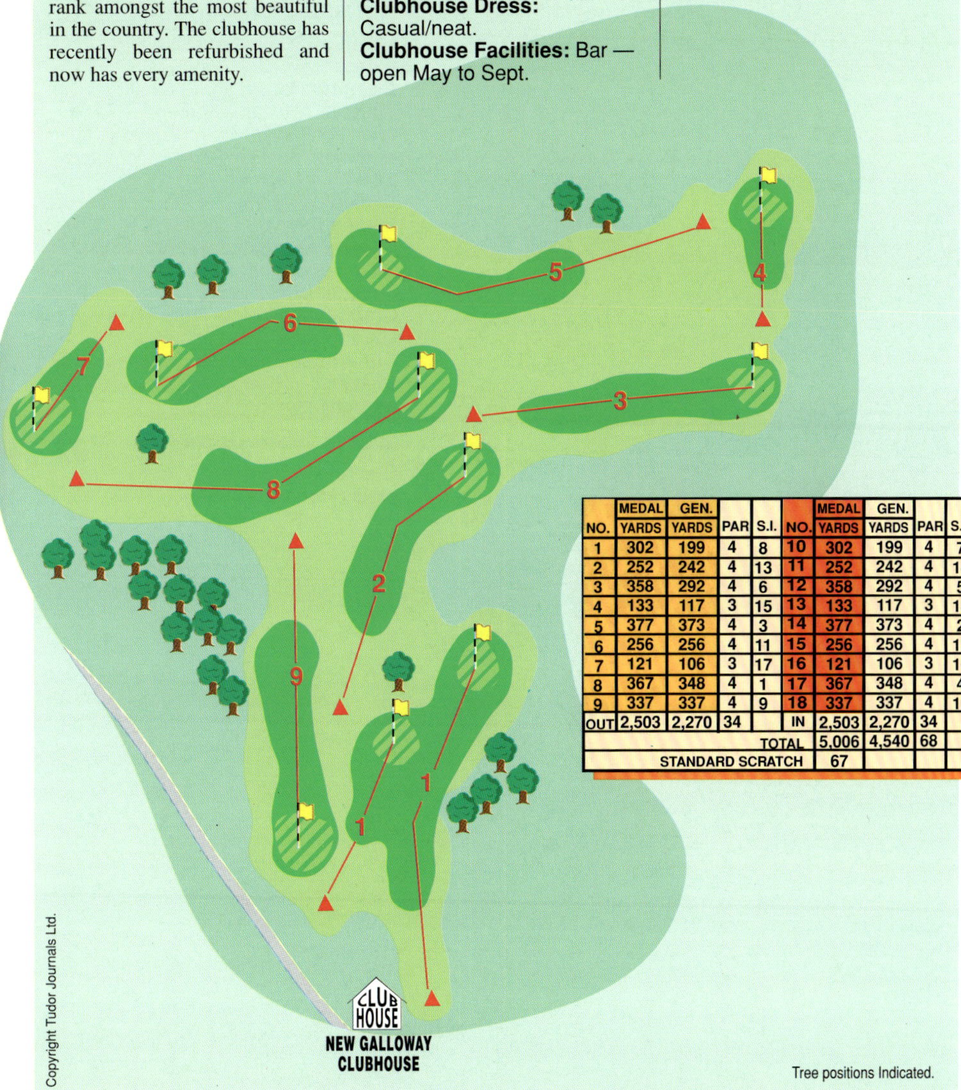

NO.	MEDAL YARDS	GEN. YARDS	PAR	S.I.	NO.	MEDAL YARDS	GEN. YARDS	PAR	S.I.
1	302	199	4	8	10	302	199	4	7
2	252	242	4	13	11	252	242	4	14
3	358	292	4	6	12	358	292	4	5
4	133	117	3	15	13	133	117	3	18
5	377	373	4	3	14	377	373	4	2
6	256	256	4	11	15	256	256	4	12
7	121	106	3	17	16	121	106	3	16
8	367	348	4	1	17	367	348	4	4
9	337	337	4	9	18	337	337	4	10
OUT	2,503	2,270	34		IN	2,503	2,270	34	
					TOTAL	5,006	4,540	68	
					STANDARD SCRATCH	67			

Tree positions Indicated.

	MEDAL YARDS	GEN. YARDS	PAR	S.I.		MEDAL YARDS	GEN. YARDS	PAR	S.I.
	328	346	4	7		328	346	4	8
	132	154	3	17		132	154	3	18
	348	360	4	13		348	360	4	14
	382	396	4	3		382	396	4	4
	385	405	4	2		385	405	4	1
	306	328	4	10		306	328	4	9
	328	345	4	6		328	345	4	5
	155	164	3	15		155	164	3	16
	317	325	4	12		317	325	4	11
OUT	2,681	2,823	34		IN	2,681	2,823	34	
					TOTAL	5,362	5,646	68	
		STANDARD SCRATCH				66	67		

Newton Stewart Golf Club,
Kirroughtree Avenue,
Minnigaff, Newton Stewart.
Tel: (01671) 402172.

LOCATION: Newton Stewart on A75.
SECRETARY: D.C. Matthewson.

Parkland course which is not too undulating. There are no very long holes which gives the beginner a gentle introduction but does not take away the natural challenge of the course.

COURSE INFORMATION

Par 68; SSS 67; Length 5,646 Yards.
Opening Hours: 9am – Dusk.
Visitors: Welcome, except avoid open competition days; Tuesday evenings; Sat/Sun 9am – 10am and 12noon – 1.30pm.
Ladies: Welcome.
Ladies Day: Tuesday.
Green Fees: Monday–Friday £13; Saturday/Sunday £15.
Juveniles: Welcome.
Clubhouse Hours: 11am – 11pm.
Clubhouse Dress: Informal.
Clubhouse Facilities: Catering available – snacks; meals by arrangement.

CONVENIENT HOTELS

Creebridge House;
Mabie House, Dumfries.

Bunker and tree positions indicated.

PORTPATRICK (DUNSKEY)

SOUTH

Portpatrick Dunskey Golf Club,
Golf Course Road,
Portpatrick,
Wigtownshire. DG9 8SU.
Tel: (01776) 810273.

LOCATION: 8 miles south west of Stranraer.
SECRETARY: J.A. Horberry.
Fax & Answerphone: (01776) 810811.

Undulating links type, set on cliffs overlooking the Irish Sea. A good test of golf when the wind blows, yet a very enjoyable course for a days golf off the forward tees for visitors. Three par 3's of great character.

COURSE INFORMATION

Par 70; SSS 68; Length 5,798/5,882 Yards.
Opening Hours: 8am.
Visitors: Welcome. Handicap certificate and prior arrangement required.
Avoid: Members time – Mon – Fri: 9am–9.30am; 1pm–2pm. Saturday / Sunday 8.30am–10am; 12noon–2pm.
Ladies Day: Tues 9.30am–10am; 5pm–6pm.
Green Fees: Mon – Fri £15 per round, £22 per day. Sat/Sun £18 per round, £27 per day.
Juveniles: Only with an adult unless handicap 24 or under.

Clubhouse Hours: 7.45am – 11pm in season.
Clubhouse Dress: Smart/Casual.
Clubhouse Facilities: Catering available from 7.45am – 9pm.
Open Competitions: March: Ladies & Gents Open; May: Gents Open; July & August Ladies & Gents Open; September: 36 Scratch Open & Ladies or Gents Open.

CONVENIENT HOTELS

Fernhill Hotel;
Portpatrick Hotel;
Crown Golf Hotel;
Ihrbour House Hotel.

NO.	MEDAL YARDS	GEN. YARDS	PAR	S.I.	NO.	MEDAL YARDS	GEN. YARDS	PAR	S.I.
1	393	387	4	5	10	329	319	4	10
2	375	331	4	9	11	163	138	3	14
3	544	534	5	1	12	390	370	4	2
4	160	156	3	17	13	293	285	4	16
5	376/405	365	4	3	14	293	293	4	6
6	382	345	4	7	15	101	99	3	18
7	165	160	3	13	16	393	379	4	4
8	294/349	288	4	11	17	301	285	4	12
9	311	298	4	15	18	535	506	5	8
OUT	3,000/ 3,084	2,864	35		IN	2,798	2,674	35	
					TOTAL	5,798/	5,538	70	
STANDARD SCRATCH – 68						5,882	67		

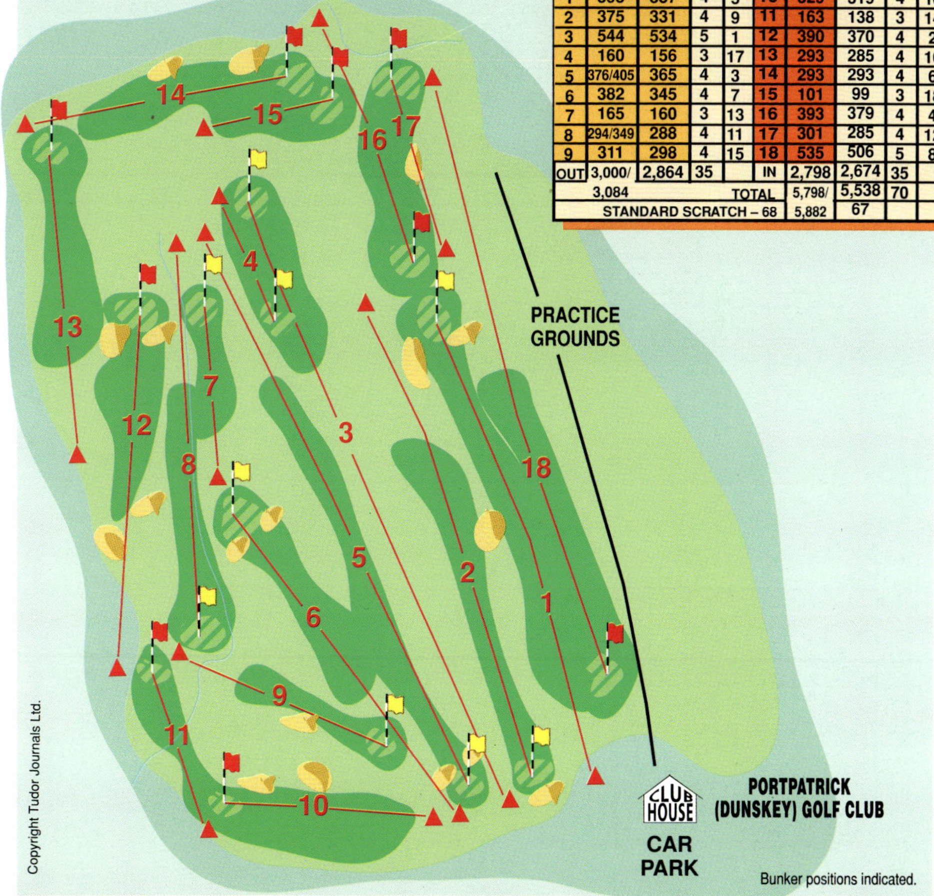

Powfoot Golf Club,
Cummertrees, Annan,
Dumfriesshire.
Tel: (01461) 770227.

LOCATION: 4 miles west of Annan.
SECRETARY: Norman Wilson.
Tel: (01461) 700276.
PROFESSIONAL: Gareth Dick.
Tel: (01461) 700327.
ARCHITECT: James Braid.

Powfoot Golf Club is a semi–links championship course on the Solway shore with outstanding views to the south and west.

COURSE INFORMATION

Par 71; SSS 71; Length 6,283 Yards.
Opening Hours: 8am – 11pm.
Visitors: Welcome Mon – Fri; No visitors at weekends.
Avoid: Ladies day Tues. and Gents Medals (1st Wed. of each month). First tee on weekdays 8.45am – 10am & noon – 1pm for members only.
Ladies: Welcome.
Green Fees: £18 per round; £25 per day Weekdays.
Juveniles: Welcome.
Clubhouse Hours: 9am–11pm.
Clubhouse Dress: Casual/Neat – No jeans, t–shirts or shellsuits allowed.
Clubhouse Facilities: Full bar and catering facilities available.

CONVENIENT HOTELS

Powfoot Golf Hotel;
Mabie House, Dumfries;
Cairndale Hotel, Dumfries.

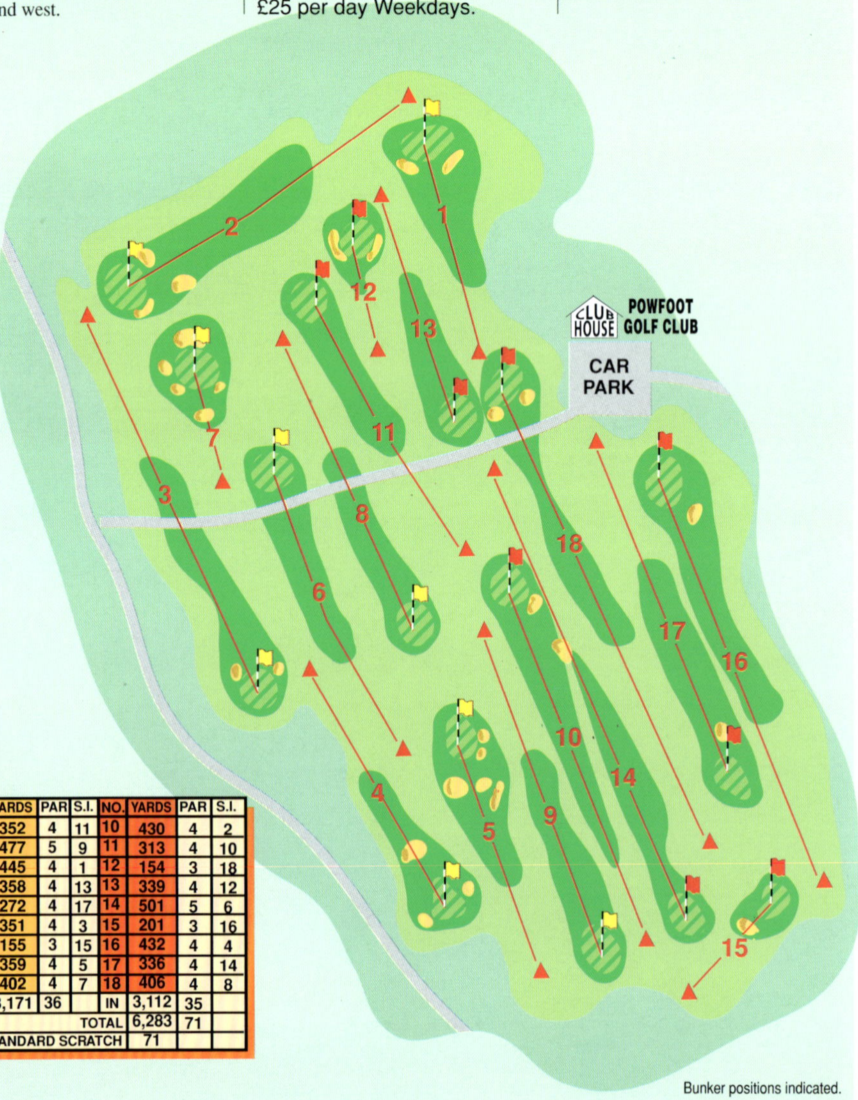

NO.	YARDS	PAR	S.I.	NO.	YARDS	PAR	S.I.
1	352	4	11	10	430	4	2
2	477	5	9	11	313	4	10
3	445	4	1	12	154	3	18
4	358	4	13	13	339	4	12
5	272	4	17	14	501	5	6
6	351	4	3	15	201	3	16
7	155	3	15	16	432	4	4
8	359	4	5	17	336	4	14
9	402	4	7	18	406	4	8
OUT	3,171	36		IN	3,112	35	
				TOTAL	6,283	71	
STANDARD SCRATCH					71		

Bunker positions indicated.

NO.	MEDAL YARDS	GEN. YARDS	PAR	S.I.	NO.	MEDAL YARDS	GEN. YARDS	PAR	S.I.
1	259	232	4	13	10	259	232	4	14
2	444	399	4	1	11	444	399	4	2
3	384	380	4	5	12	384	380	4	6
4	314	310	4	9	13	314	310	4	10
5	294	286	4	11	14	294	286	4	12
6	149	138	3	17	15	149	138	3	18
7	332	325	4	7	16	332	325	4	8
8	156	149	3	15	17	156	149	3	16
9	465	451	5	3	18	465	451	5	4
OUT	2,797	2,670	35		IN	2,797	2,670	35	
				TOTAL		5,594	5,340	70	
	STANDARD SCRATCH					70	70		

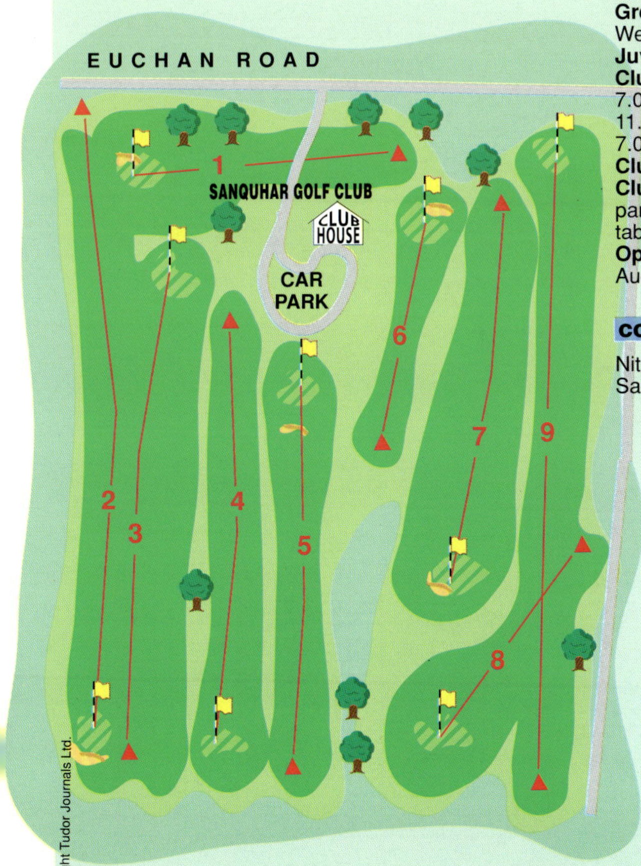

Sanquhar Golf Club, Blackaddie Road, Sanquhar, Dumfriesshire. Tel: (01659) 58181.

LOCATION: 1/2 mile West of Sanquhar by A76. Dumfries 30 miles. Prestwick Airport 30 Miles.
SECRETARY: Mrs. J. Murray.
TeL: (01659) 58181.
ARHITECTS: William Fernie.

Situated on the undulating right bank of the River Nith. Commanding views of great beauty in all directions. Nine tricky holes suitable for the beginner.

COURSE INFORMATION

Par 70; SSS 68; Length 5,594 Yards.
Opening Hours: Dawn – dusk.
Visitors: Welcome — avoid Thurs & Sun after 5.00pm.
Ladies: Welcome — Ladies day Tues after 5.00pm.
Green Fees: £10 Weekdays; £12 Weekends.
Juveniles: Welcome — £2.
Clubhouse Hours: Mon to Sat 7.00pm–11.00pm; Sun 11.30am–2.30pm & 7.00pm–11.00pm.
Clubhouse Dress: Casual.
Clubhouse Facilities: Catering for parties on request, full sized snooker table, pool, bowls, darts etc.
Open Competitions: June, July, August, September & ladies — May.

CONVENIENT HOTELS

Nithsdale Guest House, Glasgow Rd, Sanquhar.

Bunker and tree positions indicated.

Southerness Golf Club,
Southerness, Dumfries.
DG2 8AZ.
Tel: (01387) 88677.

Location: 16 miles south west of Dumfries off A710.
Secretary: Mr W. D. Ramage.
Architect: MacKenzie Ross.

Genuine and natural links course which has held Scottish and British Championships. Large area of gorse and heather add to difficulty of long par 4's. Days without wind are unusual and subtle changes of angles of directions to the holes keeps the golfer on his guard throughout. A burn comes into play at 4 holes and although there are only 65 bunkers these are well placed.

COURSE INFORMATION

Par 69; SSS 73; Length 6,566 Yards.
Opening Hours: 8am – 11pm.
Visitors: Welcome. Avoid: Mon, Tuesday, Wed, Fri 10am – 12 noon; 2pm – 4.30pm; Thurs 11am–1pm; 2.00pm – 4.30pm; Sat/Sun 10am – 11.30am and 2.30pm – 4.30pm.
Ladies: Welcome; Ladies day Thurs.
Green Fees: Mon – Fri £24; Sat/Sun £32.
Juveniles: Welcome.
Clubhouse Hours: 8am – 11pm; Bar 11am – 11pm.
Clubhouse Dress: Smart/Casual (no jeans).
Clubhouse Facilities: Full catering facilities available 7 days a week.
Open Competitions: Mens Opens June & November. Ladies Opens June & September. Mixed Opens July & September.

CONVENIENT HOTELS

Cavens House Hotel;
Clonyard Hotel;
Barons Craig Hotel;
Cairndale Hotel.
Mabie House, Dumfries.

NO.	MEDAL YARDS	GEN. YARDS	PAR	S.I.	NO.	MEDAL YARDS	GEN. YARDS	PAR	S.I.
1	393	372	4	7	10	168	141	3	16
2	450	405	4	3	11	390	371	4	12
3	408	383	4	9	12	421	387	4	6
4	169	132	3	17	13	467	436	4	2
5	496	479	5	11	14	458	418	4	8
6	405	367	4	5	15	217	195	3	14
7	215	215	3	15	16	433	414	4	4
8	371	342	4	13	17	175	164	3	18
9	435	404	4	1	18	495	480	5	10
OUT	3,342	3,099	35		IN	3,224	3,006	34	
					TOTAL	6,566	6,105	69	
					STANDARD SCRATCH	73	70		

Bunker and tree positions indicated.

St. Medan Golf Club, Monreith, Newton Stewart Wigtownshire
Tel: (0198 87) 358.

LOCATION: 4 miles south of Port William on the A747
SECRETARY: D. O'Neill.
Tel: (01988) 500555.

A seaside links course with panoramic views to the Mull of Galloway and the Isle of Man. Claimed as the most southerly golf course in Scotland.

COURSE INFORMATION

Par 64; SSS 62; Length 4,554 Yards.
Opening Hours: Course open all day.
Visitors: Welcome, except during competition days and Wed. afternoon. (medal day).
Ladies: Welcome; Ladies day Friday afternoon.
Green Fees: 9 holes £7; 18 holes £12; Daily £15; Weekly £45.
Juveniles: Welcome.

Clubhouse Hours: 11am/11pm.
Clubhouse Dress: No shorts after 7pm.
Clubhouse Facilities: Catering available from 11.30am - 9pm.
Open Competitions: Lagganharrie - May; Drape Quaich - June; Kirkmaiden - July; Portwilliam - August.

CONVENIENT HOTELS

Monreith Arms Hotel; Corsemalzie Hotel.

NO.	MEDAL YARDS	GEN. YARDS	PAR	S.I.	NO.	MEDAL YARDS	GEN. YARDS	PAR	S.I.
1	220	210	3	16	10	220	210	3	15
2	270	270	4	4	11	270	270	4	3
3	205	207	3	12	12	205	207	3	11
4	274	235	4	10	13	274	235	4	9
5	276	270	4	6	14	276	270	4	5
6	340	310	4	2	15	340	310	4	1
7	273	270	4	8	16	273	270	4	7
8	233	230	3	14	17	233	230	3	13
9	186	104	3	18	18	186	104	3	17
OUT	2,227	2,106	32		IN	2,227	2,106	32	
					TOTAL	4,554	4,212	64	
					STANDARD SCRATCH	62	62		

Stranraer Golf Club, Creachmore by Stranaer. D69 0LF.
Tel: (01776) 870 245.

LOCATION: 3 miles from Stranraer on A718 to Kirkcolm.
SECRETARY: W.I. Wilson M.B.E., C.A..
Tel: (01776) 70 3539.
ARHITECT: James Braid.

A superb 18 hole championship, parkland/seaside course, playable all year. Panoramic views over Loch Ryan and the countryside.

COURSE INFORMATION

Par 70; SSS 72; Length 6,308 Yds.
Opening Hours: 9.30am - 11.00pm.
Visitors: Welcome – avoid members times 12.30pm – 1.30pm & 5.00pm - 6.00pm weekdays; 11.45am – 1.45pm & 5.00pm – 6.00pm weekends.
Ladies: Welcome.
Green Fees: £17.50 Weekdays; £23 Weekends.
Juveniles: Only with an adult & 1/2 adult rate.
Clubhouse Dress: Smart dress, collars, no shorts or tracksuits.
Clubhouse Facilities: Full catering and bar facilities.

CONVENIENT HOTELS

North West Castle, Stranraer; Fernhill Hotel, Portpatrick Portpatrick Hotel.

NO.	MEDAL YARDS	GEN. YARDS	PAR	S.I.	NO.	MEDAL YARDS	GEN. YARDS	PAR	S.I.
1	319	281	4	16	10	346	336	4	11
2	338	330	4	14	11	377	372	4	3
3	420	403	4	4	12	185	180	3	13
4	324	317	4	12	13	335	325	4	17
5	397	382	4	6	14	513	496	5	7
6	160	149	3	10	15	165	162	3	9
7	381	369	4	8	16	470	441	4	1
8	315	308	4	18	17	462	452	4	5
9	458	417	4	2	18	343	336	4	15
OUT	3,112	2,956	35		IN	3,196	3,100	35	
					TOTAL	6,308	6,056	70	
					STANDARD SCRATCH	72	69		

Bunker and tree positions indicated.

THORNHILL (Blacknest)

Thornhill Golf Club, Black Nest, Thornhill, Dumfriesshire, DG3 5DW.
Tel: (01848) 330546.

Location: 14 miles north of Dumfries.
Secretary: R.L. Kerr.
Tel: (01848) 330546.

Set in a very picturesque in Mid-Nithsdale, Thornhill welcomes visitors. Parkland course with attractive features, and a clubhouse which welcomes visitors for meals and a drink.

COURSE INFORMATION

Par 71; SSS 69; Length 6,011 Yds.
Opening Hours: Dawn – Dusk.
Visitors: Welcome – avoid competition days.
Avoid: Club Medals between 4pm – 6pm.
Ladies: Welcome.
Green Fees: Weekdays – £16; Weekends – £20 per day.
Juveniles: Welcome.
Clubhouse Hours: 9.00am – 10.30pm.
Clubhouse Dress: No sleeveless shirts or shorts.
Clubhouse Facilities: Catering and full bar facilities available.

CONVENIENT HOTELS

Gillbank Guest House;
Trigony Hotel;
George Hotel;
Buccleuch & Queensberry Hotel;
Mabie House, Dumfries;
Drumbringan Guest House, Sanquhar.

NO.	YARDS	PAR	S.I.	NO.	YARDS	PAR	S.I.
1	149	3	17	10	396	4	4
2	477	5	6	11	342	4	12
3	359	4	9	12	363	4	8
4	426	4	1	13	407	4	2
5	267	4	13	14	156	3	18
6	421	4	3	15	497	5	5
7	317	4	11	16	191	3	16
8	160	3	15	17	266	4	14
9	332	4	7	18	485	5	10
OUT	2,908	35		IN	3,103	36	
				TOTAL	6,011	71	
				STANDARD SCRATCH	69		

Bunker and tree positions indicated.

Wigtownshire County Golf Club, Mains of Park, Glenluce, Newton Stewart. Tel: (01581) 300420.

LOCATION: 8 miles east of Stranraer on A75.
SECRETARY: R. McKnight. Tel: (01581) 300532.

"County" is the only true links course between Turnberry and Southerness. A trying test of golf enjoyed by both beginners and low handicap golfers.

COURSE INFORMATION

Par 70; SSS 68; Length 5,823 Yards.
Opening Hours: Dawn – Dusk.
Visitors: Welcome — parties should book in advance.
Avoid: Competition days and daily members' priority times.
Ladies: Welcome.
Green Fees: Weekday £16 per round & £20 per day; Weekend £18 per round & £22 per day.
Juveniles: Welcome.

Clubhouse Hours: 9am – 11pm (summertime), 9am – 5pm (Winter).
Clubhouse Dress: Neat – no shorts, vests or Headwear.
Clubhouse Facilities: Full catering all day. Refurbished clubhouse with changing and shower facilities.

CONVENIENT HOTELS

The Glenbay, Glenluce; The Kelvin, Glenluce; The Northwest Castle, Stranraer; The Portpatrick Hotel, Portpatrick.

NO.	MEDAL YARDS	GEN. YARDS	PAR	S.I.	NO.	MEDAL YARDS	GEN. YARDS	PAR	S.I.
1	332	324	4	9	10	332	326	4	6
2	294	294	4	15	11	294	283	4	12
3	402	358	4	2	12	392	385	4	1
4	296	284	4	11	13	152	141	3	17
5	162	154	3	18	14	341	319	4	8
6	491	481	5	7	15	376	329	4	5
7	355	349	4	3	16	314	307	4	14
8	300	294	4	13	17	196	187	3	16
9	341	330	4	10	18	397	346	4	4
OUT	3,029	2,868	36		IN	3,029	2,623	34	
				TOTAL		5,823	5,491	70	
				STANDARD SCRATCH		68	67		

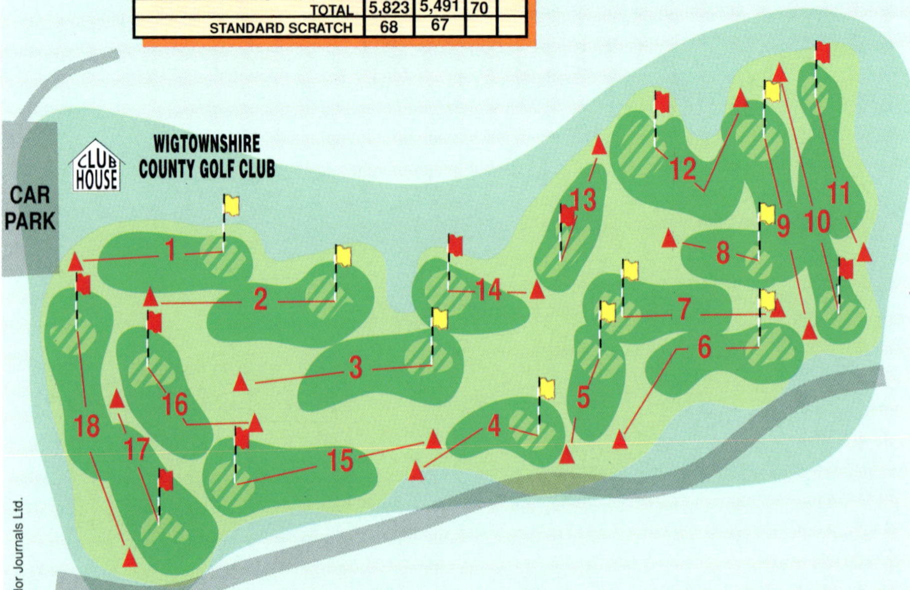

GOLF DAYS™ SCOTLAND

STIRLINGSHIRE

NO.	MEDAL YARDS	GEN. YARDS	PAR	S.I.	NO.	MEDAL YARDS	GEN. YARDS	PAR	S.I.
1	324	263	4	10	10	127	113	3	17
2	357	331	4	2	11	384	319	4	1
3	363	302	4	6	12	148	133	3	15
4	271	256	4	8	13	156	146	3	13
5	225	181	3	14	14	421	373	4	5
6	157	141	3	18	15	327	282	4	9
7	310	277	4	4	16	358	318	4	11
8	162	134	3	16	17	356	336	4	3
9	389	273	4	12	18	382	347	4	7
OUT	2,558	2,158	33		IN	2,659	2,367	33	
					TOTAL	5,217	4,525	66	
					STANDARD SCRATCH	66	68		

Aberfoyle Golf Club,
Aberfoyle, Stirlingshire.
Tel: (01877) 382493.

LOCATION: Braeval, Aberfoyle.
SECRETARY: R.D. Steele.
Tel: (01877) 382638.

A testing heathland course with magnificent views, small greens and tight fairways.

COURSE INFORMATION

Par 66; SSS 66; Length 5,217 Yards.

Opening Hours: Sunrise to Sunset.
Visitors: Welcome, weekends restricted.
Avoid: Weekends before 11.30am.
Ladies: Welcome.
Green Fees:Mon – Fri Round £12 £16 per day; Weekend £16 per round £24 per day.
Juveniles: Welcome.
Clubhouse Hours: 11.30am to 11.30pm.
Clubhouse Dress: Casual.
Clubhouse Facilities: 9.00am to 9.00pm.

CONVENIENT HOTEL

Rob Roy Motel.

Fürstenberg
Irish
Showjumping
Champion
1990

The final approach. Eric Thorburn.

Buchanan Castle Golf Club, Drymen, Stirlingshire, Glasgow. G63 0HY.
Tel: (01360) 660369.

LOCATION: 18 miles northwest of Glasgow.
SECRETARY: R. Kinsella. Tel (01360) 660307.
PROFESSIONAL: Keith Baxter. Tel: (01360) 660330.
ARCHITECT: James Braid.

A low lying parkland course with mature trees.

COURSE INFORMATION

Par 70; SSS 69; Length; 6,086 Yards.
Opening Hours: Dawn – Dusk.
Visitors: Welcome by appointment. No visitors at weekends unless staying at the Buchanan Hotel.
Avoid: Tuesdays & Saturdays.
Ladies: Welcome, avoid Saturdays. Ladies day, Tuesday.
Green Fees: Round £25; £35 per day.
Juveniles: Over 12's welcome.
Clubhouse Hours: 07.00am to 11.00pm (Summer), 08.00am to 6.00pm (Winter).
Clubhouse Dress: Jacket and tie. Weekends Smart/Casual.
Clubhouse Facilities: Full catering facilities available.

CONVENIENT HOTEL

Buchanan Highland Hotel.

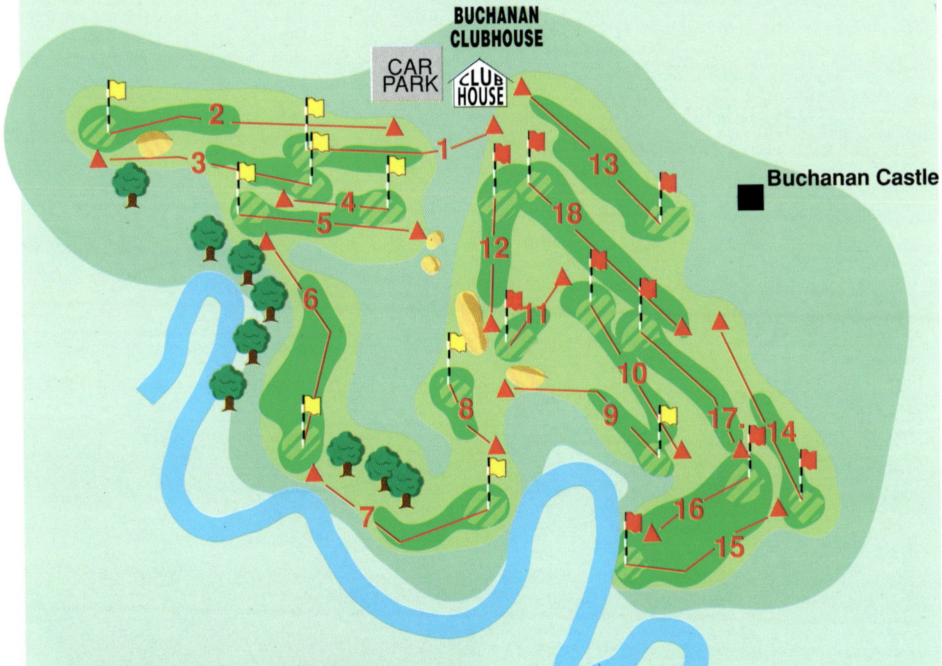

NO.	MEDAL YARDS	GEN. YARDS	PAR	S.I.	NO.	MEDAL YARDS	GEN. YARDS	PAR	S.I.
1	395	381	4	9	10	334	324	4	12
2	394	347	4	11	11	140	122	3	18
3	410	375	4	3	12	318	306	4	14
4	146	140	3	17	13	434	400	4	4
5	268	257	4	13	14	482	425	5	2
6	476	435	5	5	15	354	339	4	8
7	433	389	4	1	16	183	174	3	16
8	152	138	3	15	17	368	332	4	10
9	389	348	4	7	18	410	401	4	6
OUT	3,063	2,810	35		IN	3,023	2,823	35	
					TOTAL	6,086	5,633	70	
STANDARD SCRATCH						69	67		

Bunker and tree positions indicated.

Callander Golf Club,
Aveland Road, Callander,
Perthshire.
Tel: (01877) 330090.

LOCATION: Off the A84 at the east end of Callander.
SECRETARY: Mr Scott.
Tel: (01877) 330090.
PROFESSIONAL: W. Kelly.
Tel: (01877) 330975.
ARCHITECT: Tom Morris.

Pleasant heathland course with scenic views.

COURSE INFORMATION

Par 66; SSS 66; Length 5,125 Yards.
Visitors: Welcome (Handicap certificates required on Wednesdays and Sundays).
Opening Hours: 7am onwards.
Avoid: Wednesday 4.30pm–7.00pm & Sundays 7.00am–10.00am.
Ladies: Welcome.
Ladies Day: Tuesdays Medal.
Green Fees: Weekdays–£18 per day & £14 per round: Weekends–£22 per day & £18 per round.
Juveniles: Restricted on Sundays.
Clubhouse Hours: 11am – 12 midnight.
Clubhouse Dress: Smart / Casual.
Clubhouse Facilities: Bar and full catering.

CONVENIENT HOTELS

Wolsely Park Hotel, Stirling Road, Callander; Dalgair Hotel, Main Street, Callander.

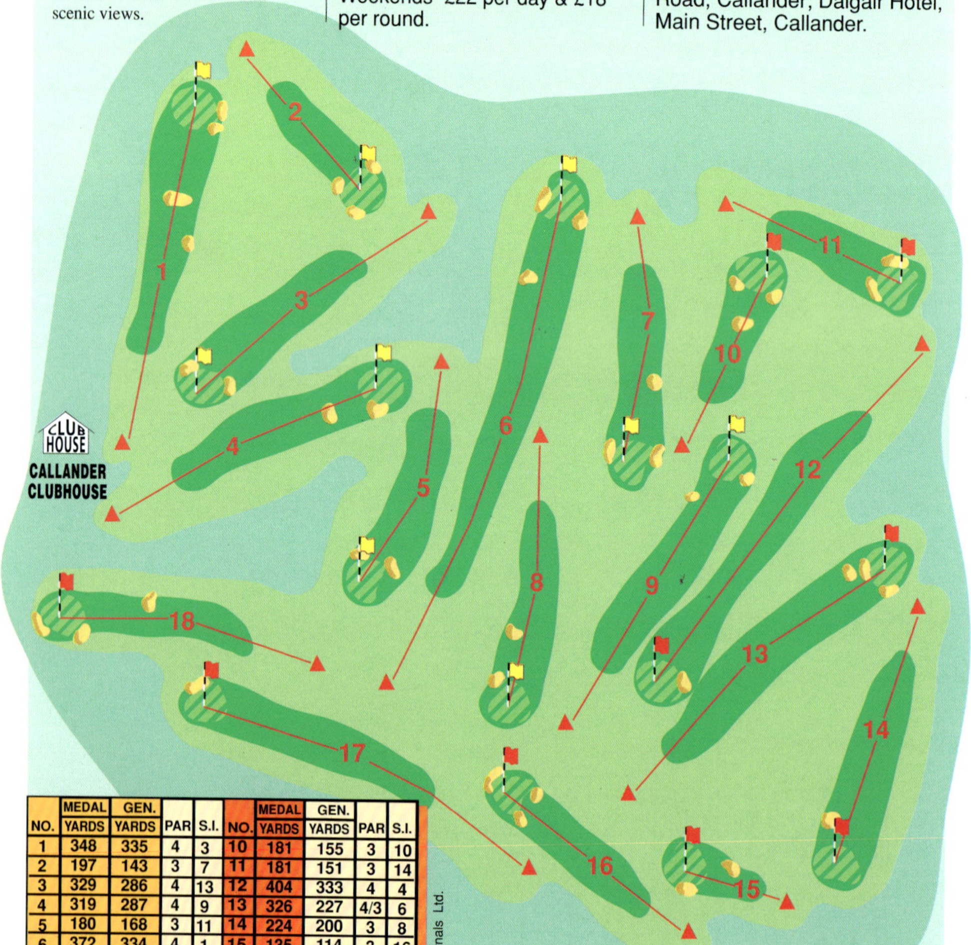

NO.	MEDAL YARDS	GEN. YARDS	PAR	S.I.	NO.	MEDAL YARDS	GEN. YARDS	PAR	S.I.
1	348	335	4	3	10	181	155	3	10
2	197	143	3	7	11	181	151	3	14
3	329	286	4	13	12	404	333	4	4
4	319	287	4	9	13	326	227	4/3	6
5	180	168	3	11	14	224	200	3	8
6	372	334	4	1	15	135	114	3	16
7	257	228	4/3	17	16	365	293	4	2
8	261	251	4	15	17	481	398	5/4	12
9	232	224	3	5	18	333	323	4	18
OUT	2,495	2,256	33/32		IN	2,630	2,194	33/31	
					TOTAL	5,125	4,450	66/63	
					STANDARD SCRATCH	66	63		

Bunker positions indicated.

Dunblane Golf Club, Dunblane, Perthshire. FK15 0LJ.
Tel: (01786) 823711.

LOCATION: 6 miles north of Stirling.
SECRETARY: J. Dunsmore.
Tel: (01786) 823711.
PROFESSIONAL: R.M. Jamieson.
Tel: (01786) 823711.

The course is an undulating parkland with no internal out of bounds. The clubhouse is attractive and the Professional's shop is well stocked.

COURSE INFORMATION

Par 69; SSS 69; Length; 5,939 Yards.
Opening Hours: 8.00 am – Dusk.
Visitors: Welcome, except weekends.
Avoid: Weekends, and weekdays from 9.30am to 12 noon; 2.30pm to 4.30pm.
Ladies: Welcome, ladies day Tuesday.
Green Fees: £16 per round; £23 per day.
Juveniles: Welcome.
Clubhouse Hours: 9.00am - 11.00pm (Summer) 9.00am to 9.30pm (Winter).
Clubhouse Dress: Smart/Casual.
Clubhouse Facilities: Full catering facilities available.

CONVENIENT HOTELS

Stirling Arms Hotel.
Dunblane Hydro Hotel.

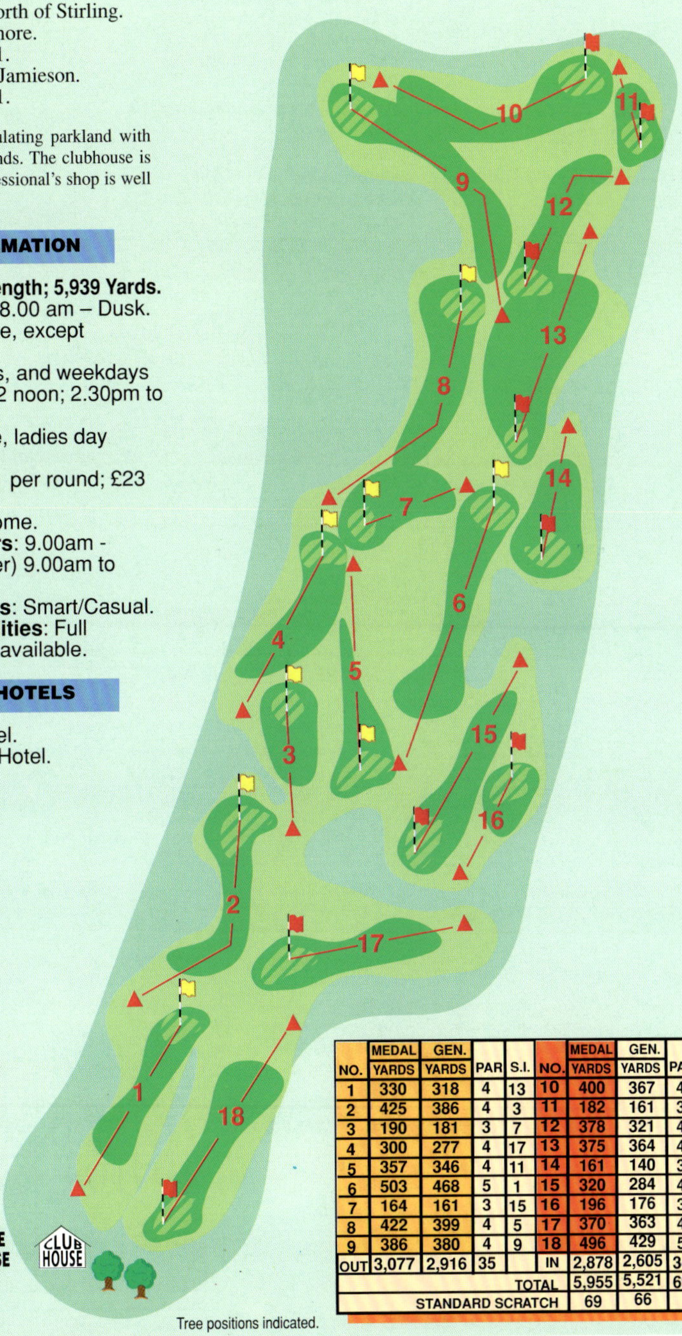

Tree positions indicated.

NO.	MEDAL YARDS	GEN. YARDS	PAR	S.I.	NO.	MEDAL YARDS	GEN. YARDS	PAR	S.I.
1	330	318	4	13	10	400	367	4	8
2	425	386	4	3	11	182	161	3	18
3	190	181	3	7	12	378	321	4	2
4	300	277	4	17	13	375	364	4	10
5	357	346	4	11	14	161	140	3	14
6	503	468	5	1	15	320	284	4	4
7	164	161	3	15	16	196	176	3	16
8	422	399	4	5	17	370	363	4	6
9	386	380	4	9	18	496	429	5	12
OUT	3,077	2,916	35		IN	2,878	2,605	34	
TOTAL						5,955	5,521	69	
STANDARD SCRATCH						69	66		

Falkirk Golf Club, Stirling Road, Camelon, Falkirk. FK2 7RS. Tel: (01324) 611061 or 612219.

LOCATION: 2 miles west of Falkirk, half way between Edinburgh and Glasgow.
SECRETARY: John Elliot. Tel: (01324) 634118.
ARCHITECT: The first nine holes were designed by James Braid.
GOLF PROFESSIONAL: Colin Gillies.

Parkland course, fairly flat and undulating.

COURSE INFORMATION

Par 71; SSS 69; Length 6,282 Yards.
Visitors: Welcome, before 4.30pm Mondays – Fridays. Parties phone to book.
Opening Hours: Dawn – Dusk.
Avoid: Thursday evenings & Saturdays.
Ladies: Welcome.
Ladies Day: Thursday.
Green Fees: Weekdays – £13 per round, £18 per day; Sunday – £25 per day.
Juveniles: Must be accompanied by an adult.
Clubhouse Hours: 11am – 11pm.
Clubhouse Dress: Smart / Casual.
Clubhouse Facilities: Catering every day. Parties catered for by arrangement.
Open Competitions: Senior Open (over 55) – May; Open Mixed 4's – July; Mens' Open – August.

CONVENIENT HOTELS

Park Hotel, Falkirk; Station Hotel, Larbert.

Bunker and tree positions indicated.

NO.	MEDAL YARDS	GEN. YARDS	PAR	S.I.	NO.	MEDAL YARDS	GEN. YARDS	PAR	S.I.
1	495	425	5	5	10	396	355	4	6
2	365	355	4	13	11	154	134	3	16
3	329	329	4	15	12	519	498	5	2
4	390	380	4	3	13	207	192	3	14
5	174	159	3	17	14	359	349	4	12
6	356	326	4	1	15	390	380	4	8
7	194	179	3	11	16	183	178	3	18
8	482	476	5	9	17	459	449	4	4
9	355	330	4	7	18	502	488	5	10
OUT	3,140	2,959	36		IN	3,142	3,025	35	
					TOTAL	6,282	5,984	71	
					STANDARD SCRATCH	70	70		

Falkirk Tryst Golf Club, 86 Burnhead Road, Larbert, Stirlingshire.
Tel: (01324) 562415.

LOCATION: On north edge of village of Stenhousemuir.
SECRETARY: R.D. Wallace. Tel (01324) 562054.
PROFESSIONAL: Steven Dunsmore. Tel: (01324) 562091.

Established in 1885 on the site of the famous 'Falkirk Tryst' or cattle markets, of the 18th century. 'Tryst' is probably derived from the old Scots word "Triste", meaning trust. The course boasts excellent greens with sandy sub soil surfaces allowing a smooth putting surface.

COURSE INFORMATION

Par 70; SSS 69; Length; 6,053 Yards.

Opening Hours: 8.00am — dusk.
Visitors: Welcome; Monday – Friday only.
Avoid: Mid week competition dates.
Ladies: Welcome.
Green Fees: Round £15; £20 per day.
Juveniles: Under 16's £2.50.

Clubhouse Hours: 12.00 noon to 11.00pm.
Clubhouse Dress: Smart/Casual, no tracksuits/collarless shirts.
Clubhouse Facilities: Catering available from 12 noon to 2.30pm. Bar lunches, high tea on request 5.00pm to 7.00pm.

CONVENIENT HOTELS

The Red Lion, Larbert.
The Station Hotel, Larbert.
The Commercial, Larbert.
Plough Hotel, Stenholisemuir.

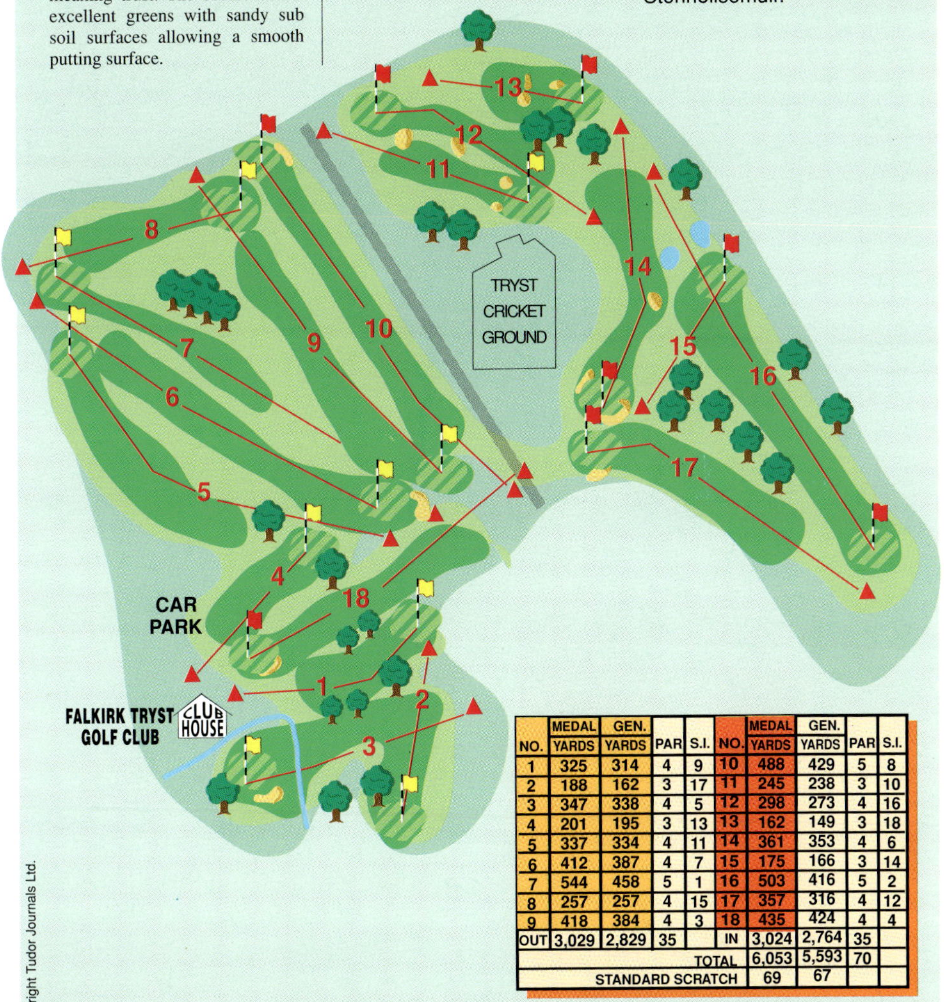

NO.	MEDAL YARDS	GEN. YARDS	PAR	S.I.	NO.	MEDAL YARDS	GEN. YARDS	PAR	S.I.
1	325	314	4	9	10	488	429	5	8
2	188	162	3	17	11	245	238	3	10
3	347	338	4	5	12	298	273	4	16
4	201	195	3	13	13	162	149	3	18
5	337	334	4	11	14	361	353	4	6
6	412	387	4	7	15	175	166	3	14
7	544	458	5	1	16	503	416	5	2
8	257	257	4	15	17	357	316	4	12
9	418	384	4	3	18	435	424	4	4
OUT	3,029	2,829	35		IN	3,024	2,764	35	
					TOTAL	6,053	5,593	70	
					STANDARD SCRATCH	69	67		

Bunker and tree positions indicated.

GLENBERVIE

**Glenbervie Golf Club Ltd,
Stirling Road, Larbert,
Stirlingshire.
Tel: (01324) 562605.**

Location: 1/2 way between Falkirk and Stirling.
Secretary: Mrs M. Purves.
Tel: (01324) 562605.
Professional: John Chillas.
Tel: (01324) 562725.
Architect: James Braid.

Parkland course with many trees. Used for qualifing rounds for the British Open and as host for many other prestigious tournaments.

NO.	MEDAL YARDS	GEN. YARDS	PAR	S.I.	NO.	MEDAL YARDS	GEN. YARDS	PAR	S.I.
1	356	346	4	11	10	168	149	3	12
2	534	493	5	5	11	331	270	4	18
3	311	294	4	15	12	424	403	4	2
4	153	148	3	17	13	198	172	3	8
5	386	360	4	9	14	407	395	4	4
6	401	375	4	3	15	506	472	5	16
7	211	180	3	7	16	373	356	4	10
8	339	316	4	13	17	500	486	5	14
9	436	419	4	1	18	368	327	4	6
OUT	3,127	2,931	35		IN	3,275	3,030	36	
					TOTAL	6,402	5,961	71	
					STANDARD SCRATCH	70			

COURSE INFORMATION

Par 71; SSS 70; Length 6,402 Yards.
Visitors: Welcome (phone to book).
Opening Hours: 8am – Dusk.
Avoid: No visitors on weekends or after 4pm weekdays.
Ladies: Welcome.
Green Fees: £25 per round £35 per day.
Juveniles: Permitted.
Clubhouse Hours: 10am – 11pm.
Clubhouse Dress: Jackets, collar and tie.
Clubhouse Facilities: Catering from 10am – 8pm; Parties catered by arrangement.
Open Competitions: Phone to check dates.

CONVENIENT HOTELS

Park Hotel, Falkirk;
Airth Castle, Airth;
Powfoulis, Airth.

Bunker and tree positions indicated.

Grangemouth Golf Club,
Polomonthill, Polmont,
Stirlingshire.
Tel: (01324) 714355.

LOCATION: 3 miles east of Falkirk, exit no.4 on the M9.
SECRETARY: I. Hutton. Tel (01324) 712585.
PROFESSIONAL: Stuart J. Campbell. Tel: (01324) 714355.
ARCHITECT: Sportswork.

A very demanding golf test on the front nine, relaxing a shade on the back nine. A well laid out course with pleasant views, wide fairways and large greens which are well bunkered. Being a municipal course it tends to be rather busy and is well patronised.

COURSE INFORMATION

Par 71; SSS 71; Length; 6,314 Yards.

Opening Hours: Dawn til dusk.
Visitors: Welcome.
Avoid: Saturdays club medals 8.00am to 4.30pm.
Ladies: Welcome, ladies day, Tuesday.
Green Fees: Round £6.00; £8.50 per day.
Weekends: Round £7.60; £10.20 per day.
Juveniles: Welcome, after 4.30pm.
Clubhouse Hours: Locker room; all day. Bar; 11.00am to 11.00pm.
Clubhouse Dress: Smart/Casual (no shorts).
Clubhouse Facilities: Catering available during bar hours.

CONVENIENT HOTEL

Inchrya Grange Hotel.

NO.	MEDAL YARDS	GEN. YARDS	PAR	S.I.	NO.	MEDAL YARDS	GEN. YARDS	PAR	S.I.
1	390	365	4	11	10	310	302	4	4
2	313	299	4	15	11	479	459	5	4
3	418	403	4	9	12	185	174	3	3
4	412	391	4	7	13	512	491	5	5
5	513	485	5	1	14	350	339	4	4
6	298	289	4	17	15	167	154	3	3
7	207	183	3	13	16	172	162	3	3
8	407	399	4	5	17	336	326	4	4
9	433	409	4	3	18	412	401	4	5
OUT	3,391	3,223	36		IN	2,923	2,808	35	35
					TOTAL	6,314	6,031	71	73
					STANDARD SCRATCH	71	70		

Polmont Golf Club,
Manuelrigg, Maddiston,
Stirlingshire.
Tel: (01324) 711277.

LOCATION: 4 miles south of Falkirk.
SECRETARY: P. Lees.
Tel (01324) 713811.

Course is hilly with tree lined fairways, the greens are small and tricky to hold.

COURSE INFORMATION

Par 72; SSS 69; Length; 6,062 Yards.

Opening Hours: Dawn until dusk.
Visitors: Welcome, except Saturday.
Avoid: Saturdays & after 5.30pm Mon-Fri.
Ladies: Welcome, ladies day Tuesday.

Green Fees: Mon – Sat £7; Sun £12 . (18 holes).
Juveniles: Welcome, after 4.30pm, except Sat.
Clubhouse Hours: 9.00am to 11.00pm.
Clubhouse Dress: Casual.
Clubhouse Facilities: Catering available on request.

CONVENIENT HOTEL

Inchrya Grange Hotel, Polmont.

NO.	GEN. YARDS	PAR	S.I.	NO.	GEN. YARDS	PAR	S.I.
1	340	4	13	10	340	4	14
2	318	4	9	11	318	4	10
3	187	3	17	12	187	3	18
4	455	5	3	13	455	5	4
5	376	4	5	14	376	4	6
6	318	4	11	15	318	4	12
7	197	3	15	16	197	3	16
8	368	4	1	17	368	4	2
9	482	5	7	18	182	5	8
OUT	3,031	36		IN	3,031	36	
				TOTAL	6,062	72	
STANDARD SCRATCH					69		

Bunker and tree positions indicated.

Stirling Golf Club, King's Park, Queen's Road, Stirling. FK8 3AA.
Tel: (01786) 473801.

LOCATION: Within 1 mile of Stirling town centre, and 1 1/2 miles from Jct.10 of the M9.
SECRETARY: Walter C. McArthur Tel: (01786) 464098.
PROFESSIONAL: Ian Collins. Tel: (01786) 471490.
ARCHITECT: James Braid & Henry Cotton.

An undulating parkland course, with superb views of Stirling Castle, Ochil Hills and Grampian Mountains.

COURSE INFORMATION

Par 72; SSS 71; Length; 6,438 Yards.
Opening Hours: 08.00am to 23.30pm.
Visitors: Welcome - contact Pro. Shop.
Ladies: Welcome (Tuesday ladies day).

Green Fees: £17 per round, £25 per day.
Juveniles: Welcome.
Clubhouse Hours: 8.00am to 23.30pm.
Clubhouse Dress: Casual.
Clubhouse Facilities: Full catering available by arrangement.

CONVENIENT HOTELS

Garfield Hotel.
Golden Lion Hotel.
Terraces Hotel.

NO.	MEDAL YARDS	GEN. YARDS	PAR	S.I.	NO.	MEDAL YARDS	GEN. YARDS	PAR	S.I.
1	478	462	5	5	10	175	170	3	16
2	293	268	4	15	11	410	400	4	12
3	320	300	4	13	12	378	367	4	4
4	361	344	4	9	13	527	483	5	8
5	509	489	5	3	14	172	152	3	18
6	155	138	3	17	15	384	365	4	2
7	432	432	4	7	16	331	297	4	14
8	192	180	3	11	17	373	361	4	10
9	434	418	4	1	18	514	497	5	6
OUT	3,174	3,031	36		IN	3,264	3,092	36	
					TOTAL	6,438	6,123	72	
					STANDARD SCRATCH	71	69		

GOLF CLUBS IN SCOTLAND
(Listed Alphabetically)

ACKNOWLEDGEMENTS

Golf Days would like to record its thanks and appreciation to the many golf clubs and staff who greatly assisted the publishers in compiling this book.

PUBLISHERS NOTE

This is the second edition of Golf Days Scotland and in compiling the information we are aware that it is not possible to ensure complete accuracy. We woud welcome comments from readers and observations from club officials to assist us in our continuous programme of updating Golf Days.

NOTES

NOTES